SQL Server T-SQL Recipes

Fourth Edition

Jason Brimhall

Jonathan Gennick

Wayne Sheffield

Apress®

SQL Server T-SQL Recipes

ISBN-13 (pbk): 978-1-4842-0062-9

ISBN-13 (electronic): 978-1-4842-0061-2

Managing Director: Welmoed Spahr
Lead Editor: Jonathan Gennick
Technical Reviewer: Louis Davidson
Editorial Board: Steve Anglin, Mark Beckner, Gary Cornell, Louise Corrigan, Jim DeWolf, Jonathan Gennick, Robert Hutchinson, Michelle Lowman, James Markham, Susan McDermott, Matthew Moodie, Jeffrey Pepper, Douglas Pundick, Ben Renow-Clarke, Gwenan Spearing, Matt Wade, Steve Weiss
Coordinating Editor: Jill Balzano
Copy Editor: April Rondeau
Compositor: SPi Global
Indexer: SPi Global
Artist: SPi Global
Cover Designer: Anna Ishchenko

Distributed to the book trade worldwide by Springer Science+Business Media New York, 233 Spring Street, 6th Floor, New York, NY 10013. Phone 1-800-SPRINGER, fax (201) 348-4505, e-mail orders-ny@springer-sbm.com, or visit www.springeronline.com. Apress Media, LLC is a California LLC and the sole member (owner) is Springer Science + Business Media Finance Inc (SSBM Finance Inc). SSBM Finance Inc is a Delaware corporation.

For information on translations, please e-mail rights@apress.com, or visit www.apress.com.

Apress and friends of ED books may be purchased in bulk for academic, corporate, or promotional use. eBook versions and licenses are also available for most titles. For more information, reference our Special Bulk Sales–eBook Licensing web page at www.apress.com/bulk-sales.

Any source code or other supplementary material referenced by the author in this text is available to readers at www.apress.com. For detailed information about how to locate your book's source code, go to www.apress.com/source-code/.

I dedicate this book to the memory of my recently-departed grandfather Dan L Greenland who was an inspiration and example in so many ways. He was a great leader and a very loving grandfather to me.

—Jason L Brimhall

Contents at a Glance

Contents

About the Authors

Jason Brimhall is first and foremost a family man. He has 15+ yrs experience in IT and has worked with SQL Server starting with SQL Server 6.5. He has worked for both large and small companies in varied industries. He has experience in performance tuning, high transaction environments, large environments, and VLDBs. He is currently a Principal Consultant, Microsoft Certified Master, and an MVP for SQL Server. Jason regularly volunteers for PASS and has been the VP of the Las Vegas User Group (SSSOLV). You can read more from Jason on his blog at: http://jasonbrimhall.info.

Jonathan Gennick is an Apress Assistant Editorial Director with responsibility for database topics. He is line-leader for Apress' Oracle and SQL Server lines. He also publishes carefully-chosen database books of a general nature. He maintains a keen interest in books across all lines that touch upon relational databases.

Outside of the day-job Jonathan looks to family and community. He serves actively in his local church as First Elder. He is an avid mountain-biker and trail builder, and a member of the Munising Bay Trail Network. For several years he served his local community as an Emergency Medical Technician for the Alger County Ambulance Service.

Wayne Sheffield, a Microsoft Certified Master in SQL Server, started working with xBase databases in the late 80's. With over 25 years in IT, he has worked with SQL Server (since version 6.5 in the late 90's) in various developer and administration roles, with an emphasis on performance tuning. He is the author of several articles at www.sqlservercentral.com, and enjoys sharing his knowledge by presenting at SQL PASS events and blogging at http://blog.waynesheffield.com/wayne.

About the Technical Reviewer

Louis Davidson has been in the IT industry for more than 15 years as a corporate database developer and architect. He has spent the majority of his career working with Microsoft SQL Server, beginning from the early days of version 1.0. He has a bachelor s degree from the University of Tennessee at Chattanooga in computer science, with a minor in mathematics. Louis is the data architect for Compass Technology (Compass.net) in Chesapeake, Virginia, leading database development on their suite of nonprofit oriented CRM products, built on the Microsoft CRM platform and SQL Server technologies.

Acknowledgments

I am grateful for the opportunity to have worked on this book. I appreciate very much the opportunity to work with my coauthors – Jonathan Gennick, Wayne Sheffied, and the authors from the previous edition. I love working with SQL Server and doing what I can to share that enthusiasm with fellow SQL Server professionals.

Much gratitude is due to my wife Krista and our children. Krista and ATW Photography were gracious enough to provide photography services to me for this book – thank you! I am thankful to Jerry and Sheila Hurst who were influential to me. Many thanks to extended family and friends who also contributed in many different ways while I worked on this book (mostly unknowingly)!

Thanks to Louis Davidson (technical reviewer for this edition) for his hard work in reading the chapters, testing the code, and providing feedback to improve the work. And, finally, thanks to Joe Sack for allowing me to continue this book and keep it going with the new editions of SQL Server.

—Jason Brimhall

Once again I'm honored by my coauthors for their continued toleration of my presence in their book. Writing SQL is fun, and I enjoy immensely my few chapters of contribution to Jason's and Wayne's excellent work.

Jonathan Gennick Several years ago, I found out that I really enjoy sharing my knowledge about SQL Server with others. Working on this book has been an extension of this sharing; an experience that I have very much enjoyed, primarily because of the great team that we had. From the entire staff at Apress working diligently behind the scenes to ensure that everything flows smoothly toward publication, to my coauthors (Jonathan Gennick and Jason Brimhall), and our technical reviewer, Louis Davidson (who had to read every word of this book and test all the code), it has been great working with this team on this book, and I hope that the work that we have all put into it is appreciated by all who read it.

Throughout the years, there have been many people that have been influential to me, usually without knowing just how influenced I was by them. Thanks to all of you for all that you have done for me.

Last, but not least, I thank my wife Karen. Without your support, I would not have been able to participate in this book. Telling you "thank you" is so inadequate in conveying my appreciation for all that you have done to help me while I've been working on this book. Now it's time for us to do something special!

—Wayne Sheffield

Introduction

Sometimes all one wants is a good example.

T-SQL is fundamental to working with SQL Server. Almost everything you do, from querying a table to creating indexes to backing up and recovering, ultimately comes down to T-SQL statements being issued and executed. Sometimes a utility executes statements on your behalf; other times you must write them yourself.

And when you have to write them yourself, you're probably going to be in a hurry. Information technology is like that. It's a field full of stress and deadlines, and don't we all just want to get home for dinner with our families?

We sure do want to be home for dinner, and that brings us full circle to the example-based format you'll find in this book. If you have a job to do that's covered in this book, you can count on a clear code example and very few words to waste your time. We put the code first! And explain it afterward. We hope our examples are clear enough that you can just crib from them and get on with your day, but the detailed explanations are there if you need them.

We've missed a few dinners from working on this book. We hope it helps you avoid the same fate.

Who This Book Is For

SQL Server T-SQL Recipes is aimed at developers deploying applications against Microsoft SQL Server 2012 and 2014. The book also helps database administrators responsible for managing those databases. Any developer or administrator valuing good code examples will find something of use in this book.

Conventions

Throughout the book, we've tried to keep to a consistent style for presenting SQL and results. Where a piece of code, a SQL reserved word, or a fragment of SQL is presented in the text, it is presented in fixed-width Courier font, such as this example:

```
SELECT * FROM HumanResources.Employee;
```

Where we discuss the syntax and options of SQL commands, we use a conversational style so you can quickly reach an understanding of the command or technique. We have chosen not to duplicate complex syntax diagrams that are best left to the official, vendor-supplied documentation. Instead, we take an example-based approach that is easy to understand and adapt.

Downloading the Code

The code for the examples shown in this book is available on the Apress web site, `www.apress.com`. A link can be found on the book's information page (`www.apress.com/9781484200629`) on the Source Code/Downloads tab. This tab is located in the Related Titles section of the page.

CHAPTER 1

Getting Started with SELECT

by Jonathan Gennick

Transact-SQL is a proprietary implementation of the SQL language. It is often referred to simply as T-SQL, and you'll see us calling it by that shorter name throughout this book. The T-SQL language extends SQL by adding procedural syntax that is useful in programming both application and business logic to run inside the database server. There's much to learn, and it all begins right here with SELECT.

Tip You can find and download various editions of the Adventure Works example database from http://msftdbprodsamples.codeplex.com/.

1-1. Connecting to a Database

Problem

You are working from the command line, or maybe you just prefer to work using commands, even from the SQL Server Management Studio GUI, and you wish to connect to a specific database. For example, you wish to connect to the example database used throughout this book.

Solution

Execute the USE statement and specify the name of your target database. The following example connects to the Adventure Works example database used in this book:

```
USE AdventureWorks2014;
```

```
Command(s) completed successfully.
```

The success message indicates a successful connection. You may now execute queries against tables and views in the database without having to qualify those object names by specifying the database name each time.

1

How It Works

When you first launch SQL Server Management Studio you are connected to a default database that your administrator has associated with your login. By default, that default database is the so-called *master* database. Being connected to the master is usually not convenient, and you shouldn't be storing your data in that database. Executing a USE statement lets you more easily access tables and views in the database you're intending to use, and there is the added benefit of your being less likely to mistakenly create objects in the master database.

1-2. Checking the Database Server Version

Problem

You've connected to a database instance and have no idea whether that instance represents SQL Server 2014, SQL Server 2012, or something even more ancient from the Prekatmai or Precambrian eras.

Solution

Query the instance for its version information. Do that by invoking the @@VERSION function. For example:

```
SELECT @@VERSION;
```

```
--------------------------------------------------
Microsoft SQL Server 2014 - 12.0.2000.8 (X64)
...
```

How It Works

There's no getting around it. You can see that we're running Community Technolgy Preview 2 (CTP2) while revising the book. That's because we want the book to be done shortly after the production release. We write against CTP2, and we test a second time against the Release to Manufacturing (RTM) just prior to publication. We then run every example again after the RTM is released to be sure nothing has changed.

1-3. Checking the Database Name

Problem

You want to determine via a query which database you are connected to. You can look up at the title bar when running SQL Server Management Studio, but today you happen to be running sqlcmd from the Windows command prompt. You want to be reminded of which database you specified in your most recent USE command.

Solution

Query for the name of the database currently being used. For example:

```
select DB_NAME();
```

```
------
master
```

How It Works

I surprised myself when generating the solution example in this recipe. I had thought I was using the Adventure Works database. I came in this morning and woke my PC from sleep, remembering that I had been in Adventure Works yesterday evening. Management Studio threw up a Connect to Server dialog, and I reflexively hit the Connect button while still in that first-cup-of-coffee state of mind. Mentally, I was still set in Adventure Works. But in reality, I had just connected to the master database by default. The sleep/wake cycle had broken my connection from yesterday, and I was genuinely surprised at seeing the result from this recipe's example.

So be careful!

Keep track of what database you are using as your default. Keep an eye on the title bar when executing queries from SQL Server Management Studio. Query as shown in this recipe if you're ever not sure and are executing from the command line. It's not fun to unleash a SQL statement against the wrong database, and it's especially not fun when said statement actually executes.

■ **Note**   You'll learn more about sqlcmd in Chapter 2. It's a utility that's useful for executing T-SQL in batch mode.

1-4. Checking Your Username

Problem

You want to access your current username from SQL, either to remind yourself of who you are logged in as, or to record the name as part of a logging solution.

Solution

There are actually three names to be concerned about. There is your login name that you used when authenticating to SQL Server. There is your database username that you are associated with upon successfully logging in. Lastly, there is the username providing the credentials under which any queries are executed. Query for the names by invoking the ORIGINAL_LOGIN(), CURRENT_USER, and SYSTEM_USER functions respectively, as follows:

```
SELECT ORIGINAL_LOGIN(), CURRENT_USER, SYSTEM_USER;
```

```
------------------------------ -------- ------------------------------

GennickT410\JonathanGennick dbo     GennickT410\JonathanGennick
```

How It Works

The example shows that I authenticated to SQL Server using the name GennickT410\JonathanGennick. That's my Windows login, made up from my PC name followed by my Windows username. The path-like syntax is typical of what you will see when Windows authentication is used. Otherwise, if you see just a simple name having no path-like syntax, you can be reasonably certain that SQL Server authentication was used, and that the login name and password were authenticated, not by Windows, but by the database engine.

After authenticating to SQL Server, you are then associated with a database username. This is the username that matters for object permissions. In the example, my database username is given as dbo.

Database administrators sometimes impersonate other users when testing queries. When doing that, the SYSTEM_USER function returns the name of the user being impersonated. However, the call to ORIGINAL_LOGIN() always returns the name used when first authenticating to the instance.

■ **Caution** Use of T-SQL's EXECUTE AS syntax to impersonate another user will cause SYSTEM_USER and CURRENT_USER to return the login name and database name of the user who is being impersonated. That is done by design, and is something to be aware of.

1-5. Querying a Table

Problem

You have a table or a view. You wish to retrieve data from specific columns.

Solution

Write a SELECT statement. List the columns you wish returned following the SELECT keyword. For example:

```
SELECT NationalIDNumber,
       LoginID,
       JobTitle
FROM HumanResources.Employee;
```

NationalIDNumber	LoginID	JobTitle
295847284	adventure-works\ken0	Chief Executive Officer
245797967	adventure-works\terri0	Vice President of Engineering
509647174	adventure-works\roberto0	Engineering Manager
...		

Specify an asterisk (*) instead of a list to return all of the columns. Here's an example showing that syntax:

```
SELECT  *
FROM  HumanResources.Employee;
```

```
BusinessEntityID NationalIDNumber LoginID                    OrganizationNode ...
---------------- ---------------- ------------------------   ---------------- ...
1                295847284        adventure-works\ken0       0x               ...
2                245797967        adventure-works\terri0     0x58             ...
3                509647174        adventure-works\roberto0   0x5AC0           ...
...
```

How It Works

The FROM clause names the table to be queried. Data is returned from that table. The comma-delimited list following the SELECT keyword specifies the columns to be returned. Whitespace doesn't matter. You can list the columns one per line as in the example, or you can list them all on the same line.

Specifying an asterisk (*) instead of a column list returns all columns of the table you are querying. Using that syntax is handy when writing ad-hoc queries and executing them from Management Studio. Don't use it from program code though. Doing so can put your program at risk of failure due to future column additions to the table, and even due to a simple rearranging of the existing columns. You're also likely to negatively impact performance by returning more data over the network than is needed. Protect yourself from both problems by listing only those columns that are really needed by the program you're writing. Don't return anything unnecessary.

1-6. Returning Specific Rows

Problem

You want to restrict query results to a subset of rows in the table that interest you.

Solution

Specify a WHERE clause that gives the conditions that rows must meet in order to be returned. For example, the following query returns only rows in which the person's title is "Ms."

```
SELECT  Title, FirstName, LastName
FROM Person.Person
WHERE Title = 'Ms.';
```

```
Title    FirstName    LastName
-------- -----------  -----------
Ms.      Gail         Erickson
Ms.      Janice       Galvin
Ms.      Jill         Williams
...
```

You may combine multiple conditions in one clause through the use of the logical operators AND and OR. The following query looks specifically for Ms. Antrim's data:

```
SELECT  Title, FirstName, LastName
FROM  Person.Person
WHERE Title = 'Ms.' AND LastName = 'Antrim';
```

```
Title    FirstName   LastName
-------- ----------- -----------
Ms.      Ramona      Antrim
```

How It Works

The WHERE clause provides search conditions that determine the rows to be returned by the query. Search conditions are written as predicates, which are expressions that evaluate to TRUE, FALSE, or UNKNOWN. Only rows for which the final evaluation of the WHERE clause is TRUE are returned. Table 1-1 lists some of the commonly used comparison operators that are available.

Table 1-1. *Operators*

Operator	Description
!=	Tests two expressions not being equal to each other.
!>	Tests that the left condition is not greater than the expression to the right.
!<	Tests that the right condition is not less than the expression to the right.
<	Tests the left condition as less than the right condition.
<=	Tests the left condition as less than or equal to the right condition.
<>	Tests two expressions not being equal to each other.
=	Tests equality between two expressions.
>	Tests the left condition being greater than the expression to the right.
>=	Tests the left condition being greater than or equal to the expression to the right.

Don't think of a WHERE clause as going out and retrieving rows that match the conditions. Think of it as a fish net or a sieve. All the possible rows are dropped into the net. Unwanted rows fall through. When a query is done executing, the rows remaining in the net are those that match the predicates you listed. Database engines will optimize execution, but the fish-net metaphor is a useful one when initially crafting a query.

You may combine multiple search conditions by utilizing the AND and OR logical operators. The AND logical operator joins two or more search conditions and returns rows only when each of the search conditions is TRUE. The OR logical operator joins two or more search conditions and returns rows when any one of the conditions are true. The second solution example shows the following AND operation. Both search conditions must be true for a row to be returned in the result set. Thus, only the row for Ms. Antrim is returned.

```
WHERE Title = 'Ms.' AND LastName = 'Antrim'
```

Use the OR operator to specify alternate choices. Use parentheses to clarify the order of operations. The following example shows an OR expression involving two LastName values. It is the result from that OR expression that is passed to the AND expression.

```
WHERE Title = 'Ms.' AND
    (LastName = 'Antrim' OR LastName = 'Galvin')
```

UNKNOWN values can make their appearance when NULL data is accessed in the search condition. A NULL value doesn't mean that the value is blank or zero—only that the value is unknown. Recipe 1-15 later in this chapter shows how to identify rows either having or not having NULL values.

1-7. Listing the Available Tables

Problem

You want to programmatically list the names of available tables in a schema. You can see the tables from Management Studio, but you want them from T-SQL as well.

Solution

One approach is to query the information schema views. This is an ISO standard approach. For example, execute the following query to see a list of all the tables and views in the HumanResources schema:

```
SELECT table_name, table_type
FROM information_schema.tables
WHERE table_schema = 'HumanResources';
```

TABLE_NAME	TABLE_TYPE
Shift	BASE TABLE
Department	BASE TABLE
...	
vJobCandidate	VIEW
vJobCandidateEmployment	VIEW

You may also choose to forget about following ISO standard, and query the system catalog instead. The relevant views are sys.tables for tables and sys.views for views. For example

```
SELECT name
FROM sys.tables
WHERE SCHEMA_NAME(schema_id)='HumanResources';
```

name
Shift
Department
Employee
...

How It Works

The information schema views are designed to be friendly toward interactive querying. They also have the advantage of conforming to the ISO standard. There are a number of such views. The one queried in the example is information_schema.tables. It returns information about tables, and also about views.

There are also system catalog views. These are more detailed than the information schema views, and they can be a bit less friendly to query. For example, the sys.tables view doesn't return a schema name in friendly text form as information_schema.tables does. Instead, you get a schema ID number. That's why the second solution example had to invoke the function SCHEMA_NAME(..) in the WHERE clause, so as to translate the ID into a readable name:

```
where schema_name(schema_id)='HumanResources'
```

The information schema treats a view as a subtype of a table. The term *base table* refers to what in SQL Server is a table, and a *view* is a stored query referencing the base tables, and possibly other views. SQL Server's system catalog returns information about views and tables through separate catalog views. The first solution example returns table and view names, whereas the second returns only table names.

Why might you wish for programmatic access to metadata? One use of such access is to write SQL statements that create groups of news statements to be executed. Say, for example, that you wish to drop all the tables in the human resources schema. You can choose to create all the DROP statements through a query:

```
SELECT 'DROP ' + table_schema + '.' + table_name + ';'
FROM information_schema.tables
WHERE table_schema = 'HumanResources'
  AND table_type = 'BASE TABLE';
```

```
--------------------------------
DROP HumanResources.Shift;
DROP HumanResources.Department;
...
```

Then you can copy the results, paste them in as the next query batch, and hit execute, and your tables are gone.

Using PowerShell might sometimes be a better way to get the job when needing to operate on groups of objects all in one go, in a set-oriented manner. However, the quick-and-dirty technique of using SQL to write SQL can be handy too.

1-8. Naming the Output Columns

Problem

You don't like the column names returned by a query. You wish to change the names for clarity in reporting, or to be compatible with an already-written program that is consuming the results from the query.

Solution

Designate what are called *column aliases*. Use the AS clause for that purpose. For example:

```
SELECT BusinessEntityID AS "Employee ID",
   VacationHours AS "Vacation",
   SickLeaveHours AS "Sick Time"
FROM HumanResources.Employee;
```

```
Employee ID Vacation Sick Time
----------- -------- ---------
          1       99        69
          2        1        20
          3        2        21
```

How It Works

Each column in a result set is given a name. The name appears in the column heading when you execute a query ad-hoc using Management Studio. The name is also the name by which any program code must reference the column when consuming the results from a query. You can specify any name you like for a column via the AS clause. Such a name is termed a *column alias*.

There are some syntax alternatives to be aware of, which you might encounter when looking over existing code written by others. The following lines show these variations, and all have the same effect:

```
BusinessEntityID AS "Employee ID"
BusinessEntityID "Employee ID"
BusinessEntityID AS [Employee ID]
```

The first two lines show ISO standard syntax. The third is syntax specific to SQL Server. The first line shows the use of the AS clause, which represents the latest thinking in the standard, and thus we recommend that approach.

■ **Note** You can omit the enclosing quotes around a column alias when there are no spaces involved.

1-9. Providing Shorthand Names for Tables

Problem

You are writing a complicated WHERE clause, or a SELECT list, mixing column names from many tables, and it is becoming tedious to properly qualify each column name with its associated table and schema name.

Solution

Specify a table alias for each table in your query. Use the AS keyword to do that. For example:

```
SELECT E.BusinessEntityID AS "Employee ID",
    E.VacationHours AS "Vacation",
    E.SickLeaveHours AS "Sick Time"
FROM HumanResources.Employee AS E
WHERE E.VacationHours > 40;
```

How It Works

Specify table aliases using the AS clause. Place an AS clause immediately following each table name in the query's FROM clause. The solution example provides the alias, or alternate name, E for the table HumanResources.Employee. As far as the rest of the query is concerned, the table is now named E. By extension, you must now yourself refer to the table only as E.

Table aliases make it easy to qualify column names in a query. It is much easier to type

```
E.BusinessEntityID
```

than it is to type

```
HumanResources.Employee.BusinessEntityID
```

In real-life use, and especially in large queries, it is helpful to make your aliases more readable than the ones in our example. For example, specify Emp instead of E as the alias for the Employee table. It is easier to remember later what Emp means than to struggle over the single letter E.

Table aliases work much like column aliases, so be sure to read Recipe 1-8 as well. The syntax alternatives described in that recipe also apply when designating table aliases.

1-10. Computing New Columns from Existing Data

Problem

You are querying a table that lacks the precise bit of information you need. However, you are able to write an expression to generate the result that you are after. For example, you want to report on total time off available to employees. Your database design divides time off into separate buckets for vacation time and sick time. You however, wish to report a single value.

Solution

Write an expression involving the existing columns in the table, and then place the expression into your SELECT list. Place it there as you would any other column. Provide a column alias by which the program executing the query can reference the computed column. For example:

```
SELECT BusinessEntityID AS "EmployeeID",
    VacationHours + SickLeaveHours AS "AvailableTimeOff"
FROM HumanResources.Employee;
```

EmployeeID	AvailableTimeOff
1	168
2	21
3	23
...	

How It Works

You can specify any expression you like in the SELECT list, and the value of that expression will be returned as a column in the query results. Most of the time you'll be referring to at least one table column from such an expression, but there are actually useful expressions that can be written that stand alone, that do not take other columns as input.

Recipe 1-8 introduces column aliases. It's especially important to provide them for computed columns. That's because if you don't provide an alias for a computed column, one is not created for you, and thus there is no name by which to refer to the column, nor is there a name to place in the output heading when executing the query ad-hoc from Management Studio.

1-11. Negating a Search Condition

Problem

You are finding it easier to describe those rows that you do *not* want rather than those that you *do* want.

Solution

Describe the rows that you do not want. Then use the NOT operator to essentially reverse the description so that you get those rows that you do want. The NOT logical operator negates the expression that follows it. For example, you can retrieve all employees having a title of anything but "Ms." by executing the following query:

```
SELECT  Title, FirstName, LastName
FROM  Person.Person
WHERE NOT Title = 'Ms.';
```

Title	FirstName	LastName
Mr.	Jossef	Goldberg
Mr.	Hung-Fu	Ting
...		
Sr.	Humberto	Acevedo
Sra.	Pilar	Ackerman
...		

How It Works

NOT specifies the reverse of a search condition, in this case specifying that only rows that don't have the Title equal to "Ms." be returned. You can apply the NOT operator to individual expressions in a WHERE clause. You can also apply it to a group of expressions. For example:

```
WHERE NOT (Title = 'Ms.' OR Title = 'Mr.')
```

Think in terms of finding all the rows having "Ms." or "Mr." and then returning everything else except those rows. The parentheses force evaluation of the OR condition first. Then all rows not meeting that condition are returned by the query.

1-12. Keeping the WHERE Clause Unambiguous

Problem

You are writing several expressions in a WHERE clause that are linked together using AND and OR, and sometimes NOT. You worry that future maintainers of your query will misconstrue your intentions.

Solution

Enclose expressions in parentheses to make clear your intent. For example:

```
SELECT Title, FirstName, LastName
FROM   Person.Person
WHERE  Title = 'Ms.' AND
       (FirstName = 'Catherine' OR
       LastName = 'Adams');
```

How It Works

You can write multiple operators (AND, OR, NOT) in a single WHERE clause, but it is important to make your intentions clear by properly embedding your ANDs and ORs in parentheses. The NOT operator takes precedence (is evaluated first) over AND. The AND operator takes precedence over the OR operator. Using both AND and OR operators in the same WHERE clause without parentheses can return unexpected results.

Consider the solution query and pretend for a moment that there are no parentheses. Is the intention to return results for all rows with a Title of "Ms.," and of those rows, only include those with a FirstName of Catherine or a LastName of Adams? Or did the query author wish to search for all people titled "Ms." with a FirstName of Catherine, as well as anyone with a LastName of Adams? The parentheses make the author's intentions crystal clear.

It is good practice to use parentheses to clarify exactly what rows should be returned. Even if you are fully conversant with the rules of operator precedence, those who come after you may not be. Make judicious use of parentheses to remove all doubt as to your intentions.

1-13. Testing for Existence

Problem

You want to know whether something is true, but you don't really care to see the data that proves it. For example, you want to know the answer to the following business question: "Are there really employees having more than 80 hours of sick time?"

Solution

One solution is to execute a query to return one row in the event that what you care about is true, and to return no rows otherwise. The following example returns the value 1 in the event of any employee having more than 80 hours of sick time:

```
SELECT TOP(1) 1
FROM HumanResources.Employee
WHERE SickLeaveHours > 80;
```

```
- - - - - - - - - -

(0 row(s) affected)
```

Another approach is to write an EXISTS predicate. For example, and testing for 40 hours this time:

```
SELECT 1
WHERE  EXISTS (
    SELECT *
    FROM HumanResources.Employee
    WHERE SickLeaveHours > 40
);
```

```
- - - - - - - - - -
         1

(1 row(s) affected)
```

How It Works

The first solution makes use of T-SQL's TOP(n) syntax to end the query when the first row is found matching the condition. No rows were found in the example. You will find one though, if you lower the hour threshold to 40. There are employees having more than 40 hours of sick time, but none that have more than 80 hours.

The second solution achieves the same result, but through an EXISTS predicate. The outer query returns the value 1 as a single row and column to indicate that rows exist for the query listed in the EXISTS predicate. Otherwise, the outer query returns no row at all.

Avoid an ORDER BY clause when testing for existence like this recipe shows. You want query execution to stop as soon as possible. You can solve a different type of problem by using ORDER BY in conjunction with TOP.

1-14. Specifying a Range of Values

Problem

You wish to specify a range of values as a search condition. For example, you are querying a table having a date column. You wish to return rows having dates only in a specified range of interest.

Solution

Write a predicate involving the BETWEEN operator. That operator allows you to specify a range of values, in this case date values. For example, to find sales orders placed between the dates 7/23/2005 and 7/24/2005:

```
SELECT SalesOrderID, ShipDate
FROM Sales.SalesOrderHeader
WHERE ShipDate BETWEEN '2005-07-23 00:00:00.0' AND '2005-07-24 23:59:59.0';
```

```
SalesOrderID ShipDate
------------ -----------------------
       43758 2005-07-23 00:00:00.000
       43759 2005-07-23 00:00:00.000
       43760 2005-07-23 00:00:00.000
       ...
```

How It Works

This recipe demonstrates the BETWEEN operator, which tests whether a column's value falls between two values that you specify. The value range is inclusive of the two endpoints.

Notice that we designated the specific time in hours, minutes, and seconds as well. The time-of-day defaults to 00:00:00, which is midnight at the start of a date. In this example, we wanted to include all of 7/24/2005. Thus, we specified the last possible second of that day.

However, there is an issue you must be aware of when using BETWEEN with date-time values: What if the shipment date is 2005-07-23 23:59:59.456? A safer approach is to test for dates being greater than or equal to the starting point, and less than the earliest time just after the end point. For example:

```
SELECT SalesOrderID, ShipDate
FROM Sales.SalesOrderHeader
WHERE ShipDate >= '2005-07-23' AND ShipDate < '2005-07-25';
```

This solution is safer, because it's trivial to specify the earliest possible time on the 25th, and then to test for ShipDate being less than that. It is not so easy to know the maximum possible fractional seconds value to specify for the BETWEEN approach. Should those be 59.997? 59.9999? 59.999999? How many nines? Don't waste time trying to figure that out. Just take the safer approach unless you are certain that your data never includes fractional seconds.

■ **Caution** You encounter the same issue with decimal digits when using BETWEEN with decimal and floating-point values as with date-time values.

1-15. Checking for Null Values

Problem

Some of the values in a column might be NULL. You wish to identify rows having or not having NULL values.

Solution

Make use of the IS NULL and IS NOT NULL tests to identify rows having or not having NULL values in a given column. For example, the following query returns any rows for which the value of the product's weight is unknown:

```
SELECT  ProductID, Name, Weight
FROM    Production.Product
WHERE   Weight IS NULL;
```

```
ProductID Name                    Weight
----------- --------------------  ------
        1 Adjustable Race          NULL
        2 Bearing Ball             NULL
        3 BB Ball Bearing          NULL
        4 Headset Ball Bearings    NULL
...
```

How It Works

NULL values cannot be identified using operators such as = and <> that are designed to compare two values and return a TRUE or FALSE result. NULL actually indicates the *absence* of a value. For that reason, neither of the following predicates can be used to detect a NULL value:

Weight = NULL yields the value UNKNOWN, which is neither TRUE nor FALSE

Weight <> NULL also yields UNKNOWN

IS NULL, however, is specifically designed to return TRUE when a value is NULL. Likewise, the expression IS NOT NULL returns TRUE when a value is not NULL. Predicates involving IS NULL and IS NOT NULL enable you to filter for rows having or not having NULL values in one or more columns.

■ **Caution** Improper handling of nulls is one of the most prevalent sources of query mistakes. See Chapter 3 for guidance and techniques that can help you avoid trouble and get the results you want.

1-16. Writing an IN-List

Problem

You are searching for matches to a specific list of values. You could write a string of predicates joined by OR operators, but you prefer a more easily readable and maintainable solution.

Solution

Create a predicate involving the IN operator, which allows you to specify an arbitrary list of values. For example, the IN operator in the following query tests the equality of the Color column to a list of expressions:

```
SELECT  ProductID, Name, Color
FROM Production.Product
WHERE Color IN ('Silver', 'Black', 'Red');
```

```
ProductID Name              Color
----------- ----------------- ---------
        317 LL Crankarm       Black
        318 ML Crankarm       Black
        319 HL Crankarm       Black
        320 Chainring Bolts   Silver
        321 Chainring Nut     Silver
...
```

How It Works

Use the IN operator any time you have a specific list of values. You can think of IN as shorthand for multiple OR expressions. For example, the following two WHERE clauses are semantically equivalent:

```
WHERE Color IN ('Silver', 'Black', 'Red')
```

```
WHERE Color = 'Silver' OR Color = 'Black' OR Color = 'Red'
```

You can see that an IN-list becomes less cumbersome than a string of OR'd-together expressions. This is especially true as the number of values grows. You can also write NOT IN to find rows having values other than those in your list.

■ **Caution** Take care when writing NOT IN. If just one value in the in-list is null, your NOT IN expression will always return UNKNOWN, and no rows will be selected. You won't have that problem when writing an in-list of literal values, such as in the example, but the problem can occur easily when your in-list is made up of variables or table columns.

1-17. Performing Wildcard Searches

Problem

You don't have a specific value or list of values to find. What you do have is a general pattern, and you want to find all values that match that pattern.

Solution

Make use of the LIKE predicate, which provides a set of basic pattern-matching capabilities. Create a string using so-called wildcards to serve as a search expression. Table 1-2 shows the wildcards available in SQL Server 2014.

Table 1-2. *Wildcards for the LIKE predicate*

Wildcard	Usage
%	The percent sign. Represents a string of zero or more characters
_	The underscore. Represents a single character
[...]	A list of characters enclosed within square brackets. Represents a single character from among any in the list.
[^...]	A list of characters enclosed within square brackets and preceded by a caret. Represents a single character from among any not in the list.

The following example demonstrates using the LIKE operation with the % wildcard, searching for any product with a name beginning with the letter B:

```
SELECT ProductID, Name
FROM Production.Product
WHERE Name LIKE 'B%';
```

This query returns the following results:

```
ProductID Name
----------- ----------------------
          3 BB Ball Bearing
          2 Bearing Ball
        877 Bike Wash - Dissolver
        316 Blade
```

How It Works

Wildcards allow you to search for patterns in character-based columns. In the example from this recipe, the % sign is used to represent a string of zero or more characters:

```
WHERE Name LIKE 'B%'
```

If searching for a literal that would otherwise be interpreted by SQL Server as a wildcard, you can use the ESCAPE clause. For example, you can search for a literal percentage sign in the Name column:

```
WHERE Name LIKE '%/%%' ESCAPE '/'
```

A slash embedded in single quotes is put after the ESCAPE clause in this example. This designates the slash symbol as the escape character for the associated expression string. Any wildcard preceded by a slash is then treated as just a regular character.

■ **Tip**   If you ever find yourself making extensive use of LIKE, especially in finding words or phrases within large text columns, be sure to become familiar with SQL Server's full-text search feature. *Pro Full-Text Search in SQL Server 2008* by Hilary Cotter and Michael Coles is a good resource on that feature and its use.

1-18. Sorting Your Results

Problem

You are executing a query, and you wish the results to come back in a specific order.

Solution

Write an ORDER BY clause into your query. Specify the columns on which to sort. Place the clause at the very end of your query. For example:

```
SELECT p.Name, h.EndDate, h.ListPrice
FROM   Production.Product p
INNER JOIN Production.ProductListPriceHistory h ON
         p.ProductID = h.ProductID
ORDER BY p.Name, h.EndDate;
```

This query returns results as follows:

Name	EndDate	ListPrice
All-Purpose Bike Stand	NULL	159.00
AWC Logo Cap	NULL	8.99
AWC Logo Cap	2006-06-30 00:00:00.000	8.6442
AWC Logo Cap	2007-06-30 00:00:00.000	8.6442
Bike Wash - Dissolver	NULL	7.95
Cable Lock	2007-06-30 00:00:00.000	25.00
...		

Notice the results are first sorted by Name. Within Name, they are sorted by EndDate.

How It Works

Although queries sometimes appear to return data properly without an ORDER BY clause, you should never depend upon any ordering that is accidental. You must write an ORDER BY into your query if the order of the result set is critical. You can designate one or more columns in your ORDER BY clause, so long as the columns do not exceed 8,060 bytes in total.

We can't stress enough the importance of ORDER BY when order matters. Grouping operations and indexing sometimes make it seem that ORDER BY is superfluous. It isn't. Trust us: there are enough corner cases that sooner or later you'll be caught out. If the sort order matters, then say so explicitly in your query by writing an ORDER BY clause.

■ **Note**   The solution query implements what is known as a *join* between two tables. There's a lot to be said about joins, and you'll learn more about them in Chapter 4.

The default sort order is an ascending sort. You can specify ascending or descending explicitly by writing either ASC and DESC, as follows:

```
ORDER BY p.Name ASC, h.EndDate DESC
```

NULL values are considered lower than everything else. They sort to the top in an ascending sort. They sort to the bottom in a descending sort.

You need not return a column in order to sort by it. For example, you can group results by color to help break any ties:

```
ORDER BY p.Name, h.EndDate, p.Color
```

It doesn't matter that Color is not returned by the query. SQL Server can sort on the column without returning it.

1-19. Specifying the Case-Sensitivity of a Sort

Problem

You want to specify whether a sort is performed in a binary manner, or whether it is case-sensitive or case-insensitive.

Solution

Add a COLLATE clause to each column specification in your ORDER BY clause that you are concerned about. Following is a repeat of the query from Recipe 1-18, but this time a binary sort is specified for the p.Name column.

```
SELECT p.Name, h.EndDate, h.ListPrice
FROM Production.Product p
INNER JOIN Production.ProductListPriceHistory h ON
      p.ProductID = h.ProductID
ORDER BY p.Name COLLATE Latin1_General_BIN ASC,
         h.EndDate DESC;
```

We've tampered with one of the product names in our copy of the Adventure Works database in order to demonstrate the effect of this query and its collation. Look at where frame size 42 occurs in the following output.

```
...
HL Headset                      2007-06-30 00:00:00.000        124.73
HL MOUNTAIN FRAME - BLACK, 42   2007-06-30 00:00:00.000       1226.9091
HL MOUNTAIN FRAME - BLACK, 42   2006-06-30 00:00:00.000       1191.1739
HL MOUNTAIN FRAME - BLACK, 42   NULL                          1349.60
HL Mountain Frame - Black, 38   2007-06-30 00:00:00.000       1226.9091
HL Mountain Frame - Black, 38   2006-06-30 00:00:00.000       1191.1739
HL Mountain Frame - Black, 38   NULL                          1349.60
HL Mountain Frame - Black, 44   2006-06-30 00:00:00.000       1349.60
...
```

The default collation in the example database produces a different result:

```
...
HL Headset                      2007-06-30 00:00:00.000                  124.73
HL Mountain Frame - Black, 38   2007-06-30 00:00:00.000               1226.9091
HL Mountain Frame - Black, 38   2006-06-30 00:00:00.000               1191.1739
HL Mountain Frame - Black, 38   NULL                                    1349.60
HL MOUNTAIN FRAME - BLACK, 42   2007-06-30 00:00:00.000               1226.9091
HL MOUNTAIN FRAME - BLACK, 42   2006-06-30 00:00:00.000               1191.1739
HL MOUNTAIN FRAME - BLACK, 42   NULL                                    1349.60
HL Mountain Frame - Black, 44   2006-06-30 00:00:00.000                 1349.60
...
```

How It Works

You have the option to specify a non-default collation for each column listed in an ORDER BY clause. You can of course explicitly specify the default collation too, but typically you would add a COLLATE clause because you want something other than the default.

SQL Server supports thousands of collations, each providing a different set of sorting rules. You can obtain a complete list by executing the following query:

```
SELECT Name, Description
FROM fn_helpcollations();
```

The list is long. It helps to narrow your search. You can get an idea as to the languages that are supported by executing the following query:

```
SELECT DISTINCT SUBSTRING(Name, 1, CHARINDEX('_', Name)-1)
FROM fn_helpcollations();
```

Then you can list the collations for just one language. For example, here is how to list collations for Ukrainian:

```
SELECT Name, Description
FROM fn_helpcollations()
WHERE Name LIKE 'Ukrainian%';
```

Each language's collation set generally provides the ability for you to choose whether any of the following matter when sorting rows: case, accents, kanatype, and character width. Kanatype matters for Japanese text. Character width comes into play in some situations in which Unicode provides the same character in, for example, single-byte or double-byte form.

A binary collation such as the Latin1_General_BIN used in the example is what you need in order to return a case-sensitive sort in the way that many programmers think of such as sort as being done. There is also a Latin1_General_CS_AS collation that is described as being case-sensitive and accent-sensitive. And that is true! But the sorting is done according to Unicode rules, and the results sometimes appear to match those from the insensitive Latin1_General_CI_AI.

Unicode sorting rules view uppercase as being greater than lowercase. Thus, "BLUE" sorts after "blue" when a case-sensitive sort is being performed. However "BLUE" will sort prior to "red" in either case, because Unicode rules only look at the case when it is needed in order to break a tie. If your column contains all distinct values such as "BLUE" and "Red," then they will sort the same no matter whether you use Latin1_General_CS_AS or Latin1_General_CI_AI, and that can be disconcerting at first. It is when you have values such as "reD," "Red," and "RED" that you will see a difference in results between case-sensitive and case-insensitive sorts done under Unicode sorting rules.

■ **Note** Visit http://www.unicode.org/reports/tr10/ to read about Unicode's collation algorithm in extreme detail.

1-20. Sorting Nulls High or Low

Problem

You are a refugee from Oracle Database, and you miss the ability to specify NULLS FIRST and NULLS LAST when writing ORDER BY clauses.

Solution

Add a semaphore expression to your ORDER BY clause for the column in question. Then specify ASC or DSC to make the nulls sort first or last as desired. The following example adds such an expression for the Weight column in order to sort that column with nulls last.

```
SELECT  ProductID, Name, Weight
FROM    Production.Product
ORDER BY ISNULL(Weight, 1) DESC, Weight;
```

```
 ProductID Name                   Weight
----------- ---------------------- -------
       826 LL Road Rear Wheel     1050.00
       827 ML Road Rear Wheel     1000.00
       818 LL Road Front Wheel     900.00
...
       504 Cup-Shaped Race           NULL
       505 Cone-Shaped Race          NULL
       506 Reflector                 NULL

(504 row(s) affected)
```

How It Works

SQL Server doesn't implement syntax for you to use in specifying whether nulls sort first or last. The solution works around that omission by evaluating the following expression during the sort:

```
ISNULL(Weight, 1)
```

A null weight yields a result of 1. Otherwise, the expression is itself null. Those are the only two possible results: 1 or null. It's a simple matter to then append ASC or DESC to specify whether the rows returning 1 sort last or first.

If you find it confusing to evaluate ISNULL in your head, then you can get the same effect through the IIF function:

```
SELECT  ProductID, Name, Weight
FROM    Production.Product
ORDER BY IIF(Weight IS NULL, 1, 0), Weight;
```

The result from IIF in this example is 1 for null and zero otherwise. The normal sort order is ascending. Rows causing the expression to evaluate to zero have non-null weights and are sorted first. The null weights trigger IIF to return a 1, and they sort last.

1-21. Forcing Unusual Sort Orders

Problem

You wish to force a sort order not directly supported by the data. For example, you wish to retrieve only the colored products, and you further wish to force the color red to sort first.

Solution

Write an expression to translate values in the data to values that will give the sort order you are after. Then order your query results by that expression. Following is one approach to the problem of retrieving colored parts and listing the red ones first:

```
SELECT p.ProductID, p.Name, p.Color
FROM Production.Product AS p
WHERE p.Color IS NOT NULL
ORDER BY CASE p.Color
WHEN 'Red' THEN NULL ELSE p.COLOR END;
```

ProductID	Name	Color
706	HL Road Frame - Red, 58	Red
707	Sport-100 Helmet, Red	Red
725	LL Road Frame - Red, 44	Red
...		
790	Road-250 Red, 48	Red
791	Road-250 Red, 52	Red
792	Road-250 Red, 58	Red
793	Road-250 Black, 44	Black
794	Road-250 Black, 48	Black
795	Road-250 Black, 52	Black

How It Works

The solution takes advantage of the fact that SQL Server sorts nulls first. The CASE expression returns NULL for red-colored items, thus forcing those first. Other colors are returned unchanged. The result is all the red items appear first in the list, and then red is followed by other colors in their natural sort order.

You don't have to rely upon nulls sorting first. You can translate "Red" to any value you like, such as, for example, to a single space character. Then that space character would sort before all the spelled-out color names.

1-22. Paging Through a Result Set

Problem

You wish to present an ordered result set to an application user N rows at a time.

Solution

Make use of the query-paging feature that was introduced in SQL Server 2012. Do this by adding OFFSET and FETCH clauses to your query's ORDER BY clause. For example, the following query uses OFFSET and FETCH to retrieve the first ten rows of results:

```
SELECT ProductID, Name
FROM Production.Product
ORDER BY Name
OFFSET O ROWS FETCH NEXT 10 ROWS ONLY;
```

Results from this query will be the first ten rows, as ordered by product name:

```
ProductID Name
----------- ------------------------
          1 Adjustable Race
        879 All-Purpose Bike Stand
        712 AWC Logo Cap
          3 BB Ball Bearing
          2 Bearing Ball
        877 Bike Wash - Dissolver
        316 Blade
        843 Cable Lock
        952 Chain
        324 Chain Stays
```

Changing the offset from 0 to 8 will fetch another ten rows. The offset will skip the first eight rows. There will be a two-row overlap with the preceding result set. Here is the query:

```
SELECT ProductID, Name
FROM Production.Product
ORDER BY Name
OFFSET 8 ROWS FETCH NEXT 10 ROWS ONLY;
```

And here are the results:

```
ProductID Name
----------- --------------------
        952 Chain
        324 Chain Stays
        322 Chainring
        320 Chainring Bolts
        321 Chainring Nut
        866 Classic Vest, L
        865 Classic Vest, M
        864 Classic Vest, S
        505 Cone-Shaped Race
        323 Crown Race
```

Continue modifying the offset each time, paging through the result until the user is finished.

How It Works

OFFSET and FETCH turn a SELECT statement into a query fetching a specific window of rows from those that are possible. Use OFFSET to specify how many rows to skip from the beginning of the possible result set. Use FETCH to set the number of rows to return. You can change either value as you wish from one execution to the next.

Be sure to specify a deterministic set of sort columns in your ORDER BY clause. Each SELECT to get the next page of results is a separate query and a separate sort operation. Make sure that your data sorts the same way each time. Do not leave ambiguity.

■ **Note** The word *deterministic* means that the same inputs always give the same outputs. Specify your sort such that the same set of input rows will always yield the same ordering in the query output.

Each execution of a paging query is a separate execution from the others. Consider executing sequences of paging queries from within a transaction providing snapshot or serializable isolation. Chapter 12 discusses such transactions in detail. However, you can begin and end such a transaction as follows:

```
SET TRANSACTION ISOLATION LEVEL SNAPSHOT;
BEGIN TRANSACTION;
    /* Queries go here */
COMMIT;
/* Return to default */
SET TRANSACTION ISOLATION LEVEL READ COMMITTED;
```

Anomalies are possible without isolation. For example:

- You might see a row twice. In the solution example, if another user inserted eight new rows with names sorting earlier than "Adjustable Race," then the second query results would be the same as the first.

- You might miss rows. If another user quickly deleted the first eight rows, then the second solution query would miss everything from "Chainring" to "Crown Race."

You may decide to risk the default isolation level. If your target table is read-only, or if it is updated in batch-mode only at night, then you might be justified in leaving the isolation level at its default because the risk of change during the day is low to non-existent. Possibly you might choose not to worry about the issue at all. However, make sure that whatever you do is the result of thinking things through and making a conscious choice.

■ **Note** It may seem rash for us to even hint at not allowing the possibility of inconsistent results. We advocate making careful and conscious decisions. Some applications—Facebook is a well-known example—trade away some consistency in favor of performance. (We routinely see minor inconsistencies on our Facebook walls). We are not saying you should do the same. We simply acknowledge the possibility of such a choice.

1-23. Sampling a Subset of Rows

Problem

You are getting familiar with a table, and you want to review a representative sampling of the data.

Solution

Query the table and limit the results using the TABLESAMPLE clause. You can specify an approximate percentage of rows to retrieve:

```
SELECT *
FROM Purchasing.PurchaseOrderHeader
TABLESAMPLE (5 PERCENT);
```

Or you can specify an approximate quantity of rows:

```
SELECT *
FROM Purchasing.PurchaseOrderHeader
TABLESAMPLE (200 ROWS);
```

How It Works

The TABLESAMPLE clause is available from SQL Server 2008 R2 forward. Use it to get an idea of what the data looks like in a table without having to page through all of the table's data.

The values specified for rows and percentages should be thought of as approximate values. If you specify a low enough value for rows, such as 20 rows in the example queries, you might not get any data back at all. That's because at some point during processing, the number or percentage of rows you specify is translated into some integer number of data pages relative to all the pages that are allocated to the table. That number of pages is randomly chosen from among all the pages, and all rows that happen to be on the selected pages are returned. The actual distribution of rows across the pages can affect the results, as can the rounding to an integer number of pages.

CHAPTER 2

Elementary Programming

by Jonathan Gennick

In this chapter, you'll find recipes showing several of the basic programming constructs available in T-SQL. The chapter is not a complete tutorial for the language, however. You'll need to read other books for that. A good tutorial, if you need one that begins with first principles, is *Beginning T-SQL* by Kathi Kellenberger and Scott Shaw (Apress, 2014).

2-1. Executing T-SQL from a File

Problem

You want to execute a script of T-SQL commands that you've stored in a file.

Solution

Invoke your script via the `sqlcmd` utility. For example, say that you create a file named `CreateColorTable.sql` having the following T-SQL statements:

```
USE AdventureWorks2014;
GO

/* Drop constraint and table to allow for the script to be rerun at will. */
ALTER TABLE Production.Product
    DROP CONSTRAINT FK_Product_Color;
GO

DROP TABLE Production.ProdColor;
GO

CREATE TABLE Production.ProdColor (
    Color NVARCHAR(15),
    CONSTRAINT PK_ProdColor_Color
        PRIMARY KEY (Color)
);
```

```
INSERT INTO Production.ProdColor (Color)
    SELECT DISTINCT Color
    FROM Production.Product
    WHERE Color IS NOT NULL;
GO

ALTER TABLE Production.Product ADD
    CONSTRAINT FK_Product_Color
    FOREIGN KEY (Color)
    REFERENCES Production.ProdColor;
```

You can execute this file of T-SQL statements by invoking `sqlcmd` as follows. Note that the invocation is done over two lines. The caret character (^) indicates to the command interpreter that the second line is a continuation of the first. If you enter the command as one long line that wraps, then omit the caret.

```
sqlcmd -e -S JONATHAN-T410\JG01 -i \a\CreateColorTable.sql ^
    -o \a\CreateColorTableOutput.txt
```

The script will execute. You'll find the output in the `.txt` file.

How It Works

The utility `sqlcmd` is a console utility for use in executing T-SQL statements from the Windows command prompt. It's invoked in the example with the following parameters:

-e	Echo T-SQL statements to the output file as they are executed.
-S	Connect to a named instance (JG01) on a server (JONATHAN-T410).
-i	Read T-SQL statements from the specified file.
-o	Write any output from executing the statements to the named file.

The statements in the example script are divided by the GO command into what are termed batches. Each GO command terminates a batch. The use of GO commands is useful for allowing script execution to continue after a statement fails.

An error in executing a statement typically terminates execution of the batch containing that statement. If the entire script is a single batch, then an error on any statement likely terminates execution of the script. Otherwise, only the current batch terminates, and the next batch is executed. The GO commands in the example make it possible for the script to continue execution even when the objects to be dropped at the beginning of the script do not exist.

■ **Note** GO is a command to the `sqlcmd` utility, and not a T-SQL statement. It is a command that has meaning for the `sqlcmd` utility, and also for SQL Server Management Studio. It is not a statement recognized by the database engine.

2-2. Retrieving Values into Variables

Problem

You want to retrieve a value from the database to put into a variable for use in later T-SQL code.

Solution

Declare variables to hold whatever values you need. Issue a query that returns zero or one rows. Specify the primary key, or a unique key, of the target row in your WHERE clause. Assign the column values to the variables, as shown in the following example:

```
DECLARE @AddressLine1 NVARCHAR(60);
DECLARE @AddressLine2 NVARCHAR(60);
SELECT @AddressLine1 = AddressLine1, @AddressLine2 = AddressLine2
FROM Person.Address
WHERE AddressID = 66;
SELECT @AddressLine1 AS Address1, @AddressLine2 AS Address2;
```

The results are as follows:

```
Address1           Address2
-----------------  --------
4775 Kentucky Dr.  Unit E
```

How It Works

The solution begins by declaring two variables. Each is prefixed by the @ symbol and followed by the defining data type. You may specify any data type that is valid for a table column.

The solution query next retrieves the two address lines for address #66. Because AddressID is the table's primary key, there can be only one row with ID #66. A query that can return at most one row, such as that in the example, is sometimes termed a *singleton select*.

■ **Caution**   Make sure to write queries that can return at most one row. One way to be sure is to specify either a primary key or a unique key in the WHERE clause.

An integral element is the following pattern in the SELECT list for assigning values returned by the query to variables that you declare:

```
@VariableName = ColumnName
```

What if your query returns no rows? In that case, your target variables will be left unchanged. For example, execute the following query block:

```
DECLARE @AddressLine1 NVARCHAR(60) = 'Alger County Sheriff'
DECLARE @AddressLine2 NVARCHAR(60) = '101 E. Varnum'
SELECT @AddressLine1 = AddressLine1, @AddressLine2 = AddressLine2
FROM Person.Address
WHERE AddressID = 49862;
SELECT @AddressLine1, @AddressLine2;
```

You will get the following results:

```
--------------------    -------------
Alger County Sheriff    101 E. Varnum
```

You can test whether values were actually assigned using the global variable @@ROWCOUNT. Here's an example:

```
DECLARE @AddressLine1 NVARCHAR(60) = 'Alger County Sheriff'
DECLARE @AddressLine2 NVARCHAR(60) = '101 E. Varnum'
SELECT @AddressLine1 = AddressLine1, @AddressLine2 = AddressLine2
FROM Person.Address
WHERE AddressID = 49862;
IF @@ROWCOUNT = 1
   SELECT @AddressLine1, @AddressLine2
ELSE
   SELECT 'Either no rows or too many rows found.';
```

If @@ROWCOUNT is 1, then the singleton select is successful. Any other value indicates a problem. A @@ROWCOUNT of zero indicates that no row was found. A @@ROWCOUNT greater than zero indicates that more than one row was found. If multiple rows are found, you will arbitrarily be given the values from the last row in the result set. That is rarely desirable behavior and is the reason for our strong admonition to query by either the primary key or a unique key.

2-3. Writing Expressions

Problem

You want to write an expression involving some variables. For example, you wish to concatenate the two address lines from Recipe 2-2.

Solution

Issue the statement SET to evaluate an expression and assign its result to a variable. The following example uses SET to concatenate the two address lines into one, separating them by a semicolon:

```
DECLARE @AddressLine1 NVARCHAR(60);
DECLARE @AddressLine2 NVARCHAR(60);
DECLARE @OneLine NVARCHAR(120);
```

```
SELECT @AddressLine1 = AddressLine1, @AddressLine2 = AddressLine2
FROM Person.Address
WHERE AddressID = 66;
SET @OneLine = @AddressLine1 + '; ' + @AddressLine2;
SELECT @OneLine;
```

Results are as follows:

```
--------------------------
4775 Kentucky Dr.; Unit E
```

How It Works

You saw in Recipe 1-10 how to write expressions in a query's SELECT list. You can write the same sort of expressions in SET commands and then assign their results to variables that you've previously declared.

The solution example is modified from that given in Recipe 2-2. In this version, a variable named @OneLine is declared. Then a SET statement is executed to concatenate the two address lines and place the resulting single line into the @OneLine variable. A semicolon followed by a space separates what were originally two lines.

Remember to precede variable names with the @ character. Doing so is necessary even in SET statements.

Take care with data conversions. It's a good practice to make your conversions explicit, which you can do using the CAST function. For example:

```
DECLARE @piChar NVARCHAR(4) = '3.14';
DECLARE @piNum DECIMAL (3,2);
SET @piNum = CAST(@piChar AS DECIMAL(3,2));
```

You have access in SET to the full range of operators as supported by SQL Server. You also have access to the built-in functions. Some of the more useful functions are described in Chapter 9 (strings), Chapter 10 (dates), and Chapter 11 (numbers). Examples in these chapters also show common conversions between the various types.

2-4. Deciding Between Two Execution Paths

Problem

You want control over which of two possible code paths is taken.

Solution

Write an IF statement as shown in the following example. Wrap each portion of the statement in a BEGIN...END sequence. The example here demonstrates executing a query conditionally based on the value of a local variable:

```
DECLARE @QuerySelector int = 3;
IF @QuerySelector = 1
BEGIN
```

```
    SELECT TOP 3 ProductID, Name, Color
    FROM Production.Product
    WHERE Color = 'Silver'
    ORDER BY Name;
END
    ELSE
BEGIN
    SELECT TOP 3 ProductID, Name, Color
    FROM Production.Product
    WHERE Color = 'Black'
    ORDER BY Name;
END;
```

This IF...THEN...ELSE execution returns the following results:

```
ProductID Name                     Color
--------- ------------------------ --------
      322 Chainring                Black
      863 Full-Finger Gloves, L    Black
      862 Full-Finger Gloves, M    Black
```

How It Works

An integer local variable is created called @QuerySelector. That variable is set to the value of 3. Then the IF statement begins by evaluating whether @QuerySelector is equal to 1:

```
IF @QuerySelector = 1
```

If @QuerySelector were indeed 1, the first BEGIN...END sequence of statements would be executed:

```
BEGIN
    SELECT TOP 3 ProductID, Name, Color
    FROM Production.Product
    WHERE Color = 'Silver'
    ORDER BY Name
END
```

Because @QuerySelector is not set to 1, the BEGIN...END sequence following the ELSE keyword is executed:

```
BEGIN
    SELECT TOP 3 ProductID, Name, Color
    FROM Production.Product
    WHERE Color = 'Black'
    ORDER BY Name
END;
```

Because the solution example is written with only one statement in each block, you can omit the `BEGIN...END` syntax:

```
DECLARE @QuerySelector int = 3;
IF @QuerySelector = 1
    SELECT TOP 3 ProductID, Name, Color
    FROM Production.Product
    WHERE Color = 'Silver'
    ORDER BY Name;
ELSE
    SELECT TOP 3 ProductID, Name, Color
    FROM Production.Product
    WHERE Color = 'Black'
    ORDER BY Name;
```

`BEGIN` is optional for single statements following `IF`, but for multiple statements that must be executed as a group, `BEGIN` and `END` must be used. As a best practice, it is easier to use `BEGIN...END` for single statements too, so that you don't forget to do so if or when the code is changed at a later time.

2-5. Detecting Whether Rows Exist

Problem

You want to write an `IF...THEN...ELSE` statement, but you want it based on whether a given query returns any rows. For example, you prefer silver-color bicycle parts but will accept a listing of black parts if no silver ones are available.

Solution

Use the `IF EXISTS (...)` syntax. Place a query inside the parentheses. The query in the following example tests for the existence of parts that are silver in color:

```
IF EXISTS (
    SELECT * FROM Production.Product
    WHERE Color = 'Silver')
BEGIN
    SELECT TOP 3 ProductID, Name, Color
    FROM Production.Product
    WHERE Color = 'Silver'
    ORDER BY Name;
END
    ELSE
BEGIN
    SELECT TOP 3 ProductID, Name, Color
    FROM Production.Product
    WHERE Color = 'Black'
    ORDER BY Name;
END;
```

Results from executing this IF...THEN...ELSE statement are as follows:

```
ProductID Name                                             Color
----------- ----------------                               -------
        952 Chain                                          Silver
        320 Chainring Bolts                                Silver
        321 Chainring Nut                                  Silver
```

If you're following along by executing these examples yourself, try substituting "Orange" in place of "Silver" and running the example again.

How It Works

Whatever query you place in the parentheses following IF EXISTS is executed just to the point of the database engine being able to determine whether the query returns any rows. If at least one row is returned, then the first BEGIN...END block is executed. If no rows are returned, then the BEGIN...END block following the ELSE keyword is executed. You can easily reverse the logic by writing IF NOT EXISTS.

Obviously the use of IF EXISTS results in an additional query execution, and the performance of the query inside the parentheses is something to consider. With respect to the solution example, it would be best if there were an index on the Color column of the Production.Product table. It's trivial and fast for the database engine to test such an index to see whether a given color exists in the table. Without an index, it might be necessary for the database engine to read the entire table before it can know the answer.

2-6. Going to a Label in a Transact-SQL Batch

Problem

You want to label a specific point in a T-SQL batch. Then you want the ability to have processing jump directly to that point in the code that you have identified by your label.

Solution

Create a label using the following syntax, which is simply to provide a label name followed by a colon:

```
LabelName:
```

Then write a GOTO statement to branch directly to the point in the code that you have labeled. Here's an example:

```
GOTO LabelName;
```

The following example checks whether a department name is already in use by an existing department. If so, the INSERT is bypassed using GOTO. If not, the INSERT is performed.

```
DECLARE @Name nvarchar(50) = 'Engineering';
DECLARE @GroupName nvarchar(50) = 'Research and Development';
DECLARE @Exists bit = 0;
```

```
IF EXISTS (
    SELECT Name
    FROM HumanResources.Department
    WHERE Name = @Name)
BEGIN
    SET @Exists = 1;
    GOTO SkipInsert;
END;

INSERT INTO HumanResources.Department
    (Name, GroupName)
    VALUES(@Name , @GroupName);

SkipInsert: IF @Exists = 1
BEGIN
    PRINT @Name + ' already exists in HumanResources.Department';
END
ELSE
BEGIN
  PRINT 'Row added';
END;
```

There is, in fact, a department named Engineering defined in the example database. So if you execute this code example, you should get the following result:

```
Engineering already exists in HumanResources.Department
```

How It Works

In this recipe's example, a variable named @Exists is defined to hold a bit value. This value acts as a flag to mark whether a row already exists in the table. For example:

```
DECLARE @Exists bit = 0;
```

Then an IF statement checks for the existence of rows for a given department. If rows exist, the bit variable is set to 1, and the GOTO command is invoked. GOTO references the label name that you want to skip to, in this case called SkipInsert.

The target label appears in the code as follows:

```
SkipInsert: IF @Exists = 1
...
```

It is also possible to, and perfectly reasonable to, write the label on a line by itself:

```
SkipInsert:
IF @Exists = 1
...
```

This recipe introduces the PRINT statement. Use it when you just want to return a message or the value of a variable, and you don't want that message or value to be interpreted by the calling application as being part of a query result set.

As a best practice, when given a choice between using GOTO and other control-of-flow methods, you should choose something other than GOTO. GOTO can decrease the clarity of the code because you'll have to jump around the batch or stored procedure code in order to understand the original intention of the query author.

■ **Tip** Going to a label at the end of a block can be a useful way to exit a block. This is especially the case when you have cleanup code that must be executed. In such a case, put the cleanup code following the exit label and then jump to that label whenever you need to exit the block. This use case is an example of when GOTO can actually add clarity rather than decrease it.

2-7. Trapping and Throwing Errors

Problem

You want better control over errors that occur during execution of a script such as that from Recipe 2-1. Specifically, you want to be able to ignore some errors while terminating the script's execution in response to others.

Solution

Place any statements that might fail inside a TRY...CATCH block. Use the CATCH side of that block to trap any errors. Issue THROW statements as needed to terminate the script's execution.

Following is a variation of the script from Recipe 2-1 that's been designed specifically to fail in order to demonstrate how to trap and throw errors:

```
USE AdventureWorks2014;
GO

BEGIN TRY
    ALTER TABLE Production.Product
        DROP CONSTRAINT FK_Trap_Color;
END TRY
BEGIN CATCH
    PRINT 'Ignore this failure.';
END CATCH;
GO
BEGIN TRY
    DROP TABLE Production.TrapColor;
END TRY
BEGIN CATCH
    PRINT 'Ignore this failure.';
END CATCH;
GO
```

```
CREATE TABLE Production.TrapColor (
    Color NVARCHAR(15),
    CONSTRAINT PK_TrapColor_Color
        PRIMARY KEY (Color)
);
GO

BEGIN TRY
    INSERT INTO Production.TrapColor (Color)
        SELECT DISTINCT Color
        FROM Production.Product;
END TRY
BEGIN CATCH
    PRINT 'Fail!';
    DROP TABLE Production.TrapColor;
    THROW;
END CATCH;
GO

ALTER TABLE Production.Product ADD
    CONSTRAINT FK_Trap_Color
    FOREIGN KEY (Color)
    REFERENCES Production.TrapColor;
```

Place this script into a file named TrapExample.sql. Then write a batch file as follows, naming it TrapExample.bat. Note the use of the -b option to sqlcmd.

```
echo off
sqlcmd -e -S JONATHAN-T410\JG01 -i \a\TrapExample.sql ^
    -b -o \a\TrapExampleOutput.lis
if errorlevel 1 goto script_failure
echo "Script Succeeded?"
exit
:script_failure
echo "Script Failed!"
```

Execute the batch file as follows:

C:\a>TrapExample

And your results should appear as:

```
C:\a>echo off
"Script Failed!"
```

The script has failed, and the failure has been detected at the Windows command prompt.

How It Works

Chapter 22 goes deeply into error handling and how to trap and respond to errors in your scripts. This recipe provides just a rudimentary example to get you started and to help when executing scripts from the command line.

There are two points in the script where errors are likely to occur. First are the two query batches for dropping objects that are created by the script:

```
BEGIN TRY
   ALTER TABLE Production.Product
      DROP CONSTRAINT FK_Trap_Color;
END TRY
BEGIN CATCH
   PRINT 'Ignore this failure.';
END CATCH;
GO
BEGIN TRY
   DROP TABLE Production.TrapColor;
END TRY
BEGIN CATCH
   PRINT 'Ignore this failure.';
END CATCH;
GO
```

The two statements that drop objects are each enclosed on the TRY side of a TRY...CATCH block. They will of course fail, and control goes to the CATCH side of each block when the respective failure occurs. The CATCH side displays a simple message, and nothing more. The errors are trapped and dealt with entirely inside the TRY...CATCH blocks. So far as the database engine is concerned, the blocks have executed successfully. The errors that are caught are not reported further up the call stack.

Next is the point at which the newly created table is to be populated with the existing color values. The INSERT statement to ostensibly populate the target table has purposely been written to fail in this example due to the presence of nulls in the data:

```
BEGIN TRY
   INSERT INTO Production.TrapColor (Color)
      SELECT DISTINCT Color
      FROM Production.Product;
END TRY
BEGIN CATCH
   PRINT 'Fail!';
   DROP TABLE Production.TrapColor;
   THROW;
END CATCH;
GO
```

The INSERT statement fails. Control transfers to the CATCH side of the TRY...CATCH block. A failure message is displayed. The previously created target table is dropped. This is done as a bit of cleanup so that unused tables don't clutter our schema. Next comes a THROW statement. The THROW statement transfers the error up the call stack, causing the database engine to "see" the error. The block has now failed, because it has returned (thrown) an error.

The sqlcmd utility sends each query batch to the database engine for execution. When the preceding batch fails, the engine reports that failure to sqlcmd. Normally, sqlcmd would simply execute the next query batch. In this example, however, we've specified the -b command-line option, and that option causes sqlcmd to immediately terminate after any failure of a query batch.

When sqlcmd terminates, it reports an error level to the command prompt. An error level of zero is universally used in the Windows command-line world to indicate success. However, our example results in failure, so sqlcmd returns an error level of 1. The remainder of the batch file tests the reported error level and responds accordingly.

2-8. Returning from the Current Execution Scope

Problem

You want to discontinue execution of a stored procedure or T-SQL batch, possibly including a numeric return code.

Solution #1: Exit with No Return Value

Write an IF statement to specify the condition under which to discontinue execution. Execute a RETURN in the event the condition is true. For example, the second query in the following code block will not execute because there are no pink bike parts in the Product table:

```
IF NOT EXISTS
   (SELECT ProductID
    FROM Production.Product
    WHERE Color = 'Pink')
BEGIN
   RETURN;
END;

SELECT ProductID
FROM Production.Product
WHERE Color = 'Pink';
```

Solution #2: Exit and Provide a Value

You have the option to provide a status value to the invoking code. First, create a stored procedure along the following lines. Notice the RETURN statements in particular.

```
CREATE PROCEDURE ReportPink AS
IF NOT EXISTS
   (SELECT ProductID
    FROM Production.Product
    WHERE Color = 'Pink')
BEGIN
   --Return the value 100 to indicate no pink products
   RETURN 100;
END;
```

```
SELECT ProductID
FROM Production.Product
WHERE Color = 'Pink';

--Return the value 0 to indicate pink was found
RETURN 0;
```

With this procedure in place, execute the following:

```
DECLARE @ResultStatus int;
EXEC @ResultStatus = ReportPink;
PRINT @ResultStatus;
```

You will get the following result:

100

This is because no pink products exist in the example database. And that's sad, because pink bicycle parts can be stunning when done right.

How It Works

RETURN exits the current Transact-SQL batch, query, or stored procedure immediately. RETURN exits only the code executing in the current scope; if you have called stored procedure B from stored procedure A and if stored procedure B issues a RETURN, stored procedure B stops immediately, but stored procedure A continues as though B had completed successfully.

The solution examples show how RETURN can be invoked with or without a return code. Use whichever approach makes sense for your application. Passing a RETURN code does allow the invoking code to determine why you have returned control, but it is not always necessary to allow for that.

The solution examples also show how it sometimes makes sense to invoke RETURN from an IF statement and other times makes sense to invoke RETURN as a stand-alone statement. Again, use whichever approach best facilitates what you are working to accomplish.

2-9. Writing a Simple CASE Expression

Problem

You have a scalar expression, table column, or variable that can take on a well-defined set of possible values. You want to specify an output value for each possible input value. For example, you want to translate department names into conference room assignments.

Solution

Write a CASE expression associating each value with its own code path. Optionally, include an ELSE clause to provide a code path for any unexpected values.

For example, the following code block uses CASE to assign departments to specific conference rooms. Departments not specifically named are lumped together by the ELSE clause into Room D.

```
SELECT DepartmentID AS DeptID, Name, GroupName,
       CASE GroupName
           WHEN 'Research and Development' THEN 'Room A'
           WHEN 'Sales and Marketing' THEN 'Room B'
           WHEN 'Manufacturing' THEN 'Room C'
       ELSE 'Room D'
       END AS ConfRoom
FROM HumanResources.Department;
```

Results from this query show the different conference room assignments as specified in the CASE expression.

DeptID	Name	GroupName	ConfRoom
1	Engineering	Research and Development	Room A
2	Tool Design	Research and Development	Room A
3	Sales	Sales and Marketing	Room B
4	Marketing	Sales and Marketing	Room B
5	Purchasing	Inventory Management	Room D
...			

How It Works

Use a CASE expression whenever you need to translate one set of defined values into another. In the case of the solution example, the expression translates group names into a set of conference room assignments. The effect is essentially a mapping of groups to rooms.

The general format of the CASE expression in the example is as follows:

```
CASE ColumnName
   WHEN OneValue THEN AnotherValue
   ...
ELSE CatchAllValue
END AS ColumnAlias
```

The ELSE clause in the expression is optional. In the example, it's used to assign any unspecified groups to Room D. Otherwise, those unspecified groups would cause the CASE expression to return NULL.

The result from a CASE expression in a SELECT statement is a column of output. It's good practice to name that column by providing a column alias. The solution example specifies AS ConfRoom to give the name ConfRoom to the column of output holding the conference room assignments, which is the column generated by the CASE expression.

2-10. Writing a Searched CASE Expression

Problem

You want to evaluate a series of Boolean expressions. When an expression is true, you want to specify a corresponding return value.

Solution

Write a so-called searched CASE expression, which you can loosely think of as being similar to multiple IF statements strung together. The following is a variation on the query from Recipe 2-9. This time, the department name is evaluated in addition to other values, such as the department identifier and the first letter of the department name.

```
SELECT DepartmentID, Name,
      CASE
          WHEN Name = 'Research and Development' THEN 'Room A'
          WHEN (Name = 'Sales and Marketing' OR DepartmentID = 10) THEN 'Room B'
          WHEN Name LIKE 'T%'THEN 'Room C'
      ELSE 'Room D' END AS ConferenceRoom
FROM HumanResources.Department;
```

Execute this query, and your results should look as follows:

DepartmentID	Name	ConferenceRoom
12	Document Control	Room D
1	Engineering	Room D
16	Executive	Room D
14	Facilities and Maintenance	Room D
10	Finance	Room B
...		

How It Works

CASE offers an alternative syntax that doesn't use an initial input expression. Instead, one or more Boolean expressions are evaluated. (A Boolean expression is a comparison expression returning either true or false or null).

The general form of a searched CASE as used in the example is as follows:

```
CASE
   WHEN Boolean_expression_1 THEN result_expression_1
   ...
   WHEN Boolean_expression_n THEN result_expression_n
   ELSE CatchAllValue
END AS ColumnAlias
```

The Boolean expressions are evaluated in the order you list them until one is found that evaluates as true. The corresponding result is then returned. If none of the expressions evaluates as true, then the optional ELSE value is returned. (The default ELSE value, should you not specify one, is null). The ability to evaluate Boolean expressions of arbitrary complexity in this flavor of CASE provides additional flexibility beyond the simple CASE expression you saw in the previous recipe.

2-11. Repeatedly Executing a Section of Code

Problem

You want to repeatedly execute a section of code until a condition is no longer true.

Solution

Write a WHILE statement using the following example as a template. In the example, the system-stored procedure sp_spaceused is used to return the table-space usage for each table in the @AWTables table variable.

```
-- Declare variables
DECLARE @AWTables TABLE (SchemaTable varchar(100));
DECLARE @TableName varchar(100);

-- Insert table names into the table variable
INSERT @AWTables (SchemaTable)
    SELECT TABLE_SCHEMA + '.' + TABLE_NAME
    FROM INFORMATION_SCHEMA.tables
    WHERE TABLE_TYPE = 'BASE TABLE'
    ORDER BY TABLE_SCHEMA + '.' + TABLE_NAME;

-- Report on each table using sp_spaceused
WHILE (SELECT COUNT(*) FROM @AWTables) > 0
BEGIN
    SELECT TOP 1 @TableName = SchemaTable
    FROM @AWTables
    ORDER BY SchemaTable;

    EXEC sp_spaceused @TableName;
    DELETE @AWTables
    WHERE SchemaTable = @TableName;
END;
```

Execute this code, and you will get multiple result sets—one for each table—similar to the following:

name	rows	reserved	data	index_size	unused
AWBuildVersion	1	16 KB	8 KB	8 KB	0 KB

name	rows	reserved	data	index_size	unused
DatabaseLog	1597	6656 KB	6544 KB	56 KB	56 KB

...

How It Works

WHILE will repeatedly execute a set of T-SQL statements while a Boolean expression remains true. In the case of the example, the Boolean expression tests the result of a query against the value zero. The query returns the number of values in a table variable. Looping continues until all values have been processed and no values remain.

In the example, the table variable @AWTABLES is populated with all the table names in the database by using the following INSERT statement:

```
INSERT @AWTables (SchemaTable)
    SELECT TABLE_SCHEMA + '.' + TABLE_NAME
    FROM INFORMATION_SCHEMA.tables
    WHERE TABLE_TYPE = 'BASE TABLE'
    ORDER BY TABLE_SCHEMA + '.' + TABLE_NAME;
```

The WHILE loop is then started, looping as long as there are rows remaining in the @AWTables table variable:

```
WHILE (SELECT COUNT(*) FROM @AWTables) > 0
```

Within the WHILE, the @TableName local variable is populated with the TOP 1 table name from the @AWTables table variable:

```
SELECT TOP 1 @TableName = SchemaTable
FROM @AWTables
ORDER BY SchemaTable;
```

Then EXEC sp_spaceused is executed against that table name:

```
EXEC sp_spaceused @TableName;
```

Lastly, the row for the reported table is deleted from the table variable:

```
DELETE @AWTables
WHERE SchemaTable = @TableName;
```

WHILE will continue to execute sp_spaceused until all rows are deleted from the @AWTables table variable.

2-12. Controlling Iteration in a Loop

Problem

You are writing a WHILE loop. Your logic requires that sometimes the loop is aborted completely, and that at other times a single iteration of the loop is terminated early while still allowing subsequent iterations to take place.

Solution

Issue a BREAK statement when you want to terminate execution of a loop with no further iterations. For example, the following is an example of BREAK in action so as to prevent an infinite loop:

```
WHILE (1=1)
BEGIN
   PRINT 'Endless While, because 1 always equals 1.';
   IF 1=1
      BEGIN
         PRINT 'But we won''t let the endless loop happen!';
         BREAK; --Because this BREAK statement terminates the loop.
      END;
END;
```

If you just want to terminate a single iteration early, then issue the CONTINUE statement as in this next example:

```
DECLARE @n int = 1;
WHILE @n = 1
BEGIN
   SET @n = @n + 1;
   IF @n > 1
      CONTINUE;
   PRINT 'You will never see this message.';
END;
```

This is a contrived example in which the PRINT statement is never executed.

How It Works

Two special statements that you can execute from within a WHILE loop are BREAK and CONTINUE. Execute a BREAK statement to exit a loop. Execute the CONTINUE statement to skip the remainder of the current iteration.

```
WHILE (1=1)
BEGIN
   PRINT 'Endless While, because 1 always equals 1.';
   IF 1=1
      BEGIN
         PRINT 'But we won''t let the endless loop happen!';
         BREAK; --Because this BREAK statement terminates the loop.
      END;
END;
```

And next is an example of CONTINUE:

```
DECLARE @n int = 1;
WHILE @n = 1
BEGIN
    SET @n = @n + 1;
    IF @n > 1
        CONTINUE;
    PRINT 'You will never see this message.';
END;
```

This example will execute with one loop iteration, but no message is displayed. Why? It's because the first iteration moves the value of @n to be greater than 1, triggering execution of the CONTINUE statement. CONTINUE causes the remainder of the BEGIN...END block to be skipped. The WHEN condition is reevaluated. Because @n is no longer 1, the loop terminates.

2-13. Pausing Execution for a Period of Time

Problem

You want to pause execution for an amount of time or until a given time of day.

Solution

Execute the WAITFOR statement For example, you can delay for a specific number of hours, minutes, and seconds:

```
WAITFOR DELAY '00:00:10';
BEGIN
    SELECT TransactionID, Quantity
    FROM Production.TransactionHistory;
END;
```

You can also wait until a specific time is reached, as in this next example:

```
WAITFOR TIME '12:22:00';
BEGIN
    SELECT COUNT(*)
    FROM Production.TransactionHistory;
END;
```

The query in this example will execute at 22 minutes past noon.

How It Works

WAITFOR provides for two options: DELAY and TIME. Specify DELAY when you want to pause for a duration of time. Specify TIME when you want to pause until a given time of day is reached. For example, DELAY '12:22:00' pauses execution for 12 hours and 22 minutes, whereas TIME '12:22:00' pauses until the next time it is 12:22 p.m.

■ **Caution** If you specify TIME `'12:22:00'` at, say 12:24 p.m., then you will be waiting almost 24 hours until execution resumes. That's because the times are on a 24-hour clock.

2-14. Looping through Query Results a Row at a Time

Problem

You need to implement row-by-row processing in your application. You don't want to fire off a single UPDATE or SELECT statement and let the database engine do the work. Instead, you want to "touch" each row and process it individually.

Solution

Implement cursor-based processing. A T-SQL cursor allows you to write row-by-row processing into your application, thus giving you full control over exactly what is done.

■ **Caution** Cursors can eat up instance memory, reduce concurrency, decrease network bandwidth, lock resources, and often require an excessive amount of code compared to a set-based alternative. Think carefully about whether you can avoid the need for a cursor by taking a set-based approach to the problem at hand.

Although we recommend avoiding cursors whenever possible, using cursors for ad hoc, periodic database administration information gathering, as demonstrated in this next example, is usually perfectly justified.

The following code block demonstrates a cursor that loops through each session ID currently active on the SQL Server instance. The block executes SP_WHO on each session to see each session's logged-in user name and other data.

```
-- Do not show rowcounts in the results
SET NOCOUNT ON;

DECLARE @session_id smallint;

-- Declare the cursor
DECLARE session_cursor CURSOR FORWARD_ONLY READ_ONLY FOR
    SELECT session_id
    FROM sys.dm_exec_requests
    WHERE status IN ('runnable', 'sleeping', 'running');

-- Open the cursor
OPEN session_cursor;

-- Retrieve one row at a time from the cursor
FETCH NEXT
    FROM session_cursor
    INTO @session_id;
```

```
-- Process and retrieve new rows until no more are available
WHILE @@FETCH_STATUS = 0
BEGIN
    PRINT 'Spid #: ' + STR(@session_id);
    EXEC ('sp_who ' + @session_id);

    FETCH NEXT
        FROM session_cursor
        INTO @session_id;
END;

-- Close the cursor
CLOSE session_cursor;

-- Deallocate the cursor
DEALLOCATE session_cursor;
```

Execute the code block. You'll get output as follows:

```
Spid #:          10
   spid   ecid status              loginame                 ...
   ------ ------ --------          ---------------------    ...
       10      0 sleeping          sa                       ...
...
Spid #:          52
   spid   ecid status              loginame                 ...
   ------ ------ ---------         ---------------------    ...
       52      0 runnable          Jonathan-T410\Jonathan   ...
```

How It Works

Query authors who have programming backgrounds are often more comfortable using Transact-SQL cursors than the set-based alternatives for retrieving or updating rows. For example, a programmer may decide to loop through one row at a time, updating rows in a singleton fashion, instead of updating an entire set of rows in a single operation. Often it's better to find a set-based solution, but there are some cases, as in the example, in which using a cursor is justifiable.

The code example illustrates the general life cycle of a T-SQL cursor, which is as follows:

1. A cursor variable is declared and associated with a SQL statement.

    ```
    DECLARE session_cursor CURSOR FORWARD_ONLY READ_ONLY FOR
        SELECT session_id
        FROM sys.dm_exec_requests
        WHERE status IN ('runnable', 'sleeping', 'running');
    ```

2. The cursor is then opened for use.

    ```
    OPEN session_cursor;
    ```

3. Rows can then be fetched one at a time.

```
FETCH NEXT
    FROM session_cursor
    INTO @session_id;
```

4. Typically a WHILE loop is used to process and fetch as long as rows remain.

```
WHILE @@FETCH_STATUS = 0
BEGIN
    ... Processing goes here ...

    FETCH NEXT
        FROM session_cursor
        INTO @session_id;
END;
```

5. The cursor is then closed.

```
CLOSE session_cursor;
```

6. And, finally, you should deallocate the cursor and associated memory.

```
DEALLOCATE session_cursor;
```

The @@FETCH_STATUS function used in the example returns a code indicating the results from the preceding FETCH. Possible result codes are as follows:

0: The fetch operation was successful. You now have a row to process.

-1: You have fetched beyond the end of the cursor or otherwise have attempted to fetch a row not included in the cursor's result set.

-2: You have fetched what should be a valid row, but the row has been deleted since you first opened the cursor, or the row has been modified such that it is no longer part of the cursor's query results.

Most often when doing row-by-row processing, you'll just process and fetch until the status is no longer zero. That's the precise approach taken in the solution example. The other codes come into play when you are executing variations on FETCH that allow you to specify specific result-set rows by their absolute or relative positions in the set.

The difference between closing and deallocating a cursor is that closing a cursor retains the definition. You are able to reopen the cursor. Once you deallocate a cursor, the definition and resources are gone, as if you had never declared it in the first place.

CHAPTER 3

■ ■ ■

Working with NULLS

by Wayne Sheffield

A NULL value represents the absence of data or, in other words, data that is missing or unknown. When coding queries, stored procedures, or any other T-SQL, it is important to keep in mind the nullability of data because it will affect many aspects of your logic. For example, the default result of most operators (such as, +, -, AND, and OR) is NULL when either operand is NULL.

- NULL + 10 = NULL

- NULL AND TRUE = NULL

- NULL OR FALSE = NULL

The exception occurs when using the OR operator in a NULL OR TRUE test. Since one side of the equation is TRUE, the OR operator will return TRUE even if the other side is NULL.

Many functions will also return NULL when an input is NULL. This chapter discusses how to use SQL Server's built-in functions and other common logic to overcome some of the hurdles associated with working with NULL values. Table 3-1 describes some of the functions that SQL Server provides for working with NULL values.

Table 3-1. *NULL Functions*

Function	Description
ISNULL	ISNULL validates whether an expression is NULL and, if so, replaces the NULL value with an alternate value.
COALESCE	The COALESCE function returns the first non-NULL value from a provided list of expressions.
NULLIF	NULLIF returns a NULL value when the two provided expressions have the same value. Otherwise, the first expression is returned.

The next few recipes will demonstrate these functions in action.

3-1. Replacing NULL with an Alternate Value

Problem

You are selecting rows from a table, and your results contain NULL values. You would like to replace the NULL values with an alternate value.

Solution

The ISNULL function validates whether an expression is NULL and, if so, replaces the NULL value with an alternate value. In this example, any NULL value in the CreditCardApprovalCode column will be replaced with the value 0:

```
SELECT   h.SalesOrderID,
         h.CreditCardApprovalCode,
         CreditApprovalCode_Display = ISNULL(h.CreditCardApprovalCode,
                                             '**NO APPROVAL**')
FROM     Sales.SalesOrderHeader h
WHERE    h.SalesOrderID BETWEEN 43735 AND 43740;
```

This returns the following results:

SalesOrderID	CreditCardApprovalCode	CreditApprovalCode_Display
43735	1034619Vi33896	1034619Vi33896
43736	1135092Vi7270	1135092Vi7270
43737	NULL	**NO APPROVAL**
43738	631125Vi62053	631125Vi62053
43739	NULL	**NO APPROVAL**
43740	834624Vi94036	834624Vi94036

How It Works

In this example, the column CreditCardApprovalCode contains NULL values for rows where there is no credit approval. This query returns the original value of CreditCardApprovalCode in the second column. In the third column, the query uses the ISNULL function to evaluate each CreditCardApprovalCode. If the value is NULL, the value passed to the second parameter of ISNULL—**NO APPROVAL**—is returned.

It is important to note that the return type of ISNULL is the same as the input type of the first parameter. To illustrate this, view the following SELECT statements and their results. The first statement attempts to return a string when the first input to ISNULL is an integer:

```
SELECT  ISNULL(CAST(NULL AS INT), 'String Value') ;
```

This query returns the following:

```
Msg 245, Level 16, State 1, Line 1
Conversion failed when converting the varchar value 'String Value' to data type int.
```

The second example attempts to return a string that is longer than the defined length of the first input:

```
SELECT  ISNULL(CAST(NULL AS CHAR(10)), '20 characters*******') ;
```

This query returns the following:

```
----------
20 charact
```

Note that the 20-character string is truncated to 10 characters. This behavior can be tricky, because the type of the second parameter is not checked until it is used. For example, if the first example is modified so that the non-NULL value is supplied in the first parameter, no error is generated.

```
SELECT  ISNULL(1, 'String Value') ;
```

This query returns the following:

```
-----------
1
```

No error is generated in this query because the second parameter is not used. When testing your use of ISNULL, it is important both to test the conditions where NULL and non-NULL values are supplied to the first parameter and to make sure that any string values are not truncated.

3-2. Returning the First Non-NULL Value from a List

Problem

You have a list of values that may contain NULLs, and you would like to return the first non-NULL value from your list.

Solution

The COALESCE function returns the first non-NULL value from a provided list of expressions. The syntax is as follows:

```
COALESCE ( expression [ ,...n ] )
```

This recipe demonstrates how to use COALESCE to return the first occurrence of a non-NULL value:

```
SELECT  c.CustomerID,
        SalesPersonPhone = spp.PhoneNumber,
        CustomerPhone = pp.PhoneNumber,
        PhoneNumber = COALESCE(pp.PhoneNumber, spp.PhoneNumber, '**NO PHONE**')
FROM    Sales.Customer c
        LEFT OUTER JOIN Sales.Store s
            ON c.StoreID = s.BusinessEntityID
```

```
        LEFT OUTER JOIN Person.PersonPhone spp
            ON s.SalesPersonID = spp.BusinessEntityID
        LEFT OUTER JOIN Person.PersonPhone pp
            ON c.CustomerID = pp.BusinessEntityID
ORDER BY CustomerID ;
```

This returns the following (abridged) results:

CustomerID	SalesPersonPhone	CustomerPhone	PhoneNumber
1	340-555-0193	697-555-0142	697-555-0142
2	740-555-0182	819-555-0175	819-555-0175
3	517-555-0117	212-555-0187	212-555-0187
...			
292	517-555-0117	NULL	517-555-0117
293	330-555-0120	747-555-0171	747-555-0171
294	883-555-0116	NULL	883-555-0116
...			
11000	NULL	608-555-0117	608-555-0117
11001	NULL	637-555-0123	637-555-0123
11002	NULL	683-555-0161	683-555-0161
...			
20778	NULL	NULL	**NO PHONE**
20779	NULL	NULL	**NO PHONE**
20780	NULL	NULL	**NO PHONE**
...			

How It Works

In this recipe, you know that a customer is either a customer in the Person table or the SalesPerson associated with a Store. You would like to return the phone numbers associated with all of your customers. You use the COALESCE function to return the customer's PhoneNumber if it exists; otherwise, you return the SalesPerson's PhoneNumber. Note that a third value was added to the COALESCE function: '** NO PHONE **'. This third value is of course one that will never be NULL, because we have specified it as a string literal. It serves to provide a non-NULL value as a failsafe. If there is no customer phone number on record, and there is also no sales person phone number on record, then the function will return '** NO PHONE **'. You'll never get a NULL in that particular column of output.

3-3. Choosing Between ISNULL and COALESCE in a SELECT Statement

Problem

You are coding a SELECT statement, and the calling application expects that NULL values will be replaced with non-NULL alternates. You know that you can choose between ISNULL and COALESCE to perform the operation but cannot decide which option is best.

Solution

There are generally two camps when it comes to making one's mind up between ISNULL and COALESCE.

- ISNULL is easier to spell, and the name makes more sense; use COALESCE only if you have more than two arguments, and even then consider chaining your calls to ISNULL to avoid COALESCE, like so: ISNULL(value1, ISNULL(value2, ISNULL(value3, ''))).

- COALESCE is more flexible and is part of the ANSI-standard SQL, so it is a more portable function if a developer is writing SQL on more than one platform.

At their cores, both functions essentially accomplish the same task; however, the functions have some subtle differences, and being aware of them may assist in any debugging efforts.

On the surface, ISNULL is simply a version of COALESCE that is limited to two parameters; however, ISNULL is a function that is built into the SQL Server engine and is evaluated at query-processing time, and COALESCE is expanded into a CASE expression during query compilation.

One difference between the two functions is the data type returned by the function when the parameters are of different data types. Take the following example:

```
DECLARE @sql NVARCHAR(MAX) = '
    SELECT  ISNULL(''5'', 5),
            ISNULL(5, ''5''),
            COALESCE(''5'', 5),
            COALESCE(5, ''5'') ;
    ' ;

EXEC sp_executesql @sql ;

SELECT  column_ordinal,
        is_nullable,
        system_type_name
FROM    master.sys.dm_exec_describe_first_result_set(@sql, NULL, 0) a ;
```

■ **Note** This example introduces some concepts that have not yet been discussed in this book. In the example, we would like to execute a query but also retrieve metadata about the query. The procedure sp_executesql accepts an NVARCHAR parameter and executes that string as a T-SQL batch. This is a useful tactic when building and executing dynamic queries in your applications. For further information on sp_executesql, please refer to the SQL Server books online at http://msdn.microsoft.com/en-us/library/ms188001.aspx.

To describe the results of the query, we use the table-valued function dm_exec_describe_first_result_set. Table-valued functions are described in the "User Defined Functions" chapter, and this function in particular is documented in SQL Server books online at http://msdn.microsoft.com/en-us/library/ff878236.aspx.

The following is the result of this set of statements:

```
---- ----------- ----------- -----------
5    5           5           5
column_ordinal is_nullable system_type_name
-------------- ----------- ------------------
1              0           varchar(1)
2              0           int
3              1           int
4              0           int
```

Note that the type returned from ISNULL changes depending on the order of the input parameters, while COALESCE returns the data type of highest precedence regardless of argument order. So long as an implicit conversion exists between the value selected by the ISNULL or COALESCE function and the return type selected, the function will implicitly cast the return value to the return type. However, be aware that if an implicit conversion does not exist between the return type and value to be returned, SQL Server will raise an error. For example:

■ **Note**   For a complete list of data types in SQL Server, listed in order of precedence, refer to SQL Server books online at http://msdn.microsoft.com/en-us/library/ms190309(v=sql.110).aspx.

```sql
SELECT  COALESCE('five', 5) ;
```

This returns the following:

```
Msg 245, Level 16, State 1, Line 1
Conversion failed when converting the varchar value 'five' to data type int.
```

Here is another example:

```sql
DECLARE @i INT = NULL ;
SELECT  ISNULL(@i, 'five') ;
```

This returns the following:

```
Msg 245, Level 16, State 1, Line 2
Conversion failed when converting the varchar value 'five' to data type int.
```

The nullability of the return value may be different as well. Consider an application that requests the LastName, FirstName, and MiddleName columns from a table. The application expects the NULL values in the MiddleName columns to be replaced with an empty string. The following SELECT statement uses both

ISNULL and COALESCE to convert the values, so the differences can be observed by describing the result set. See here:

```
DECLARE @sql NVARCHAR(MAX) = '
SELECT TOP 10
        FirstName,
        LastName,
        MiddleName_ISNULL = ISNULL(MiddleName, ''''),
        MiddleName_COALESCE = COALESCE(MiddleName, '''')
FROM    Person.Person ;
        ' ;

EXEC sp_executesql @sql ;

SELECT  column_ordinal,
        name,
        is_nullable
FROM    master.sys.dm_exec_describe_first_result_set(@sql, NULL, 0) a ;
```

The preceding statements return the two result sets:

FirstName	LastName	MiddleName_ISNULL	MiddleName_COALESCE
Syed	Abbas	E	E
Catherine	Abel	R.	R.
Kim	Abercrombie		
Kim	Abercrombie		
Kim	Abercrombie	B	B
Hazem	Abolrous	E	E
Sam	Abolrous		
Humberto	Acevedo		
Gustavo	Achong		
Pilar	Ackerman		

column_ordinal	name	is_nullable
1	FirstName	0
2	LastName	0
3	MiddleName_ISNULL	0
4	MiddleName_COALESCE	1

The nullability of ISNULL will always be false if at least one of the inputs is not nullable. COALESCE's nullability will be false only if all inputs are not nullable.

■ **Tip** This is a fairly subtle difference and may or may not affect you. Where I have seen these differences creep up is in application code where you may have a data-access library or object-relational-mapping layer that makes data-type decisions based on the nullability of columns in your result set.

How It Works

It is important to understand the nuances of the function you are using and how the data returned from ISNULL and COALESCE will be used. To eliminate the confusion that may occur with implicit type conversions, type precedence rules, and nullability rules, it is good practice to explicitly cast all inputs to the same type prior to being inputted into ISNULL or COALESCE.

■ **Note**   There are a number of discussions regarding the performance of ISNULL versus COALESCE. For most uses of these functions, the performance differences are negligible. There are some cases—when using correlated subqueries—where ISNULL and COALESCE will cause the query optimizer to generate different query plans, with COALESCE generating a suboptimal plan as compared to ISNULL.

3-4. Looking for NULLs in a Table

Problem

You have a table with a nullable column. You would like to return rows either where that column is NULL or where that column is not NULL.

Solution

The first hurdle to overcome when working with NULLs is to remove this WHERE clause from your mind: WHERE SomeColumn = NULL. The second hurdle is to remove this clause: WHERE SomeCol <> NULL. NULL is an "unknown" value. SQL Server cannot evaluate any operator where an input to the operator is unknown.

- What is NULL + 1? NULL?
- What is NULL * 5? NULL?
- Does NULL = 1? NULL?
- Is NULL <> 1? NULL?

To search for NULL values, use IS NULL and IS NOT NULL. Specifically, IS NULL returns TRUE if the operand is NULL, and IS NOT NULL returns TRUE if the operand is defined as (NOT NULL). Take the following statement:

```
DECLARE @value INT = NULL;

SELECT  CASE WHEN @value = NULL THEN 1
             WHEN @value <> NULL THEN 2
             WHEN @value IS NULL THEN 3
             ELSE 4
        END ;
```

This simple CASE expression demonstrates that the NULL value stored in the variable @value cannot be evaluated with traditional equality operators. The IS NULL operator evaluates to TRUE, and the result of the statement is the following:

```
3
```

So, how does this apply to searching for NULL values in a table? Say an application requests all rows in the Person table with a NULL value for MiddleName:

```
SELECT TOP 5
       LastName, FirstName, MiddleName
FROM   Person.Person
WHERE  MiddleName IS NULL ;
```

The result of this statement is as follows:

```
LastName             FirstName          MiddleName
-------------------- ------------------ -----------
Abercrombie          Kim                NULL
Abercrombie          Kim                NULL
Abolrous             Sam                NULL
Acevedo              Humberto           NULL
Achong               Gustavo            NULL
```

How It Works

The IS NULL operator evaluates one operand and returns TRUE if the value is unknown. The IS NOT NULL operator evaluates one operand and returns TRUE if the value is defined.

Previous recipes in this chapter introduced the ISNULL and COALESCE functions. The ISNULL function is often confused with the IS NULL operator. After all, the names differ by only one space. Functionally, the ISNULL function may be used in a WHERE clause; however, there are some differences in how the SQL Server query plan optimizer decides how to execute statements with IS NULL versus ISNULL when those used in a WHERE clause predicate.

Look at the following three statements that query the JobCandidate table and return the JobCandidate rows that have a non-NULL BusinessEntityID. All three statements return the same rows, but there is are differences in the execution plans.

The first statement uses ISNULL to return 1 for NULL values and returns all rows where ISNULL does not return 1.

```
SET SHOWPLAN_TEXT ON ;
GO

SELECT  JobCandidateID,
        BusinessEntityID
FROM    HumanResources.JobCandidate
WHERE   ISNULL(BusinessEntityID, 1) <> 1 ;
GO

SET SHOWPLAN_TEXT OFF ;
```

Here's the execution plan that results:

```
|--Index Scan(OBJECT:([AdventureWorks2008R2].[HumanResources].[JobCandidate].
[IX_JobCandidate_BusinessEntityID]),  WHERE:(isnull([AdventureWorks2008R2].
[HumanResources].[JobCandidate].[BusinessEntityID],(1))<>(1)))
```

The execution plan contains an index scan. In this case, SQL Server will look at every row in the index to satisfy the results. Maybe the reason for this is the inequality operator (<>). The query may be rewritten as follows:

```
SET SHOWPLAN_TEXT ON ;
GO

SELECT  JobCandidateID,
        BusinessEntityID
FROM    HumanResources.JobCandidate
WHERE   ISNULL(BusinessEntityID, 1) = BusinessEntityID ;
GO

SET SHOWPLAN_TEXT OFF ;
```

And here is the new execution plan:

```
|--Index Scan(OBJECT:([AdventureWorks2008R2].[HumanResources].[JobCandidate].
[IX_JobCandidate_BusinessEntityID]),  WHERE:(isnull([AdventureWorks2008R2].
[HumanResources].[JobCandidate].[BusinessEntityID],(1))=[AdventureWorks2008R2].
[HumanResources].[JobCandidate].[BusinessEntityID]))
```

Again, the query optimizer chooses to use an index scan to satisfy the query. What happens when the IS NULL operator is used instead of the ISNULL function?

```
SET SHOWPLAN_TEXT ON ;
GO

SELECT  JobCandidateID,
        BusinessEntityID
FROM    HumanResources.JobCandidate
WHERE   BusinessEntityID IS NOT NULL ;
GO

SET SHOWPLAN_TEXT OFF ;
```

Now the execution looks like this:

```
|--Index Seek(OBJECT:([AdventureWorks2008R2].[HumanResources].[JobCandidate].
[IX_JobCandidate_BusinessEntityID]), SEEK:([AdventureWorks2008R2].[HumanResources].
[JobCandidate].[BusinessEntityID] IsNotNull) ORDERED FORWARD)
```

By using the IS NULL operator, SQL Server is able to seek on the index instead of scanning the index. ISNULL() is a function; whenever a column is passed into a function, SQL Server must evaluate that function for every row and is not able to seek on an index to satisfy the WHERE clause.

3-5. Removing Values from an Aggregate

Problem

You are attempting to understand production delays and have decided to report on the average variance between the ActualStartDate and the ScheduledStartDate of operations in your production sequence. You would like to understand the following:

- What is the variance for all operations?

- What is the variance for all operations where the variance is not 0?

Solution

NULLIF returns a NULL value when the two provided expressions have the same value; otherwise, the first expression is returned:

```
SELECT  r.ProductID,
        r.OperationSequence,
        StartDateVariance = AVG(DATEDIFF(day, ScheduledStartDate,
                                         ActualStartDate)),
        StartDateVariance_Adjusted = AVG(NULLIF(DATEDIFF(day,
                                                 ScheduledStartDate,
                                                 ActualStartDate), 0))
FROM    Production.WorkOrderRouting r
WHERE   r.ProductID BETWEEN 514 AND 516
GROUP BY r.ProductID,
        r.OperationSequence
ORDER BY r.ProductID,
        r.OperationSequence ;
```

The query returns the following results:

ProductID	OperationSequence	StartDateVariance	StartDateVariance_Adjusted
514	6	4	8
514	7	4	8
515	6	0	NULL
515	7	0	NULL
516	6	4	8

How It Works

The query includes two columns that use the aggregate function AVG to return the average difference in days between the scheduled and actual start dates of a production sequence for a given product. The column StateDateVariance includes all of the rows in the aggregate. The column StartDateVariance_Adjusted eliminates rows where the variance is 0 by using the NULLIF function. The NULLIF function accepts the result of DATEDIFF as the first parameter and compares this result to the value 0 that we passed to the second parameter. If DATEDIFF returns 0, NULLIF returns NULL, and the NULL value is then eliminated from the AVG aggregate.

3-6. Enforcing Uniqueness with NULL Values

Problem

You have a table that contains a column that allows NULLs. There may be many rows with NULL values, but any non-NULL value must be unique.

Solution

For this recipe, create a table called Product where CodeName may be NULL:

```
USE tempdb;
CREATE TABLE dbo.Product
    (
      ProductId INT NOT NULL
                  CONSTRAINT PK_Product PRIMARY KEY CLUSTERED,
      ProductName NVARCHAR(50) NOT NULL,
      CodeName NVARCHAR(50)
    ) ;
GO
```

Create a unique nonclustered index on CodeName:

```
CREATE UNIQUE INDEX UX_Product_CodeName ON dbo.Product (CodeName) ;
GO
```

Test the unique index by adding some rows to the table:

```
INSERT INTO dbo.Product (ProductId, ProductName, CodeName) VALUES  (1, 'Product 1', 'Shiloh');
INSERT INTO dbo.Product (ProductId, ProductName, CodeName) VALUES  (2, 'Product 2', 'Sphynx');
INSERT INTO dbo.Product (ProductId, ProductName, CodeName) VALUES  (3, 'Product 3', NULL);
INSERT INTO dbo.Product (ProductId, ProductName, CodeName) VALUES  (4, 'Product 4', NULL);
GO
```

Here is the result of the insert statements:

```
(1 row(s) affected)

(1 row(s) affected)

(1 row(s) affected)
Msg 2601, Level 14, State 1, Line 13
Cannot insert duplicate key row in object 'dbo.Product' with unique index
'UX_Product_CodeName'. The duplicate key value is (<NULL>).
The statement has been terminated.
```

A unique index may be built on a nullable column; however, the unique index can contain only one NULL. SQL Server allows filtered indexes where the index is created only for a subset of the data in the table. Drop the unique index created earlier and create a new, unique, nonclustered, filtered index on CodeName so as to index (and enforce uniqueness) only on rows that have a defined CodeName. See the following:

```
DROP INDEX dbo.Product.UX_Product_CodeName;
GO

CREATE UNIQUE INDEX UX_Product_CodeName ON dbo.Product (CodeName) WHERE CodeName IS NOT NULL
GO
```

Test the new index by adding some rows:

```
INSERT INTO dbo.Product (ProductId, ProductName, CodeName) VALUES (4, 'Product 4', NULL);
INSERT INTO dbo.Product (ProductId, ProductName, CodeName) VALUES (5, 'Product 5', NULL);
```

The results show two rows were added successfully:

```
(1 row(s) affected)

(1 row(s) affected)
```

If a row is added that violates the unique constraint on the CodeName, a constraint violation will be raised:

```
INSERT INTO dbo.Product (ProductId, ProductName, CodeName) VALUES (6, 'Product 6', 'Shiloh');
```

Here are the results:

```
Msg 2601, Level 14, State 1, Line 1
Cannot insert duplicate key row in object 'dbo.Product' with unique index
'UX_Product_CodeName'. The duplicate key value is (Shiloh).
The statement has been terminated.
```

A select from the Product table will show that multiple NULLs have been added to the CodeName column; however, uniqueness has been maintained on defined CodeName values. See the following:

```
SELECT  *
FROM    dbo.Product;
```

The SELECT statement yields the following:

ProductId	ProductName	CodeName
1	Product 1	Shiloh
2	Product 2	Sphynx
3	Product 3	NULL
4	Product 4	NULL
5	Product 5	NULL. See the following:

How It Works

Unique constraints and unique indexes will, by default, enforce uniqueness in the same way with respect to NULL values. Indexes allow for the use of index filtering, and the filter will be created only on the rows that meet the filter criteria. There are many benefits to filtered indexes, as discussed in the "Managing Indexes" chapter.

3-7. Enforcing Referential Integrity on Nullable Columns

Problem

You have a table with a foreign key defined so as to enforce referential integrity. You want to enforce the foreign key where values are defined but allow NULL values into the foreign-key column.

Solution

The default behavior of a foreign-key constraint is to enforce referential integrity on non-NULL values but allow NULL values, even though there may not be a corresponding NULL value in the primary-key table. This example uses a Category table and an Item table. The Item table includes a nullable CategoryId column that references the CategoryId of the Category table.

First, create the Category table and add some values:

```
CREATE TABLE dbo.Category
    (
    CategoryId INT NOT NULL
                    CONSTRAINT PK_Category PRIMARY KEY CLUSTERED,
    CategoryName NVARCHAR(50) NOT NULL
    ) ;
GO
```

```
INSERT INTO dbo.Category (CategoryId, CategoryName)
VALUES  (1, 'Category 1'),
        (2, 'Category 2'),
        (3, 'Category 3') ;

GO
```

Next, create the Item table and add the foreign key to the Category table:

```
CREATE TABLE dbo.Item
        (
        ItemId INT NOT NULL
                    CONSTRAINT PK_Item PRIMARY KEY CLUSTERED,
        ItemName NVARCHAR(50) NOT NULL,
        CategoryId INTEGER NULL
                    CONSTRAINT FK_Item_Category REFERENCES Category(CategoryId)
        ) ;
GO
```

Now, attempt to insert three rows into the Item table. The first row contains a valid reference to the Category table. The second row will fail with a foreign-key violation. The third row will insert successfully, because the CategoryId is NULL:

```
INSERT INTO dbo.Item (ItemId, ItemName, CategoryId) VALUES  (1, 'Item 1', 1);
INSERT INTO dbo.Item (ItemId, ItemName, CategoryId) VALUES  (2, 'Item 2', 4);
INSERT INTO dbo.Item (ItemId, ItemName, CategoryId) VALUES  (3, 'Item 3', NULL);
```

These INSERT statements generate the following results:

```
(1 row(s) affected)
Msg 547, Level 16, State 0, Line 5
The INSERT statement conflicted with the FOREIGN KEY CONSTRAINT "FK_Item_Category".
The conflict occurred in database "AdventureWorks2014", table "dbo.Category", column
'CategoryId'.
The statement has been terminated.
(1 row(s) affected)
```

How It Works

If a table contains a foreign-key reference on a nullable column, NULL values are allowed in the foreign-key table. If the foreign key is on multiple nullable columns, a NULL value would be allowed in any of the nullable columns. To enforce the referential integrity on all rows, the foreign-key column must be declared as non-nullable. Foreign keys are discussed in detail in the "Managing Tables" chapter.

3-8. Joining Tables on Nullable Columns

Problem

You need to join two tables but have NULL values in one or both sides of the join.

Solution

When joining on a nullable column, remember that the equality operator returns FALSE for NULL = NULL. Let's see what happens when you have NULL values on both sides of a join. Create two tables with sample data:

```
CREATE TABLE dbo.Test1
    (
        TestValue NVARCHAR(10) NULL
    );
CREATE TABLE dbo.Test2
    (
        TestValue NVARCHAR(10) NULL
    ) ;
GO

INSERT INTO dbo.Test1
VALUES ('apples'),
       ('oranges'),
       (NULL),
       (NULL) ;

INSERT INTO dbo.Test2
VALUES (NULL),
       ('oranges'),
       ('grapes'),
       (NULL) ;
GO
```

If an inner join is attempted on these tables, like so:

```
SELECT  t1.TestValue,
        t2.TestValue
FROM    dbo.Test1 t1
        INNER JOIN dbo.Test2 t2
            ON t1.TestValue = t2.TestValue ;
```

the query returns the following:

```
TestValue  TestValue
---------- ----------
oranges    oranges
```

How It Works

Predicates in the join condition evaluate NULLs the same way as predicates do in the WHERE clause. When SQL Server evaluates the condition t1.TestValue = t2.TestValue, the equals operator returns FALSE if one or both of the operands is NULL; therefore, the only rows that will be returned from an INNER JOIN are rows where neither side of the join is NULL and those non-NULL values are equal.

CHAPTER 4

Querying from Multiple Tables

by Jonathan Gennick

It is the rare database that has all its data in a single table. Data tends to be spread over multiple tables in ways that optimize storage and ensure consistency and integrity. Part of your job when writing a query is to deploy and link together T-SQL operations that can operate across tables in order to generate needed business results.

4-1. Correlating Parent and Child Rows

Problem

You want to bring together data from parent and child tables. For example, you have a list of people in a parent table named `Person`, and a list of phone numbers in a child table named `PersonPhone`. Each person may have zero, one, or several phone numbers. You want to return a list of each person having at least one phone number, along with all their numbers.

Note   It is also possible to return *all* persons, including those having zero phone numbers. Recipe 4-3 shows how.

Solution

Write an *inner join* to bring related information from two tables together into a single result set. Begin with a FROM clause and one of the tables:

```
FROM Person.Person
```

Add the keywords `INNER JOIN` followed by the second table:

```
FROM    Person.Person
        INNER JOIN Person.PersonPhone
```

Follow with an ON clause to specify the *join condition*. The join condition identifies the row combinations of interest. It is the BusinessEntityID that identifies a person. That same ID indicates the phone numbers for a person. For this example, you want all combinations of Person and PersonPhone rows sharing the same value for BusinessEntityID. The following ON clause gives that result:

```
FROM    Person.Person
        INNER JOIN Person.PersonPhone
            ON Person.BusinessEntityID = PersonPhone.BusinessEntityID
```

Specify the columns you wish to see in the output. All columns from both tables are available. The following final version of the query returns two columns from each table:

```
SELECT  PersonPhone.BusinessEntityID,
        FirstName,
        LastName,
        PhoneNumber
FROM    Person.Person
        INNER JOIN Person.PersonPhone
            ON Person.BusinessEntityID = PersonPhone.BusinessEntityID
ORDER BY LastName,
        FirstName,
        Person.BusinessEntityID;
```

The ORDER BY clause sorts the results so that all phone numbers for a given person group together. Results are as follows:

```
BusinessEntityID FirstName   LastName     PhoneNumber
---------------- ----------  ------------ -------------
             285 Syed        Abbas        926-555-0182
             293 Catherine   Abel         747-555-0171
              38 Kim         Abercrombie  208-555-0114
             295 Kim         Abercrombie  334-555-0137
            2170 Kim         Abercrombie  919-555-0100
             211 Hazem       Abolrous     869-555-0125
            2357 Sam         Abolrous     567-555-0100
             297 Humberto    Acevedo      599-555-0127
...
```

How It Works

The inner join is fundamental. Imagine the following, very simplified, two tables:

```
Person                                   PersonPhone
BusinessEntityID FirstName   LastName     BusinessEntityID PhoneNumber
---------------- ----------  --------     ---------------- ------------
             285 Syed        Abbas        285              926-555-0182
             293 Catherine   Abel         293              747-555-0171
```

From a conceptual standpoint, an inner join begins with all possible combinations of rows from the two tables. Some combinations make sense. Some do not. The set of all possible combinations is called the *Cartesian product*. Notice the bold rows in the following Cartesian product.

```
BusinessEntityID FirstName   LastName BusinessEntityID PhoneNumber
---------------- ----------  -------- ---------------- ------------
             285 Syed        Abbas    285              926-555-0182
             285 Syed        Abbas    293              747-555-0171
             293 Catherine   Abel     293              747-555-0171
             293 Catherine   Abel     285              926-555-0182
```

It makes sense to have Syed's name in the same row as his phone number. Likewise, it is sensible to list Catherine with her phone number. There's no logic at all in listing Syed's name with Catherine's number, or vice versa. Thus, the join condition is very sensibly written to specify the case in which the two BusinessEntityID values are the same:

```
ON Person.BusinessEntityID = PersonPhone.BusinessEntityID
```

The Cartesian product gives all possible results from an inner join. Picture the Cartesian product in your mind. Bring in the fishnet analogy from Recipe 1-4. Then write join conditions to trap the rows that you care about as the rest of the Cartesian product falls through your net.

■ **Note** Database engines do not materialize the entire Cartesian product when executing an inner join. There are more efficient approaches for SQL Server to take. However, regardless of approach, the results will always be in line with the conceptual description given here in this recipe.

THE TERM "RELATIONAL"

One sometimes hears the claim that the word *relational* in *relational database* refers to the fact that one table can "relate" to another, in the sense that one joins the two tables together, as described in Recipe 4-1. That explanation sounds so very plausible, yet it is incorrect.

The term *relation* comes from set theory, and you can read in detail about what a relation is by visiting Wikipedia's article on *finitary relations*:

http://en.wikipedia.org/wiki/Finitary_relation

The key statement from the current version of this article reads as follows (emphasis added):

"Typically, the property [a relation] describes a possible connection *between the components of a k-tuple*."

The words "between the components of" tell the tale. A tuple's analog is the row. The components of a tuple are its values, and thus the database analog would be the values in a row. The term *relation* speaks to a relationship, not between tables, but between the values in a row.

We encourage you to read the Wikipedia article. Then if you really want to dive deeper into set theory and how it can help you work with data, we recommend you read the book *Applied Mathematics for Database Professionals* by Lex de Haan and Toon Koppelaars (Apress, 2007).

4-2. Querying Many-to-Many Relationships

Problem

You have a many-to-many relationship with two detail tables on either side of an intersection table. You want to resolve the relationship across all three tables.

Solution

String two inner joins together. The following example joins three tables in order to return discount information on a specific product:

```
SELECT  p.Name,
        s.DiscountPct
FROM    Sales.SpecialOffer s
        INNER JOIN Sales.SpecialOfferProduct o
            ON s.SpecialOfferID = o.SpecialOfferID
        INNER JOIN Production.Product p
            ON o.ProductID = p.ProductID
WHERE   p.Name = 'All-Purpose Bike Stand';
```

The results of this query are as follows:

Name	DiscountPct
All-Purpose Bike Stand	0.00

How It Works

A join starts after the first table in the FROM clause. In this example, three tables are joined together: Sales.SpecialOffer, Sales.SpecialOfferProduct, and Production.Product. The first table referenced in the FROM clause, Sales.SpecialOffer, contains a lookup of sales discounts:

```
FROM Sales.SpecialOffer s
```

Notice the letter s that trails the table name. This is a *table alias*. Once you begin using more than one table in a query, it is important to explicitly identify the data source of the individual columns. If the same column names exist in two different tables, you can get an error from the SQL compiler asking you to clarify which column you really want to return.

As a best practice, it is a good idea to use aliases whenever column names are specified in a query. For each of the referenced tables, an alias is used to symbolize the table name, saving you the trouble of spelling it out each time. This query uses a single character as a table alias, but you can use any valid identifier. A table alias, aside from allowing you to shorten or clarify the original table name, allows you to swap out the base table name if you ever have to replace it with a different table or view, or if you need to self-join the tables. Table aliases are optional, but recommended when your query has more than one table. (Because table aliases are optional, you can instead specify the entire table name every time you refer to the column in that table.)

Getting back to the example, the INNER JOIN keywords follow the first table reference, and then the table being joined to it is named, followed by its alias:

```
INNER JOIN Sales.SpecialOfferProduct o
```

After that, the ON keyword prefaces the column joins:

```
ON
```

This particular INNER JOIN is based on the equality of two columns, one from the first table and another from the second:

```
s.SpecialOfferID = o.SpecialOfferID
```

Next, the Production.Product table is inner joined as well:

```
INNER JOIN Production.Product p
    ON o.ProductID = p.ProductID
```

Finally, a WHERE clause is used to filter rows returned in the final result set:

```
WHERE    p.Name = 'All-Purpose Bike Stand';
```

4-3. Making One Side of a Join Optional

Problem

You want rows returned from one table in a join even when there are no corresponding rows in the other table. For example, you want to list states and provinces and their tax rates. Sometimes no tax rate is on file. In those cases, you still want to list the state or province.

Solution

Write an *outer join* rather than the inner join that you have seen in the recipes so far. You can designate an outer join as being either *left* or *right*. Following is a left outer join that produces a list of all states and provinces, including tax rates when they are available.

```
SELECT    s.CountryRegionCode,
          s.StateProvinceCode,
          t.TaxType,
          t.TaxRate
FROM      Person.StateProvince s
          LEFT OUTER JOIN Sales.SalesTaxRate t
              ON s.StateProvinceID = t.StateProvinceID;
```

This returns the following results:

CountryRegionCode	StateProvinceCode	TaxType	TaxRate
CA	AB	1	14.00
CA	AB	2	7.00
US	AK	NULL	NULL
US	AL	NULL	NULL
US	AR	NULL	NULL
AS	AS	NULL	NULL
US	AZ	1	7.75
CA	BC	3	7.00
...			

How It Works

A left outer join causes the table named first to become the nonoptional table, or what I often term as the *anchor table*. The word "left" derives from the fact that English is written left to right. The left outer join in the solution makes StateProvince the anchor table, so all states are returned. The sales tax side of the join is then the optional side, and the database engine supplies nulls for the sales tax columns when no corresponding row exists for each state in question.

Change the join type in the solution from LEFT OUTER to INNER, and you'll get only those rows for states that have tax rates defined in the SalesTaxRate table. This is because an inner join requires a row from each table involved. By making the join a left outer join, you make the right-hand table optional. Rows from the left-hand table are returned regardless of whether corresponding rows exist in the other table. Thus, you get *all* states and provinces; lack of a tax rate does not prevent a state or province from appearing in the results.

It is common to write outer joins with one optional table as left outer joins. However, you do have the option of looking at things from the other direction. For example:

```
FROM    Sales.SalesTaxRate t
        RIGHT OUTER JOIN Person.StateProvince s
```

This right outer join will yield the same results as the left outer join in the solution example. That's because the order of the tables has been flipped. StateProvince is now on the right-hand side, and it is the anchor table once again because this time a right outer join is used.

■ **Tip** Experiment! Take time to execute the solution query. Then change the join clause to read INNER JOIN. Note the difference in results. Then change the entire FROM clause to use a right outer join with the StateProvince table on the right-hand side. You should get the same results as you got from the solution query.

4-4. Making Both Sides of a Join Optional

Problem

You want the effect of a left and a right outer join at the same time.

Solution

Write a full outer join. Do that using the keywords FULL OUTER JOIN. For example:

```
SELECT  soh.SalesOrderID,
        sr.SalesReasonID,
        sr.Name
FROM    Sales.SalesOrderHeader soh
        FULL OUTER JOIN Sales.SalesOrderHeaderSalesReason sohsr
            ON soh.SalesOrderID = sohsr.SalesOrderID
        FULL OUTER JOIN Sales.SalesReason sr
            ON sr.SalesReasonID = sohsr.SalesReasonID;
```

This query follows the same pattern as that seen in Recipe 4-3 on querying many-to-many relationships. Only the join type and tables are different.

How It Works

The solution query returns sales orders and their associated reasons. The full outer join in the query guarantees the following:

- All the results from an inner join

- One additional row for each order not associated with a sale

- One additional row for each sales reason not associated with an order

The additional rows have nulls from one side of the join or the other. If there is no order associated with a reason, then there is no value available for the SalesOrderID column in the result, and the value is null. Likewise, the SalesReasonID and Name values are null in the case of an order having no reason.

Results are as follows for orders associated with reasons:

```
SalesOrderID SalesReasonID Name
------------ ------------- -------------
       43697             5 Manufacturer
       43697             9 Quality
       43702             5 Manufacturer
...
```

Any reasons not associated with an order will come back with nulls in the order columns:

```
SalesOrderID SalesReasonID Name
------------ ------------- ----------------------
        NULL               3 Magazine Advertisement
        NULL               7 Demo Event
        NULL               8 Sponsorship
...
```

Any orders not given a reason will likewise come back with nulls in the reason columns:

```
SalesOrderID SalesReasonID Name
------------ ------------- ----
       45889          NULL NULL
       48806          NULL NULL
       51723          NULL NULL
...
```

All the preceding results will come back as a single result set.

4-5. Generating All Possible Row Combinations

Problem

You want to generate all possible combinations of rows from two tables. You want to generate the Cartesian product described in Recipe 4-1.

Solution

Write a *cross join*. In this example, the Person.StateProvince and Sales.SalesTaxRate tables are cross joined to generate all possible combinations of rows from the two tables:

```
SELECT  s.CountryRegionCode,
        s.StateProvinceCode,
        t.TaxType,
        t.TaxRate
FROM    Person.StateProvince s
        CROSS JOIN Sales.SalesTaxRate t;
```

This returns the following (abridged) results:

```
CountryRegionCode StateProvinceCode TaxType         TaxRate
----------------- ----------------- ------- ----------------
CA                AB                1                  14.00
US                AK                1                  14.00
US                AL                1                  14.00
...
```

How It Works

A cross join is essentially a join with no join conditions. Every row from one table is joined to every row in the other table, regardless of whether the resulting combination of values makes any sense. The result is termed a *Cartesian product*.

The solution results show StateProvince and SalesTaxRate information that doesn't logically go together. Because the Person.StateProvince table had 181 rows, and the Sales.SalesTaxRate had 29 rows, the query returned 5249 rows.

4-6. Selecting from a Result Set

Problem

You find it easier to think in terms of selecting a set of rows, and then selecting again from that result set.

Solution

Create a *derived table* in your FROM clause by enclosing a SELECT statement within parentheses. For example, the following query joins SalesOrderHeader to the results from a query against SalesOrderDetail:

```
SELECT DISTINCT
        s.PurchaseOrderNumber
FROM    Sales.SalesOrderHeader s
        INNER JOIN (SELECT  SalesOrderID
                    FROM    Sales.SalesOrderDetail
                    WHERE   UnitPrice BETWEEN 1000 AND 2000
                   ) d
            ON s.SalesOrderID = d.SalesOrderID;
```

This returns the following abridged results:

```
PurchaseOrderNumber
-------------------
PO1595126190
PO9077115532
PO013340115824
PO011861162351
PO9222123146

...
```

How It Works

Derived tables are SELECT statements that act as tables in the FROM clause. A derived table is a separate query in itself and doesn't require the use of a temporary table to store its results. Thus, queries that use derived tables can sometimes perform significantly better than the process of building a temporary table and querying from it, as you eliminate the steps needed for SQL Server to create and allocate a temporary table prior to use.

This example's query returns the PurchaseOrderNumber from the Sales.SalesOrderHeader table for any order containing products with a UnitPrice between 1000 and 2000. The query joins a table to a derived table using an inner join operation. The derived table query is encapsulated in parentheses and is followed by a table alias.

4-7. Introducing New Columns

Problem

You are writing a query that returns an expression, and you seem to be stuck repeating the expression in multiple clauses of the query. You'd prefer to state the computation just one time.

■ **Note** Thanks to Brad Schulz for graciously allowing us to copy the example in this recipe from his blog post about CROSS APPLY. It's a wonderful post. We encourage you to read it at: http://bradsruminations. blogspot.com/2011/04/t-sql-tuesday-017-it-slices-it-dices-it.html

---

Solution

There's a clever way to use CROSS APPLY that can sometimes help you avoid the need to redundantly write the expression for a computed column. For example, the following is a GROUP BY query with a computed column. You can see how part of the expression behind the column appears in the query redundantly three times:

```
SELECT
   DATENAME(MONTH,
      DATEADD(MONTH,
         DATEDIFF(MONTH,'19000101',OrderDate),
         '19000101')
   ) AS Mth,
   SUM(TotalDue) AS Total
FROM Sales.SalesOrderHeader
WHERE OrderDate>='20120101'
  AND OrderDate<'20140101'
GROUP BY DATEADD(MONTH,
            DATEDIFF(MONTH,'19000101',OrderDate),
            '19000101')
ORDER BY DATEADD(MONTH,
            DATEDIFF(MONTH,'19000101',OrderDate),
            '19000101');
```

Redundancy is undesirable. It clutters the query and increases the chance of error. Any change or correction to the expression logic must be repeated three times or else the query won't produce correct results. You can eliminate the undesired redundancy by placing the expression logic into a cross-joined subquery. Here's how to do that:

```
SELECT DATENAME(MONTH,FirstDayOfMth) AS Mth,
       SUM(TotalDue) AS Total
FROM Sales.SalesOrderHeader
CROSS APPLY (
   SELECT DATEADD(MONTH,
            DATEDIFF(MONTH,'19000101',OrderDate),
            '19000101') AS FirstDayOfMth
   ) F_Mth
where OrderDate>='20120101'
   and OrderDate<'20140101'
group by FirstDayOfMth
order by FirstDayOfMth
```

How It Works

The queries in this example each group the sales by month. Results in both cases are:

```
Mth                             Total
-----------------------------   --------------------
January                             1462448.8986
February                            2749104.6546
March                               2350568.1264
April                               1727689.5793
May                                  3299799.233
June                                1920506.6177
July                                3253418.7629
August                              4663508.0154
September                           3638980.3689
October                            2488758.6715
November                           3809633.4035
December                           3099432.1035
```

The second query simplifies the logic by placing the column expression into a subquery. The execution plan is the same in both cases, so there is no performance impact, only an increase in readability and maintainability.

The subquery is a correlated subquery returning one row. Each individual row from the main query is cross-joined to the subquery. All possible combinations of one row and one row work out to be just one row. The same number of rows are thus returned, but those rows now each contain the computed column. Then the results are grouped and summed by month.

4-8. Testing for the Existence of a Row

Problem

You are writing a WHERE clause. You want to return rows from the table you are querying based upon the existence of related rows in some other table.

Solution

One solution is to write a subquery in conjunction with the EXISTS predicate:

```
SELECT   s.PurchaseOrderNumber
FROM     Sales.SalesOrderHeader s
WHERE    EXISTS ( SELECT SalesOrderID
                  FROM   Sales.SalesOrderDetail sod
                  WHERE  sod.UnitPrice BETWEEN 1000 AND 2000
                  AND sod.SalesOrderID = s.SalesOrderID );
```

This returns the following abridged results.

```
PurchaseOrderNumber
-------------------
PO12586178184
PO10440182311
PO13543119495
PO12586169040
PO2146113582
...
```

How It Works

The critical piece in the solution example is the subquery in the WHERE clause, which checks for the existence of SalesOrderIDs that have products with a UnitPrice between 1000 and 2000. A JOIN is essentially written into the WHERE clause of the subquery by stating sod.SalesOrderID = s.SalesOrderID. The subquery uses the SalesOrderID from each returned row in the outer query.

The subquery in this recipe is known as a *correlated subquery*. It is so called because the subquery accesses values from the parent query. It is certainly possible to write an EXISTS predicate with a noncorrelated subquery, however, it is unusual to do so.

Look back at Recipe 4-6. It solves the same problem and generates the same results, but uses a derived table in the FROM clause. Often you can solve such problems multiple ways. Pick the one that performs best. If performance is equal, then pick the approach with which you are most comfortable.

4-9. Testing Against the Result from a Query

Problem

You are writing a WHERE clause and wish to write a predicate involving the result from another query. For example, you wish to compare a value in a table against the maximum value in a related table.

Solution

Write a *noncorrelated* subquery. Make sure it returns a single value. Put the query where you would normally refer to the value. For example:

```
SELECT  BusinessEntityID,
        SalesQuota AS CurrentSalesQuota
FROM    Sales.SalesPerson
WHERE   SalesQuota = (SELECT    MAX(SalesQuota)
                      FROM      Sales.SalesPerson
                      );
```

This returns the three salespeople who reached the maximum sales quota of 300,000:

```
BusinessEntityID    CurrentSalesQuota
----------------    ---------------------
             275           300000.00
             279           300000.00
             284           300000.00
Warning: Null value is eliminated by an aggregate or other SET operation.
```

How It Works

There is no WHERE clause in the subquery, and the subquery does not reference values from the parent query. It is therefore not a correlated subquery. Instead, the maximum sales quota is retrieved once. That value is used to evaluate the WHERE clause for all rows tested by the parent query.

Ignore the warning message in the results. That message simply indicates that some of the SalesQuota values fed into the MAX function were null. You can avoid the message by adding WHERE SalesQuota IS NOT NULL to the subquery. You can also avoid the message by issuing the command set ANSI_WARNINGS OFF. However, there is no real need to avoid the message unless it offends your sense of tidiness to see it.

4-10. Stacking Two Row Sets Vertically

Problem

You are querying the same data from two different sources. You wish to combine the two sets of results. For example, you wish to combine current with historical sales quotas.

Solution

Write two queries. Glue them together with the UNION ALL operator. For example:

```
SELECT  BusinessEntityID,
        GETDATE() QuotaDate,
        SalesQuota
FROM    Sales.SalesPerson
WHERE   SalesQuota > 0
UNION ALL
SELECT  BusinessEntityID,
        QuotaDate,
        SalesQuota
FROM    Sales.SalesPersonQuotaHistory
WHERE   SalesQuota > 0
ORDER BY BusinessEntityID DESC,
        QuotaDate DESC;
```

Results are as follows.

```
BusinessEntityID QuotaDate                       SalesQuota
---------------- ----------------------- ----------------------
             290 2012-02-09 00:04:39.420          250000.00
             290 2008-04-01 00:00:00.000          908000.00
             290 2008-01-01 00:00:00.000          707000.00
             290 2007-10-01 00:00:00.000         1057000.00
...
```

How It Works

The solution query appends two result sets into a single result set. The first result set returns the BusinessEntityID, the current date, and the SalesQuota. Because GETDATE()is a function, it doesn't naturally generate a column name, so a QuotaDate column alias was used in its place:

```
SELECT  BusinessEntityID,
        GETDATE() QuotaDate,
        SalesQuota
FROM    Sales.SalesPerson
```

The WHERE clause filters data for those salespeople with a SalesQuota greater than zero:

```
WHERE   SalesQuota > 0
```

The next part of the query is the UNION ALL operator, which appends all results from the second query:

```
UNION ALL
```

The second query pulls data from the Sales.SalesPersonQuotaHistory, which keeps the history for a salesperson's sales quota as it changes through time:

```
SELECT   BusinessEntityID,
         QuotaDate,
         SalesQuota
FROM     Sales.SalesPersonQuotaHistory
```

The ORDER BY clause sorts the result set by BusinessEntityID and QuotaDate, both in descending order. The ORDER BY clause, when needed, must appear at the bottom of the entire statement. In the solution query, the clause is:

```
ORDER BY BusinessEntityID DESC,
         QuotaDate DESC;
```

You cannot write individual ORDER BY clauses for each of the SELECTs that you UNION together. ORDER BY can only appear once at the end, and applies to the combined result set.

Column names in the final, combined result set derive from the first SELECT in the overall statement. Thus, the ORDER BY clause should only refer to column names from the *first* result set.

■ **Tip**   UNION ALL is more efficient than UNION (described in the next recipe), because UNION ALL does not force a sort or similar operation in support of duplicate elimination. Use UNION ALL whenever possible, unless you really do need duplicate rows in the result set to be eliminated.

4-11. Eliminating Duplicate Values from a Union

Problem

You are writing a UNION query and prefer not to have duplicate rows in the results. For example, you wish to generate a list of unique surnames from among employees and salespersons.

Solution

Write a union query, but omit the ALL keyword and write just UNION instead. For example:

```
SELECT  P1.LastName
FROM    HumanResources.Employee E
        INNER JOIN Person.Person P1
            ON E.BusinessEntityID = P1.BusinessEntityID
UNION
SELECT  P2.LastName
FROM    Sales.SalesPerson SP
        INNER JOIN Person.Person P2
            ON SP.BusinessEntityID = P2.BusinessEntityID;
```

Results are as follows.

```
LastName
------------
Abbas
Abercrombie
Abolrous
Ackerman
Adams
...
```

How It Works

The behavior of the UNION operator is to remove all duplicate rows. The solution query uses that behavior to generate a list of unique surnames from among the combined group of employees and salespersons.

For large result sets, deduplication can be a very costly operation. It very often involves a sort. If you don't need to deduplicate your data, or if your data is naturally distinct, write UNION ALL instead and your queries will run more efficiently. (See Recipe 4-10 for an example of UNION ALL).

■ **Caution**   Do you need your results sorted? Then be sure to write an ORDER BY clause. The solution results appear sorted, but that is a side effect from the deduplication operation. You should not count on such a side effect. The database engine might not drive the sort to completion. Other deduplication logic can be introduced in a future release and break your query. If you need ordering, write an ORDER BY clause into your query.

4-12. Subtracting One Row Set from Another

Problem

You want to subtract one set of rows from another. For example, you want to subtract component ID numbers from a list of product ID numbers so as to find those products that are at the top of the heap and are not themselves part of some larger product.

Solution

Write a union query involving the EXCEPT operator. Subtract products that are components from the total list of products, leaving only those products that are not components. For example:

```
SELECT  P.ProductID
FROM    Production.Product P
EXCEPT
SELECT  BOM.ComponentID
FROM    Production.BillOfMaterials BOM;
```

```
ProductID
-----------
        378
        710
        879
        856
...
```

How It Works

EXCEPT begins with the first query and eliminates any rows that are also found in the second. It is considered to be a union operator, although the operation is more along the lines of a subtraction.

In the Adventure Works database, the BillOfMaterials table describes products that are made up of other products. The component products are recorded in the ComponentID column. Thus, subtracting the ComponentID values from the ProductID values in the Product table leaves only those products that are at the top and are not themselves part of some larger product.

■ **Note** The EXCEPT operator implicitly deduplicates the final result set.

4-13. Finding Rows in Common Between Two Row Sets

Problem

You have two queries. You want to discover which rows are returned by both. For example, you wish to find products that have incurred both good and poor reviews.

Solution

Write a union query using the INTERSECT keyword. For example:

```
SELECT  PR1.ProductID
FROM    Production.ProductReview PR1
WHERE   PR1.Rating >= 4
INTERSECT
SELECT  PR1.ProductID
FROM    Production.ProductReview PR1
WHERE   PR1.Rating <= 2;
```

Results from this query show the one product that has both good and bad reviews:

```
ProductID
-----------
        937
```

How It Works

The INTERSECT operator finds rows in common between two row sets. The solution example defines a good review as one with a rating of 4 and above. A bad review is a rating of 2 and lower. It's easy to write a separate query to identify products falling into each case. The INTERSECT operator takes the results from both of those simple queries and returns a single result set showing the products—just one in this case—that both queries return.

■ **Note**   Like the EXCEPT operator, INTERSECT implicitly deduplicates the final results.

Sometimes you'll find yourself wanting to include other columns in an INTERSECT query, and those columns cause the intersection operation to fail because that operation is performed taking all columns into account. One solution is to treat the intersection query as a derived table and join it to the Product table. For example:

```
SELECT  PR3.ProductID,
        PR3.Name
FROM    Production.Product PR3
        INNER JOIN (SELECT  PR1.ProductID
                    FROM    Production.ProductReview PR1
                    WHERE   PR1.Rating >= 4
                    INTERSECT
                    SELECT  PR1.ProductID
                    FROM    Production.ProductReview PR1
                    WHERE   PR1.Rating <= 2
                   ) SQ
           ON PR3.ProductID = SQ.ProductID;
```

```
ProductID Name
----------- ------------------
        937 HL Mountain Pedal
```

Another approach is to move the intersection subquery into the WHERE clause and use it to generate an in-list. For example:

```
SELECT  ProductID,
        Name
FROM    Production.Product
WHERE   ProductID IN (SELECT    PR1.ProductID
                      FROM      Production.ProductReview PR1
                      WHERE     PR1.Rating >= 4
                      INTERSECT
                      SELECT    PR1.ProductID
                      FROM      Production.ProductReview PR1
                      WHERE     PR1.Rating <= 2);
```

```
ProductID Name
----------- ------------------
        937 HL Mountain Pedal
```

In this version of the query, the subquery generates a list of product ID numbers. The database engine then treats that list as input into the IN predicate. There is only one product in this case, so you can think loosely in terms of the database engine ultimately executing a statement such as the following:

```
SELECT  ProductID,
        Name
FROM    Production.Product
WHERE   ProductID IN (937);
```

You can actually write an IN predicate that gives a list of hard-coded values, or you can choose to generate that list of values from a SELECT statement, as in this recipe.

4-14. Finding Rows that Are Missing

Problem

You want to find rows in one table or result set that have no corresponding rows in another. For example, you want to find all products in the Product table with no corresponding special offers.

Solution

Different approaches are possible, one of which is to write a query involving EXCEPT:

```
SELECT  ProductID
FROM    Production.Product
EXCEPT
SELECT  ProductID
FROM    Sales.SpecialOfferProduct;
```

```
 ProductID
-----------
         1
         2
         3
...
```

If you want to see more than just a list of ID numbers, you can write a query involving NOT EXISTS and a correlated subquery. For example:

```
SELECT   P.ProductID,
         P.Name
FROM     Production.Product P
WHERE    NOT EXISTS ( SELECT *
                      FROM   Sales.SpecialOfferProduct SOP
                      WHERE  SOP.ProductID = P.ProductID );
```

```
 ProductID Name
----------- --------------------------------------------------
         1 Adjustable Race
         2 Bearing Ball
         3 BB Ball Bearing
...
```

How It Works

The solution involving EXCEPT is simple to write and easy to understand. The top query generates a list of all possible products. The bottom query generates a list of products that have been given special offers. EXCEPT subtracts the second list from the first and returns a list of products having no corresponding rows in SpecialOfferProduct. The downside is that this approach limits the final results to just a list of ID numbers.

The second solution involves a NOT EXISTS predicate. You first read about EXISTS in Recipe 4-8. NOT EXISTS is a variation on that theme. Rather than testing for existence, the predicate tests for nonexistence. The parent query then returns all product rows not having corresponding special offers. You are able to include any columns that you desire from the Product table in the query results.

4-15. Comparing Two Tables

Problem

You have two copies of a table. You want to test for equality. Do both copies have the same row and column values?

Solution

Begin by creating a copy of the table. For purposes of example in this recipe, use the Password table

```
SELECT   *
INTO     Person.PasswordCopy
FROM     Person.Password;
```

Then execute the following UNION query to compare the data between the two tables and report on the differences.

```
SELECT  *,
        COUNT(*) DupeCount,
        'Password' TableName
FROM    Person.Password P
GROUP BY BusinessEntityID,
        PasswordHash,
        PasswordSalt,
        rowguid,
        ModifiedDate
HAVING  NOT EXISTS ( SELECT *,
                            COUNT(*)
                     FROM   Person.PasswordCopy PC
                     GROUP BY BusinessEntityID,
                            PasswordHash,
                            PasswordSalt,
                            rowguid,
                            ModifiedDate
                     HAVING PC.BusinessEntityID = P.BusinessEntityID
                            AND PC.PasswordHash = P.PasswordHash
                            AND PC.PasswordSalt = P.PasswordSalt
                            AND PC.rowguid = P.rowguid
                            AND PC.ModifiedDate = P.ModifiedDate
                            AND COUNT(*) = COUNT(ALL P.BusinessEntityID) )
UNION
SELECT  *,
        COUNT(*) DupeCount,
        'PasswordCopy' TableName
FROM    Person.PasswordCopy PC
GROUP BY BusinessEntityID,
        PasswordHash,
        PasswordSalt,
        rowguid,
        ModifiedDate
HAVING  NOT EXISTS ( SELECT *,
                            COUNT(*)
                     FROM   Person.Password P
                     GROUP BY BusinessEntityID,
                            PasswordHash,
                            PasswordSalt,
                            rowguid,
                            ModifiedDate
                     HAVING PC.BusinessEntityID = P.BusinessEntityID
                            AND PC.PasswordHash = P.PasswordHash
                            AND PC.PasswordSalt = P.PasswordSalt
                            AND PC.rowguid = P.rowguid
                            AND PC.ModifiedDate = P.ModifiedDate
                            AND COUNT(*) = COUNT(ALL PC.BusinessEntityID) );
```

The result from this query will be zero rows. That is because the tables are unchanged. You've made a copy of Password, but haven't changed values in either table.

Now make some changes to the data in the two tables. BusinessEntityID numbers are in the range 1, . . . , 19972. Following are some statements to change data in each table, and to create one duplicate row in the copy:

```
UPDATE  Person.PasswordCopy
SET     PasswordSalt = 'Munising!'
WHERE   BusinessEntityID IN (9783, 221);

UPDATE  Person.Password
SET     PasswordSalt = 'Marquette!'
WHERE   BusinessEntityID IN (42, 4242);

INSERT  INTO Person.PasswordCopy
        SELECT  *
        FROM    Person.PasswordCopy
        WHERE   BusinessEntityID = 1;
```

Having changed the data, reissue the previous UNION query to compare the two tables. This time there are results indicating the differences just created:

```
BusinessEntityID PasswordHash   ... PasswordSalt ... DupeCount TableName
---------------- -------------  ... ------------ ... --------- ------------
               1 pbFwXWE99vobT ... bE3XiWw=      ...         1 Password
              42 HSLAA7MxklY4d ... Marquette!    ...         1 Password
             221 DFSEDLoy3em1I ... 5nzaMoQ=      ...         1 Password
            4242 YITAXaCQCapPi ... Marquette!    ...         1 Password
            9783 1gvO8vLyjlhQY ... YcAxsQQ=      ...         1 Password
               1 pbFwXWE99vobT ... bE3XiWw=      ...         2 PasswordCopy
              42 HSLAA7MxklY4d ... uTuRBuI=      ...         1 PasswordCopy
             221 DFSEDLoy3em1I ... Munising!     ...         1 PasswordCopy
            4242 YITAXaCQCapPi ... mj6TQG4=      ...         1 PasswordCopy
            9783 1gvO8vLyjlhQY ... Munising!     ...         1 PasswordCopy
```

These results indicate rows from each table that are not found in the other. They also indicate differences in duplication counts.

How It Works

The solution query is intimidating at first, and it is a lot to type. But it is a rote query once you get the hang of it, and the two halves are essentially mirror images of each other.

The grouping and counting is there to handle the possibility of duplicate rows. Each of the queries begins by grouping all columns and generating a duplication count. For example, the second subquery examines PasswordCopy:

```
SELECT  *,
        COUNT(*) DupeCount,
        'PasswordCopy' TableName
```

```
FROM    Person.PasswordCopy PC
GROUP BY BusinessEntityID,
        PasswordHash,
        PasswordSalt,
        rowguid,
        ModifiedDate;
```

```
BusinessEntityID PasswordHash         DupeCount TableName
---------------- ------------- ...    ---------- ------------
               1 pbFwXWE99vobT ...            2 PasswordCopy
               2 bawRVNrZQYQo5 ...            1 PasswordCopy
...
```

Here, you can see that there are two rows containing the same set of values. Both rows are associated with BusinessEntityID 1. The DupeCount for that ID is 2.

Next comes a subquery in the HAVING clause to restrict the results to only those rows not also appearing in the Password table:

```
HAVING  NOT EXISTS ( SELECT *,
                            COUNT(*)
                     FROM   Person.PasswordCopy PC
                     GROUP BY BusinessEntityID,
                            PasswordHash,
                            PasswordSalt,
                            rowguid,
                            ModifiedDate
                     HAVING PC.BusinessEntityID = P.BusinessEntityID
                            AND PC.PasswordHash = P.PasswordHash
                            AND PC.PasswordSalt = P.PasswordSalt
                            AND PC.rowguid = P.rowguid
                            AND PC.ModifiedDate = P.ModifiedDate
                            AND COUNT(*) = COUNT(ALL P.BusinessEntityID) )
```

This HAVING clause is tedious to write, but it is conceptually simple. It compares all columns, looking for equality. It compares row counts to check for differences in the number of times a row is duplicated in either of the tables. The results are a list of rows in PasswordCopy that do not also exist the same number of times in Password.

Both queries do the same thing from different directions. The first query in the UNION finds rows in Password that are not also in PasswordCopy. The second query reverses things and finds rows in PasswordCopy that are not also in Password. Both queries will detect differences in duplication counts.

There is one row that is reported in the solution results because it occurs twice in the copy and once in the original. See here:

```
BusinessEntityID PasswordHash   ... PasswordSalt ... DupeCount TableName
---------------- ------------- ... ------------ ... --------- ------------
               1 pbFwXWE99vobT ... bE3XiWw=     ...         1 Password
...
               1 pbFwXWE99vobT ... bE3XiWw=     ...         2 PasswordCopy
...
```

The `TableName` column lets you see that `Password` contains just one row for `BusinessEntityID` 1. That makes sense, because that column is the primary key. The `PasswordCopy` table, however, has no primary key. Somehow, someone has duplicated the row for `BusinessEntityID` 1. That table has two copies of the row. Because the number of copies is different, the tables do not compare as being equal.

The solution query reports differences between the two tables. An empty result set indicates that the two tables contain the same rows, which have the same values and occur the same number of times.

CHAPTER 5

■ ■ ■

Aggregations and Grouping

by Wayne Sheffield

Aggregate functions are used to perform a calculation on one or more values, and the result is a single value. If your query has any columns with nonwindowed aggregate functions, then a GROUP BY clause is required for the query. Table 5-1 shows the various aggregate functions.

Table 5-1. *Aggregate Functions*

Function Name	Description
AVG	The AVG aggregate function calculates the average of non-NULL values in a group.
CHECKSUM_AGG	The CHECKSUM_AGG function returns a checksum value based on a group of rows, allowing you to potentially track changes to a table. For example, adding a new row or changing the value of a column that is being aggregated will usually result in a new checksum integer value. The reason I say "usually" is because there is a possibility that the checksum value does not change even if values are modified.
COUNT	The COUNT aggregate function returns an integer data type showing the count of rows in a group, including rows with NULL values.
COUNT_BIG	The COUNT_BIG aggregate function returns a bigint data type showing the count of rows in a group, including rows with NULL values.
GROUPING	
MAX	The MAX aggregate function returns the highest value in a set of non-NULL values.
MIN	The MIN aggregate function returns the lowest value in a group of non-NULL values.
STDEV	The STDEV function returns the standard deviation of all values provided in the expression based on a sample of the data population.
STDEVP	The STDEVP function also returns the standard deviation for all values in the provided expression, but does so based upon the entire data population.
SUM	The SUM aggregate function returns the summation of all non-NULL values in an expression.
VAR	The VAR function returns the statistical variance of values in an expression based upon a sample of the provided population.
VARP	The VARP function returns the statistical variance of values in an expression, but does so based upon the entire data population.

■ **Note** Window functions—and using aggregate functions with window functions—are discussed in Chapter 7.

The STDEV, STDEVP, VAR, and VARP are statistical functions. The use of these functions requires knowledge of how statistics works, which is beyond the scope of this book.

With the exception of the COUNT and COUNT_BIG functions, all of the aggregate functions have the same syntax (the syntax and usage of these functions will be discussed in a recipe later on in this chapter).

```
aggregate_function_name ( { [ [ ALL | DISTINCT ] expression ] } )
```

where expression is a series of expressions and operations that returns a single value (but does not include aggregate functions or subqueries) that the aggregate function will be calculated over. If the optional keyword DISTINCT is used, then only distinct values will be considered. If the optional keyword ALL is used, then all values will be considered. If neither is specified, then ALL is used by default. Aggregate functions and subqueries are not allowed for the expression parameter.

Frequently when aggregating data, you will want to perform the aggregation based upon a grouping of a set of columns in the query. Grouping is primarily performed in SQL Server by using the GROUP BY clause within a SELECT query to determine in which group the rows should be put. Grouping can also be performed at the column level with the use of window functions. Data is aggregated by using the appropriate aggregation function. The simplified syntax is as follows:

```
SELECT Column1, <aggregate_function>(Column2)
FROM table_list
[WHERE search_conditions]
GROUP BY Column1
```

GROUP BY follows the optional WHERE clause and is most often used when aggregate functions are being utilized in the SELECT statement.

5-1. Computing an Aggregation

Problem

You want to perform several aggregations on the ratings of your products.

Solution

Use the appropriate aggregation function to determine each aggregation:

```
SELECT  MIN(Rating)     Rating_Min,
        MAX(Rating)     Rating_Max,
        SUM(Rating)     Rating_Sum,
        AVG(Rating)     Rating_Avg
FROM    Production.ProductReview;
```

This query produces the following result set:

Rating_Min	Rating_Max	Rating_Sum	Rating_Avg
2	5	16	4

How It Works

For the non-NULL values in the table in the Rating column, the MIN function calculates the lowest of these values; the MAX function calculates the highest of these values; the SUM function calculates the total of the ratings; and the AVG aggregate function calculates the average of the values. To demonstrate the use of DISTINCT, let's compare the previous query with the columns returned from the following query:

```
SELECT  AVG(Grade) AS AvgGrade,
        AVG(DISTINCT Grade) AS AvgDistinctGrade
FROM    (VALUES (1, 100),
                (1, 100),
                (1, 100),
                (1, 100),
                (1, 100),
                (1, 30)
        ) dt (StudentId, Grade);
```

This query produces the following result set:

AvgGrade	AvgDistinctGrade
88	65

In this example, we have a student with six grades—five perfect grades of 100 and one failing grade of 30; the average of all of the grades is 88. Within these grades are two distinct grades, and the average of these distinct grades is 65.

When utilizing the AVG function, the expression parameter must be one of the numeric data types.

5-2. Creating Aggregations Based upon the Values of the Data

Problem

You want to aggregate one or more columns, with the aggregations applied to a set of columns whenever the data in those columns change. For example, for each order, you want to see the number of line items, as well as the average, minimum, maximum, and total for those line items.

Solution

The SalesOrderID column is included in the query in order to make the results meaningful (e.g. which order is this for?). Each desired aggregation is performed against the LineTotal column. Finally, the query utilizes the GROUP BY clause in order to group the data by the SalesOrderID. See the following:

```
SELECT  TOP (10)
        SalesOrderID,
        SUM(LineTotal)      AS OrderTotal,
        MIN(LineTotal)      AS MinLine,
        MAX(LineTotal)      AS MaxLine,
        AVG(LineTotal)      AS AvgLine,
        COUNT(LineTotal)    AS CountLine
FROM    [Sales].[SalesOrderDetail]
GROUP BY SalesOrderID
ORDER BY SalesOrderID;
```

This query returns the following result set:

SalesOrderID	OrderTotal	MinLine	MaxLine	AvgLine	CountLine
43659	20565.620600	10.373000	6074.982000	1713.801716	12
43660	1294.252900	419.458900	874.794000	647.126450	2
43661	32726.478600	20.746000	8099.976000	2181.765240	15
43662	28832.528900	178.580800	5248.764000	1310.569495	22
43663	419.458900	419.458900	419.458900	419.458900	1
43664	24432.608800	28.840400	8099.976000	3054.076100	8
43665	14352.771300	10.373000	4049.988000	1435.277130	10
43666	5056.489600	356.898000	2146.962000	842.748266	6
43667	6107.082000	17.100000	2039.994000	1526.770500	4
43668	35944.156200	20.186500	5248.764000	1239.453662	29

How It Works

To determine the groups that rows should be put in, the GROUP BY clause is used in a SELECT query. When grouping a result set, the GROUP BY clause can specify multiple columns, and all columns listed in the SELECT clause must be either used in an aggregate function or referenced in the GROUP BY clause. If the query returns both aggregated and non-aggregated columns, and the GROUP BY clause doesn't specify all of the non-aggregated columns, then the following error will be raised (this error was generated by removing the GROUP BY clause from the example in this recipe):

```
Msg 8120, Level 16, State 1, Line 9
Column 'Sales.SalesOrderDetail.SalesOrderID' is invalid in the select list because
it is not contained in either an aggregate function or the GROUP BY clause.
```

This error is raised because any column being returned by the query that is not used in an aggregate function in the SELECT list must be listed in the GROUP BY clause for the query.

5-3. Counting the Rows in a Group

Problem

You want to see the number of rows for each value of a column—for instance, the number of products you have in inventory on each shelf for your first five shelves.

Solution

Utilize the COUNT or COUNT_BIG function to return the count of rows in a group:

```
SELECT  TOP (5)
        Shelf,
        COUNT(ProductID) AS ProductCount,
        COUNT_BIG(ProductID) AS ProductCountBig
FROM    Production.ProductInventory
GROUP BY Shelf
ORDER BY Shelf;
```

This query returns the following result set:

Shelf	ProductCount	ProductCountBig
A	81	81
B	36	36
C	55	55
D	50	50
E	85	85

The results of this query show each shelf and the number of products on each of those shelves.

How It Works

The COUNT and COUNT_BIG functions are utilized to return a count of the number of items in a group. The difference between these functions is the data type returned: COUNT returns an INTEGER, while COUNT_BIG returns a BIGINT. You should utilize COUNT_BIG if you will be counting more rows than the INTEGER data type supports ($2^{31}-1$). Throughout this book, the COUNT function will be used. The syntax for these functions is as follows:

```
COUNT | COUNT_BIG ( { [ [ ALL | DISTINCT ] expression ] | * } )
```

The difference between this syntax and the other aggregate functions is the optional asterisk (*) that can be specified. The use of COUNT(*) specifies that all rows should be counted so as to return the total number of rows within a table; conversely, if COUNT(<nullable column>) is used, then rows where that column is NULL will not be counted. COUNT(*) does not use any parameters, so it does not use any information about any column.

When utilizing the COUNT or COUNT_BIG functions, the expression parameter can be of any data type except for the text, image, or ntext data types. For instance, for the following table variable:

```
DECLARE @test TABLE (col1 TEXT);
```

this query:

```
SELECT COUNT(col1) FROM @test;
```

will return the following error:

```
Msg 8117, Level 16, State 1, Line 4
Operand data type text is invalid for count operator.
```

However, you can utilize COUNT(*) instead:

```
SELECT COUNT(*) FROM @test;
```

which returns this result set:

```
--
0
```

If you are using the COUNT function and you exceed the capacity for an integer, then the following error will be generated:

```
Msg 8115, Level 16, State 2, Line 1
Arithmetic overflow error converting expression to data type int.
```

5-4. Detecting Changes in a Table

Problem

You need to determine whether any changes have been made to the data in a column.

Solution

Utilize the CHECKSUM_AGG function to detect changes in a table. For example:

```
IF OBJECT_ID('tempdb.dbo.[#Recipe5.4]') IS NOT NULL DROP TABLE [#Recipe5.4];
CREATE TABLE [#Recipe5.4]
(
    StudentID INTEGER,
    Grade     INTEGER
);
```

```
INSERT INTO [#Recipe5.4] (StudentID, Grade)
VALUES   (1, 100),
         (1, 95)

SELECT  StudentID, CHECKSUM_AGG(Grade) AS GradeChecksumAgg
FROM    [#Recipe5.4]
GROUP BY StudentID;

UPDATE  [#Recipe5.4]
SET     Grade = 99
WHERE   Grade = 95;

SELECT  StudentID, CHECKSUM_AGG(Grade) AS GradeChecksumAgg
FROM    [#Recipe5.4]
GROUP BY StudentID;
```

These queries return the following result sets:

StudentID	GradeChecksumAgg
1	59

StudentID	GradeChecksumAgg
1	7

How It Works

The CHECKSUM_AGG function returns the checksum of the values in the group, in this case the values from the Grade column. In the second query, the last grade is changed, and when the first query is rerun, the aggregated checksum returns a different value.

When utilizing the CHECKSUM_AGG function, the expression parameter must be of an integer data type.

■ **Note**   Because of the hashing algorithm being used, it is possible for the CHECKSUM_AGG function to return the same value with different data. You should use this function only if your application can tolerate occasionally missing a change.

5-5. Restricting a Result Set to Groups of Interest

Problem

You do not want to return all of the rows that could be returned by an aggregation; instead, you want only the rows where the aggregation itself is filtered. For example, you want to report on the reasons that the product was scrapped, but only for the reasons that have more than 50 occurrences.

Solution

Specify a HAVING clause, giving the conditions that the aggregated rows must meet in order to be returned.

This example queries two tables: Production.ScrapReason and Production.WorkOrder. The Production.ScrapReason table is a lookup table that contains manufacturing failure reasons, and the Production.WorkOrder table contains the manufacturing work orders that control which products are manufactured in the quantity and time period required in order to meet inventory and sales needs. A report is needed that shows which of the "failure reasons" have occurred more than 50 times, which can be achieved by the following code:

```
SELECT  s.Name,
        COUNT(w.WorkOrderID) AS Cnt
FROM    Production.ScrapReason s
        INNER JOIN Production.WorkOrder w
            ON s.ScrapReasonID = w.ScrapReasonID
GROUP BY s.Name
HAVING  COUNT(*) > 50;
```

This query returns the following result set:

Name	Cnt
Gouge in metal	54
Stress test failed	52
Thermoform temperature too low	63
Trim length too long	52
Wheel misaligned	51

How It Works

The HAVING clause of the SELECT statement allows you to specify a search condition on a query that uses GROUP BY and/or an aggregated value. The syntax is as follows:

```
SELECT select_list
FROM table_list
[ WHERE search_conditions ]
[ GROUP BY group_by_list ]
[ HAVING search_conditions ]
```

The HAVING clause is used to qualify the results after the GROUP BY has been applied. The WHERE clause, in contrast, is used to qualify the rows that are returned from the tables specified in the FROM clause before the data is aggregated or grouped. HAVING qualifies the aggregated data after the data has been grouped.

In this recipe, the SELECT clause requests a count of WorkOrderIDs by failure name:

```
SELECT  s.Name,
        COUNT(w.WorkOrderID) AS Cnt
```

Two tables are joined by the ScrapReasonID column:

```
FROM    Production.ScrapReason s
        INNER JOIN Production.WorkOrder w
            ON s.ScrapReasonID = w.ScrapReasonID
```

Because an aggregate function is used in the SELECT clause, the nonaggregated columns must appear in the GROUP BY clause:

```
GROUP BY s.Name
```

Lastly, using the HAVING query ensures that, of the selected and grouped data, only those rows in the result set with a count of more than 50 will be returned:

```
HAVING COUNT(*)>50
```

5-6. Performing Aggregations against Unique Values Only

Problem

You need to know the quantity of unique values per date.

Solution

Add the DISTINCT clause to the COUNT function:

```
SELECT  [RateChangeDate],
        COUNT([Rate]) AS [Count],
        COUNT(DISTINCT Rate) AS [DistinctCount]
FROM    [HumanResources].[EmployeePayHistory]
WHERE   RateChangeDate >= '2008-12-01'
        AND RateChangeDate < '2008-12-10'
GROUP BY RateChangeDate;
```

This query returns the following result set:

RateChangeDate	Count	DistinctCount
2008-12-01 00:00:00.000	2	2
2008-12-02 00:00:00.000	3	2
2008-12-03 00:00:00.000	1	1
2008-12-04 00:00:00.000	3	3
2008-12-05 00:00:00.000	1	1
2008-12-06 00:00:00.000	2	2
2008-12-07 00:00:00.000	5	3
2008-12-08 00:00:00.000	2	2
2008-12-09 00:00:00.000	3	3

How It Works

This query utilizes two COUNT functions; the second one also uses the DISTINCT clause. This forces the COUNT function to count only the distinct values in the specified column, in this case the Rate column. To further understand the difference, let's examine the data for a date where the two functions are returning different values—2008-12-02:

```
SELECT  RateChangeDate, Rate
FROM    HumanResources.EmployeePayHistory
WHERE   RateChangeDate = '2008-12-02';
```

This query returns the following three rows:

```
RateChangeDate              Rate
----------------------      -----
2008-12-02 00:00:00.000     6.50
2008-12-02 00:00:00.000     10.00
2008-12-02 00:00:00.000     10.00
```

When looking at the data, you can see that for this date there are three rows; however, there are two distinct values in the Rate column. Therefore, the COUNT function returned 3, while COUNT(DISTINCT) returned 2.

5-7. Creating Hierarchical Summaries

Problem

You need to return a data set with the detail data as well as with subtotal rows and a grand total row based upon the GROUP BY clause.

Solution

You need to include the ROLLUP argument after the GROUP BY clause. This example uses the ROLLUP argument to produce subtotal lines at the Shelf level, as well as a grand total line:

```
SELECT  i.Shelf,
        p.Name,
SUM(i.Quantity) AS Total
FROM    Production.ProductInventory i
INNER JOIN Production.Product p
ON i.ProductID = p.ProductID
WHERE   i.Shelf IN ('A','B')
AND     p.Name LIKE 'Metal%'
GROUP BY ROLLUP(i.Shelf, p.Name);
```

This query returns the following result set:

```
Shelf       Name        Total
----------  ----------- -----
A           Metal Angle 404
A           Metal Bar 1 353
A           Metal Bar 2 622
A           NULL        1379
B           Metal Angle 355
B           Metal Bar 1 403
B           Metal Bar 2 497
B           NULL        1255
NULL        NULL        2634
```

How It Works

The order in which you place the columns in the GROUP BY ROLLUP clause affects how data is aggregated. ROLLUP in this query aggregates the total quantity for each change in Shelf. Notice the row with shelf A and the NULL name; this holds the total quantity for shelf A. Also notice that the final row is the grand total of all product quantities. Whereas CUBE creates a result set that aggregates all combinations for the selected columns, ROLLUP generates the aggregates for a hierarchy of values.

```
GROUP BY ROLLUP (i.Shelf, p.Name)
```

ROLLUP aggregated both a grand total and totals by shelf. Totals were not generated for the product name, but would have been had CUBE been designated instead.

ROLLUP uses a slightly different syntax than previous versions of SQL Server used. ROLLUP comes directly after the GROUP BY clause, instead of trailing the GROUP BY clause with a WITH ROLLUP clause. Notice also that the column lists are contained within parentheses.

■ **Note**   The GROUP BY WITH ROLLUP feature does not follow the ISO standard, and it will be removed in a future version of Microsoft SQL Server. You should avoid using this feature in any new development work, and you should modify any applications that currently use this feature to use the ROLLUP argument instead.

In this example, I've shown how the ROLLUP clause works across a set of columns. Let's examine another scenario now: we want to include the LocationID column in the output, and then we want to perform the ROLLUP at just the name level. This would be performed with the following query:

```
SELECT  i.Shelf,
        i.LocationID,
        p.Name,
SUM(i.Quantity) AS Total
FROM    Production.ProductInventory i
INNER JOIN Production.Product p
ON i.ProductID = p.ProductID
```

```
WHERE    i.Shelf IN ('A','B')
AND      p.Name LIKE 'Metal%'
GROUP BY i.Shelf, i.LocationID, ROLLUP(i.Shelf, p.Name)
ORDER BY i.Shelf, i.LocationID;
```

This is accomplished by grouping by Shelf and LocationID and then applying ROLLUP.

5-8. Creating Summary Totals and Subtotals

Problem

You need to return a data set with the detail data as well as with the data summarized on each combination of columns specified in the GROUP BY clause.

Solution

You need to include the CUBE argument after the GROUP BY clause. This example uses the CUBE argument to produce subtotal lines at both the Shelf and LocationID levels, as well as a grand total line:

```
SELECT  Shelf,
        LocationID,
SUM(Quantity) AS Total
FROM    Production.ProductInventory
WHERE   Shelf IN ('A','B')
AND     LocationID IN (10, 20)
GROUP BY CUBE(Shelf, LocationID);
```

This query produces several levels of totals, the first being by LocationID.

Shelf	LocationID	Total
A	10	1379
B	10	1648
NULL	10	3027
A	20	1680
B	20	355
NULL	20	2035
NULL	NULL	5062
A	NULL	3059
B	NULL	2003

How It Works

By using the CUBE argument, the query groups by the specified columns, and it creates additional rows that provide totals for each combination of the columns specified in the GROUP BY clause. The rows with NULL values indicate a totaling at either the subtotal or total level. When all of the columns specified in the GROUP BY CUBE are NULL, then this row is the total row. Rows with one or more, but not all, of the columns specified in the GROUP BY CUBE set to NULL are subtotals at the level of the non-null columns. See recipes 5-12 and 5-13 for differing these groups from data when the columns specified in the GROUP BY CUBE clause contain legitimate NULL values.

CUBE uses a slightly different syntax than in previous versions of SQL Server: CUBE comes after the GROUP BY clause instead of trailing the GROUP BY clause with a WITH CUBE. Notice also that the column lists are contained within parentheses.

■ **Note** The GROUP BY WITH CUBE feature does not follow the ISO standard, and it will be removed in a future version of Microsoft SQL Server. You should avoid using this feature in any new development work, and you should modify any applications that currently use this feature to use the CUBE argument instead.

As with the ROLLUP feature, CUBE allows to you first group by columns, then a cube. For example:

```
SELECT   Shelf,
         LocationID,
         SUM(i.Quantity) AS Total
FROM     Production.ProductInventory
WHERE    Shelf in ('A','B')
AND      LocationID in (10,20)
GROUP BY shelf, CUBE(Shelf, LocationID);
```

5-9. Creating Custom Summaries

Problem

You need to have one result set with multiple custom aggregations.

Solution

You must include the GROUPING SETS argument after the GROUP BY clause and also include each of the custom aggregations that you want performed.

SQL Server gives you the ability to define your own grouping sets within a single query result set without having to resort to multiple UNION ALL queries. GROUPING SETS also provides you with more control over what is aggregated, as compared to the previously demonstrated CUBE and ROLLUP operations. This is performed by using the GROUPING SETS operator.

First, let's define a business requirement for a query, which is to have a single result set that contains three different aggregate quantity summaries. Specifically, I would like to see quantity totals by shelf, quantity totals by both shelf and product name, and then also quantity totals by location and name.

We'll use the GROUPING SETS operator to define the various aggregations we would like to have returned in a single result set:

```
SELECT   i.Shelf,
         i.LocationID,
         p.Name,
         SUM(i.Quantity) AS Total
```

```
FROM     Production.ProductInventory i
         INNER JOIN Production.Product p
             ON i.ProductID = p.ProductID
WHERE    Shelf IN ('A', 'C')
         AND Name IN ('Chain', 'Decal', 'Head Tube')
GROUP BY GROUPING SETS((i.Shelf), (i.Shelf, p.Name), (i.LocationID, p.Name));
```

This returns the following results:

Shelf	LocationID	Name	Total
NULL	1	Chain	236
NULL	5	Chain	192
NULL	50	Chain	161
NULL	20	Head Tube	544
A	NULL	Chain	353
A	NULL	Head Tube	544
A	NULL	NULL	897
C	NULL	Chain	236
C	NULL	NULL	236

How It Works

The new GROUPING SETS operator allows you to define varying aggregate groups in a single query while avoiding having multiple queries attached together using the UNION ALL operator. The core of this recipe's example is the following line of code:

```
GROUP BY GROUPING SETS ((i.Shelf), (i.Shelf, p.Name), (i.LocationID, p.Name))
```

Notice that, unlike a regular aggregated query, the GROUP BY clause is not followed by a list of columns. Instead, it is followed by GROUPING SETS. GROUPING SETS is then followed by parentheses and the groupings of column names, each of which is also encapsulated in parentheses.

To achieve this in previous versions of SQL Server, you would have needed to use the UNION ALL operator with multiple queries, as follows:

```
SELECT   NULL AS Shelf,
         i.LocationID,
         p.Name,
         SUM(i.Quantity) AS Total
FROM     Production.ProductInventory i
         INNER JOIN Production.Product p
             ON i.ProductID = p.ProductID
WHERE    Shelf IN ('A', 'C')
         AND Name IN ('Chain', 'Decal', 'Head Tube')
GROUP BY i.LocationID,
         p.Name
```

```
UNION ALL
SELECT  i.Shelf,
        NULL,
        NULL,
        SUM(i.Quantity) AS Total
FROM    Production.ProductInventory i
        INNER JOIN Production.Product p
            ON i.ProductID = p.ProductID
WHERE   Shelf IN ('A', 'C')
        AND Name IN ('Chain', 'Decal', 'Head Tube')
GROUP BY i.Shelf
UNION ALL
SELECT  i.Shelf,
        NULL,
        p.Name,
        SUM(i.Quantity) AS Total
FROM    Production.ProductInventory i
        INNER JOIN Production.Product p
            ON i.ProductID = p.ProductID
WHERE   Shelf IN ('A', 'C')
        AND Name IN ('Chain', 'Decal', 'Head Tube')
GROUP BY i.Shelf,
        p.Name;
```

This query returns the following result set, which has the same results as when using grouping sets (just ordered slightly differently by the database engine):

Shelf	LocationID	Name	Total
NULL	1	Chain	236
NULL	5	Chain	192
NULL	50	Chain	161
NULL	20	Head Tube	544
A	NULL	NULL	897
C	NULL	NULL	236
A	NULL	Chain	353
C	NULL	Chain	236
A	NULL	Head Tube	544

As you can see, GROUPING SETS allows for quite a bit simpler code for the complex requirements. GROUPING SETS also allows you to use CUBE and ROLLUP as one of the sets.

5-10. Identifying Rows Generated by the GROUP BY Arguments

Problem

You need to differentiate between the rows that actually have stored NULL data and the total or subtotal rows generated by the GROUP BY arguments that have a NULL value generated for that column.

Solution

You need to utilize the GROUPING function in your query.

The following query uses a CASE statement to evaluate whether each row is a total by the ReorderPoint, total by Size, or a regular, noncubed row:

```
SELECT  CASE WHEN GROUPING(ReorderPoint) = 1 THEN '--GROUP--'
             ELSE CONVERT(VARCHAR(15), ReorderPoint)
        END AS ReorderPointCalc,
        ReorderPoint,
        CASE WHEN GROUPING(Size) = 1 THEN '--GROUP--'
             ELSE CONVERT(VARCHAR(15), Size)
        END AS SizeCalc,
        Size,
        CASE WHEN GROUPING(ReorderPoint) = 0 AND GROUPING(Size) = 1 THEN 'Size Total'
             WHEN GROUPING(ReorderPoint) = 1 AND GROUPING(Size) = 0 THEN 'ReorderPoint
             Total'
             WHEN GROUPING(ReorderPoint) = 1 AND GROUPING(Size) = 1 THEN 'Grand Total'
             ELSE 'Regular Row'
        END AS RowType,
        SUM(StandardCost) AS Total
FROM    Production.Product
WHERE   ReorderPoint = 3
GROUP BY CUBE(ReorderPoint, Size);
```

This query returns the following result set:

ReorderPointCalc	ReorderPoint	SizeCalc	Size	RowType	Total
3	3	NULL	NULL	Regular Row	290.7344
--GROUP--	NULL	NULL	NULL	ReorderPoint Total	290.7344
3	3	70	70	Regular Row	20.5663
--GROUP--	NULL	70	70	ReorderPoint Total	20.5663
3	3	L	L	Regular Row	254.3789
--GROUP--	NULL	L	L	ReorderPoint Total	254.3789
3	3	M	M	Regular Row	254.3789
--GROUP--	NULL	M	M	ReorderPoint Total	254.3789
3	3	S	S	Regular Row	247.6203
--GROUP--	NULL	S	S	ReorderPoint Total	247.6203
3	3	XL	XL	Regular Row	104.8105
--GROUP--	NULL	XL	XL	ReorderPoint Total	104.8105
--GROUP--	NULL	--GROUP--	NULL	Grand Total	1172.4893
3	3	--GROUP--	NULL	Size Total	1172.4893

How It Works

Notice how the rows grouped in the previous recipes have NULL values in the columns that aren't participating in the aggregate totals. For example, when shelf C is totaled up in the previous recipe, the location and product name columns are NULL:

```
C  NULL  NULL  236
```

If the data contains NULL values, then it can become difficult to differentiate the NULL values from the data, and NULL values from the grouping. To address this issue, you can use the GROUPING function. This allows you to differentiate and act upon those rows that are generated automatically for aggregates using CUBE, ROLLUP, and GROUPING SETS. In this example, the SELECT statement evaluates whether the data in the column is NULL due to the grouping; if so, it returns "–GROUP–". The SELECT statement also calculates for each row whether it is a regular row (a row that contains data from the table), or whether it is added to the result set as the result of the grouping. If it is the result of the grouping, it determines which grouping (Size, ReorderPoint, or Grand Total) that the row represents.

■ **Tip** For more on CASE, see Chapter 2.

When GROUPING returns a 1 value (true), it means the column NULL is not an actual data value but rather is a result of the aggregate operation, standing in for the value all. So, for example, if the ReorderPoint value is not NULL and the Size is NULL because of the CUBE aggregation process and not the data itself, the string Size Total is returned:

```
CASE WHEN GROUPING(ReorderPoint) = 0 AND GROUPING(Size) = 1 THEN 'Size Total'
```

The statement continues with similar logic, only this time if the ReorderPoint value is NULL because of the CUBE aggregation process but the Size is not null, a ReorderPoint total is provided:

```
WHEN GROUPING(ReorderPoint) = 1 AND GROUPING(Size) = 0 THEN 'ReorderPoint Total'
```

The last WHEN states that when both ReorderPoint and Size are NULL because of the CUBE aggregation process, then the row contains the grand total for the result set:

```
WHEN GROUPING(ReorderPoint) = 1 AND GROUPING(Size) = 1 THEN 'Grand Total'
```

Notice that the first two rows returned in this result set have a value of NULL for the Size. For the row where the ReorderPoint is 3, the NULL is from the actual data. Without the GROUPING function, it would be difficult to determine by looking at the data returned whether the NULL was from the data or from the grouping.

GROUPING returns only a 1 or a 0; however, you also have the option of using GROUPING_ID to compute grouping at a finer grain, as demonstrated in the next recipe.

5-11. Identifying Summary Levels

Problem

You need to identify which columns are being considered in the grouping rows added to the result set; however, using the GROUPING function on the multiple columns being grouped is making the query complex and difficult to understand.

Solution

You need to utilize the GROUPING_ID function in your query.

The following query uses the GROUPING_ID function to return those columns used in the grouping of that particular row:

```
SELECT  Shelf,
        LocationID,
        Bin,
        CASE GROUPING_ID(Shelf, LocationID, Bin)
          WHEN 1 THEN 'Shelf/Location Total'
          WHEN 2 THEN 'Shelf/Bin Total'
          WHEN 3 THEN 'Shelf Total'
          WHEN 4 THEN 'Location/Bin Total'
          WHEN 5 THEN 'Location Total'
          WHEN 6 THEN 'Bin Total'
          WHEN 7 THEN 'Grand Total'
          ELSE 'Regular Row'
        END AS GroupingType,
        SUM(Quantity) AS Total
FROM    Production.ProductInventory
WHERE   LocationID IN (3)
        AND Bin IN (1, 2)
GROUP BY CUBE(Shelf, LocationID, Bin)
ORDER BY Shelf,
         LocationID,
         Bin;
```

The result set returned from this query has descriptions of the various aggregations that resulted from using CUBE.

Shelf	LocationID	Bin	GroupingType	Total
NULL	NULL	NULL	Grand Total	90
NULL	NULL	1	Bin Total	49
NULL	NULL	2	Bin Total	41
NULL	3	NULL	Location Total	90
NULL	3	1	Location/Bin Total	49
NULL	3	2	Location/Bin Total	41
A	NULL	NULL	Shelf Total	90
A	NULL	1	Shelf/Bin Total	49
A	NULL	2	Shelf/Bin Total	41
A	3	NULL	Shelf/Location Total	90
A	3	1	Regular Row	49
A	3	2	Regular Row	41

How It Works

■ **Note** This recipe assumes an understanding of the binary/base-2 number system.

Identifying which rows belong to which type of aggregate becomes progressively more difficult for each new column you add to the GROUP BY clause and for each unique data value that can be grouped and aggregated. For example, this query shows the quantity of products in location 3 within bins 1 and 2:

```
SELECT   Shelf,
         LocationID,
         Bin,
         Quantity
FROM     Production.ProductInventory
WHERE    LocationID IN (3)
AND      Bin IN (1, 2);
```

This query returns only two rows:

Shelf	LocationID	Bin	Quantity
A	3	2	41
A	3	1	49

Now, what if we needed to report aggregations based on the various combinations of Shelf, Location, and Bin? We could use CUBE to give summaries of all these potential combinations:

```
SELECT  Shelf,
        LocationID,
        Bin,
        SUM(Quantity) AS Total
FROM    Production.ProductInventory
WHERE   LocationID IN (3)
AND     Bin IN (1, 2)
GROUP BY CUBE(Shelf, LocationID, Bin)
ORDER BY Shelf,
        LocationID,
        Bin;
```

Although the query returns the various aggregations expected from CUBE, the results are difficult to decipher.

Shelf	LocationID	Bin	Total
NULL	NULL	NULL	90
NULL	NULL	1	49
NULL	NULL	2	41
NULL	3	NULL	90
NULL	3	1	49
NULL	3	2	41
A	NULL	NULL	90
A	NULL	1	49
A	NULL	2	41
A	3	NULL	90
A	3	1	49
A	3	2	41

This is where GROUPING_ID comes in handy. Using this function, we can determine the level of grouping for the row. This function is more complicated than GROUPING, however, because GROUPING_ID takes one or more columns as its input and then returns the integer equivalent of the base-2 (binary) number calculation on the columns.

Stepping through this, the query starts off with the list of the three nonaggregated columns to be returned in the result set:

```
SELECT i.Shelf,
       i.LocationID,
       i.Bin,
```

Next, a CASE statement evaluates the return value of GROUPING_ID for the list of the three columns:

```
CASE GROUPING_ID(i.Shelf, i.LocationID, i.Bin)
```

Since there are three columns in the GROUP BY CUBE, the various potential aggregations are represented in the following WHENs/THENs:

```
CASE GROUPING_ID(i.Shelf,i.LocationID, i.Bin)
     WHEN 1 THEN 'Shelf/Location Total'
     WHEN 2 THEN 'Shelf/Bin Total'
     WHEN 3 THEN 'Shelf Total'
     WHEN 4 THEN 'Location/Bin Total'
     WHEN 5 THEN 'Location Total'
     WHEN 6 THEN 'Bin Total'
     WHEN 7 THEN 'Grand Total'
ELSE 'Regular Row'
END,
```

Each potential combination of aggregations is handled in the CASE statement. The rest of the query involves using an aggregate function on quantity and then using CUBE to find the various aggregation combinations for the shelf, location, and bin:

```
     SUM(i.Quantity) AS Total
  FROM Production.ProductInventory i
 WHERE i.LocationID IN (3)
   AND i.Bin IN (1, 2)
 GROUP BY CUBE (i.Shelf, i.LocationID, i.Bin)
 ORDER BY i.Shelf, i.LocationID, i.Bin;
```

To illustrate the concept of a base-2 conversion to an integer, let's start by including the results of the GROUPING_ID function (for the set of columns defined above) and the individual GROUPING function outputs (for each of the three columns) to the query. The updated query that will be used is:

```
SELECT  Shelf,
        LocationID,
        Bin,
        CASE GROUPING_ID(Shelf, LocationID, Bin)
          WHEN 1 THEN 'Shelf/Location Total'
          WHEN 2 THEN 'Shelf/Bin Total'
          WHEN 3 THEN 'Shelf Total'
          WHEN 4 THEN 'Location/Bin Total'
          WHEN 5 THEN 'Location Total'
          WHEN 6 THEN 'Bin Total'
          WHEN 7 THEN 'Grand Total'
          ELSE 'Regular Row'
        END AS GroupingType,
        GROUPING_ID(Shelf, LocationID, Bin) AS [G_ID],
        GROUPING(Shelf) AS [G_Shelf],
        GROUPING(LocationID) AS [G_Loc],
        GROUPING(Bin) AS [G_Bin],
        (GROUPING(Shelf)*4) + (GROUPING(LocationID)*2) + GROUPING(Bin) AS [G_Total],
        SUM(Quantity) AS Total
```

```
FROM      Production.ProductInventory
WHERE     LocationID IN (3)
          AND Bin IN (1, 2)
GROUP BY CUBE(Shelf, LocationID, Bin)
ORDER BY Shelf,
LocationID,
Bin;
```

This query returns the following result set:

Shelf	LocationID	Bin	GroupingType	G_ID	G_Shelf	G_Loc	G_Bin	G_Total	Total
NULL	NULL	NULL	Grand Total	7	1	1	1	7	90
NULL	NULL	1	Bin Total	6	1	1	0	6	49
NULL	NULL	2	Bin Total	6	1	1	0	6	41
NULL	3	NULL	Location Total	5	1	0	1	5	90
NULL	3	1	Location/Bin Total	4	1	0	0	4	49
NULL	3	2	Location/Bin Total	4	1	0	0	4	41
A	NULL	NULL	Shelf Total	3	0	1	1	3	90
A	NULL	1	Shelf/Bin Total	2	0	1	0	2	49
A	NULL	2	Shelf/Bin Total	2	0	1	0	2	41
A	3	NULL	Shelf/Location Total	1	0	0	1	1	90
A	3	1	Regular Row	0	0	0	0	0	49
A	3	2	Regular Row	0	0	0	0	0	41

In this query, the GROUPING function is used for each column in the same order as they are called in the GROUPING_ID function, and the results display a bit map for those three columns. Starting from the rightmost column, the G_Bin column is taken as is. By their locations in the bit map, the G_Loc column has its value multiplied by two, and the G_Shelf column has its value multiplied by 4. The sum of these numbers is returned in the G_Total column, and you can see that it matches up exactly with the G_ID column.

It is possible to obtain the same information utilizing just the GROUPING function. If we modify the original query to also determine the Grouping Type by the GROUPING function, the query would become:

```
SELECT  i.Shelf,
        i.LocationID,
        i.Bin,
CASE GROUPING_ID(i.Shelf, i.LocationID, i.Bin)
WHEN 1 THEN 'Shelf/Location Total'
WHEN 2 THEN 'Shelf/Bin Total'
WHEN 3 THEN 'Shelf Total'
WHEN 4 THEN 'Location/Bin Total'
WHEN 5 THEN 'Location Total'
WHEN 6 THEN 'Bin Total'
WHEN 7 THEN 'Grand Total'
ELSE 'Regular Row'
END AS GroupingType,
CASE WHEN GROUPING(Shelf) = 0 AND GROUPING(LocationID) = 0 AND GROUPING(Bin) = 1
THEN 'Shelf/Location Total'
WHEN GROUPING(Shelf) = 0 AND GROUPING(LocationID) = 1 AND GROUPING(Bin) = 0
THEN 'Shelf/Bin Total'
```

```
WHEN GROUPING(Shelf) = 0 AND GROUPING(LocationID) = 1 AND GROUPING(Bin) = 1
THEN 'Shelf Total'
WHEN GROUPING(Shelf) = 1 AND GROUPING(LocationID) = 0 AND GROUPING(Bin) = 0
THEN 'Location/Bin Total'
WHEN GROUPING(Shelf) = 1 AND GROUPING(LocationID) = 0 AND GROUPING(Bin) = 1
THEN 'Location Total'
WHEN GROUPING(Shelf) = 1 AND GROUPING(LocationID) = 1 AND GROUPING(Bin) = 0
THEN 'Bin Total'
WHEN GROUPING(Shelf) = 1 AND GROUPING(LocationID) = 1 AND GROUPING(Bin) = 1
THEN 'Grand Total'
ELSE 'Regular Row'
END,
SUM(i.Quantity) AS Total
FROM      Production.ProductInventory i
WHERE     i.LocationID IN (3)
AND i.Bin IN (1, 2)
GROUP BY CUBE(i.Shelf, i.LocationID, i.Bin)
ORDER BY i.Shelf,
         i.LocationID,
         i.Bin;
```

When run, this query produces the following result set:

Shelf	LocationID	Bin	GroupingType	GroupingTypeMod	Total
NULL	NULL	NULL	Grand Total	Grand Total	90
NULL	NULL	1	Bin Total	Bin Total	49
NULL	NULL	2	Bin Total	Bin Total	41
NULL	3	NULL	Location Total	Location Total	90
NULL	3	1	Location/Bin Total	Location/Bin Total	49
NULL	3	2	Location/Bin Total	Location/Bin Total	41
A	NULL	NULL	Shelf Total	Shelf Total	90
A	NULL	1	Shelf/Bin Total	Shelf/Bin Total	49
A	NULL	2	Shelf/Bin Total	Shelf/Bin Total	41
A	3	NULL	Shelf/Location Total	Shelf/Location Total	90
A	3	1	Regular Row	Regular Row	49
A	3	2	Regular Row	Regular Row	41

It can be seen that the same results can be produced utilizing just the GROUPING function. For either function, as you increase the number of columns that the grouping is being performed on, each additional column doubles the number of values being returned (and thus it doubles the number of WHEN expressions needed in the CASE statement). However, if you are utilizing the GROUPING function, then each column that you add also needs to be added into the WHEN expression, quickly making the use of the GROUPING_ID function simpler—with just the three columns being grouped on in this example, the section utilizing the GROUPING_ID function is already simpler to read and understand. Using the GROUPING_ID function is also more efficient; notice that there is just one call to the GROUPING_ID function, while there are twenty-one calls to the GROUPING function. Each call does take some additional CPU time—even if the GROUPING function call is extremely efficient, there will be a hit.

CHAPTER 6

Advanced Select Techniques

by Wayne Sheffield

It's easy to return data from a table. What's not so easy is getting the data you need how you need it, utilizing fast, set-based methods. This chapter will show you some of the advanced techniques that can be used when selecting data.

6-1. Avoiding Duplicate Results

Problem

You need to see all of the dates on which any employee was hired. However, you have hired multiple employees on the same dates, and you want to see each relevant date only once.

Solution #1

Utilize the DISTINCT clause of the SELECT statement to remove duplicate values:

```
SELECT  DISTINCT TOP (10) HireDate
FROM    HumanResources.Employee
ORDER BY HireDate;
```

This query returns the following result set:

```
HireDate
----------
2006-06-30
2007-01-26
2007-11-11
2007-12-05
2007-12-11
2007-12-20
2007-12-26
2008-01-06
2008-01-07
2008-01-24
```

Solution #2

Utilize the GROUP BY clause of the SELECT statement to remove duplicate values:

```
SELECT  TOP (10) HireDate
FROM    HumanResources.Employee
GROUP BY HireDate
ORDER BY HireDate;
```

This query returns the same result set.

How It Works

The default behavior of a SELECT statement is to use the ALL keyword (however, because it is the default, you'll rarely see this being spelled out in a query), meaning that all rows will be retrieved and displayed if they exist. Using the DISTINCT keyword instead of ALL allows you to return only unique rows (across columns selected) in your results.

When utilizing the GROUP BY clause, all unique values are grouped together. If all columns in the query are in the GROUP BY clause, the output will not have any duplicate rows.

Please see the next recipe for how the TOP clause affects the result set.

6-2. Returning the Top *N* Rows

Problem

You want to return only the last five dates on which any employee was hired.

Solution

Utilize the TOP clause of the SELECT statement, together with an ORDER BY clause, to return the five most recent dates on which an employee was hired:

```
SELECT  TOP (5) HireDate
FROM    HumanResources.Employee
GROUP BY HireDate
ORDER BY HireDate DESC;
```

This query returns the following result set:

```
HireDate
----------
2013-05-30
2013-03-14
2012-09-30
2012-05-30
2012-04-16
```

How It Works

The TOP keyword allows you to return the first *n* number of rows from a query that is based on the number of rows or percentage of rows that you define. The first rows returned are also impacted by how your query is ordered. In this example, we are ordering the results by HireDate descending, so only the first five most recent dates are returned. Note that if you utilize TOP without an ORDER BY clause, the database engine will return the specified number of rows in the quickest manner by which it can find any rows matching the predicate—which means that they will likely be returned in a random order.

The TOP keyword also allows for returning a percentage. To return the top 5 percent of the most recent dates any employee was hired, add the PERCENT keyword to the previous query:

```
SELECT  TOP (5) PERCENT HireDate
FROM    HumanResources.Employee
GROUP BY HireDate
ORDER BY HireDate DESC;
```

This query returns the following result set:

```
HireDate
----------
2013-05-30
2013-03-14
2012-09-30
2012-05-30
2012-04-16
2011-05-31
2011-02-25
2011-02-15
2011-02-14
```

■ **Note** The parentheses surrounding the expression are required in INSERT, UPDATE, DELETE, and MERGE statements. To maintain backward compatibility, they are optional in SELECT statements, though it is recommended that they be used in order to be consistent across all of the statements in which they are used.

6-3. Renaming a Column in the Output

Problem

Your query has a column that is the result of a function, and you need to assign the column a name. Or, your query joins multiple tables together, and you are returning columns from multiple tables, and each column has the same name.

Solution

Utilize a column alias to specify an alternate name for a column in the result set:

```
SELECT ss.name AS SchemaName,
       TableName = st.name,
       st.object_id ObjectId
FROM   sys.schemas AS ss
       JOIN sys.tables st
       ON ss.schema_id = st.schema_id
ORDER BY SchemaName, TableName;
```

This query returns the following (abridged) result set:

SchemaName	TableName	ObjectId
dbo	AWBuildVersion	469576711
dbo	DatabaseLog	245575913
dbo	ErrorLog	277576027
dbo	MyTestTable	1159675179
dbo	Person	1975678086
dbo	PersonPhone	2039678314
dbo	PhoneNumberType	2007678200

■ **Note** The ObjectId values returned may be different on your server.

How It Works

In this example, two system views are being queried. Each system view contains a name column. To prevent ambiguity, each column is supplied a column alias.

There are a few different methods of creating a column alias. These can be shown as:

```
expression [AS] column_alias
expression [AS] [column_alias]
expression [AS] "column_alias"
expression [AS] 'column_alias'
column_alias = expression
'column_alias' = expression
```

The solution showed three of these methods. In the first line, the column is aliased by specifying the column being returned, followed by the optional AS keyword, and then followed by the column alias. In the second line, the column alias is specified first, followed by an equals sign, which is followed by the column being returned. The third column utilizes the first method without the optional AS keyword. Any of these methods will work in SQL Server.

It should be noted that the AS method is the ANSI standard for column aliases. Also note that the last method listed, where the column alias is in a string followed by the equals sign and the column or expression to be aliased, is to be removed in a future version of SQL Server. You should use one of the other methods for creating a column alias.

6-4. Retrieving Data Directly into Variables

Problem

You need to retrieve data with a query directly into a variable for subsequent use.

Solution

Utilize the SELECT statement to retrieve data from a table and populate a variable with that data:

```
DECLARE @FirstHireDate DATE,
        @LastHireDate  DATE;

SELECT  @FirstHireDate = MIN(HireDate),
        @LastHireDate = MAX(HireDate)
FROM    HumanResources.Employee;

SELECT  @FirstHireDate AS FirstHireDate,
        @LastHireDate AS LastHireDate;
```

This query returns the following result set:

FirstHireDate	LastHireDate
2006-06-30	2013-05-30

How It Works

The variables are initially declared. The first query retrieves the first and last hire dates and populates the variables with these values. The final query returns these variables to be displayed. If the query operates on multiple rows, the variable will be populated with the contents of the last row. The following example shows how the query operates on multiple rows and how the value in the variable is the value from the last record operated on:

```
DECLARE @LastHireDate DATE;

SELECT  @LastHireDate = HireDate
FROM    HumanResources.Employee
ORDER BY HireDate DESC;

SELECT  TOP (1) HireDate
FROM    HumanResources.Employee
ORDER BY HireDate DESC;

SELECT  @LastHireDate AS LastHireDate;
```

This query returns the following result set:

```
HireDate
----------
2013-05-30

LastHireDate
------------
```

6-5. Creating a New Table with the Results from a Query

Problem

You need to have the result set from a query put into a new table.

Solution

Utilize the INTO clauses of the SELECT statement to create and populate a new table with the results from this query:

```
IF OBJECT_ID('dbo.Sales') IS NOT NULL DROP TABLE dbo.Sales;
SELECT  *
INTO    dbo.Sales
FROM    Sales.SalesOrderDetail
WHERE   ModifiedDate = '2011-06-01T00:00:00.000';

SELECT  COUNT(*) AS QtyOfRows
FROM    dbo.Sales;
```

This query returns the following result set:

```
QtyOfRows
-----------
4
```

How It Works

The SELECT...INTO statement creates a new table in the default filegroup and then inserts the result set from the query into it. In this example, the rows from the Sales.SalesOrderDetail table that were modified on June 1, 2011, are put into the new table, dbo.Sales. You can use a three-part naming sequence to create the table in a different database on the same SQL Server instance. The columns created are in the order of the columns returned in the query, and they have the names of the columns as specified in the query (meaning that if you use a column alias, the column alias will be the name of the column). The data types for the columns will be the data types of the underlying columns.

There are some limitations to the use of this syntax, as follows:

- You cannot create a new table on a different instance or server.

- You cannot create a table variable or a partitioned table.

- Only data and columns are copied; indexes, constraints, and triggers are not copied.

- Use of the ORDER BY clause does not guarantee that the rows will be inserted in that order.

- If a computed column is selected, the column in the new table will not be a computed column. The data in this column will be the result of the computed column.

- New columns that originate from a sparse column will not have the sparse property set.

- The Identity property of a column is applied to the new column, unless one of the following conditions is true:

  - Multiple select statements are joined by using UNION.

  - The identity column is part of an expression.

  - The identity column is listed more than once in the select list.

  - The SELECT statement contains a join.

  - The identity column is from a remote data source.

If the database is in the simple or bulk-logged recovery model, then the SELECT...INTO statement is minimally logged. For more information about minimally logged operations, see http://msdn.microsoft.com/en-us/library/ms190925.aspx#MinimallyLogged.

6-6. Filtering the Results from a Subquery

Problem

You need to filter the results from one query based upon the results from another query. For instance, you want to retrieve all of the purchase order numbers for any order where there is a line-item unit price between $1,900 and $2,000.

Solution

Utilize a query with a subquery, where the subquery has the results that will be filtered by the outer query:

```
SELECT   s.PurchaseOrderNumber
FROM     Sales.SalesOrderHeader s
WHERE    EXISTS ( SELECT SalesOrderID
                  FROM   Sales.SalesOrderDetail
                  WHERE  UnitPrice BETWEEN 1900 AND 2000
                         AND SalesOrderID = s.SalesOrderID )
ORDER BY s.PurchaseOrderNumber;
```

This query returns the following result set:

```
PurchaseOrderNumber
------------------------
PO10440182311
PO12586169040
PO12586178184
PO13543119495
PO2146113582
PO5858172038
PO7569171528
```

How It Works

In this example, the `PurchaseOrderNumber` column is retrieved from the `Sales.SalesOrderHeader` table. The individual line items for each order are in the `Sales.SalesOrderDetail` table. The subquery returns a row if there is a `Sales.SalesOrderDetail` record with a `UnitPrice` between $1,900 and $2,000 for the `SalesOrderId`. If a record exists in the subquery, the outer query will return the `PurchaseOrderNumber` for that order. If you look at the last line of the subquery, you can see that the `SalesOrderId` is being related to the `SalesOrderId` column from the `Sales.SalesOrderHeader` table. This is an example of a correlated subquery: the values returned depend upon the values of the outer query.

Subqueries can frequently be rewritten into a query with a `JOIN` condition. You should evaluate each query to see which method achieves the best performance. For instance, the example shown in this recipe can be rewritten in the following format, which returns the same result set:

```
SELECT DISTINCT sh.PurchaseOrderNumber
FROM Sales.SalesOrderHeader AS sh
    JOIN Sales.SalesOrderDetail AS sd
    ON sh.SalesOrderID = sd.SalesOrderID
WHERE sd.UnitPrice BETWEEN 1900 AND 2000;
```

6-7. Selecting from the Results of Another Query

Problem

You have a query that needs to be used as a data source that is input into another query.

Solution

Make the query into a derived table, and use it in the `FROM` clause of the second query:

```
SELECT DISTINCT
        s.PurchaseOrderNumber
FROM    Sales.SalesOrderHeader s
        JOIN (SELECT  SalesOrderID
              FROM     Sales.SalesOrderDetail
              WHERE    UnitPrice BETWEEN 1900 AND 2000
             ) dt
        ON s.SalesOrderID = dt.SalesOrderID
ORDER BY s.PurchaseOrderNumber;
```

This query returns the following result set:

```
PurchaseOrderNumber
------------------------
PO10440182311
PO12586169040
PO12586178184
PO13543119495
PO2146113582
PO5858172038
PO7569171528
```

How It Works

This example's query searches for the PurchaseOrderNumber from the Sales.SalesOrderHeader table for any order that contains products from the Sales.SalesOrderDetails table with a UnitPrice between 1,900 and 2,000. The query joins the Sales.SalesOrderHeader table to a derived table (which is itself a query), which is encapsulated in parentheses and is followed by a table alias (dt).

Since the derived table doesn't require a temporary table to store the results, it frequently performs better than temporary tables, since you eliminate the steps that SQL Server takes to create, allocate, populate, and destroy the temporary table.

6-8. Passing Rows Through a Function

Problem

You have a table-valued function that you want to utilize in your query.

Solution

Use the APPLY operator in the FROM clause of a query to invoke a table-valued function:

```
IF OBJECT_ID('dbo.fn_WorkOrderRouting') IS NOT NULL DROP FUNCTION dbo.fn_WorkOrderRouting;
GO

CREATE FUNCTION dbo.fn_WorkOrderRouting (@WorkOrderID INT)
RETURNS TABLE
AS
RETURN
        SELECT    WorkOrderID,
                  ProductID,
                  OperationSequence,
                  LocationID
        FROM      Production.WorkOrderRouting
        WHERE     WorkOrderID = @WorkOrderID;
GO
```

```
SELECT TOP (5)
        w.WorkOrderID,
        w.OrderQty,
        r.ProductID,
        r.OperationSequence
FROM    Production.WorkOrder w
        CROSS APPLY dbo.fn_WorkOrderRouting(w.WorkOrderID) AS r
ORDER BY w.WorkOrderID,
        w.OrderQty,
        r.ProductID;
```

This query returns the following result set:

WorkOrderID	OrderQty	ProductID	OperationSequence
13	4	747	1
13	4	747	2
13	4	747	3
13	4	747	4
13	4	747	6

How It Works

First, a table-valued function is created that returns work-order routing information for the WorkOrderId passed to it. The query then selects the first five records from the Production.WorkOrder table that contain two columns from the table-valued function. The next part of the SELECT statement is the key piece of this recipe: in the FROM clause, for each row from the Production.WorkOrder table, the WorkOrderId column is passed to the new fn_WorkOrderRouting function using the CROSS APPLY operator.

Both the left and right operands of the APPLY operator are table sources; the difference is that the right operand can be a table-valued function that accepts a parameter from the left operand. (The left operand can be a table-valued function, but it cannot accept a parameter from the right operand.) The APPLY operator works by applying the right operand against each row of the left operand. Similar to JOIN operators, the columns being returned from the left operand will be duplicated for each row returned by the right operand.

The CROSS and OUTER clauses of the APPLY operator are used to control how rows are returned in the final result of the two operands when the APPLY operator does not return any rows. Similar to an INNER JOIN, if CROSS APPLY is utilized and the right operand does not return any rows, then that row from the left operand is removed from the result set. And like an OUTER JOIN, if OUTER APPLY is utilized and the right operand does not return any rows, then that row from the left operand is returned with the values of the columns that come from the right operand being set to NULL.

To illustrate the difference between CROSS APPLY and OUTER APPLY, let's add a record to the Production.WorkOrder table.

```
INSERT  INTO Production.WorkOrder
        (ProductID,
         OrderQty,
         ScrappedQty,
         StartDate,
         EndDate,
```

```
        DueDate,
        ScrapReasonID,
        ModifiedDate)
VALUES  (1,
        1,
        1,
        GETDATE(),
        GETDATE(),
        GETDATE(),
        1,
        GETDATE());
```

Because this is a new row and the Production.WorkOrder table has an IDENTITY column for the WorkOrderId, the new row will have the maximum WorkOrderId value in the table. Additionally, the new row will not have an associated value in the Production.WorkOrderRouting table because it was just added.

Next, the previous CROSS APPLY query is executed, filtering it to return data for the newly inserted row only.

```
SELECT  w.WorkOrderID,
        w.OrderQty,
        r.ProductID,
        r.OperationSequence
FROM    Production.WorkOrder AS w
        CROSS APPLY dbo.fn_WorkOrderRouting(w.WorkOrderID) AS r
WHERE   w.WorkOrderID IN (SELECT    MAX(WorkOrderID)
                          FROM      Production.WorkOrder);
```

This query returns the following result set:

```
WorkOrderID OrderQty    ProductID   OperationSequence
----------- ----------- ----------- -----------------
```

Since there isn't a row in the Production.WorkOrderRouting table, a row isn't returned by the function. Since a CROSS APPLY is being utilized, the absence of a row from the function removes the row from the left operand, resulting in no rows being returned by the query.

Now, change the CROSS APPLY to an OUTER APPLY.

```
SELECT  w.WorkOrderID,
        w.OrderQty,
        r.ProductID,
        r.OperationSequence
FROM    Production.WorkOrder AS w
        OUTER APPLY dbo.fn_WorkOrderRouting(w.WorkOrderID) AS r
WHERE   w.WorkOrderID IN (SELECT    MAX(WorkOrderID)
                          FROM      Production.WorkOrder);
```

This query returns the following result set:

WorkOrderID	OrderQty	ProductID	OperationSequence
72592	1	NULL	NULL

You may have noticed that I have described the left and right operands of the APPLY operator as table sources. This means that you do not have to utilize a table-valued function for the right operand; you can use anything that returns a table, such as a derived table. For example, the following query returns the same result set as the first example in this recipe, but without the use of the table-valued function:

```
SELECT TOP (5)
        w.WorkOrderID,
        w.OrderQty,
        r.ProductID,
        r.OperationSequence
FROM    Production.WorkOrder w
        CROSS APPLY (SELECT WorkOrderID,
                            ProductID,
                            OperationSequence,
                            LocationID
                     FROM    Production.WorkOrderRouting
                     WHERE   WorkOrderID = w.WorkOrderId
                    ) AS r
ORDER BY w.WorkOrderID,
        w.OrderQty,
        r.ProductID;
```

In this example, we are utilizing the CROSS APPLY operator against a correlated subquery instead of against a table-valued function. The only difference with the correlated subquery is that the variable in the WHERE clause has been replaced with the column name from the table that was being passed into the table-valued function.

6-9. Returning Random Rows from a Table

Problem

You want to return a sampling of rows from a table.

Solution

Utilize the TABLESAMPLE clause of the SELECT statement:

```
SELECT  FirstName,
        LastName
FROM    Person.Person
TABLESAMPLE SYSTEM (2 PERCENT);
```

This query returns the following (abridged) result set:

FirstName	LastName
Madeline	King
Marcus	King
Maria	King
Anton	Kirilov
Anton	Kirilov
Sandra	Kitt
Christian	Kleinerman
Christian	Kleinerman
Andrew	Kobylinski
Reed	Koch
Reed	Koch
Reed	Koch

■ **Note** Because of the random nature of this clause, you will see different results than what is shown.

How It Works

TABLESAMPLE allows you to extract a sampling of rows from a table specified in the FROM clause. This sampling can be based on either a percentage or a number of rows. You can use TABLESAMPLE when only a sampling of rows is necessary for the application instead of a full result set. TABLESAMPLE also provides you with a somewhat randomized result set. Because of this, if you rerun the previous example, you will get different results.

TABLESAMPLE works by extracting a sample of rows from the query result set. In this example, 2 percent of rows were sampled from the Person.Person table. However, don't let the "percent" fool you. That percentage is the *percentage of the table's data pages*. Once the sample pages are selected, all rows for the selected pages are returned. Since the fill state of pages can vary, the number of rows returned will also vary—you'll notice this in the row count returned. If you designate the number of rows, this is actually converted by SQL Server into a percentage, and then the same method is used by SQL Server to identify the percentage of data pages to be used.

6-10. Converting Rows into Columns

Problem

Your database stores information about your employees, including what department they are assigned to and what shift they work in. You need to produce a report that shows how many employees by department are assigned to each shift for selected departments, with each department having a separate column in the result set.

Solution

Use the PIVOT operator to pivot the department column into columns for each department, and count the employees in each department by shift.

How It Works

We start off this example by first examining the data before it is pivoted:

```
SELECT   s.Name AS ShiftName,
         h.BusinessEntityID,
         d.Name AS DepartmentName
FROM     HumanResources.EmployeeDepartmentHistory h
         INNER JOIN HumanResources.Department d
             ON h.DepartmentID = d.DepartmentID
         INNER JOIN HumanResources.Shift s
             ON h.ShiftID = s.ShiftID
WHERE    EndDate IS NULL
         AND d.Name IN ('Production', 'Engineering', 'Marketing')
ORDER BY ShiftName;
```

This query returns the following (abridged) result set:

ShiftName	BusinessEntityID	DepartmentName
Day	6	Engineering
Day	14	Engineering
Day	15	Engineering
Day	16	Marketing
Day	17	Marketing
Day	18	Marketing
Day	25	Production
Day	27	Production
Day	28	Production
...		
Evening	145	Production
Evening	146	Production
Evening	147	Production
...		
Night	71	Production
Night	72	Production
Night	73	Production

In this result set, we can see that all of the departments are listed in one column. The next step is to pivot the department values returned from this query into columns, along with a count of employees by shift.

```
SELECT  ShiftName,
        Production,
        Engineering,
        Marketing
FROM    (SELECT s.Name AS ShiftName,
                h.BusinessEntityID,
                d.Name AS DepartmentName
         FROM   HumanResources.EmployeeDepartmentHistory h
                INNER JOIN HumanResources.Department d
                    ON h.DepartmentID = d.DepartmentID
                INNER JOIN HumanResources.Shift s
                    ON h.ShiftID = s.ShiftID
         WHERE  EndDate IS NULL
                AND d.Name IN ('Production', 'Engineering', 'Marketing')
        ) AS a
PIVOT
(
 COUNT(BusinessEntityID)
 FOR DepartmentName IN ([Production], [Engineering], [Marketing])
) AS b
ORDER BY ShiftName;
```

This query returns the following result set:

ShiftName	Production	Engineering	Marketing
Day	79	6	9
Evening	54	0	0
Night	46	0	0

In this second query, we utilized the PIVOT operator to shift the specified departments into columns, while simultaneously performing a COUNT aggregation by the shift. The syntax for the PIVOT operator is as follows:

```
FROM  table_source
PIVOT   ( aggregate_function ( value_column )
        FOR pivot_column
        IN ( <column_list>)
        ) table_alias
```

Table 6-1 shows the arguments for the PIVOT operator.

Table 6-1. *PIVOT Arguments*

Argument	Description
table_source	The table where the data will be pivoted.
aggregate_function	The aggregate function that will be used against the specified column. COUNT(*) is not allowed.
value_column	The column that will be used in the aggregate function.
pivot_column	The column that will be used to create the column headers.
column_list	The values to pivot from the pivot column.
table_alias	The table alias of the pivoted result set.

Prior to the introduction of the PIVOT operator, a pivot would be performed through aggregations, calculated columns, and the GROUP BY operator. The query that uses the PIVOT operator can be replicated using this method:

```
SELECT   s.Name AS ShiftName,
         SUM(CASE WHEN d.Name = 'Production' THEN 1 ELSE 0 END) AS Production,
         SUM(CASE WHEN d.Name = 'Engineering' THEN 1 ELSE 0 END) AS Engineering,
         SUM(CASE WHEN d.Name = 'Marketing' THEN 1 ELSE 0 END) AS Marketing
FROM     HumanResources.EmployeeDepartmentHistory h
         INNER JOIN HumanResources.Department d
             ON h.DepartmentID = d.DepartmentID
         INNER JOIN HumanResources.Shift s
             ON h.ShiftID = s.ShiftID
WHERE    h.EndDate IS NULL
         AND d.Name IN ('Production', 'Engineering', 'Marketing')
GROUP BY s.Name;
```

This query returns the same result set as the query utilizing the PIVOT operator.

One key item to point out regarding pivoting queries is that the values being pivoted must be known in advance. If the values are not known in advance, then the queries have to be constructed dynamically. In looking at the query utilizing the PIVOT operator, the dynamically generated name needs to be used in two places: in the column_list from the outer query and then again in the PIVOT operator. In this second place, the value needs to have the [] brackets for qualifying a name. In the second example (that doesn't utilize the PIVOT operator), the value is used twice, in the same line. When constructing a dynamic pivot, many developers find it easier to work with the strategy in the second example than that in the first. (This comparison ignores the department names hard-coded in the WHERE clause in both examples; if the values aren't known, then you would not be utilizing the values.)

6-11. Converting Columns into Rows

Problem

You have a table that has multiple columns for various phone numbers. You want to normalize this data by converting the columns into rows.

Solution

Utilize the UNPIVOT operator to convert multiple columns for a row to a row for each column:

```
IF OBJECT_ID('tempdb.dbo.#Contact') IS NOT NULL DROP TABLE #Contact;
CREATE TABLE #Contact
        (
        EmployeeID INT NOT NULL,
        PhoneNumber1 BIGINT,
        PhoneNumber2 BIGINT,
        PhoneNumber3 BIGINT
        )
GO

INSERT  #Contact
        (EmployeeID, PhoneNumber1, PhoneNumber2, PhoneNumber3)
VALUES  (1, 2718353881, 3385531980, 5324571342),
        (2, 6007163571, 6875099415, 7756620787),
        (3, 9439250939, NULL, NULL);

SELECT  EmployeeID,
        PhoneType,
        PhoneValue
FROM    #Contact c
UNPIVOT
(
 PhoneValue
 FOR PhoneType IN ([PhoneNumber1], [PhoneNumber2], [PhoneNumber3])
) AS p;
```

This query returns the following result set:

EmployeeID	PhoneType	PhoneValue
1	PhoneNumber1	2718353881
1	PhoneNumber2	3385531980
1	PhoneNumber3	5324571342
2	PhoneNumber1	6007163571
2	PhoneNumber2	6875099415
2	PhoneNumber3	7756620787
3	PhoneNumber1	9439250939

How It Works

The UNPIVOT operator does *almost* the opposite of the PIVOT operator by changing columns into rows. It uses the same syntax as the PIVOT operator, only using UNPIVOT instead of PIVOT.

This example utilizes UNPIVOT to remove column-repeating groups frequently found in denormalized tables. The first part of this example creates and populates a denormalized table, which has incrementing phone number columns.

The UNPIVOT operator is then utilized to convert the numerous phone number columns into a more normalized form of reusing a single PhoneValue column and having a PhoneType column to identify the type of phone number, instead of repeating the phone number column multiple times.

The UNPIVOT operator starts off with an opening parenthesis. A new column called PhoneValue is created to hold the values from the specified columns. The FOR clause specifies the pivot column (PhoneType) that will be created, and its value will be the name of the column. This is followed by the IN clause, which specifies the columns from the original table that will be consolidated into a single column. Finally, a closing parenthesis is specified, and the UNPIVOT operation is aliased with an arbitrary table alias.

Prior to the introduction of the UNPIVOT operator, an unpivot would have had to be performed by running multiple queries that are UNIONed together. For example, the above could be performed with the following query:

```
SELECT   EmployeeID,
         'PhoneNumber1' AS PhoneType,
         c.PhoneNumber1 AS PhoneValue
FROM     #Contact c
WHERE    c.PhoneNumber1 IS NOT NULL
UNION ALL
SELECT   EmployeeID,
         'PhoneNumber2' AS PhoneType,
         c.PhoneNumber2 AS PhoneValue
FROM     #Contact c
WHERE    c.PhoneNumber2 IS NOT NULL
UNION ALL
SELECT   EmployeeID,
         'PhoneNumber3' AS PhoneType,
         c.PhoneNumber3 AS PhoneValue
FROM     #Contact c
WHERE    c.PhoneNumber3 IS NOT NULL
ORDER BY EmployeeID, PhoneType;
```

6-12. Reusing Common Subqueries in a Query

Problem

You have a query that utilizes the same subquery multiple times. You have noticed that changes to the subquery are becoming problematic because you occasionally miss making a change to one of the subquery instances.

Solution

Utilize a common table expression to define the query once, and reference it in place of the subqueries in your query:

```
WITH cte AS
(
SELECT SalesOrderID
FROM   Sales.SalesOrderDetail
WHERE  UnitPrice BETWEEN 1900 AND 2000
)
SELECT  s.PurchaseOrderNumber
FROM    Sales.SalesOrderHeader s
WHERE   EXISTS (SELECT SalesOrderID
               FROM cte
               WHERE SalesOrderID = s.SalesOrderID );
```

This query returns the following result set:

```
PurchaseOrderNumber
------------------------
PO12586178184
PO10440182311
PO13543119495
PO12586169040
PO2146113582
PO7569171528
PO5858172038
```

How It Works

A common table expression, commonly referred to by its acronym CTE, is similar to a view or a derived query, allowing you to create a temporary query that can be referenced within the scope of a SELECT, INSERT, UPDATE, DELETE, or MERGE statement. Unlike a derived query, you don't need to copy the query definition multiple times, for each time it is used. You can also use local variables within a CTE definition—something you can't do in a view definition. The syntax for a CTE is as follows:

```
WITH expression_name [ ( column_name [ ,...n ] ) ] AS ( CTE_query_definition ) [ ,...n ]
```

The arguments of a CTE are described in Table 6-2.

Table 6-2. *CTE Arguments*

Argument	Description
expression_name	The name of the common table expression
column_name [,...n]	The unique column names of the expression
CTE_query_definition	The SELECT query that defines the common table expression

There are two forms of CTEs. A *recursive* CTE is one where the query for the CTE references itself. A recursive CTE will be shown in the next recipe. A *nonrecursive* CTE does not reference itself.

In this example, a nonrecursive CTE is created that selects the SalesOrderId column from all records from the Sales.SalesOrderDetail table that have a UnitPrice between 1,900 and 2,000. Later in the query, this CTE is referenced in the EXISTS clause. If this query had used this subquery multiple times, you would have simply referenced the CTE where necessary, while the logic for the subquery was contained just once in the definition of the CTE.

Each time a CTE is referenced, the entire query that makes up the CTE is executed; a CTE does not perform the action once and leave the results available for all references to the CTE. If you desire this capability, investigate the Temporary Storage options discussed in Chapter 13. To illustrate that CTEs are called each time that they are referenced, let's look at the following queries:

```
SET STATISTICS IO ON;
RAISERROR('CTE #1', 10, 1) WITH NOWAIT;
WITH VendorSearch(RowNumber, VendorName, AccountNumber) AS
(
SELECT     ROW_NUMBER() OVER (ORDER BY Name) RowNum,
           Name,
           AccountNumber
FROM       Purchasing.Vendor
)
SELECT *
FROM VendorSearch;

RAISERROR('CTE #2', 10, 1) WITH NOWAIT;
WITH VendorSearch(RowNumber, VendorName, AccountNumber) AS
(
SELECT     ROW_NUMBER() OVER (ORDER BY Name) RowNum,
           Name,
           AccountNumber
FROM       Purchasing.Vendor
)
SELECT RowNumber,
       VendorName,
       AccountNumber
FROM   VendorSearch
WHERE  RowNumber BETWEEN 1 AND 5
UNION
SELECT RowNumber,
       VendorName,
       AccountNumber
FROM   VendorSearch
WHERE  RowNumber BETWEEN 100 AND 104;
SET STATISTICS IO OFF;
```

In this example, I/O statistics are turned on, and then the same CTE is used in two queries. In the first query, the CTE is referenced once. In the second query, it is referenced twice. A message is also displayed at the start of each query. Ignoring the returned result sets, the I/O statistics returned are as follows:

```
CTE #1
Table 'Vendor'. Scan count 1, logical reads 4, physical reads 0, read-ahead reads 0, lob
logical reads 0, lob physical reads 0, lob read-ahead reads 0.
CTE #2
Table 'Vendor'. Scan count 2, logical reads 8, physical reads 0, read-ahead reads 0, lob
logical reads 0, lob physical reads 0, lob read-ahead reads 0.
```

As shown, the first use of the CTE scans the Vendor table once, for four logical reads. The second CTE scans the Vendor table twice, for eight logical reads.

Multiple CTEs can be utilized within one WITH clause; they just need to be separated from each other with a comma. A CTE can reference previously defined CTEs, but not CTEs that have not yet been defined. Every column in a CTE must have a unique column name. This can be accomplished by specifying the column alias either as the columns are introduced into the query or as a comma-delimited list after the CTE name is defined. For instance:

```
WITH CTE(N) AS
(
SELECT TOP (5) object_id
FROM sys.objects
)
SELECT N FROM CTE;
```

In this example, the object_id column has been aliased to N (at WITH CTE(N)) If column aliases are not defined with the CTE declaration, then the column names from the query will be utilized.

■ **Caution**   If the CTE is not the first statement in a batch of statements, the previous statement must be terminated with a semicolon.

■ **Note**   Terminating an SQL statement with a semicolon is part of the ANSI specifications. Currently, SQL Server does not require most statements to be terminated with a semicolon; however, this practice is deprecated, and its usage will be required in a future version of SQL Server. To make a future upgrade easier, you should start terminating all statements with a semicolon.

6-13. Querying Recursive Tables

Problem

You have a table with hierarchal data where one column references another column in the same table on a different row. You need to query the data so as to return data for each record from the parent row. For instance, the following builds a company table that contains an entry for each company in a (hypothetical) giant mega-conglomerate:

```
IF OBJECT_ID('tempdb.dbo.#Company') IS NOT NULL DROP TABLE #Company;
CREATE TABLE #Company
        (
        CompanyID INT NOT NULL
                        PRIMARY KEY,
        ParentCompanyID INT NULL,
        CompanyName VARCHAR(25) NOT NULL
        );

INSERT  #Company
        (CompanyID, ParentCompanyID, CompanyName)
VALUES  (1, NULL, 'Mega-Corp'),
        (2, 1, 'Mediamus-Corp'),
        (3, 1, 'KindaBigus-Corp'),
        (4, 3, 'GettinSmaller-Corp'),
        (5, 4, 'Smallest-Corp'),
        (6, 5, 'Puny-Corp'),
        (7, 5, 'Small2-Corp');
```

Solution

Utilize a *recursive* CTE to create the hierarchy tree.

```
WITH  CompanyTree(ParentCompanyID, CompanyID, CompanyName, CompanyLevel) AS
(
-- Anchor Member
SELECT  ParentCompanyID,
        CompanyID,
        CompanyName,
        0 AS CompanyLevel
FROM    #Company
WHERE   ParentCompanyID IS NULL
UNION ALL
-- Recursive Member
SELECT  c.ParentCompanyID,
        c.CompanyID,
        c.CompanyName,
        p.CompanyLevel + 1
```

```
FROM      #Company c
          INNER JOIN CompanyTree p
              ON c.ParentCompanyID = p.CompanyID
)
SELECT ParentCompanyID,
       CompanyID,
       CompanyName,
       CompanyLevel
FROM   CompanyTree;
```

This query returns the following result set:

ParentCompanyID	CompanyID	CompanyName	CompanyLevel
NULL	1	Mega-Corp	0
1	2	Mediamus-Corp	1
1	3	KindaBigus-Corp	1
3	4	GettinSmaller-Corp	2
4	5	Smallest-Corp	3
5	6	Puny-Corp	4
5	7	Small2-Corp	4

How It Works

A recursive CTE is created by creating an *anchor* member and then performing a UNION ALL of the anchor member to the *recursive* member. The anchor member defines the base of the recursion—in this case, the top level of the corporate hierarchy. The anchor is defined first, and this query is joined to the next query through a UNION ALL set operation.

In this example, the anchor definition includes three columns from the Company table and a CompanyLevel column to display how many levels deep a particular company is in the company hierarchy.

The recursive member is defined next. The same three columns are returned from the Company table. The recursion is next; the query is joined to the anchor member by referencing the name of the CTE and specifying the join condition. In this case, the join condition is the expression c.ParentCompanyID = p.CompanyId. Finally, in the column list for this query, the CompanyLevel from the CTE is incremented for the hierarchy level.

After the recursive CTE has been defined, the columns from the CTE are returned in the final query.

Multiple anchor members and recursive members can be defined. All anchor members must be defined before any recursive members are. Multiple anchor members can utilize the UNION, UNION ALL, INTERSECT, and EXCEPT set operators. The UNION ALL set operator must be used between the last anchor member and the first recursive member. All recursive members must use the UNION ALL set operator.

If the recursive member contains a value in the joining column that is also found in the anchor member, then an infinite loop is created. You can utilize the MAXRECURSION query hint to limit the depth of recursions. By default, the serverwide recursion depth default is 100 levels. The value you utilize in the query hint should be based upon your understanding of the data. For example, if you know that your data should not go beyond ten levels deep, then you should set the MAXRECURSION query hint to that value.

6-14. Hard-Coding the Results from a Query

Problem

In your query, you have a set of constant values that you want to use as a source of data.

Solution

Utilize the VALUES clause to create a table-value constructor:

How It Works

The VALUES clause can be used as a source of data in INSERT statements, as the source table in a MERGE statement, and as a derived table in a SELECT statement. An example of using the VALUES clause in an INSERT statement can be seen in Recipe 6-13 when populating the Company table.

An example of using the VALUES clause in a SELECT statement would be if you always referred to the first ten presidents of the United States:

```
SELECT *
FROM (VALUES ('George', 'Washington'),
             ('Thomas', 'Jefferson'),
             ('John', 'Adams'),
             ('James', 'Madison'),
             ('James', 'Monroe'),
             ('John Quincy', 'Adams'),
             ('Andrew', 'Jackson'),
             ('Martin', 'Van Buren'),
             ('William', 'Harrison'),
             ('John', 'Tyler')
    ) dtPresidents(FirstName, LastName);
```

This query returns the following result set:

FirstName	LastName
George	Washington
Thomas	Jefferson
John	Adams
James	Madison
James	Monroe
John Quincy	Adams
Andrew	Jackson
Martin	Van Buren
William	Harrison
John	Tyler

The syntax for the VALUES clause is as follows:

```
VALUES ( <row value expression list> ) [ ,...n ]

<row value expression list> ::=
  {<row value expression> } [ ,...n ]

<row value expression> ::=
  { DEFAULT | NULL | expression }
```

The VALUES keyword introduces the row-value expression list. Each list must start and end with a parenthesis, and multiple lists must be separated by a comma. Inside the parentheses is the value for each column, with each column being separated by a comma. A column's value can be specified as NULL, or if the table-value constructor is being using in an INSERT statement, the keyword DEFAULT can be used to use that column's default value (if the column does not have a default, NULL will be the inserted value). The maximum number of rows that can be constructed using a table-value constructor is 1,000. The table value constructor is equivalent to each list being a separate SELECT statement that is subsequently used with the UNION ALL set operator to make a single result set out of multiple SELECT statements. The number of values specified in each list must be the same, and they follow the data-type conversion properties of the UNION ALL set operator, for which unmatched data types between rows are implicitly converted to a type of the next higher precedence. If the conversion cannot be implicitly converted, then an error is returned.

CHAPTER 7

Windowing Functions

by Wayne Sheffield

SQL Server is designed to work best on sets of data. By definition, sets of data are unordered; it is not until the query's ORDER BY clause that the final results of the query become ordered. Windowing functions allow your query to look at a subset of the rows being returned by your query before applying the function to just those rows. In doing so, the functions allow you to specify an order for your unordered subset of data so as to evaluate that data in a particular order. This is performed before the final result is ordered (and in addition to it). This allows for processes that previously required self-joins, the use of inefficient inequality operators, or non-set-based row-by-row (iterative) processing to use more efficient set-based processing.

The key to windowing functions is in controlling the order in which the rows are evaluated, when the evaluation is restarted, and what set of rows within the result set should be considered for the function (the window of the data set that the function will be applied to). These actions are performed with the OVER clause.

There are three groups of functions that the OVER clause can be applied to; in other words, there are three groups of functions that can be windowed. These groups are the aggregate functions, the ranking functions, and the analytic functions. Additionally, the sequence object's NEXT VALUE FOR function can be windowed. The functions that can have the OVER clause applied to them are shown in the following tables:

Table 7-1. *Aggregate Functions*

AVG	CHECKSUM_AGG	COUNT	COUNT_BIG	MAX	MIN
STDEV	STDEVP		SUM	VAR	VARP

Ranking functions allow you to return a ranking value that is associated with each row in a partition of a result set. Depending on the function used, multiple rows may receive the same value within the partition, and there may be gaps between assigned numbers.

Table 7-2. *Ranking Functions*

Function	Description
ROW_NUMBER	ROW_NUMBER returns an incrementing integer for each row within a partition of a set. ROW_NUMBER will return a unique number within each partition, starting with 1.
RANK	Similar to ROW_NUMBER, RANK increments its value for each row within a partition of the set. The key difference is that if rows with tied values exist within the partition, they will receive the same rank value, and the next value will receive the rank value as if there had been no ties, producing a gap between assigned numbers.
DENSE_RANK	The difference between DENSE_RANK and RANK is that DENSE_RANK doesn't have gaps in the rank values when there are tied values; the next value has the next rank assignment.
NTILE	NTILE divides the result set into a specified number of groups, based on the ordering and optional partition clause.

Analytic functions (introduced in SQL Server 2012) compute an aggregate value on a group of rows. In contrast to the aggregate functions, they can return multiple rows for each group.

Table 7-3. *Analytic Functions*

Function	Description
CUME_DIST	CUME_DIST calculates the cumulative distribution of a value in a group of values. The cumulative distribution is the relative position of a specified value in a group of values.
FIRST_VALUE	Returns the first value from an ordered set of values.
LAG	Retrieves data from a previous row in the same result set as specified by a row offset from the current row.
LAST_VALUE	Returns the last value from an ordered set of values.
LEAD	Retrieves data from a subsequent row in the same result set as specified by a row offset from the current row.
PERCENTILE_CONT	Calculates a percentile based on a continuous distribution of the column value. The value returned may or may not be equal to any of the specific values in the column.
PERCENTILE_DISC	Computes a specific percentile for sorted values in the result set. The value returned will be the value with the smallest CUME_DIST value (for the same sort specification) that is greater than or equal to the specified percentile. The value returned will be equal to one of the values in the specific column.
PERCENT_RANK	Computes the relative rank of a row within a set.

Many people will break down these functions into two groups: the LAG, LEAD, FIRST_VALUE, and LAST_VALUE functions are considered to be offset functions, and the remaining functions are called analytic functions. These functions come in complementary pairs, and many of the recipes will cover them in this manner.

The syntax for the OVER clause is as follows:

```
OVER (
    [ <PARTITION BY clause> ]
    [ <ORDER BY clause> ]
    [ <ROW or RANGE clause> ]
)
```

The PARTITION BY clause is used to restart the calculations when the values in the specified columns change. It specifies columns from the tables in the FROM clause of the query, scalar functions, scalar subqueries, or variables. If a PARTITION BY clause isn't specified, the entire data set will be the partition.

The ORDER BY clause defines the order in which the OVER clause evaluates the data subset for the function. It can only refer to columns that are in the FROM clause of the query.

The ROWS | RANGE clause defines a subset of rows that the window function will be applied to within the partition. If ROWS is specified, this subset is defined with the position of the current row relative to the other rows within the partition by position. If RANGE is specified, this subset is defined by the value(s) of the column(s) in the current row relative to the other rows within the partition. This range is defined as a beginning point and an ending point. For both ROWS and RANGE, the beginning point can be UNBOUNDED PRECEDING or CURRENT ROW, and the ending point can be UNBOUNDED FOLLOWING or CURRENT ROW, where UNBOUNDED PRECEDING means the first row in the partition, UNBOUNDED FOLLOWING means the last row in the partition, and CURRENT ROW is just that—the current row. Additionally, when ROWS is specified, an offset can be specified with <X> PRECEDING or <X> FOLLOWING, which is simply the number of rows prior to or following the current row. Additionally, there are two methods to specify the subset range—you can specify just the beginning point (which will use the default CURRENT ROW as the default ending point), or you can specify both with the BETWEEN <starting point> AND <ending point> syntax. Finally, the entire ROWS | RANGE clause itself is optional; if it is not specified, the default ROWS | RANGE clause will default to RANGE BETWEEN UNBOUNDED PRECEDING AND CURRENT ROW.

Each of the windowing functions permits and requires various clauses from the OVER clause.

With the exception of the CHECKSUM, GROUPING, and GROUPING_ID functions, all of the aggregate functions can be windowed through the use of the OVER clause, as shown in Table 7-1 above. Additionally, the ROWS | RANGE clause allows you to perform running aggregations and sliding (moving) aggregations.

The first four recipes in this section utilize the following table and data:

```
CREATE TABLE #Transactions
    (
        AccountId INTEGER,
        TranDate DATE,
        TranAmt NUMERIC(8, 2)
    );
INSERT  INTO #Transactions
SELECT  *
FROM    ( VALUES ( 1, '2011-01-01', 500),
                 ( 1, '2011-01-15', 50),
                 ( 1, '2011-01-22', 250),
                 ( 1, '2011-01-24', 75),
                 ( 1, '2011-01-26', 125),
                 ( 1, '2011-01-26', 175),
                 ( 2, '2011-01-01', 500),
                 ( 2, '2011-01-15', 50),
                 ( 2, '2011-01-22', 25),
                 ( 3, '2011-01-22', 5000),
```

```
                    ( 3, '2011-01-27', 550),
                    ( 3, '2011-01-27', 95 ),
                    ( 3, '2011-01-30', 2500)
            ) dt (AccountId, TranDate, TranAmt);
```

Note that within AccountIDs 1 and 3, there are two rows that have the same TranDate value. This duplicate date will be used to highlight the differences in some of the clauses used in the OVER clause in subsequent recipes.

7-1. Calculating Totals Based upon the Prior Row

Problem

You need to calculate the total of a column, where the total is the sum of the column values through the current row. For instance, for each account, calculate the total transaction amount to date in date order.

Solution

Utilize the SUM function with the OVER clause to perform a running total:

```
SELECT  AccountId,
        TranDate,
        TranAmt,
        -- running total of all transactions
        RunTotalAmt = SUM(TranAmt) OVER (PARTITION BY AccountId ORDER BY TranDate)
FROM    #Transactions AS t
ORDER BY AccountId,
        TranDate;
```

This query returns the following result set:

AccountId	TranDate	TranAmt	RunTotalAmt
1	2011-01-01	500.00	500.00
1	2011-01-15	50.00	550.00
1	2011-01-22	250.00	800.00
1	2011-01-24	75.00	875.00
1	2011-01-26	125.00	1175.00
1	2011-01-26	175.00	1175.00
2	2011-01-01	500.00	500.00
2	2011-01-15	50.00	550.00
2	2011-01-22	25.00	575.00
3	2011-01-22	5000.00	5000.00
3	2011-01-27	550.00	5645.00
3	2011-01-27	95.00	5645.00
3	2011-01-30	2500.00	8145.00

How It Works

The OVER clause, when used in conjunction with the SUM function, allows us to perform a running total of the transaction. Within the OVER clause, the PARTITION BY clause is specified so as to restart the calculation every time the AccountId value changes. The ORDER BY clause is specified and determines in which order the rows should be calculated. Since the ROWS | RANGE clause is not specified, the default RANGE BETWEEN UNBOUNDED PRECEDING AND CURRENT ROW is utilized. When the query is executed, the TranAmt column from all of the rows prior to and including the current row is summed up and returned.

In this example, for the first row for each AccountID value, the RunTotalAmt returned is simply the value from the TotalAmt column from the row. For subsequent rows, this value is incremented by the value in the current row's TotalAmt column. When the AccountID value changes, the running total is reset and recalculated for the new AccountID value. So, for AccountID = 1, the RunTotalAmt value for TranDate 2011-01-01 is 500 (the value of that row's TranAmt column). For the next row (TranDate 2011-01-1), the TranAmt of 50 is added to the 500 for a running total of 550. In the next row (TranDate 2011-01-22), the TranAmt of 250 is added to the 550 for a running total of 800.

Note the duplicate TranDate value within each AccountID value—the running total did not increment in the way that you would expect it to. Since this query did not specify a ROWS | RANGE clause, the default of RANGE BETWEEN UNBOUNDED PRECEDING AND CURRENT ROW was utilized. RANGE does not work on a row-position basis; instead, it works off of the values in the columns. For the rows with the duplicate TranDate, the TranAmt for all of the rows with that duplicate value were summed together. To see the data in the manner in which you would most likely want to see a running total, modify the query to include an additional column that performs the same running total calculation with the ROWS clause:

```
SELECT   AccountId,
         TranDate,
         TranAmt,
         -- running total of all transactions
         RunTotalAmt =   SUM(TranAmt) OVER (PARTITION BY AccountId ORDER BY TranDate),
         -- "Proper" running total by row position
         RunTotalAmt2 =  SUM(TranAmt) OVER (PARTITION BY AccountId
                                           ORDER BY TranDate
                                           ROWS UNBOUNDED PRECEDING)
FROM     #Transactions AS t
ORDER BY AccountId,
         TranDate;
```

This query produces these more desirable results in the RunTotalAmt2 column:

AccountId	TranDate	TranAmt	RunTotalAmt	RunTotalAmt2
1	2011-01-01	500.00	500.00	500.00
1	2011-01-15	50.00	550.00	550.00
1	2011-01-22	250.00	800.00	800.00
1	2011-01-24	75.00	875.00	875.00
1	2011-01-26	125.00	1175.00	1000.00
1	2011-01-26	175.00	1175.00	1175.00
2	2011-01-01	500.00	500.00	500.00
2	2011-01-15	50.00	550.00	550.00
2	2011-01-22	25.00	575.00	575.00
3	2011-01-22	5000.00	5000.00	5000.00
3	2011-01-27	550.00	5645.00	5550.00
3	2011-01-27	95.00	5645.00	5645.00
3	2011-01-30	2500.00	8145.00	8145.00

Running aggregations can be performed over the other aggregate functions. In this next example, the query is modified to perform running averages, counts, and minimum/maximum calculations.

```
SELECT  AccountId,
        TranDate,
        TranAmt,
        -- running average of all transactions
        RunAvg = AVG(TranAmt) OVER (PARTITION BY AccountId ORDER BY TranDate),
        -- running total # of transactions
        RunTranQty = COUNT(*) OVER (PARTITION BY AccountId ORDER BY TranDate),
        -- smallest of the transactions so far
        RunSmallAmt = MIN(TranAmt) OVER (PARTITION BY AccountId ORDER BY TranDate),
        -- largest of the transactions so far
        RunLargeAmt = MAX(TranAmt) OVER (PARTITION BY AccountId ORDER BY TranDate),
        -- running total of all transactions
        RunTotalAmt = SUM(TranAmt) OVER (PARTITION BY AccountId ORDER BY TranDate)
FROM    #Transactions AS t
WHERE   AccountID = 1
ORDER BY AccountId, TranDate;
```

This query returns the following result set:

AccountId	TranDate	TranAmt	RunAvg	RunTranQty	RunSmallAmt	RunLargeAmt	RunTotalAmt
1	2011-01-01	500.00	500.000000	1	500.00	500.00	500.00
1	2011-01-15	50.00	275.000000	2	50.00	500.00	550.00
1	2011-01-22	250.00	266.666666	3	50.00	500.00	800.00
1	2011-01-24	75.00	218.750000	4	50.00	500.00	875.00
1	2011-01-26	125.00	195.833333	6	50.00	500.00	1175.00
1	2011-01-26	175.00	195.833333	6	50.00	500.00	1175.00

7-2. Calculating Totals Based upon a Subset of Rows

Problem

When performing these aggregations, you want only the current row and the two previous rows to be considered for the aggregation.

Solution

Utilize the ROWS clause of the OVER clause:

```
SELECT AccountId,
       TranDate,
       TranAmt,
       -- average of the current and previous 2 transactions
       SlideAvg = AVG(TranAmt)
```

```
                    OVER (PARTITION BY AccountId
                              ORDER BY TranDate
                              ROWS BETWEEN 2 PRECEDING AND CURRENT ROW),
      -- total # of the current and previous 2 transactions
      SlideQty  = COUNT(*)
                    OVER (PARTITION BY AccountId
                              ORDER BY TranDate
                              ROWS BETWEEN 2 PRECEDING AND CURRENT ROW),
      -- smallest of the current and previous 2 transactions
      SlideMin = MIN(TranAmt)
                    OVER (PARTITION BY AccountId
                              ORDER BY TranDate
                              ROWS BETWEEN 2 PRECEDING AND CURRENT ROW),
      -- largest of the current and previous 2 transactions
      SlideMax = MAX(TranAmt)
                    OVER (PARTITION BY AccountId
                              ORDER BY TranDate
                              ROWS BETWEEN 2 PRECEDING AND CURRENT ROW),
      -- total of the current and previous 2 transactions
      SlideTotal = SUM(TranAmt)
                    OVER (PARTITION BY AccountId
                              ORDER BY TranDate
                              ROWS BETWEEN 2 PRECEDING AND CURRENT ROW)
FROM    #Transactions AS t
ORDER BY AccountId, TranDate;
```

This query returns the following result set:

```
AccountId   TranDate    TranAmt SlideAvg      SlideQty SlideMin SlideMax SlideTotal
----------- ----------  ------- -----------   -------- -------- -------- ----------
1           2011-01-01  500.00  500.000000    1        500.00   500.00   500.00
1           2011-01-15  50.00   275.000000    2        50.00    500.00   550.00
1           2011-01-22  250.00  266.666666    3        50.00    500.00   800.00
1           2011-01-24  75.00   125.000000    3        50.00    250.00   375.00
1           2011-01-26  125.00  150.000000    3        75.00    250.00   450.00
1           2011-01-26  175.00  125.000000    3        75.00    175.00   375.00
2           2011-01-01  500.00  500.000000    1        500.00   500.00   500.00
2           2011-01-15  50.00   275.000000    2        50.00    500.00   550.00
2           2011-01-22  25.00   191.666666    3        25.00    500.00   575.00
3           2011-01-22  5000.00 5000.000000   1        5000.00  5000.00  5000.00
3           2011-01-27  550.00  2775.000000   2        550.00   5000.00  5550.00
3           2011-01-27  95.00   1881.666666   3        95.00    5000.00  5645.00
3           2011-01-30  2500.00 1048.333333   3        95.00    2500.00  3145.00
```

How It Works

The ROWS clause is added to the OVER clause of the aggregate functions to specify that the aggregate functions should look only at the current row and the previous two rows for their calculations. As you look at each column in the result set, you can see that the aggregation was performed over just these rows (the window of rows that the aggregation is applied to). As the query progresses through the result set, the window slides to encompass the specified rows relative to the current row.

Let's examine the results row by row for AccountID 1. Remember that we are applying a subset (ROWS clause) to be the current row and the two previous rows. For TranDate 2011-01-01, there are no previous rows. For the COUNT calculation, there is just one row, so SlideQty returns 1. For each of the other columns (SlideAvg, SlideMin, SlideMax, SlideTotal), there are no previous rows, so the current row's TranAmt is returned as the AVG, MIN, MAX, and SUM values.

For the second row (TranDate 2011-01-15), there are now two rows "visible" in the subset of data, starting from the first row. The COUNT calculation sees these two and returns 2 for the SlideQty. The AVG calculation of these two rows is 275: (500 + 50) / 2. The MIN of these two values (500, 50) is 50. The MAX of these two values is 500. And finally, the SUM (total) of these two values is 550. These are the values returned in the SlideAvg, SlideMin, SlideMax, and SlideTotal columns.

For the third row (TranDate 2011-01-15), there are now three rows "visible" in the subset of data, starting from the first row. The COUNT calculation sees these three and returns 3 for the SlideQty. The AVG calculation of the TranAmt column for these three rows is 266.66: (500 + 50 + 250) / 3. The MIN of these three values (500, 50, 250) is still 50, and the MAX of these three values is still 500. And finally, the SUM (total) of these three values is 800. These are the values returned in the SlideAvg, SlideMin, SlideMax, and SlideTotal columns.

For the fourth row (TranDate 2011-01-24), we still have three rows "visible" in the subset of data; however, we have started our sliding / moving aggregation window—the window starts with the second row and goes through the current (fourth) row. The COUNT calculation still sees that we are applying the function to only three rows, so it returns 3 in the SlideQty column. The AVG calculation of the TranAmt column for the three rows is applied over the values (50, 250, 75), which produces an average of 125: (50 + 250 + 75) / 3. The MIN of the three values is still 50, while the MAX of these three values is now 250. The SUM total of these three values is 375. Again, these are the values returned in the SlideAvg, SlideMin, SlideMax, and SlideTotal columns.

As we progress to the fifth row (TranDate 2011-01-26 and TranAmt 125.00), the window slides again. We are still looking at only three rows (the third row through the fifth row), so SlideQty still returns 3. The other calculations are looking at the TranAmt values of 250, 75, 125 for these three rows, so the AVG, MIN, MAX, and SUM calculations are 150, 75, 250, and 450.

For the sixth row, the window again slides, and the calculations are recalculated for the new subset of data. For the seventh row, we now have the AccountID changing from 1 to 2. Since the query has a PARTITION BY clause set on the AccountID column, the calculations are reset. The seventh row of the result set is the first row for this partition (AccountID), so the SlideQty is 1, and the other columns will have for the AVG, MIN, MAX, and SUM calculations the value of the TranAmt column. The sliding window continues as defined above.

7-3. Calculating a Percentage of Total

Problem

With each row in your result set, you want to have the data included so that you are able to calculate what percentage of the total the row is.

Solution

Use the SUM function with the OVER clause without specifying any ordering so as to have each row return the total for that partition:

```
SELECT  AccountId,
        TranDate,
        TranAmt,
        AccountTotal = SUM(TranAmt) OVER (PARTITION BY AccountId),
        AmountPct = TranAmt / SUM(TranAmt) OVER (PARTITION BY t.AccountId)
FROM    #Transactions AS t
```

This query returns the following result set (AmountPct column truncated at 7 decimals for brevity):

AccountId	TranDate	TranAmt	AccountTotal	AmountPct
1	2011-01-01	500.00	1175.00	0.4255319
1	2011-01-15	50.00	1175.00	0.0425531
1	2011-01-22	250.00	1175.00	0.2127659
1	2011-01-24	75.00	1175.00	0.0638297
1	2011-01-26	125.00	1175.00	0.1063829
1	2011-01-26	175.00	1175.00	0.1489361
2	2011-01-01	500.00	575.00	0.8695652
2	2011-01-15	50.00	575.00	0.0869565
2	2011-01-22	25.00	575.00	0.0434782
3	2011-01-22	5000.00	8145.00	0.6138735
3	2011-01-27	550.00	8145.00	0.0675260
3	2011-01-27	95.00	8145.00	0.0116635
3	2011-01-30	2500.00	8145.00	0.3069367

How It Works

When the SUM function is utilized with the OVER clause, and the OVER clause does not contain the ORDER BY clause, then the SUM function will return the total amount for the partition. The current row's value can be divided by this total to obtain the percentage of the total that the current row is. If the ORDER BY clause had been included, then a ROWS | RANGE clause would have been used; if one wasn't specified, then the default RANGE BETWEEN UNBOUNDED PRECEDING AND CURRENT ROW would have been used, as shown in recipe 7-1.

If you wanted to get the total for the entire result set instead of the total for each partition (in this example, AccountId), you would use:

```
SELECT  AccountId,
        TranDate,
        TranAmt,
        Total = SUM(TranAmt) OVER (),
        AmountPct = TranAmt / SUM(TranAmt) OVER ()
FROM    #Transactions AS t
ORDER BY AccountId, TranDate;
```

7-4. Calculating a "Row X of Y"

Problem

You want your result set to display a "Row X of Y," where X is the current row number and Y is the total number of rows.

Solution

Use the ROW_NUMBER function to obtain the current row number, and the COUNT function with the OVER clause to obtain the total number of rows:

```
SELECT  AccountId,
        TranDate,
        TranAmt,
        AcctRowID = ROW_NUMBER() OVER (PARTITION BY AccountId ORDER BY AccountId, TranDate),
        AcctRowQty = COUNT(*) OVER (PARTITION BY AccountId),
        RowID = ROW_NUMBER() OVER (ORDER BY AccountId, TranDate),
        RowQty = COUNT(*) OVER ()
FROM    #Transactions AS t
ORDER BY AccountId, TranDate;;
```

This query returns the following result set:

AccountId	TranDate	TranAmt	AcctRowID	AcctRowQty	RowID	RowQty
1	2011-01-01	500.00	1	6	1	13
1	2011-01-15	50.00	2	6	2	13
1	2011-01-22	250.00	3	6	3	13
1	2011-01-24	75.00	4	6	4	13
1	2011-01-26	125.00	5	6	5	13
1	2011-01-26	175.00	6	6	6	13
2	2011-01-01	500.00	1	3	7	13
2	2011-01-15	50.00	2	3	8	13
2	2011-01-22	25.00	3	3	9	13
3	2011-01-22	5000.00	1	4	10	13
3	2011-01-27	550.00	2	4	11	13
3	2011-01-27	95.00	3	4	12	13
3	2011-01-30	2500.00	4	4	13	13

How It Works

The ROW_NUMBER function is used to get the current row number within a partition, and the COUNT function is used to get the total number of rows within a partition. Both the ROW_NUMBER and COUNT functions are used twice, once with a PARTITION BY clause and once without. The ROW_NUMBER function returns a sequential number (as ordered by the specified ORDER BY clause in the OVER clause) for each row that has the partition specified. In the AcctRowID column, this is partitioned by the AccountId, so the sequential numbering will restart upon each change in the AccountId column; in the RowID column, a PARTITION BY is not specified, so this will return a sequential number for each row with the entire result set. Likewise for the COUNT function: the AcctRowQty column is partitioned by the AccountID column, so this will return, for each row, the number of rows within this partition (AccountId). The RowQty column is not partitioned, so this will return the total number of rows in the entire result set. The corresponding columns (AcctRowID, AcctRowQty and RowID, RowQty) utilize the same PARTITION BY clause (or lack of) in order to make the results meaningful.

For each row for AccountID = 1, the AcctRowID column will return a sequential number for each row, and the AcctRowQty column will return 6 (since there are 6 rows for this account). In a similar way, the RowID column will return a sequential number for each row in the result set, and the RowQty will return the total number of rows in the result set (13), since both of these are calculated without a PARTITION BY clause. For the first row where AccountId = 1, this will be row 1 of 6 within AccountId 1, and row 1 of 13 within the entire result set. The second row will be 2 of 6 and 2 of 13, and this proceeds through the remaining rows for this AccountId. When we get to AccountId = 2, the AcctRowID and AcctRowQty columns reset (due to the PARTITION BY clause), and return row 1 of 3 for the AccountId, and row 7 of 13 for the entire result set.

7-5. Using a Logical Window

Problem

You want the rows being considered by the OVER clause to be affected by the value in the column instead of the row positioning as determined by the ORDER BY clause in the OVER clause.

Solution

In the OVER clause, utilize the RANGE clause instead of the ROWS option:

```
CREATE TABLE #Test
        (
        RowID INT IDENTITY,
        FName VARCHAR(20),
        Salary SMALLINT
        );

INSERT INTO #Test (FName, Salary)
VALUES ('George',      800),
       ('Sam',         950),
       ('Diane',      1100),
       ('Nicholas',   1250),
       ('Samuel',     1250),   --<< duplicate value of above row
       ('Patricia',   1300),
       ('Brian',      1500),
       ('Thomas',     1600),
       ('Fran',       2450),
       ('Debbie',     2850),
       ('Mark',       2975),
       ('James',      3000),
       ('Cynthia',    3000),   --<< duplicate value of above row
       ('Christopher', 5000);
```

```
SELECT RowID,
       FName,
       Salary,
       SumByRows = SUM(Salary) OVER (ORDER BY Salary ROWS UNBOUNDED PRECEDING),
       SumByRange = SUM(Salary) OVER (ORDER BY Salary RANGE UNBOUNDED PRECEDING)
FROM   #Test
ORDER BY RowID;
```

This query returns the following result set:

RowID	FName	Salary	SumByRows	SumByRange
1	George	800	800	800
2	Sam	950	1750	1750
3	Diane	1100	2850	2850
4	Nicholas	1250	4100	5350
5	Samuel	1250	5350	5350
6	Patricia	1300	6650	6650
7	Brian	1500	8150	8150
8	Thomas	1600	9750	9750
9	Fran	2450	12200	12200
10	Debbie	2850	15050	15050
11	Mark	2975	18025	18025
12	James	3000	21025	24025
13	Cynthia	3000	24025	24025
14	Christopher	5000	29025	29025

How It Works

When utilizing the RANGE clause, the SUM function adjusts its window based upon the values in the specified column. The window is sized upon the beginning- and ending-point boundaries specified; in this case, the beginning point of UNBOUNDED PRECEDING (the first row in the partition) was specified, and the default ending boundary of CURRENT ROW was used. This example shows the salary of your employees, and the SUM function is performing a running total of the salaries in order of the salary. For comparison purposes, the running total is being calculated with both the ROWS and RANGE clauses. Within this dataset, there are two groups of employees that have the same salary: RowIDs 4 and 5 are both 1,250, and 12 and 13 are both 3,000. When the running total is calculated with the ROWS clause, you can see that the salary of the current row is being added to the prior total of the previous rows. However, when the RANGE clause is used, all of the rows that contain the value of the current row are totaled and added to the total of the previous value. The result is that for rows 4 and 5, both employees with a salary of 1,250 are added together for the running total (and this action is repeated for rows 12 and 13).

■ **Tip** If you need to perform running aggregations, and there is the possibility that you can have multiple rows with the same value in the columns specified by the ORDER BY clause, you should use the ROWS clause instead of the RANGE clause.

7-6. Generating an Incrementing Row Number

Problem

You need to have a query return total sales information. You need to include a row number for each row that corresponds to the order of the date of the purchase (so as to show the sequence of the transactions), and the numbering needs to start over for each account number.

Solution

Utilize the ROW_NUMBER function to assign row numbers to each row:

```
SELECT TOP 10
        AccountNumber,
        OrderDate,
        TotalDue,
        ROW_NUMBER() OVER (PARTITION BY AccountNumber ORDER BY OrderDate) AS RowNumber
FROM    AdventureWorks2014.Sales.SalesOrderHeader
ORDER BY AccountNumber;
```

This query returns the following result set:

AccountNumber	OrderDate	TotalDue	RN
10-4020-000001	2005-08-01 00:00:00.000	12381.0798	1
10-4020-000001	2005-11-01 00:00:00.000	22152.2446	2
10-4020-000001	2006-02-01 00:00:00.000	31972.1684	3
10-4020-000001	2006-05-01 00:00:00.000	29418.5269	4
10-4020-000002	2006-08-01 00:00:00.000	8727.1055	1
10-4020-000002	2006-11-01 00:00:00.000	4682.6908	2
10-4020-000002	2007-02-01 00:00:00.000	1485.918	3
10-4020-000002	2007-05-01 00:00:00.000	1668.3751	4
10-4020-000002	2007-08-01 00:00:00.000	3478.1096	5
10-4020-000002	2007-11-01 00:00:00.000	3941.9843	6

How It Works

The ROW_NUMBER function is utilized to generate a row number for each row in the partition. The PARTITION_BY clause is utilized to restart the number generation for each change in the AccountNumber column. The ORDER_BY clause is utilized to order the numbering of the rows by the value in the OrderDate column.

You can also utilize the ROW_NUMBER function to create a virtual numbers, or tally, table. (A numbers, or tally, table is simply a table of sequential numbers, and it can be utilized to eliminate loops. Use your favorite Internet search tool to find information about what the numbers or tally table is and how it can replace loops. One excellent article is found at www.sqlservercentral.com/articles/T-SQL/62867/.)

For instance, the sys.all_columns system view has more than 8,000 rows. You can utilize this to easily build a numbers table with this code:

```
SELECT  ROW_NUMBER() OVER (ORDER BY (SELECT NULL)) AS RN
FROM    sys.all_columns;
```

This query will produce a row number for each row in the sys.all_columns view. In this instance, the ordering doesn't matter, but it is required, so the ORDER BY clause is specified as "(SELECT NULL)". If you need more records than what are available in this table, you can simply cross join this table to itself, which will produce more than 64 million rows.

In this example, a table scan is required. Another method is to produce the numbers or tally table by utilizing constants. The following example creates a one-million-row virtual tally table without incurring any disk I/O operations:

```
WITH
TENS      (N) AS (SELECT 0 UNION ALL SELECT 0 UNION ALL SELECT 0 UNION ALL
                  SELECT 0 UNION ALL SELECT 0 UNION ALL SELECT 0 UNION ALL
                  SELECT 0 UNION ALL SELECT 0 UNION ALL SELECT 0 UNION ALL SELECT 0),
THOUSANDS (N) AS (SELECT 1 FROM TENS t1 CROSS JOIN TENS t2 CROSS JOIN TENS t3),
MILLIONS  (N) AS (SELECT 1 FROM THOUSANDS t1 CROSS JOIN THOUSANDS t2),
TALLY     (N) AS (SELECT ROW_NUMBER() OVER (ORDER BY (SELECT 0)) FROM MILLIONS)
SELECT N
FROM    TALLY;
```

7-7. Returning Rows by Rank
Problem

You want to calculate a ranking of your data based upon specified criteria. For instance, you want to rank your salespeople based upon their sales quotas on a specific date.

Solution

Utilize the RANK or DENSE_RANK functions to rank your salespeople:

```
SELECT  BusinessEntityID,
        SalesQuota,
        RANK() OVER (ORDER BY SalesQuota DESC) AS RankWithGaps,
        DENSE_RANK() OVER (ORDER BY SalesQuota DESC) AS RankWithoutGaps,
        ROW_NUMBER() OVER (ORDER BY SalesQuota DESC) AS RowNumber
FROM    Sales.SalesPersonQuotaHistory
WHERE   QuotaDate = '2014-03-01'
AND     SalesQuota < 500000;
```

This query returns the following result set:

BusinessEntityID	SalesQuota	RankWithGaps	RankWithoutGaps	RowNumber
284	497000.00	1	1	1
286	421000.00	2	2	2
283	403000.00	3	3	3
278	390000.00	4	4	4
280	390000.00	4	4	5
274	187000.00	6	5	6
285	26000.00	7	6	7
287	1000.00	8	7	8

How It Works

RANK and DENSE_RANK both assign a ranking value to each row within a partition. If multiple rows within the partition tie with the same value, they are assigned the same ranking value. When there is a tie, RANK will assign the following ranking value as if there had not been any ties, and DENSE_RANK will assign the next ranking value. If there are no ties in the partition, the ranking value assigned is the same as if the ROW_NUMBER function had been used with the same OVER clause definition.

In this example, we have eight rows returned, and the RowNumber column shows these rows with their sequential numbering. The fourth and fifth rows have the same SalesQuota value, so for both RANK and DENSE_RANK, these are ranked as 4. The sixth row has a different value, so it continues with the ranking values. It is with this row that we can see the difference between the functions—with RANK, the ranking continues with 6, which is the ROW_NUMBER that was assigned (as if there had not been a tie). With DENSE_RANK, the ranking continues with 5—the next value in this ranking.

With this example, we can see that RANK produces a gap between the ranking values when there is a tie, and DENSE_RANK does not. The decision of which function to utilize will depend upon whether gaps are allowed or not. For instance, when ranking sports teams, you would want the gaps.

7-8. Sorting Rows into Buckets

Problem

You want to split your salespeople up into four groups based upon their sales quotas.

Solution

Utilize the NTILE function and specify the number of groups to divide the result set into:

```
SELECT  BusinessEntityID,
        QuotaDate,
        SalesQuota,
        NTILE(4) OVER (ORDER BY SalesQuota DESC) AS [NTILE]
FROM    Sales.SalesPersonQuotaHistory
WHERE   SalesQuota BETWEEN 266000.00 AND 319000.00;
```

This query produces the following result set:

BusinessEntityID	QuotaDate	SalesQuota	NTILE
280	2007-07-01 00:00:00.000	319000.00	1
284	2007-04-01 00:00:00.000	304000.00	1
280	2006-04-01 00:00:00.000	301000.00	1
282	2007-01-01 00:00:00.000	288000.00	2
283	2007-04-01 00:00:00.000	284000.00	2
284	2007-01-01 00:00:00.000	281000.00	2
278	2008-01-01 00:00:00.000	280000.00	3
283	2006-01-01 00:00:00.000	280000.00	3
283	2006-04-01 00:00:00.000	267000.00	4
278	2006-01-01 00:00:00.000	266000.00	4

How It Works

The NTILE function divides the result set into the specified number of groups based upon the partitioning and ordering specified in the OVER clause. Notice that the first two groups have three rows in each group, and the final two groups have two. If the number of rows in the result set is not evenly divisible by the specified number of groups, then the leading groups will have one extra row assigned to those groups until the remainder has been accommodated. Additionally, if you do not have as many buckets as were specified, all of the buckets will not be assigned.

7-9. Grouping Logically Consecutive Rows Together
Problem

You need to group logically consecutive rows together so that subsequent calculations can treat those rows identically. For instance, your manufacturing plant utilizes RFID tags to track the movement of your products. During the manufacturing process, a product may be rejected and sent back to an earlier part of the process to be corrected. You want to track the number of trips that a tag makes to an area. The manufacturing plant has four rooms. The first room has two sensors in it. An RFID tag is affixed to a part of the item being manufactured. As the item moves about room 1, the RFID tag affixed to it can be picked up by the different sensors. As long as the consecutive entries (when ordered by the time the sensor was read) for this RFID tag are in room 1, then this RFID tag is to be considered to be in its first trip to room 1. Once the RFID tag leaves room 1 and goes to room 2, the sensor in room 2 will pick up the RFID tag and place an entry into the database—this will be the first trip into room 2 for this RFID tag. The RFID tag subsequently is moved into room 3, where the sensor in that room detects the RFID tag and places an entry into the database—the first trip into room 3. While in room 3, the item is rejected and is sent back into room 2 for corrections. As it enters room 2, it is picked up by the sensor in room 2 and entered into the system. Since there is a different room between the two entries for room 2, the entries for room 2 are not consecutive, which makes this the second trip into room 2. Subsequently, when the item is corrected and is moved back into room 3, the sensor in room 3 enters a second entry for the item. Since the item was in room 2 between the two sensor readings in room 3, this is the second trip into room 3. The item subsequently is moved to room 4. What we are looking to produce from the query for this tag is:

```
Tag #   Room #  Trip #
1       1       1
1       1       1
1       2       1
1       3       1
1       2       2
1       3       2
1       4       1
```

This recipe will utilize the following data:

```
CREATE TABLE #RFID_Location (
    TagId           INTEGER,
    Location        VARCHAR(25),
    SensorReadTime  DATETIME);
INSERT INTO #RFID_Location
        (TagId, Location, SensorReadTime)
VALUES  (1, 'Room1', '2012-01-10T08:00:01'),
        (1, 'Room1', '2012-01-10T08:18:32'),
        (1, 'Room2', '2012-01-10T08:25:42'),
        (1, 'Room3', '2012-01-10T09:52:48'),
        (1, 'Room2', '2012-01-10T10:05:22'),
        (1, 'Room3', '2012-01-10T11:22:15'),
        (1, 'Room4', '2012-01-10T14:18:58'),
        (2, 'Room1', '2012-01-10T08:32:18'),
        (2, 'Room1', '2012-01-10T08:51:53'),
        (2, 'Room2', '2012-01-10T09:22:09'),
        (2, 'Room1', '2012-01-10T09:42:17'),
        (2, 'Room1', '2012-01-10T09:59:16'),
        (2, 'Room2', '2012-01-10T10:35:18'),
        (2, 'Room3', '2012-01-10T11:18:42'),
        (2, 'Room4', '2012-01-10T15:22:18');
```

Solution

The goal of this recipe is to introduce the concept of an "island" of data, where rows that are desired to be sequential are compared to other values to determine if they are in fact sequential. This is accomplished by utilizing two ROW_NUMBER functions, differing only in that one uses an additional column in the PARTITION BY clause. This gives us one ROW_NUMBER function returning a sequential number per RFID tag (PARTITION BY TagId), and the second ROW_NUMBER function returning a number that is desired to be sequential

(PARTITION BY TagId, Location) The difference between these results will group logically consecutive rows together. See the following:

```
WITH cte AS
(
SELECT TagId, Location, SensorReadTime,
       ROW_NUMBER() OVER (PARTITION BY TagId ORDER BY SensorReadTime) -
       ROW_NUMBER() OVER (PARTITION BY TagId, Location ORDER BY SensorReadTime) AS Grp
FROM   #RFID_Location
)
SELECT TagId, Location, SensorReadTime, Grp,
       DENSE_RANK() OVER (PARTITION BY TagId, Location ORDER BY Grp) AS TripNbr
FROM   cte
ORDER BY TagId, SensorReadTime;
```

This query returns the following result set:

TagId	Location	SensorDate	Grp	TripNbr
1	Room1	2012-01-10 08:00:01.000	0	1
1	Room1	2012-01-10 08:18:32.000	0	1
1	Room2	2012-01-10 08:25:42.000	2	1
1	Room3	2012-01-10 09:52:48.000	3	1
1	Room2	2012-01-10 10:05:22.000	3	2
1	Room3	2012-01-10 11:22:15.000	4	2
1	Room4	2012-01-10 14:18:58.000	6	1
2	Room1	2012-01-10 08:32:18.000	0	1
2	Room1	2012-01-10 08:51:53.000	0	1
2	Room2	2012-01-10 09:22:09.000	2	1
2	Room1	2012-01-10 09:42:17.000	1	2
2	Room1	2012-01-10 09:59:16.000	1	2
2	Room2	2012-01-10 10:35:18.000	4	2
2	Room3	2012-01-10 11:18:42.000	6	1
2	Room4	2012-01-10 15:22:18.000	7	1

How It Works

This recipe introduces the concept of islands, where the data is logically grouped together based upon the values in the rows. As long as the values are sequential, they are part of the same island. A gap in the values separates one island from another. Islands are created by subtracting a value from each row that is *desired* to be sequential for the ordering column(s) from a value from that row that *is* sequential for the ordering column(s). In this example, we utilized two ROW_NUMBER functions to generate these numbers (if the columns had contained either of these numbers, then the associated ROW_NUMBER function could have been removed and that column itself used instead). The first ROW_NUMBER function partitions the result set by the TagId and assigns the row number as ordered by the SensorDate. This provides us with the sequential numbering within the TagId. The second ROW_NUMBER function partitions the result set by the TagId and Location and assigns the row number, as ordered by the SensorDate. This provides us with the numbering that is desired to be sequential. The difference between these two calculations will assign consecutive rows in the same location to the same Grp number. The previous results show that consecutive entries in the same location are indeed assigned the same Grp number. The following query breaks down the ROW_NUMBER functions into individual columns so that you can see how this is performed:

```
WITH cte AS
(
SELECT TagId, Location, SensorReadTime,
       -- For each tag, number each sensor reading by its timestamp
       ROW_NUMBER()OVER (PARTITION BY TagId ORDER BY SensorReadTime) AS RN1,
       -- For each tag and location, number each sensor reading by its timestamp.
       ROW_NUMBER() OVER (PARTITION BY TagId, Location ORDER BY SensorReadTime) AS RN2
FROM   #RFID_Location
)
SELECT TagId, Location, SensorReadTime,
       -- Display each of the row numbers,
       -- Subtract RN2 from RN1
       RN1, RN2, RN1-RN2 AS Grp
FROM   cte
ORDER BY TagId, SensorReadTime;
```

This query returns the following result set:

TagId	Location	SensorDate	RN1	RN2	Grp
1	Room1	2012-01-10 08:00:01.000	1	1	0
1	Room1	2012-01-10 08:18:32.000	2	2	0
1	Room2	2012-01-10 08:25:42.000	3	1	2
1	Room3	2012-01-10 09:52:48.000	4	1	3
1	Room2	2012-01-10 10:05:22.000	5	2	3
1	Room3	2012-01-10 11:22:15.000	6	2	4
1	Room4	2012-01-10 14:18:58.000	7	1	6
2	Room1	2012-01-10 08:32:18.000	1	1	0
2	Room1	2012-01-10 08:51:53.000	2	2	0
2	Room2	2012-01-10 09:22:09.000	3	1	2
2	Room1	2012-01-10 09:42:17.000	4	3	1
2	Room1	2012-01-10 09:59:16.000	5	4	1
2	Room2	2012-01-10 10:35:18.000	6	2	4
2	Room3	2012-01-10 11:18:42.000	7	1	6
2	Room4	2012-01-10 15:22:18.000	8	1	7

With this query, you can see that for each TagId, the RN1 column is sequentially numbered from 1 to the total number of rows for that TagId. For the RN2 column, the Location is added to the PARTITION BY clause, resulting in the assigned row numbers being restarted every time the location changes.

Let's walk through what is going on with TagId #1. For the first sensor reading, RN1 is 1 (the first reading for this tag). This sensor was located in Room1. For RN2, this is the first sensor reading for this Tag/Location. The difference between these two values is 0.

For the second row, RN1 is 2 (the second reading for this tag). The sensor reading is still from Room1, so RN2 returns a 2. Again, the difference between these two values is 0.

For the third row, this is the third reading for this tag, so RN1 is 3. This sensor reading is from Room2. Since RN2 is calculated with a PARTITION BY clause that includes the location, this resets the numbering and RN2 returns a 1. The difference between these two values is 2.

For the fourth row, this is the fourth reading for this tag, so RN1 is 4. This sensor reading is from Room3, so RN2 is reset again and returns a 1. The difference between the two values is 3.

For the fifth row, RN1 will return 5. This sensor reading is from Room2, and looking at just the values for Room2, this is the second row for Room2, so RN2 will return a 2. The difference between these two values is 3.

For the sixth row, RN1 will return 6. This is from the second time in Room3, so RN2 will return a 2. The difference between these two values is 4.

For the seventh and last row, RN1 will return 7. This reading is from Room4 (the first reading from this location), so RN2 will return a 1. The difference between these two values is 6.

In looking at the data sequentially, as long as we are in the same location, then the difference between the two values will be the same. A subsequent trip to this location, after having been picked up by a second location first, will return a value that is higher than this difference. If we were to have multiple return trips to a location, each time this difference would be a higher value than what was returned for the last time in this location. This difference does not need to be sequential at this stage (that will be handled in the next step); what is important is that a return trip *to this location* will generate a difference that is higher than the previous difference, and that multiple consecutive readings in the same location will generate the same difference.

In considering this difference (the Grp column) for all of the rows *within the same location*, as long as this difference is the same, those rows with the same difference value are in the same trip to that location. If the difference changes for that location, then you are in a subsequent trip to this location. To handle calculating the trips, the DENSE_RANK function is utilized so that there will not be any gaps, using the ORDER BY clause against this difference (the Grp column). The following query takes the first example and adds in both the DENSE_RANK and RANK functions to illustrate the difference that these would have on the results:

```
WITH cte AS
(
SELECT TagId, Location, SensorReadTime,
       ROW_NUMBER() OVER (PARTITION BY TagId ORDER BY SensorReadTime) -
       ROW_NUMBER() OVER (PARTITION BY TagId, Location ORDER BY SensorReadTime) AS Grp
FROM   #RFID_Location
)
SELECT TagId, Location, SensorReadTime, Grp,
       DENSE_RANK() OVER (PARTITION BY TagId, Location ORDER BY Grp) AS TripNbr,
       RANK() OVER (PARTITION BY TagId, Location ORDER BY Grp) AS TripNbrRank
FROM   cte
ORDER BY TagId, SensorReadTime;
```

This query returns the following result set:

TagId	Location	SensorDate	Grp	TripNbr	TripNbrRank
1	Room1	2012-01-10 08:00:01.000	0	1	1
1	Room1	2012-01-10 08:18:32.000	0	1	1
1	Room2	2012-01-10 08:25:42.000	2	1	1
1	Room3	2012-01-10 09:52:48.000	3	1	1
1	Room2	2012-01-10 10:05:22.000	3	2	2
1	Room3	2012-01-10 11:22:15.000	4	2	2
1	Room4	2012-01-10 14:18:58.000	6	1	1
2	Room1	2012-01-10 08:32:18.000	0	1	1
2	Room1	2012-01-10 08:51:53.000	0	1	1
2	Room2	2012-01-10 09:22:09.000	2	1	1

2	Room1	2012-01-10 09:42:17.000 1	2	3
2	Room1	2012-01-10 09:59:16.000 1	2	3
2	Room2	2012-01-10 10:35:18.000 4	2	2
2	Room3	2012-01-10 11:18:42.000 6	1	1
2	Room4	2012-01-10 15:22:18.000 7	1	1

In this result, the first two rows are both in Room1, and they both produced the Grp value of 0, so they are both considered as Trip1 for this location. For the next two rows, the tag was in locations Room2 and Room3. These were both the first times in these locations, so each of these is considered as Trip1 for their respective locations. You can see that both the RANK and DENSE_RANK functions produced this value.

For the fifth row, the tag was moved back into Room2. This produced the Grp value of 3. This location had a previous Grp value of 2, so this is a different island for this location. Since this is a higher value, its RANK and DENSE_RANK value is 2, indicating the second trip to this location.

You can follow this same logic for the remaining rows for this tag. When we move to the second tag, you can see how the RANK function returns the wrong trip number for TagId 2 for the second trip to Room1 (the fourth and fifth rows for this tag). Since in this example we are looking for no gaps, DENSE_RANK would be the proper function to use, and we can see that DENSE_RANK did return that this is trip 2 for that location.

7-10. Accessing Values from Other Rows

Problem

You need to write a sales summary report that shows the total due from orders by year and quarter. You want to include a difference between the current quarter and prior quarter, as well as a difference between the current quarter of this year and the same quarter of the previous year.

Solution

Aggregate the total due by year and quarter, and utilize the LAG function to look at the previous records:

```
WITH cte AS
(
-- Break the OrderDate down into the Year and Quarter
SELECT  DATEPART(QUARTER, OrderDate) AS Qtr,
        DATEPART(YEAR, OrderDate) AS Yr,
        TotalDue
FROM    Sales.SalesOrderHeader
), cteAgg AS
(
-- Aggregate the TotalDue, Grouping on Year and Quarter
SELECT  Yr,
        Qtr,
        SUM(TotalDue) AS TotalDue
FROM    cte
GROUP BY Yr, Qtr
)
```

```
SELECT  Yr,
        Qtr,
        TotalDue,
        -- Get the total due from the prior quarter
        TotalDue - LAG(TotalDue, 1, NULL) OVER (ORDER BY Yr, Qtr) AS DeltaPriorQtr,
        -- Get the total due from 4 quarters ago.
        -- This will be for the prior Year, same Quarter.
        TotalDue - LAG(TotalDue, 4, NULL) OVER (ORDER BY Yr, Qtr) AS DeltaPriorYrQtr
FROM    cteAgg
ORDER BY Yr, Qtr;
```

This query returns the following result set:

Yr	Qtr	TotalDue	DeltaPriorQtr	DeltaPriorYrQtr
2005	3	5203127.8807	NULL	NULL
2005	4	7490122.7457	2286994.865	NULL
2006	1	6562121.6796	-928001.0661	NULL
2006	2	6947995.43	385873.7504	NULL
2006	3	11555907.1472	4607911.7172	6352779.2665
2006	4	9397824.1785	-2158082.9687	1907701.4328
2007	1	7492396.3224	-1905427.8561	930274.6428
2007	2	9379298.7027	1886902.3803	2431303.2727
2007	3	15413231.8434	6033933.1407	3857324.6962
2007	4	14886562.6775	-526669.1659	5488738.499
2008	1	12744940.3554	-2141622.3221	5252544.033
2008	2	16087078.2305	3342137.8751	6707779.5278
2008	3	56178.9223	-16030899.3082	-15357052.9211

How It Works

The first CTE is utilized to retrieve the year and quarter from the OrderDate column and to pass the TotalDue column to the rest of the query. The second CTE is used to aggregate the TotalDue column, grouping on the extracted Yr and Qtr columns. The final SELECT statement returns these aggregated values and then makes two calls to the LAG function. The first call retrieves the TotalDue column from the previous row in order to compute the difference between the current quarter and the previous quarter. The second call retrieves the TotalDue column from four rows prior to the current row in order to compute the difference between the current quarter and the same quarter one year ago.

The syntax for the LAG and LEAD functions is as follows:

```
LAG | LEAD (scalar_expression [,offset] [,default])
  OVER ( [ partition_by_clause ] order_by_clause )
```

The scalar_expression is an expression of any type that returns a scalar value (typically a column), offset is the number of rows to offset the current row by, and default is the value to return if the value returned is NULL. The default value for offset is 1, and the default value for default is NULL.

7-11. Finding Gaps in a Sequence of Numbers

Problem

You have a table with a series of numbers that has gaps in the series. You want to find these gaps.

Solution

Utilize the LEAD function in order to compare the next row with the current row to look for a gap:

```
CREATE TABLE #Gaps (col1 INTEGER PRIMARY KEY CLUSTERED);

INSERT INTO #Gaps (col1)
VALUES (1), (2), (3),
       (50), (51), (52), (53), (54), (55),
       (100), (101), (102),
       (500),
       (950), (951), (952),
       (954);

-- Compare the value of the current row to the next row.
-- If > 1, then there is a gap.
WITH cte AS
(
SELECT  col1 AS CurrentRow,
        LEAD(col1, 1, NULL) OVER (ORDER BY col1) AS NextRow
FROM    #Gaps
)
SELECT  cte.CurrentRow + 1 AS [Start of Gap],
        cte.NextRow - 1 AS [End of Gap]
FROM    cte
WHERE   cte.NextRow - cte.CurrentRow > 1;
```

This query returns the following result set:

Start of Gap	End of Gap
4	49
56	99
103	499
501	949
953	953

How It Works

The LEAD function works in a similar manner to the LAG function, which was covered in the previous recipe. In this example, a table is created that has gaps in the column. The table is then queried, comparing the value in the current row to the value in the next row. If the difference is greater than 1, then a gap exists and is returned in the result set.

163

To explain this in further detail, let's look at all of the rows, with the next row being returned:

```
SELECT  col1 AS CurrentRow,
        LEAD(col1, 1, NULL) OVER (ORDER BY col1) AS NextRow
FROM    #Gaps;
```

This query returns the following result set:

CurrentRow	NextRow
1	2
2	3
3	50
50	51
51	52
52	53
53	54
54	55
55	100
100	101
101	102
102	500
500	950
950	951
951	952
952	954
954	NULL

For the current row of 1, we can see that the next value for this column is 2. For the current row value of 2, the next value is 3. For the current row value of 3, the next value is 50. At this point, we have a gap. Since we have the values of 3 and 50, the gap is from 4 through 49—or, as is coded in the first query, CurrentRow+1 to NextRow−1. Adding the WHERE clause for where the difference is greater than 1 results in only the rows with a gap being returned.

7-12. Accessing the First or Last Value from a Partition

Problem

You need to write a report that shows, for each customer, the date that they placed their least and most expensive orders.

Solution

Utilize the FIRST_VALUE and LAST_VALUE functions:

```
SELECT DISTINCT TOP (5)
       CustomerID,
       -- Get the date for the customer's least expensive order
       FIRST_VALUE(OrderDate)
```

```
       OVER (PARTITION BY CustomerID
                ORDER BY TotalDue
                  ROWS BETWEEN UNBOUNDED PRECEDING AND UNBOUNDED FOLLOWING) AS OrderDateLow,
       -- Get the date for the customer's most expensive order
       LAST_VALUE(OrderDate)
       OVER (PARTITION BY CustomerID
                ORDER BY TotalDue
                  ROWS BETWEEN UNBOUNDED PRECEDING AND UNBOUNDED FOLLOWING) AS OrderDateHigh
FROM    Sales.SalesOrderHeader
ORDER BY CustomerID;
```

This query returns the following result set for the first five customers:

```
CustomerID  OrderDateLow            OrderDateHigh
----------  ----------------------  ----------------------
11000       2013-06-20 00:00:00.000 2011-06-21 00:00:00.000
11001       2014-05-12 00:00:00.000 2011-06-17 00:00:00.000
11002       2013-06-02 00:00:00.000 2011-06-09 00:00:00.000
11003       2013-06-07 00:00:00.000 2011-05-31 00:00:00.000
11004       2013-06-24 00:00:00.000 2011-06-25 00:00:00.000
```

How It Works

The FIRST_VALUE and LAST_VALUE functions are used to return a scalar expression (typically a column) from the first and last rows in the partition; in this example they are returning the OrderDate column. The window is set to a partition of the CustomerID, ordered by the TotalDue, and the ROWS clause is used to specify all of the rows for the partition. The syntax for the FIRST_VALUE and LAST_VALUE functions is as follows:

```
FIRST_VALUE | LAST_VALUE ( scalar_expression )
  OVER ( [ partition_by_clause ] order_by_clause [ rows_range_clause ] )
```

where scalar_expression is an expression of any type that returns a scalar value (typically a column).

Let's prove that this query is returning the correct results by examining the data for the first customer:

```
SELECT CustomerID, TotalDue, OrderDate
FROM    Sales.SalesOrderHeader
WHERE   CustomerID = 11000
ORDER BY TotalDue;
```

```
CustomerID  TotalDue               OrderDate
----------  ---------------------  ----------------------
11000       2587.8769              2013-06-20 00:00:00.000
11000       2770.2682              2013-10-03 00:00:00.000
11000       3756.989               2011-06-21 00:00:00.000
```

With these results, you can easily see that the date for the least expensive order was 2013-06-20, and the date for the most expensive order was 2011-06-21. This matches up with the data returned in the previous query.

7-13. Calculating the Relative Position or Rank of a Value within a Set of Values

Problem

You want to know the relative position and rank of a customer's order by the total of the order in respect to the total of all of the customers' orders.

Solution

Utilize the CUME_DIST and PERCENT_RANK functions to obtain the relative position and the relative rank of a value:

```
SELECT CustomerID,
       TotalDue,
       CUME_DIST()
       OVER (PARTITION BY CustomerID
               ORDER BY TotalDue) AS CumeDistOrderTotalDue,
       PERCENT_RANK()
       OVER (PARTITION BY CustomerID
               ORDER BY TotalDue) AS PercentRankOrderTotalDue
FROM   Sales.SalesOrderHeader
WHERE  CustomerID IN (11439, 30116)
ORDER BY CustomerID, TotalDue;
```

This code returns the following result set:

CustomerID	TotalDue	CumeDistOrderTotalDue	PercentRankOrderTotalDue
11439	858.9607	0.166666666666667	0
11439	2288.9187	0.333333333333333	0.2
11439	2591.1808	0.5	0.4
11439	2673.0613	0.833333333333333	0.6
11439	2673.0613	0.833333333333333	0.6
11439	2715.3497	1	1
30116	47520.583	0.25	0
30116	51390.8958	0.5	0.333333333333333
30116	55317.9431	0.75	0.666666666666667
30116	57441.8455	1	1

How It Works

The CUME_DIST function returns the cumulative distribution of a value within a set of values (that is, the relative position of a specific value within a set of values), while the PERCENT_RANK function returns the relative rank of a value in a set of values (that is, the relative standing of a value within a set of values). NULL values will be included, and the value returned will be the lowest possible value. There are two basic differences between these functions—first, CUME_DIST checks to see how many values are less than *or equal to* the current value, while PERCENT_RANK checks to see how many values are less than the current value only. Secondly, CUME_DIST divides this number by the number of rows in the partition, while PERCENT_RANK divides this number by the number of *other* rows in the partition.

The syntax of these functions is as follows:

```
CUME_DIST() | PERCENT_RANK( )
  OVER ( [ partition_by_clause ] order_by_clause )
```

The result returned by CUME_DIST will be a float(53) data type, with the value being greater than 0 and less than or equal to 1 (0 < x <= 1). CUME_DIST returns a percentage defined as the number of rows with a value less than or equal to the current value, divided by the total number of rows within the partition.

PERCENT_RANK also returns a float(53) data type, and the value being returned will be greater than or equal to 0, and less than or equal to 1 (0 <= x <= 1). PERCENT_RANK returns a percentage defined as the number of rows with a value less than the current row divided by the number of other rows in the partition. The first value returned by PERCENT_RANK will always be zero, since there will always be zero rows with a smaller value, and zero divided by anything will always be zero.

In examining the results from this query, we see that for the first row for the first CustomerID, the TotalDue value is 858.9607. For CUME_DIST, there is 1 row that has this value or less, and there are 6 total rows, so 1/6 = 0.1667. For PERCENT_RANK, there are 0 rows that have a value lower than this, and there are 5 other rows, so 0/5 = 0.

Regarding the second row's (TotalDue value of 2288.9187) CUME_DIST column, there are 2 rows with this value or less, which will return a CUME_DIST value of 2/6, or 0.333. For PERCENT_RANK, there is 1 row with a value lower than this TotalDue value, and there are 5 other rows, so this will return a PERCENT_RANK value of 1/5, or 0.2.

When we get down to the fourth row, we see that the fourth and fifth rows have the same TotalDue value. For CUME_DIST, there are 5 rows with this value or less, so 5/6 = 0.833 for both of these rows. For PERCENT_RANK, for both rows, there are 3 rows with a value less than the current value, so 3/5 = 0.6 for both rows. Note that for PERCENT_RANK, we are counting the number of other rows that are not the current row, not the number of other rows with a different value.

7-14. Calculating Continuous or Discrete Percentiles

Problem

You want to see both the median salary and the 75th percentile salary for all employees per department.

Solution

Utilize the PERCENTILE_CONT and PERCENTILE_DISC functions to return percentile calculations based upon a value at a specified percentage:

```
DECLARE @Employees TABLE
        (
         EmplId INT PRIMARY KEY CLUSTERED,
         DeptId INT,
         Salary NUMERIC(8, 2)
        );
```

```
INSERT INTO @Employees
VALUES (1, 1, 10000),
       (2, 1, 11000),
       (3, 1, 12000),
       (4, 2, 25000),
       (5, 2, 35000),
       (6, 2, 75000),
       (7, 2, 100000);

SELECT  EmplId,
        DeptId,
        Salary,
        PERCENTILE_CONT(0.5)
            WITHIN GROUP (ORDER BY Salary ASC)
            OVER (PARTITION BY DeptId) AS MedianCont,
        PERCENTILE_DISC(0.5)
            WITHIN GROUP (ORDER BY Salary ASC)
            OVER (PARTITION BY DeptId) AS MedianDisc,
        PERCENTILE_CONT(0.75)
            WITHIN GROUP (ORDER BY Salary ASC)
            OVER (PARTITION BY DeptId) AS Percent75Cont,
        PERCENTILE_DISC(0.75)
            WITHIN GROUP (ORDER BY Salary ASC)
            OVER (PARTITION BY DeptId) AS Percent75Disc,
        CUME_DIST()
            OVER (PARTITION BY DeptId
                    ORDER BY Salary) AS CumeDist
FROM    @Employees
ORDER BY DeptId, EmplId;
```

This query returns the following result set:

EmplId	DeptId	Salary	MedianCont	MedianDisc	Percent75Cont	Percent75Disc	CumeDist
1	1	10000.00	11000	11000.00	11500	12000.00	0.333333333333333
2	1	11000.00	11000	11000.00	11500	12000.00	0.666666666666667
3	1	12000.00	11000	11000.00	11500	12000.00	1
4	2	25000.00	55000	35000.00	81250	75000.00	0.25
5	2	35000.00	55000	35000.00	81250	75000.00	0.5
6	2	75000.00	55000	35000.00	81250	75000.00	0.75
7	2	100000.00	55000	35000.00	81250	75000.00	1

How It Works

PERCENTILE_CONT calculates a percentile based upon a continuous distribution of values of the specified column, while PERCENTILE_DISC calculates a percentile based upon a discrete distribution of the column values. The syntax for these functions is as follows:

```
PERCENTILE_CONT ( numeric_literal) | PERCENTILE_DISC ( numeric_literal )
    WITHIN GROUP ( ORDER BY order_by_expression [ ASC | DESC ] )
    OVER ( [ <partition_by_clause> ] )
```

For PERCENTILE_CONT, this is performed by using the specified percentile value (SP) and the number of rows in the partition (N), and by computing the row number of interest (RN) after the ordering has been applied. The row number of interest is computed from the formula RN = (1 + (SP * (N − 1))). The result returned is the average of the values from the rows at CRN = CEILING(RN) and FRN = FLOOR(RN). The value returned may or may not exist in the partition being analyzed. In looking at DeptId 1, with the specified percentile of 50%, we see that the RN = (1 + (0.5 * (3 − 1))). Working from the inside out, this goes to (1 + (0.5 * 2)), then to (1 + 1), with a final result of 2. The CRN and FRN of this value is the same: 2.

When we look at DeptId 2, we see it has 4 rows. This changes the calculation to (1 + (0.5 * (4 − 1))), to (1 + (0.5 * 3)) to (1 + 1.5) to 2.5. In this case, the CRN of this value is 3, and the FRN of this value is 2.

When we use the 75th percentile, for DeptId 1 we get (1 + (.75 * (3 − 1))), which evaluates to RN = 2.5, CRN = 3 and FRN = 2. For DeptID 2, we get (1 + (.75 * (4 − 1))), which evaluates to RN = 3.25, CRN = 4, and FRN = 3.

The next step is to return a linear interpolation of the values at these two row numbers. If CRN = FRN = RN, then return the value at RN. Otherwise, use the calculation ((CRN − RN) * (value at FRN)) + ((RN − FRN) * (value at CRN)). Starting with DeptId 1, for the 50th percentile, since CRN = FRN = RN, the value at RN (11,000) is returned. For the 75th percentile, the values of interest are those at rows 2 and 3. The more complicated calculation is used: ((3 − 2.5) * 11000) + ((2.5 − 2) * 12000) = (.5 * 11000) + (.5 * 12000) = (5500 + 6000) = 11500. Notice that this value does not exist in the data set.

When we evaluate DeptId 2, at the 50% percentile, we are looking at rows 2 and 3. The linear interpolation of these values is ((3 − 2.5) * 35000) + ((2.5 − 2) * 75000) = (.5 * 35000) + (.5 * 75000) = (17500 + 37500) = 55000. For the 75% percentile, we are looking at rows 3 and 4. The linear interpolation of these values is ((4 − 3.25) * 75000) + ((3.25-3) * 100000) = (.75 * 75000) + (.25 * 100000) = (56250 + 25000) = 81250. Again, notice that neither of these values exists in the data set.

For PERCENTILE_DISC, and for the specified percentile (P), the values of the partition are sorted, and the value returned will be from the row with the smallest CUME_DIST value (with the same ordering) that is greater than or equal to P. The value returned will exist in one of the rows in the partition being analyzed. Since the result for this function is based on the CUME_DIST value, that function was included in the previous query in order to show its value.

In the example, PERCENTILE_DISC(0.5) is utilized to obtain the median value. For DeptId = 1, there are three rows, so the CUME_DIST is split into thirds. The row with the smallest CUME_DIST value that is greater than or equal to the specified value is the middle row (0.667), so the median value is the value from the middle row (after sorting), or 11000. For DeptId = 2, there are four rows, so the CUME_DIST is split into fourths. For the second row, its CUME_DIST value matches the specified percentile, so the value used is the value from that row.

When looking at the 75th percentile, for DeptId 1 the row with the smallest CUME_DIST that is greater than or equal to .75 is the last row, which has a CUME_DIST value of 1, so the salary value from that row (12000) is returned for each row. For DeptId 2, the third row has a CUME_DIST that matches the specified percentile, so the salary value from that row (75000) is returned for each row. Notice that PERCENTILE_DISC always returns a value that exists in the partition.

7-15. Assigning Sequences in a Specified Order

Problem

You are inserting multiple student grades into a table. Each record needs to have a sequence assigned, and you want the sequences to be assigned in order of the grades.

Solution

Utilize the OVER clause of the NEXT VALUE FOR function, specifying the desired order.

```
IF EXISTS (SELECT *
            FROM sys.sequences AS seq
                JOIN sys.schemas AS sch
                  ON seq.schema_id = sch.schema_id
            WHERE sch.name = 'dbo'
            AND   seq.name = 'CH7Sequence')
   DROP SEQUENCE dbo.CH7Sequence;

CREATE SEQUENCE dbo.CH7Sequence AS INTEGER START WITH 1;

DECLARE @ClassRank TABLE
        (
         StudentID TINYINT,
         Grade TINYINT,
         SeqNbr INTEGER
        );
INSERT INTO @ClassRank (StudentId, Grade, SeqNbr)
SELECT StudentId,
       Grade,
       NEXT VALUE FOR dbo.CH7Sequence OVER (ORDER BY Grade ASC)
FROM   (VALUES (1, 100),
               (2, 95),
               (3, 85),
               (4, 100),
               (5, 99),
               (6, 98),
               (7, 95),
               (8, 90),
               (9, 89),
               (10, 89),
               (11, 85),
               (12, 82)) dt(StudentId, Grade);

SELECT StudentId, Grade, SeqNbr
FROM   @ClassRank;
```

This query returns the following result set:

```
StudentID Grade SeqNbr
--------- ----- ------
12        82    1
3         85    2
11        85    3
10        89    4
9         89    5
8         90    6
7         95    7
2         95    8
6         98    9
5         99    10
1         100   11
4         100   12
```

How It Works

The optional OVER clause of the NEXT VALUE FOR function is utilized to specify the order in which the sequence should be applied. The syntax is as follows:

```
NEXT VALUE FOR [ database_name . ] [ schema_name . ]  sequence_name
   [ OVER (<over_order_by_clause>) ]
```

Sequences are used to create an incrementing number. While similar to an identity column, they are not bound to any table, can be reset, and can be used across multiple tables. Sequences are discussed in detail in recipe 13-22. Sequences are assigned by calling the NEXT VALUE FOR function, and multiple values can be assigned simultaneously. The order of these assignments can be controlled by the use of the optional OVER clause of the NEXT VALUE FOR function.

CHAPTER 8

Inserting, Updating, Deleting

by Wayne Sheffield

In this chapter, I will cover how to modify data using the Transact-SQL INSERT, UPDATE, DELETE, and MERGE statements. I'll review the basics of each statement and cover specific techniques such as inserting data returned from a stored procedure and outputting the affected rows of a data modification.

Before going into the new features, let's start by reviewing basic INSERT concepts.

The simplified syntax for the INSERT command is as follows:

```
INSERT [ INTO]
table_or_view_name [ ( column_list ) ]
table_source
```

Where `table_source` can be

```
VALUES (({DEFAULT | NULL | expression } [ ,...n ]) [ ,...n ])
derived_tables (any SELECT statement that returns rows of data)
execute_statement (calling a stored procedure that returns results)
dml_table_source
DEFAULT VALUES
```

Table 8-1 describes the arguments of this command.

Table 8-1. INSERT Command Arguments

Argument	Description
table_or_view_name	The name of the table or updateable view into which you are inserting the data
column_list	The explicit comma-separated list of columns on the insert table that will be populated with values
({DEFAULT | NULL | expression } [,...n])	The comma-separated list of values to be inserted as a row into the table. You can insert multiple rows in a single statement. Each value can be an expression, NULL value, or DEFAULT value (if a default was defined for the column).

8-1. Inserting a New Row

Problem

You need to insert one row into a table using a set of defined values.

Solution

A simple use of the INSERT statement accepts a list of values in the VALUES clause that are mapped to a list of columns specified in the INTO clause. In this recipe, we will add a new row to the Production.Location table, as follows:

```
INSERT  INTO Production.Location
        (Name, CostRate, Availability)
VALUES  ('Wheel Storage', 11.25, 80.00) ;
```

This returns the following:

```
(1 row(s) affected)
```

To verify the row has been inserted correctly, let's query the Location table for the new row:

```
SELECT  Name,
        CostRate,
        Availability
FROM    Production.Location
WHERE   Name = 'Wheel Storage' ;
```

This returns the following:

Name	CostRate	Availability
Wheel Storage	11.25	80.00

How It Works

In this recipe, a new row was inserted into the Production.Location table. The query began with the INSERT statement and the name of the table receiving the inserted data (the INTO keyword is optional):

```
INSERT INTO Production.Location
```

Next, we explicitly listed the columns of the destination table receiving the supplied values:

```
(Name, CostRate, Availability)
```

A comma must separate each column. Columns don't need to be listed in the same order as they appear in the base table, but the values supplied in the VALUES clause must exactly match the order of the column list. Column lists are not necessary if the VALUES clause specifies values for all of the columns in the base table and if these values are specified in the same order in which they are defined in that table. However, using column lists is recommended, because explicitly listing columns allows you to add new columns to the base table without changing your INSERT statements (assuming the new column has a default value).

The next line of code is the VALUES clause and contains a comma-separated list of values (expressions) to insert:

```
VALUES ('Wheel Storage', 11.25, 80.00)
```

The values in this list must be provided in the same order as the corresponding columns are listed, or if no columns are listed, the VALUES clause must contain values for all of the table's columns in the same order as they appear in the table definition.

8-2. Specifying Default Values

Problem

You need to insert one row into a table, and you want to use a table's default values for some columns.

Solution

In the previous recipe, we inserted a row into the Production.Location table. The Production.Location table has two other columns that are not explicitly referenced in the INSERT statement. If you look at the definition of Production.Location listed in Table 8-2, you will see that there is also a LocationID column and a ModifiedDate column that we did not include in the INSERT statement.

Table 8-2. Production.Location Table Definition

Column Name	Data Type	Nullability	Default Value	Identity Column?
LocationID	smallint	NOT NULL		Yes
Name	dbo.Name (user-defined data type)	NOT NULL		No
CostRate	smallmoney	NOT NULL	0.00	No
Availability	decimal(8,2)	NOT NULL	0.00	No
ModifiedDate	datetime	NOT NULL	GETDATE() (function to return the current date and time)	No

■ **Note**   See the "Managing Tables" chapter for more information on the CREATE TABLE command, IDENTITY columns, and DEFAULT values.

The ModifiedDate column has a default value of GETDATE(). If an INSERT statement does not explicitly supply a value for the ModifiedDate column of a new row in the Production.Location table, SQL Server will execute the GETDATE() function to populate the column with the current date and time. The INSERT could have been written to supply a value and override the default value. Here's an example:

```
INSERT   Production.Location
         (Name,
          CostRate,
          Availability,
          ModifiedDate)
VALUES   ('Wheel Storage 2',
          11.25,
          80.00,
          '4/1/2012') ;
```

When a column has a default value specified, you can use the DEFAULT keyword in the VALUES clause to explicitly use the default value. Here's an example:

```
INSERT   Production.Location
         (Name,
          CostRate,
          Availability,
          ModifiedDate)
VALUES   ('Wheel Storage 3',
          11.25,
          80.00,
          DEFAULT) ;
```

When a column has no default value specified, you can use the DEFAULT keyword in the VALUES clause to explicitly use the default of the column's type. Here's an example:

```
INSERT   INTO Person.Address
         (AddressLine1,
          AddressLine2,
          City,
          StateProvinceID,
          PostalCode)
VALUES   ('15 Wake Robin Rd',
          DEFAULT,
          'Sudbury',
          30,
          '01776') ;
```

In this case, the Person.Address table has no default value specified for the AddressLine2 column, so SQL Server uses the default value for the NVARCHAR type, which is NULL.

■ **Note**   The rowversion data type (also known as timestamp) automatically generates unique binary numbers. An INSERT that specifies either DEFAULT or NULL will generate this binary number.

If each column in the table uses defaults for all columns, you can perform an INSERT that inserts a row using only the defaults for each column by including the DEFAULT VALUES option. For example, the following table has default values for all of its columns:

```
CREATE TABLE #ExampleTable
(
    RowID       INTEGER IDENTITY,
    RowColID    UNIQUEIDENTIFIER DEFAULT NEWID(),
    RowDate     DATETIME DEFAULT GETDATE()
);
```

A row can be inserted into this table using the DEFAULT VALUES option:

```
INSERT INTO #ExampleTable DEFAULT VALUES;
```

When the row is selected out, we can see that each of the columns has had its assigned default value assigned to it:

```
SELECT * FROM #ExampleTable;
```

RowID	RowColID	RowDate
1	AB728BF2-ED5C-4A93-A2D9-A2B125E9A8D6	2015-01-19 15:13:53.147

How It Works

The DEFAULT keyword allows you to explicitly set a column's default value in an INSERT statement. If all columns are to be set to their default values, the DEFAULT VALUES keywords can be used. If the table definition contains no default value for a column, the type's default value will be used.

The LocationID column from the Production.Location table and the RowID column from the #ExampleTable table, however, are IDENTITY columns (not defaulted columns). An IDENTITY property on a column causes the value in that column to automatically populate with an incrementing numeric value. Because LocationID is an IDENTITY column, the database manages inserting the values for this row; an INSERT statement cannot normally specify a value for an IDENTITY column. If you want to specify a certain value for an IDENTITY column, you need to follow the procedure outlined in the next recipe.

8-3. Overriding an IDENTITY Column

Problem

You have a table with an IDENTITY column defined. You need to override the IDENTITY property and insert explicit values into the IDENTITY column.

Solution

A column using an IDENTITY property automatically increments based on a numeric seed and increment value for every row inserted into the table. IDENTITY columns are often used as surrogate keys (a *surrogate key* is a unique key generated by the database that holds no business-level significance other than to ensure uniqueness within the table).

177

In data load or recovery scenarios, you may find that you need to manually insert explicit values into an IDENTITY column. For example, a row with the key value of 4 is deleted accidentally, and you need to manually reconstruct that row and preserve the original value of 4 with the original business information.

To explicitly insert a numeric value into a column defined with an IDENTITY property, you must use the SET IDENTITY_INSERT command. The syntax is as follows:

```
SET IDENTITY_INSERT [database_name.[schema_name].]table { ON | OFF }
```

Table 8-3 shows the arguments of this command.

Table 8-3. SET IDENTITY_INSERT Command

Argument	Description
[database_name.[schema_name].]table	The optional database name, optional schema name, and required table name for which an INSERT statement will be allowed to explicitly specify IDENTITY values.
ON	OFF	When set ON, explicit value inserts are allowed. When set OFF, explicit value inserts are *not* allowed.

This recipe will demonstrate how to explicitly insert the value of an IDENTITY column into a table. The following query demonstrates what happens if you try to explicitly insert into an IDENTITY column without first using IDENTITY_INSERT:

```
INSERT INTO HumanResources.Department (DepartmentID, Name, GroupName)
VALUES (17, 'Database Services', 'Information Technology');
```

This returns an error, keeping you from inserting an explicit value for the IDENTITY column:

```
Msg 544, Level 16, State 1, Line 2
Cannot insert explicit value for identity column in table 'Department' when
IDENTITY_INSERT is set to OFF.
```

Using SET IDENTITY_INSERT removes this barrier:

```
SET IDENTITY_INSERT HumanResources.Department ON;

INSERT HumanResources.Department (DepartmentID, Name, GroupName)
VALUES (17, 'Database Services', 'Information Technology');

SET IDENTITY_INSERT HumanResources.Department OFF;
```

How It Works

In the recipe, IDENTITY_INSERT was set ON prior to the INSERT:

```
SET IDENTITY_INSERT HumanResources.Department ON ;
```

The INSERT was then performed using a value of 17. When inserting into an IDENTITY column, you must also explicitly list the column names after the INSERT table_name clause:

```
INSERT  HumanResourcesDepartment
        (DepartmentID,
         Name,
         GroupName)
VALUES  (17,
         'Database Services',
         'Information Technology') ;
```

If the inserted value is greater than the current IDENTITY value, new inserts to the table will automatically use this new value as the IDENTITY seed.

IDENTITY_INSERT should be set OFF once you are finished explicitly inserting values:

```
SET IDENTITY_INSERT HumanResources.Department OFF;
```

Only one table in a session can have IDENTITY_INSERT ON at a time. If you were to explicitly insert IDENTITY values into multiple tables, the pattern would look something like the following:

```
SET IDENTITY_INSERT TableA ON ;
INSERT INTO TableA (...) VALUES (...);
INSERT INTO TableA (...) VALUES (...);
INSERT INTO TableA (...) VALUES (...);
SET IDENTITY_INSERT TableA OFF ;

SET IDENTITY_INSERT TableB ON ;
INSERT INTO TableB (...) VALUES (...);
INSERT INTO TableB (...) VALUES (...);
INSERT INTO TableB (...) VALUES (...);
SET IDENTITY_INSERT TableB OFF ;

SET IDENTITY_INSERT TableC ON ;
INSERT INTO TableC (...) VALUES (...);
INSERT INTO TableC (...) VALUES (...);
INSERT INTO TableC (...) VALUES (...);
SET IDENTITY_INSERT TableC OFF ;
```

Closing a connection will reset the IDENTITY_INSERT property to OFF for any table on which it is currently set to ON.

8-4. Generating a Globally Unique Identifier (GUID)

Problem

A column in your table is defined with the type UNIQUEIDENTIFIER. You need to insert a new row into the table and generate a new GUID for the row you are inserting.

■ **Note** For further information regarding the UniqueIdentifier data type, please refer to the SQL Server product documentation at http://msdn.microsoft.com/en-us/library/ms187942.aspx.

Solution

The NEWID system function generates a new GUID that can be inserted into a column defined with UNIQUEIDENTIFIER:

```
INSERT   Purchasing.ShipMethod
         (Name,
          ShipBase,
          ShipRate,
          rowguid)
VALUES   ('MIDDLETON CARGO TS1',
          8.99,
          1.22,
          NEWID()) ;

SELECT   rowguid,
         Name
FROM     Purchasing.ShipMethod
WHERE    Name = 'MIDDLETON CARGO TS1';
```

This returns the following (note that your rowguid value will be different from that in this example):

rowguid	Name
02F47979-CC55-4C4B-B4AA-ECD3F5CC85AF	MIDDLETON CARGO TS1

How It Works

The rowguid column in the Purchasing.ShipMethod table is a UNIQUEIDENTIFIER data-type column. Here is an excerpt from the table definition:

```
rowguid uniqueidentifier ROWGUIDCOL NOT NULL DEFAULT (NEWID ()),
```

To generate a new uniqueidentifier data-type value for this inserted row, the NEWID() function was used in the VALUES clause:

```
VALUES('MIDDLETON CARGO TS1', 8.99, 1.22, NEWID())
```

Selecting the new row that was just created, the rowguid was given a uniqueidentifier value of 174BE850-FDEA-4E64-8D17-C019521C6C07 (although when you test it yourself, you'll get a different value because NEWID creates a new value each time it is executed).

Note that the table is defined with a default value of NEWID( ). If a value is not specified for the rowguid column, SQL Server will use the NEWID function to generate a new GUID for the row.

8-5. Inserting Results from a Query

Problem

You need to insert multiple rows into a table based on the results of a query.

Solution

The previous recipes showed how to insert a single row of data. This recipe demonstrates how to insert multiple rows into a table using the INSERT...SELECT form of the INSERT statement. The syntax for performing an INSERT...SELECT is as follows:

```
INSERT [INTO]
table_or_view_name[(column_list)] SELECT column_list FROM data_source
```

The syntax for using INSERT...SELECT is almost identical to that for inserting a single row. Instead of using the VALUES clause, designate a SELECT query that is formatted to return rows with a column definition that matches the column list specified in the INSERT INTO clause of the statement. The SELECT query can be based on one or more data sources, so long as the column list conforms to the expected data types of the destination table.

For the purposes of this example, this recipe creates a new table for storing the result of a query. The example populates values from the HumanResources.Shift table into the new dbo.Shift_Archive table:

```
CREATE TABLE dbo.Shift_Archive
      (
      ShiftID          TINYINT NOT NULL,
      Name             Name NOT NULL,
      StartTime        DATETIME NOT NULL,
      EndTime          DATETIME NOT NULL,
      ModifiedDate     DATETIME NOT NULL
                            CONSTRAINT DF_ShiftModDate DEFAULT (GETDATE()),
      CONSTRAINT PK_Shift_ShiftID PRIMARY KEY CLUSTERED (ShiftID ASC)
      );
GO
```

Next, an INSERT...SELECT is performed:

```
INSERT  INTO dbo.Shift_Archive
        (ShiftID,
         Name,
         StartTime,
         EndTime,
         ModifiedDate)
        SELECT  ShiftID,
```

```
            Name,
            StartTime,
            EndTime,
            ModifiedDate
    FROM    HumanResources.Shift
    ORDER BY ShiftID ;
```

The results show that three rows were inserted:

```
(3 row(s) affected)
```

Next, a query is executed to confirm the inserted rows in the Shift_Archive table:

```
SELECT  ShiftID,
        Name
FROM    dbo.Shift_Archive ;
```

This returns:

```
ShiftID Name
------- -------
1       Day
2       Evening
3       Night
```

How It Works

The INSERT...SELECT form of the INSERT statement instructs SQL Server to insert multiple rows into a table based on a SELECT query. Just like regular, single-value INSERTs, you begin by using INSERT INTO table_name and specifying the list of columns to be inserted:

```
INSERT INTO dbo.Shift_Archive (ShiftID, Name, StartTime, EndTime, ModifiedDate)
```

The next clause is the query used to populate the table. The SELECT statement must return columns in the same order as the columns appear in the INSERT column list, and these columns must have data-type compatibility with the associated columns in the column list:

```
SELECT ShiftID
     , Name
     , StartTime
     , EndTime
     , ModifiedDate
  FROM HumanResources.Shift
 ORDER BY ShiftID
```

When the column lists aren't designated, the SELECT statement must provide values for *all* the columns of the table into which the data is being inserted.

8-6. Inserting Results from a Stored Procedure

Problem

You want to insert multiple rows into a table based on the results of a stored procedure.

Solution

A *stored procedure* groups one or more Transact-SQL statements into a logical unit and stores it as an object in a SQL Server database. Stored procedures allow for more sophisticated result-set creation (for example, you can use several intermediate result sets built in temporary tables before returning the final result set). Stored procedures that return a result set can be used with the INSERT...EXEC form of the INSERT statement.

This recipe demonstrates how to add rows to a table from the output of a stored procedure. A stored procedure can be used in this manner if it returns data via a SELECT statement from within the procedure definition, and if the result set (or multiple result sets) matches the column list specified in the INSERT INTO clause of the INSERT statement.

■ **Note**   For more information on stored procedures, see the "Stored Procedures" chapter.

The syntax for inserting data from a stored procedure is as follows:

```
INSERT [INTO] table_or_view_name [(column_list)] EXEC stored_procedure_name
```

The syntax is almost identical to that of the INSERT...SELECT form, only this time the data is populated via a stored-procedure execution and not a SELECT statement.

For this example, create a stored procedure that returns rows from the Production.TransactionHistory table, where the start and end dates are between the values passed to the stored procedure as parameters and the row does not already exist in the archive table:

```
CREATE PROCEDURE dbo.usp_SEL_Production_TransactionHistory
        @ModifiedStartDT DATETIME,
        @ModifiedEndDT DATETIME
AS
        SELECT    TransactionID,
                  ProductID,
                  ReferenceOrderID,
                  ReferenceOrderLineID,
                  TransactionDate,
                  TransactionType,
                  Quantity,
                  ActualCost,
                  ModifiedDate
        FROM      Production.TransactionHistory
        WHERE     ModifiedDate BETWEEN @ModifiedStartDT
                          AND      @ModifiedEndDT
                  AND TransactionID NOT IN (
                  SELECT  TransactionID
                  FROM    Production.TransactionHistoryArchive) ;
GO
```

Test the stored procedures to check that the results are returned as expected:

```
EXEC dbo.usp_SEL_Production_TransactionHistory '2013-09-01', '2013-09-02';
```

This returns 648 rows based on the date range passed to the procedure. Next, use this stored procedure to insert the 648 rows into the Production.TransactionHistoryArchive table:

```
INSERT   Production.TransactionHistoryArchive
         (TransactionID,
          ProductID,
          ReferenceOrderID,
          ReferenceOrderLineID,
          TransactionDate,
          TransactionType,
          Quantity,
          ActualCost,
          ModifiedDate)
         EXEC dbo.usp_SEL_Production_TransactionHistory '2013-09-01', '2013-09-02' ;
```

Executing this statement yields the following results:

```
(648 row(s) affected)
```

How It Works

This example demonstrated using a stored procedure to populate a table using INSERT and EXEC. The INSERT began with the name of the table into which rows were to be inserted:

```
INSERT Production.TransactionHistoryArchive
```

Next was the list of columns to be inserted into:

```
(TransactionID,
 ProductID,
 ReferenceOrderID,
 ReferenceOrderLineID,
 TransactionDate,
 TransactionType,
 Quantity,
 ActualCost,
 ModifiedDate)
```

Finally, the EXEC statement executed the stored procedure with the supplied parameters:

```
EXEC dbo.usp_SEL_Production_TransactionHistory '2013-09-01', '2013-09-02'
```

8-7. Inserting Multiple Rows at Once from Supplied Values

Problem

You are creating a script that adds multiple rows into a table one at a time. You want to optimize the size and speed of the script by reducing the number of statements executed.

Solution

SQL Server includes the ability to insert multiple rows using a single INSERT statement without requiring a subquery or stored-procedure call. This allows the application to reduce the code required to add multiple rows and also to reduce the number of individual statements executed by the script. The VALUES clause is repeated once for each row inserted.

First, create a table to receive the rows:

```
CREATE TABLE HumanResources.Degree
    (
    DegreeID INT NOT NULL
                IDENTITY(1, 1)
                PRIMARY KEY,
    DegreeName VARCHAR(30) NOT NULL,
    DegreeCode VARCHAR(5) NOT NULL,
    ModifiedDate DATETIME NOT NULL
    ) ;
GO
```

Next, insert multiple rows into the new table:

```
INSERT  INTO HumanResources.Degree
        (DegreeName, DegreeCode, ModifiedDate)
VALUES  ('Bachelor of Arts', 'B.A.', GETDATE()),
        ('Bachelor of Science', 'B.S.', GETDATE()),
        ('Master of Arts', 'M.A.', GETDATE()),
        ('Master of Science', 'M.S.', GETDATE()),
        ('Associate" s Degree', 'A.A.', GETDATE()) ;
GO
```

This returns the following query output:

```
(5 row(s) affected)
```

How It Works

This recipe demonstrated inserting multiple rows from a single INSERT statement. I started by creating a new table to contain college degree types. Then I inserted rows using the standard INSERT...VALUES form of the INSERT statement. The column list was specified as in all forms of the INSERT statement:

```
INSERT HumanResources.Degree (DegreeName, DegreeCode, ModifiedDate)
```

Next, in the VALUES clause, I designated a new row for each degree type. Each row had three columns, and these columns were encapsulated in parentheses:

```
VALUES  ('Bachelor of Arts', 'B.A.', GETDATE()),
        ('Bachelor of Science', 'B.S.', GETDATE()),
        ('Master of Arts', 'M.A.', GETDATE()),
        ('Master of Science', 'M.S.', GETDATE()),
        ('Associate" s Degree', 'A.A.', GETDATE()) ;
```

This feature allows a developer or DBA to insert multiple rows without needing to retype the initial INSERT table name and column list. This is a great way to populate the lookup tables of a database with a set of initial values. Rather than hand-code 50 INSERT statements in your setup script, create a single INSERT with multiple rows. Not only does this help the script development, but it also optimizes the script execution because there is only one statement to compile and execute instead of 50.

■ **Note**   This is otherwise known as a "Table-Value Constructor." In addition to being able to be used in an INSERT statement, it can also be used in the USING clause of the MERGE statement, as well as in the FROM clause of the definition of a derived table.

8-8. Inserting Rows and Returning the Inserted Rows

Problem

You are inserting a row into a table, and that table contains some default or identity values. You want to return the resulting values to the calling application so as to update the user interface.

Solution

The OUTPUT clause adds a result set to the INSERT statement. This result set contains a specified set of columns and the set of rows that were inserted. For example, to add three rows to the Purchasing. ShipMethod table:

```
INSERT  Purchasing.ShipMethod
        (Name, ShipBase, ShipRate)
OUTPUT  INSERTED.ShipMethodID, INSERTED.Name,
        INSERTED.rowguid, INSERTED.ModifiedDate
VALUES  ('MIDDLETON CARGO TS11', 10, 10),
        ('MIDDLETON CARGO TS12', 10, 10),
        ('MIDDLETON CARGO TS13', 10, 10) ;
```

The output of this INSERT statement will be as follows:

ShipMethodID	Name	rowguid	ModifiedDate
12	MIDDLETON CARGO TS11	F5D01C2C-59D8-4360-8F2F-C46AECCA5187	2015-01-20 14:10:38.630
13	MIDDLETON CARGO TS12	10665CA4-F864-42E9-B559-4DA7DBA95580	2015-01-20 14:10:38.630
14	MIDDLETON CARGO TS13	7BD4E041-C822-4166-BB35-AD06B42D65BA	2015-01-20 14:10:38.630

Note that the results contain values for ShipMethodID, rowguid, and ModifiedDate, three columns for which the query did not specify values explicitly. For the rowguid and ModifiedDate columns, these are default values; for the ShipMethodID column this is an identity value.

How It Works

The OUTPUT clause of the INSERT statement was added directly after the column_list of the INSERT statement (or the table_name if the column_list is not specified explicitly). As rows were inserted into the table, they were exposed to the OUTPUT clause through the virtual table inserted. In this example, the query outputted all columns from the inserted virtual table and returned them as a result set:

```
INSERT Purchasing.ShipMethod (Name, ShipBase, ShipRate)
OUTPUT  inserted.*
VALUES  ('MIDDLETON CARGO TS14', 10, 10),
        ('MIDDLETON CARGO TS15', 10, 10),
        ('MIDDLETON CARGO TS16', 10, 10) ;
```

It is also possible to output information from the INSERT statement to a table or table variable for further processing. In this case, the IDs of the inserted rows are output to a table variable:

```
DECLARE @insertedShipMethodIDs TABLE
(
    ShipMethodID INTEGER
);
INSERT Purchasing.ShipMethod (Name, ShipBase, ShipRate)
OUTPUT inserted.ShipMethodID INTO @insertedShipMethodIDs
VALUES  ('MIDDLETON CARGO TS17', 10, 10),
        ('MIDDLETON CARGO TS18', 10, 10),
        ('MIDDLETON CARGO TS19', 10, 10);
```

These examples use a table value constructor to perform the INSERT operations. The OUTPUT clause will work with any form of INSERT statement, such as INSERT ... SELECT and INSERT ... EXEC.

8-9. Updating a Single Row or Set of Rows

Problem

You need to modify a set of columns in rows that already exist in a table.

Solution

The UPDATE statement modifies data that already exists in a table. The UPDATE statement applies changes to single or multiple columns of single or multiple rows in a table.

The basic syntax for the UPDATE statement is as follows:

```
UPDATE  <table_or_view_name>
SET     column_name = {expression | DEFAULT | NULL} [ ,...n ]
WHERE   <search_condition>
```

Table 8-4 describes the arguments of this command.

Table 8-4. *UPDATE Command Arguments*

Argument	Description
table_or_view_name	The table or updateable view containing data to be updated.
column_name = {expression | DEFAULT | NULL}	The name of the column or columns to be updated. Followed by the expression to assign to the column. Instead of an explicit expression, DEFAULT or NULL may be specified.
search_condition	The search condition that defines *which* rows are modified. If this isn't included, all rows from the table or updateable view will be modified.

In this example, a single row is updated by designating the SpecialOfferID, which is the primary key of the table (for more on primary keys, see the "Managing Tables" chapter).

Before performing the update, first query the specific row that the update statement will modify:

```
SELECT  DiscountPct
FROM    Sales.SpecialOffer
WHERE   SpecialOfferID = 10 ;
```

This returns the following:

```
DiscountPct
0.50
```

Next, perform the modification:

```
UPDATE  Sales.SpecialOffer
SET     DiscountPct = 0.15
WHERE   SpecialOfferID = 10 ;
```

Querying the modified row after the update confirms that the value of DiscountPct was indeed modified:

```
SELECT   DiscountPct
FROM     Sales.SpecialOffer
WHERE    SpecialOfferID = 10 ;
```

This returns the following:

```
DiscountPct
0.15
```

How It Works

In this example, the query started off with UPDATE and the table name—Sales.SpecialOffer:

```
UPDATE Sales.SpecialOffer
```

Next, the SET clause was used, followed by a list of column assignments:

```
SET DiscountPct = 0.15
```

Had this been the end of the query, *all* of the rows in the Sales.SpecialOffer table would have been modified. Just as a SELECT statement with no WHERE clause returns all the rows in a table, an UPDATE statement with no WHERE clause will update all rows in a table. But the intention of this query was to update the discount percentage for only a specific product. The WHERE clause was used in order to achieve this:

```
WHERE SpecialOfferID = 10 ;
```

After executing this query, only one row was modified. Had there been multiple rows that met the search condition in the WHERE clause, those rows would have been modified as well. For example, the following statement will update the rows with the three specified SpecialOfferID values:

```
UPDATE   Sales.SpecialOffer
SET      DiscountPct = 0.15
WHERE    SpecialOfferID IN (10, 11, 12) ;
```

■ **Tip** Performing a SELECT query with the FROM and WHERE clauses of an UPDATE, prior to the UPDATE, allows you to see what rows you will be updating (an extra validation that you are updating the proper rows). This is also a good opportunity to use a transaction to allow for rollbacks in the event that your modifications are undesired. For more on transactions, see the "Transactions, Locking, Blocking, Deadlocking" chapter.

8-10. Updating While Using a Second Table as the Data Source

Problem

You need to update rows in a table, but either your filter condition requires a second table or you need to use data from a second table as the source of your update.

Solution

The UPDATE statement can modify rows based on a FROM clause and associated WHERE clause search conditions. The basic syntax for this form of the UPDATE statement is as follows:

```
UPDATE <table_or_view_name | table_or_view_alias>
SET    column_name = {expression | DEFAULT | NULL} [ ,...n ]
FROM   <table_source>
WHERE  <search_condition>
```

The FROM and WHERE clauses are not mandatory; however, you will find that they are almost always implemented in order to specify exactly which rows are to be modified based on joins against one or more tables.

In this example, assume that a specific product, "Full-Finger Gloves, M," from the Production.Product table has a customer purchase limit of two units per customer. For this query's requirement, any shopping cart with a quantity of more than two units for this product should immediately be adjusted back to the limit of 2:

```
UPDATE  c
SET     Quantity = 2,
        ModifiedDate = GETDATE()
FROM    Sales.ShoppingCartItem c
        INNER JOIN Production.Product p
            ON c.ProductID = p.ProductID
WHERE   p.Name = 'Full-Finger Gloves, M '
AND     c.Quantity > 2 ;
```

How It Works

Stepping through the code, the first line showed the table (or table alias) to be updated:

```
UPDATE c
```

Next, the columns to be updated were designated in the SET clause:

```
SET Quantity =2,
   ModifiedDate = GETDATE()
```

Next came the FROM clause where the Sales.ShoppingCartltem and Production.Product tables were joined by ProductID. When joining multiple tables, the object to be updated must be referenced in the FROM clause:

```
FROM  Sales.ShoppingCartItem c
INNER JOIN Production.Product p
ON    c.ProductID = p.ProductID
```

Using the updated table in the FROM clause allowed joins between multiple tables. Presumably, the joined tables will be used to filter the updated rows or to provide values for the updated rows.

The WHERE clause specified that only the "Full-Finger Gloves, M" product in the Sales.ShoppingCartItem should be modified, and only if the Quantity is greater than 2 units:

```
WHERE p.Name = 'Full-Finger Gloves, M '
AND   c.Quantity > 2 ;
```

8-11. Updating Data and Returning the Affected Rows

Problem

You are required to audit rows that have changed in a given table. Each time the DiscountPct is updated on the Sales.SpecialOffer table, the SpecialOfferID as well as the old and new values of the DiscountPct column should be recorded.

Solution

The OUTPUT clause adds to the UPDATE statement a result set that contains a specified set of columns for the set of rows that were updated. For example, say all Customer discounts are increased by 5 percent:

```
UPDATE  Sales.SpecialOffer
SET     DiscountPct *= 1.05
OUTPUT  inserted.SpecialOfferID,
        deleted.DiscountPct AS old_DiscountPct,
        inserted.DiscountPct AS new_DiscountPct
WHERE   Category = 'Customer' ;
```

This update statement returns the following results:

SpecialOfferID	old_DiscountPct	new_DiscountPct
10	0.15	0.1575
15	0.50	0.525

How It Works

The OUTPUT clause of the UPDATE statement was added directly after the SET clause of the UPDATE statement. As rows are updated in the table, they are exposed to the OUTPUT clause through the virtual tables inserted and deleted. In this example, the query outputted all old and new DiscountPct column values for a changed SpecialOrderID and returned them as a result set:

```
UPDATE  Sales.SpecialOffer
SET     DiscountPct *= 1.05
OUTPUT  inserted.SpecialOfferID,
            deleted.DiscountPct AS old_DiscountPct,
            inserted.DiscountPct AS new_DiscountPct
WHERE   Category = 'Customer' ;
```

For columns that did not change (SpecialOfferID) in this case, either the inserted or deleted table could be used to retrieve values.

It is also possible to output information from the UPDATE statement to a table or table variable for further processing. If there were a table variable named @updatedOffers defined prior to the UPDATE statement (this query will return an error because this table variable is not defined), the query would read as follows:

```
UPDATE  Sales.SpecialOffer
SET     DiscountPct *= 1.05
OUTPUT  inserted.SpecialOfferID,
        deleted.DiscountPct AS old_DiscountPct,
        inserted.DiscountPct AS new_DiscountPct
        INTO @updatedOffers
WHERE   Category = 'Customer' ;
```

8-12. Updating Large-Value Columns

Problem

You have a large-value data-type column and want to update a portion of the data in that column without updating the entire column.

Solution

Updates can be made to large-value data-type column values without rewriting the entire column value. SQL Server introduced new large-value data types in SQL Server 2005, which replace the deprecated text, ntext, and image data types. These data types include the following:

- varchar(max), which holds non-Unicode variable-length data

- nvarchar(max), which holds Unicode variable-length data

- varbinary(max), which holds variable-length binary data

These data types can store up to $2^{31}-1$ bytes of data, or 2 giga-bytes.

■ **Note** For more information on using large-value types in SQL Server, see the SQL Server product documentation at http://msdn.microsoft.com/en-us/library/ms130896.aspx.

A major drawback of text and image data types is that they require separate functions, such as WRITETEXT and UPDATETEXT, to manipulate the image/text data. The new large-value data types allow modifications through standard INSERT and UPDATE statements.

The syntax for inserting a large-value data type is no different from that for a regular INSERT. The large-value data type can be modified in its entirety using the UPDATE statement as you would for other data types. The UPDATE statement additionally allows you to update a portion of the large-value data type through the WRITE method of the large-value data type:

```
UPDATE <table_or_view_name>
SET    column_name.WRITE (expression, (@Offset, @Length)
FROM   <table_source>
WHERE  <search_condition>
```

Table 8-5 describes the parameters of the WRITE method.

Table 8-5. UPDATE Command with WRITE Method in the SET Clause

Argument	Description
Expression	Expression defines the chunk of text to be placed in the column.
@Offset	@Offset determines the starting position in the existing column value where the new text should be placed. If @Offset is NULL, the new expression will be appended to the end of the column (also ignoring the second @Length parameter).
@Length	@Length determines the length of the section to overlay.

Create a new table called RecipeChapter to hold the large-value data type:

```
CREATE TABLE dbo.RecipeChapter
        (
        ChapterID INT NOT NULL CONSTRAINT PK_RecipeChapter PRIMARY KEY CLUSTERED,
        Chapter VARCHAR(MAX) NOT NULL
        ) ;
GO
```

Next, insert a row into the table. Notice that there is nothing special about the string being inserted into the Chapter column:

```
INSERT  INTO dbo.RecipeChapter
        (ChapterID,
         Chapter)
VALUES  (1,
        'At the beginning of each chapter you will notice
that basic concepts are covered first.') ;
```

Next, update the inserted row by adding a sentence to the end of the column value:

```
UPDATE  dbo.RecipeChapter
SET     Chapter.WRITE('In addition to the basics, this chapter will also provide recipes
that can be used in your day to day development and administration.',
                      NULL, NULL)
WHERE   ChapterID = 1 ;
```

Replace the first instance of the phrase "day to day" with the single word "daily":

```
UPDATE   dbo.RecipeChapter
SET      Chapter.WRITE('daily', CHARINDEX('day to day', Chapter) - 1,
                         LEN('day to day'))
WHERE    ChapterID = 1 ;
```

■ **Note**   For further information on CHARINDEX and LEN, please see the "Working with Strings" chapter.

Finally, review the resulting string:

```
SELECT   Chapter
FROM     dbo.RecipeChapter
WHERE    ChapterID = 1;
```

This returns the following:

```
Chapter
----------------------------------------
At the beginning of each chapter you will notice that basic concepts are covered first. In
addition to the basics, this chapter will also provide recipes that can be used in your
daily development and administration.
```

How It Works

The recipe began by creating a table where book chapter descriptions were to be held. The Chapter column used a varchar(max) data type:

```
CREATE TABLE dbo.RecipeChapter
        (
        ChapterID INT NOT NULL CONSTRAINT PK_RecipeChapter PRIMARY KEY CLUSTERED,
        Chapter VARCHAR(MAX) NOT NULL
        ) ;
GO
```

Next, a new row was inserted. Notice that the syntax for inserting a large-object data type doesn't differ from inserting data into a regular non-large-value data type:

```
INSERT   INTO dbo.RecipeChapter
         (ChapterID,
          Chapter)
VALUES   (1,
          'At the beginning of each chapter you will notice
that basic concepts are covered first.') ;
```

An UPDATE was performed against the RecipeChapter table to add a second sentence after the end of the first sentence:

```
UPDATE dbo.RecipeChapter
```

The SET clause was followed by the name of the column to be updated (Chapter) and the new .WRITE method, which took three parameters. The first parameter was the sentence to be appended. The second and third parameters were NULL, indicating that the new text should be appended to the column and not inserted into the middle. See the following:

```
SET    Chapter.WRITE ('In addition to the basics, this chapter will also provide
recipes that can be used in your day to day development and administration.'
                        , NULL, NULL)
```

The WHERE clause specified that the Chapter column for a single row matching ChapterID = 1 was to be modified:

```
WHERE ChapterID = 1 ;
```

The next example of .WRITE demonstrates replacing data within the body of the column. In the example, the expression "day to day" was replaced with "daily." The bigint value of @Offset and @Length are measured in bytes for the varbinary(max) and varchar(max) data types. For nvarchar(max), these parameters measure the actual number of characters. For this example, .WRITE has a value for @Offset (181 bytes into the text) and @Length (10 bytes long):

```
UPDATE  dbo.RecipeChapter
SET     Chapter.WRITE('daily', CHARINDEX('day to day', Chapter) - 1,
                        LEN('day to day'))
WHERE   ChapterID = 1 ;
```

In the recipe example, string functions were used to find the required offset and length. These values may also be specified explicitly if they are known:

```
UPDATE dbo.RecipeChapter
    SET    Chapter .WRITE('daily', 181, 10)
WHERE  ChapterID = 1 ;
```

To build on this recipe, consider the case of inserting data or removing data from the column value instead of replacing a set of characters:

```
-- insert the string '*test value* ' before the word 'beginning'
UPDATE dbo.RecipeChapter
SET    Chapter.WRITE('*test value* ', 7, 0)
WHERE  ChapterID = 1 ;
```

The following select statement will show the string "*test value*" inserted into the chapter text:

```
SELECT Chapter
FROM   dbo.RecipeChapter ;
```

This query returns the following:

```
Chapter
-------------------------------------------------------------------------
At the *test value* beginning of each chapter you will notice
that basic concepts are covered first. In addition to the basics, this chapter will also
provide recipes that can be used in your daily development and administration.
```

Because a length of 0 is specified, no data in the original column will be overlaid by the string that is to be inserted. Now let's remove that data:

```
-- remove the string '*test value* ' before the word 'beginning'
UPDATE dbo.RecipeChapter
SET    Chapter.WRITE('', 7, 13)
WHERE  ChapterID = 1 ;
```

The following SELECT statement will show the string '*test value*' removed from the chapter text:

```
SELECT Chapter
FROM   dbo.RecipeChapter ;
```

This query returns the following:

```
Chapter
-------------------------------------------------------------------------
At the beginning of each chapter you will notice
that basic concepts are covered first. In addition to the basics, this chapter will also provide
recipes that can be used in your daily development and administration.
```

Because the empty string ' ' is used along with a length of 13, 13 characters in the source value will be replaced by the empty string, effectively deleting 13 characters from the column.

■ **Note**   So, why not update the entire value of the column? Let's say that instead of a 200- or 300-character string, the column contains 10MB or 1GB of data. By updating just the few bytes that need to change, only the changed pages will be required to be logged. If the entire value were updated, the entire value will be logged, which would be much less efficient.

8-13. Deleting Rows

Problem

You need to remove one or more rows from a table.

Solution

The DELETE statement removes one or more rows from a table. First, create an example table and populate it with rows:

```
SELECT *
INTO    Production.Example_ProductProductPhoto
FROM    Production.ProductProductPhoto ;
```

```
(504 row(s) affected)
```

■ **Note** The SELECT...INTO <table_name> form of the SELECT statement (covered in the "Advanced SELECT Techniques" chapter) creates a new table with the name <table_name> and column definitions that conform to the columns returned from the SELECT clause. In the case of a SELECT * from a single table, the resulting table will have the same column definitions as the base table; however, no defaults, constraints, indexes, or keys are copied from the base table.

Next, delete all rows from the table:

```
DELETE Production.Example_ProductProductPhoto ;
```

This returns the following:

```
(504 row(s) affected)
```

Next, use a DELETE statement with a WHERE clause. Let's say the relationship of keys between two tables was dropped, and the users were able to delete data from the primary-key table, but the data in the foreign key tables is not deleted (see the "Managing Tables" chapter for a review of primary and foreign keys). We now need to delete rows in the foreign-key tables that are missing a corresponding entry in the Product table. In this example, no rows meet this criteria:

```
-- Repopulate the Example_ProductProductPhoto table
INSERT  Production.Example_ProductProductPhoto
SELECT  *
FROM    Production.ProductProductPhoto ;

DELETE  Production.Example_ProductProductPhoto
WHERE   ProductID NOT IN (SELECT     ProductID
                          FROM       Production.Product) ;
```

The INSERT followed by the DELETE returns the following:

```
(504 row(s) affected)
(0 row(s) affected)
```

This third example demonstrates the same functionality of the previous example, except the DELETE has been rewritten to use a FROM clause instead of a subquery:

```
DELETE
FROM    ppp
FROM    Production.Example_ProductProductPhoto ppp
        LEFT OUTER JOIN Production.Product p
            ON ppp.ProductID = p.ProductID
WHERE   p.ProductID IS NULL ;
```

This delete statement returns: (0 row(s) affected)

How It Works

In the first example of the recipe, all rows were deleted from the Example_ProductProductPhoto table:

```
DELETE Production.Example_ProductProductPhoto
```

This is because there was no WHERE clause to specify which rows would be deleted. In the second example, the WHERE clause was used to specify rows to be deleted based on a subquery lookup to another table:

```
WHERE ProductID NOT IN (SELECT ProductID FROM Production.Product)
```

The third example used a LEFT OUTER JOIN instead of a subquery, joining the ProductID of the two tables:

```
DELETE
FROM    ppp -- the alias of the table to be modified
--
-- use a FROM clause and JOIN to specify the table to be modified
-- and any joins used to filter the delete
--
FROM    Production.Example_ProductProductPhoto ppp
        LEFT OUTER JOIN Production.Product p
            ON ppp.ProductID = p.ProductID
--
-- and filters to select the rows to be deleted from the table to be modified
--
WHERE   p.ProductID IS NULL ;
```

Because a LEFT OUTER JOIN was used, if any rows did *not* match between the left and right tables, the fields selected from the right table would be represented by NULL values. To delete rows in Production. Example_ProductProductPhoto that did not have a matching ProductID in the Production.Product table, I qualified the Production.Product as follows:

```
WHERE  p.ProductID IS NULL
```

Any rows without a match to the Production.Product table would then be deleted from the Production.Example_ProductProductPhoto table.

In this last example, it looks like there were two FROM clauses. The first time the FROM keyword was used, it was specifying the table that the DELETE was going to be targeting. The second time it was used was the actual FROM clause. The first use of FROM is optional. The second use is required if you are joining another table to the target table. Note that you could avoid the second use by using a subquery in the WHERE clause instead.

8-14. Deleting Rows and Returning the Deleted Rows

Problem

You need to delete a number of rows from a table and return the ID of the deleted rows to the client application.

Solution

A DELETE statement may contain an OUTPUT clause. The OUTPUT clause of the DELETE statement instructs SQL Server to return specified columns from the deleted rows.

First, create a sample table:

```
SELECT *
INTO   HumanResources.Example_JobCandidate
FROM   HumanResources.JobCandidate ;
```

This statement will output the following:

```
(13 row(s) affected)
```

Next, delete rows from the table and return the IDs of the deleted rows:

```
DELETE
FROM   HumanResources.Example_JobCandidate
OUTPUT deleted.JobCandidateID
WHERE  JobCandidateID < 5 ;
```

The DELETE statement returns these results:

```
JobCandidateID
--------------
1
2
3
4
```

How It Works

The OUTPUT clause adds a result set that contains the columns in the OUTPUT clause to the DELETE statement. The DELETE, FROM, WHERE, and any of the JOIN clauses work the same as any other DELETE statement. The OUTPUT clause allows access to the deleted virtual table. The virtual table is a temporary view of the rows affected by the DELETE statement. See here:

```
DELETE
  FROM HumanResources.Example_JobCandidate
OUTPUT deleted.JobCandidateID
 WHERE JobCandidateID < 5
```

The output may be redirected to a destination table or table variable using the OUTPUT ... INTO form of the OUTPUT clause. For example, if a table variable @deletedCandidates had been declared in a stored procedure or script, the output of the DELETE statement would be inserted in the table variable with the statement:

```
DELETE
  FROM HumanResources.Example_JobCandidate
OUTPUT deleted.JobCandidateID INTO @deletedCandidates
 WHERE JobCandidateID < 5
```

8-15. Deleting All Rows Quickly (Truncating)

Problem

You need to remove all rows from a table quickly with minimal logging.

Solution

The TRUNCATE statement deletes all rows from a table in a minimally logged fashion that results in a much quicker delete than a standard DELETE statement if you have very large tables. The DELETE statement should be used for operations that must be fully logged; however, for test or throwaway data, TRUNCATE is a fast technique for removing large amounts of data from the database. "Minimal logging" refers to how much recoverability information is written to the database's transaction log. The syntax for TRUNCATE is as follows:

```
TRUNCATE TABLE table_name ;
```

This statement takes just the table name to truncate. Since TRUNCATE always removes *all* rows from a table, there is no FROM or WHERE clause.

First, populate a sample table:

```
SELECT *
INTO    Production.Example_TransactionHistory
FROM    Production.TransactionHistory ;
```

The INSERT statement returns the following:

```
(113443 row(s) affected)
```

Next, truncate ALL rows from the example table:

```
TRUNCATE TABLE Production.Example_TransactionHistory ;
```

Next, the table's row count is queried:

```
SELECT COUNT(*)
FROM   Production.Example_TransactionHistory ;
```

This returns the following:

0

How It Works

The TRUNCATE TABLE statement, like the DELETE statement, can delete rows from a table. Unlike the DELETE statement, which logs each row deleted in the transaction log, TRUNCATE TABLE deallocates the pages allocated to the table, which is considerably faster than deleting each of the rows. Thus, all that is logged in the transaction log is the page deallocations, making TRUNCATE TABLE a minimally logged operation. Unlike DELETE, however, the TRUNCATE TABLE always removes ALL rows in the table (so there is never a WHERE clause).

Although TRUNCATE TABLE is a faster way to delete rows, you cannot use it if the table columns are referenced by a foreign-key constraint (see the "Managing Tables" chapter for more information on foreign keys), if the table is published using transactional or merge replication, or if the table participates in an indexed view (see the "Managing Views" chapter for more information). Also, if the table has an IDENTITY column, keep in mind that the column will be reset to the seed value defined for the column (if no seed was explicitly set, it is set to 1).

The TRUNCATE TABLE statement is a Data Definition Lanugage (DDL) statement; as such, its usage will require elevated permissions.

8-16. Merging Data (Inserting, Updating, and/or Deleting Values)

Problem

You have a table that contains the ID of the last order placed by a customer. Each time a customer places an order, you need to either insert a new record if this is the first order placed by that customer or update an existing row if the customer had placed an order previously.

Solution

The MERGE statement accepts a row or set of rows and, for each row, determines whether that row exists in a target table. The statement allows different actions to be taken based on this determination. The basic syntax for the MERGE statement is as follows:

```
MERGE
    [ INTO ] <target_table> [ [ AS ] table_alias ]
    USING <table_source> [ [ AS ] table_alias ]
    ON <merge_search_condition>
```

201

```
[ WHEN MATCHED [ AND <clause_search_condition> ]
    THEN <merge_matched> ] [ ...n ]
[ WHEN NOT MATCHED [ BY TARGET ] [ AND <clause_search_condition> ]
    THEN <merge_not_matched> ]
[ WHEN NOT MATCHED BY SOURCE [ AND <clause_search_condition> ]
    THEN <merge_matched> ] [ ...n ]
```

Table 8-6 describes the elements of the MERGE statement:

Table 8-6. *MERGE Statement*

Argument	Definition
target_table	The table or updateable view that the MERGE statement will update, insert into, or delete from.
table_source	The data source that will be matched to the target table. The MERGE statement will execute updates, inserts, or deletes against the target table based on the result of this match.
merge_search_condition	Specifies the conditions by which the source table will be matched against the target table.
clause_search_condition	The MERGE statement can choose from multiple WHEN MATCHED and WHEN NOT MATCHED clauses. If, for example, multiple WHEN MATCHED clauses exist, the MERGE statement will choose the first WHEN MATCHED clause found that matches the search condition specified.
merge_matched	Specifies an UPDATE or DELETE to be executed against the target_table.
	In the case where the MERGE statement will update a row, this looks like this:
	UPDATE SET column_name = {expression | DEFAULT | NULL} [,...n } } [,...n]
	Note, this looks just like the update statement's column-assignment list. There is no WHERE clause or table name specified here, as this context has been set previously in target_table and merge_search_condition.
	When the MERGE statement should execute a delete, the syntax is simply DELETE.
merge_not_matched	Specifies an INSERT to be executed against the target_table. The INSERT operation looks like this:
	INSERT [(column_list)] ({DEFAULT | NULL | expression }[,...n])
	Note, the arguments to this statement follow the same rules as the INSERT statement syntax described in Table 8-1.

This example will track the latest customer order information in the following table:

```
CREATE TABLE Sales.LastCustomerOrder
    (
    CustomerID INT,
    SalesOrderID INT,
    CONSTRAINT pk_LastCustomerOrder PRIMARY KEY CLUSTERED (CustomerId)
    ) ;
```

Executing this CREATE TABLE statement returns the following:

```
Command(s) completed successfully.
```

The following statements will declare variables representing the customer and order IDs and then use the MERGE statement to INSERT into or UPDATE the Sales.LastCustomerOrder table:

```
DECLARE @CustomerID INT = 100,
        @SalesOrderID INT = 101 ;

MERGE INTO Sales.LastCustomerOrder AS tgt
    USING
        (SELECT @CustomerID AS CustomerID,
                @SalesOrderID AS SalesOrderID
        ) AS src
    ON tgt.CustomerID = src.CustomerID
    WHEN MATCHED
        THEN UPDATE
          SET        SalesOrderID = src.SalesOrderID
    WHEN NOT MATCHED
        THEN INSERT (
                    CustomerID,
                    SalesOrderID
                    )
        VALUES      (src.CustomerID,
                    src.SalesOrderID) ;
```

Executing these statements will return the following:

```
(1 row(s) affected)
```

Check to see whether the record was inserted successfully:

```
SELECT  *
FROM    Sales.LastCustomerOrder ;
```

This SELECT statement returns the following:

```
CustomerID  SalesorderID
----------- ------------
100         101
```

Using the following table, substitute values for the variables @CustomerID and @SalesOrderID. For each row in the table, update the script with the appropriate values and rerun the DECLARE and MERGE statements.

@CustomerID	@SalesOrderID
101	101
100	102
102	103
100	104
101	105

Now rerun the SELECT statement to check the results:

```
SELECT   *
FROM     Sales.LastCustomerOrder ;
```

The SELECT statement returns the following:

```
CustomerID  SalesorderID
----------- ------------
100         104
101         105
102         103
```

As new orders are created for a customer, a new row is added to the table if this is the first order for that customer; however, if that customer had already placed an order, the existing row is updated.

A new requirement has just been sent to us, and not only do we need to track the LastCustomerOrder, but we also need to track the LargestCustomerOrder. We need to populate a new table and insert a row for the first order a customer places, updating the row only if a new order from that customer is larger than the previously recorded order.

First, create a table to track the order information:

```
CREATE TABLE Sales.LargestCustomerOrder
     (
      CustomerID INT,
      SalesOrderID INT,
           TotalDue MONEY,
      CONSTRAINT pk_LargestCustomerOrder PRIMARY KEY CLUSTERED (CustomerId)
     );
```

Executing this CREATE TABLE statement returns the following:

```
Command(s) completed successfully.
```

The following statements will declare variables representing the customer and order IDs as well as the TotalDue for the order. They will then use the MERGE statement to INSERT into or UPDATE the Sales. LastCustomerOrder table:

```
DECLARE @CustomerID INT = 100,
        @SalesOrderID INT = 101 ,
        @TotalDue MONEY = 1000.00;

MERGE INTO Sales.LargestCustomerOrder AS tgt
    USING
        (SELECT @CustomerID AS CustomerID,
                @SalesOrderID AS SalesOrderID,
                @TotalDue AS TotalDue
        ) AS src
    ON tgt.CustomerID = src.CustomerID
    WHEN MATCHED AND tgt.TotalDue < src.TotalDue
        THEN UPDATE
            SET      SalesOrderID = src.SalesOrderID
                , TotalDue = src.TotalDue
    WHEN NOT MATCHED
        THEN INSERT (
                    CustomerID,
                    SalesOrderID,
                    TotalDue
                    )
            VALUES  (src.CustomerID,
                    src.SalesOrderID,
                    src.TotalDue);
```

Check to see whether the record was inserted successfully:

```
SELECT  *
FROM    Sales.LargestCustomerOrder;
```

This SELECT statement returns the following:

CustomerID	SalesorderID	TotalDue
100	101	1000.00

Using the following table, substitute values for the variables @CustomerID and @SalesOrderID and @TotalDue. For each row in the table, update the script with the appropriate values and rerun the DECLARE and MERGE statements.

@CustomerID	@SalesOrderID	@TotalDue
101	101	1000.00
100	102	1100.00
100	104	999.00
101	105	999.00

Now, rerun the SELECT statement to check the results:

```
SELECT  *
FROM    Sales.LargestCustomerOrder;
```

The SELECT statement returns the following:

CustomerID	SalesorderID	TotalDue
100	102	1100.00
101	101	1000.00

Note that the final two orders did not update any rows, and the results indicate the correct largest orders of 1,100.00 and 1,000.00.

How It Works

In this example, we used the MERGE statement to insert new rows into a table or update rows that already existed in that table. The basic structure of the two examples is the same, so let's look at the elements of the Sales.LargestCustomerOrder example, which adds one twist.

The first two statements in the example created a table to hold the customer order information and declared variables that were used in the MERGE statement. The meat of the example is the MERGE statement itself.

First, we specified the table that was to be the "target" of the MERGE statement, in this case Sales.LargestCustomerOrder. We aliased this table as tgt for reference throughout the statement. We were merging into a table in this case, but we could also have specified an updateable view. See here:

```
MERGE INTO Sales.LargestCustomerOrder AS tgt
```

Next, we specified the data that we wanted to merge into the target table. In this case, we used a SELECT statement as a derived table, but this clause can take a number of forms. We could have used any one of the following:

- Table or view

- Row set function such as OPENROWSET

- User-defined table function

- Call to OPENXML

- Derived table

The USING clause may also include inner and outer joins so as to involve multiple tables and sources.

In the example we used a derived table that returned one row by mapping variable values to columns in our result set. This is a common pattern when using the MERGE statement with the stored-procedure parameter values as the source of the merge:

```
USING
    (SELECT @CustomerID AS CustomerID,
            @SalesOrderID AS SalesOrderID,
            @TotalDue AS TotalDue
    ) AS src
```

Once we had specified a source and target, we needed to instruct the MERGE statement how to match the source row(s) with the rows in the target table. This was effectively a JOIN condition between the source and target:

```
ON tgt.CustomerID = src.CustomerID
```

For each source row processed by the MERGE statement, it may either:

- Exist in both the source and target (MATCHED)

- Exist in the source but not the target (NOT MATCHED)

- Exist in the target but not the source (NOT MATCHED BY SOURCE)

In this example, we used WHEN MATCHED with a filter so that only rows that met the join condition and the filter condition were updated in the target table. For these rows, we updated the TotalDue column of the target table:

```
WHEN MATCHED AND tgt.TotalDue < src.TotalDue
    THEN UPDATE
    SET        SalesOrderID = src.SalesOrderID
           , TotalDue = src.TotalDue
```

The WHEN NOT MATCHED clause indicates that a row exists in the source that does not exist in the target. In this example, we wanted to insert a new row in the target when this occurs:

```
WHEN NOT MATCHED
    THEN INSERT (
                 CustomerID,
                 SalesOrderID,
                 TotalDue
                 )
    VALUES     (src.CustomerID,
                 src.SalesOrderID,
                 src.TotalDue) ;
```

The MERGE statement accommodates multiple instances of the WHEN MATCHED, WHEN NOT MATCHED, and WHEN NOT MATCHED BY SOURCE clauses. Let's say that we would like to track the last customer order and the largest customer order in the same table. We may have these clauses:

```
WHEN MATCHED AND tgt.TotalDue < src.TotalDue
    THEN UPDATE
    SET        SalesOrderID = src.SalesOrderID
           , TotalDue = src.TotalDue
WHEN MATCHED
    THEN UPDATE
    SET        SalesOrderID = src.SalesOrderID
```

The order of these clauses is important. The MERGE statement will choose the first clause that evaluates as true. In this case, if the MERGE statement found a match that had a TotalDue that was greater than the existing largest TotalDue for a customer, then the first clause was chosen. The second clause was chosen for all other matches. If we reversed the order of these clauses, then the WHEN MATCHED with no filter would execute for all matched rows, and the filtered clause would never be chosen.

Like the INSERT, UPDATE, and DELETE statements described earlier, the MERGE statement contains an OUTPUT clause. The only difference is that the MERGE statement adds a new $ACTION keyword that indicates whether an INSERT, UPDATE, or DELETE operation occurred against the target table. This T-SQL batch is the same as the batch described throughout this chapter; however, the OUTPUT clause with the $ACTION column has been added to the MERGE statement:

```
DECLARE @CustomerID INT = 100,
        @SalesOrderID INT = 201 ,
        @TotalDue MONEY = 1200.00;

MERGE INTO Sales.LargestCustomerOrder AS tgt
    USING
        (SELECT @CustomerID AS CustomerID,
                @SalesOrderID AS SalesOrderID,
                @TotalDue AS TotalDue
        ) AS src
    ON tgt.CustomerID = src.CustomerID
    WHEN MATCHED AND tgt.TotalDue < src.TotalDue
        THEN UPDATE
            SET       SalesOrderID = src.SalesOrderID
                  , TotalDue = src.TotalDue
    WHEN NOT MATCHED
        THEN INSERT (
                    CustomerID,
                    SalesOrderID,
                    TotalDue
                    )
            VALUES   (src.CustomerID,
                    src.SalesOrderID,
                    src.TotalDue)
    OUTPUT
        $ACTION,
        DELETED.*,
        INSERTED.*;
```

This MERGE statement returns the following:

$ACTION	CustomerID	SalesorderID	TotalDue	CustomerID	SalesorderID	TotalDue
UPDATE	100	102	1100.00	100	201	2000.00

The $ACTION keyword indicates that this set of values resulted in an update to the target table, and the columns that follow represent the version, of the record both before and after the update.

8-17. Inserting Output Data

Problem

You have an INSERT, UPDATE, DELETE, or MERGE operation with output data that you want to insert into another table.

Solution

In what is perhaps one of the more complicated uses of the INSERT statement, the INSERT statement allows for the use of a "dml table source" to accept the rows that are used in an output clause from a nested Data Manipulation Language (DML) operation (INSERT, UPDATE, DELETE, or MERGE), rows that it will then insert into another table.

For example, let's use the last MERGE statement from the previous recipe as an example. For the sample data, we'll use a CustomerID of 100, a SalesOrderID of 205, and a TotalDue of 2500.00. The output data (the merge action, and the values from the inserted and deleted virtual tables) will be inserted into a table variable. See the following:

```
-- Create a table variable to hold the output data
-- This could be a temporary or a permanent table.
DECLARE @dml_output TABLE (
    MergeAction             VARCHAR(6),
    DeletedCustomerID       INTEGER,
    DeletedSalesOrderID     INTEGER,
    DeletedTotalDue         MONEY,
    InsertedCustomerID      INTEGER,
    InsertedSalesOrderID    INTEGER,
    InsertedTotalDue        MONEY
    );
-- Insert into the holding table
INSERT INTO @dml_output
        (MergeAction,
         DeletedCustomerID,
         DeletedSalesOrderID,
         DeletedTotalDue,
         InsertedCustomerID,
         InsertedSalesOrderID,
         InsertedTotalDue
        )
-- SELECT from a table source
SELECT  *
-- The FROM clause needs to be a derived table
-- The output columns are its output. FROM (
        MERGE INTO Sales.LargestCustomerOrder AS tgt
            USING
                (SELECT 100 AS CustomerID,
                        205 AS SalesOrderID,
                        2500.00 AS TotalDue
                ) AS src
            ON tgt.CustomerID = src.CustomerID
            WHEN MATCHED AND tgt.TotalDue < src.TotalDue
                THEN UPDATE
                    SET      SalesOrderID = src.SalesOrderID
                            , TotalDue = src.TotalDue
            WHEN NOT MATCHED
                THEN INSERT (
                            CustomerID,
                            SalesOrderID,
```

```
                            TotalDue
                         )
                VALUES   (src.CustomerID,
                          src.SalesOrderID,
                          src.TotalDue)
            OUTPUT
                $ACTION,
                DELETED.*,
                INSERTED.*
-- Define the derived table's output column
        ) dt(MergeAction,
            DeletedCustomerID,
            DeletedSalesOrderID,
            DeletedTotalDue,
            InsertedCustomerID,
            InsertedSalesOrderID,
            InsertedTotalDue);


SELECT  *
FROM    @dml_output;
```

This query returns the following result set:

UPDATE	100	201	1200.00	100	205	2500.00

How It Works

We started off by creating a table variable to hold the results (a temporary table or permanent table would also work):

```
DECLARE @dml_output TABLE (
    MergeAction             VARCHAR(6),
    DeletedCustomerID       INTEGER,
    DeletedSalesOrderID     INTEGER,
    DeletedTotalDue         MONEY,
    InsertedCustomerID      INTEGER,
    InsertedSalesOrderID    INTEGER,
    InsertedTotalDue        MONEY
    );
```

Next, we inserted into this table variable the output results from the MERGE statement:

```
INSERT INTO @dml_output
        (MergeAction,
         DeletedCustomerID,
         DeletedSalesOrderID,
         DeletedTotalDue,
         InsertedCustomerID,
         InsertedSalesOrderID,
         InsertedTotalDue
        )
```

```
SELECT  *
FROM    ( <dml statement with output clause>
        ) <derived table alias>
          (MergeAction,
           DeletedCustomerID,
           DeletedSalesOrderID,
           DeletedTotalDue,
           InsertedCustomerID,
           InsertedSalesOrderID,
           InsertedTotalDue);
```

Note that the INSERT statement is written as an INSERT INTO / SELECT statement, and that the MERGE statement, with the output clause, is written as a derived table for the SELECT statement. Since this is a derived table for the SELECT statement, you can have a WHERE clause defined (not shown here) to filter the records being inserted based upon any of the columns being returned in the OUTPUT clause of the nested DML statement.

There are some restrictions to the table that is the target of the outer INSERT statement:

- It cannot be a view or a remote table.

- It cannot have any triggers defined on it.

- It cannot participate in any Primary Key/Foreign Key relationships.

- It cannot participate in merge replication or updateable subscriptions.

There are also restrictions to the table that is the target of the nested DML statement:

- It cannot be a remote table or a partitioned view.

- The DML statement for the nested DML statement cannot contain a "DML table source" clause.

Other notes about using a DML table source:

- The entire operation is atomic—either the outer INSERT statement and the nested DML operations both succeed, or neither do.

- The OUTPUT INTO clause is not supported for INSERT statements containing a dml table source (OUTPUT INTO does not expose the output columns where they could be used as columns in a derived table).

- @@ROWCOUNT returns the rows inserted by the outer INSERT statement.

- @@IDENTITY, SCOPE_IDENTITY, and IDENT_CURRENT return identity values generated by the nested DML statement.

- The SELECT statement for the DML table source cannot contain subqueries, aggregate functions, ranking functions, Full-Text predicates, user-defined functions that perform data access, or the TEXTPTR function.

CHAPTER 9

■ ■ ■

Working with Strings

by Wayne Sheffield

This next set of recipes demonstrates SQL Server's many string functions. String functions provide a multitude of options for your Transact-SQL programming, allowing for string cleanup, conversion between ASCII and regular characters, pattern searches, removal of trailing blanks, and much more. Table 9-1 lists the different string functions available in SQL Server.

Table 9-1. *String Functions*

Function Name(s)	Description
CONCAT	The CONCAT function concatenates a variable list of string values into one larger string.
ASCII and CHAR	The ASCII function takes the leftmost character of a character expression and returns the ASCII code. The CHAR function converts an integer value for an ASCII code to a character value instead.
CHARINDEX and PATINDEX	The CHARINDEX function is used to return the starting position of a string within another string. The PATINDEX function is similar to CHARINDEX, except that PATINDEX allows the use of wildcards when specifying the string for which to search.
DIFFERENCE and SOUNDEX	DIFFERENCE and SOUNDEX both work with character strings to evaluate those that sound similar. SOUNDEX assigns a string a four-digit code, and DIFFERENCE evaluates the level of similarity between the SOUNDEX outputs for two separate strings.
FORMAT	The FORMAT function returns locale-aware formatting of date/time and number values as strings.
LEFT and RIGHT	The LEFT function returns a part of a character string, beginning at the specified number of characters from the left. The RIGHT function is like the LEFT function, only it returns a part of a character string beginning at the specified number of characters from the right.

(*continued*)

Table 9-1. (*continued*)

Function Name(s)	Description
LEN and DATALENGTH	The LEN function returns the number of characters in a string expression, excluding any blanks after the last character (trailing blanks). DATALENGTH, however, returns the number of bytes used for an expression. LEN works for any data type that can be implicitly converted to a string; DATALENGTH works on any data type.
LOWER and UPPER	The LOWER function returns a character expression in lowercase, and the UPPER function returns a character expression in uppercase.
LTRIM and RTRIM	The LTRIM function removes leading blanks, and the RTRIM function removes trailing blanks.
NCHAR and UNICODE	The UNICODE function returns the Unicode integer value for the first character of the character or input expression. The NCHAR function takes an integer value that designates a Unicode character and converts it to its character equivalent.
QUOTENAME	The QUOTENAME function returns a UNICODE string with added delimiters so as to make a valid identifier for SQL Server.
REPLACE	The REPLACE function replaces all instances of a provided string within a specified string with a new string.
REPLICATE	The REPLICATE function repeats a given character expression a designated number of times.
REVERSE	The REVERSE function takes a character expression and outputs the expression with each character position displayed in reverse order.
SPACE	The SPACE function returns a string of repeated blank spaces, based on the integer you designate for the input parameter.
STR	The STR function converts numerical data to a string.
STUFF	The STUFF function deletes a specified length of characters and inserts a designated string at the specified starting point.
SUBSTRING	The SUBSTRING function returns a defined chunk of a specified expression.

This chapter will demonstrate examples of how these string functions are used.

9-1. Concatenating Multiple Strings

Problem/+

You have a set of string values that you would like to concatenate into one string value. This is often a requirement when formatting names or addresses. In the database, the name may be stored as separate first, middle, and last names; however, you may wish to execute a query that returns "Last Name, First Name" and even adds the middle initial if it exists.

Solution

For this example, create a FullName column from the FirstName, MiddleName, and LastName columns of the Person.Person table:

```
SELECT  TOP (5)
        FullName = CONCAT(LastName, ', ', FirstName, ' ', MiddleName)
FROM    Person.Person p;
```

The results of this query are:

```
FullName
-----------------------------------
Abbas, Syed E
Abel, Catherine R.
Abercrombie, Kim
Abercrombie, Kim
Abercrombie, Kim B
```

How It Works

The CONCAT function accepts a variable list of string values (at least two are required) and concatenates them into one string. A difference between the CONCAT function and using the + operator is how nulls are handled. The operator + will return NULL if either the left or right side of the operator is NULL. The CONCAT function will convert NULL arguments to an empty string prior to the concatenation.

Take the following SELECT statement that concatenates a FullName with three different approaches:

```
SELECT  TOP (5)
        FullName = CONCAT(LastName, ', ', FirstName, ' ', MiddleName),
        FullName2 = LastName + ', ' + FirstName + ' ' + MiddleName,
        FullName3 = LastName + ', ' + FirstName +
                            IIF(MiddleName IS NULL, '', ' ' + MiddleName)
FROM    Person.Person p
WHERE   MiddleName IS NULL;
```

This query yields the following results:

FullName	FullName2	FullName3
Abercrombie, Kim	NULL	Abercrombie, Kim
Abercrombie, Kim	NULL	Abercrombie, Kim
Abolrous, Sam	NULL	Abolrous, Sam
Acevedo, Humberto	NULL	Acevedo, Humberto
Achong, Gustavo	NULL	Achong, Gustavo

The FullName column used the CONCAT function as seen in the recipe. FullName2 uses the + operator. The + operator will always return NULL if one of its operands is NULL—since MiddleName is NULL for all rows, then FullName2 is NULL for all rows. Finally, the FullName3 column shows the logic that is encapsulated in the CONCAT function. In this recipe's example, three columns and two string literals were concatenated together using the CONCAT function. The MiddleName column was NULL for some rows in the table, but no additional NULL-handling logic is required when using CONCAT to generate the FullName string.

9-2. Finding a Character's ASCII Value

Problem

Your application requires the ASCII values of a string's characters, or passes you ASCII values that you must then assemble into a string.

Solution

This first example demonstrates how to convert characters into the integer ASCII value:

```
SELECT  ASCII('H'),
        ASCII('e'),
        ASCII('l'),
        ASCII('l'),
        ASCII('o');
```

This returns:

72	101	108	108	111

Next, the CHAR function is used to convert the integer values back into characters again:

```
SELECT  CHAR(72),
        CHAR(101),
        CHAR(108),
        CHAR(108),
        CHAR(111) ;
```

This returns:

H	e	l	l	o

How It Works

The ASCII function takes the leftmost character of a character expression and returns the ASCII code. The CHAR function converts the integer value of an ASCII code to a character value. The ASCII function only converts the first character of the supplied string. If the string is empty or NULL, ASCII will return NULL (note that an empty string is a zero-length string, so a blank-space character is represented by a value of 32).

In this recipe, the word "Hello" was deconstructed into five characters and then converted into the numeric ASCII values using the ASCII function. In the second T-SQL statement, the process was reversed and the ASCII values were converted back into characters using the CHAR function.

9-3. Returning Integer and Character Unicode Values

Problem

Your application requires the Unicode values of a string's characters, or passes you Unicode values that you must assemble into a string.

Solution

The UNICODE function returns the Unicode integer value for the first character of the character or input expression. The NCHAR function takes an integer value designating a Unicode character and converts it to its character equivalent.

This first example converts single characters into an integer value representing the Unicode standard character code:

```
SELECT  UNICODE('G'),
        UNICODE('o'),
        UNICODE('o'),
        UNICODE('d'),
        UNICODE('!');
```

This returns:

71	111	111	100	33

Next, the Unicode integer values are converted back into characters:

```
SELECT  NCHAR(71),
        NCHAR(111),
        NCHAR(111),
        NCHAR(100),
        NCHAR(33) ;
```

This returns

G	o	o	d	!

How It Works

In this example, the string "Good!" was deconstructed one character at a time, and then each character was converted into an integer value using the UNICODE function. In the second example, the integer values were reversed back into characters by using the NCHAR function.

9-4. Locating Characters in a String

Problem

You need to find out where a string segment or character pattern starts within the context of a larger string. For example, you need to find all of the street addresses that match a pattern you are looking for.

Solution

This example demonstrates how to find the starting position of a string within another string:

```
SELECT CHARINDEX('string to find','This is the bigger string to find something in.');
```

This returns

20

That is, the first character of the first instance of the string "string to find" is the 20th character of the string that we are searching.

In some cases a character pattern must be found within a string. The following example returns all rows from the address table that contain the digit 0 preceding the word "Olive"

```
SELECT TOP 10
        AddressID,
        AddressLine1,
        PATINDEX('%[0]%Olive%', AddressLine1)
FROM    Person.Address
WHERE   PATINDEX('%[0]%Olive%', AddressLine1) > 0;
```

The results of this statement are:

AddressID	AddressLine1	
29048	1201 Olive Hill	3
11768	1201 Olive Hill	3
15417	1206 Olive St	3
24480	1480 Oliveria Road	4
19871	1480 Oliveria Road	4
12826	1803 Olive Hill	3
292	1803 Olive Hill	3
29130	2309 Mt. Olivet Ct.	3
23767	2309 Mt. Olivet Ct.	3
23875	3280 Oliveria Road	4

How It Works

The CHARINDEX function is used to return the starting position of a string within another string. The syntax is as follows:

```
CHARINDEX ( expressionToFind ,expressionToSearch[ , start_location ] )
```

CHARINDEX will search the string passed to expressionToSearch for the first instance of expressionToFind that exists after the optionally specified start_location.

This function returned the starting character position, in this case the 20th character, where the first argument expression was found in the second expression. Wildcards are not supported with CHARINDEX.

To use wildcards when searching for a substring, use the PATINDEX function. While similar to CHARINDEX, PATINDEX allows the use of wildcards in the string you are searching for. The syntax for PATINDEX is as follows:

```
PATINDEX ( '%pattern%' ,expression )
```

PATINDEX returns the start position of the first occurrence of the search pattern, but unlike CHARINDEX, it does not contain a starting position option. Both CHARINDEX and PATINDEX return 0 if the search expression is not found in the expression to be searched.

■ **Note**   In this example we showed a small example of the wildcard searches that may be used within PATINDEX. PATINDEX supports the same wildcard functionality as the LIKE operator. For further information, see the Performing Wildcard Searches recipe in "Getting Started with SELECT" chapter.

9-5. Determining the Similarity of Strings

Problem

You are designing a call-center application to help the agents look up customers by last name while speaking with the customer on the phone. The agents would like to guess at the spelling of the name to narrow the search results and then work with the customer to determine the appropriate spelling.

Solution

The two functions SOUNDEX and DIFFERENCE both work with character strings and evaluate the strings based on English phonetic rules.

Take the example where an agent hears the name "Smith." SOUNDEX may be used to return all of the names that contain the same SOUNDEX value as the string "Smith":

```
SELECT  DISTINCT
        SOUNDEX(LastName),
        SOUNDEX('Smith'),
        LastName
FROM    Person.Person
WHERE   SOUNDEX(LastName) = SOUNDEX('Smith');
```

This query returns the following results:

		LastName
S530	S530	Schmidt
S530	S530	Smith
S530	S530	Smith-Bates
S530	S530	Sneath

Note that "Smith" is returned, but so are a number of names that may sound like the last name "Smith."

Another way to look at the data would be to view the names that had the "least difference" from the search expression. The SQL Server DIFFERENCE function evaluates the phonetic similarity of two strings and returns a value from 0 (low similarity) to 4 (high similarity). If we look for last names with a phonetic similarity to "Smith":

```
SELECT  DISTINCT
        SOUNDEX(LastName),
        SOUNDEX('Smith'),
        DIFFERENCE(LastName, 'Smith'),
        LastName
FROM    Person.Person
WHERE   DIFFERENCE(LastName, 'Smith') = 4;
```

This query returns:

			LastName
S530	S530	4	Smith
S530	S530	4	Smith-Bates
S530	S530	4	Sneath
S550	S530	4	Simon
S553	S530	4	Samant
S553	S530	4	Swaminathan

Note that the name "Schmidt" contains the same SOUNDEX value as Smith, so it is returned with the first query. It is absent from the second query since the DIFFERNCE between "Schmidt" and "Smith" is 3, not 4:

```
SELECT DIFFERENCE('Smith','Schmidt');
```

How It Works

The SOUNDEX function follows a set of rules originally created to categorize names based on the phonetic characteristics of the name rather than the spelling of that name. The soundex of a name consists of a letter–the first letter of that name–followed by three digits representing the predominant consonant sounds of that name.

DIFFERENCE uses a variation of the soundex algorithm to return a rather coarse determination of the phonetic similarity of two strings–a range from 0 representing very low similarity to 4 representing very high similarity.

9-6. Returning the Leftmost or Rightmost Portion of a String

Problem

You have a string value and only need the first or last part of the string. For example, you have a report that will list a set of products, but you only have room on the report to display the first ten characters of the product name.

Solution

This recipe demonstrates how to return a subset of the leftmost and rightmost parts of a string. First, take the leftmost (first) ten characters of a string:

```
SELECT LEFT('I only want the leftmost 10 characters.', 10);
```

This returns:

```
I only wan
```

Next, take the rightmost (last) ten characters of a string:

```
SELECT RIGHT('I only want the rightmost 10 characters.', 10);
```

This returns:

```
haracters.
```

The example in the problem statement describes taking the left ten characters of the product name for a report. The following query is an example of how to accomplish this:

```
SELECT  TOP (5)
        ProductNumber,
        ProductName = LEFT(Name, 10)
FROM    Production.Product;
```

This query yields the following:

```
ProductNumber             ProductName
------------------------  -----------
AR-5381                   Adjustable
BA-8327                   Bearing Ba
BE-2349                   BB Ball Be
BE-2908                   Headset Ba
BL-2036                   Blade
```

221

It is common that a string needs to be "padded" on one side or another. For example, the AccountNumber column in the Sales.Customer table is ten characters consisting of "AW" plus eight digits. The eight digits include the CustomerID column padded with zeros. A customer with the CustomerID 123 would have the account number "AW00000123." See the following:

```
SELECT  TOP (5)
        CustomerID,
        AccountNumber = CONCAT('AW', RIGHT(REPLICATE('0', 8)
                                + CAST(CustomerID AS VARCHAR(10)), 8))
FROM    Sales.Customer;
```

This returns:

CustomerID	AccountNumber
1	AW00000001
2	AW00000002
7	AW00000007
19	AW00000019
20	AW00000020

How It Works

The LEFT function returns the segment of the supplied character string that starts at the beginning of the string and ends at the specified number of characters from the beginning of the string. The RIGHT function returns the segment of the supplied character string that starts at the specified number of characters from the end of the string and ends at the end of the string.

This recipe demonstrated three examples of using LEFT and RIGHT. The first two examples demonstrated how to return the leftmost or the rightmost characters of a string value. The third example demonstrated how to pad a string in order to conform to some expected business or reporting format.

When presenting data to end users or exporting data to external systems, you may sometimes need to preserve or add leading values, such as leading zeros to fixed-length numbers or spaces to varchar fields. CustomerID was zero-padded by first concatenating eight zeros in a string to the converted varchar(10) value of the CustomerID. Then, outside of this concatenation, RIGHT was used to grab the last eight characters of the concatenated string (thus taking leading zeros from the left side with it when the CustomerID fell short of eight digits).

9-7. Returning Part of a String

Problem

You are creating a call-center report that includes aggregations of data by area code and exchange of phone numbers in the system. You need to look at characters 1 to 3 and 5 to 7 of a phone number string.

Solution

Use the left and substring functions to pull out the desired characters of the phone number.

```
SELECT  TOP (3)
        PhoneNumber,
        AreaCode = LEFT(PhoneNumber, 3),
        Exchange = SUBSTRING(PhoneNumber, 5, 3)
FROM    Person.PersonPhone
WHERE   PhoneNumber LIKE '[0-9][0-9][0-9]-[0-9][0-9][0-9]-[0-9][0-9][0-9][0-9]';
```

PhoneNumber	AreaCode	Exchange
100-555-0115	100	555
100-555-0124	100	555
100-555-0137	100	555

How It Works

The SUBSTRING function returns a defined segment of a specified string expression. The syntax is as follows:

```
SUBSTRING ( expression, start, length )
```

The first argument of this function is the character expression that contains the desired segment. The second argument defines the starting position of the segment to return from within "expression." The third argument is the length, in characters, of the segment to be returned.

In this recipe, the SUBSTRING function was used to extract digits 5 to 7 from a longer phone number. The first parameter was the phone number. The second parameter was the starting position of the string–the fifth character in the string. The third parameter indicated how many characters to extract– three.

There were multiple phone number formats stored in the database, and we were only interested in the format XXX-XXX-XXXX. The WHERE clause of the SELECT statement used wildcards with the LIKE operator to filter the results to only numbers that met this format.

9-8. Counting Characters or Bytes in a String

Problem

Your application requires you to return the length or size (in bytes) of strings that you return from a stored procedure.

Solution

This first example returns the number of characters in the Unicode string (Unicode data takes two bytes for each character, whereas ASCII takes only one), with trailing spaces excluded:

```
SELECT LEN(N'She sells sea shells by the sea shore.  ');
```

This returns:

This next example returns the number of bytes in the Unicode string:

```
SELECT DATALENGTH(N'She sells sea shells by the sea shore.  ');
```

This returns:

```
80
```

How It Works

The LEN function returns the number of characters in a string expression, excluding any blanks after the last character (trailing blanks). DATALENGTH returns the number of bytes used for an expression (including trailing blanks).

This recipe uses a Unicode string that is defined by prefixing the string with an N:

```
N'She sells sea shells by the sea shore.  '
```

The number of characters for this string is 38 according to LEN, as there are 38 characters starting with the "S" in "She" and ending with the period. The spaces following the "." are not counted by LEN. DATALENGTH returns 80 bytes. SQL Server uses the Unicode UCS-2 encoding form, which consumes two bytes per character stored, and the trailing spaces are counted: (38 + 2) * 2.

■ **Note** We typically use DATALENGTH to find the number of bytes in a string; however, DATALENGTH will determine the length of any data type. Take the following query, for example:

```
SELECT  DATALENGTH(123),
        DATALENGTH(123.0),
        DATALENGTH(GETDATE());
```

We pass an int, a numeric, and a datetime value into DATALENGTH, and DATALENGTH returns 4, 5, and 8, respectively.

9-9. Replacing Part of a String

Problem

You need to replace all instances of a string value within a larger string value. For example, the name of a product has changed and you must update product descriptions with the new product name.

Solution

This example replaces all instances of the string "Classic" with the word "Vintage":

```
SELECT REPLACE('The Classic Roadie is a stunning example of the bikes that AdventureWorks
have been producing for years - Order your classic Roadie today and experience
AdventureWorks history.', 'Classic', 'Vintage');
```

This returns:

The Vintage Roadie is a stunning example of the bikes that AdventureWorks have been producing for years - Order your Vintage Roadie today and experience AdventureWorks history.

How It Works

The REPLACE function searches a source string for all instances of a provided search pattern and replaces them with the supplied replacement string. One strength of REPLACE is that unlike PATINDEX and CHARINDEX that return one location where a pattern is found, REPLACE finds and replaces all instances of the search string within a specific character string. The syntax for REPLACE is as follows:

```
REPLACE ( string_expression , search_string , replacement_string );
```

The first argument, string_expression, is the string that will be searched. The second argument, search_string, is the string to be removed from the original string. The third argument, replacement_string, is the string to use as a replacement for the search string.

In this example we searched the product description for all instances of the string "Classic" and replaced them with the string "Vintage."

REPLACE can also be used to remove portions of a string. If the replacement_string parameter is an empty string (''), REPLACE will remove search_string from string_expression and replace it with 0 characters.

■ **Note:** In this case this is an empty string ('') not a NULL value. If replacement_string is NULL the output of REPLACE will always be NULL.

9-10. Stuffing a String into a String
Problem
You need to insert a string into another string.

Solution
This example replaces a part of a string and inserts a new expression into the string body:

```
SELECT STUFF ( 'My cat''s name is X. Have you met him?', 18, 1, 'Edgar' );
```

This returns:

My cat's name is Edgar. Have you met him?

■ **Note** Do you notice the two single quotes in the query above? This is not double quote but rather is an "escaped" apostrophe. String literals in SQL Server are identified by single quotes. To specify an apostrophe in a string literal you need to "escape" the apostrophe by placing two apostrophes next to each other. You can see in the results listing: "cat"s" is displayed as "cat's."

How It Works

The STUFF function deletes a specified length of characters and inserts a designated string at the specified starting point. The syntax is as follows:

```
STUFF ( character_expression, start, length, character_expression )
```

The first argument of this function is the character expression to be modified. The second argument is the starting position of the string to be inserted. The third argument is the number of characters to delete within the string in the first argument. The fourth argument is the actual character expression that you want to insert.

The first character expression in this recipe was "My cat's name is X. Have you met him?" The start value was 18, meaning the replacement was to occur at the 18th character in the string ("X"). The length parameter was 1, meaning only one character at position 18 was to be deleted. The last character expression was Edgar. This was the value to stuff into the string.

If a 0 length parameter is specified, the STUFF function simply inserts the second string into the first string before the character specified with the start argument. For example:

```
SELECT STUFF ( 'My cat''s name is X. Have you met him?', 18, 0, 'Edgar' );
```

This returns:

```
My cat's name is EdgarX. Have you met him?
```

If an empty string (") is specified for the second character expression, the STUFF function deletes the characters starting with the character specified by the start argument and continuing for the number of characters specified by the length argument. For example:

```
SELECT STUFF ( 'My cat''s name is X. Have you met him?', 18, 8, '' );
```

This returns:

```
My cat's name is you met him?
```

9-11. Changing Between Lowercase and Uppercase

Problem

You have some text that, for reporting purposes, you would like to return as all uppercase or all lowercase.

Solution

The following query shows the value of DocumentSummary for a specific row in the Production.Document table:

```
SELECT  DocumentSummary
FROM    Production.Document
WHERE   FileName = 'Installing Replacement Pedals.doc';
```

This returns the following sentence-case value:

```
DocumentSummary
----------------------------------------------------------Detailed instructions for
replacing pedals with Adventure Works Cycles replacement pedals.  Instructions are
applicable to all Adventure Works Cycles bicycle models and replacement pedals. Use only
Adventure Works Cycles parts when replacing worn or broken components.
```

This first example demonstrates setting values to lowercase:

```
SELECT  LOWER(DocumentSummary)
FROM    Production.Document
WHERE   FileName = 'Installing Replacement Pedals.doc';
```

This returns:

```
detailed instructions for replacing pedals with adventure works cycles replacement pedals.
instructions are applicable to all adventure works cycles bicycle models and replacement
pedals. use only adventure works cycles parts when replacing worn or broken components.
```

Now for uppercase:

```
SELECT  UPPER(DocumentSummary)
FROM    Production.Document
WHERE   FileName = 'Installing Replacement Pedals.doc';
```

This returns:

```
DETAILED INSTRUCTIONS FOR REPLACING PEDALS WITH ADVENTURE WORKS CYCLES REPLACEMENT PEDALS.
INSTRUCTIONS ARE APPLICABLE TO ALL ADVENTURE WORKS CYCLES BICYCLE MODELS AND REPLACEMENT
PEDALS. USE ONLY ADVENTURE WORKS CYCLES PARTS WHEN REPLACING WORN OR BROKEN COMPONENTS.
```

How It Works

The LOWER function returns a character expression in lowercase, and the UPPER function returns a character expression in uppercase. If a character in the string is not case-convertible, the character is returned with no conversion. For example, look at a string with Thai characters:

```
SELECT UPPER (N'เป็นสายอักขระ unicode');
```

This returns:

เป็นสายอักขระ UNICODE

Because there is no upper- or lowercase distinction for the Thai characters, the UPPER and LOWER functions have no effect on them.

The first example demonstrated the LOWER function and returned a character expression in lowercase. The second example demonstrated the UPPER function and returned a character expression in uppercase. In both cases the function took a single argument: the character expression containing the case to be converted to either upper- or lowercase.

9-12. Removing Leading and Trailing Blanks

Problem

You have text entered through an application that may contain leading or trailing blanks, and you would like to remove these blanks before storing the data.

Solution

This first example demonstrates removing leading blanks from a string:

```
SELECT CONCAT('''', LTRIM('    String with leading and trailing blanks.    '), '''' );
```

This returns:

'String with leading and trailing blanks.   '

This second example demonstrates removing trailing blanks from a string:

```
SELECT CONCAT('''', RTRIM('    String with leading and trailing blanks.    '), '''' );
```

This returns:

'   String with leading and trailing blanks.'

This final example shows that LTRIM and RTRIM may be used together to remove blanks from both ends of a string:

```
SELECT CONCAT('''', LTRIM(RTRIM('   String with leading and trailing blanks.   ')), '''' );
```

This returns:

```
'String with leading and trailing blanks.'
```

How It Works

Both LTRIM and RTRIM take a single argument—a character expression that is to be trimmed. The function then trims the leading or trailing blanks. Note that there is not a TRIM function (as seen in other programming languages) that can be used to remove both leading and trailing characters. To do this, you must use both LTRIM and RTRIM in the same expression.

9-13. Repeating an Expression N Times

Problem

Often when testing an application's user interface, you will need to populate sample data into a database, and that sample data must fill the database columns to the maximum length of character data allowed so as to ensure that the UI will properly display larger strings. Generally, the character "W" is used, as it is a wide character.

Solution

Use the REPLICATE function to produce a string of 30 W characters:

```
SELECT REPLICATE ('W', 30) ;
```

This returns:

```
WWWWWWWWWWWWWWWWWWWWWWWWWWWWWW
```

Use the REPLICATE function to produce a string of 30 repetitions of the string 'Z_':

```
SELECT REPLICATE ('W_', 30) ;
```

This returns:

```
W_W_W_W_W_W_W_W_W_W_W_W_W_W_W_W_W_W_W_W_W_W_W_W_W_W_W_W_W_W_
```

How It Works

The REPLICATE function repeats a given character expression a designated number of times. The syntax is as follows:

```
REPLICATE ( character_expression,integer_expression )
```

The first argument is the character expression to be repeated. The second argument is the integer value representing the number of times the character expression is to be repeated.

In this recipe's first example the letter "W" was supplied as the character expression and was repeated 30 times. The second example showed that REPLICATE can repeat string values, and not only single characters. Use REPLICATE to repeat values rather than having to enter the string literals manually.

Please note that if the value being returned from the REPLICATE function is longer than 8,000 characters, it will be truncated to 8,000 characters unless the character expression being replicated is explicitly cast to a VARCHAR(MAX) or NVARCHAR(MAX) data type.

9-14. Repeating a Blank Space N Times

Problem

You are formatting a set of values for display and you would like the values to be returned as a one-column result set and be aligned in 20-character columns.

Solution

This example demonstrates how to repeat a blank space a defined number of times so as to align the values onto 20-character boundaries:

```
DECLARE @animals TABLE
    (
     string1 VARCHAR(20),
     string2 VARCHAR(20),
     string3 VARCHAR(20)
    );
INSERT  @animals
VALUES  ('elephant', 'dog', 'giraffe'),
        ('kitty', 'puppy', 'ant'),
        ('chicken', 'fish', 'marmacet');

SELECT  CONCAT(string1, SPACE(20 - LEN(string1)),
               string2, SPACE(20 - LEN(string2)),
               string3, SPACE(20 - LEN(string3)))
            AS formatted_string
FROM    @animals;
```

This returns:

```
formatted_string
--------------------------------------------------
elephant            dog             giraffe
kitty               puppy           ant
chicken             fish            marmacet
```

How It Works

The SPACE function returns a string of repeated blank spaces based on the integer you designate for the input parameter. This is the same functionality as the REPLICATE function, only the character to replicate is always a space.

In this recipe there were values that had to be returned in one column of text aligned to 20-character boundaries. Each value was concatenated with a number of spaces equal to 20–the length of the string.

The maximum length for the return value for the SPACE function is 8,000 characters. If you need to return more than 8,000 characters, or to include spaces in Unicode data, use the REPLICATE function instead.

9-15. Reversing the Order of Characters in a String

Problem

You wish to return a string with the characters in the reverse order from the string.

Solution

Utilize the REVERSE function to perform this. As a simple example:

```
SELECT REVERSE('Hello World');
```

Returns:

```
dlroW olleH
```

As you can see, the string has been reversed (essentially a mirror of the input string). Now, while this may show us how the REVERSE function works, it doesn't really help us understand why we would want to return a string reversed.

Let's say that you want to separate the file name and path from a fully qualified file name. In the catalog view sys.database_files, the column physical_name has the fully qualified file name for each database file that is part of the current database. Let's use the REVERSE function to find the last backslash ('\') character in the string and use that position as the basis for the boundary between path and file name.

```
SELECT  Path = LEFT(physical_name, LEN(physical_name) -
                CHARINDEX('\', REVERSE(physical_name)) + 1),
        FileName = RIGHT(physical_name, CHARINDEX('\', REVERSE(physical_name)) - 1)
FROM    sys.database_files;
```

This example returns the following results. (In this example the paths and file names will differ depending on the database file names and locations used on your system.)

```
Path                            FileName
----------------------------    ------------------------------
E:\SqlDatabases\                AdventureWorks2014_Data.mdf
E:\SqlDatabases\                AdventureWorks2014_log.ldf
```

How It Works

The REVERSE function takes a character expression and outputs the expression with each character position displayed in reverse order.

In this example, by using CHARINDEX on the reversed string, instead of finding the first occurrence of the character, the last occurrence was returned. LEFT and RIGHT were used to split the string at the identified location.

CHAPTER 10

■ ■ ■

Working with Dates and Times

by Wayne Sheffield

SQL Server has several different date and time data types, which have varying levels of range and precision (and corresponding varying levels of storage requirement space). SQL Server also has numerous functions to retrieve, modify, and validate the data from these data types in their various formats. This chapter focuses on these functions. Table 10-1 shows the various date/time data types.

Table 10-1. *SQL Server Date/Time Data Types*

Data Type	Format	Range	Accuracy	Storage Size (Bytes)
Time	hh:mm:ss[.nnnnnnn]	00:00:00.0000000 through 23:59:59.9999999	100 nanoseconds	3 to 5
Date	YYYY-MM-DD	0001-01-01 through 9999-12-31	1 day	3
Smalldatetime	YYYY-MM-DD hh:mm:ss	1900-01-01 through 2079-06-06	1 minute	4
Datetime	YYYY-MM-DD hh:mm:ss[.nnn]	1753-01-01 through 9999-12-31	0.00333 second	8
datetime2	YYYY-MM-DD hh:mm:ss[.nnnnnnn]	0001-01-01 00:00:00.0000000 through 9999-12-31 23:59:59.9999999	100 nanoseconds	6 to 8
Datetimeoffset	YYYY-MM-DD hh:mm:ss[.nnnnnnn] [+|-]hh:mm	0001-01-01 00:00:00.0000000 through 9999-12-31 23:59:59.9999999 (in UTC)	100 nanoseconds	8 to 10

10-1. Returning the Current Date and Time

Problem

You need to use the current date and time in your query.

Solution

Use the GETDATE, GETUTCDATE, CURRENT_TIMESTAMP, SYSDATETIME, SYSUTCDATETIME, or SYSDATETIMEOFFSET function to return the current time.

```
SELECT 'GETDATE()' AS [Function],           GETDATE() AS [Value];
SELECT 'CURRENT_TIMESTAMP'AS [Function],    CURRENT_TIMESTAMP AS [Value];
SELECT 'GETUTCDATE()' AS [Function],        GETUTCDATE() AS [Value];
SELECT 'SYSDATETIME()' AS [Function],       SYSDATETIME() AS [Value];
SELECT 'SYSUTCDATETIME()' AS [Function],    SYSUTCDATETIME() AS [Value];
SELECT 'SYSDATETIMEOFFSET()' AS [Function], SYSDATETIMEOFFSET() AS [Value];
```

This query returns the following results (with the redundant headers omitted):

```
Function              Value
------------------    ---------------------------------------
GETDATE()             2015-01-23 23:47:39.170
CURRENT_TIMESTAMP     2015-01-23 23:47:39.170
GETUTCDATE()          2015-01-24 04:47:39.170
SYSDATETIME()         2015-01-23 23:47:39.1728701
SYSUTCDATETIME()      2015-01-24 04:47:39.1728701
SYSDATETIMEOFFSET()   2015-01-23 23:47:39.1728701 -05:00
```

■ **Note** Many of the recipes in this chapter call one or more functions that return a value based upon the current date and time. When you run these recipes on your system, you will get a different result that will be based upon the date and time as set on the computer running your instance of SQL Server.

How It Works

The GETDATE and CURRENT_TIMESTAMP functions return the local date and time in a date/time data type. The GETUTCDATE function returns UTC time, also in a date/time data type. SYSDATETIME returns the local date and time in a datetime2 data type. SYSUTCDATETIME returns UTC time, also in a datetime2 data type. Finally, SYSDATETIMEOFFSET returns the local time, plus the number of hours and minutes offset from UTC, in a datetimeoffset data type.

10-2. Converting Between Time Zones

Problem

You need to convert a date/time value from one time zone to another.

Solution

Use the SWITCHOFFSET function to convert date/time values in one time zone to corresponding values in a different time zone.

```
SELECT SWITCHOFFSET(SYSDATETIMEOFFSET(), '+03:00');
```

This query returns the following result:

```
2015-01-24 07:50:54.0050138 +03:00
```

How It Works

The SWITCHOFFSET function converts a datetimeoffset value (or a value that can be implicitly converted to a datetimeoffset value) to a different time zone, adjusting the date, hours, and minutes as necessary. The returned value will be the same UTC time as the supplied value.

■ **Note**   The SWITCHOFFSET function is not aware of daylight saving time (DST). As such, the conversions it makes are not adjusted for DST.

10-3. Converting a Date/Time Value to a Datetimeoffset Value

Problem

You need to convert a date/time value to a datetimeoffset value for use in the SWITCHOFFSET function.

■ **Note**   A datetimeoffset is a data type that was introduced in SQL Server 2008. It is based upon a 24-hour clock and is aware of the time zone. It has the same precision as a datetime2 data type. See Table 10-1 for more information.

Solution

Use the TODATETIMEOFFSET function. This example converts the system's current date/time value to the current time in the Eastern Time Zone (without DST adjustments). It then displays both that time and the current system time in a datetimeoffset format.

```
SELECT  TODATETIMEOFFSET(GETDATE(), '-05:00') AS [Eastern Time Zone Time],
        SYSDATETIMEOFFSET() [Current System Time];
```

This query returns the following result:

Eastern Time Zone Time	Current System Time
2015-01-23 23:53:00.520 -05:00	2015-01-23 23:53:00.5222502 -05:00

How It Works

The TODATETIMEOFFSET function converts a datetime2 value (or a value that can be implicitly converted into a datetime2 value) to a datetimeoffset value of the specified time zone.

■ **Note**   The TODATETIMEOFFSET function is not aware of Daylight Saving Time (DST). As such, the conversions it makes are not adjusted for DST.

10-4. Incrementing or Decrementing a Date's Value

Problem

You need to add an interval to a date or time portion of a date/time value.

Solution

Use the DATEADD function to add any quantity of any portion of a date or time value.

```
SELECT DATEADD(YEAR, -1, '2009-04-02T00:00:00');
```

This query returns the following result:

```
2008-04-02 00:00:00.000
```

How It Works

The DATEADD function has three parameters. The first parameter is the part of the date to modify, or datepart, and it can be any of the names or abbreviations shown in Table 10-2.

Table 10-2. *Datepart Boundaries*

Datepart	Abbreviations
Year	yy, yyyy
quarter	qq, q
month	mm, m
dayofyear	dy, y
Day	dd, d
week	wk, ww
weekday	dw, w
hour	hh
minute	mi, n
second	ss, s
millisecond	ms
microsecond	mcs
nanosecond	ns

The second parameter is a numeric value for the number of datepart units that you are adding to the date. If the value is negative, these units will be subtracted from the date. Finally, the third parameter is the date being modified.

10-5. Finding the Difference Between Two Dates

Problem

You need to calculate the difference between two dates.

Solution

Use the DATEDIFF function to calculate the difference between any two dates.

```
SELECT   TOP (5)
         ProductID,
         GETDATE() AS Today,
         EndDate,
         DATEDIFF(MONTH, EndDate, GETDATE()) AS ElapsedMonths
FROM     Production.ProductCostHistory
WHERE    EndDate IS NOT NULL
ORDER BY ProductID;
```

237

This query returns the ProductID, the current date/time, the product's EndDate, and the number of months between the EndDate and today's date. The first five records in this table are as follows:

ProductID	Today	EndDate	ElapsedMonths
707	2015-01-23 23:56:52.880	2012-05-29 00:00:00.000	32
707	2015-01-23 23:56:52.880	2013-05-29 00:00:00.000	20
708	2015-01-23 23:56:52.880	2012-05-29 00:00:00.000	32
708	2015-01-23 23:56:52.880	2013-05-29 00:00:00.000	20
709	2015-01-23 23:56:52.880	2012-05-29 00:00:00.000	32

How It Works

The DATEDIFF function accepts three parameters; the first is the datepart (from Table 10-2), which identifies whether you are counting the difference in terms of days, hours, minutes, months, and so on. The last two parameters are the two dates you want to compare.

Notice that the DATEDIFF function returns the number of datepart boundaries crossed; this is not the same as the elapsed time between the two dates, however. For instance, for the following query, each column returns the quantity of one datepart boundary crossed for each of the specified dateparts, even though the difference between these two date/time values is 100 nanoseconds (.000001 seconds).

```
WITH cteDates (StartDate, EndDate) AS
(
SELECT  CONVERT(DATETIME2, '2010-12-31T23:59:59.9999999'),
        CONVERT(DATETIME2, '2011-01-01T00:00:00.0000000')
)
SELECT  StartDate,
        EndDate,
        DATEDIFF(YEAR, StartDate, EndDate) AS Years,
        DATEDIFF(QUARTER, StartDate, EndDate) AS Quarters,
        DATEDIFF(MONTH, StartDate, EndDate) AS Months,
        DATEDIFF(DAY, StartDate, EndDate) AS Days,
        DATEDIFF(HOUR, StartDate, EndDate) AS Hours,
        DATEDIFF(MINUTE, StartDate, EndDate) AS Minutes,
        DATEDIFF(SECOND, StartDate, EndDate) AS Seconds,
        DATEDIFF(MILLISECOND, StartDate, EndDate) AS Milliseconds,
        DATEDIFF(MICROSECOND, StartDate, EndDate) AS MicroSeconds
FROM    cteDates;
```

10-6. Finding the Elapsed Time Between Two Dates

Problem

You need to find the elapsed time between two dates.

Solution

You need to calculate the number of datepart boundaries crossed at the smallest precision level that you are interested in. Then, calculate the higher datepart boundaries from that number. For example, the following code determines the elapsed time down to the seconds:

```
DECLARE @StartDate DATETIME2 = '2012-01-01T18:25:42.9999999',
        @EndDate   DATETIME2 = '2012-06-15T13:12:11.8675309';

WITH cte AS
(
SELECT  DATEDIFF(SECOND, @StartDate, @EndDate) AS ElapsedSeconds,
        DATEDIFF(SECOND, @StartDate, @EndDate)/60 AS ElapsedMinutes,
        DATEDIFF(SECOND, @StartDate, @EndDate)/3600 AS ElapsedHours,
        DATEDIFF(SECOND, @StartDate, @EndDate)/86400 AS ElapsedDays
)
SELECT  @StartDate AS StartDate,
        @EndDate AS EndDate,
        CONVERT(VARCHAR(10), ElapsedDays) + ':' +
        CONVERT(VARCHAR(10), ElapsedHours%24) + ':' +
        CONVERT(VARCHAR(10), ElapsedMinutes%60) + ':' +
        CONVERT(VARCHAR(10), ElapsedSeconds%60) AS [ElapsedTime (D:H:M:S)]
FROM    cte;
```

This query returns the following result:

StartDate	EndDate	ElapsedTime (D:H:M:S)
2012-01-01 18:25:42.9999999	2012-06-15 13:12:11.8675309	165:18:46:29

How It Works

Since we are interested in knowing the elapsed time down to the second, we start off by getting the number of SECOND datepart boundaries that are crossed between these two dates. There are 60 seconds in a minute, so we then take the number of seconds and divide by 60 to get the number of minutes. There are 3,600 seconds in an hour (60 x 60), so we then divide the number of seconds by 3,600 to get the number of hours. And there are 86,400 seconds in a day (60 x 60 x 24), so we divide the number of seconds by 86,400 to get the number of days.

However, these are not quite the numbers we are looking for; we need to express this as the number of that particular datepart boundary after the next highest boundary; for example, the number of hours past the number of whole days. So, we then use the modulo operator to get the remaining number of hours that don't make up an entire day (hours modulo 24), the remaining number of minutes that don't make up an entire hour (minutes modulo 60), and the remaining number of seconds that don't make up an entire minute (seconds modulo 60). Since all of these divisions are occurring with an integer, the fractional remainder will be truncated, so we do not have to worry about this floating down to the next lower datepart boundary calculation.

You can easily adapt this method for a finer precision (milliseconds, and so on). However, to get a less fine precision (for example, years), you need to start looking at whether a year is a leap year, so you will need to apply leap year criteria to your calculation.

10-7. Displaying the String Value for Part of a Date

Problem

You need to return the name of the month and the day of the week for a specific date.

Solution

Use the DATENAME function to get the name of the datepart portion of the date.

```
SELECT  TOP (5)
        ProductID,
        EndDate,
        DATENAME(MONTH, EndDate) AS MonthName,
        DATENAME(WEEKDAY, EndDate) AS WeekDayName
FROM    Production.ProductCostHistory
WHERE   EndDate IS NOT NULL
ORDER BY ProductID;
```

This query returns the following results:

ProductID	EndDate	MonthName	WeekDayName
707	2012-05-29 00:00:00.000	May	Tuesday
707	2013-05-29 00:00:00.000	May	Wednesday
708	2012-05-29 00:00:00.000	May	Tuesday
708	2013-05-29 00:00:00.000	May	Wednesday
709	2012-05-29 00:00:00.000	May	Tuesday

How It Works

The DATENAME function returns a character string representing the datepart specified. While any of the dateparts listed in Table 10-2 can be used, only the month and weekday dateparts convert to a name; the other dateparts return the value as a string.

10-8. Displaying the Integer Representations for Parts of a Date

Problem

You need to separate a date into individual columns for year, month, and date.

Solution

Use the DATEPART function to retrieve the datepart specified from a date as an integer.

```
SELECT   TOP (5)
         ProductID,
         EndDate,
         DATEPART(YEAR, EndDate) AS [Year],
         DATEPART(MONTH, EndDate) AS [Month],
         DATEPART(DAY, EndDate) AS [Day]
FROM     Production.ProductCostHistory
WHERE    EndDate IS NOT NULL
ORDER BY ProductID;
```

This query returns the following results:

ProductID	EndDate	Year	Month	Day
707	2012-05-29 00:00:00.000	2012	5	29
707	2013-05-29 00:00:00.000	2013	5	29
708	2012-05-29 00:00:00.000	2012	5	29
708	2013-05-29 00:00:00.000	2013	5	29
709	2012-05-29 00:00:00.000	2012	5	29

How It Works

The DATEPART function retrieves the specified datepart from the date as an integer. Any of the dateparts in Table 10-2 can be utilized.

■ **Note** The YEAR, MONTH, and DAY functions are synonyms for the DATEPART function, with the appropriate datepart specified.

10-9. Determining Whether a String Is a Valid Date

Problem

You need to determine whether the value of a string is a valid date.

Solution

You need to utilize the ISDATE function in your query.

```
SELECT   MyData,
         ISDATE(MyData) AS IsADate
FROM     ( VALUES ( 'IsThisADate'),
                  ( '2012-02-14'),
                  ( '2012-01-01T00:00:00'),
                  ( '2012-12-31T23:59:59.9999999') ) dt (MyData);
```

This query returns the following results:

```
MyData                          IsADate
--------------------------      -----------
IsThisADate                     0
2012-02-14                      1
2012-01-01T00:00:00             1
2012-12-31T23:59:59.9999999     0
```

How It Works

The ISDATE function checks to see whether the expression passed to it is a valid date, time, or date/time value. If the expression is a valid date, a true (1) will be returned; otherwise, a false (0) will be returned. Because the last record is a datetime2 data type, it does not pass this check.

10-10. Determining the Last Day of the Month

Problem

You need to determine what the last day of the month is for a date you are working with.

Solution

Use the EOMONTH function to determine the last day of the month for a given date.

```
SELECT  MyData,
        EOMONTH(MyData) AS LastDayOfThisMonth,
        EOMONTH(MyData, 1) AS LastDayOfNextMonth
FROM    (VALUES ('2012-02-14T00:00:00' ),
                ('2012-01-01T00:00:00'),
                ('2012-12-31T23:59:59.9999999')) dt(MyData);
```

This query returns the following results:

```
MyData                          LastDayOfThisMonth LastDayOfNextMonth
--------------------------      ------------------ ------------------
2012-02-14T00:00:00             2012-02-29         2012-03-31
2012-01-01T00:00:00             2012-01-31         2012-02-29
2012-12-31T23:59:59.9999999     2012-12-31         2013-01-31
```

How It Works

The EOMONTH function returns the last day of the month for the specified date. It has an optional parameter that will add the specified number of months to the specified date.

■ **Note** Prior to this function being added to SQL Server 2012, you would have had to first determine the first day of the month that the specified date was in (see Recipe 10-12), add one month (see Recipe 10-4), and finally subtract one day (see Recipe 10-4) to obtain the last day of the month.

10-11. Creating a Date from Numbers

Problem

You need to create a date from numbers representing the various parts of the date. For example, you have data for the year, month, and day parts of a specific day, and you need to make a date out of those numbers.

Solution

Use the DATEFROMPARTS functionto build a date from the numbers representing the year, month, and day.

```
SELECT  'DateFromParts' AS ConversionType,
        DATEFROMPARTS(2012, 8, 15) AS [Value];
SELECT  'TimeFromParts' AS ConversionType,
        TIMEFROMPARTS(18, 25, 32, 5, 1) AS [Value];
SELECT  'SmallDateTimeFromParts' AS ConversionType,
        SMALLDATETIMEFROMPARTS(2012, 8, 15, 18, 25) AS [Value];
SELECT  'DateTimeFromParts' AS ConversionType,
        DATETIMEFROMPARTS(2012, 8, 15, 18, 25, 32, 450) AS [Value];
SELECT  'DateTime2FromParts' AS ConversionType,
        DATETIME2FROMPARTS(2012, 8, 15, 18, 25, 32, 5, 7) AS [Value];
SELECT  'DateTimeOffsetFromParts' AS ConversionType,
        DATETIMEOFFSETFROMPARTS(2012, 8, 15, 18, 25, 32, 5, 4, 0, 7) AS [Value];
```

This query returns the following result set (with redundant headers removed):

```
ConversionType          Value
--------------          ----------
DateFromParts           2012-08-15
TimeFromParts           18:25:32.5
SmallDateTimeFromParts  2012-08-15 18:25:00
DateTimeFromParts       2012-08-15 18:25:32.450
DateTime2FromParts      2012-08-15 18:25:32.0000005
DateTimeOffsetFromParts 2012-08-15 18:25:32.0000005 +04:00
```

How It Works

The functions demonstrated earlier build an appropriate date/time value in the specified data type from the parts that make up that data type.

The TIMEFROMPARTS, DATETIME2FROMPARTS, and DATETIMEOFFSETFROMPARTS functions each have a fraction parameter and a precision parameter. For the latter two, the fraction is the seventh parameter (in the previous example, the numeral 5), and the precision parameter is the last parameter (the numeral 7). For the TIMEFROMPARTS function, these parameters are the last two parameters listed. These parameters work together to control what degree of precision the fraction is applied to. This is best demonstrated with the following query:

```
SELECT TIMEFROMPARTS(18, 25, 32, 5, 1);
SELECT TIMEFROMPARTS(18, 25, 32, 5, 2);
SELECT TIMEFROMPARTS(18, 25, 32, 5, 3);
SELECT TIMEFROMPARTS(18, 25, 32, 5, 4);
SELECT TIMEFROMPARTS(18, 25, 32, 5, 5);
SELECT TIMEFROMPARTS(18, 25, 32, 5, 6);
SELECT TIMEFROMPARTS(18, 25, 32, 5, 7);
SELECT TIMEFROMPARTS(18, 25, 32, 50, 2);
SELECT TIMEFROMPARTS(18, 25, 32, 500, 3);
```

These queries return the following result set (with the header lines removed):

```
18:25:32.5
18:25:32.05
18:25:32.005
18:25:32.0005
18:25:32.00005
18:25:32.000005
18:25:32.0000005
18:25:32.50
18:25:32.500
```

10-12. Finding the Beginning Date of a Datepart

Problem

You need to determine what the first day of a datepart boundary is for a specified date. For example, you want to know what the first day of the current quarter is based on the specified date.

Solution #1

Use the DATEADD and DATEDIFF functions to perform this calculation.

```
DECLARE @MyDate DATETIME2 = '2012-01-01T18:25:42.9999999',
        @Base   DATETIME =  '1900-01-01T00:00:00',
        @Base2  DATETIME =  '2000-01-01T00:00:00';

-- Solution 1
SELECT  MyDate,
        DATEADD(YEAR,    DATEDIFF(YEAR,    @Base, MyDate), @Base) AS [FirstDayOfYear],
        DATEADD(MONTH,   DATEDIFF(MONTH,   @Base, MyDate), @Base) AS [FirstDayOfMonth],
        DATEADD(QUARTER,DATEDIFF(QUARTER, @Base, MyDate), @Base) AS [FirstDayOfQuarter]
```

```
FROM    (VALUES ('1981-01-17T00:00:00'),
                ('1961-11-23T00:00:00'),
                ('1960-07-09T00:00:00'),
                ('1980-07-11T00:00:00'),
                ('1983-01-05T00:00:00'),
                ('2006-11-27T00:00:00'),
                ('2013-08-03T00:00:00')) dt (MyDate);

SELECT  'StartOfHour' AS ConversionType,
        DATEADD(HOUR,   DATEDIFF(HOUR,   @Base, @MyDate), @Base) AS DateResult
UNION ALL
SELECT  'StartOfMinute',
        DATEADD(MINUTE, DATEDIFF(MINUTE, @Base, @MyDate), @Base)
UNION ALL
SELECT  'StartOfSecond',
        DATEADD(SECOND, DATEDIFF(SECOND, @Base2, @MyDate), @Base2);
```

This query returns the following:

```
MyDate              FirstDayOfYear          FirstDayOfMonth         FirstDayOfQuarter
------------------  ----------------------  ----------------------  ----------------------
1981-01-17T00:00:00 1981-01-01 00:00:00.000 1981-01-01 00:00:00.000 1981-01-01 00:00:00.000
1961-11-23T00:00:00 1961-01-01 00:00:00.000 1961-11-01 00:00:00.000 1961-10-01 00:00:00.000
1960-07-09T00:00:00 1960-01-01 00:00:00.000 1960-07-01 00:00:00.000 1960-07-01 00:00:00.000
1980-07-11T00:00:00 1980-01-01 00:00:00.000 1980-07-01 00:00:00.000 1980-07-01 00:00:00.000
1983-01-05T00:00:00 1983-01-01 00:00:00.000 1983-01-01 00:00:00.000 1983-01-01 00:00:00.000
2006-11-27T00:00:00 2006-01-01 00:00:00.000 2006-11-01 00:00:00.000 2006-10-01 00:00:00.000
2013-08-03T00:00:00 2013-01-01 00:00:00.000 2013-08-01 00:00:00.000 2013-07-01 00:00:00.000


ConversionType DateResult
-------------- -----------------------
StartOfHour    2012-01-01 18:00:00.000
StartOfMinute  2012-01-01 18:25:00.000
StartOfSecond  2012-01-01 18:25:42.000
```

Solution #2

Break the date down into the appropriate parts, then use the DATETIMEFROMPARTS function to build a new date, with the parts that are being truncated set to 1 (for months/dates) or zero (for hours/minutes/seconds/milliseconds).

```
SELECT  MyDate,
        DATETIMEFROMPARTS(ca.Yr, 1,     1, 0, 0, 0, 0) AS FirstDayOfYear,
        DATETIMEFROMPARTS(ca.Yr, ca.Mn, 1, 0, 0, 0, 0) AS FirstDayOfMonth,
        DATETIMEFROMPARTS(ca.Yr, ca.Qt, 1, 0, 0, 0, 0) AS FirstDayOfQuarter
FROM    (VALUES ('1981-01-17T00:00:00'),
                ('1961-11-23T00:00:00'),
                ('1960-07-09T00:00:00'),
                ('1980-07-11T00:00:00'),
```

```
                    ('1983-01-05T00:00:00'),
                    ('2006-11-27T00:00:00'),
                    ('2013-08-03T00:00:00')) dt (MyDate)
CROSS APPLY (SELECT DATEPART(YEAR, dt.MyDate) AS Yr,
                    DATEPART(MONTH, dt.MyDate) AS Mn,
                    ((CEILING(MONTH(dt.MyDate)/3.0)*3)-2) AS Qt
            ) ca;
WITH cte AS
(
SELECT  DATEPART(YEAR, @MyDate) AS Yr,
        DATEPART(MONTH, @MyDate) AS Mth,
        DATEPART(DAY, @MyDate) AS Dy,
        DATEPART(HOUR, @MyDate) AS Hr,
        DATEPART(MINUTE, @MyDate) AS Mn,
        DATEPART(SECOND, @MyDate) AS Sec
)
SELECT  'StartOfHour' AS ConversionType,
        DATETIMEFROMPARTS(cte.Yr, cte.Mth, cte.Dy, cte.Hr, 0, 0, 0) AS DateResult
FROM    cte
UNION ALL
SELECT  'StartOfMinute',
        DATETIMEFROMPARTS(cte.Yr, cte.Mth, cte.Dy, cte.Hr, cte.Mn, 0, 0)
FROM    cte
UNION ALL
SELECT  'StartOfSecond',
        DATETIMEFROMPARTS(cte.Yr, cte.Mth, cte.Dy, cte.Hr, cte.Mn, cte.Sec, 0)
FROM    cte;
```

Solution #3

Use the FORMAT function to format the date, using default values for the parts to be truncated.

```
SELECT  CONVERT(CHAR(10), ca.MyDate, 121) AS MyDate,
        CAST(FORMAT(ca.MyDate, 'yyyy-01-01') AS DATETIME) AS FirstDayOfYear,
        CAST(FORMAT(ca.MyDate, 'yyyy-MM-01') AS DATETIME) AS FirstDayOfMonth
FROM    (VALUES ('1981-01-17T00:00:00'),
                ('1961-11-23T00:00:00'),
                ('1960-07-09T00:00:00'),
                ('1980-07-11T00:00:00'),
                ('1983-01-05T00:00:00'),
                ('2006-11-27T00:00:00'),
                ('2013-08-03T00:00:00')) dt (MyDate)
CROSS APPLY (SELECT CAST(dt.MyDate AS DATE)) AS ca(MyDate);

SELECT  'StartOfHour' AS ConversionType,
        FORMAT(@MyDate, 'yyyy-MM-dd HH:00:00.000') AS DateResult
UNION ALL
SELECT  'StartOfMinute',
        FORMAT(@MyDate, 'yyyy-MM-dd HH:mm:00.000')
UNION ALL
SELECT  'StartOfSecond',
        FORMAT(@MyDate, 'yyyy-MM-dd HH:mm:ss.000');
```

How It Works #1

In order to find the datepart boundary that you are interested in, you use the DATEDIFF function to return the number of boundaries between a known date and the date that you are comparing to. You then use the DATEADD function to add this number of boundaries back to the known date. Keep in mind that DATEDIFF returns an integer, so you need to choose your known date so that you don't cause a numeric overflow. This can become problematic when you work with the SECOND datepart boundary (or one of the fractional second datepart boundaries).

How It Works #2

The year, month, and beginning month of the quarter are calculated in the CROSS APPLY operator. The parts to keep are passed in to the DATETIMETOPARTS function, and default values are passed in for the remaining parts so as to generate the desired dates. For the second part of this solution, the year, month, day, hour, minute, and second parts are extracted, and then the desired parts are passed in to the DATETIMETOPARTS function, with the parts of the time to be truncated set to zero. This solution produces the same results as Solution #1.

How It Works #3

The FORMAT function utilizes the .NET 4.0 formatting capabilities to format the date as a string, and then the CAST function is utilized to change the string back into a DATETIME data type. The parts of the time that are to be truncated are set to zero, while for the first day of calculations, the day and month are set to 1 where appropriate. With the exception of FirstDayOfQuarter, this solution returns the same results as Solution #1.

■ **Tip** In my performance testing of these solutions, Solution #1 is the fastest. Solution #2 (as coded earlier, where the date/time parts need to be extracted) takes about twice the time to run as Solution #1. However, if the parts of the dates are already available, then this solution is slightly faster than Solution #1. Solution #3 is by far the slowest, coming in at about 100 times slower than either of the other solutions.

10-13. Include Missing Dates

Problem

You are producing a report that breaks down expenses by category and that sums up the expenses at the month level. One of your categories does not have expenses for every month, so those months are missing values in the report. You want those missing months to be reported with a value of zero for the expense amount.

Solution

Utilize a calendar table to generate the missing months.

```
DECLARE @Base DATETIME = '1900-01-01T00:00:00';
WITH cteExpenses AS
(
SELECT  ca.FirstOfMonth,
        SUM(ExpenseAmount) AS MonthlyExpenses
```

```
FROM     ( VALUES ('2012-01-15T00:00:00', 1250.00),
                  ('2012-01-28T00:00:00', 750.00),
                  ('2012-03-01T00:00:00', 1475.00),
                  ('2012-03-23T00:00:00', 2285.00),
                  ('2012-04-01T00:00:00', 1650.00),
                  ('2012-04-22T00:00:00', 1452.00),
                  ('2012-06-15T00:00:00', 1875.00),
                  ('2012-07-23T00:00:00', 2125.00) ) dt (ExpenseDate, ExpenseAmount)
CROSS APPLY (SELECT DATEADD(MONTH,
                  DATEDIFF(MONTH, @Base, ExpenseDate), @Base) ) ca (FirstOfMonth)
GROUP BY  ca.FirstOfMonth
), cteMonths AS
(
SELECT  DATEFROMPARTS(2012, M, 1) AS FirstOfMonth
FROM     ( VALUES (1), (2),  (3),  (4),
                  (5), (6),  (7),  (8),
                  (9), (10), (11), (12) ) Months (M)
)
SELECT  CAST(FirstOfMonth AS DATE) AS FirstOfMonth,
        MonthlyExpenses
FROM    cteExpenses
UNION ALL
SELECT  m.FirstOfMonth,
        0
FROM    cteMonths M
        LEFT JOIN cteExpenses e
            ON M.FirstOfMonth = e.FirstOfMonth
WHERE   e.FirstOfMonth IS NULL
ORDER BY FirstOfMonth;
```

This query produces the following results:

```
FirstOfMonth MonthlyExpenses
------------ ---------------
2012-01-01   2000.00
2012-02-01   0.00
2012-03-01   3760.00
2012-04-01   3102.00
2012-05-01   0.00
2012-06-01   1875.00
2012-07-01   2125.00
2012-08-01   0.00
2012-09-01   0.00
2012-10-01   0.00
2012-11-01   0.00
2012-12-01   0.00
```

How It Works

The cteExpenses common table expression builds a derived table of expense dates and amounts. The CROSS APPLY operator converts each date to the date for the beginning of the month. The expenses are then summed up and grouped by this beginning of the month date. If we run just this portion of the query, we get the following results:

```
FirstOfMonth             MonthlyExpenses
-----------------------  ----------------
2012-01-01 00:00:00.000  2000.00
2012-03-01 00:00:00.000  3760.00
2012-04-01 00:00:00.000  3102.00
2012-06-01 00:00:00.000  1875.00
2012-07-01 00:00:00.000  2125.00
```

As you can see, several months are missing. To include these missing months, the cteMonths common table expression is created, which uses the DATEFROMPARTS function to build the first day of the month for each month. Running just this portion of the query returns the following results:

```
FirstOfMonth
------------
2012-01-01
2012-02-01
2012-03-01
2012-04-01
2012-05-01
2012-06-01
2012-07-01
2012-08-01
2012-09-01
2012-10-01
2012-11-01
2012-12-01
```

Finally, the expenses are returned from the first part of the query. This expenses result set is unioned to a second result set that returns the months left-joined to the expenses. This second result set is filtered to return only the months that do not exist in the expenses, before joining with the expenses result set. The result is that all months are shown in the result set, with the months without data having a zero value.

In this recipe, a virtual calendar table was created that contains the first day of each month in the year. Frequently, calendar tables will contain days for every day in the year, with additional columns to hold other information, such as the first day of the month, the day of the week for the date, and whether this is a weekday or a weekend date or a holiday. Using a prebuilt calendar table can greatly simplify many calculations that would need to be performed.

10-14. Finding Arbitrary Dates

Problem

You need to find the date of an arbitrary date, such as the third Thursday in November or the date for last Friday.

Solution

Use a calendar table with additional columns to query the desired dates.

```
CREATE TABLE dbo.Calendar (
              [Date] DATE CONSTRAINT PK_Calendar PRIMARY KEY CLUSTERED,
              FirstDayOfYear DATE,
              LastDayOfYear DATE,
              FirstDayOfMonth DATE,
              LastDayOfMonth DATE,
              FirstDayOfWeek DATE,
              LastDayOfWeek DATE,
              DayOfWeekName NVARCHAR(20),
              IsWeekDay BIT,
              IsWeekEnd BIT);
GO
DECLARE @Base  DATETIME = '1900-01-01T00:00:00',
        @Start DATETIME = '2000-01-01T00:00:00';
INSERT INTO dbo.Calendar
SELECT  TOP (9497)
              ca.Date,
              cy.FirstDayOfYear,
              cyl.LastDayOfYear,
              cm.FirstDayOfMonth,
              cml.LastDayOfMonth,
              cw.FirstDayOfWeek,
              cwl.LastDayOfWeek,
              cd.DayOfWeekName,
              cwd.IsWeekDay,
              CAST(cwd.IsWeekDay - 1 AS BIT) AS IsWeekEnd
FROM        (SELECT ROW_NUMBER() OVER (ORDER BY (SELECT 0))
              FROM sys.all_columns t1
              CROSS JOIN sys.all_columns t2) dt (RN)
CROSS APPLY (SELECT DATEADD(DAY, RN-1, @Start)) AS ca(Date)
CROSS APPLY (SELECT DATEADD(YEAR, DATEDIFF(YEAR, @Base, ca.Date), @Base)) AS cy(FirstDayOfYear)
CROSS APPLY (SELECT DATEADD(DAY, -1, DATEADD(YEAR, 1, cy.FirstDayOfYear))) AS cyl(LastDayOfYear)
CROSS APPLY (SELECT DATEADD(MONTH, DATEDIFF(MONTH, @Base, ca.Date), @Base)) AS
cm(FirstDayOfMonth)
CROSS APPLY (SELECT DATEADD(DAY, -1, DATEADD(MONTH, 1, cm.FirstDayOfMonth))) AS
cml(LastDayOfMonth)
CROSS APPLY (SELECT DATEADD(DAY,-(DATEPART(weekday ,ca.Date)-1),ca.Date)) AS cw(FirstDayOfWeek)
CROSS APPLY (SELECT DATEADD(DAY, 6, cw.FirstDayOfWeek)) AS cwl(LastDayOfWeek)
```

```
CROSS APPLY (SELECT DATENAME(weekday, ca.Date)) AS cd(DayOfWeekName)
CROSS APPLY (SELECT CASE WHEN cd.DayOfWeekName
                        IN ('Monday', 'Tuesday', 'Wednesday', 'Thursday', 'Friday')
                        THEN 1
                        ELSE 0
                    END) AS cwd(IsWeekDay);
GO

WITH cte AS
(
SELECT  FirstDayOfMonth,
        Date,
        RN = ROW_NUMBER() OVER (PARTITION BY FirstDayOfMonth ORDER BY Date)
FROM    dbo.Calendar
WHERE   DayOfWeekName = 'Thursday'
)
SELECT  Date
FROM    cte
WHERE   RN = 3
AND     FirstDayOfMonth = '2012-11-01T00:00:00';

SELECT  c1.Date
FROM    dbo.Calendar c1 -- prior week
        JOIN dbo.Calendar c2 -- current week
            ON c1.FirstDayOfWeek = DATEADD(DAY, -7, c2.FirstDayOfWeek)
WHERE   c1.DayOfWeekName = 'Friday'
AND     c2.Date = CAST(GETDATE() AS DATE);
```

This query returns the following result sets:

```
Date
----------
2012-11-15

Date
----------
2015-01-16
```

How It Works

This recipe creates a calendar table with columns for extra information—the first and last days of the year, the month and week, the weekday name for the date, and whether this date is a weekday or weekend. This table is then populated for all the dates between January 1, 2000, and December 31, 2025.

The first date that is retrieved is the third Thursday in November. The query gets all of the Thursdays, along with the first day of the month. It then calculates a row number for that date in that month. Finally, the date for the third Thursday in November is returned.

The second date that is retrieved is the Friday of the previous week. The query starts off by performing a self-join to the calendar table. On the current week side of the join, the first day of the week for today's date is obtained and is used to join to the previous week by subtracting seven days. This gets the first day of the previous week. It then returns the date for that week that has a weekday name of Friday.

As you can see, calendar tables can be easily adjusted to suit your needs. A column of IsWorkingDay could be added and populated, and then it would be easy to find the date five working days in the future. Holidays can be tracked, as can fiscal accounting periods, especially those that don't follow the norm of the calendar year.

Calendar tables are typically sized to hold several years' worth of data. It takes less than 10,000 records to hold every date between January 1, 2000, and December 31, 2025. Because of its small size and static nature, this is one of those tables that benefits from being heavily indexed to provide covering indexes for all the queries you would run against it.

10-15. Querying for Intervals

Problem

You want to count the number of employees that were employed during each month.

Solution

Use a calendar table to get the months employees were active and then aggregate the data.

```
WITH cte AS
(
SELECT  edh.BusinessEntityID,
        c.FirstDayOfMonth
FROM    HumanResources.EmployeeDepartmentHistory AS edh
        JOIN dbo.Calendar AS c
            ON c.Date BETWEEN edh.StartDate
                AND ISNULL(edh.EndDate, GETDATE())
GROUP BY edh.BusinessEntityID,
        c.FirstDayOfMonth
)
SELECT  FirstDayOfMonth,
        COUNT(*) AS EmployeeQty
FROM    cte
GROUP BY FirstDayOfMonth
ORDER BY FirstDayOfMonth;
```

This query returns the following (abridged) result set:

```
FirstDayOfMonth EmployeeQty
--------------- -----------
2006-06-01      1
2006-07-01      1
2006-08-01      1
2006-09-01      1
2006-10-01      1
2006-11-01      1
...
2014-07-01      290
2014-08-01      290
2014-09-01      290
2014-10-01      290
2014-11-01      290
2014-12-01      290
2015-01-01      290
```

How It Works

Using the 25-year calendar table created in Recipe 10-14, the beginning of the month and employee identifier are returned for each employee who is active between the start date and end date (or current date, if null). The GROUP BY clause is utilized to eliminate duplicates created by each date within a month. The employees are then counted per month.

10-16. Working with Dates and Times Across National Boundaries

Problem

When exchanging data with a company in a different country, dates either are converted incorrectly or generate an error when being imported.

Solution

Use one of the ISO-8601 date formats to ensure that the date/time value is unambiguous.

```
SELECT 'sysdatetime' AS ConversionType, 126 AS Style,
       CONVERT(varchar(30), SYSDATETIME(), 126) AS [Value] UNION ALL
SELECT 'sysdatetime', 127,
       CONVERT(varchar(30), SYSDATETIME(), 127) UNION ALL
SELECT 'getdate', 126,
       CONVERT(varchar(30), GETDATE(), 126) UNION ALL
SELECT 'getdate', 127,
        CONVERT(varchar(30), GETDATE(), 127);
```

This code returns the following result set:

```
ConversionType Style        Value
-------------- -----------  ------------------------------
sysdatetime    126          2015-01-24T00:44:45.5308465
sysdatetime    127          2015-01-24T00:44:45.5308465
getdate        126          2015-01-24T00:44:45.530
getdate        127          2015-01-24T00:44:45.530
```

How It Works

When working with dates that cross national boundaries, you frequently run into data-conversion issues. For instance, take the date 02/04/2012: in the United States, this is February 4, 2012, while in the United Kingdom, this is April 2, 2012. In this example, the date is converted improperly. Another example is 12/25/2012: in the United States, this is December 25, 2012; in the United Kingdom, computers would attempt to convert it into the 12th day of the 25th month of 2012, and since there aren't 25 months, it would generate an error.

Any date with the month and day values both being less than or equal to 12 is ambiguous (unless the values are the same). Any date with a number greater than 12 may generate an error when attempting to convert it to a date data type.

To work with this date-conversion issue, an international standard was created. This standard is ISO-8601: "Data elements and interchange formats – Information interchange – Representation of dates and times." There are two formats that are allowed to represent date with time:

```
YYYY-MM-DDThh:mm:ss[.nnnnnnn][{+|-}hh:mm]
YYYY-MM-DDThh:mm:ss[.nnnnnnn]Z (UTC, Coordinated Universal Time)
```

The following are examples of using these formats:

```
2012-07-28T16:45:33
2012-07-28T16:45:33.1234567+07:00
2012-07-28T16:45:33.1234567Z
```

To properly use the ISO-8601 format, the date and time portions must be specified, including the separators, meaning the *T*, the colons (:), the + or –, and the periods (.). The brackets indicate that the fractional seconds and time-zone-offset portions of the time are optional. The time is specified using the 24-hour clock format. The *T* is used to indicate the start of the time portion of the date/time value in the string. The *Z* indicates that the time is in UTC time.

The date/time values that are specified in this format are unambiguous. The SET DATEFORMAT and SET LANGUAGE default language settings do not affect the results.

When querying dates and times, the CONVERT function has two styles (126 and 127) that convert a date/time data type into the ISO-8601 date format with time values.

In this chapter, and throughout this book, examples with dates use the ISO-8601 standard.

CHAPTER 11

■ ■ ■

Working with Numbers

by Jonathan Gennick

SQL Server supports integer, decimal, and floating-point numbers. Working with numbers requires an understanding of the types of numbers available and what they are capable of doing. Implicit conversion rules sometimes lead to surprising results from seemingly simple-to-understand expressions. The recipes in this chapter show some of the more common operations as well as techniques for guarding against unexpected and unwanted results.

11-1. Representing Integers

Problem

You are writing T-SQL or creating a table and want to represent integer data in a binary format.

Solution

Choose one of the four integer data types provided in SQL Server. Here is a code block showing the four types and their range of valid values:

```
DECLARE @bip bigint, @bin bigint
DECLARE @ip int, @in int
DECLARE @sip smallint, @sin smallint
DECLARE @ti tinyint

SET @bip =   9223372036854775807   /*  2^63-1 */
SET @bin =  -9223372036854775808   /* -2^63   */
SET @ip  =            2147483647   /*  2^31-1 */
SET @in  =           -2147483648   /* -2^31   */
SET @sip =                 32767   /*  2^15-1 */
SET @sin =                -32768   /* -2^15   */
SET @ti  =                   255   /*  2^8-1  */
```

```
SELECT 'bigint' AS type_name, @bip AS max_value, @bin AS min_value
UNION ALL
SELECT 'int', @ip, @in
UNION ALL
SELECT 'smallint', @sip, @sin
UNION ALL
SELECT 'tinyint', @ti, 0
ORDER BY max_value DESC;
```

How It Works

SQL Server supports four integer data types. Each allocates a specific number of bytes for use in representing integer values. From largest to smallest, the types are as follows:

- bigint (eight bytes)
- int (four bytes)
- smallint (two bytes)
- tinyint (one byte)

The results from the solution example show the range of values supported by each of the types:

type_name	max_value	min_value
bigint	9223372036854775807	-9223372036854775808
int	2147483647	-2147483648
smallint	32767	-32768
tinyint	255	0

Attempts to store an out-of-range value result in an overflow error. For example, decrement the minimum value for smallint by 1, and attempt to store that value, and you'll get the following results:

```
DECLARE @sin smallint
SET @sin =              -32769
Msg 220, Level 16, State 1, Line 2
Arithmetic overflow error for data type smallint, value = -32769.
```

tinyint is a single byte limited to positive values only. The other three types do take negative values. SQL Server does not provide for unsigned versions of bigint, int, and smallint.

Choose from among the integer types based upon the range of values that you are working with. Don't forget to allow for future growth. If storing the national debt, for example, you might want to jump straight to the bigint data type. Any of the types may also be used in CREATE TABLE statements. You can create table columns based upon the four types, as well as upon T-SQL variables, as shown in the example.

■ **Note**   The absolute value range in the negative direction is one greater than in the positive direction. That is because of the two's-complement notation used internally by the database engine. If you're curious, you can read more about two's-complement in the following Wikipedia article:

http://en.wikipedia.org/wiki/Two%27s_complement.

11-2. Creating Single-Bit Integers

Problem

Your application requires several on/off flags that you wish to store in the smallest possible space.

Solution

Store the flags using the type bit. For example:

```
DECLARE @SunnyDayFlag bit

SET @SunnyDayFlag = 1;
SET @SunnyDayFlag = 'true'

SELECT @SunnyDayFlag;
```

How It Works

Integers decrease in size from eight bytes to one byte as you move from bigint to tinyint. Using the bit type, you can define a column or variable that can be set to 1, 0, or null.

The values 'true' and 'false' (case-insensitive) equate to 1 and 0, respectively. SQL Server coalesces bit variables into groups of eight or fewer, storing up to eight values in a single byte.

■ **Caution**   While the official documentation lumps bit with the integer types, it is a type better suited for true/false flags than for numeric values you want to use in expressions.

11-3. Representing Decimal and Monetary Amounts

Problem

You are working with decimal data, such as monetary amounts, for which precise, base-10 representation is critical. You want to create a variable or table column of an appropriate type.

Solution

Use the decimal data type. Specify the total number of digits needed. Also specify how many of those digits are to the right of the decimal point. Here's an example:

```
DECLARE @x0 decimal(7,0) = 1234567.
DECLARE @x1 decimal(7,1) = 123456.7
DECLARE @x2 decimal(7,2) = 12345.67
DECLARE @x3 decimal(7,3) = 1234.567
DECLARE @x4 decimal(7,4) = 123.4567
DECLARE @x5 decimal(7,5) = 12.34567
DECLARE @x6 decimal(7,6) = 1.234567
DECLARE @x7 decimal(7,7) = .1234567
```

The first parameter to decimal indicates the overall number of digits. The second parameter indicates how many of those digits are to the right of the decimal place.

How It Works

Choose the decimal type whenever the accurate representation of decimal values is important. You'll be able to accurately represent values to the number of digits you specify, with none of the rounding or imprecision that often results from floating-point types and their use of base-2.

The two parameters to a decimal declaration are termed *precision* and *scale*. Precision refers to the overall number of digits. Scale refers to the location of the decimal point in respect to those digits. The default precision and scale are 18 and 0.

The number of digits of precision in the solution example is held constant at seven. The changing location of the decimal point indicates the effect of different values for scale.

■ **Tip** Monetary values are a particularly good application of the decimal type. For example, a declaration of decimal(11,2) allows a range of values from -$999,999,999.99 to $999,999,999.99.

11-4. Representing Floating-Point Values

Problem

You are performing scientific calculations and need the ability to represent floating-point values.

Solution

Choose one of the floating-point types supported by SQL Server. As a practical matter, you have the following choices:

```
DECLARE @x1 real  /* same as float(24) */
DECLARE @x2 float /* same as float(53) */
DECLARE @x3 float(53)
DECLARE @x4 float(24)
```

How It Works

Table 11-1 gives the absolute-value ranges supported by the declarations in this solution. For example, the largest magnitude real number is 3.40E+38. That value can, of course, be either positive or negative. The least magnitude value other than zero that you can represent is 1.18E-38. If you must represent a value of smaller magnitude, such as 1.18E-39, you would need to look toward the float type.

All values in Table 11-1 can be either positive or negative. Storing zero is also always an option.

Table 11-1. *Floating-Point Value Ranges*

Declaration	Minimum Absolute Value	Maximum Absolute Value
real	1.18E-38	3.40E+38
float	2.23E-308	1.79E+308
float(53)	2.23E-308	1.79E+308
float(24)	1.18E-38	3.40E+38

You can specify float(n) using any n from 1 to 53. However, any value n from 1..24 is treated as 24. Likewise, any value n from 25..53 is treated as 53. A declaration of float(25) is thus the same as float(53).

Types real and float(24) are equivalent and require 7 bytes of storage. Types float and float(53) are equivalent and require 15 bytes of storage.

11-5. Writing Mathematical Expressions

Problem

You are working with number values and want to write expressions to compute new values.

Solution

Write any expression you like, making use of SQL Server's supported operators and functions. For example, the expression in the following code block computes the new balance of a home loan after a payment of $500. The loan balance is $94,235.49. The interest rate is 6 percent. Twelve monthly payments are made per year.

```
DECLARE @cur_bal decimal(7,2) = 94235.49
DECLARE @new_bal decimal(7,2)

SET @new_bal = @cur_bal - (500.00 - ROUND(@cur_bal * 0.06 / 12.00, 2))
SELECT @new_bal;
```

The result will be 94206.67.

How It Works

You can write expressions of arbitrary length involving combinations of values, function calls, and operators. In doing so, you must be aware of and respect the rules of operator precedence. For example, multiplication occurs before addition, as is standard in mathematics.

Table 11-2 lists operators in order of their evaluation priority. The table lists all operators, including the nonmathematical ones.

Table 11-2. *Operator Precedence in SQL Server*

Priority Level	Operator	Description
1	~	Bitwise NOT
2	*, /, %	Multiply, divide, modulo
3	+, -	Positive sign, negative sign
3	+, -	Add, subtract
3	+	String concatenate
3	&, ^, |	Bitwise AND, Bitwise exclusive OR, Bitwise OR
4	=, <, <=, !<, >, >=, !>, <>, !=	Equals, less than, less than or equal, not less than, greater than, greater than or equal, not greater than, not equal, not equal
5	NOT	Logical NOT
6	AND	Logical AND
7	ALL, ANY, BETWEEN, IN, LIKE, OR, SOME	Logical OR and others
8	=	Assignment

Use parentheses to override the default priority. The solution example includes parentheses to force the monthly interest amount to be subtracted from the $500 monthly payment, leaving the amount to be applied to the principal.

```
(500.00 - ROUND(@cur_bal * 0.06 / 12.00 ,2))
```

Omit the outer parentheses, and you'll get a very different result.

■ **Tip**   It's a reasonable practice to include parentheses for clarity, especially when using operators other than the fundamental four: +, -, *, and /. Not everyone has the precedence table memorized. You can make it easy on your successors and clarify your intentions by including parentheses in cases where misinterpretation is likely.

Another issue to contend with is data-type precedence and the presence or absence of implicit conversions. Recipe 11-6, coming next, helps you guard against incorrect results from mixing data types within an expression.

11-6. Casting Between Data Types

Problem

You want to guard against trouble when writing an expression involving values from more than one data type.

Solution

Consider explicitly converting values between types to maintain full control over your expressions and their results. For example, invoke CAST and CONVERT as follows to change values from one type to another:

```
SELECT 6/100,
       CAST(6 AS DECIMAL(1,0)) / CAST(100 AS DECIMAL(3,0)),
       CAST(6.0/100.0 AS DECIMAL(3,2));

SELECT 6/100,
       CONVERT(DECIMAL(1,0), 6) / CONVERT(DECIMAL(3,0), 100),
       CONVERT(DECIMAL(3,2), 6.0/100.0);
```

The results from both these queries are as follows:

```
--- ----------- ------
  0    0.060000   0.06
```

Choose either CAST or CONVERT depending upon the importance you attach to complying with the ISO SQL standard. CAST is a standard function. CONVERT is specific to SQL Server. My opinion is to favor CAST unless you have some specific need for functionality offered by CONVERT.

How It Works

One of the most common implicit conversion errors in SQL Server is actually the result of an implicit conversion not occurring in a specific case when a cursory glance would lead one to expect it to occur. That case involves the division of numeric values written as integers, such as 6/100.

Recall the solution example from Recipe 11-5. Instead of writing the six percent interest rate as 0.06, write it as 6/100 inside parentheses. Make just that one change, and the resulting code is as follows:

```
DECLARE @cur_bal decimal(7,2) = 94235.49
DECLARE @new_bal decimal(7,2)

SET @new_bal = @cur_bal - (500.00 - ROUND(@cur_bal * (6/100) / 12.00 ,2))
SELECT @new_bal;
```

Execute this code, and the result changes from the correct result of 94206.67 as given in Recipe 11-5 to the incorrect result of 93735.49. Why the change? It's because 6 and 100 are written with no decimal points, so they are treated as integers. Integer division then ensues. The uninitiated expects 6/100 to evaluate to 0.06, but integer division leads to a result of zero. The interest rate evaluates to zero, and too much of the loan payment is applied to the principal.

■ **Caution** Keep in mind that numeric constants written without a decimal point are treated as integers. When writing an expression involving constants along with decimal values, include decimal points in your constants so they are also treated as decimals—unless, of course, you are certain you want them written as integers.

The solution in this case is to recognize that the expression requires decimal values and write either 0.06 or 6.0/100.0 instead. For example, the following version of the expression will yield the same correct results as in Recipe 11-5:

```
SET @new_bal = @cur_bal - (500.00 - ROUND(@cur_bal * (6.0/100.0) / 12.00 ,2))
```

What of the values 500.00 and 12.00? Can they be written as 500 and 12? It turns out that they *can* be written that way. The following expression yields correct results:

```
SET @new_bal = @cur_bal - (500 - ROUND(@cur_bal * (6.0/100.0) / 12 ,2))
```

You can get away in this case with 500 and 12, because SQL Server applies data type precedence. In the case of 500, the value being subtracted is a decimal value. Thus, the database engine implicitly converts 500 to a decimal. For much the same reason, the integer 12 is also promoted to a decimal. That conversion makes sense in this particular case, but it may not always be what you want.

Table 11-3 lists data types by precedence. Any time an operator works on values of two different types, the type lower on the scale is promoted to the type higher on the scale. If such a conversion is not what you want, or if you just want to clearly specify the conversion to remove any doubt, invoke either the CAST or the CONVERT function.

Table 11-3. *Data-Type Precedence in SQL Server*

Precedence Level	Data Type	Precedence Level	Data Type
1	Any user-defined type	16	int
2	sql_variant	17	smallint
3	xml	18	tinyint
4	datetimeoffset	19	bit
5	datetime2	20	ntext
6	datetime	21	text
7	smalldatetime	22	image
8	date	23	timestamp
9	time	24	unique
10	float	25	nvarchar
11	real	26	nchar
12	decimal	27	varchar
13	money	28	char
14	smallmoney	29	varbinary
15	bigint	30	binary

The following is one last restatement of Recipe 11-5's solution. The original solution used ROUND to force the interest amount to two decimal places, but what was the resulting data type? Do you know? Perhaps it is better to be certain. The following code casts the result of the interest computation to the type decimal(7,2). The rounding still occurs, but this time as part of the casting operation.

```
DECLARE @cur_bal decimal(7,2) = 94235.49
DECLARE @new_bal decimal(7,2)

SET @new_bal = @cur_bal - (500.00 - CAST(@cur_bal * (6.0/100.0) / 12.00 AS decimal(7,2)))
SELECT @new_bal;
```

The result is 94206.67.

Remember in particular the tricky case of integer division in instances such as 6/100. That behavior is unintuitive and leads to many errors. Otherwise, the implicit conversions implied by the precedence levels in Table 11-3 tend to make sense and produce reasonable results. Whenever values from two types are involved in the same expression, the value of the type having the lower precedence is converted into an instance of the type having the higher precedence. Even so, I recommend explicit conversions in all but the most obvious cases. If you aren't absolutely certain at a glance just what is occurring within an expression, then make the conversions explicit.

11-7. Converting Numbers to Text

Problem

You have numeric values that you want to represent in human-readable form.

Solution

Make use of the CONVERT function to specify one of the character types as being the target data type. The following example converts product prices and weights to strings of type NVARCHAR:

```
SELECT ProductID, Name,
       CONVERT(NVARCHAR, ListPrice, 1) AS 'Price',
       CONVERT(NVARCHAR, Weight) AS 'Weight'
FROM Production.Product
WHERE ListPrice > 0 AND Weight IS NOT NULL;
```

How It Works

You saw CONVERT used in Recipe 11-6 to convert from one number type to another, but it can also convert to text. The output from the solution example is as follows:

```
ProductID Name                       Price     Weight
--------- -------------------------- --------- ------
...
      719 HL Road Frame - Red, 48    1,431.50 2.16
      720 HL Road Frame - Red, 52    1,431.50 2.20
      721 HL Road Frame - Red, 56    1,431.50 2.24
      722 LL Road Frame - Black, 58   337.22  2.46
      723 LL Road Frame - Black, 60   337.22  2.48
      724 LL Road Frame - Black, 62   337.22  2.50
...
```

An optional third parameter provides limited control over the specific textual format that is used. Table 11-4 describes the available styles and their parameter values. The first set of style numbers applies to floating-point and real-input values; the second set applies to values in one of the monetary types.

Table 11-4. *Style Values for Use with the CONVERT Function*

Type Family	Style Number	Result
Floating-point	0	Gives zero to six digits and scientific notation when needed. This is the default style when floating-point values are converted to text.
	1	Gives eight digits and scientific notation.
	2	Gives 16 digits and scientific notation.
Money	0	Allows two decimal digits. No commas used between digit groups. This is the default style for non-floating-point conversions.
	1	Allows two decimal digits and includes commas between digit groups.
	2	Allows four decimal digits, but no commas.

11-8. Converting from Text to a Number

Problem

You want to compute a human-readable representation of a number to one of the binary equivalents used by SQL Server to store numeric types.

Solution

Invoke the CONVERT function and specify a numeric type as the first parameter. For example:

```
SELECT 0-CONVERT(DECIMAL, NationalIDNumber) AS 'Negative ID'
FROM HumanResources.Employee;
```

This query converts national ID numbers from text to decimal, and arbitrarily makes them negative. Results are as follows:

```
Negative ID
----------
 -10708100
-109272464
-112432117
...
```

How It Works

In Recipe 11-7 you saw CONVERT used to represent numeric values in their textual form. You can also go the opposite direction. Specify the name of your desired numeric type as the first parameter, and pass a valid text representation as the second.

11-9. Rounding

Problem

You want to round a number value to a specific number of decimal places.

Solution

Invoke the ROUND function. Here's an example:

```
SELECT EndOfDayRate,
       ROUND(EndOfDayRate,0) AS EODR_Dollar,
       ROUND(EndOfDayRate,2) AS EODR_Cent
FROM Sales.CurrencyRate;
```

The results are as follows:

EndOfDayRate	EODR_Dollar	EODR_Cent
1.0002	1.00	1.00
1.55	2.00	1.55
1.9419	2.00	1.94
1.4683	1.00	1.47
8.2784	8.00	8.28

...

How It Works

Invoke ROUND to round a number to a specific number of decimal places, as specified by the second argument. The solution example shows rounding both to the nearest integer (zero decimal places) and to the nearest hundredth (two decimal places).

■ **Note**   Digit values of 5 and higher round upward. Rounding 0.5 to the nearest integer yields 1.0 as a result.

You can invoke ROUND with a negative argument to round to the left of the decimal place. The following is an example that rounds product inventories to the nearest 10 units and to the nearest 100 units:

```
SELECT ProductID, SUM(Quantity) AS Quantity,
      SUM(ROUND(Quantity,-1)) as Q10,
      SUM(ROUND(Quantity,-2)) as Q100
FROM Production.ProductInventory
GROUP BY ProductID;
```

The results show the effects of rounding away from the decimal place:

ProductID	Quantity	Q10	Q100
1	1085	1080	1100
2	1109	1110	1100
3	1352	1350	1300
4	1322	1320	1300

...

ROUND usually returns a value. However, there is one case to beware of. It comes about because ROUND returns its result in the same data type as the input value. The following three statements illustrate the instance in which ROUND will throw an error:

```
SELECT ROUND(500,-3);
SELECT ROUND(500.0,-4);
SELECT ROUND(500.0,-3);
```

The first and second statements will return 1000 and 0.0, respectively. But the third query will throw an error as follows:

```
Msg 8115, Level 16, State 2, Line 2
Arithmetic overflow error converting expression to data type numeric.
```

ROUND(500,-3) succeeds because the input value is an integer constant. (No decimal point means that 500 is considered as an integer.) The result is thus also an integer, and an integer is large enough to hold the value 1000.

ROUND(500.0,-4) returns zero. The input value indicates a type of decimal(4,1). The value rounds to zero because the value is being rounded too far to the left. Zero fits into the four-digit precision of the implied data type.

ROUND(500.0,-3) fails because the result is 1000. The value 1000 will not fit into the implied data type of decimal(4,1). You can get around the problem by casting your input value to a larger precision. Here's an example:

```
SELECT ROUND(CAST(500.0 as DECIMAL(5,1)),-3)
```

```
-------------------------------------------
                    1000.0
```

This time, the input value is explicitly made to be decimal(5,1). The five digits of precision leave four to the left of the decimal place. Those four are enough to represent the value 1000.

11-10. Rounding Always Up or Down

Problem

You want to force a result to an integer value. You want to always round either up or down.

Solution

Invoke CEILING to always round up to the next integer value. Invoke FLOOR to always round down to the next lowest integer value. Here's an example:

```
SELECT CEILING(-1.23), FLOOR (-1.23), CEILING(1.23), FLOOR(1.23);
```

The results are as follows:

```
------- ------- ------- -------
    -1      -2       2       1
```

How It Works

CEILING and FLOOR don't give quite the same flexibility as ROUND. You can't specify a number of decimal places. The functions simply round up or down to the nearest integer, period.

You can work around the nearest integer limitation using a bit of math. For example, to invoke CEILING to the nearest cent and to the nearest hundred, use this:

```
SELECT CEILING(123.0043*100.0)/100.0 AS toCent,
       CEILING(123.0043/100.0)*100.0 AS toHundred;
```

toCent	toHundred
123.010000	200.0

We don't trust this technique for binary floating-point values. However, it should work fine on decimal values so long as the extra math doesn't push those values beyond the bounds of precision and scale that the decimal can support.

11-11. Discarding Decimal Places

Problem

You want to just "chop off" the digits past the decimal point. You don't care about rounding at all. You just want zeros.

Solution

Invoke the ROUND function using a third parameter that is nonzero. Here's an example:

```
SELECT ROUND(123.99,0,1), ROUND(123.99,1,1), ROUND(123.99,-1,1);
```

```
------- ------- -------
 123.00  123.90  120.00
```

Do be aware that Management Studio will by default display two digits past the decimal point. You can see however, how the third parameter is causing the ROUND function to round downward to zero.

How It Works

Some database brands (Oracle, for example) implement a TRUNCATE function to eliminate values past the decimal point. SQL Server accomplishes that task using the ROUND function. Make the third parameter anything but zero, and the function will truncate rather than round.

11-12. Testing Equality of Binary Floating-Point Values

Problem

You are testing two binary floating-point values for equality, but the imprecision inherent in floating-point representation is causing values that you consider equal to be rejected as not equal.

Solution

Decide on a difference threshold below which you will consider the two values to be equal. Then test the absolute value of the difference to see whether it is less than your threshold. For example, the following example assumes a threshold of 0.000001 (one one-millionth):

```
DECLARE @r1 real = 0.95
DECLARE @f1 float = 0.95
IF ABS(@r1-@f1) < 0.000001
   SELECT 'Equal'
ELSE
   SELECT 'Not Equal'
```

The difference is less than the threshold, so the values are considered to be equal. The result is as follows:

```
-----
Equal
```

How It Works

Not all decimal values can be represented precisely in binary floating-point. In addition, different expressions that should in theory yield identical results sometimes differ by tiny amounts. The following is a query block to illustrate the problem:

```
DECLARE @r1 real = 0.95
DECLARE @f1 float = 0.95
SELECT @r1, @f1, @r1-@f1;
```

Both values are the same but not really. The results are as follows:

```
------------  ---------------------  ---------------------
       0.95                    0.95  -1.19209289106692E-08
```

The 00 fundamental problem is that the base-2 representation of 0.95 is a never-ending string of bits. The float type is larger, allowing for more bits, which is the reason for the nonzero difference. By applying the threshold method shown in the solution, you can pretend that the tiny difference does not exist.

■ **Caution** The solution in this recipe represents a conscious decision to disregard small differences in order to treat two values as being equal. Make that decision while keeping in mind the context of how the values are derived and the context of the problem that is being solved.

11-13. Treating Nulls as Zeros

Problem

You are writing expressions with numeric values that might be null. You want to treat nulls as zero.

Solution

Invoke the COALESCE function to supply a value of zero in the event of a null. For example, the following query returns the MaxQty column from Sales.SpecialOffer. That column is nullable. COALESCE is used to supply a zero as an alternate value.

```
SELECT SpecialOfferID, MaxQty, COALESCE(MaxQty, 0) AS MaxQtyAlt
FROM Sales.SpecialOffer;
```

The results are as follows:

SpecialOfferID	MaxQty	MaxQtyAlt
1	NULL	0
2	14	14
3	24	24
4	40	40
5	60	60
6	NULL	0
7	NULL	0

...

How It Works

COALESCE is an ISO standard function that takes as its input any number of values. It returns the first non-null value in the resulting list. The solution example invokes COALESCE to return a zero in the event MaxQty is null.

SQL Server also implements an ISNULL function, which is propriety and takes only two arguments, but otherwise is similar to COALESCE in that it returns the first non-null value in the list. You can implement the solution example using ISNULL as follows and get the same results:

```
SELECT SpecialOfferID, MaxQty, ISNULL(MaxQty, 0) AS MaxQtyAlt
FROM Sales.SpecialOffer;
```

It's generally good practice to avoid invoking either COALESCE or ISNULL within a WHERE clause predicate. Applying functions to a column mentioned in a WHERE clause can inhibit the use of an index on the column. Here's an example of what we try to avoid:

```
SELECT SpecialOfferID
FROM Sales.SpecialOffer
WHERE COALESCE(MaxQty,0) = 0;
```

In a case like this, we prefer to write an IS NULL predicate, as follows:

```
SELECT SpecialOfferID
FROM Sales.SpecialOffer
WHERE MaxQty = 0 OR MaxQty IS NULL;
```

We believe the IS NULL approach preserves the greatest amount of flexibility for the optimizer.

11-14. Generating a Row Set of Sequential Numbers

Problem

You need to generate a row set with an arbitrary number of rows. For example, you want to generate one row per day in the year so that you can join to another table that might be missing rows for some of the days, with the goal of ultimately creating a row set that has one row per day.

Solution

Many row-generator queries are possible. The following is one solution I particularly like. It is a variation on a technique introduced to me by database expert Vladimir Przyjalkowski in 2004. It returns rows in power-of-ten increments controlled by the number of joins that you write in the outer query's FROM clause. This particular example returns 10,000 rows numbered from 0 to 9999.

```
WITH ones AS (
    SELECT *
    FROM (VALUES (0), (1), (2), (3), (4),
                 (5), (6), (7), (8), (9)) AS numbers(x)
)
SELECT 1000*o1000.x + 100*o100.x + 10*o10.x + o1.x x
FROM ones o1, ones o10, ones o100, ones o1000
ORDER BY x;
```

The results are as follows:

```
          x
-----------
          0
          1
          2
          3
...
       9997
       9998
       9999
```

If you like, you can restrict the number of rows returned by wrapping the main query inside of an enclosing query that restricts the results. Be sure to keep the WITH clause first. Also specify an alias for the new, enclosing query. The following example specifies n as the alias:

```
WITH ones AS (
    SELECT *
    FROM (VALUES (0), (1), (2), (3), (4),
                 (5), (6), (7), (8), (9)) AS numbers(x)
)
SELECT n.x FROM (
    SELECT 1000*o1000.x + 100*o100.x + 10*o10.x + o1.x x
    FROM ones o1, ones o10, ones o100, ones o1000
) n
WHERE n.x < 5000
ORDER BY x;
```

This version returns 5,000 rows numbered from 0 through 4999.

How It Works

Row sets of sequential numbers are handy for data densification. Data densification refers to the filling in of missing rows, such as in time series data. Imagine, for example, that you want to generate a report showing how many employees were hired on each day of the year. A quick test of the data shows that hire dates are sparse—there are only a few days in a given year on which employees have been hired. Here's an example:

```
SELECT DISTINCT HireDate
FROM HumanResources.Employee
WHERE HireDate >= '2012-01-01'
  AND HireDate < '2013-01-01'
ORDER BY HireDate;
```

The results indicate that hires occur sparsely throughout the year:

```
HireDate
----------
2012-04-16
2012-05-30
2012-09-30
```

Using the solution query, you can create a sequence table to use in densifying the data so as to return one row per day, regardless of number of hires. Begin by creating a 1,000-row table using a form of the solution query:

```
WITH ones AS (
    SELECT *
    FROM (VALUES (0), (1), (2), (3), (4),
                 (5), (6), (7), (8), (9)) AS numbers(x)
)
SELECT 100*o100.x + 10*o10.x + o1.x x
INTO SeqNum
FROM ones o1, ones o10, ones o100;
```

Now it's possible to join against SeqNum and use that table as the basis for generating one row per day in the year. Here's an example:

```
SELECT DATEADD(day, x, '2012-01-01'), HireDate
FROM SeqNum LEFT OUTER JOIN HumanResources.Employee
    ON DATEADD(day, x, '2012-01-01') = HireDate
WHERE x < DATEDIFF (day, '2012-01-01', '2013-01-01')
ORDER BY x;
```

The results are as follows. The `HireDate` column is non-null for days on which a hire was made.

```
                            HireDate
----------------------- ----------
2012-01-01 00:00:00.000 NULL
2012-01-02 00:00:00.000 NULL
...
2012-04-15 00:00:00.000 NULL
2012-04-16 00:00:00.000 2012-04-16
2012-04-17 00:00:00.000 NULL
...
```

Add a simple GROUP BY operation to count the hires per date, and we're done! Here's the final query:

```
SELECT DATEADD(day, x, '2012-01-01'), COUNT(HireDate)
FROM SeqNum LEFT OUTER JOIN HumanResources.Employee
    ON DATEADD(day, x, '2012-01-01') = HireDate
WHERE x < DATEDIFF (day, '2012-01-01', '2013-01-01')
GROUP BY x
ORDER BY x;
```

Results now show the number of hires per day. The following are results for the same days as in the previous output. This time, the count of hires is zero on all days having only null hire dates. The count is 1 on May 18, 2006, for the one person hired on that date.

```
----------------------- -----------
2012-01-01 00:00:00.000           0
2012-01-02 00:00:00.000           0
...
2012-04-15 00:00:00.000           0
2012-04-16 00:00:00.000           1
2012-04-17 00:00:00.000           0
...
```

You'll receive a warning message upon executing the final query. The message is nothing to worry about. It reads as follows:

```
Warning: Null value is eliminated by an aggregate or other SET operation.
```

This message simply indicates that the COUNT function was fed null values, and indeed that is the case. Null hire dates were fed into the COUNT function. Those nulls were ignored and not counted, which is precisely the behavior wanted in this case.

11-15. Generating Random Integers in a Row Set

Problem

You want each row returned by a query to include a random integer value. You further want to specify the range within which those random values will fall. For example, you want to generate a random number between 900 and 1,000 for each product.

Solution

Invoke the built-in RAND() function, as shown in the following example:

```
DECLARE @rmin int, @rmax int;
SET @rmin = 900;
SET @rmax = 1000;
SELECT Name,
       CAST(RAND(CHECKSUM(NEWID())) * (@rmax-@rmin) AS INT) + @rmin
FROM Production.Product;
```

You'll get results as follows, except that your random numbers might be different from mine:

```
Name
-------------------------------------------------- -----------
Adjustable Race                                            939
All-Purpose Bike Stand                                     916
AWC Logo Cap                                               914
BB Ball Bearing                                           992
Bearing Ball                                              975
```

How It Works

RAND() returns a random float value between 0 exclusive and 1 exclusive. RAND() accepts a seed parameter, and any given seed will generate the same result. These are two characteristics you must keep in mind and compensate for as you use the function.

The following is the simplest possible invocation of RAND() in a query against Production.Product. The resulting "random" number is not very random at all. SQL Server treats the function as deterministic because of the lack of a parameter, invokes the function just one time, and applies the result of that invocation to all rows returned by the query.

```
SELECT Name, RAND()
FROM Production.Product;
```

```
Name
-------------------------------------------------- ---------------------
Adjustable Race                                    0.472241415009636
All-Purpose Bike Stand                             0.472241415009636
AWC Logo Cap                                       0.472241415009636
BB Ball Bearing                                    0.472241415009636
Bearing Ball                                       0.472241415009636
```

What's needed is a seed value that changes for each row. A common and useful approach is to base the seed value on a call to NEWID(). NEWID() returns a value in a type not passable to RAND(). You can work around that problem by invoking CHECKSUM() on the NEWID() value to generate an integer value acceptable as a seed. Here's an example:

```
SELECT Name, RAND(CHECKSUM(NEWID()))
FROM Production.Product;
```

Name	
Adjustable Race	0.943863936349248
All-Purpose Bike Stand	0.562297100626295
AWC Logo Cap	0.459806720686023
BB Ball Bearing	0.328415563433923
Bearing Ball	0.859439320073147

The NEWID() function generates a globally unique identifier. Because the result must be globally unique, no two invocations of NEWID() will return the same result. The function is therefore not deterministic, and the database engine thus invokes the RAND(CHECKSUM(NEWID())) expression anew for each row.

Now comes some math. It's necessary to shift the random values from their just-greater-than-zero to less-than-one range into the range, in this case, of 900 to 1000. Begin by multiplying the result from RAND() by the magnitude of the range. Do that by multiplying the random values by 100, which is the difference between the upper and lower bounds of the range. Here's an example:

```
DECLARE @rmin int, @rmax int;
SET @rmin = 900;
SET @rmax = 1000;
SELECT Name,
       RAND(CHECKSUM(NEWID())) * (@rmax-@rmin)
FROM Production.Product;
```

Name	
Adjustable Race	12.5043506882683
All-Purpose Bike Stand	46.3611080374763
AWC Logo Cap	17.1908607269767
BB Ball Bearing	89.5318634996859
Bearing Ball	50.74511276104
...	

Next is to shift the spread of values so that they appear in the desired range. Do that by adding the minimum value as shown in the following query and its output. The result is a set of random values beginning at just above 900 and going to just less than 1000.

```
DECLARE @rmin int, @rmax int;
SET @rmin = 900;
SET @rmax = 1000;
SELECT Name,
       RAND(CHECKSUM(NEWID())) * (@rmax-@rmin) + @rmin
FROM Production.Product;
```

Name	
Adjustable Race	946.885865947398
All-Purpose Bike Stand	957.087533428096
AWC Logo Cap	924.321027483594
BB Ball Bearing	988.996724323006
Bearing Ball	943.797723186947

11-16. Reducing Space Used by Decimal Storage

Problem

You have very large tables with a great many decimal columns holding values notably smaller than their precisions allow. You want to reduce the amount of space to better reflect the actual values stored rather than the possible maximums.

■ **Note** The solution described in this recipe is available only in the Enterprise Edition of SQL Server.

Solution

Enable vardecimal storage for your database. Do that by invoking sp_db_vardecimal_storage_format, as follows:

```
EXEC sp_db_vardecimal_storage_format 'AdventureWorks2012', 'ON'
```

Then estimate the amount of space to be saved per table. For example, issue the following call to sp_estimated_rowsize_reduction_for_vardecimal to determine the average row length before and after vardecimal is enabled on the Production.BillOfMaterials table:

```
EXEC sys.sp_estimated_rowsize_reduction_for_vardecimal 'Production.BillOfMaterials'
```

Your results should be similar to the following:

avg_rowlen_fixed_format	avg_rowlen_vardecimal_format	row_count
57.00	56.00	2679

A one-byte-per-row savings is hardly worth pursuing. However, pursue it anyway by enabling vardecimal storage on the table:

```
sp_tableoption 'Production.BillOfMaterials', 'vardecimal storage format', 1
```

Be aware that converting to vardecimal is an offline operation. Be sure you can afford to take the table offline for the duration of the process.

How It Works

By switching on vardecimal storage for a table, you allow the engine to treat decimal values as variable length in much the same manner as variable-length strings are treated, trading an increase in CPU time for a reduction in storage from not having to store unused bytes. You enable the use of the option at the database level. Then you can apply the option on a table-by-table basis.

While the vardecimal option sounds great on the surface, we recommend some caution. Make sure that the amount of disk space saved makes it really worth the trouble of enabling the option. Remember that there is a CPU trade-off. The example enables the option for a 2,679-row table and would save about one byte per row on average. Such a savings is fine for a book example, but it's hardly worth pursing in real life. Go for a big win, or don't play at all.

You can generate a list of databases on your server that shows which ones have vardecimal is enabled. Issue the following command to do that:

```
EXEC sp_db_vardecimal_storage_format
```

Your results should resemble the following. The Database Name values may be displayed extremely wide in Management Studio. You may need to scroll left and right to see the Vardecimal State values. I've elided much of the space between the columns in this output for the sake of readability.

Database Name	Vardecimal State
master	OFF
tempdb	OFF
model	OFF
msdb	OFF
AdventureWorks2012	ON

Similarly, you can issue the following query to generate a list of tables within a database for which the option is enabled. (Increase the VARCHAR size in the CAST if your table or schema names combine to be longer than 40 characters.)

```
SELECT CAST(ss.name + '.' + so.name AS VARCHAR(40)) AS 'Table Name',
       CASE objectproperty(so.object_id, N'TableHasVarDecimalStorageFormat')
            WHEN 1 then 'ON' ELSE 'OFF'
            END AS 'Vardecimal State'
FROM sys.objects so JOIN sys.schemas ss
    ON so.schema_id = ss.schema_id
WHERE so.type_desc = 'USER_TABLE'
ORDER BY ss.name, so.name;
```

Your results should be similar to the following:

```
Table Name                               Vardecimal State
---------------------------------------- ----------------
dbo.AWBuildVersion                       OFF
dbo.DatabaseLog                          OFF
dbo.ErrorLog                             OFF
...
Production.BillOfMaterials               ON
...
```

To disable vardecimal storage on a table, invoke the sp_tableoption procedure with a third parameter of 0 rather than 1. Disable the option at the database level by first disabling it for all tables and then by executing sp_db_vardecimal_storage_format with a second parameter of 'OFF'.

■ ■ ■

Transactions, Locking, Blocking, and Deadlocking

by Jason Brimhall

In this chapter, I'll review recipes for handling transactions, lock monitoring, blocking, and deadlocking. I'll review the SQL Server table option that allows you to either disable lock escalation or enable it for a partitioned table. I'll demonstrate the snapshot isolation level, as well as Dynamic Management Views (DMVs), which are used to monitor and troubleshoot blocking and locking.

Transaction Control

Transactions are an integral part of a relational database system, and they help define a single unit of work. This unit of work can include one or more Transact-SQL statements, which are either committed or rolled back as a group. This all-or-none functionality helps prevent partial updates or inconsistent data states. A partial update occurs when one part of an interrelated process is rolled back or cancelled without rolling back or reversing all of the other parts of the interrelated processes.

A transaction is bound by the four properties of the ACID test. ACID stands for Atomicity, Consistency, Isolation (or Independence), and Durability.

- *Atomicity* means that the transactions are an all-or-nothing entity—carrying out all the steps or none at all.

- *Consistency* ensures that the data is valid both before and after the transaction. Data integrity must be maintained (foreign key references, for example), and internal data structures need to be in a valid state.

- *Isolation* is a requirement that transactions not be dependent on other transactions that may be taking place concurrently (either at the same time or overlapping). One transaction can't see another transaction's data that is in an intermediate state, but instead sees the data as it was either before the transaction began or after the transaction completes.

- *Durability* means that the transaction's effects are fixed after the transaction has committed, and any changes will be recoverable after system failures.

In this chapter, I'll demonstrate and review the SQL Server functionality and mechanisms that are used to ensure ACID test compliance, namely: locking and transactions.

There are three possible transaction types in SQL Server: autocommit, explicit, or implicit.

Autocommit is the default behavior for SQL Server, where each separate Transact-SQL statement you execute is automatically committed after it is finished. For example, it is possible for you to have two INSERT statements, with the first one failing and the second one succeeding; the second change is maintained, because each INSERT is automatically contained in its own transaction. Although this mode frees the developer from having to worry about explicit transactions, depending on this mode for transactional activity can be a mistake. For example, if you have two transactions, one that credits an account and another that debits it, and the first transaction failed, you'll have a debit without the credit. This may make the bank happy, but not necessarily the customer, who had his account debited. Autocommit is even a bit dangerous for ad hoc administrative changes; for example, if you accidentally delete all rows from a table, you don't have the option of rolling back the transaction after you've realized the mistake.

Implicit transactions occur when the SQL Server session automatically opens a new transaction when one of the following statements is first executed: ALTER TABLE, FETCH, REVOKE, CREATE, GRANT, SELECT, DELETE, INSERT, TRUNCATE TABLE, DROP, OPEN, and UPDATE.

A new transaction is automatically created (opened) once any of the aforementioned statements are executed and remains open until either a ROLLBACK or COMMIT statement is issued. The initiating command is included in the open transaction. Implicit mode is activated by executing the following command in your query session:

```
SET IMPLICIT_TRANSACTIONS ON;
```

To turn this off (back to explicit mode), execute the following:

```
SET IMPLICIT_TRANSACTIONS OFF;
```

Implicit mode can be *very* troublesome in a production environment, because application designers and end users could forget to commit transactions, leaving them open to block other connections (more on blocking later in this chapter).

Explicit transactions are those you define yourself. This is by far the recommended mode of operation when performing data modifications for your database application. This is because you explicitly control which modifications belong to a single transaction, as well as the actions that are performed if an error occurs. Modifications that must be grouped together are done using your own instruction.

Explicit transactions use the Transact-SQL commands and keywords described in Table 12-1.

Table 12-1. *Explicit Transaction Commands*

Command	Description
BEGIN TRANSACTION	Sets the starting point of an explicit transaction.
ROLLBACK TRANSACTION	Restores original data modified by a transaction and brings data back to the state it was in at the start of the transaction. Resources held by the transaction are freed.
COMMIT TRANSACTION	Ends the transaction if no errors were encountered and makes changes permanent. Resources held by the transaction are freed.
BEGIN DISTRIBUTED TRANSACTION	Allows you to define the beginning of a distributed transaction to be managed by Microsoft Distributed Transaction Coordinator (MSDTC). MSDTC must be running both locally and remotely.
SAVE TRANSACTION	Issues a savepoint within a transaction, which allows you to define a location to which a transaction can return if part of the transaction is cancelled. A transaction must be rolled back or committed immediately after being rolled back to a savepoint.
@@TRANCOUNT	Returns the number of active transactions for the connection. BEGIN TRANSACTION increments @@TRANCOUNT by 1, while ROLLBACK TRANSACTION resets @@TRANCOUNT to 0 while COMMIT TRANSACTION decrements @@TRANCOUNT by 1. ROLLBACK TRANSACTION to a savepoint has no impact.

12-1. Using Explicit Transactions

Problem

You are attempting to implement explicit transactions within your code and need to be able to commit the data changes only upon meeting certain criteria; otherwise, the data changes should not occur.

Solution

You can use explicit transactions to COMMIT or ROLLBACK a data modification depending on the return of an error in a batch of statements. See the following:

```
USE AdventureWorks2014;
GO
/* -- Before count */
SELECT BeforeCount = COUNT(*)
FROM HumanResources.Department;
/* -- Variable to hold the latest error integer value */
DECLARE @Error int;
BEGIN TRANSACTION
INSERT INTO HumanResources.Department (Name, GroupName)
    VALUES ('Accounts Payable', 'Accounting');
SET @Error = @@ERROR;
IF (@Error<> 0)
    GOTO Error_Handler;
```

```
INSERT INTO HumanResources.Department (Name, GroupName)
    VALUES ('Engineering', 'Research and Development');
SET @Error = @@ERROR;
IF (@Error <> 0)
    GOTO Error_Handler;
COMMIT TRANSACTION
Error_Handler:
IF @Error <> 0
BEGIN
ROLLBACK TRANSACTION;
END
/* -- After count */
SELECT AfterCount = COUNT(*)
FROM HumanResources.Department;
GO
```

This query returns the following:

```
BeforeCount 16
(1 row(s) affected)


(1 row(s) affected)
Msg 2601, Level 14, State 1, Line 14
Cannot insert duplicate key row in object 'HumanResources.Department'
with unique index 'AK_Department_Name'.
The duplicate key value is (Engineering).
The statement has been terminated.
AfterCount 16
(1 row(s) affected)
```

How It Works

The first statement in this example validated the count of rows in the HumanResources.Department table, returning 16 rows:

```
-- Before count
SELECT BeforeCount = COUNT(*)
FROM HumanResources.Department;
```

A local variable was created to hold the value of the @@ERROR function (which captures the latest error state of a SQL statement):

```
-- Variable to hold the latest error integer value
DECLARE @Error int
```

Next, an explicit transaction was started:

```
BEGIN TRANSACTION
```

The next statement attempted an INSERT into the HumanResources.Department table. There was a unique key on the department name, but because the department name didn't already exist in the table, the insert succeeded. See here:

```
INSERT INTO HumanResources.Department (Name, GroupName)
    VALUES ('Accounts Payable', 'Accounting');
```

Next was an error handler for the INSERT:

```
SET @Error = @@ERROR
IF (@Error <> 0) GOTO Error_Handler
```

This line of code evaluates the @@ERROR function. The @@ERROR system function returns the last error number value for the last-executed statement within the scope of the current connection. The IF statement says *if* an error occurs, the code should jump to the Error_Handler section of the code (using GOTO).

GOTO is a keyword that helps you control the flow of statement execution. The identifier after GOTO, Error_Handler, is a user-defined code section.

Next, another insert is attempted, this time for a department that already exists in the table. Because the table has a unique constraint on the Name column, this insert will fail:

```
INSERT INTO HumanResources.Department (Name, GroupName)
    VALUES ('Engineering', 'Research and Development');
```

The failure will cause the @@ERROR following this INSERT to be set to a nonzero value. The IF statement will then evaluate to TRUE, which will invoke the GOTO, thus skipping over the COMMIT TRAN to the Error_Handler section:

```
SET @Error = @@ERROR;
IF (@Error <> 0)
    GOTO Error_Handler;
COMMIT TRAN
```

Following the Error_Handler section is a ROLLBACK TRANSACTION.

```
Error_Handler:
IF @Error <> 0
BEGIN
ROLLBACK TRANSACTION;
END
```

Another count is performed after the rollback, and again, there are only 16 rows in the database. This is because both INSERTs were in the same transaction and one of the INSERTs failed. Since a transaction is all-or-nothing, no rows were inserted. See here:

```
/* -- After count */
SELECT AfterCount = COUNT(*)
FROM HumanResources.Department;
```

The following are some thoughts and recommendations regarding how to handle transactions in your Transact-SQL code or through your application:

- Keep transaction time as short as possible for the business process at hand. Transactions that remain open can hold locks on resources for an extended period of time, which can block other users from performing work or reading data.

- Minimize resources locked by the transaction. For example, update only tables that are related to the transaction at hand. If the data modifications are logically dependent on each other, they belong in the same transaction. If not, the unrelated updates belong in their own transactions.

- Add only *relevant* Transact-SQL statements to a transaction. Don't add extra lookups or updates that are not germane to the specific transaction. Executing a SELECT statement within a transaction can create locks on the referenced tables, which can in turn block other users or sessions from performing work or reading data.

- Do not open new transactions that require user or external feedback within the transaction. Open transactions can hold locks on resources, and user feedback can take an indefinite amount of time to receive. Instead, gather user feedback *before* issuing an explicit transaction.

12-2. Displaying the Oldest Active Transaction

Problem

Your transaction log is growing, and a backup of the log is not alleviating the issue. You fear an uncommitted transaction may be the cause of the transaction-log growth.

Solution

Use the DBCC OPENTRAN command to identify the oldest active transactions in a database. If a transaction remains open in the database, intentionally or not, this transaction can block other processes from performing activities against the modified data. Also, backups of the transaction log can only truncate the inactive portion of a transaction log, so open transactions can cause the log to grow (or reach the physical limit) until that transaction is committed or rolled back.

This example demonstrates using DBCC OPENTRAN to identify the oldest active transaction in the database:

```
USE AdventureWorks2014;
GO
BEGIN TRANSACTION
DELETE Production.ProductProductPhoto
WHERE ProductID = 317;

DBCC OPENTRAN('AdventureWorks2014');

ROLLBACK TRANSACTION;
GO
```

This query returns the following:

```
(1 row(s) affected)
Transaction information for database 'AdventureWorks2014'.

Oldest active transaction:
      SPID (server process ID): 54
      UID (user ID) : -1
      Name : user_transaction
      LSN :     (41:1021:39)
      Start time    : Dec 24 2014 12:45:53:780AM
      SID : 0x01050000000000000515000000a065cf7e784b9b5fe77c8770375a2900
DBCC execution completed. If DBCC printed error messages,
contact your system administrator.
```

How It Works

The recipe started by opening a new transaction and then deleting a specific row from the Production.
ProductProductPhoto table. Next, the DBCC OPENTRAN was executed, with the database name in parentheses:

```
DBCC OPENTRAN('AdventureWorks2014');
```

These results showed information regarding the oldest active transaction, including the server process ID, user ID, and start time of the transaction. The key pieces of information from the results are the server process ID (SPID) and start time.

Once you have this information, you can validate the Transact-SQL being executed using DMVs, figure out how long the process has been running, and, if necessary, shut down the process. DBCC OPENTRAN is useful for troubleshooting orphaned connections (connections still open in the database but disconnected from the application or client) and for identifying transactions missing a COMMIT or ROLLBACK statement.

This command also returns the oldest distributed and undistributed replicated transactions, if any exist within the database. If there are no active transactions, no session-level data will be returned.

12-3. Querying Transaction Information by Session

Problem

There is an active transaction that you want to investigate because of reported timeouts.

Solution

This recipe demonstrates how to find out more information about an active transaction by querying the sys.dm_tran_session_transactions DMV. To demonstrate, I'll describe a common scenario: Your application is encountering a significant number of blocks with a high duration. You've been told that this application always opens an explicit transaction prior to each query.

To illustrate this scenario, I'll execute the following SQL (representing the application code that is causing the concurrency issue):

```
SET TRANSACTION ISOLATION LEVEL SERIALIZABLE;
GO
USE AdventureWorks2014;
GO
BEGIN TRAN
SELECT *
FROM  HumanResources.Department
INSERT INTO HumanResources.Department (Name, GroupName)
    VALUES ('Test', 'QA');
```

In a new SQL Server Management Studio query window, I would like to identify all open transactions by querying the sys.dm_tran_session_transactions DMV:

```
SELECT session_id, transaction_id, is_user_transaction, is_local
FROM sys.dm_tran_session_transactions
WHERE is_user_transaction = 1;
GO
```

This results in the following (your actual session IDs and transaction IDs will vary):

session_id	transaction_id	is_user_transaction	is_local
51	145866	1	1

Now that I have a session ID to work with (again, the session_id you receive may be different), I can dig into the details about the most recent query executed by querying sys.dm_exec_connections and sys.dm_exec_sql_text:

```
SELECT s.text
FROM sys.dm_exec_connections c
CROSS APPLY sys.dm_exec_sql_text(c.most_recent_sql_handle) s
WHERE c.most_recent_session_id = 51;--use the session_id returned by the previous query
GO
```

This returns the last statement executed. (I could have also used the sys.dm_exec_requests DMV for an ongoing and active session; however, nothing was currently executing for my example transaction, so no data would have been returned.) See here:

```
text
-------------------------------------------------------------
BEGIN TRAN
SELECT *
FROM  HumanResources.Department
INSERT INTO HumanResources.Department (Name, GroupName)
      VALUES ('Test', 'QA');
```

Since I also have the transaction ID from the first query against `sys.dm_tran_session_transactions`, I can use `sys.dm_tran_active_transactions` to learn more about the transaction itself:

```
SELECT transaction_begin_time
,tran_type = CASE transaction_type
    WHEN 1 THEN 'Read/write transaction'
    WHEN 2 THEN 'Read-only transaction'
    WHEN 3 THEN 'System transaction'
    WHEN 4 THEN 'Distributed transaction'
    END
,tran_state = CASE transaction_state
    WHEN 0 THEN 'not been completely initialized yet'
    WHEN 1 THEN 'initialized but has not started'
    WHEN 2 THEN 'active'
    WHEN 3 THEN 'ended (read-only transaction)'
    WHEN 4 THEN 'commit initiated for distributed transaction'
    WHEN 5 THEN 'transaction prepared and waiting resolution'
    WHEN 6 THEN 'committed'
    WHEN 7 THEN 'being rolled back'
    WHEN 8 THEN 'been rolled back'
    END
FROM sys.dm_tran_active_transactions
WHERE transaction_id = 12969598; -- change this value to the transaction_id returned in the first
--query of this recipe
GO
```

This returns information about the transaction start time, the type of transaction, and the state of the transaction:

transaction_begin_time	tran_type	tran_state
2014-12-07 10:03:26.520	Read/write transaction	active

How It Works

This recipe demonstrated how to use various DMVs to troubleshoot and investigate a long-running, active transaction. The columns you decide to use depend on the issue you are trying to troubleshoot. In this scenario, I used the following troubleshooting path:

- I queried `sys.dm_tran_session_transactions` in order to display a mapping between the session ID and the transaction ID (identifier of the individual transaction).

- I queried `sys.dm_exec_connections` and `sys.dm_exec_sql_text` in order to find the latest command executed by the session (referencing the `most_recent_sql_handle` column).

- Lastly, I queried `sys.dm_tran_active_transactions` in order to determine how long the transaction was open, the type of transaction, and the state of the transaction.

Using this troubleshooting technique allows you to go back to the application and pinpoint query calls for abandoned transactions (opened but never committed) and transactions that are inappropriate because they run too long or are unnecessary from the perspective of the application. Before proceeding, you should revisit the first query window and issue the following command to ensure the transaction is no longer running:

```
ROLLBACK TRANSACTION;
```

Locking

Locking is a normal and necessary part of a relational database system, ensuring the integrity of the data by not allowing concurrent updates to the same data or the viewing of data that is in the middle of being updated. SQL Server manages locking dynamically; however, it is still important to understand how Transact-SQL queries impact locking in SQL Server. Before proceeding to the recipes, I'll briefly describe SQL Server locking fundamentals.

Locks help prevent concurrency problems from occurring. Concurrency problems (discussed in detail in the next section, "Transaction, Locking, and Concurrency") can happen when one user attempts to read data that another is modifying, to modify data that another is reading, or to modify data that another transaction is trying to modify.

Locks are placed against SQL Server resources. How a resource is locked is called its *lock mode*. Table 12-2 reviews the main lock modes that SQL Server has at its disposal.

Table 12-2. *SQL Server Lock Modes*

Name	Description
Shared lock	Shared locks are issued during read-only, nonmodifying queries. They allow data to be read but not updated by other processes while being held.
Intent lock	Intent locks effectively create a lock queue, designating the order of connections and their associated right to update or read resources. SQL Server uses intent locks to show future intention of acquiring locks on a specific resource.
Update lock	Update locks are acquired prior to modifying the data. When the row is modified, this lock is escalated to an exclusive lock. If not modified, it is downgraded to a shared lock. This lock type prevents deadlocks (discussed later in this chapter) if two connections hold a shared lock on a resource and attempt to convert to an exclusive lock but cannot because they are each waiting for the other transaction to release the shared lock.
Exclusive lock	This type of lock issues a lock on the resource that bars any kind of access (reads or writes). It is issued during INSERT, UPDATE, and DELETE statements.
Schema modification	This type of lock is issued when a DDL statement is executed.
Schema stability	This type of lock is issued when a query is being compiled. It keeps DDL operations from being performed on the table.
Bulk update	This type of lock is issued during a bulk-copy operation. Performance is increased for the bulk copy operation, but table concurrency is reduced.
Key-range	Key-range locks protect a range of rows (based on the index key)—for example, protecting rows in an UPDATE statement with a range of dates from 1/1/2014 to 12/31/2014. Protecting the range of data prevents row inserts into the date range that would be missed by the current data modification.

You can lock all manner of resources in SQL Server, from a single row in a database to a table to the database itself. Lockable resources vary in granularity, from small (at the row level) to large (the entire database). Small-grain locks allow for greater database concurrency, because users can execute queries against specified unlocked rows. Each lock placed by SQL Server requires memory, however, so thousands of individual row locks can also affect SQL Server performance. Larger-grained locks reduce concurrency but take up fewer resources. Table 12-3 details the resources SQL Server can apply locks to.

Table 12-3. *SQL Server Lock Resources*

Resource Name	Description
Allocation unit	A set of related pages grouped by data type; for example, data rows, index rows, and large object data rows
Application	An application-specified resource
Database	An entire database lock
Extent	Allocation unit of eight contiguous 8 KB data or index pages
File	The database file
HOBT	A heap (table without a clustered index) or B-tree
Metadata	System metadata
Key	Index-row lock, helping prevent phantom reads. Also called a *key-range lock*, this lock type uses both a range and a row component. The range represents the range of index keys between two consecutive index keys. The row component represents the lock type on the index entry
Object	A database object; for example, a table, view, stored procedure, or function
Page	An 8 KB data or index page
RID	Row identifier, designating a single table row
Table	A resource that locks entire table, data, and indexes

Not all lock types are compatible with each other. For example, no other locks can be placed on a resource that has already been locked by an exclusive lock. The other transaction must wait, or time out, until the exclusive lock is released. A resource locked by an update lock can have a shared lock placed on it only by another transaction. A resource locked by a shared lock can have other shared or update locks placed on it.

Locks are allocated and escalated automatically by SQL Server. Escalation means that finer-grain locks (row or page locks) are converted into coarse-grain table locks. SQL Server will attempt to initialize escalation when a single Transact-SQL statement has more than 5,000 locks on a single table or index or if the number of locks on the SQL Server instance exceeds the available memory threshold. Locks take up system memory, so converting many locks into one larger lock can free up memory resources. The drawback to freeing up the memory resources, however, is reduced concurrency.

■ **Note**   SQL Server has a table option that allows you to disable lock escalation or enable lock escalation at the partition (instead of table) scope. I'll demonstrate this in Recipe 12-5.

12-4. Viewing Lock Activity

Problem

You want to check the current locking activity in SQL Server.

Solution

This recipe shows you how to monitor locking activity in the database using the SQL Server `sys.dm_tran_locks` DMV. The example query being monitored by this DMV will use a table locking hint.

In the first part of this recipe, a new query editor window is opened, and the following command is executed:

```
USE AdventureWorks2014;
BEGIN TRAN
SELECT ProductID, ModifiedDate
FROM Production.ProductDocument WITH (TABLOCKX);
```

In a second query editor window, the following query is executed:

```
SELECT sessionid = request_session_id ,
ResType = resource_type ,
ResDBID = resource_database_id ,
ObjectName = OBJECT_NAME(resource_associated_entity_id, resource_database_id) ,
RMode = request_mode ,
RStatus = request_status
FROM sys.dm_tran_locks
WHERE resource_type IN ('DATABASE', 'OBJECT');
GO
```

■ **Tip**   This recipe narrows down the result set to two SQL Server resource types of DATABASE and OBJECT for clarity. Typically, you'll monitor several types of resources. The resource type determines the meaning of the `resource_associated_entity_id` column, as I'll explain in the "How It Works" section of this recipe.

The query returned information about the locking session identifier (server process ID, or SPID), the resource being locked, the database, the object, the resource mode, and the lock status:

sessionid	ResType	ResDBID	ObjectName	RMode	RStatus
53	DATABASE	8	NULL	S	GRANT
52	DATABASE	8	NULL	S	GRANT
52	OBJECT	8	ProductDocument	X	GRANT

How It Works

The example began by starting a new transaction and executing a query against the Production. ProductDocument table using a TABLOCKX locking hint (this hint places an exclusive lock on the table). To monitor which locks were open for the current SQL Server instance, the sys.dm_tran_locks DMV was queried. It returned a list of active locks found in the AdventureWorks2014 database. The exclusive lock on the ProductDocument table could be seen in the last row of the results.

The first three columns define the session lock, resource type, and database ID:

```
SELECT sessionid = request_session_id ,
ResType = resource_type ,
ResDBID = resource_database_id ,
```

The next column uses the OBJECT_NAME function. Notice that it uses two parameters (object ID and database ID) in order to specify which name to access:

```
ObjectName = OBJECT_NAME(resource_associated_entity_id, resource_database_id) ,
```

I also query the locking request mode and status:

```
RMode = request_mode ,
RStatus = request_status
```

Lastly, the FROM clause references the DMV, and the WHERE clause designates two resource types:

```
FROM sys.dm_tran_locks
WHERE resource_type IN ('DATABASE', 'OBJECT');
```

The resource_type column designates what the locked resource represents (for example, DATABASE, OBJECT, FILE, PAGE, KEY, RID, EXTENT, METADATA, APPLICATION, ALLOCATION_UNIT, or HOBT type). The resource_associated_entity_id depends on the resource type, determining whether the ID is an object ID, allocation unit ID, or HOBT ID:

- If the resource_associated_entity_id column contains an object ID (for a resource type of OBJECT)), you can translate the name using the sys.objects catalog view.

- If the resource_associated_entity_id column contains an allocation unit ID (for a resource type of ALLOCATION_UNIT), you can reference sys.allocation_units and reference the container_id. Container_id can then be joined to sys.partitions where you can then determine the object ID.

- If the resource_associated_entity_id column contains a HOBT ID (for a resource type of KEY, PAGE, ROW, or HOBT), you can directly reference sys.partitions and look up the associated object ID.

- For resource types such as DATABASE, EXTENT, APPLICATION, or METADATA, the resource_associated_entity_id column will be 0.

Use sys.dm_tran_locks to troubleshoot unexpected concurrency issues, such as a query session that may be holding locks longer than desired or be issuing a lock resource granularity or lock mode that you hadn't expected (perhaps a table lock instead of a finer-grained row or page lock). Understanding what is happening at the locking level can help you troubleshoot query concurrency more effectively.

12-5. Controlling a Table's Lock-Escalation Behavior

Problem

You want to alter how SQL Server behaves with regard to lock escalation.

Solution

Each lock that is created in SQL Server consumes memory resources. When the number of locks increases, memory decreases. If the percentage of memory being used for locks exceeds a certain threshold, SQL Server can convert fine-grained locks (page or row) into coarse-grained locks (table locks). This process is called *lock escalation*. Lock escalation reduces the overall number of locks being held on the SQL Server instance, thus reducing lock memory usage.

While finer-grained locks do consume more memory, they also can improve concurrency, because multiple queries can access unlocked rows. Introducing table locks may reduce memory consumption, but can also introduce blocking, because a single query holds an entire table. Depending on the application using the database, this behavior may not be desired, and you may want to exert more control over when SQL Server performs lock escalations.

SQL Server has the ability to control lock escalation at the table level using the ALTER TABLE command. You are now able to choose from the following three settings:

- TABLE, which is the default behavior used in SQL Server. When configured, lock escalation is enabled at the table level for both partitioned and nonpartitioned tables.

- AUTO enables lock escalation at the partition level (heap or B-tree) if the table is partitioned. If it is not partitioned, escalation will occur at the table level.

- DISABLE removes lock escalation at the table level. Note that you still may see table locks because of TABLOCK hints or for queries against heaps using a serializable isolation level.

This recipe demonstrates how to modify a table so as to use the AUTO and DISABLE settings:

```
USE AdventureWorks2014;
GO
ALTER TABLE Person.Address
    SET ( LOCK_ESCALATION = AUTO );

SELECT lock_escalation,lock_escalation_desc
FROM sys.tables WHERE name='Address';
GO
```

This query returns the following:

lock_escalation	lock_escalation_desc
2	AUTO

Next, I'll disable escalation:

```
USE AdventureWorks2014;
GO
ALTER TABLE Person.Address
SET ( LOCK_ESCALATION = DISABLE);

SELECT lock_escalation,lock_escalation_desc
FROM sys.tables WHERE name='Address';
GO
```

This query returns the following:

lock_escalation	lock_escalation_desc
1	DISABLE

How It Works

This recipe demonstrated enabling two SQL Server table options that control locking escalation. The command began with a standard ALTER TABLE statement designating the table name to modify:

```
ALTER TABLE Person.Address
```

The second line designated the SET command along with the LOCK_ESCALATION configuration to be used:

```
SET ( LOCK_ESCALATION = AUTO )
```

After changing the configuration, I was able to validate the option by querying the lock_escalation_ desc column from the sys.tables catalog view:

Once the AUTO option is enabled, if the table is partitioned, lock escalation will occur at the partitioned level, which improves concurrency if there are multiple sessions acting against separate partitions.

■ **Note**   For further information on partitioning, see Chapter 16.

If the table is not partitioned, table-level escalation will occur as usual. If you designate the DISABLE option, table-level lock escalation will not occur. This can help improve concurrency but could result in increased memory consumption if your requests are accessing a large number of rows or pages.

Transaction, Locking, and Concurrency

One of the ACID properties is *Isolation*. Transaction isolation refers to the extent to which changes made by one transaction can be seen by other transactions occurring in the database (in other words, under conditions of concurrent database access). At the highest possible degree of isolation, each transaction occurs as if it were the only transaction taking place at that time. No changes made by other transactions are visible to it. At the lowest level, anything done in one transaction, whether committed or not, is visible by another transaction.

The ANSI/ISO SQL standard defines four types of interactions between concurrent transactions.

- *Dirty reads*: These occur while a transaction is updating a row, and a second transaction reads the row before the first transaction is committed. If the original update rolls back, the uncommitted changes will be read by the second transaction, even though they are never committed to the database. This is the definition of a dirty read.

- *Nonrepeatable reads*: These occur when one transaction is updating data and a second is reading the same data while the update is in progress. The data retrieved before the update will not match the data retrieved after the update.

- *Phantom reads*: These occur when a transaction issues two reads, and between the two reads, the underlying data is updated with data being inserted or deleted. This causes the results of each query to differ. Rows returned in one query that do not appear in the other are called *phantom rows*.

- *Lost updates*: This occurs when two transactions update a row's value and the transaction to last update the row "wins." Thus, the first update is lost.

SQL Server uses locking mechanisms to control the competing activity of simultaneous transactions. To avoid concurrency issues such as dirty reads, nonrepeatable reads, and so on, it implements locking to control access to database resources and to impose a certain level of transaction isolation. Table 12-4 describes the available isolation levels in SQL Server.

Table 12-4. *SQL Server Isolation Levels*

ISOLATION LEVEL	DESCRIPTION
READ COMMITTED (this is the default behavior of SQL Server)	While READ COMMITTED is used, uncommitted data modifications can't be read. Shared locks are used during a query, and data cannot be modified by other processes while the query is retrieving the data. Data inserts and modifications to the same table are allowed by other transactions, so long as the rows involved are not locked by the first transaction.
READ UNCOMMITTED	This is the least restrictive isolation level, issuing no locks on the data selected by the transaction. This provides the highest concurrency but the lowest amount of data integrity, because the data you read can be changed while you read it (as mentioned previously, these reads are known as *dirty reads*), or new data can be added or removed that would change your original query results. This option allows you to read data without blocking others, but with the danger of reading data "in flux" that could be modified during the read itself (including reading data changes from a transaction that ends up getting rolled back). For relatively static and unchanging data, this isolation level can potentially improve performance by instructing SQL Server not to issue unnecessary locking on the accessed resources.

(continued)

Table 12-4. (*continued*)

ISOLATION LEVEL	DESCRIPTION
REPEATABLE READ	When enabled, dirty and nonrepeatable reads are not allowed. This is achieved by placing shared locks on all read resources. New rows that may fall into the range of data returned by your query can, however, still be inserted by other transactions.
SERIALIZABLE	When enabled, this is the most restrictive setting. Range locks are placed on the data based on the search criteria used to produce the result set. This ensures that actions such as the insertion of new rows, the modification of values, or the deletion of existing rows that would have been returned within the original query and search criteria are not allowed.
SNAPSHOT	This isolation level allows you to read a transactionally consistent version of the data as it existed at the *beginning* of a transaction. Data reads do not block data modifications. However, the SNAPSHOT session will not detect changes being made.

Transactions and locking go hand in hand. Depending on your application design, your transactions can significantly impact database concurrency and performance. Concurrency refers to how many people can query and modify the database and database objects at the same time. For example, the READ UNCOMMITTED isolation level allows the greatest amount of concurrency, since it issues no locks—with the drawback that you can encounter a host of data-isolation anomalies (dirty reads, for example). The SERIALIZABLE mode, however, offers very little concurrency with other processes when querying a larger range of data.

12-6. Configuring a Session's Transaction-Locking Behavior

Problem

You want to change the default transaction-locking behavior for Transact-SQL statements used in a connection.

Solution

Use the SET TRANSACTION ISOLATION LEVEL command to set the default transaction-locking behavior for Transact-SQL statements used in a connection. You can have only one isolation level set at a time, and the isolation level does not change unless explicitly set. SET TRANSACTION ISOLATION LEVEL allows you to change the locking behavior for a specific database connection. The syntax for this command is as follows:

```
SET TRANSACTION ISOLATION LEVEL { READ UNCOMMITTED | READ COMMITTED
REPEATABLE READ
SNAPSHOT | SERIALIZABLE }
```

In this first example, SERIALIZABLE isolation is used to query the contents of a table. In the first query editor window, the following code is executed:

```
USE AdventureWorks2014;
GO
SET TRANSACTION ISOLATION LEVEL SERIALIZABLE;
GO
BEGIN TRANSACTION

SELECT  AddressTypeID, Name
FROM Person.AddressType
WHERE AddressTypeID BETWEEN 1 AND 6;
GO
```

This query returns the following results (while still leaving a transaction open for the query session):

AddressTypeID	Name
1	Billing
2	Home
3	Main Office
4	Primary
5	Shipping
6	Archive

In a second query editor, the following query is executed to view the kinds of locks generated by the SERIALIZABLE isolation level:

```
SELECT resource_associated_entity_id, resource_type,
request_mode, request_session_id
FROM sys.dm_tran_locks;
GO
```

This shows several key locks being held for request_session_id 52 (which is the other session's ID):

resource_associated_entity_id	resource_type	request_mode	request_session_id
0	DATABASE	S	52
0	DATABASE	S	53
72057594043039744	PAGE	IS	52
101575400	OBJECT	IS	52
72057594043039744	KEY	RangeS-S	52
72057594043039744	KEY	RangeS-S	52
72057594043039744	KEY	RangeS-S	52
72057594043039744	KEY	RangeS-S	52
72057594043039744	KEY	RangeS-S	52
72057594043039744	KEY	RangeS-S	52
72057594043039744	KEY	RangeS-S	52

Back in the first query editor window, execute the following code to end the transaction and remove the locks:

```
COMMIT TRANSACTION;
```

In contrast, the same query is executed again in the first query editor window, this time using the READ UNCOMMITTED isolation level to read the range of rows:

```
USE AdventureWorks2014;
GO
SET TRANSACTION ISOLATION LEVEL READ UNCOMMITTED;
GO
BEGIN TRANSACTION

SELECT  AddressTypeID, Name
FROM Person.AddressType
WHERE AddressTypeID BETWEEN 1 AND 6;
GO
```

In a second query editor, the following query is executed to view the kinds of locks generated by the READ UNCOMMITTED isolation level:

```
SELECT resource_associated_entity_id, resource_type,
request_mode, request_session_id
FROM sys.dm_tran_locks;
GO
```

This returns the following (abridged) results:

resource_associated_entity_id	resource_type	request_mode	request_session_id
0	DATABASE	S	52
0	DATABASE	S	53

Unlike SERIALIZABLE, the READ UNCOMMITTED isolation level creates no additional locks on the keys of the Person.AddressType table.

Returning to the first query editor with the READ UNCOMMITTED query, the transaction is ended for cleanup purposes:

```
COMMIT TRANSACTION;
```

I'll demonstrate the SNAPSHOT isolation level next. In the first query editor window, the following code is executed:

```
ALTER DATABASE AdventureWorks2014
SET ALLOW_SNAPSHOT_ISOLATION ON;
GO
USE AdventureWorks2014;
GO
SET TRANSACTION ISOLATION LEVEL SNAPSHOT;
GO
```

```
BEGIN TRANSACTION
SELECT  CurrencyRateID,EndOfDayRate
FROM Sales.CurrencyRate
WHERE CurrencyRateID = 8317;
```

This query returns the following:

CurrencyRateID	EndOfDayRate
8317	0.6862

In a second query editor window, the following query is executed:

```
USE AdventureWorks2014;
GO
UPDATE Sales.CurrencyRate
SET EndOfDayRate = 1.00
WHERE CurrencyRateID = 8317;
GO
```

Now back to the first query editor; the following query is executed once more:

```
SELECT  CurrencyRateID,EndOfDayRate
FROM Sales.CurrencyRate
WHERE CurrencyRateID = 8317;
GO
```

This query returns the following:

CurrencyRateID	EndOfDayRate
8317	0.6862

The same results are returned as before, even though the row was updated by the second query editor query. The SELECT was not blocked from reading the row, nor was the UPDATE blocked from making the modification.

Now, return to the first query window to commit the transaction and reissue the query:

```
COMMIT TRANSACTION;
SELECT  CurrencyRateID,EndOfDayRate
FROM Sales.CurrencyRate
WHERE CurrencyRateID = 8317;
GO
```

This returns the updated value:

CurrencyRateID	EndOfDayRate
8317	1.00

How It Works

In this recipe, I demonstrated how to change the locking isolation level of a query session by using SET TRANSACTION ISOLATION LEVEL. Executing this command isn't necessary if you want to use the default SQL Server isolation level, which is READ COMMITTED. Otherwise, once you set an isolation level, it remains in effect for the connection until explicitly changed again.

The first example in the recipe demonstrated using the SERIALIZABLE isolation level:

```
SET TRANSACTION ISOLATION LEVEL SERIALIZABLE;
GO
```

An explicit transaction was then started, and a query was executed against the Person.AddressType table for all rows that fell within a specific range of AddressTypeID values:

```
BEGIN TRANSACTION
SELECT  AddressTypeID, Name
FROM Person.AddressType
WHERE AddressTypeID BETWEEN 1 AND 6;
```

In a separate connection, a query was then executed against the sys.dm_tran_locks DMV, which returned information about active locks being held for the SQL Server instance. In this case, we saw a number of key range locks, which served the purpose of prohibiting other connections from inserting, updating, or deleting data that would cause different results in the query's search condition (WHERE AddressTypeID BETWEEN 1 AND 6).

In the second example, the isolation level was set to READ UNCOMMITTED:

```
SET TRANSACTION ISOLATION LEVEL READ UNCOMMITTED;
GO
```

Querying sys.dm_tran_locks again, we saw that this time no row, key, or page locks were held at all on the table, allowing other transactions to potentially modify the queried rows while the original transaction remained open. With this isolation level, the query performs dirty reads, meaning that the query could read data with in-progress modifications, whether or not the actual modification is committed or rolled back later.

In the third example from the recipe, the database setting ALLOW_SNAPSHOT_ISOLATION was enabled for the database:

```
ALTER DATABASE AdventureWorks2014
SET ALLOW_SNAPSHOT_ISOLATION ON;
GO
```

This option had to be ON in order to start a SNAPSHOT transaction. In the next line of code, the database context was changed, and SET TRANSACTION ISOLATION LEVEL was set to SNAPSHOT:

```
USE AdventureWorks2014;
GO
SET TRANSACTION ISOLATION LEVEL SNAPSHOT;
GO
```

A transaction was then opened, and a query against Sales.CurrencyRate was performed:

```
BEGIN TRANSACTION
SELECT  CurrencyRateID,EndOfDayRate
FROM Sales.CurrencyRate
WHERE CurrencyRateID = 8317;
```

In the second query editor session, the same Sales.CurrencyRate row being selected in the first session query was modified:

```
USE AdventureWorks2014;
GO
UPDATE Sales.CurrencyRate
SET EndOfDayRate = 1.00
WHERE CurrencyRateID = 8317;
GO
```

Back at the first query editor session, although the EndOfDayRate was changed to 1.0 in the second session, executing the query again in the SNAPSHOT isolation level showed that the value of that column was still 0.6862. This new isolation level provided a consistent view of the data as of the beginning of the transaction. After committing the transaction, reissuing the query against Sales.CurrencyRate revealed the latest value.

What if you decide to UPDATE a row in the SNAPSHOT session that was updated in a separate session? Had the SNAPSHOT session attempted an UPDATE against CurrencyRateID 8317 instead of a SELECT, an error would have been raised, warning you that an update was made against the original row while in SNAPSHOT isolation mode.

```
Msg 3960, Level 16, State 1, Line 2
Cannot use snapshot isolation to access table 'Sales.CurrencyRate'
directly or indirectly in database 'AdventureWorks2014'.
Snapshot transaction aborted due to update conflict.
Retry transaction.
```

Blocking

Blocking occurs when one transaction in a database session is locking resources that one or more other session transactions want to read or modify. Short-term blocking is usually okay and is expected for busy applications. However, poorly designed applications can cause long-term blocking, unnecessarily keeping locks on resources and blocking other sessions from reading or updating them.

In SQL Server, a blocked process remains blocked indefinitely or until it times out (based on SET LOCK_TIMEOUT), the server goes down, the process is killed, the connection finishes its updates, or something happens to the original transaction to cause it to release its locks on the resource.

Here are some reasons why long-term blocking can happen:

- Excessive row locks on a table without an index can cause SQL Server to acquire a table lock, blocking out other transactions.

- Applications open a transaction and then request user feedback or interaction while the transaction stays open. This is usually when an end user is allowed to enter data in a GUI while a transaction remains open. While open, any resources referenced by the transaction may be held with locks.

- Transactions BEGIN and then look up data that could have been referenced prior to the transaction starting.

- Queries use locking hints inappropriately; for example, if the application needs only a few rows but uses a table-lock hint instead.

- The application uses long-running transactions that update many rows or many tables within one transaction (chunking large updates into smaller update transactions can help improve concurrency).

12-7. Identifying and Resolving Blocking Issues

Problem

You need to identify any blocking processes, and associated TSQL being executed, within your database.

Solution

In this recipe, I'll demonstrate how to identify a blocking process, view the Transact-SQL being executed by the process, and then forcibly shut down the active session's connection (thus rolling back any open work not yet committed by the blocking session). First, however, let's look at a quick background of the commands used in this example.

This recipe demonstrates how to identify blocking processes with the SQL Server DMV sys.dm_os_waiting_tasks. This view is intended to be used in lieu of the sp_who2 system-stored procedure, which was used in previous versions of SQL Server.

After identifying the blocking process, this recipe will then use the sys.dm_exec_sql_text dynamic management function and sys.dm_exec_connections DMV used earlier in the chapter to identify the SQL text of the query that is being executed—and then, as a last resort, forcefully end the process.

To forcefully shut down a wayward active query session, the KILL command is used. KILL should be used only if other methods are not available, including waiting for the process to stop on its own or shutting down or canceling the operation via the calling application. The syntax for KILL is as follows:

```
KILL {SPID | UOW} [WITH STATUSONLY]
```

Table 12-5 describes the arguments for this command.

Table 12-5. *KILL Command Arguments*

Argument	Description
SPID	This indicates the session ID associated with the active database connection to be shut down.
UOW	This is the unit-of-work identifier for a distributed transaction, which is the unique identifier of a specific distributed transaction process.
WITH STATUSONLY	Some KILL statements take longer to roll back a transaction than others (depending on the scope of updates being performed by the session). To check the status of a rollback, you can use WITH STATUSONLY to get an estimate of rollback time.

Beginning the example, the following query is executed in the first query editor session in order to set up a blocking process:

```
USE AdventureWorks2014;
GO
BEGIN TRAN
UPDATE Production.ProductInventory
SET Quantity = 400
WHERE ProductID = 1 AND LocationID = 1;
```

Next, in a second query editor window, the following query is executed:

```
USE AdventureWorks2014;
GO
BEGIN TRAN
UPDATE Production.ProductInventory
SET Quantity = 406
WHERE ProductID = 1 AND LocationID = 1;
```

Now, in a third query editor window, this next query is executed:

```
SELECT blocking_session_id, wait_duration_ms, session_id
FROM sys.dm_os_waiting_tasks
WHERE blocking_session_id IS NOT NULL;
GO
```

This query returns the following (your results will vary):

blocking_session_id	wait_duration_ms	session_id
53	27371	52

This query identified that session 53 is blocking session 52.

To see what session 53 is doing, execute the following query in the same window as the previous query:

```
SELECT t.text
FROM sys.dm_exec_connections c
CROSS APPLY sys.dm_exec_sql_text (c.most_recent_sql_handle) t
WHERE c.session_id = 53; --use the blocking_session_id from the previous query
GO
```

This query returns the following:

```
text
BEGIN TRAN
UPDATE Production.ProductInventory
SET Quantity = 400
WHERE ProductID = 1 AND LocationID = 1;
```

Next, to forcibly shut down the session, execute this query:

```
KILL 53;
```

This results in the following:

```
Command(s) completed successfully.
```

The second session's UPDATE is then allowed to proceed once the first session's connection is removed.

How It Works

The recipe demonstrated blocking by executing an UPDATE against the Production.ProductInventory table that had a transaction that had been opened but *not* committed. In a different session, a similar query was executed against the same table and the same row. Because the other connection's transaction never committed, the second connection must wait in line indefinitely before it has a chance to update the record.

In a third query editor window, the sys.dm_os_waiting_tasks DMV was queried, returning information on the session being blocked by another session.

When troubleshooting blocks, you'll want to see exactly what the blocking session_id is doing. To view this, the recipe used a query against sys.dm_exec_connections and sys.dm_exec_sql_text. The sys.dm_exec_connections DMV was used to retrieve the most_recent_sql_handle column for session_id 53. This is a pointer to the SQL text in memory and was used as an input parameter for the sys.dm_exec_sql_text dynamic management function. The text column is returned from sys.dm_exec_sql_text, displaying the SQL text of the blocking process.

■ **Note** Often blocks *chain*, and you must work your way through each blocked process up to the original blocking process using the blocking_session_id and session_id columns.

KILL was then used to forcibly end the blocking process, but in a production scenario, you'll want to see whether the process is valid and, if so, whether it should be allowed to complete or whether it can be shut down or cancelled using the application (by the application end user, for example). Prior to stopping the process, be sure you are not stopping a long-running transaction that is critical to the business, like a payroll update, for example. If there is no way to stop the transaction (for example, the application that spawned it cannot commit the transaction), you can use the KILL command (followed by the SPID to terminate).

12-8. Configuring How Long a Statement Will Wait for a Lock to Be Released

Problem

You need to extend how long a transaction can wait if it is blocked by another transaction.

Solution

When a transaction or statement is being blocked, it is waiting for a lock on a resource to be released. This recipe demonstrates the SET LOCK_TIMEOUT option, which specifies how long the blocked statement should wait for a lock to be released before returning an error.

The syntax is as follows:

```
SET LOCK_TIMEOUT timeout_period
```

The timeout period is the number of milliseconds before a locking error will be returned. To set up this recipe's demonstration, I will execute the following batch:

```
USE AdventureWorks2014;
GO
BEGIN TRAN
UPDATE Production.ProductInventory
SET Quantity = 400
WHERE ProductID = 1 AND LocationID = 1;
```

In a second query window, I will execute the following code, which demonstrates setting up a lock timeout period of one second (1,000 milliseconds):

```
USE AdventureWorks2014;
GO
SET LOCK_TIMEOUT 1000;
UPDATE Production.ProductInventory
SET Quantity = 406
WHERE ProductID = 1 AND LocationID = 1;
```

After one second (1,000 milliseconds), I will receive the following error message:

```
Msg 1222, Level 16, State 51, Line 4
Lock request time out period exceeded.
The statement has been terminated.
```

How It Works

In this recipe, the lock timeout is set to 1000 milliseconds (1 second). This setting doesn't impact how long a resource can be *held* by a process, only how long it has to wait for another process to release access to the resource. Before proceeding, you should revisit the first query window and issue the following command to ensure the transaction is no longer running:

```
ROLLBACK TRANSACTION;
```

Deadlocking

Deadlocking occurs when one user session (let's call it Session 1) has locks on a resource that another user session (let's call it Session 2) wants to modify, and Session 2 has locks on resources that Session 1 needs to modify. Neither Session 1 nor Session 2 can continue until the other releases its respective locks, so SQL Server chooses one of the sessions in the deadlock as the *deadlock victim*.

■ **Note** A deadlock victim has its session killed, and its transactions are rolled back.

Here are some reasons why deadlocks can happen:

- The application accesses tables in a different order in each session. For example, Session 1 updates Customers and then Orders, whereas Session 2 updates Orders and then Customers. This increases the chance of two processes deadlocking, rather than accessing and updating a table in a serialized (in order) fashion.

- The application uses long-running transactions, updating many rows or many tables within one transaction. This increases the surface area of rows that can cause deadlock conflicts.

- In some situations, SQL Server issues several row locks, which it later decides must be escalated to a table lock. If these rows exist on the same data pages, and two sessions are both trying to escalate the lock granularity on the same page, a deadlock can occur.

12-9. Identifying Deadlocks with a Trace Flag

Problem

You are experiencing a high volume of deadlocks within your database. You need to find out what is causing the deadlocks.

Solution

If you are having deadlock trouble in your SQL Server instance, you can use this recipe to make sure deadlocks are logged to the SQL Server log appropriately using the DBCC TRACEON, DBCC TRACEOFF, and DBCC TRACESTATUS commands. These functions enable, disable, and check the status of trace flags.

■ **Tip** There are other methods in SQL Server for troubleshooting deadlocks, such as using SQL Profiler, but since this book is Transact-SQL focused, I will be focusing on Transact-SQL based options.

Trace flags are used within SQL Server to enable or disable specific behaviors for the SQL Server instance. By default, SQL Server doesn't return significant logging when a deadlock event occurs. Using trace flag 1222, information about locked resources and types participating in a deadlock are returned in an XML format, helping you troubleshoot the event.

The DBCC TRACEON command enables trace flags. The syntax is as follows:

```
DBCC TRACEON ( trace# [ ,...n ][ ,-1 ] ) [ WITH NO_INFOMSGS ]
```

Table 12-6 describes the arguments for this command.

Table 12-6. *DBCC TRACEON Command Arguments*

Argument	Description
trace#	This specifies one or more trace flag numbers to enable.
-1	When -1 is designated, the specified trace flags are enabled globally.
WITH NO_INFOMSGS	When included in the command, WITH NO_INFOMSGS suppresses informational messages from the DBCC output.

The DBCC TRACESTATUS command is used to check on the status (enabled or disabled) for a specific flag or flags. The syntax is as follows:

```
DBCC TRACESTATUS ( [ [ trace# [ ,...n ] ][ , ][ -1 ] ] ) [ WITH NO_INFOMSGS ]
```

Table 12-7 describes the arguments for this command.

Table 12-7. *DBCC TRACESTATUS Command Arguments*

Argument	Description
trace# [,...n]]	This specifies one or more trace flag numbers to check the status of.
-1	This shows globally enabled flags.
WITH NO_INFOMSGS	When included in the command, WITH NO_INFOMSGS suppresses informational messages from the DBCC output.

The DBCC TRACEOFF command disables trace flags. The syntax is as follows:

```
DBCC TRACEOFF ( trace# [ ,.. .n ] [ , -1 ] ) [ WITH NO_INFOMSGS ]
```

Table 12-8 describes the arguments for this command.

Table 12-8. *DBCC TRACEOFF Command Arguments*

Argument	Description
trace#	This indicates one or more trace flag numbers to disable.
-1	This disables the globally set flags.
WITH NO_INFOMSGS	When included in the command, WITH NO_INFOMSGS suppresses informational messages from the DBCC output.

To demonstrate this recipe, a deadlock will be simulated. In a new query editor window, the following query is executed:

```
USE AdventureWorks2014;
GO
SET NOCOUNT ON;
WHILE 1=1
BEGIN
BEGIN TRANSACTION
UPDATE Purchasing.Vendor
SET CreditRating = 1
WHERE BusinessEntityID = 1494;
UPDATE Purchasing.Vendor
SET CreditRating = 2
WHERE BusinessEntityID = 1492;
COMMIT TRANSACTION
END
```

In a second query editor window, the following query is executed:

```
USE AdventureWorks2014;
GO
SET NOCOUNT ON;
WHILE 1=1
BEGIN
BEGIN TRANSACTION
UPDATE Purchasing.Vendor
SET CreditRating = 2
WHERE BusinessEntityID = 1492;
UPDATE Purchasing.Vendor
SET CreditRating = 1
WHERE BusinessEntityID = 1494;
COMMIT TRANSACTION
END
```

After a few seconds, check each query editor window until the following error message appears on one of the query editors:

```
Msg 1205, Level 13, State 51, Line 9
Transaction (Process ID 52) was deadlocked on lock resources with another process and has
been chosen as the deadlock victim. Rerun the transaction.
```

Looking at the SQL log found in SQL Server Management Studio, the deadlock event was not logged. I'll now open a third query editor window and execute the following command:

```
DBCC TRACEON (1222, -1)
GO
DBCC TRACESTATUS
```

DBCC TRACESTATUS shows the active traces running for both the local session and globally:

```
TraceFlag      Status Global  Session
1222           110    1       1
```

To simulate another deadlock, I'll restart the "winning" connection query (the one that wasn't killed in the deadlock), and then the deadlock "losing" session, causing another deadlock after a few seconds.

After the deadlock has occurred, I will stop the other executing query. Now the SQL log in SQL Server Management Studio contains a detailed error message from the deadlock event, including the database and object involved, the lock mode, and the Transact-SQL statements involved in the deadlock.

When deadlocks occur, you'll want to find out the queries that are involved so you can troubleshoot them accordingly. The following excerpt from the log shows a deadlocked query:

```
05/08/2012 20:20:00,spid16s,Unknown,
UPDATE [Purchasing].[Vendor] set [CreditRating] = @1
WHERE [BusinessEntityID]=@2
```

From this we can tell which query was involved in the deadlocking, which is often enough to get started with a solution. Other important information you can retrieve by using trace 1222 includes the login name of the deadlocked process, the client application used to submit the query, and the isolation level used for its connection (letting you know whether that connection is using an isolation level that doesn't allow for much concurrency). See the following log:

```
... clientapp=Microsoft SOL Server Management Studio - Query hostname=LesRois hostpid=2388
loginname=LesRois\Administrator isolationlevel=serializable (4) xactid=1147351 currentdb=8
lockTimeout=4294967295 clientoption1=673187936 clientoption2=390200
```

After examining the SQL log, disable the trace flag in the query editor:

```
DBCC TRACEOFF (1222, -1)
GO
DBCC TRACESTATUS
```

Before proceeding, you should now revisit the first query window and issue the following command to ensure the transaction is no longer running:

```
ROLLBACK TRANSACTION;
```

How It Works

In this recipe, I simulated a deadlock using two separate queries that updated the same rows repeatedly, but in the opposite order. When a deadlock occurred, the error message was returned to the query editor window, but nothing was written to the SQL log.

To enable deadlock logging to the SQL log, the recipe enabled trace flag 1222. Trace 1222 returns detailed deadlock information to the SQL log. The -1 flag indicated that trace flag 1222 should be enabled globally for all SQL Server connections. To turn on a trace flag, DBCC TRACEON was used, with the 1222 flag in parentheses:

```
DBCC TRACEON (1222, -1)
```

To verify that the flag was enabled, DBCC TRACESTATUS was executed:

```
DBCC TRACESTATUS
```

After encountering another deadlock, the deadlock information was logged in the SQL log. The flag was then disabled using DBCC TRACEOFF:

```
DBCC TRACEOFF (1222, -1)
```

12-10. Identifying Deadlocks with Extended Events

Problem

You are experiencing a high volume of deadlocks within your database. You need to find out the causes of the deadlocks.

Solution

If you are having deadlock trouble in your SQL Server instance, follow this recipe to make sure deadlocks are logged to a file on the filesystem for later review by the DBA team.

To demonstrate this recipe, a deadlock will be simulated. In a new query editor window, I will reuse the code from the previous section (relisted here) to cause a deadlock:

```
USE AdventureWorks2014;
GO
SET NOCOUNT ON;
SET TRANSACTION ISOLATION LEVEL SERIALIZABLE;
WHILE 1=1
BEGIN
BEGIN TRAN
UPDATE Purchasing.Vendor
SET CreditRating = 1
WHERE BusinessEntityID = 1494;
UPDATE Purchasing.Vendor
SET CreditRating = 2
WHERE BusinessEntityID = 1492;
COMMIT TRAN
END
```

In a second query editor window, the following query is executed:

```
USE AdventureWorks2014;
GO
SET NOCOUNT ON;
WHILE 1=1
BEGIN
BEGIN TRANSACTION
UPDATE Purchasing.Vendor
SET CreditRating = 2
WHERE BusinessEntityID = 1492;
UPDATE Purchasing.Vendor
SET CreditRating = 1
WHERE BusinessEntityID = 1494;
COMMIT TRANSACTION
END
```

In a third query editor window, the following query is executed to create the extended event session so as to trap the deadlock information. This session should be created prior to running the deadlock scenario that I just relisted from Recipe 12-9. See the following:

```
CREATE EVENT SESSION [Deadlock] ON SERVER
ADD EVENT sqlserver.lock_deadlock(
ACTION(sqlserver.database_name,sqlserver.plan_handle,sqlserver.sql_text)),
ADD EVENT sqlserver.xml_deadlock_report
ADD TARGET package0.event_file(SET filename=N'C:\Database\XE\Deadlock.xel')
--Ensure the file path exists and permissions are set or change the path.
WITH (STARTUP_STATE=ON)
GO

ALTER EVENT SESSION Deadlock
ON SERVER
STATE = START;
```

With this Extended Event (XE or XEvent) session created, when the deadlock scripts are executed the deadlock graph with pertinent information from the winning and losing sessions involved in the deadlock will be trapped to the output file at C:\Database\XE\Deadlock.xel. Having encountered a deadlock, I will now run the next script to see what has been captured for the deadlock:

```
/* read the captured data */

SELECT TargetData AS DeadlockGraph
FROM
(SELECT CAST(event_data AS xml) AS TargetData
            FROM sys.fn_xe_file_target_read_file('C:\Database\XE\Deadlock*.xel',NULL,NULL, NULL)
                )AS Data
WHERE TargetData.value('(event/@name)[1]', 'varchar(50)') = 'xml_deadlock_report';
```

This will output the deadlock graph in a basic XML format.

How It Works

In this recipe, I simulated a deadlock using two separate queries that updated the same rows repeatedly, but updating two rows in the opposite order. When a deadlock occurred, the error message was logged to the query editor window, but nothing was written to the SQL log.

To enable deadlock logging to a file on the file system, the recipe enabled an XE session to trap the deadlock graph. This session will trap the SQL statements for each of the sessions involved in the deadlock, along with the associated plan handle and database source.

With the flexibility of Extended Events, this session could be altered to include more or less data while still offering a lightweight means to capture the deadlock for effective troubleshooting.

12-11. Setting Deadlock Priority

Problem

While trying to resolve deadlock issues, you have determined that certain query sessions are less critical, and you want to increase the chance of those sessions being chosen as the deadlock victim.

Solution

You can increase a query session's chance of being chosen as a deadlock victim by using the SET DEADLOCK_PRIORITY command. The syntax for this command is as follows:

```
SET DEADLOCK_PRIORITY { LOW | NORMAL | HIGH | <numeric-priority> }
```

Table 12-9 describes the arguments for this command.

Table 12-9. SET DEADLOCK_PRIORITY *Command Arguments*

Argument	Description
LOW	LOW makes the current connection the likely deadlock victim.
NORMAL	NORMAL lets SQL Server decide based on which connection seems least expensive to roll back.
HIGH	HIGH lessens the chances of the connection being chosen as the victim, unless the other connection is also HIGH or has a numeric priority greater than 5.
<numeric-priority>	The numeric priority allows you to use a range of values from -10 to 10, where -10 is the most likely deadlock victim, up to 10 being the least likely to be chosen as a victim. The higher number between two participants in a deadlock wins.

For example, had the first query from the previous recipe used the following deadlock priority command, it would almost certainly have been chosen as the victim (normally, the default deadlock victim is the connection SQL Server deems least expensive to cancel and roll back):

```
USE AdventureWorks2014;
GO
SET NOCOUNT ON;
SET DEADLOCK_PRIORITY LOW;
```

```
WHILE 1=1
BEGIN
BEGIN TRANSACTION
UPDATE Purchasing.Vendor
SET CreditRating = 1
WHERE BusinessEntityID = 1492;
UPDATE Purchasing.Vendor
SET CreditRating = 2
WHERE BusinessEntityID = 1494;
COMMIT TRANSACTION
END
GO
```

How It Works

You can also set the deadlock priority to HIGH and NORMAL. HIGH means that unless the other session is of the same priority, it will not be chosen as the victim. NORMAL is the default behavior and will be chosen if the other session is HIGH, but will not be chosen if the other session is LOW. If both sessions have the same priority, the least expensive transaction to roll back will be chosen.

■ ■ ■

Managing Tables

by Wayne Sheffield

Almost all databases have one thing in common: they use tables to store data. In this chapter, I'll present recipes that demonstrate table creation and manipulation. Tables are used to store data in the database and are the central unit upon which most SQL Server database objects depend. Tables are uniquely named within a database and schema and contain one or more columns. Each column has an associated data type that defines the kind of data that can be stored within it.

A table can have up to 1,024 columns (with the exception of sparse columns) but can't exceed a total of 8,060 actual used bytes per row. A data page size is 8KB, including the header, which stores information about the page. This byte limit is not applied to the large object data types—varchar(max), nvarchar(max), varbinary(max), text, image, xml—or any CLR data type based upon these formats, such as the geography or geometry data types.

Another exception to the 8,060-byte limit rule is SQL Server's *row overflow* functionality for regular varchar, nvarchar, varbinary, and sql_variant data types, or any CLR data type based upon these formats, such as the HierarchyId data type. If the lengths of these individual data types do not exceed 8,000 bytes, but the combined width of more than one of these columns together in a table exceeds the 8,060-byte row limit, the column with the largest width will be dynamically moved to another 8KB page and replaced in the original table with a 24-byte pointer. Row overflow provides extra flexibility for managing large row sizes, but you should still limit your potential maximum variable data-type length in your table definition when possible, because page overflow may decrease query performance, since more data pages need to be retrieved by a single query.

13-1. Creating a Table

Problem

You need to create a table to store data.

Solution

Use the CREATE TABLE statement to create a new table.

```
CREATE TABLE dbo.Person (
  PersonID INT IDENTITY CONSTRAINT PK_Person PRIMARY KEY CLUSTERED,
  BusinessEntityId INT NOT NULL
      CONSTRAINT FK_Person REFERENCES Person.BusinessEntity (BusinessEntityID),
  First_Name VARCHAR(50) NOT NULL);
```

How It Works

This recipe creates a relatively simple table of three columns. The first column (`PersonID`) has an integer data type, is automatically populated by having the `IDENTITY` property set, and has a clustered primary key constraint on it. Since primary key constraints do not allow columns to be nullable, this column is implicitly set to not allow NULL values.

The second column (`BusinessEntityId`) has an integer data type, and it has been specified that NULL values are not to be inserted into it. This column has a foreign key constraint on it that references a second table; this foreign key constraint enforces that whatever value is in this column must have a corresponding value in the referenced table. The value in the referenced table must exist prior to adding the value in this table, and before a value can be deleted from the referenced table, there must be no corresponding values in this table.

The third column (`First_Name`) has a varchar(50) data type, and it has been specified that NULL values are not allowed. The length of the name can be up to 50 characters.

Note that this format allows you to create constraints on a single column. If you need to build a constraint that encompasses multiple columns, you would need to use the following format for those columns:

```
CREATE TABLE dbo.Test (
  Column1 INT NOT NULL,
  Column2 INT NOT NULL,
  CONSTRAINT PK_Test PRIMARY KEY CLUSTERED (Column1, Column2));
```

■ **Note**   To create a table variable, you need to use the `DECLARE` statement instead of the `CREATE TABLE` statement. See Recipe 13-23 for more details about using table variables.

13-2. Adding a Column

Problem

You need to add a new column to an existing table.

Solution

Use the `ALTER TABLE` statement to add new columns to a table.

```
ALTER TABLE dbo.Person
ADD Last_Name VARCHAR(50) NULL;
```

How It Works

The `ALTER TABLE` statement is used to make modifications to existing tables, including adding new columns. The first line of code specifies which table is to be modified, and the next line adds a new column (`Last_Name`) with a varchar(50) data type. For all of the existing rows, the value of this column is NULL.

13-3. Adding a Column that Requires Data

Problem

You need to add a new column to an existing table, and you need to create it so as to have NOT NULL values.

Solution

Use the ALTER TABLE statement to add new columns to a table and simultaneously specify a *default constraint*.

```
ALTER TABLE dbo.Person
ADD IsActive BIT NOT NULL
CONSTRAINT DF_Person_IsActive DEFAULT (0);
```

How It Works

The ALTER TABLE statement is used to add the new column. The first line specifies the table to be modified, the second line specifies the column to be added with the NOT NULL specification, and the third line specifies a default constraint with a value of 0. SQL Server will add the column to the table with the NOT NULL attribute and will set the value of this column to 0 for all existing rows in this table. Any new rows that do not specify a value for this column will also default to 0.

■ **Note**   See Recipe 13-13 for how a *default constraint* works.

13-4. Changing a Column

Problem

You need to modify the data type or properties of an existing column in a table.

Solution

Use the ALTER TABLE statement to modify existing columns in a table.

```
ALTER TABLE dbo.Person
ALTER COLUMN Last_Name VARCHAR(75) NULL;
```

How It Works

The ALTER TABLE statement is used to make modifications to existing tables, including modifying existing columns. The first line of code specifies which table is to be modified, and the next line specifies the modification of an existing column (Last_Name), followed by the column's new definition.

■ **Note**   If the existing column is specified with the NOT NULL attribute, you must specify NOT NULL for the new column definition as well in order to retain the NOT NULL attribute on the column. Additionally, if the existing column already has data in it, and the data is not able to be implicitly converted to the new data type, then the ALTER TABLE statement will fail.

13-5. Creating a Computed Column

Problem

You need to save a calculation used when querying a table.

Solution

Use the ALTER TABLE statement to add a computed column to an existing table, or use the CREATE TABLE statement to create a computed column as the table is created:

```
ALTER TABLE Production.TransactionHistory
ADD CostPerUnit AS (ActualCost/Quantity);

CREATE TABLE HumanResources.CompanyStatistic (
  CompanyID int NOT NULL,
  StockTicker char(4) NOT NULL,
  SharesOutstanding int NOT NULL,
  Shareholders int NOT NULL,
  AvgSharesPerShareholder AS (SharesOutstanding/Shareholders) PERSISTED);
```

How It Works

The ALTER TABLE statement is used to add a new computed column to an existing table.

In the first example, a new computed column (CostPerUnit) is added to a table. When querying this table, this column will be returned with the results of the calculation specified. The calculation results themselves are not physically stored in the table.

If you were to run the following query:

```
SELECT  TOP (1) CostPerUnit, Quantity, ActualCost
FROM    Production.TransactionHistory
WHERE   Quantity > 10
ORDER BY ActualCost DESC;
```

you would get the following results:

CostPerUnit	Quantity	ActualCost
132.0408	13	1716.5304

Computed columns can't be used within a DEFAULT or FOREIGN KEY constraint. A calculated column can't be explicitly updated or inserted into (since its value is always derived).

Computed columns can be used within indexes but must meet certain requirements, such as being deterministic (always returning the same result for a given set of inputs) and precise (not containing float values).

In the second example, a new table is created with a computed column. Since this calculated column is specified as PERSISTED, the calculation results are physically stored in the table (but the calculation is still performed by SQL Server). This means that any changes to the columns involved in the computation will result in the computed column being recalculated and updated. The stored data still can't be modified directly—the data is still computed. Storing the data does mean, however, that the column can be used to partition a table (see the "Managing Large Tables" chapter), or it can be used in an index with an imprecise (float-based) value—unlike its nonpersisted version.

13-6. Removing a Column

Problem

You need to remove a column from a table.

Solution

Use the ALTER TABLE statement to drop an existing column from a table.

```
ALTER TABLE dbo.Person
DROP COLUMN Last_Name;
```

How It Works

The first line of code specifies the table that is being modified. The second line of code specifies to drop the Last_Name column.

■ **Note** You can drop a column only if it isn't being used in a PRIMARY KEY, FOREIGN KEY, UNIQUE, or CHECK CONSTRAINT (these constraint types are all covered in this chapter). You also can't drop a column being used in an index or one that has a DEFAULT value bound to it.

13-7. Removing a Table

Problem

You need to remove a table from the database.

Solution

Use the DROP TABLE statement to drop an existing table from the database.

```
DROP TABLE dbo.Person;
```

How It Works

The code specifies to remove the table definition and data for the specified table from the database.

■ **Note**   The DROP TABLE statement will fail if any other table is referencing the table to be dropped through a foreign key constraint. If there are foreign key references, you must drop them first before dropping the primary key table.

13-8. Reporting on a Table's Definition

Problem

You need to see information about the metadata for a table.

Solution

Use the system-stored procedure sp_help to report a table's metadata information.

```
EXECUTE sp_help 'Person.Person';
```

How It Works

The sp_help system-stored procedure returns several different result sets with useful information regarding the specific object (in this example, it returns data about the table Person.Person). This system-stored procedure can be used to gather information regarding other database object types as well. The results of this example include numerous columns and multiple result sets; therefore, the results are not being shown. Some of information in the results includes information about the columns in the table, what filegroup the table is located on, all indexes and the columns that are part of those indexes, information about all constraints, and whether the table is referenced by any foreign keys or views.

13-9. Reducing Storage Used by NULL Columns

Problem

You have a table with hundreds (or even thousands) of columns (for example, a table in a SharePoint site that stores data about uploaded documents, where different columns are used for data about different file types), and most of these columns are NULL. However, this table still consumes extremely large amounts of storage space. You need to reduce the storage needs of this table.

Solution

Specify the SPARSE column attribute for each of these nullable columns.

How It Works

Sparse columns are a storage optimization improvement that enables zero-byte storage of NULL values. Consequently, this allows a large number of sparse columns to be defined for a table (as of this writing, 30,000 sparse columns are allowed). This improvement is ideal for database designs and applications requiring a high number of infrequently populated columns or for tables having sets of columns related only with a subset of the data stored in the table.

To define a sparse column, you need add only the SPARSE storage attribute after the column definition within a CREATE or ALTER TABLE command, as the following query demonstrates:

```
CREATE TABLE dbo.WebsiteProduct (
    WebsiteProductID int NOT NULL PRIMARY KEY IDENTITY(1,1),
    ProductNM varchar(255) NOT NULL,
    PublisherNM varchar(255) SPARSE NULL,
    ArtistNM varchar(150) SPARSE NULL,
    ISBNNBR varchar(30) SPARSE NULL,
    DiscsNBR int SPARSE NULL,
    MusicLabelNM varchar(255) SPARSE NULL);
```

The previous table takes a somewhat abnormal approach to creating columns that apply only to specific product types. For example, the PublisherNM and ISBNNBR columns apply to a book product, whereas DiscsNBR, ArtistNM, and MusicLabelNM will more often apply to a music product. When a product row is stored, the sparse columns that do not apply to it will *not* incur a storage cost for each NULL value.

Let's now insert two new rows into the table, one representing a book and one a music album:

```
INSERT dbo.WebsiteProduct (ProductNM, PublisherNM, ISBNNBR)
  VALUES ('SQL Server Transact-SQL Recipes', 'Apress', '9781484200629');
INSERT dbo.WebsiteProduct (ProductNM, ArtistNM, DiscsNBR, MusicLabelNM)
  VALUES ('Etiquette', 'Casiotone for the Painfully Alone', 1, 'Tomlab');
```

Returning just the appropriate columns for book products is accomplished with the following query:

```
SELECT ProductNM, PublisherNM,ISBNNBR FROM dbo.WebsiteProduct WHERE ISBNNBR IS NOT NULL;
```

This query returns the following result set:

ProductNM	PublisherNM	ISBNNBR
SQL Server Transact-SQL Recipes	Apress	9781484200629

If your table has a large number of columns and you want to return all the columns that have NOT NULL values, then you can utilize a COLUMN SET. A COLUMN SET allows you to logically group all sparse columns defined for the table. This column (with a data type of xml) allows for SELECTs and data modification and is defined by designating COLUMN_SET FOR ALL_SPARSE_COLUMNS after the column definitions. You can have only one COLUMN SET for a single table, and you also can't add one to a table that already has sparse columns defined in it. If you attempt to add a COLUMN SET to the dbo.WebsiteProduct table (which already has sparse columns) with the ALTER TABLE statement:

```
ALTER TABLE dbo.WebsiteProduct
ADD ProductAttributeCS XML COLUMN_SET FOR ALL_SPARSE_COLUMNS;
```

the following error is returned:

```
Msg 1734, Level 16, State 1, Line 1
Cannot create the sparse column set 'ProductAttributeCS' in the table 'WebsiteProduct'
because the table already contains one or more sparse columns. A sparse column set cannot
be added to a table if the table contains a sparse column.
```

Taking the previous table, this code will re-create it with a sparse column:

```
IF OBJECT_ID('dbo.WebsiteProduct', 'U') IS NOT NULL
   DROP TABLE dbo.WebsiteProduct;
CREATE TABLE dbo.WebsiteProduct (
   WebsiteProductID int NOT NULL PRIMARY KEY IDENTITY(1,1),
   ProductNM varchar(255) NOT NULL,
   PublisherNM varchar(255) SPARSE NULL,
   ArtistNM varchar(150) SPARSE NULL,
   ISBNNBR varchar(30) SPARSE NULL,
   DiscsNBR int SPARSE NULL,
   MusicLabelNM varchar(255) SPARSE NULL,
   ProductAttributeCS xml COLUMN_SET FOR ALL_SPARSE_COLUMNS);
```

After re-inserting the data by running the prior two INSERT statements, you can now query the table using this COLUMN SET (instead of the individual columns in the table), as demonstrated here:

```
SELECT  ProductNM, ProductAttributeCS
FROM    dbo.WebsiteProduct
WHERE   ISBNNBR IS NOT NULL;
```

This query returns the following result set:

ProductNM	ProductAttributeCS
SQL Server Transact-SQL Recipes	\<PublisherNM>Apress\</PublisherNM>\<ISBNNBR>9781484200629\</ISBNNBR>

You can also execute INSERT and UPDATE statements against the COLUMN SET columns.

```
INSERT dbo.WebsiteProduct (ProductNM, ProductAttributeCS)
VALUES ('Roots & Echoes',
        '<ArtistNM>The Coral</ArtistNM>
        <DiscsNBR>1</DiscsNBR>
        <MusicLabelNM>Deltasonic</MusicLabelNM>');
```

■ **Caution** Any columns not specified will be set to NULL. If you use an UPDATE statement, data in existing columns will be set to NULL if the columns were not specified.

Once a column set is defined for a table, performing a SELECT * query no longer returns each individual sparse column, as the following query demonstrates (it returns only nonsparse columns and then the column set):

```
SELECT * FROM dbo.WebsiteProduct;
```

This query returns the following result set:

WebsiteProductID	ProductNM	ProductAttributeCS
1	SQL Server Transact-SQL Recipes	<PublisherNM>Apress</PublisherNM> <ISBNNBR>9781484200629</ISBNNBR>
2	Etiquette	<ArtistNM>Casiotone for the Painfully Alone</ArtistNM> <DiscsNBR>1</DiscsNBR> <MusicLabelNM>Tomlab</MusicLabelNM>
3	Roots & Echoes	<ArtistNM>The Coral</ArtistNM> <DiscsNBR>1</DiscsNBR> <MusicLabelNM>Deltasonic</MusicLabelNM>

It turns out that using the SPARSE attribute of a column is not free—non-NULL values use an extra 4 bytes per column per row. Therefore, the amount of space savings that you will see depends upon the data types being used for the columns, and the percentage of values in the column that are NULL. The Books Online article "Using Sparse Columns" at https://msdn.microsoft.com/en-us/library/cc280604.aspx has a chart that shows, for a specific data type, what percentage of rows need to be NULL in order to save 40% space. However, let's take our WebsiteProduct table as an example and show the difference. Here we'll make two identical tables, one with sparse columns and one without, and add 500,000 rows to each table. Then we'll look at the size of the table using the sp_spaceused stored procedure:

```
IF OBJECT_ID('dbo.WebsiteProduct') IS NOT NULL DROP TABLE dbo.WebsiteProduct;
IF OBJECT_ID('dbo.WebsiteProduct_sparse') IS NOT NULL DROP TABLE dbo.WebsiteProduct_sparse;
CREATE TABLE dbo.WebsiteProduct (
    WebsiteProductID int NOT NULL PRIMARY KEY ,
    ProductNM varchar(255) NOT NULL,
    PublisherNM varchar(255) NULL,
    ArtistNM varchar(150) NULL,
    ISBNNBR varchar(30) NULL,
    DiscsNBR int NULL,
    MusicLabelNM varchar(255) NULL);
CREATE TABLE dbo.WebsiteProduct_sparse (
    WebsiteProductID int NOT NULL PRIMARY KEY ,
    ProductNM varchar(255) NOT NULL,
    PublisherNM varchar(255) SPARSE NULL,
    ArtistNM varchar(150) SPARSE NULL,
    ISBNNBR varchar(30) SPARSE NULL,
    DiscsNBR int SPARSE NULL,
    MusicLabelNM varchar(255) SPARSE NULL);
```

```
GO
WITH Tens    (N) AS (SELECT 1 UNION ALL SELECT 1 UNION ALL SELECT 1 UNION ALL
                     SELECT 1 UNION ALL SELECT 1 UNION ALL SELECT 1 UNION ALL
                     SELECT 1 UNION ALL SELECT 1 UNION ALL SELECT 1 UNION ALL SELECT 1),
    Hundreds(N) AS (SELECT 1 FROM Tens t1, Tens t2),
    Millions(N) AS (SELECT 1 FROM Hundreds t1, Hundreds t2, Hundreds t3),
     Tally  (N) AS (SELECT ROW_NUMBER() OVER (ORDER BY (SELECT NULL)) FROM Millions)
INSERT INTO dbo.WebsiteProduct (WebsiteProductID, ProductNM)
SELECT  TOP (500000) N, 'Product#' + CONVERT(VARCHAR(15), N)
FROM    Tally;

INSERT INTO dbo.WebsiteProduct_sparse (WebsiteProductID, ProductNM)
SELECT  WebsiteProductID, ProductNM
FROM    dbo.WebsiteProduct;

EXECUTE sp_spaceused 'dbo.WebsiteProduct';
EXECUTE sp_spaceused 'dbo.WebsiteProduct_sparse';
```

The sp_spaceused results are:

name	rows	reserved	data	index_size	unused
WebsiteProduct	500000	17288 KB	17208 KB	72 KB	8 KB

name	rows	reserved	data	index_size	unused
WebsiteProduct_sparse	500000	15304 KB	15224 KB	64 KB	16 KB

The space savings across five sparse columns over 500,000 rows can be seen above. In this case, all of the sparse columns are NULL; however, as you add more columns and more rows, this savings will continue to increase.

13-10. Adding a Constraint to a Table

Problem

You need to add one or more constraints (PRIMARY KEY, UNIQUE, or FOREIGN KEY) to a table in order to enforce referential integrity rules on the table or between tables.

Solution

Use the ALTER TABLE statement to add PRIMARY KEY, UNIQUE, or FOREIGN KEY constraints to enforce referential integrity rules on this table. The following statements create a table and then create PRIMARY KEY, UNIQUE, and FOREIGN KEY constraints on it:

```
CREATE TABLE dbo.Person (
  PersonID INT IDENTITY NOT NULL,
  BusinessEntityId INT NOT NULL,
```

```
First_Name VARCHAR(50) NULL,
Last_Name VARCHAR(50) NULL);

ALTER TABLE dbo.Person
  ADD CONSTRAINT PK_Person PRIMARY KEY CLUSTERED (PersonID),
      CONSTRAINT FK_Person FOREIGN KEY (BusinessEntityId)
         REFERENCES Person.BusinessEntity (BusinessEntityID),
      CONSTRAINT UK_Person_Name UNIQUE (First_Name, Last_Name);
```

How It Works

The ALTER TABLE statement allows you to modify an existing table, including by adding constraints to it. You can also use the CREATE TABLE statement to both create the table and add the constraints to it simultaneously:

```
IF OBJECT_ID('dbo.Person','U') IS NOT NULL
   DROP TABLE dbo.Person;
CREATE TABLE dbo.Person (
  PersonID INT IDENTITY NOT NULL,
  BusinessEntityId INT NOT NULL,
  First_Name VARCHAR(50) NULL,
  Last_Name VARCHAR(50) NULL,
  CONSTRAINT PK_Person PRIMARY KEY CLUSTERED (PersonID),
  CONSTRAINT FK_Person FOREIGN KEY (BusinessEntityId)
      REFERENCES Person.BusinessEntity (BusinessEntityID),
  CONSTRAINT UK_Person_Name UNIQUE (First_Name, Last_Name) );
```

Constraints place limitations on the data that can be entered into a column or columns. A constraint on a single column can be created as either a *table constraint* or a *column constraint*; constraints being implemented on more than one column must be created as table constraints.

A column constraint is specified in the CREATE TABLE statement as part of the definition of the column. A column constraint applies to only the single column. In comparison, a table constraint is specified in the CREATE TABLE statement after the comma separating the columns. Although not required, table constraints are generally placed after all column definitions. In the previous example, the constraints are created as table constraints. The same table, with column constraints used for the single-column constraints, is shown here:

```
IF OBJECT_ID('dbo.Person','U') IS NOT NULL
   DROP TABLE dbo.Person;
CREATE TABLE dbo.Person (
  PersonID INT IDENTITY NOT NULL
      CONSTRAINT PK_Person PRIMARY KEY CLUSTERED (PersonID),
  BusinessEntityId INT NOT NULL
      CONSTRAINT FK_Person FOREIGN KEY (BusinessEntityId)
         REFERENCES Person.BusinessEntity (BusinessEntityID),
  First_Name VARCHAR(50) NULL,
  Last_Name VARCHAR(50) NULL,
  CONSTRAINT UK_Person_Name UNIQUE (First_Name, Last_Name) );
```

A *primary key* is a special type of constraint that identifies a single column or a set of columns, which in turn uniquely identifies all rows in the table.

A primary key enforces *entity integrity,* meaning that rows are guaranteed to be unambiguous and unique. Best practices for database normalization dictate that every table has a primary key. A primary key provides a way to access the record and ensures that the key is unique. A primary key column can't contain NULL values.

Only one primary key is allowed for a table, and when a primary key is designated, an underlying table *index* is automatically created, defaulting to a clustered index type (index types are reviewed in the "Managing Indexes" chapter). You can also explicitly designate that a nonclustered index will be created when the primary key is created, if you have a better use for the single clustered index allowed for a table. An index created on the primary key counts against the 1,000 total indexes allowed for a table.

A *composite primary key* is the unique combination of *more* than one column in the table. To define a composite primary key, you must use a *table constraint* instead of a *column constraint.*

In the prior example, a PRIMARY KEY constraint is created on the PersonID column.

You can have only one primary key defined on a table. If you want to enforce uniqueness on other nonprimary key columns, you can use a UNIQUE constraint. A unique constraint, by definition, creates an alternate key. Unlike a PRIMARY KEY constraint, you can create multiple UNIQUE constraints for a single table, and you are also allowed to designate a UNIQUE constraint for columns that allow NULL values (although only one NULL value is allowed for a single-column key per table). Like primary keys, UNIQUE constraints enforce entity integrity by ensuring that rows can be uniquely identified.

The UNIQUE constraint creates an underlying table index when it is created. This index can be CLUSTERED or NONCLUSTERED (although you can't create the index as CLUSTERED if a clustered index already exists for the table).

As with PRIMARY KEY constraints, you can define a UNIQUE constraint when a table is created, either on the column-definition or the table-constraint level.

You can have only one NULL value for a single-column UNIQUE constraint. For a multiple-column UNIQUE constraint, you can have only a single NULL value in that column for the values of the remaining columns in the UNIQUE constraint. Consider the following code that inserts data into the previous table, which has a UNIQUE constraint defined on the nullable First_Name and Last_Name columns:

```
INSERT INTO dbo.Person (BusinessEntityId, First_Name) VALUES (1, 'MyName');
INSERT INTO dbo.Person (BusinessEntityId, First_Name) VALUES (1, 'MyName2');
INSERT INTO dbo.Person (BusinessEntityId) VALUES (1);
```

In the first two INSERT statements, NULL values are being inserted into the Last_Name column. You can have multiple NULL values in the Last_Name column as long as the First_Name column is different. Both of these statements are allowed once. Trying to run either of these a second time will generate an error:

```
Msg 2627, Level 14, State 1, Line 1
Violation of UNIQUE KEY constraint 'UK_Person_Name'. Cannot insert duplicate key in object
'dbo.Person'. The duplicate key value is (MyName2, <NULL>).
```

■ **Note**   Starting with SQL Server 2012, the constraint violation error messages have been enhanced to show the values that are causing the error. As such, you can tell that the previous error statement comes from the second INSERT statement.

In the third INSERT statement, NULL values are being inserted into both the First_Name and Last_Name columns. Again, this is allowed just once. Subsequent attempts will generate the same error (except that the values being displayed will be different).

Foreign key constraints establish and enforce relationships between tables and help maintain referential integrity, which means that every value in the foreign key column(s) must exist in the corresponding column(s) for the referenced table. Foreign key constraints also help define domain integrity, in that they define the range of potential and allowed values for a specific column or columns. Domain integrity defines the validity of values in a column. Foreign key constraints can be defined only by referencing a table that has a constraint enforcing entity integrity, either a PRIMARY KEY or UNIQUE constraint.

Foreign key constraints can be created as a table constraint or, if the constraint is on a single column, as a column constraint. In the prior example, a FOREIGN KEY constraint is created between the BusinessEntityId column in the table being created and the BusinessEntityId column in the Person. BusinessEntity table.

You can create multiple FOREIGN KEY constraints on a table. Creating a FOREIGN KEY constraint does not create any indexes on the table.

When there is a FOREIGN KEY constraint between tables, SQL Server restricts the ability to delete a row from the referenced table or update the column to a different value, unless the referencing table does not contain that value. Furthermore, SQL Server restricts the ability to insert a row into the referencing table unless there is also a row with that value in the referenced table. Since SQL Server must check for this existence in the referencing table when updating or deleting records in the referenced table, it can be advantageous to create an index in the referencing table on the foreign key column(s) to support this lookup.

13-11. Creating a Recursive Foreign Key

Problem

You need to ensure that the values in a column exist in a different column in the same table. For example, an employee table might contain a column for employee_id and another column for manager_id. The data in manager_id column must exist in the employee_id column.

Solution

Create a recursive foreign key:

```
CREATE TABLE dbo.Employees (
    employee_id INT IDENTITY PRIMARY KEY CLUSTERED,
    manager_id INT NULL REFERENCES dbo.Employees (employee_id));
```

■ **Note** Some people will call a recursive foreign key a *self-referencing foreign key*. Use whichever you want; they mean the same thing.

How It Works

The table is created with two columns. The first column is employee_id, and it is an identity column, with a primary key created as a column constraint. The second column is manager_id. It is defined as nullable, and it has a foreign key that is referencing the employee_id column in the same table.

■ **Tip**   When creating a FOREIGN KEY *column constraint*, the keywords FOREIGN KEY are optional.

Now let's insert some data by running the following statements, then we'll query the results:

```
INSERT INTO dbo.Employees DEFAULT VALUES;
INSERT INTO dbo.Employees (manager_id) VALUES (1);
SELECT * FROM dbo.Employees;
```

This query returns the following results:

```
employee_id manager_id
----------- -----------
1           NULL
2           1
```

If we then run the following statement:

```
INSERT INTO dbo.Employees (manager_id) VALUES (10);
```

SQL Server will generate an error since there is no employee_id with a value of 10:

```
Msg 547, Level 16, State 0, Line 9
The INSERT statement conflicted with the FOREIGN KEY SAME TABLE constraint
"FK__Employees__manag__6EE06CCD". The conflict occurred in database
"AdventureWorks2008R2", table "dbo.Employees", column 'employee_id'.
```

13-12. Allowing Data Modifications to Foreign Key Columns in the Referenced Table to Be Reflected in the Referencing Table

Problem

You need to change the value of a column on a table that is involved in a foreign key relationship as the referenced table, and there are rows in the referencing table using this value.

Solution

Create the foreign key with *cascading* changes.

How It Works

Foreign keys restrict the values that can be placed within the foreign key column or columns. If the associated primary key or unique value does not exist in the reference table, the INSERT or UPDATE to the table row fails. This restriction is bidirectional in that if an attempt is made to delete a primary key but one or more rows that reference that specific key exist in the foreign key table, an error will be returned. All referencing foreign key rows must be deleted prior to deleting the targeted primary key or unique value; otherwise, an error will be raised.

SQL Server provides an automatic mechanism for handling changes in the primary key/unique key column, called *cascading changes*. In previous examples, cascading options weren't used. You can allow cascading changes for deletions or updates using ON DELETE and ON UPDATE. The basic syntax for cascading options is as follows:

```
[ ON DELETE { NO ACTION | CASCADE | SET NULL | SET DEFAULT }    ]
[ ON UPDATE { NO ACTION | CASCADE | SET NULL | SET DEFAULT }    ]
[ NOT FOR REPLICATION ]
```

Table 13-1 details these arguments.

Table 13-1. Cascading Change Arguments

Argument	Description
NO ACTION	The default setting for a new foreign key is NO ACTION, meaning if an attempt to delete a row on the primary key/unique column occurs when there is a referencing value in a foreign key table, the attempt will raise an error and prevent the statement from executing.
CASCADE	For ON DELETE, if CASCADE is chosen, foreign key rows referencing the deleted primary key are also deleted. For ON UPDATE, foreign key rows referencing the updated primary key are also updated.
SET NULL	If the primary key row is deleted, the foreign key referencing row(s) can also be set to NULL (assuming NULL values are allowed for that foreign key column).
SET DEFAULT	If the primary key row is deleted, the foreign key referencing row(s) can also be set to a DEFAULT value. The new cascade SET DEFAULT option assumes the column has a default value set for a column. If not, and if the column is nullable, a NULL value is set.
NOT FOR REPLICATION	The NOT FOR REPLICATION option is used to prevent foreign key constraints from being enforced by SQL Server Replication Agent processes (allowing data to arrive via replication potentially out of order from the primary key data).

In this example, two parent tables are created and populated, and a third table is created using cascading options in the foreign key definitions to these parent tables. Data is then inserted into the third table. The data in the third table is selected. Finally, one of the rows in a parent table is deleted (causing a cascade delete), a row in the other parent table is modified (causing a cascade update to NULL), and the data in the third table is again selected.

```
IF OBJECT_ID('dbo.PersonPhone','U') IS NOT NULL DROP TABLE dbo.PersonPhone;
IF OBJECT_ID('dbo.PhoneNumberType','U') IS NOT NULL DROP TABLE dbo.PhoneNumberType;
IF OBJECT_ID('dbo.Person','U') IS NOT NULL DROP TABLE dbo.Person;

CREATE TABLE dbo.Person (
  BusinessEntityId INT PRIMARY KEY,
  FirstName VARCHAR(25),
  LastName  VARCHAR(25));
```

```
CREATE TABLE dbo.PhoneNumberType (
  PhoneNumberTypeId INT PRIMARY KEY,
  Name VARCHAR(25));

INSERT INTO dbo.PhoneNumberType
SELECT  PhoneNumberTypeId, Name
FROM    Person.PhoneNumberType;

INSERT INTO dbo.Person
SELECT BusinessEntityId, FirstName, LastName
FROM Person.Person
WHERE BusinessEntityID IN (1,2);

CREATE TABLE dbo.PersonPhone (
        [BusinessEntityID] [int] NOT NULL,
        [PhoneNumber] [dbo].[Phone] NOT NULL,
        [PhoneNumberTypeID] [int] NULL,
        [ModifiedDate] [datetime] NOT NULL,
    CONSTRAINT [UQ_PersonPhone_BusinessEntityID_PhoneNumber_PhoneNumberTypeID]
        UNIQUE CLUSTERED
            ([BusinessEntityID], [PhoneNumber], [PhoneNumberTypeID]),
    CONSTRAINT [FK_PersonPhone_Person_BusinessEntityID]
        FOREIGN KEY ([BusinessEntityID])
        REFERENCES [dbo].[Person] ([BusinessEntityID])
        ON DELETE CASCADE,
    CONSTRAINT [FK_PersonPhone_PhoneNumberType_PhoneNumberTypeID]
        FOREIGN KEY ([PhoneNumberTypeID])
        REFERENCES [dbo].[PhoneNumberType] ([PhoneNumberTypeID])
        ON UPDATE SET NULL
);


INSERT INTO dbo.PersonPhone (BusinessEntityId, PhoneNumber, PhoneNumberTypeId, ModifiedDate)
VALUES (1, '757-867-5309', 1, '2012-03-22T00:00:00'),
       (2, '804-867-5309', 2, '2012-03-22T00:00:00');

SELECT 'Initial Data', * FROM dbo.PersonPhone;

DELETE FROM dbo.Person
WHERE BusinessEntityID = 1;

UPDATE dbo.PhoneNumberType
   SET PhoneNumberTypeID = 4
 WHERE PhoneNumberTypeID = 2;

SELECT 'Final Data', * FROM dbo.PersonPhone;
```

This example produces the following results:

	BusinessEntityID	PhoneNumber	PhoneNumberTypeID	ModifiedDate
Initial Data	1	757-867-5309	1	2012-03-22 00:00:00.000
Initial Data	2	804-867-5309	2	2012-03-22 00:00:00.000

	BusinessEntityID	PhoneNumber	PhoneNumberTypeID	ModifiedDate
Final Data	2	804-867-5309	NULL	2012-03-22 00:00:00.000

In the following example, one of the foreign key constraints uses ON DELETE CASCADE in a CREATE TABLE definition:

```
CONSTRAINT [FK_PersonPhone_Person_BusinessEntityID]
    FOREIGN KEY([BusinessEntityID])
    REFERENCES [dbo].[Person] ([BusinessEntityID])
    ON DELETE CASCADE,
```

By using this cascade option, if a row is deleted in the dbo.Person table, any referencing BusinessEntityID in the dbo.PersonPhone table will also be deleted. This can be witnessed in the previous example, where the dbo.Person record for BusinessEntityId = 1 is deleted and the corresponding record in the dbo.PhoneNumber table is also deleted.

A second foreign key constraint is also defined in the CREATE TABLE statement by using ON UPDATE:

```
CONSTRAINT [FK_PersonPhone_PhoneNumberType_PhoneNumberTypeID]
  FOREIGN KEY([PhoneNumberTypeID])
  REFERENCES [dbo].[PhoneNumberType] ([PhoneNumberTypeID])
  ON UPDATE SET NULL
```

If an update is made to the primary key of the dbo.PhoneNumberType table, the PhoneNumberTypeID column in the referencing dbo.PhoneNumber table will be set to NULL. This can be seen in the previous example, where the dbo.PhoneNumberType record has the PhoneNumberTypeId value changed from 2 to 4, and the corresponding record in the dbo.PhoneNumber table has its PhoneNumberTypeId value changed to NULL.

13-13. Specifying Default Values for a Column

Problem

You need to ensure that if you don't specify a column when inserting data into the table, a default value is used to populate that column. For example, you have a column named InsertedDate that needs to contain the date/time whenever a record is added to the table.

Solution

Create a DEFAULT constraint:

```
IF OBJECT_ID('dbo.Employees', 'U') IS NOT NULL
    DROP TABLE dbo.Employees;
CREATE TABLE dbo.Employees (
    EmployeeId INT PRIMARY KEY CLUSTERED,
    First_Name VARCHAR(50) NOT NULL,
    Last_Name  VARCHAR(50) NOT NULL,
    InsertedDate DATETIME DEFAULT GETDATE());
```

How It Works

The table is created with a DEFAULT constraint that uses the GETDATE system function to return the current system date and time.

Default constraints are used only if the column is not specified in the INSERT statement. Here's an example:

```
INSERT INTO dbo.Employees (EmployeeId, First_Name, Last_Name)
VALUES (1, 'Wayne', 'Sheffield');
INSERT INTO dbo.Employees (EmployeeId, First_Name, Last_Name, InsertedDate)
VALUES (2, 'Jim', 'Smith', NULL);
SELECT * FROM dbo.Employees;
```

This query returns the following result set:

EmployeeId	First_Name	Last_Name	InsertedDate
1	Wayne	Sheffield	2015-01-26 13:41:54.980
2	Jim	Smith	NULL

> ■ **Note**   This recipe calls one or more functions that return a value based upon the current date and time. When you run this recipe on your system, you will get a different result that will be based upon the date and time as set on the computer running your instance of SQL Server.

The first INSERT statement did not specify the InsertedDate column, so the default constraint was fired, and the current system date/time was inserted into the column. The second INSERT statement did specify the InsertedDate column— a NULL value was specified. The NULL value is what was inserted into the column.

13-14. Validating Data as It Is Entered into a Column

Problem

You need to ensure that data entered into a column follows specific business rules. For example, the date in an EndingDate column must occur after the date in the StartingDate column.

Solution

Create a CHECK constraint:

```
CREATE TABLE dbo.BooksRead (
  ISBN      VARCHAR(20),
  StartDate DATETIME NOT NULL,
  EndDate   DATETIME NULL,
  CONSTRAINT CK_BooksRead_EndDate CHECK (EndDate > StartDate));
```

How It Works

A CHECK constraint is created that ensures that the EndDate is greater than the StartDate. If a value is entered into the EndDate column that is not greater than the StartDate, then the insert or update will fail.

```
INSERT INTO BooksRead (ISBN, StartDate, EndDate)
VALUES ('9781430242000', '2012-08-01T16:25:00', '2011-08-15T12:35:00 ');
```

Since the EndDate is in the previous year, this error will be generated:

```
Msg 547, Level 16, State 0, Line 7
The INSERT statement conflicted with the CHECK constraint "CK_BooksRead_EndDate".
The conflict occurred in database "AdventureWorks2014", table "dbo.BooksRead".
The statement has been terminated.
```

A CHECK constraint is used to define what format and values are allowed for a column. The syntax of the CHECK constraint is as follows:

```
CHECK ( logical_expression )
```

If the logical expression of the CHECK constraint evaluates to TRUE, then the row will be inserted or updated. If the CHECK constraint expression evaluates to FALSE, the row insert or update will fail.

In the previous example, the constraint is created as a table constraint. If the constraint references only the column it applies to, it can be created as a column constraint; otherwise, it must be created as a table constraint.

A CHECK constraint can perform any check that returns a logical value, including using a user-defined scalar function. For instance, it can perform pattern matching with the LIKE operator. As an example, the following table has a check constraint on the phone number column to ensure that it follows the U.S. standard of XXX-YYY-ZZZZ, where all positions are numbers except for the two dashes:

```
IF OBJECT_ID('dbo.Employees','U') IS NOT NULL
   DROP TABLE dbo.Employees;
CREATE TABLE dbo.Employees (
  EmployeeId INT IDENTITY,
```

```
FirstName   VARCHAR(50),
LastName    VARCHAR(50),
PhoneNumber VARCHAR(12) CONSTRAINT CK_Employees_PhoneNumber
  CHECK (PhoneNumber LIKE '[0-9][0-9][0-9]-[0-9][0-9][0-9]-[0-9][0-9][0-9][0-9]'));
```

When inserting the following rows, the first insert is successful while the second insert fails:

```
INSERT INTO dbo.Employees (FirstName, LastName, PhoneNumber)
VALUES ('Wayne', 'Sheffield', '800-555-1212');

INSERT INTO dbo.Employees (FirstName, LastName, PhoneNumber)
VALUES ('Wayne', 'Sheffield', '555-1212');
```

```
Msg 547, Level 16, State 0, Line 12
The INSERT statement conflicted with the CHECK constraint " CK_Employees_PhoneNumber".
The conflict occurred in database "AdventureWorks2014", table "dbo.Employees", column
'PhoneNumber'.
The statement has been terminated.
```

13-15. Temporarily Turning Off a Constraint

Problem

You need to temporarily turn off a constraint on a table. For instance, you are performing a bulk-load process where you don't need to verify that each row meets the constraint requirements.

Solution

Utilize the ALTER TABLE statement to disable a constraint:

```
ALTER TABLE dbo.Employees
NOCHECK CONSTRAINT CK_Employees_PhoneNumber;
```

How It Works

The ALTER TABLE statement specifies to no longer check the specified foreign key or check constraint created on the specified table. In this example, the CK_Employees_PhoneNumber check constraint that was created on the dbo.Employees table in Recipe 13-14 is disabled. If we then rerun the second insert statement from that recipe, it succeeds.

You can alternatively disable all foreign key and check constraints by replacing the constraint name with ALL. Here's an example:

```
ALTER TABLE dbo.Employees
NOCHECK CONSTRAINT ALL;
```

You can turn the constraint back on to check future data changes by the following ALTER TABLE statement:

```
ALTER TABLE dbo.Employees
CHECK CONSTRAINT CK_Employees_PhoneNumber;
```

Note that this does not verify that the data currently existing in the table meets the constraint; it merely enables the constraint for future data changes.

To enable all disabled constraints and verify that all of the data in the table meets those constraint restrictions, you would need to use the following ALTER TABLE statement:

```
ALTER TABLE dbo.Employees
WITH CHECK CHECK CONSTRAINT ALL;
```

In this case, the record inserted from the second insert statement in Recipe 13-14 causes the check to fail. This record needs to be updated to pass the constraint, or it needs to be deleted.

■ **Caution** Once a constraint has been disabled using WITH NOCHECK, SQL Server marks the constraint as non-trusted, since data can be inserted that violates the constraint. Non-trusted constraints cannot be used by the query optimizer to optimize queries, therefore the query optimizer does not consider constraints that are defined WITH NOCHECK. Such constraints are ignored until they are reenabled and verified by using ALTER TABLE <table> WITH CHECK CHECK CONSTRAINT ALL; at this point the constraint will be marked as trusted. Non-trusted constraints may cause performance degradation by not building optimal query execution plans.

13-16. Removing a Constraint

Problem

You need to remove a constraint from a table.

Solution

Utilize the ALTER TABLE statement to drop a constraint:

```
ALTER TABLE dbo.BooksRead
DROP CONSTRAINT CK_BooksRead_EndDate;
```

How It Works

The table_name designates the table you are dropping the constraint from, and the constraint_name designates the name of the constraint to be dropped. In this example, the CK_BooksRead_EndDate check constraint is dropped from the dbo.BooksRead table that was created in Recipe 13-14. Any type of constraint (PRIMARY KEY, FOREIGN KEY, UNIQUE, DEFAULT, or CHECK) can be dropped.

13-17. Creating Auto-incrementing Columns

Problem

You need to create a column that automatically increments itself.

Solution

Utilize the IDENTITYproperty of a column:

```
IF OBJECT_ID('dbo.Employees','U') IS NOT NULL
   DROP TABLE dbo.Employees;
CREATE TABLE dbo.Employees (
    employee_id INT IDENTITY PRIMARY KEY CLUSTERED,
    manager_id INT NULL REFERENCES dbo.Employees (employee_id),
    First_Name VARCHAR(50) NULL,
    Last_Name  VARCHAR(50) NULL,
    CONSTRAINT UQ_Employees_Name UNIQUE (First_Name, Last_Name));
```

How It Works

The IDENTITY column property allows you to define an automatically incrementing numeric value for a single column in a table. An IDENTITY column is most often used for surrogate primary key columns because they are more compact than non-numeric data type natural keys. When a new row is inserted into a table with an IDENTITY column property, the column is inserted with a unique incremented value. The data type for an IDENTITY column can be int, tinyint, smallint, bigint, decimal, or numeric (the decimal and numeric data types must have a scale of 0). Tables can have only one IDENTITY column defined, and the defined IDENTITY column can't have a DEFAULT or any rule settings associated with it. The IDENTITY attribute must be specified when the column is created (either through a CREATE TABLE or ALTER TABLE statement); you cannot specify to change an existing column to have the IDENTITY attribute.

■ **Note**   *Surrogate keys*, also called *artificial keys*, can be used as primary keys and have no inherent business/data meaning. Surrogate keys are independent of the data itself and are used to provide a single unique record locator in the table. A big advantage to surrogate primary keys is that they don't need to change. If you use business data to define your key (natural key), such as first name and last name, these values can change over time and change arbitrarily. Surrogate keys don't have to change, as their only meaning is within the context of the table itself.

The basic syntax for an IDENTITY property column is as follows:

```
[ IDENTITY [ ( seed ,increment ) ] [NOT FOR REPLICATION] ]
```

The IDENTITY property accepts two optional values: seed and increment. seed defines the starting number for the IDENTITY column, and increment defines the value added to the previous IDENTITY column value to get the value for the next row added to the table. The default for both seed and increment is 1. The NOT FOR REPLICATION option preserves the original values of the publisher IDENTITY column data when replicated to the subscriber, retaining any values referenced by foreign key constraints (preventing the breaking of relationships between tables that may use the IDENTITY column as a primary key and foreign key reference).

Using an IDENTITY column does not guarantee that there will not be gaps in the numbers. Identity values are never rolled back, even if the INSERT statement is in a transaction that is subsequently rolled back. Subsequent insert statements will skip those numbers. Here's an example:

```
INSERT INTO dbo.Employees (manager_id, First_Name, Last_Name)
    VALUES (NULL, 'Wayne', 'Sheffield')

BEGIN TRANSACTION
INSERT INTO dbo.Employees (manager_id, First_Name, Last_Name)
    VALUES (1, 'Jim', 'Smith');
ROLLBACK TRANSACTION;

INSERT INTO dbo.Employees (manager_id, First_Name, Last_Name)
    VALUES (1, 'Jane', 'Smith');

SELECT * FROM dbo.Employees;
```

This query produces the following result set:

employee_id	manager_id	First_Name	Last_Name
1	NULL	Wayne	Sheffield
3	1	Jane	Smith

In viewing these results, we can see that the rolled-back INSERT statement created a gap in the employee_id sequencing.

Using an IDENTITY column does not guarantee that the column will contain unique values. To guarantee this, the column needs to have a PRIMARY KEY or UNIQUE constraint on it.

When a table has an IDENTITY column, you can utilize IDENTITYCOL in a SELECT statement to return the IDENTITY column. If the SELECT statement contains more than one table in the FROM clause with an identity column, then IDENTITYCOL must be qualified with the table name or alias.

```
SELECT  IDENTITYCOL, employee_id, Last_Name
FROM    dbo.Employees
ORDER BY IDENTITYCOL;
```

This query returns the following result set:

employee_id	employee_id	Last_Name
1	1	Sheffield
3	3	Smith

As you can see, the IDENTITYCOL is just an alias for the IDENTITY column in place on this table.

13-18. Obtaining the Identity Value Used

Problem

You need to know what the value is of the identity column for the row that you just inserted into a table.

Solution

Utilize the @@IDENTITY, SCOPE_IDENTITY, or IDENT_CURRENT system functions:

```
SELECT @@IDENTITY, SCOPE_IDENTITY(), IDENT_CURRENT('dbo.Employees');
```

How It Works

The @@IDENTITY, SCOPE_IDENTIY, and IDENT_CURRENT system functions return the last identity value generated by the INSERT, SELECT INTO, or bulk copy statement. All three functions are similar in that they return the last value inserted into the IDENTITY column of a table.

    @@IDENTITY returns the last identity value generated by any table in the current session. If the insert statement fires a trigger that inserts an identity column into another table, the value returned by @@IDENTITY will be that of the table inserted into by the trigger.

    SCOPE_IDENTITY returns the last identity value generated by any table in the current session and scope. In the previous scenario, SCOPE_IDENTITY returns the identity value returned by the first insert statement, not the insert into the second table from the trigger.

    IDENT_CURRENT returns the last identity value generated for a table, in any session or scope.

13-19. Viewing or Changing the Seed Settings on an Identity Column

Problem

You need to see and/or change the seed value used on an IDENTITY column.

Solution

Utilize DBCC CHECKIDENT to view or change the IDENTITY column's seed value:

```
DBCC CHECKIDENT ('dbo.Employees');
```

How It Works

DBCC CHECKIDENT checks the current maximum value for the specified table. The syntax for this command is as follows:

```
DBCC CHECKIDENT
( 'table_name' [ , {NORESEED | { RESEED [ , new_reseed_value ] }}])
[ WITH NO_INFOMSGS ]
```

Table 13-2 details the arguments of this command.

Table 13-2. CHECKIDENT *Arguments*

Argument	Description
table_name	This indicates the name of the table to check IDENTITY values for.
NORESEED | RESEED	NORESEED means that no action is taken other than to report the maximum identity value. RESEED specifies what the current IDENTITY value should be.
new_reseed_value	This specifies the new current IDENTITY value.
WITH NO_INFOMSGS	When included in the command, WITH NO_INFOMSGS suppresses informational messages from the DBCC output.

In this solution, the IDENTITY value is checked for the dbo.Employees table (from Recipe 13-17) and returns the following results:

```
Checking identity information: current identity value '3', current column value '3'.
DBCC execution completed. If DBCC printed error messages, contact your system
administrator.
```

In Recipe 13-17, it was demonstrated how a gap can occur in an identity column. If there had been a failed insert of multiple records and new records had not been added since, we might want to reclaim those values for use. To accomplish that, we would use the RESEED option. The following code uses the example from Recipe 13-17, with the addition of resetting the IDENTITY column after the transaction was rolled back:

```
TRUNCATE TABLE dbo.Employees;
INSERT INTO dbo.Employees (manager_id, First_Name, Last_Name)
      VALUES (NULL, 'Wayne', 'Sheffield');

BEGIN TRANSACTION;
INSERT INTO dbo.Employees (manager_id, First_Name, Last_Name)
     VALUES (1, 'Jim', 'Smith');
ROLLBACK TRANSACTION;

DBCC CHECKIDENT ('dbo.Employees', RESEED, 1);
INSERT INTO dbo.Employees (manager_id, First_Name, Last_Name)
      VALUES (1, 'Jane', 'Smith');

SELECT * FROM dbo.Employees;

DBCC CHECKIDENT ('dbo.Employees');
```

■ **Tip** The TRUNCATE TABLE statement, in addition to deleting all of the data in that table, also resets the identity seed to the initial setting, which in this case is 0.

This code produces the following result set and messages:

```
Checking identity information: current identity value '2'.
DBCC execution completed. If DBCC printed error messages, contact your system administrator.

employee_id manager_id  First_Name Last_Name
----------- ----------- ---------- ---------
1           NULL        Wayne      Sheffield
2           1           Jane       Smith

Checking identity information: current identity value '2'.
DBCC execution completed. If DBCC printed error messages, contact your system
administrator.
```

You can see in the results that the gap is now omitted.

13-20. Inserting Values into an Identity Column

Problem

You have accidentally deleted some data from a table with an identity column, and you need to insert the missing data from a backup into the table. You need to keep the original identity column values.

Solution

Utilize the SET IDENTITY_INSERT ON statement to insert explicit values into an identity column.

```
SET IDENTITY_INSERT dbo.Employees ON;
INSERT INTO dbo.Employees (employee_id, manager_id, First_Name, Last_Name)
VALUES (5, 1, 'Joe', 'Smith');
SET IDENTITY_INSERT dbo.Employees OFF;
```

How It Works

The SET IDENTITY_INSERT ON statement toggles whether explicit values can be inserted into an identity column. You can have only one table at a time with the IDENTITY_INSERT property set to ON. To insert into an identity column, you must explicitly list the identity column in the list of columns being inserted into.

13-21. Automatically Inserting Unique Values

Problem

You have a database set up using merge replication to multiple subscribers at remote offices. Users at the remote offices insert data into their local database. You need to insert an automatically generated value that will be unique across all locations.

Solution

Utilize the UNIQUEIDENTIFIER data type, with a default constraint using the NEWID or NEWSEQUENTIALID system function:

```
CREATE TABLE HumanResources.BuildingAccess(
  BuildingEntryExitID uniqueidentifier ROWGUIDCOL
    CONSTRAINT DF_BuildingAccess_BuildingEntryExitID DEFAULT NEWID()
    CONSTRAINT UK_BuildingAccess_BuildingEntryExitID UNIQUE,
  EmployeeID int NOT NULL,
  AccessTime datetime NOT NULL,
  DoorID int NOT NULL);
```

How It Works

The UNIQUEIDENTIFIER data type is a 16-bit globally unique identifier (GUID) and is represented as a 32-character hexadecimal string. The total number of unique keys is 2^{122}. Since this number is so large, the chances of randomly generating the same value twice are negligible. (Microsoft claims that it will be unique for every database *networked* in the world.)

Just like an IDENTITY column, a column with the UNIQUEIDENTIFIER data type does not guarantee uniqueness; a PRIMARY KEY or UNIQUE constraint must be used to guarantee the uniqueness of the values in the column. Keep in mind that the UNIQUEIDENTIFIER data type does not generate new GUID values; it simply stores the generated values. The UNIQUE constraint is necessary where you need to ensure that the same generated value cannot be inserted into the table twice.

The ROWGUIDCOL indicates that the column is a row GUID column. There can be just one column per table designated as a ROWGUIDCOL. Using ROWGUIDCOL allows one to use the $ROWGUID synonym for the column designated as the ROWGUIDCOL.

To automatically insert values into the UNIQUEIDENTIFIER data-typed column, you need to use a default constraint with either the NEWID or NEWSEQUENTIALID system function. NEWID generates a random GUID; NEWSEQUENTIALID generates a GUID that is greater than any GUID previously generated by this function on this computer since Windows was started. Since NEWSEQUENTIALID generates an increasing value, its use can minimize page splits and fragmentation.

To show how this all works, the following statements insert one row into the previous table and then select that row:

```
INSERT HumanResources.BuildingAccess (EmployeeID, AccessTime, DoorID)
VALUES (32, GETDATE(), 2);

SELECT *
  FROM HumanResources.BuildingAccess;
SELECT $ROWGUID
  FROM HumanResources.BuildingAccess;
```

These queries return the following result sets:

BuildingEntryExitID	EmployeeID	AccessTime	DoorID
06ADA180-DC37-4AAC-9AD5-8DE5FC0B9D73	32	2015-01-26 14:30:39.320	2

BuildingEntryExitID
06ADA180-DC37-4AAC-9AD5-8DE5FC0B9D73

■ **Note** Since this example utilizes a function that is virtually guaranteed to generate unique values each time it is called, you will see different GUID values when you run this query.

13-22. Using Unique Identifiers Across Multiple Tables

Problem

You need to have a unique identifier across multiple tables that is sequentially incremented.

Solution

Utilize a SEQUENCE.

```
CREATE SEQUENCE dbo.MySequence
    AS INTEGER
        START WITH 1
        INCREMENT BY 1;
GO
```

How It Works

A SEQUENCE generates numbers in sequential order. Unlike IDENTITY columns, they are not associated with tables. The complete syntax for a SEQUENCE object is as follows:

```
CREATE SEQUENCE [schema_name . ] sequence_name
    [ AS [ built_in_integer_type | user-defined_integer_type ] ]
    [ START WITH <constant> ]
    [ INCREMENT BY <constant> ]
    [ { MINVALUE [ <constant> ] } | { NO MINVALUE } ]
    [ { MAXVALUE [ <constant> ] } | { NO MAXVALUE } ]
    [ CYCLE | { NO CYCLE } ]
    [ { CACHE [ <constant> ] } | { NO CACHE } ]
    [ ; ]
```

Table 13-3 shows the arguments for the creation of a sequence object.

Table 13-3. *Sequence-Creation Arguments*

Argument	Description
sequence_name	The unique name in the database for the sequence.
built_in_integer_type user-defined_integer_type	Sequences can be built upon any of the integer data types: tinyint, smallint, integer, bigint, or a user-defined data type that is based on one of these types. If the type is not specified, the sequence defaults to bigint.
START WITH <constant>	The first value returned by the sequence object. The default value is the minimum value for that data type for an ascending sequence or the maximum value for that data type for a descending sequence. It must lie between MINVALUE and MAXVALUE.
INCREMENT BY <constant>	The value used to increment (if positive) or decrement (if negative) the sequence object when the NEXT VALUE FOR function is called. INCREMENT BY cannot be zero; if not specified, it defaults to 1.
MINVALUE	Specifies the minimum value that the sequence object can be; if not specified, it defaults to the minimum value for the data type the sequence object is being built upon.
MAXVALUE	Specifies the maximum value that the sequence object can be; if not specified, it defaults to the maximum value for the data type the sequence object is being built upon.
CYCLE	Specifies whether the sequence should restart at the minimum value when the maximum is exceeded (for descending sequences, restart at the maximum when the minimum is exceeded). Cycling restarts the sequencing from the minimum or maximum value, not the start value. The default is NO CYCLE.
CACHE	Increases the performance of sequence objects by caching the current value and the number of values left in the cache.

To retrieve the next sequence, you need to use the NEXT VALUE FOR system function. The following code utilizes the dbo.MySequence sequence:

```
CREATE TABLE dbo.Table1 (
  Table1ID INTEGER NOT NULL,
  Table1Data VARCHAR(50));
CREATE TABLE dbo.Table2 (
  Table2ID INTEGER NOT NULL,
  Table2Data VARCHAR(50));

INSERT INTO dbo.Table1 (Table1ID, Table1Data)
VALUES (NEXT VALUE FOR dbo.MySequence, 'Ferrari'),
       (NEXT VALUE FOR dbo.MySequence, 'Lamborghini');

INSERT INTO dbo.Table2 (Table2ID, Table2Data)
VALUES (NEXT VALUE FOR dbo.MySequence, 'Apple'),
       (NEXT VALUE FOR dbo.MySequence, 'Orange');

SELECT * FROM dbo.Table1;
SELECT * FROM dbo.Table2;
```

These queries produce the following result sets:

Table1ID	Table1Data
1	Ferrari
2	Lamborghini

Table2ID	Table2Data
3	Apple
4	Orange

Like IDENTITY columns, SEQUENCE numbers are generated outside the scope of transactions; they are consumed whether the transaction is committed or rolled back. Sequences are useful over identity columns in the following scenarios:

- The application requires a number before the insert into the table is made.

- The application requires sharing a single series of numbers between multiple tables or between multiple columns within a table.

- The application must restart the number series when a specified number is reached.

- The application requires the sequence values to be sorted by another field. To accomplish this, the NEXT VALUE FOR function can apply the OVER clause to the function call. (See the "Windowing Functions" chapter for more details of using the OVER clause.)

- The application requires that multiple numbers be assigned at the same time. For instance, you need to ensure that sequential numbers are used for the data being inserted. If other processes are also getting numbers, you could acquire numbers with a gap between some. This is avoided by calling the sp_sequence_get_range stored procedure to retrieve several numbers from the sequence at once.

- You need to change the specification of the sequence, such as the increment value.

13-23. Using Temporary Storage

Problem

You need to temporarily store interim query results for further processing.

Solution #1

Utilize a temporary table.

```
CREATE TABLE #temp (
  Column1 INT,
  Column2 INT);
```

Solution #2

Utilize a table variable.

```
DECLARE @temp TABLE (
  Column1 INT,
  Column2 INT);
```

How It Works

Temporary storage can utilize either a temporary table or a table variable. Temporary tables come in two varieties: local (uses a single #) or global (uses two: ##). A global temporary table is visible to all sessions. A local temporary table is available to the current session, from the time the table is created to the time when all procedures are executed from that session after the table is created. A table variable is visible within the current batch only.

Temporary storage can be the target of any of the data manipulation language (DML) statements (INSERT, UPDATE, DELETE, SELECT, MERGE) that any permanent table can be the target of.

- Temporary storage can be useful for doing the following:

- Eliminating repeated use of a query or CTE

- Performing preaggregation or interim calculation storage

- Staging table/prevalidation table

- Gaining data access to remote servers

Both temporary tables and table variables are stored in memory and are spilled to disk only when necessary. Table 13-4 shows the differences between temporary tables and table variables.

***Table 13-4.** Temporary Table and Table Variable Differences*

Feature	Table Variables	Temporary Tables
Scope	Current batch only	Current session, available to nested stored procedure called after creation. (Global temporary tables visible to all sessions.)
Usage	User-defined functions, stored procedures, triggers, batches.	Stored procedures, triggers, batches.
Creation	DECLARE statement only.	CREATE TABLE or SELECT INTO statement.
Table name	Maximum 128 characters	Local: Maximum 116 characters. Global: Maximum 128 characters.
Column data types	Can use user-defined data types and XML collections defined in the current database.	Can use user-defined data types and XML collections defined in the tempdb database.

(*continued*)

Table 13-4. (*continued*)

Feature	Table Variables	Temporary Tables
Collation	String columns inherit collation from the current database.	String columns inherit collation from the tempdb database for regular databases or from the current database if it is a contained database.
Indexes	Can only have indexes that are automatically created with `PRIMARY KEY` and `UNIQUE` constraints as part of the `DECLARE` statement.	Indexes can be created with `PRIMARY KEY` and `UNIQUE` constraints as part of the `CREATE TABLE` statement. Indexes can be added afterward with the `CREATE INDEX` statement.
Data insertion	INSERT statement only (including `INSERT/EXEC`)	`INSERT` statement (including `INSERT/EXEC`). `SELECT INTO` statement.
Constraints	`PRIMARY KEY`, `UNIQUE`, `NULL`, `CHECK`, and `DEFAULT` constraints are allowed, but they must be incorporated into the creation of the table variable in the `DECLARE` statement. `FOREIGN KEY` constraints are not allowed.	`PRIMARY KEY`, `UNIQUE`, `NULL`, `CHECK`, and `DEFAULT` constraints are allowed. They can be created as part of the `CREATE TABLE` statement, or they can be added with the `ALTER TABLE` statement. `FOREIGN KEY` constraints are not allowed.
Truncate table	Table variables cannot use the `TRUNCATE TABLE` statement.	Temporary tables can use the `TRUNCATE TABLE` statement.
Parallelism	Supported for `SELECT` statements only	Supported for `SELECT`, `INSERT`, `UPDATE`, and `DELETE` statements.
`SET IDENTITY_INSERT`	Usage not supported	Usage is supported.
Stored procedure recompilations	Not applicable	Creating temporary tables and data inserts may cause stored procedure recompilations.
Destruction	Destroyed automatically at the end of the batch	Destroyed explicitly with the `DROP TABLE` statement. Destroyed automatically when the session ends. For global temporary tables, they will not be dropped until no other session is running a statement that accesses the table.
Implicit transactions	Implicit transactions last only for the length of the update against the table variable. Table variables use fewer resources than temporary tables.	Implicit transactions last for the length of the transaction, which requires more resources than table variables do.
Explicit transactions	Table variables are not affected by a `ROLLBACK TRANSACTION` statement.	Data is rolled back in temporary tables when a `ROLLBACK TRANSACTION` statement occurs.

(*continued*)

Table 13-4. (*continued*)

Feature	Table Variables	Temporary Tables
Statistics	The query optimizer cannot create any statistics on table variable columns, so it treats all table variables as having one record when creating execution plans.	The query optimizer can create statistics on columns, so it can use the actual row count for generating execution plans.
Parameter to stored procedures	Table variables can be passed as a parameter to stored procedures (as a predefined user-defined table type).	Temporary tables cannot be passed to stored procedures. (They are still in scope to nested stored procedures.)
Explicitly named constraints	Explicitly named constraints are not allowed on table variables.	Explicitly named constraints are allowed on temporary tables except in contained databases. The schema that the table is in can have only one constraint with that name, so beware of multiuser issues.
Dynamic SQL	Must declare and populate table variables in the dynamic SQL to be executed.	Temporary tables can be created prior to being used in the dynamic SQL. Population of the temporary table can occur prior to or within the dynamic SQL.

Since statistics are not created on table variables, the performance of table variables can suffer when the result set becomes too large, when column data cardinality is critical to the query optimization process, and even when joined to other tables. When encountering performance issues, be sure to test all alternative solutions, and don't necessarily assume that either of these options is less desirable than other.

CHAPTER 14

■ ■ ■

Managing Views

by Wayne Sheffield

Views allow you to create a virtual representation of table data and are defined by a SELECT statement. The defining SELECT statement can join one or more tables and can include one or more columns. Once created, a view can be referenced in the FROM clause of a query.

Views can be used to simplify data access for query writers, obscuring the underlying complexity of the SELECT statement. Views are also useful for managing security and protecting sensitive data. If you want to restrict direct table access by the end user, you can grant permissions exclusively to views, rather than to the underlying tables. You can also use views to expose only those columns that you want the end user to see, including just the necessary columns in the view definition. Views can even allow direct data updates under specific circumstances, which will be described later in this chapter. Views also provide a standard interface to the back-end data, which shouldn't need to change unless there are significant changes to the underlying table structures.

In addition to regular views, you can also create indexed views, which are views that actually have the index data persisted within the database (regular views do not actually store physical data). Also available are partitioned and distributed-partitioned views, which allow you to represent one logical table that is made up of multiple horizontally partitioned tables, each of which can be located on either the same or different SQL Servers. See Table 14-1 for a look at these various view types.

Table 14-1. *SQL Server View Types*

View Type	Description
Regular view	This view is defined by a Transact-SQL query. No data is actually stored in the database; only the view definition is stored.
Indexed view	This view is first defined by a Transact-SQL query, and then, after certain requirements are met, a clustered index is created on it in order to materialize the index data to be similar to table data. Once a clustered index is created, multiple nonclustered indexes can be created on the indexed view as needed.
Partitioned view	This is a view that uses UNION ALL to combine multiple, smaller tables into a single, virtual table for performance or scalability purposes.
Distributed-partitioned view	This is a partitioned view across two or more SQL Server instances.

In this chapter, I'll present recipes that create each of these types of views, and I'll also provide methods for reporting view metadata.

Regular Views

Views are a great way to filter data and columns before presenting them to end users. Views can be used to obscure numerous table joins and column selections and can also be used to implement security by allowing users authorization access only to the view, not to the actual underlying tables.

For all the usefulness of views, there are some performance shortcomings to be aware of. When considering views for your database, adhere to the following best practices:

- Performance-tune your views as you would performance-tune a SELECT query, because a regular view is essentially just a "stored" query. Poorly performing views can have a significant impact on server performance.

- Limit the nesting of views when possible. Specifically, do not define a view that calls another view, and so on. This can lead to confusion when you attempt to tune inefficient queries, and it can degrade performance with each level of view nesting.

- When possible, use stored procedures instead of views. Stored procedures can offer a performance boost, because the execution plan can be reused. Stored procedures can also reduce network traffic, allow for more sophisticated business logic, and have fewer coding restrictions than a view (see the "Stored Procedures" chapter for more information).

When a view is created, its definition is stored in the database, but the actual data that the view returns is not stored separately from the underlying tables. When creating a view, you cannot use certain SELECT elements in a view definition, including INTO, OPTION, COMPUTE, COMPUTE BY, or references to table variables or temporary tables. You also cannot use ORDER BY, unless used in conjunction with the TOP keyword.

14-1. Creating a View

Problem

You have several processes that all need to run the same query. This query needs to return multiple columns from multiple tables for a specific product category. For example, you need to return product transaction history data for all bikes.

Solution

Create a view that uses just the necessary columns, joined to the proper tables, and filtered for *Bikes*. Here's an example:

```
CREATE VIEW dbo.v_Product_TransactionHistory
AS
SELECT  p.Name AS ProductName,
        p.ProductNumber,
        pc.Name AS ProductCategory,
        ps.Name AS ProductSubCategory,
        pm.Name AS ProductModel,
```

```
            th.TransactionID,
            th.ReferenceOrderID,
            th.ReferenceOrderLineID,
            th.TransactionDate,
            th.TransactionType,
            th.Quantity,
            th.ActualCost,
            th.Quantity * th.ActualCost AS ExtendedPrice
    FROM    Production.TransactionHistory th
            INNER JOIN Production.Product p
                ON th.ProductID = p.ProductID
            INNER JOIN Production.ProductModel pm
                ON pm.ProductModelID = p.ProductModelID
            INNER JOIN Production.ProductSubcategory ps
                ON ps.ProductSubcategoryID = p.ProductSubcategoryID
            INNER JOIN Production.ProductCategory pc
                ON pc.ProductCategoryID = ps.ProductCategoryID
    WHERE   pc.Name = 'Bikes';
    GO
```

How It Works

A view was created that retrieves multiple columns from multiple tables for the product category of Bikes. You can now query this data with this SELECT statement:

```
SELECT  ProductName,
        ProductNumber,
        ReferenceOrderID,
        ActualCost
FROM    dbo.v_Product_TransactionHistory
ORDER BY ProductName;
```

This returns the following (abridged) result set:

ProductName	ProductNumber	ReferenceOrderID	ActualCost
Mountain-200 Black, 38	BK-M68B-38	53457	1652.3928
Mountain-200 Black, 38	BK-M68B-38	53463	1652.3928
...			
Touring-3000 Yellow, 62	BK-T18Y-62	67117	0.00
Touring-3000 Yellow, 62	BK-T18Y-62	70594	742.35

In this case, the view benefits anyone needing to write a query to access this data, because the user doesn't need to specify the many table joins each time the query is written.

The view definition also used column aliases, using ProductName instead of just Name, making the column name unambiguous and reducing the possible confusion with other columns called Name. Qualifying what data is returned from the view in the WHERE clause also allowed you to restrict the data that the query writer could see—in this case, only letting the query writer reference products of a specific product category.

A view is also a good example of code reuse. Multiple processes can utilize this view for performing their actions. If at a later time it is decided that Bicycles should be included along with Bikes, all that is necessary is for the WHERE clause to be modified to include Bicycles, and all of the processes would then start returning bicycles as well as bikes.

14-2. Querying a View's Definition

Problem

You have a process that needs to know the definition of a view.

Solution

Utilize the sys.sql_modules system catalog view or the OBJECT_DEFINITION function. Here's an example:

```
SELECT  definition
FROM    sys.sql_modules AS sm
WHERE   object_id = OBJECT_ID('dbo.v_Product_TransactionHistory');

SELECT  OBJECT_DEFINITION(OBJECT_ID('dbo.v_Product_TransactionHistory'));

EXECUTE sp_helptext 'dbo.v_Product_TransactionHistory';
```

How It Works

These queries return the following result set, which is the definition of the specified view:

```
CREATE VIEW dbo.v_Product_TransactionHistory
AS
SELECT  p.Name AS ProductName,
        p.ProductNumber,
        pc.Name AS ProductCategory,
        ps.Name AS ProductSubCategory,
        pm.Name AS ProductModel,
        th.TransactionID,
        th.ReferenceOrderID,
        th.ReferenceOrderLineID,
        th.TransactionDate,
        th.TransactionType,
        th.Quantity,
        th.ActualCost
FROM    Production.TransactionHistory th
        INNER JOIN Production.Product p
            ON th.ProductID = p.ProductID
```

```
INNER JOIN Production.ProductModel pm
    ON pm.ProductModelID = p.ProductModelID
INNER JOIN Production.ProductSubcategory ps
    ON ps.ProductSubcategoryID = p.ProductSubcategoryID
INNER JOIN Production.ProductCategory pc
    ON pc.ProductCategoryID = ps.ProductCategoryID
WHERE    pc.Name = 'Bikes';
```

These methods allow you to view the procedural code of all objects, including views, triggers, stored procedures, and functions. If the object is defined as encrypted or if the user does not have permission for this object, a NULL will be returned.

14-3. Obtaining a List of All Views in a Database

Problem

You need to know the names of all of the views in a database.

Solution

Query the sys.views or sys.objects system catalog view. Here's an example:

```
SELECT   OBJECT_SCHEMA_NAME(v.object_id) AS SchemaName,
         v.name
FROM     sys.views AS v ;

SELECT   OBJECT_SCHEMA_NAME(o.object_id) AS SchemaName,
         o.name
FROM     sys.objects AS o
WHERE    o.type = 'V' ;
```

How It Works

Both of these queries query a system catalog view so as to return the metadata for the name and schema for all views in the database. Each query returns the following result set:

```
SchemaName      name
---------------  --------------------------------
Person          vStateProvinceCountryRegion
Sales           vStoreWithDemographics
Sales           vStoreWithContacts
Sales           vStoreWithAddresses
Purchasing      vVendorWithContacts
Purchasing      vVendorWithAddresses
dbo             v_Product_TransactionHistory
Person          vAdditionalContactInfo
HumanResources  vEmployee
```

```
HumanResources   vEmployeeDepartment
HumanResources   vEmployeeDepartmentHistory
Sales            vIndividualCustomer
Sales            vPersonDemographics
HumanResources   vJobCandidate
HumanResources   vJobCandidateEmployment
HumanResources   vJobCandidateEducation
Production       vProductAndDescription
Production       vProductModelCatalogDescription
Production       vProductModelInstructions
Sales            vSalesPerson
Sales            vSalesPersonSalesByFiscalYears
```

Note that the sys.views and sys.objects catalog views obtain their data from the same data source. sys.views is a filtered representation of the sys.objects catalog view, for just the views, with additional columns exposed.

14-4. Obtaining a List of All Columns in a View

Problem

You need to know the names of all the columns in a view.

Solution

Query the sys.columns system catalog view. Here's an example:

```
SELECT  name,
        column_id
FROM    sys.columns
WHERE   object_id = OBJECT_ID('dbo.v_Product_TransactionHistory');
```

How It Works

In this query, the metadata of the names and column positions for the view are returned in the following result set:

```
name                   column_id
-------------------    -----------
ProductName            1
ProductNumber          2
ProductCategory        3
ProductSubCategory     4
ProductModel           5
TransactionID          6
ReferenceOrderID       7
ReferenceOrderLineID   8
```

```
TransactionDate      9
TransactionType      10
Quantity             11
ActualCost           12
ExtendedPrice        13
```

■ **Tip**   Views can reference other views or tables within the view definition. These referenced objects are called object dependencies (the view depends on them to return data). If you would like to query object dependencies for views, use the `sys.sql_expression_dependencies` catalog view, which is covered in the "Objects and Dependencies" chapter.

14-5. Refreshing the Definition of a View

Problem

You have modified the structure of one of the tables used in a view, and now the view is returning incorrect results.

Solution

Refresh the definition of the view by utilizing either the `sp_refreshview` or `sys.sp_refreshsqlmodule` system-stored procedures. Here's an example:

```
EXECUTE dbo.sp_refreshview N'dbo.v_Product_TransactionHistory';
EXECUTE sys.sp_refreshsqlmodule @name = N'dbo.v_Product_TransactionHistory';
```

How It Works

When table objects referenced by a view are changed, the view's metadata can become outdated. For instance, if you change the width of a column in a table, this change may not be reflected in the view until the metadata has been refreshed. You can refresh the view's metadata with either the `dbo.sp_refreshview` or `sys.sp_refreshsqlmodule` system-stored procedures. Both of these system-stored procedures call the same internal routine, so they are accomplishing the exact same action.

To use either procedure, you will need ALTER permission on the view. Additionally, if the view references any XML Schema Collections or CLR user-defined types, you will need the REFERENCES permission on those objects.

14-6. Modifying a View

Problem

You need to make a change to the definition of a view.

Solution

Utilize the ALTER VIEW statement to change the definition of a view.

How It Works

The ALTER VIEW statement allows you to change the definition of a view by specifying a new definition. This is performed by first removing the existing definition from the system catalogs (including any indexes, if it is an indexed view) and then adding the new definition. For example, to change the view created in the first recipe to include Bicycles, the following script would be executed:

```
ALTER VIEW dbo.v_Product_TransactionHistory
AS
SELECT  p.Name AS ProductName,
        p.ProductNumber,
        pc.Name AS ProductCategory,
        ps.Name AS ProductSubCategory,
        pm.Name AS ProductModel,
        th.TransactionID,
        th.ReferenceOrderID,
        th.ReferenceOrderLineID,
        th.TransactionDate,
        th.TransactionType,
        th.Quantity,
        th.ActualCost,
        th.Quantity * th.ActualCost AS ExtendedPrice
FROM    Production.TransactionHistory th
        INNER JOIN Production.Product p
            ON th.ProductID = p.ProductID
        INNER JOIN Production.ProductModel pm
            ON pm.ProductModelID = p.ProductModelID
        INNER JOIN Production.ProductSubcategory ps
            ON ps.ProductSubcategoryID = p.ProductSubcategoryID
        INNER JOIN Production.ProductCategory pc
            ON pc.ProductCategoryID = ps.ProductCategoryID
WHERE   pc.Name IN ('Bikes', 'Bicycles');
GO

SELECT  ProductName,
        ProductNumber,
        ReferenceOrderID,
        ActualCost
FROM    dbo.v_Product_TransactionHistory
ORDER BY ProductName;
```

This query returns the following (abridged) result set:

```
ProductName              ProductNumber ReferenceOrderID ActualCost
---------------------    ------------- ---------------- ------------
Mountain-200 Black, 38   BK-M68B-38    53457            1652.3928
Mountain-200 Black, 38   BK-M68B-38    53463            1652.3928
...
Touring-3000 Yellow, 62  BK-T18Y-62    67117            0.00
Touring-3000 Yellow, 62  BK-T18Y-62    70594            742.35
```

Since there are no entries (yet) in the Production.ProductCategory table with a name of Bicycle, the same number of rows is returned.

14-7. Modifying Data Through a View

Problem

You need to make data modifications to a table, but you only have access to the table through a view.

Solution

Provided that you are modifying columns from one base table, you can issue INSERT, UPDATE, DELETE, and MERGE statements against a view.

How It Works

INSERT, UPDATE, DELETE, and MERGE statements can be issued against a view, with the following provisions:

- Any modifications must reference columns from only one base table.

- The columns being modified in the view must directly reference the underlying data in the table. The columns cannot be derived in any way, such as through the following:

  - An aggregate function

  - A computed column

- The columns being modified are not affected by GROUP BY, HAVING, or DISTINCT clauses.

- TOP is not used together with the WITH CHECK OPTION clause anywhere in the SELECT statement of the view.

Generally, the database engine must be able to unambiguously trace modifications from the view definition to one base table.

In the view created in the first recipe of this chapter, the query references multiple tables and has a calculated column. To examine the results for `ReferenceOrderId = 53463`, the following query is issued:

```
SELECT  ProductName,
        ProductNumber,
        ReferenceOrderID,
        Quantity,
        ActualCost,
        ExtendedPrice
FROM    dbo.v_Product_TransactionHistory
WHERE   ReferenceOrderID = 53463
ORDER BY ProductName;
```

This query returns the following result set:

ProductName	ProductNumber	ReferenceOrderID	Quantity	ActualCost	ExtendedPrice
Mountain-200 Black, 38	BK-M68B-38	53463	1	1652.3928	1652.3928

It is decided to update the quantity of this record to 3, so the following query is issued:

```
UPDATE  dbo.v_Product_TransactionHistory
SET     Quantity = 3
WHERE   ReferenceOrderID = 53463;
```

Running the previous query now returns the following result set:

ProductName	ProductNumber	ReferenceOrderID	Quantity	ActualCost	ExtendedPrice
Mountain-200 Black, 38	BK-M68B-38	53463	3	1652.3928	4957.1784

What this example demonstrates is that even though the view is created against multiple tables, as long as the update is against just one of the tables, the data exposed by the view can be updated. Now, if it wasn't realized that the ExtendedPrice column is a calculated column and the UPDATE statement tries to update that column as well with this query:

```
UPDATE  dbo.v_Product_TransactionHistory
SET     Quantity = 3,
        ExtendedPrice = 4957.1784
WHERE   ReferenceOrderID = 53463;
```

then the following error is generated:

```
Msg 4406, Level 16, State 1, Line 12
Update or insert of view or function 'dbo.v_Product_TransactionHistory' failed because it
contains a derived or constant field.
```

14-8. Encrypting a View

Problem

You have a SQL Server–based commercial application, and you need to hide the definition of the view.

Solution

Encrypt the view with the WITH ENCRYPTION clause in the view definition.

How It Works

Using the WITH ENCRYPTION clause in the CREATE VIEW and ALTER VIEW statements allows you to encrypt the Transact-SQL code of the view. Once encrypted, you can no longer view the definition in the sys.sql_modules catalog view or in the OBJECT_DEFINITION system function.

Software vendors that use SQL Server as the back-end database management system often encrypt the Transact-SQL code in order to prevent tampering or reverse-engineering by clients or competitors. If you use encryption, be sure to save the original, unencrypted definition so that you can make modifications to it in the future.

The following example creates an encrypted view:

```
CREATE VIEW dbo.v_Product_TopTenListPrice
WITH ENCRYPTION
AS
SELECT TOP 10
        p.Name,
        p.ProductNumber,
        p.ListPrice
FROM    Production.Product p
ORDER BY p.ListPrice DESC;
GO
```

When the following queries are run to view the definition (as shown in the second recipe):

```
SELECT  definition
FROM    sys.sql_modules AS sm
WHERE   object_id = OBJECT_ID('dbo.v_Product_TopTenListPrice');

SELECT  OBJECT_DEFINITION(OBJECT_ID('dbo.v_Product_TopTenListPrice')) AS definition;
```

the following results are returned:

```
definition
----------
NULL

definition
----------
NULL
```

■ **Note**   Encrypting a view (or any other code in SQL Server, such as a stored procedure) is performed with an encryption method that is easily broken. In fact, there are third-party products that will decrypt the "encrypted" code. You should not rely upon this encryption to keep others from viewing the code.

Additionally, the OBJECTPROPERTY function can be used to determine if an object is encrypted, as follows:

```
SELECT  name,
        OBJECTPROPERTY(object_id, 'IsEncrypted') AS IsEncrypted
FROM    sys.views
WHERE   name = 'v_Product_TopTenListPrice'
AND     schema_id = SCHEMA_ID('dbo');
```

14-9. Indexing a View

Problem

You need to optimize the performance of a view that is defined against multiple tables, all of which have infrequent data modifications.

Solution

Create an index on the view. An indexed view will allow you to materialize the results of the view as a physical object, similar to a regular table and associated indexes. This allows the SQL Server query optimizer to retrieve results from a single physical area instead of having to process the view definition query each time it is called.

To create an indexed view, you are required to use the WITH SCHEMABINDING option, which binds the view to the schema of the underlying tables. This prevents any changes in the base table that would impact the view definition. The WITH SCHEMABINDING option also adds additional requirements to the view's SELECT definition. Object references in a schema-bound view must include the two-part schema.object naming convention, and all referenced objects have to be located in the same database.

In the following example, a view is created using the SCHEMABINDING option:

```
CREATE VIEW dbo.v_Product_Sales_By_LineTotal
WITH SCHEMABINDING
AS
SELECT  p.ProductID,
        p.Name AS ProductName,
        SUM(LineTotal) AS LineTotalByProduct,
        COUNT_BIG(*) AS LineItems
FROM    Sales.SalesOrderDetail s
        INNER JOIN Production.Product p
            ON s.ProductID = p.ProductID
GROUP BY p.ProductID,
        p.Name;
GO
```

Before creating an index, I will demonstrate querying the regular view, which returns the query I/O cost statistics using the SET STATISTICS IO command:

```
SET STATISTICS IO ON;
GO

SELECT TOP 5
        ProductName,
        LineTotalByProduct
FROM    dbo.v_Product_Sales_By_LineTotal
ORDER BY LineTotalByProduct DESC ;
GO
```

This query produces the following result set:

```
ProductName                 LineTotalByProduct
-------------------------   ------------------
Mountain-200 Black, 38      4400592.800400
Mountain-200 Black, 42      4009494.761841
Mountain-200 Silver, 38     3693678.025272
Mountain-200 Silver, 42     3438478.860423
Mountain-200 Silver, 46     3434256.941928
```

This query also returns the following I/O information reporting the various activities performed against the tables involved in the query that was run (if you are following along with the recipe, keep in mind that unless your system is identical in every way to mine, then you will probably have different statistic values returned from the following statistics):

```
Table 'Product'. Scan count 0, logical reads 10, physical reads 0, read-ahead reads 0, lob
logical reads 0, lob physical reads 0, lob read-ahead reads 0.
Table 'Worktable'. Scan count 0, logical reads 0, physical reads 0, read-ahead reads 0, lob
logical reads 0, lob physical reads 0, lob read-ahead reads 0.
Table 'Workfile'. Scan count 0, logical reads 0, physical reads 0, read-ahead reads 0, lob
logical reads 0, lob physical reads 0, lob read-ahead reads 0.
Table 'SalesOrderDetail'. Scan count 1, logical reads 1246, physical reads 2, read-ahead
reads 1284, lob logical reads 0, lob physical reads 0, lob read-ahead reads 0.
```

Now we can add the clustered and nonclustered indexes to this view:

```
CREATE UNIQUE CLUSTERED INDEX UCI_v_Product_Sales_By_LineTotal
ON dbo.v_Product_Sales_By_LineTotal (ProductID);
GO
CREATE NONCLUSTERED INDEX NI_v_Product_Sales_By_LineTotal
ON dbo.v_Product_Sales_By_LineTotal (ProductName);
GO
```

When the previous query is now run, the same results are returned. However, the statistics have changed:

```
Table 'v_Product_Sales_By_LineTotal'. Scan count 1, logical reads 5, physical reads 0,
read-ahead reads 0, lob logical reads 0, lob physical reads 0, lob read-ahead reads 0.
```

How It Works

Let's step through the process. First, a view was created that utilized the WITH SCHEMABINDING clause:

```
CREATE VIEW dbo.v_Product_Sales_By_LineTotal
WITH SCHEMABINDING
AS
```

The rest of the view was a regular SELECT statement that summed the LineTotal column and counted the number of records for the ProductID and Name grouping:

```
SELECT  p.ProductID,
        p.Name AS ProductName,
        SUM(LineTotal) AS LineTotalByProduct,
        COUNT_BIG(*) AS LineItems
FROM    Sales.SalesOrderDetail s
        INNER JOIN Production.Product p
            ON s.ProductID = p.ProductID
GROUP BY p.ProductID,
        p.Name;
```

Notice that the query referenced the COUNT_BIG aggregate function instead of the more typically used COUNT function. If the GROUP BY clause is used on an indexed view, then the COUNT_BIG function is required in order for SQL Server to maintain the number of rows in each group within the indexed view.

Once the view was successfully created with SCHEMABINDING, a unique clustered index was then created on it:

```
CREATE UNIQUE CLUSTERED INDEX UCI_v_Product_Sales_By_LineTotal
ON dbo.v_Product_Sales_By_LineTotal (ProductID);
GO
```

To index a view, you must first create a unique clustered index on it. This process materializes the view, making it have a physical existence instead of its normal virtual existence. Once this index has been built, the view data is stored in much the same way as a clustered index for a table is stored. After a clustered index is created, you can also create additional nonclustered indexes, as you would for a regular table. In the example, a nonclustered index was created on the ProductName column of the indexed view:

```
CREATE NONCLUSTERED INDEX NI_v_Product_Sales_By_LineTotal
ON dbo.v_Product_Sales_By_LineTotal (ProductName);
GO
```

Once a view is indexed, view indexes can then be used by SQL Server Enterprise Edition whenever the view or underlying tables are referenced in a query. The SET STATISTICS IO command was used to demonstrate how SQL Server performs the data page retrieval both before and after the view was indexed.

Indexed views can provide performance benefits for relatively static data. Frequently updated base tables, however, are not an ideal choice for being referenced in an indexed view, because the updates will also cause frequent updates to the view's indexes, potentially reducing the benefit of any query performance gained. This is a trade-off between data-modification speed and query speed.

Also, although indexed views can be created using any edition of SQL Server, they will be automatically considered during the query execution if you are using Enterprise Edition. To make sure SQL Server uses them in other editions, you would need to use the view hint NOEXPAND, which is reviewed in the next recipe.

14-10. Creating a Partitioned View

Problem

You have a table that has an extremely large row count and is causing performance issues. Only the current month's data is actively changing. You want to reduce the size of this table in order to improve the performance of DML operations, yet you still want to keep all of the rows in the table for your queries and to keep the same object name in your queries.

Solution

Split the table into multiple tables, and create a partitioned view with the same name as the original table name. This example will work with the fictional company MegaCorp. They want to track all of the hits to their website. Anticipating a large amount of traffic, a WebHits table is created for each month in the TSQLRecipe_A database:

```
IF DB_ID('TSQLRecipe_A') IS NULL
    CREATE DATABASE TSQLRecipe_A;
GO
USE TSQLRecipe_A;
GO
CREATE TABLE dbo.WebHits_201201
        (
        HitDt DATETIME
            NOT NULL
            CONSTRAINT PK__WebHits_201201 PRIMARY KEY
            CONSTRAINT CK__WebHits_201201__HitDt
            CHECK (HitDt >= '2012-01-01'
                    AND HitDt < '2012-02-01'),
        WebSite VARCHAR(20) NOT NULL
        );
GO
CREATE TABLE dbo.WebHits_201202
        (
        HitDt DATETIME
            NOT NULL
            CONSTRAINT PK__WebHits_201202 PRIMARY KEY
```

```
                    CONSTRAINT CK__WebHits_201202__HitDt
                    CHECK (HitDt >= '2012-02-01'
                            AND HitDt < '2012-03-01'),
              WebSite VARCHAR(20) NOT NULL
          );
GO
CREATE TABLE dbo.WebHits_201203
          (
          HitDt DATETIME
                NOT NULL
                CONSTRAINT PK__WebHits_201203 PRIMARY KEY
                CONSTRAINT CK__WebHits_201203__HitDt
                CHECK (HitDt >= '2012-03-01'
                        AND HitDt < '2012-04-01'),
              WebSite VARCHAR(20) NOT NULL
          );
GO
CREATE VIEW dbo.WebHits
AS
SELECT  HitDt,
        WebSite
FROM    dbo.WebHits_201201
UNION ALL
SELECT  HitDt,
        WebSite
FROM    dbo.WebHits_201202
UNION ALL
SELECT  HitDt,
        WebSite
FROM    dbo.WebHits_201203;
GO
```

How It Works

Partitioned views allow you to create a single, logical representation (view) of two or more horizontally partitioned tables that are located on the same SQL Server instance. While you can accomplish the same thing by using partitioned tables, that is an Enterprise Edition feature; partitioned views are available on all editions.

To set up a partitioned view, a large table is split into smaller tables based on a range of values defined in a CHECK constraint. This CHECK constraint ensures that each smaller table holds unique data that cannot be stored in the other tables. The partitioned view is then created using a UNION ALL to join each smaller table into a single result set.

The performance benefit is realized when a query is executed against the partitioned view. If the view is partitioned by a date range, for example, and a query is used to return rows that are stored only in a single table of the partition, SQL Server is smart enough to search only that one partition instead of all tables in the partitioned view.

After the tables are set up, the partitioned view can be created. There are three areas that have specific requirements that need to be met in order to create a partitioned view.

1. The SELECT list

    -   All columns in the affected tables need to be selected in the column list of the view.

    -   The columns in the same ordinal position need to be of the same type, including the collation.

    -   At least one of these columns must appear in the SELECT list in the same ordinal position. This column (in each table) must be defined so as to have a check constraint, such that any specified value for that column can satisfy at most only one of the constraints from the involved tables. This column is known as the *partitioning column*, and it may have a different name in each of the tables. The constraints need to be enabled and trusted.

    -   The same column cannot be used multiple times in the SELECT list.

2. The partitioning column

    -   The partitioning column is *part* of the PRIMARY KEY constraint for the table.

    -   It cannot be a computed, identity, default, or timestamp column.

    -   There can be only one check constraint on the partitioning column.

3. The underlying tables

    -   The same table cannot appear more than once in the set of tables in the view.

    -   The underlying tables cannot have indexes on computed columns.

    -   The underlying tables need to have their PRIMARY KEY constraints on the same number of columns.

    -   All underlying tables need to have the same ANSI padding setting.

Notice the check constraints on the HitDt columns. These check constraints create the partitioning column necessary for the view.

For the partitioned view to be able to update data in the underlying tables, the following conditions must be met:

-   INSERT statements must supply values for all the columns in the view, even if the underlying tables have a default constraint or they allow NULL values. If the column does have a default definition, the INSERT statement cannot use the DEFAULT keyword for this column.

-   The value being inserted into the partitioning column should satisfy at least one of the underlying constraints.

-   UPDATE statements cannot specify the DEFAULT keyword as a value in the SET clause.

-   Columns in the view that are identity columns in any underlying table cannot be modified by either the INSERT or UPDATE statements.

-   If any underlying table contains a TIMESTAMP (ROWVERSION) column, the data cannot be modified by using an UPDATE or INSERT statement.

- None of the underlying tables can contain a trigger or an ON UPDATE CASCADE/SET NULL/SET DEFAULT or ON DELETE CASCADE/SET NULL/SET DEFAULT constraint.

- INSERT, UPDATE, and DELETE actions are not allowed if there is a self-join with the same view or any of the underlying tables in the statement.

- Bulk importing of data from the bcp utility or the BULK INSERT and INSERT ... SELECT * FROM OPENROWSET(BULK...) statements is not supported.

Considering all of the previous requirements, the view is created in the final statement of the solution example.

Now you can insert some records into the view. If everything works correctly, they will be inserted into their underlying tables:

```
INSERT  INTO dbo.WebHits (HitDt, WebSite)
VALUES  ('2012-01-15T13:22:18.456', 'MegaCorp'),
        ('2012-02-15T13:22:18.456', 'MegaCorp'),
        ('2012-03-15T13:22:18.456', 'MegaCorp');
GO
```

To check whether the records are in the proper tables, run the following query:

```
SELECT  *
FROM    dbo.WebHits_201201;
```

This query returns the following result set:

```
HitDt                   WebSite
----------------------- ---------
2012-01-15 13:22:18.457 MegaCorp
```

Then run:

```
SELECT  *
FROM    dbo.WebHits_201202;
```

This query returns the following result set:

```
HitDt                   WebSite
----------------------- ---------
2012-02-15 13:22:18.457 MegaCorp
```

Next, run the following:

```
SELECT  *
FROM    dbo.WebHits_201203;
```

This query returns the following result set:

```
HitDt                   WebSite
----------------------- ---------
2012-03-15 13:22:18.457 MegaCorp
```

Now that you can see that the data is going into the proper tables, let's look at how SQL Server retrieves data. Run the following:

```
SET STATISTICS IO ON;
GO
SELECT  *
FROM    dbo.WebHits
WHERE   HitDt >= '2012-02-01'
        AND HitDt < '2012-03-01';
```

This query returns the following result set:

```
HitDt                   WebSite
----------------------- --------------------
2012-02-15 13:22:18.457 MegaCorp

Table 'WebHits_201202'. Scan count 1, logical reads 2, physical reads 0, read-ahead reads
0, lob logical reads 0, lob physical reads 0, lob read-ahead reads 0.
```

If SELECT statements that reference the view specify a search condition, the query optimizer uses the check constraints to determine which underlying tables contain that data, and the execution plan is built referencing only those tables. In the previous query, even though the query was being run against the view, the check constraints on the underlying tables told SQL Server that for the date range being selected, only the WebHits_201202 table would need to be accessed to retrieve data. When the execution plan was built and executed, this is exactly what happened.

There are several benefits to utilizing partitioned views. These include the following:

- Allowing easier archiving of data, without extra transaction-log activity. You don't need to move records from one table to another to archive them or even to just delete them. Moving records would require transaction-log entries for the tables being deleted from and being inserted into, potentially growing the transaction log to an undesired size.

- Assuming that data is modified only on the current month's underlying table, only the indexes on that table will need maintenance activities. Since the size of the indexes will be much smaller, the time required for the index maintenance will be shorter.

- Queries can be run against a smaller number of records.

■ **Note**   It is recommended that if all of the underlying tables are on the same SQL Server instance, a partitioned table be used instead. However, this is an Enterprise Edition and greater feature; if you are using a lesser edition, using a partitioned view may be the only choice available to you.

14-11. Creating a Distributed-Partitioned View

Problem

You need to spread the workload of a table across multiple servers.

Solution

Create a table on each instance of SQL Server, then create a distributed-partitioned view on each server so as to access the data from all of the servers. For instance, if the tables for the previous recipe were on separate instances, the following code would be used to create this view:

```
CREATE VIEW dbo.WebHits
AS
SELECT  HitDt,
        WebSite
FROM    serverName.dbName.dbo.WebHits_201201
UNION ALL
SELECT  HitDt,
        WebSite
FROM    serverName2.dbName.dbo.WebHits_201202
UNION ALL
SELECT  HitDt,
        WebSite
FROM    serverName3.dbName.dbo.WebHits_201203;
GO
```

How It Works

Distributed-partitioned views allow you to create a single logical representation (view) of two or more horizontally partitioned tables that are located on multiple SQL Server instances. Distributed-partitioned views have a few more conditions to them than partitioned views; however, the only difference between them is whether all of the underlying tables are on the same SQL Server instance or not. The additional conditions for distributed-partitioned views are as follows:

- A distributed transaction will be initiated in order to guarantee atomicity across all instances affected by the update. This will require DTC to be running on each of the servers.

- SET XACT_ABORT ON must be run in order for INSERT, UPDATE, and DELETE statements to work.

- Any smallmoney and smalldatetime columns in remote tables will be mapped as money and datetime. Therefore, the corresponding columns in the same ordinal position in the SELECT list in the local tables must be money or datetime data types.

- Linked servers utilized in the partitioned view cannot be a loopback-linked server (the linked server points to the same instance of SQL Server).

- A distributed-partitioned view cannot use the EXCEPT or INTERSECT operators.

In a distributed-partitioned view, each server has a view that references its local table(s), and the remote tables are referenced in a four-part naming schema (Server.Database.Schema.Table) and utilize a linked server.

CHAPTER 15

■ ■ ■

Managing Large Tables and Databases

by Wayne Sheffield

Very large tables (where you have row counts in the tens of millions) have special needs. All data manipulations and maintenance operations need special considerations. This chapter will deal with features in SQL Server that can help; specifically, I'll cover how partitioning a table can ease data movements and how the use of filegroups and data compression can help you improve performance by distributing data I/O across multiple drives and having a smaller amount of data to store on disk.

Table partitioning provides you with a built-in method of horizontally partitioning data within a table or index while still maintaining a single logical object. *Horizontal partitioning* involves keeping the same number of columns in each partition but reducing the number of rows. Partitioning can ease the management of very large tables or indexes; data can be loaded into a partitioned table in seconds instead of minutes or hours; query performance can be improved; and you can perform maintenance operations more quickly, allowing for smaller maintenance windows. You can also improve performance by enabling lock escalation so as to lock at the partition level before locking at the table level. The recipes in this chapter will demonstrate how to use Transact-SQL commands to create, modify, and manage partitions and to partition database objects.

This chapter will also cover *filegroup* placement. Database data files belong to filegroups. Every database has a primary filegroup, and you can add additional filegroups as needed. The addition of new filegroups to a database is often used for *very large databases* (VLDBs) because filegroups can ease backup administration and potentially improve performance by distributing data over multiple arrays. *Data compression* is used to put more data in a given amount of space, reducing disk I/O at the cost of increased CPU usage in performing the compression and decompression to work with the data.

■ **Note** Files and filegroups are covered in detail in the "Files, Filegroups, and Integrity" chapter.

The recipes in this chapter will be utilizing your company's database, MegaCorpData. The database and additional files will be created on your C: drive, in a folder named Apress. The database is created from the following script:

```
USE master;
GO

EXECUTE xp_create_subdir 'C:\Apress';
```

```
IF DB_ID('MegaCorpData') IS NOT NULL DROP DATABASE MegaCorpData;
GO

CREATE DATABASE MegaCorpData
ON PRIMARY
(NAME = 'MegaCorpData',
 FILENAME = 'C:\Apress\MegaCorpData.MDF',
 SIZE = 3MB,
 MAXSIZE = UNLIMITED,
 FILEGROWTH = 1MB)
LOG ON
(NAME = 'MegaCorpData_Log',
 FILENAME = 'C:\Apress\MegaCorpData.LDF',
 SIZE = 3MB,
 MAXSIZE = UNLIMITED,
 FILEGROWTH = 1MB);
GO
```

■ **Note**   Table partitioning is a Developer or Enterprise edition (or higher) feature.

15-1. Partitioning a Table

Problem

You are adding a table (dbo.WebSiteHits) to your company's database (MegaCorpData) to track each hit to your company's web site. This table is expected to grow very large, very quickly. Because of its potential size, you are concerned that queries will not perform very well and that database backups may take longer than what your maintenance window allows for.

Solution

Partition the table into multiple filegroups, with each filegroup having its files on a different disk.

How It Works

The first step is to create multiple filegroups:

```
ALTER DATABASE MegaCorpData ADD FILEGROUP hitfg1;
ALTER DATABASE MegaCorpData ADD FILEGROUP hitfg2;
ALTER DATABASE MegaCorpData ADD FILEGROUP hitfg3;
ALTER DATABASE MegaCorpData ADD FILEGROUP hitfg4;
```

The next step is to add files to each filegroup:

```
ALTER DATABASE MegaCorpData
ADD FILE (NAME = mchitfg1,
          FILENAME = 'C:\Apress\mc_hitfg1.ndf',
          SIZE = 1MB)
```

```
TO FILEGROUP hitfg1;
ALTER DATABASE MegaCorpData
ADD FILE (NAME = mchitfg2,
         FILENAME = 'C:\Apress\mc_hitfg2.ndf',
         SIZE = 1MB)
TO FILEGROUP hitfg2;
ALTER DATABASE MegaCorpData
ADD FILE (NAME = mchitfg3,
         FILENAME = 'C:\Apress\mc_hitfg3.ndf',
         SIZE = 1MB)
TO FILEGROUP hitfg3;
ALTER DATABASE MegaCorpData
ADD FILE (NAME = mchitfg4,
         FILENAME = 'C:\Apress\mc_hitfg4.ndf',
         SIZE = 1MB)
TO FILEGROUP hitfg4;
```

Now that we have filegroups with files ready to receive data, we need to create a partition function, which will determine how the table will have its data horizontally partitioned by mapping rows to partitions based upon the value of a specified column:

```
USE MegaCorpData;
GO
CREATE PARTITION FUNCTION HitsDateRange (datetime)
AS RANGE LEFT FOR VALUES ('2006-01-01T00:00:00', '2007-01-01T00:00:00', '2008-01-01T00:00:00');
```

The partition function specifies the name of the function, the data type, whether the range of boundaries is bound to the left or right (in this example, left was used), and the values that define the data in each boundary. You cannot specify a data type of text, ntext, image, xml, timestamp, varchar(max), varbinary(max), or nvarchar(max), nor can you use alias data types or CLR-defined data types. The number of values that you choose amounts to a total of $n + 1$ partitions. You can have up to 15,000 partitions, so you can specify up to 14,999 boundaries. If the values are not specified in order, the database engine sorts the values, creates the function, and returns a warning that the values were not provided in order. If there are any duplicate values, the database engine returns an error. The first partition contains values less than the lowest specified value, and the last partition contains values higher than the highest specified value. RANGE LEFT is used to specify that the upper boundary of each partition is the value specified; RANGE RIGHT is used to specify that the upper boundary of each partition is less than the specified value. In this case, we are specifying the first day of each year, creating yearly partitions. If you wanted to partition the data by month, you would just include values for the first of each month. Tables 15-1 and 15-2 show how the partition boundaries for the previous values are set for the specified dates.

Table 15-1. RANGE LEFT *Boundaries*

Partition #	Values
1	<= '2006-01-01'
2	> '2006-01-01' and <= '2007-01-01'
3	> '2007-01-01' and <= '2008-01-01'
4	> '2008-01-01'

Table 15-2. RANGE RIGHT Boundaries

Partition #	Values
1	< '2006-01-01'
2	>= '2006-01-01' and < '2007-01-01'
3	>= '2007-01-01' and < '2008-01-01'
4	>= '2008-01-01'

Once a partition function is created, it can be used in one or more partition schemes. A partition scheme maps the partitions defined in a partition function to actual filegroups. For example:

```
CREATE PARTITION SCHEME HitDateRangeScheme
AS PARTITION HitsDateRange
TO (hitfg1, hitfg2, hitfg3, hitfg4);
```

In this statement, you assign a name to the partition scheme and specify what partition function the scheme is bound to and which filegroups are assigned to each partition.

Now that all of the preliminary work is done, the new partitioned table can be built:

```
CREATE TABLE dbo.WebSiteHits (
    WebSiteHitID BIGINT NOT NULL IDENTITY(1, 1),
    WebSitePage VARCHAR(255) NOT NULL,
    HitDate DATETIME NOT NULL,
    CONSTRAINT PK_WebSiteHits PRIMARY KEY CLUSTERED (WebSiteHitId, HitDate)
)
ON [HitDateRangeScheme] (HitDate);
```

There are a couple of items to note about this CREATE TABLE statement. The first is the ON clause; it specifies which partition scheme to put the table on. The second item is the PRIMARY KEY constraint definition; while the primary key is unique with just the identity column (unless you deliberately add duplicate values to that column), the partitioning column has been added to it. This is because all unique indexes, including those that are automatically built from PRIMARY KEY and UNIQUE constraints, need to have the partitioning column included in the index key.

15-2. Locating Data in a Partition

Problem

You want to ensure that data is being stored in the expected partitions.

Solution

Utilize the $PARTITION function to return the partition that a row is stored in:

```
INSERT  dbo.WebSiteHits (WebSitePage, HitDate)
VALUES  ('Home Page', '2007-10-22T00:00:00'),
        ('Home Page', '2006-10-02T00:00:00'),
```

```
                ('Sales Page', '2008-05-09T00:00:00'),
                ('Sales Page', '2000-03-04T00:00:00');
SELECT   WebSitePage,
         HitDate,
         $PARTITION.HitsDateRange (HitDate) AS [Partition]
FROM     dbo.WebSiteHits;
```

This query returns the following result set:

```
WebSitePage HitDate                 Partition
----------- ----------------------- -----------
Sales Page  2000-03-04 00:00:00.000 1
Home Page   2006-10-02 00:00:00.000 2
Home Page   2007-10-22 00:00:00.000 3
Sales Page  2008-05-09 00:00:00.000 4
```

How It Works

This example starts by inserting four rows into the table. Based on the dates inserted, each row should be in a separate partition. Next, a query is run to select the data from the table, and the query utilizes the $PARTITION function to return which partition the data is in. The syntax of the $PARTITION function is as follows:

```
$PARTITION.partition_function_name(expression)
```

where partition_function_name is the name of the partition function used to partition the table, and expression is the name of the partitioning column.

The $PARTITION function evaluates each HitDate and determines which partition said data is stored in based on the partition function. This allows you to see how your data is stored and how it is distributed across the different partitions. If one partition has an uneven distribution, you can explore creating new partitions or removing existing partitions, both of which are demonstrated in the upcoming recipes.

15-3. Adding a Partition

Problem

You're into the last year that your partition scheme covers, so you need to add partitions.

Solution

Utilize the ALTER PARTITION SCHEME and ALTER PARTITION FUNCTION statements to extend the partition onto a new or existing filegroup and to create the new partition. For example:

```
ALTER PARTITION SCHEME HitDateRangeScheme NEXT USED [PRIMARY];
GO

ALTER PARTITION FUNCTION HitsDateRange () SPLIT RANGE ('2009-01-01T00:00:00');
GO
```

How It Works

This example starts by using the ALTER PARTITION SCHEME statement to designate the next partition filegroup to use. The syntax for ALTER PARTITION SCHEME is as follows:

```
ALTER PARTITION SCHEME partition_scheme_name NEXT USED [ filegroup_name ]
```

where partition_scheme_name is the name of the partition scheme to modify. NEXT USED [filegroup_name] queues the specified filegroup to be used next by the next new partition created with an ALTER PARTITION FUNCTION statement.

In a given partition scheme, you can have only one filegroup that is designated NEXT USED. The filegroup does not need to be empty to be used.

In this example, we are specifying that the PRIMARY filegroup will be the filegroup that the next partition is placed on.

Next, the example uses the ALTER PARTITION FUNCTION statement to create (split) the new partition by splitting the partition boundaries. The syntax for ALTER PARTITION FUNCTION is as follows:

```
ALTER PARTITION FUNCTION partition_function_name() {
SPLIT RANGE ( boundary_value ) | MERGE RANGE ( boundary_value ) }
```

where partition_function_name is the name of the partition function to add or remove a partition from. SPLIT RANGE is used to create a new partition by defining a new boundary value; MERGE RANGE is used to remove an existing partition at the specified boundary and to move any existing records to another partition.

The existing partition is split, using the original boundary type of LEFT or RIGHT. You can split only one partition at a time. After this split, the partition layout now looks like Table 15-3.

Table 15-3. *New RANGE LEFT Boundaries*

Partition #	Values
1	<= '2006-01-01'
2	> '2006-01-01' and <= '2007-01-01'
3	> '2007-01-01' and <= '2008-01-01'
4	> '2008-01-01' and <= '2009-01-01'
5	> '2009-01-01'

Once the new partition is created, any new row added that qualifies to go to the new partition will be stored in that partition.

```
INSERT  dbo.WebSiteHits
        (WebSitePage, HitDate)
VALUES  ('Sales Page', '2009-03-04T00:00:00');

SELECT  WebSitePage,
        HitDate,
        $PARTITION.HitsDateRange (HitDate) AS [Partition]
FROM    dbo.WebSiteHits;
```

This query returns the following result set:

```
WebSitePage HitDate                 Partition
----------- ----------------------- -----------
Sales Page  2000-03-04 00:00:00.000 1
Home Page   2006-10-02 00:00:00.000 2
Home Page   2007-10-22 00:00:00.000 3
Sales Page  2008-05-09 00:00:00.000 4
Sales Page  2009-03-04 00:00:00.000 5
```

15-4. Removing a Partition

Problem

You need to remove a partition and move the data in that partition into another partition.

Solution

Utilize the ALTER PARTITION FUNCTION statement to remove a partition and merge the data in that partition into another partition. For example:

```
ALTER PARTITION FUNCTION HitsDateRange () MERGE RANGE ('2007-01-01T00:00:00');
GO

SELECT  WebSitePage,
        HitDate,
        $PARTITION.HitsDateRange(HitDate) Partition
FROM    dbo.WebSiteHits;
```

This query returns the following result set:

```
WebSitePage HitDate                 Partition
----------- ----------------------- -----------
Sales Page  2000-03-04 00:00:00.000 1
Home Page   2007-10-22 00:00:00.000 2
Home Page   2006-10-02 00:00:00.000 2
Sales Page  2008-05-09 00:00:00.000 3
Sales Page  2009-03-04 00:00:00.000 4
```

How It Works

Recipe 15-3 showed the syntax for the ALTER PARTITION FUNCTION statement, including a description of the MERGE RANGE functionality that is used to remove an existing partition. Removing a partition merges the specified partition with the preceding partition, with the rows being moved into the new partition.

In this example, the partition with the boundary '2007-01-01' is removed. When the table is queried, you can see that the row in the year 2007 has been moved from the third partition to the second partition.

Table 15-4 shows the new partition layout.

Table 15-4. *New RANGE LEFT Boundaries*

Partition #	Values
1	<= '2006-01-01'
2	> '2006-01-01' and <= '2008-01-01'
3	> '2008-01-01' and <= '2009-01-01'
4	> '2009-01-01'

15-5. Determining Whether a Table Is Partitioned

Problem

You need to determine whether a table is partitioned.

Solution

Query the sys.partitions system view to determine the partitions on an object. For example:

```
SELECT  p.partition_id,
        p.object_id,
        p.partition_number
FROM    sys.partitions AS p
WHERE   p.partition_id IS NOT NULL
AND     p.object_id = OBJECT_ID('dbo.WebSiteHits');
```

This query returns the following result set:

```
partition_id          object_id    partition_number
--------------------  -----------  ----------------
72057594039042048     245575913    1
72057594039173120     245575913    2
72057594039238656     245575913    4
72057594039304192     245575913    3
```

■ **Note**   The partition_id and object_id values will be different on your system.

How It Works

The system view sys.partitions contains a row for each partition of a table as well as for most types of indexes. (All tables contain at least one partition, whether they are specifically partitioned or not.)

15-6. Determining the Boundary Values for a Partitioned Table

Problem

You want to determine what the existing boundaries are for a partition function.

Solution

Query the system views to obtain this information. For example:

```
SELECT  t.name AS TableName,
        i.name AS IndexName,
        p.partition_number AS [Part#],
        f.type_desc,
        CASE WHEN f.boundary_value_on_right = 1 THEN 'RIGHT' ELSE 'LEFT' END AS
        BoundaryType,
        r.boundary_id,
        r.value AS BoundaryValue
FROM    sys.tables AS t
        JOIN sys.indexes AS i
            ON t.object_id = i.object_id
        JOIN sys.partitions AS p
            ON i.object_id = p.object_id
                AND i.index_id = p.index_id
        JOIN sys.partition_schemes AS s
            ON i.data_space_id = s.data_space_id
        JOIN sys.partition_functions AS f
            ON s.function_id = f.function_id
        LEFT JOIN sys.partition_range_values AS r
            ON f.function_id = r.function_id
                AND r.boundary_id = p.partition_number
WHERE   t.object_id = OBJECT_ID('dbo.WebSiteHits')
AND     i.type <= 1
ORDER BY p.partition_number;
```

This query returns the following result set:

TableName	IndexName	Part#	type_desc	BoundaryType	boundary_id	BoundaryValue
WebSiteHits	PK_WebSiteHits	1	RANGE	LEFT	1	2006-01-01 00:00:00.000
WebSiteHits	PK_WebSiteHits	2	RANGE	LEFT	2	2008-01-01 00:00:00.000
WebSiteHits	PK_WebSiteHits	3	RANGE	LEFT	3	2009-01-01 00:00:00.000
WebSiteHits	PK_WebSiteHits	4	RANGE	LEFT	NULL	NULL

How It Works

The sys.partition_range_values system view contains the information about boundary values for a partition function. Join to the other system views to return more information, such as the table, index, partition number, and type of boundary.

15-7. Determining the Partitioning Column for a Partitioned Table

Problem

You need to determine which column is the partitioning column on a partitioned table.

Solution

Query the system views to obtain the partitioning column for a table. For example:

```
SELECT  t.object_id AS Object_ID,
        t.name AS TableName,
        ic.column_id AS PartitioningColumnID,
        c.name AS PartitioningColumnName
FROM    sys.tables AS t
        JOIN sys.indexes AS i
            ON t.object_id = i.object_id
        JOIN sys.partition_schemes AS ps
            ON ps.data_space_id = i.data_space_id
        JOIN sys.index_columns AS ic
            ON ic.object_id = i.object_id
                AND ic.index_id = i.index_id
                AND ic.partition_ordinal > 0
        JOIN sys.columns AS c
            ON t.object_id = c.object_id
                AND ic.column_id = c.column_id
WHERE   t.object_id = OBJECT_ID('dbo.WebSiteHits')
AND     i.type <= 1;
```

This query returns the following result set:

Object_ID	TableName	PartitioningColumnID	PartitioningColumnName
773577794	WebSiteHits	3	HitDate

How It Works

The system views sys.partition_schemes and sys.index_columns can be joined together and, with other system views, can be used to determine which column is the partitioning column.

15-8. Determining the NEXT USED Partition

Problem

When splitting a partition (as shown in Recipe 15-3), you started off by specifying the NEXT USED partition. However, there was a problem during the split, and you need to determine which partition is currently set to be used next.

Solution

Query the system views to determine the NEXT USED partition:

```
SELECT  PartitionSchemaName,
        NextUsedPartition = FileGroupName
FROM    (SELECT FileGroupName = FG.name,
                PartitionSchemaName = PS.name,
                RANK() OVER (PARTITION BY PS.name ORDER BY DestDS.destination_id) AS dest_rank
         FROM   sys.partition_schemes PS
                JOIN sys.destination_data_spaces AS DestDS
                    ON DestDS.partition_scheme_id = PS.data_space_id
                JOIN sys.filegroups AS FG
                    ON FG.data_space_id = DestDS.data_space_id
                LEFT JOIN sys.partition_range_values AS PRV
                    ON PRV.boundary_id = DestDS.destination_id
                        AND PRV.function_id = PS.function_id
         WHERE  PRV.value IS NULL
        ) AS a
WHERE   dest_rank = 2;
```

How It Works

When NEXT USED is specified, there will be two partitions listed in the sys. destination_data_spaces view that are not included in sys.partition_range_values (there will always be one that represents the infinity range). If there is a second one present, it represents the partition that is set to be NEXT USED. We can get the NEXT USED partition for each partition where a NEXT USED has been specified by using joins. This is achieved by first performing a JOIN to sys.partition_schemes (to acquire the partition scheme name) and to sys.destination_data_spaces and sys.filegroups (to get the filegroup name). Next, a LEFT JOIN is performed to sys.partition_range_values to get the second occurrence (via the RANK function) of its NULL value (signifying no match on the join).

15-9. Moving a Partition to a Different Partitioned Table

Problem

You want to move the older data in your partitioned table to a history table.

Solution

Utilize the ALTER TABLE statement to move partitions between tables. For example:

```
CREATE TABLE dbo.WebSiteHitsHistory
    (
    WebSiteHitID BIGINT NOT NULL IDENTITY,
    WebSitePage VARCHAR(255) NOT NULL,
    HitDate DATETIME NOT NULL,
    CONSTRAINT PK_WebSiteHitsHistory PRIMARY KEY (WebSiteHitID, HitDate)
    )
```

```
ON      [HitDateRangeScheme](HitDate);
GO

ALTER TABLE dbo.WebSiteHits SWITCH PARTITION 1 TO dbo.WebSiteHitsHistory PARTITION 1;
GO

SELECT  WebSitePage,
        HitDate,
        $PARTITION.HitsDateRange(HitDate) Partition
FROM    dbo.WebSiteHits;
SELECT  WebSitePage,
        HitDate,
        $PARTITION.HitsDateRange(HitDate) Partition
FROM    dbo.WebSiteHitsHistory;
```

These queries return the following result sets:

```
WebSitePage HitDate                 Partition
----------- ----------------------- -----------
Home Page   2007-10-22 00:00:00.000 2
Home Page   2006-10-02 00:00:00.000 2
Sales Page  2008-05-09 00:00:00.000 3
Sales Page  2009-03-04 00:00:00.000 4

WebSitePage HitDate                 Partition
----------- ----------------------- -----------
Sales Page  2000-03-04 00:00:00.000 1
```

How It Works

With SQL Server's partitioning functionality, you can transfer partitions between different tables with a minimum of effort or overhead. Partitions are transferred between tables using the ALTER TABLE...SWITCH statement. Transfers can take place in three ways: switching a partition from one partitioned table to another partitioned table (both tables need to be partitioned on the same column), transferring an entire table from a nonpartitioned table to a partitioned table, or moving a partition from a partitioned table to a nonpartitioned table. The basic syntax of the ALTER TABLE statement used to switch partitions is as follows:

```
ALTER TABLE [ schema_name. ] tablename
SWITCH [ PARTITION source_partition_number_expression ]
TO [ schema_name. ] target_table
[ PARTITION target_partition_number_expression ]
```

Table 15-5 details the arguments of this command.

Table 15-5. `ALTER TABLE...SWITCH` *Arguments*

Argument	Description
`[ schema_name. ] tablename`	The source table to move the partition from
`source_partition_number_expression`	The partition number being relocated
`[ schema_name. ] target_table`	The target table to receive the partition
`partition.target_partition_number_expression`	The destination partition number

This example starts by creating a history table (`WebSiteHitsHistory`). Next, the `ALTER TABLE` statement is used to move partition 1 from the `WebSiteHits` table to partition 1 of the `WebSiteHitsHistory` table. Finally, both tables are queried to show the data that is in each table and which partition the data is in.

Moving partitions between tables is much faster than performing a manual row operation (`INSERT...SELECT`, for example) because you aren't actually moving physical data. Instead, you are only changing the metadata regarding which table the partition is currently associated with. Also, keep in mind that the target partition of any existing table needs to be empty so as to accommodate the incoming partition. If it is a nonpartitioned table, the table must be empty.

15-10. Moving Data from a Nonpartitioned Table to a Partition in a Partitioned Table

Problem

You have just found the long-lost spreadsheet that the original web site designer saved the web hits into. You have loaded this data into a table, and you want to add it to your `WebSiteHits` table.

Solution

Utilize the `ALTER TABLE` statement to move the data from the nonpartitioned table to an empty partition in the partitioned table. For example:

```
IF OBJECT_ID('dbo.WebSiteHitsImport','U') IS NOT NULL DROP TABLE dbo.WebSiteHitsImport;
GO
CREATE TABLE dbo.WebSiteHitsImport
    (
        WebSiteHitID BIGINT NOT NULL IDENTITY,
        WebSitePage VARCHAR(255) NOT NULL,
        HitDate DATETIME NOT NULL,
        CONSTRAINT PK_WebSiteHitsImport PRIMARY KEY (WebSiteHitID, HitDate),
        CONSTRAINT CK_WebSiteHitsImport CHECK (HitDate <= '2006-01-01T00:00:00')
    )
ON hitfg1;
GO
INSERT INTO dbo.WebSiteHitsImport (WebSitePage, HitDate)
VALUES ('Sales Page', '2005-06-01T00:00:00'),
    ('Main Page', '2005-06-01T00:00:00');
GO
```

```
-- partition 1 is empty - move data to this partition
ALTER TABLE dbo.WebSiteHitsImport SWITCH TO dbo.WebSiteHits PARTITION 1;
GO

-- see the data
SELECT  WebSiteHitId,
        WebSitePage,
        HitDate,
        $PARTITION.HitsDateRange(HitDate) Partition
FROM    dbo.WebSiteHits;
SELECT  WebSiteHitId,
        WebSitePage,
        HitDate,
        $PARTITION.HitsDateRange(HitDate) Partition
FROM    dbo.WebSiteHitsImport;
```

These queries return the following result sets:

WebSiteHitId	WebSitePage	HitDate	Partition
1	Sales Page	2005-06-01 00:00:00.000	1
2	Main Page	2005-06-01 00:00:00.000	1
1	Home Page	2007-10-22 00:00:00.000	2
2	Home Page	2006-10-02 00:00:00.000	2
3	Sales Page	2008-05-09 00:00:00.000	3
5	Sales Page	2009-03-04 00:00:00.000	4

WebSiteHitId	WebSitePage	HitDate	Partition

How It Works

In this example, we first create a new, nonpartitioned table that the imported data will be loaded into and then insert some records into that table. Next, the ALTER TABLE statement is utilized to move the data from the new, nonpartitioned table into an empty partition in the partitioned table. Finally, SELECT statements are run against the two tables to show where the data is within those tables. Since the source table is not partitioned, the partition number on the source table is not specified in the ALTER TABLE statement.

To move the data from one table to the partitioned table, the table whose data is being moved must be in the same filegroup as the partition that the data is to be moved into for the partitioned table. Additionally, the table whose data is being moved must have the same structure (columns, indexes, constraints) as the partitioned table, and it must have an additional check constraint that enforces that the data in the partitioned column has the same allowable values as the corresponding partition on the partitioned table. Finally, the partition on the partitioned table that the data is being moved to must be empty. Since this is a metadata operation (assigning the existing data pages from one table to another), it makes sense that the data must exist in the same filegroup as the partition and that the partition is empty; otherwise, data would need to be moved through INSERT...SELECT statements.

■ **Caution** In this example, both tables have an identity column. If you look at the returned results, there are duplicate values for this identity column. Since the unique constraints include the partitioning column values in addition to the identity column values, these values are valid even though duplicated identity column values are not normally seen.

15-11. Moving a Partition from a Partitioned Table to a Nonpartitioned Table

Problem

You want to move all of the data in a partition of a partitioned table to a nonpartitioned table.

Solution

Utilize the ALTER TABLE statement to move the data from a partition of a partitioned table to a nonpartitioned table. For example:

```
ALTER TABLE dbo.WebSiteHits SWITCH PARTITION 1 TO dbo.WebSiteHitsImport;
GO

-- see the data
SELECT  WebSiteHitId,
        WebSitePage,
        HitDate,
        $PARTITION.HitsDateRange(HitDate) Partition
FROM    dbo.WebSiteHits;
SELECT  WebSiteHitId,
        WebSitePage,
        HitDate,
        $PARTITION.HitsDateRange(HitDate) Partition
FROM    dbo.WebSiteHitsImport;
```

These queries return the following result sets:

WebSiteHitId	WebSitePage	HitDate	Partition
1	Home Page	2007-10-22 00:00:00.000	2
2	Home Page	2006-10-02 00:00:00.000	2
3	Sales Page	2008-05-09 00:00:00.000	3
5	Sales Page	2009-03-04 00:00:00.000	4

WebSiteHitId	WebSitePage	HitDate	Partition
1	Sales Page	2005-06-01 00:00:00.000	1
2	Main Page	2005-06-01 00:00:00.000	1

How It Works

In this example, the ALTER TABLE statement is utilized to move the data from a partition of the partitioned table to an empty, nonpartitioned table. Next, SELECT statements are run against the two tables to show where the data is within those tables. Since the destination table is not partitioned, the partition number on the destination table is not specified in the ALTER TABLE statement.

To move the data from one partition of a partitioned table to the nonpartitioned table, the nonpartitioned table must be in the same filegroup as the partition from which the data is to be removed, and the nonpartitioned table must be empty. Additionally, the nonpartitioned table must have the same structure (columns, indexes, constraints) as the partitioned table. In the prior recipe, the nonpartitioned column required an additional check constraint; this additional check constraint is not necessary when moving data into a nonpartitioned table. However, if you plan on moving the data back into the partitioned table, it is a good idea to add a check constraint when you create the unpartitioned table to ensure that data that would violate the partition does not get inserted into this table,

15-12. Reducing Table Locks on Partitioned Tables

Problem

Your partitioned table is incurring an excessive number of table locks, and you want to reduce them as much as you can.

Solution

Change the lock escalation of the table so as to lock at the partition level instead of at the table level.

```
ALTER TABLE dbo.WebSiteHits SET (LOCK_ESCALATION = AUTO);
```

How It Works

Locks on a table normally go from row to table. If a query is performing all of its activity in one partition of a partitioned table, it can be beneficial to change this behavior on the partitioned table to escalate from the row to the partition. This is performed utilizing the ALTER TABLE statement, as shown earlier.

■ **Caution**   If queries that are locking different partitions need to expand their locks to other partitions, it is possible that this could increase the potential for deadlocks.

■ **Note**   See the "Transactions, Locking, Blocking, Deadlocking" chapter for more information about lock escalation.

15-13. Removing Partition Functions and Schemes

Problem

You are no longer using a specific partition function or scheme, and you want to remove it from the database.

Solution

Utilize the DROP PARTITION SCHEME and DROP PARTITION FUNCTION statements to drop the partition scheme and function. For example:

```
DROP TABLE dbo.WebSiteHits;
DROP TABLE dbo.WebSiteHitsHistory;
DROP PARTITION SCHEME HitDateRangeScheme;
DROP PARTITION FUNCTION HitsDateRange;
GO
```

How It Works

Dropping a partition scheme or function requires that they are no longer bound to a table. In this example, we removed their usage by dropping the test tables that were utilizing the partition function and scheme. If you don't want to lose this data, you should copy this data to another table. If your goal is to simply have all of the data in one partition, you can merge all of the partitions while keeping the partition scheme and function. (A partitioned table with a single partition is functionally equivalent to a nonpartitioned table.)

If you had originally created the table without any clustered indexes, you can use the CREATE INDEX DROP EXISTING option to rebuild the index without the partition scheme reference.

To remove the partition scheme, you utilize the DROP PARTITION SCHEME statement, specifying the name of the partition scheme to drop. To remove the partition function, you utilize the DROP PARTITION FUNCTION statement, specifying the name of the partition function to drop.

15-14. Easing VLDB Manageability (with Filegroups)

Problem

You have a very large database (VLDB) with some very large tables. You want to minimize the performance impact of these tables on the rest of the database.

Solution

Place the large tables on specific filegroups that are placed on different disks than the rest of the database.

How It Works

Filegroups are often used for very large databases because they can ease backup administration and potentially improve performance by distributing data over disk LUNs or arrays. When creating a table, you can specify that it be created on a specific filegroup. For example, if you have a table that you know will become very large, you can designate that it be created on a specific filegroup that can accommodate it.

The basic syntax for designating a table's filegroup is as follows:

```
CREATE TABLE ...
[ ON {filegroup | "default" }] [ { TEXTIMAGE_ON { filegroup | "default" } ]
```

Table 15-6 details the arguments of this command.

Table 15-6. *Arguments for Creating a Table on a Filegroup*

Argument	Description
filegroup	This specifies the name of the filegroup on which the table will be created.
"DEFAULT"	This sets the table to be created on the default filegroup defined for the database.
TEXTIMAGE_ON { filegroup	"DEFAULT" }	This option stores in a separate filegroup the data from text, ntext, image, xml, varchar(max), nvarchar(max), and varbinary(max) data types.

Recipe 15-1 demonstrated how to create additional filegroups in a database, and Recipe 15-9 demonstrated how to create a table on a specific filegroup.

15-15. Compressing Table Data

Problem

You want to reduce the amount of disk space required for storing data in a table.

Solution

Utilize row or page data compression.

How It Works

Two forms of compression are available in SQL Server for tables, indexes, and filegroups: row-level and page-level compression.

Row-level compression applies variable-length storage to numeric data types (for example, int, bigint, and decimal) and fixed-length types such as money and datetime. Row-level compression also applies variable-length format to fixed-character strings and doesn't store trailing blank characters or NULL and 0 values.

Page-level compression includes row-level compression and also adds prefix and dictionary compression. Prefix compression involves the storage of column prefix values that are stored multiple times in a column across rows and replaces the redundant prefixes with references to the single value. Dictionary compression occurs after prefix compression and involves finding repeated data values anywhere on the data page (not just prefixes) and then replacing the redundancies with a pointer to the single value.

To enable compression on a new table being created, utilize the DATA_COMPRESSION option in the CREATE TABLE statement and select either NONE, ROW, or PAGE.

```
CREATE TABLE dbo.DataCompressionTest
      (
      JobPostinglD INT NOT NULL IDENTITY PRIMARY KEY CLUSTERED,
      CandidatelD INT NOT NULL,
      JobDESC CHAR(2000) NOT NULL
      )
WITH (DATA_COMPRESSION = ROW);
GO
```

The following example creates a table and inserts 100,000 rows into this table consisting of a random integer in one column and a string consisting of 50 a characters. (The GO command, followed by a number, repeats that batch the specified number of times.)

```
CREATE TABLE dbo.ArchiveJobPosting
      (
      JobPostinglD INT NOT NULL IDENTITY PRIMARY KEY CLUSTERED,
      CandidatelD INT NOT NULL,
      JobDESC CHAR(2000) NOT NULL
      );
GO


INSERT  dbo.ArchiveJobPosting
        (CandidatelD,
         JobDESC)
VALUES (CAST(RAND() * 10 AS INT),
        REPLICATE('a', 50))
GO 100000
```

The sp_estimate_data_compression_savings system-stored procedure estimates the amount of disk savings if enabling row- or page-level compression. The stored procedure takes five arguments: the schema name of the table to be compressed, object name, index ID, partition number, and data-level compression method (NONE, ROW, or PAGE). The following example checks to see how much space can be saved by using row-level compression:

```
EXECUTE sp_estimate_data_compression_savings @schema_name = 'dbo', @object_name =
'ArchiveJobPosting', @index_id = NULL, @partition_number = NULL, @data_compression = 'ROW';
```

This returns the following information (results pivoted for readability):

object_name	ArchiveJobPosting
schema_name	dbo
index_id	1
partition_number	1
size_with_current_compression_setting(KB)	200752
size_with_requested_compression_setting(KB)	7344
sample_size_with_current_compression_setting(KB)	40656
sample_size_with_requested_compression_setting(KB)	1488

■ **Note**   You may receive different results on your system.

As you can see from the stored procedure results, adding row-level compression would save more than 193,000 KB with the current data set. The sample size data is based on the stored procedure loading sample data into a cloned table in tempdb and validating the compression ratio accordingly.

The following example tests to see whether there are benefits to using page-level compression:

```
EXECUTE sp_estimate_data_compression_savings @schema_name = 'dbo', @object_name =
'ArchiveJobPosting', @index_id = NULL, @partition_number = NULL, @data_compression = 'PAGE';
```

This returns the following:

object_name	ArchiveJobPosting
schema_name	dbo
index_id	1
partition_number	1
size_with_current_compression_setting(KB)	200752
size_with_requested_compression_setting(KB)	1984
sample_size_with_current_compression_setting(KB)	40392
sample_size_with_requested_compression_setting(KB)	400

■ **Note**   You may receive different results on your system.

Sure enough, the page-level compression shows additional benefits beyond row-level compression. To turn page-level compression on for the table, execute the following statement:

```
ALTER TABLE dbo.ArchiveJobPosting REBUILD WITH (DATA_COMPRESSION = PAGE);
```

Data compression can also be configured at the partition level. In the next set of commands, a new partitioning function and scheme are created and applied to a new table. The table will use varying compression levels based on the partition.

```
CREATE PARTITION FUNCTION pfn_ArchivePart(int)
AS RANGE LEFT FOR VALUES (50000, 100000, 150000);
GO
CREATE PARTITION SCHEME psc_ArchivePart
AS PARTITION pfn_ArchivePart
TO (hitfg1, hitfg2, hitfg3, hitfg4);
GO
CREATE TABLE dbo.ArchiveJobPosting_V2
      (
      JobPostingID INT NOT NULL IDENTITY PRIMARY KEY CLUSTERED,
      CandidateID INT NOT NULL,
      JobDesc CHAR(2000) NOT NULL
      )
```

```
ON      psc_ArchivePart(JobPostingID)
WITH (
    DATA_COMPRESSION = PAGE ON PARTITIONS (1 TO 3),
    DATA_COMPRESSION = ROW ON PARTITIONS (4));
GO
```

The partitions you want to apply a data compression type to can be specified as a single partition number, a range of partitions with the starting and ending partitions separated by the TO keyword, or as a comma-delimited list of partition numbers and ranges. All of these partition options can be used at the same time.

If you want to change the compression level for any of the partitions, utilize the ALTER TABLE statement. This example changes partition 4 from row-level to page-level compression:

```
ALTER TABLE dbo.ArchiveJobPosting_V2
REBUILD PARTITION = 4
WITH (DATA_COMPRESSION = PAGE);
GO
```

15-16. Rebuilding a Heap

Problem

You have a heap (a table without a clustered index) that has become severely fragmented, and you want to reduce both the fragmentation and the number of forwarded records in the table.

Solution

Utilize the REBUILD option of the ALTER TABLE statement to rebuild a heap. For example:

```
CREATE TABLE dbo.HeapTest
(
        HeapTest VARCHAR(1000)
);
GO
INSERT INTO dbo.HeapTest (HeapTest)
VALUES ('Test');
GO 10000
SELECT  index_type_desc,
        fragment_count,
        page_count,
        forwarded_record_count
FROM    sys.dm_db_index_physical_stats(DB_ID(), DEFAULT, DEFAULT, DEFAULT, 'DETAILED')
WHERE   object_id = OBJECT_ID('dbo.HeapTest');
GO
UPDATE dbo.HeapTest
SET HeapTest = REPLICATE('Test',250);
GO
SELECT  index_type_desc,
        fragment_count,
        page_count,
        forwarded_record_count
```

```
FROM     sys.dm_db_index_physical_stats(DB_ID(), DEFAULT, DEFAULT, DEFAULT, 'DETAILED')
WHERE    object_id = OBJECT_ID(' dbo.HeapTest');
GO
ALTER TABLE dbo.HeapTest REBUILD;
GO

SELECT   index_type_desc,
         fragment_count,
         page_count,
         forwarded_record_count
FROM     sys.dm_db_index_physical_stats(DB_ID(), DEFAULT, DEFAULT, DEFAULT, 'DETAILED')
WHERE    object_id = OBJECT_ID(' dbo.HeapTest');
GO
```

These queries return the following result sets:

index_type_desc	fragment_count	page_count	forwarded_record_count
HEAP	4	23	0

index_type_desc	fragment_count	page_count	forwarded_record_count
HEAP	5	1442	9934

index_type_desc	fragment_count	page_count	forwarded_record_count
HEAP	4	1430	0

■ **Note** The fragment_count value will differ on your system and will even change if you run this recipe multiple times.

How It Works

In this example, a table is created with a single VARCHAR(1000) column, and 10,000 rows are added to this table with the value Test. An UPDATE statement is then run, which expands the data in this column to be Test repeated 250 times, for a total length of 1,000, which completely fills up the column. When the data is initially populated with the INSERT statement, the data pages are filled with as many rows as can fit. When the UPDATE statement is run, most of these rows have to move to other pages because fewer rows can fit onto a page. When rows are moved on a heap, a forwarding record is left in the place of the original row, causing an even further increased need for data pages.

During this process, the physical index statistics are being computed. From the results, it is obvious that the UPDATE statement causes a massive growth in the number of pages required to hold the data and in the number of forwarded records. After the table is rebuilt, the table now uses fewer pages, and the table no longer has any forwarded records.

■ ■ ■

Managing Indexes

by Jason Brimhall

Indexes assist with query processing by speeding up access to the data stored in tables and views. Indexes allow for ordered access to data based on an ordering of data rows. These rows are ordered based upon the values stored in certain columns. These columns comprise the index key columns, and their values (for any given row) are a row's index key.

This chapter contains recipes for creating, altering, and dropping different types of indexes. I will demonstrate how indexes can be created, including the syntax for index options, support for partition schemes, the INCLUDE command, page- and row-lock disabling, index disabling, and the ability to perform online operations.

Before beginning the exercises in this chapter, you may wish to back up the AdventureWorks2014 database so that you can restore it to its original state after going through the recipes.

■ **Note** For coverage of index maintenance, reindexing, and rebuilding (ALTER INDEX), see Chapter 24. Indexed views are covered in Chapter 14. For coverage of index-performance troubleshooting and fragmentation, see Chapter 24.

Index Overview

An index is a database object that, when created, can provide faster access paths to data and can facilitate faster query execution. Indexes are used to provide SQL Server with a more efficient method of accessing data. Instead of always searching every data page in a table, an index facilitates the retrieval of specific rows without having to read a table's entire content.

By default, rows in a regular table that lacks a clustered index aren't stored in any particular order. A table in an orderless state is called a *heap*. To retrieve rows from a heap based on a matching set of search conditions, SQL Server would have to read through all the rows in the table. Even if only one row matched the search criteria and that row just happened to be the first row the SQL Server database engine read, SQL Server would still need to evaluate every single table row, because there is no other way for it to know if other matching rows exist. Such a scan for information is known as a *full-table scan*. For a large table, that might mean reading hundreds, thousands, millions, or even billions of rows just to retrieve a single row. However, if SQL Server knows that there is an index on a column (or columns) of a table, then it may be able to use that index to search for matching records more efficiently.

In SQL Server, a table is contained in one or more *partitions*. A partition is a unit of organization that allows you to separate the allocation of data horizontally within a table and/or index while still maintaining a single logical object. When a table is created, by default, all of its data is contained within a single partition. A partition contains a heap or, when a clustered index is created, a *B-tree structure*.

389

When an index is created, its index key data is stored in a B-tree structure. A B-tree structure starts with a *root node*, which is the beginning of the index. This root node has index data that contains a range of index key values, which point to the next level of index nodes, called the *intermediate leaf level*. The bottom level of the node is called the *leaf level*. The leaf level differs based on whether the actual index type is *clustered* or *nonclustered*. If it is a clustered index, the leaf level is the actual data page. If it's a nonclustered index, the leaf level contains pointers to the heap or clustered index data pages.

A clustered index determines how the actual table data is physically stored. You can designate only one clustered index per table. This index type stores the data according to the designated index key column or columns. Figure 16-1 demonstrates the B-tree structure of the clustered index. Notice that the leaf level consists of the actual data pages.

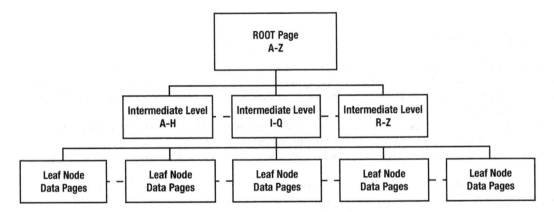

Figure 16-1. *B-tree structure of a clustered index*

Clustered index selection is a critical choice, because you can have only one clustered index for a single table. In general, good candidates for clustered indexes include columns that are queried often in range queries, because the data is then physically organized in a particular order. Range queries use the BETWEEN keyword and the greater-than (>) and less-than (<) operators. Other columns to consider are those used to order large result sets, those used in aggregate functions, and those that contain entirely unique values. Frequently updated columns and non-unique columns are usually not a good choice for a clustered index key, because the clustered index key is contained in the leaf level of all dependent nonclustered indexes, causing excessive reordering and modifications. For this same reason, you should also avoid creating a clustered index with too many or very wide (many bytes) index keys.

Nonclustered indexes store index pages separately from the physical data, with pointers to the physical data that is located in the index pages and nodes. Nonclustered index columns are stored in the order of the index key column values. You can have up to 999 nonclustered indexes on a table or indexed view. For nonclustered indexes, the leaf node level is the index key coupled to a row locator that points to either the row of a heap or the clustered index row key, as shown in Figure 16-2.

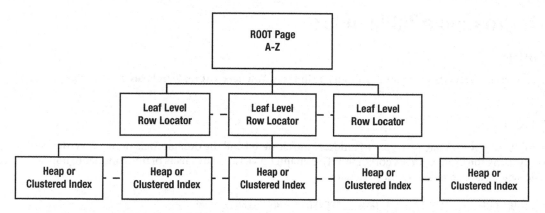

Figure 16-2. *B-tree structure of a nonclustered index*

When selecting columns to be used for nonclustered indexes, look for those columns that are frequently referenced in WHERE, JOIN, and ORDER BY clauses. Search for highly selective columns that would return smaller result sets (less than 20 percent of all rows in a table). *Selectivity* refers to how many rows exist for each unique index key value. If a column has poor selectivity, for example, containing only zeros or ones, it is unlikely that SQL Server will take advantage of that query when creating the query execution plan, because of its poor selectivity.

An index, either clustered or nonclustered, is based on one or more key values. The index key refers to columns used to define the index itself. SQL Server also has a feature that allows the addition of non-key columns to the leaf level of the index by using the INCLUDE clause, which is demonstrated later in the chapter. This feature allows more of your query's selected columns to be returned or "covered" by a single nonclustered index, thus reducing total I/O, because SQL Server doesn't have to access the clustered leaf-level data pages at all.

You can use up to 16 key columns in a single index, as long as you don't exceed 900 bytes for all index key columns combined. You can't use large-object data types within the index key, including varchar(max), nvarchar(max), varbinary(max), xml, ntext, text, and image data types.

Clustered and nonclustered indexes can be specified as either unique or non-unique. Choosing a unique index ensures that the data values inserted into the key column or columns are unique. For unique indexes using multiple keys (called a *composite index*), the combination of the key values has to be unique for every row in the table.

As noted earlier, indexes can be massively beneficial in terms of your query performance, but there are also costs associated with them. You should only add indexes based on expected query activity, and you should continually monitor whether indexes are still being used over time. If not, they should be considered for removal. Too many indexes on a table can cause performance overhead whenever data modifications are performed in the table, because SQL Server must maintain the index changes alongside the data changes. Ongoing maintenance activities such as index rebuilding and reorganization will also be prolonged with excessive indexing.

These next few recipes demonstrate how to create, modify, disable, view, and drop indexes.

■ **Note**   See Chapter 24 to learn how to view which indexes are being used for a query. Chapter 24 also covers how to view index fragmentation and identify whether an index is being used over time. To learn how to rebuild or reorganize indexes, see Chapter 24.

16-1. Creating a Table Index

Problem

You have a table that has been created without any indexes. You need to create indexes on this table.

Solution

I will show you how to create two types of indexes, one clustered and the other nonclustered. An index is created by using the CREATE INDEX command. This chapter reviews many facets of this command; however, the basic syntax used in this solution is as follows:

```
CREATE [ UNIQUE ] [ CLUSTERED | NONCLUSTERED ] INDEX index_name
ON {
[ database_name. [ schema_name ] . | schema_name. ] table_or_view_name}
( column [ ASC | DESC ] [ ,...n ] )
```

The arguments of this command are described in Table 16-1.

Table 16-1. CREATE INDEX *Command Arguments*

Argument	Description
[UNIQUE]	You can have only one primary key on each table. However, if you wish to enforce uniqueness in other non-key columns, you can designate that the index be created with the UNIQUE constraint. You can create multiple UNIQUE indexes for a single table, and you can include columns that contain NULL values (although only one NULL value is allowed per column combo).
[CLUSTERED	NONCLUSTERED]	This specifies the index type, either CLUSTERED or NONCLUSTERED. You can have only one CLUSTERED index, but up to 999 NONCLUSTERED indexes.
index_name	This defines the name of the new index.
[database_name. [schema_name] .	This indicates the table or view to be indexed.
	schema_name.] table_or_view_name}Column	This specifies the column or columns to be used as part of the index key.
[ASC	DESC]	This defines the specific column order of indexing, either ASC for ascending order or DESC for descending order.

To help demonstrate the creation of indexes for this example, I will create a new table in the AdventureWorks2014 database and intentionally exclude a PRIMARY KEY in the table definition:

```
USE AdventureWorks2014;
GO
IF NOT EXISTS (Select 1/0 from sys.objects where name = 'TerminationReason' and
SCHEMA_NAME(schema_id) = 'HumanResources')
BEGIN
CREATE TABLE HumanResources.TerminationReason(
```

```
TerminationReasonID smallint IDENTITY(1,1) NOT NULL,
TerminationReason varchar(50) NOT NULL,
DepartmentID smallint NOT NULL,
 CONSTRAINT FK_TerminationReason_DepartmentID FOREIGN KEY (DepartmentID)
REFERENCES HumanResources.Department(DepartmentID)
      );
END
```

Before I demonstrate how to use CREATE INDEX, it is important to remember that when a primary key is created on a column using CREATE TABLE or ALTER TABLE, that primary key also creates an index. Instead of defining this up front, in this example I will create a CLUSTERED index on TerminationReasonID using ALTER TABLE with ADD CONSTRAINT:

```
USE AdventureWorks2014;
GO
ALTER TABLE HumanResources.TerminationReason
ADD CONSTRAINT PK_TerminationReason PRIMARY KEY CLUSTERED (TerminationReasonID);
```

Next, I will create a nonclustered index on the Departments column:

```
USE AdventureWorks2014;
GO
CREATE NONCLUSTERED INDEX NCI_TerminationReason_DepartmentID ON HumanResources.
TerminationReason (DepartmentID);
```

How It Works

In this exercise, the TerminationReason table was created without a primary key defined, meaning that, initially, the table was a heap. The primary key was then added using ALTER TABLE. The word CLUSTERED follows the PRIMARY KEY statement, thus designating a clustered index with the new constraint. See the following:

```
ALTER TABLE HumanResources.TerminationReason
ADD CONSTRAINT PK_TerminationReason PRIMARY KEY CLUSTERED (TerminationReasonID)
```

Had the TerminationReasonID column not been chosen as the primary key, you could have still defined a clustered index on it by using CREATE INDEX:

```
USE AdventureWorks2014;
GO
CREATE CLUSTERED INDEX CI_TerminationReason_TerminationReasonID ON HumanResources.
TerminationReason (TerminationReasonID);
```

Had a nonclustered index already existed for the table, the creation of the new clustered index would have caused the nonclustered index to be rebuilt in order to swap the nonclustered leaf-level row identifier with the clustered key.

The nonclustered index in the example was created as follows:

```
USE AdventureWorks2014;
GO
CREATE NONCLUSTERED INDEX NCI_TerminationReason_DepartmentID ON HumanResources.
TerminationReason (DepartmentID);
```

The only difference in syntax between the two index types is the use of CLUSTERED or NONCLUSTERED between the keywords CREATE and INDEX.

16-2. Creating a Table Index

Problem

You have a table that needs to be created, and you need to create indexes on this table.

Solution #1

I will show you how to create a nonclustered index using two methods introduced in SQL Server 2014. In this recipe, the index is created inline while creating the table.

To help demonstrate the creation of indexes for this example, I will recreate the table from the previous recipe in the AdventureWorks2014 database, but this time with the new index being defined at the time the table is created:

```
USE AdventureWorks2014;
GO
IF EXISTS (Select 1/0 from sys.objects where name = 'TerminationReason' and SCHEMA_
NAME(schema_id) = 'HumanResources')
BEGIN
        DROP TABLE HumanResources.TerminationReason;
END
CREATE TABLE HumanResources.TerminationReason(
  TerminationReasonID smallint IDENTITY(1,1) NOT NULL,
  TerminationReason varchar(50) NOT NULL,
  DepartmentID smallint NOT NULL INDEX NCI_TerminationReason_DepartmentID NONCLUSTERED,
  CONSTRAINT FK_TerminationReason_DepartmentID FOREIGN KEY (DepartmentID)
REFERENCES HumanResources.Department(DepartmentID)
        );
/* Create a Primary Key and Clustered Index */
USE AdventureWorks2014;
GO
ALTER TABLE HumanResources.TerminationReason
ADD CONSTRAINT PK_TerminationReason PRIMARY KEY CLUSTERED (TerminationReasonID);
```

How It Works

In this solution, the TerminationReason table was created without a primary key defined, just like in the previous exercise. The difference here is that the table was created with an index at the same time. The index in this example was created as follows:

```
DepartmentID smallint NOT NULL INDEX NCI_TerminationReason_DepartmentID NONCLUSTERED,
```

Solution #2

An alternate approach to creating indexes at the time of table creation is to define the index so as to be created after the list of columns, as follows:

```
USE AdventureWorks2014;
GO
IF EXISTS (Select 1/0 from sys.objects where name = 'TerminationReason' and SCHEMA_
NAME(schema_id) = 'HumanResources')
BEGIN
        DROP TABLE HumanResources.TerminationReason;
END

CREATE TABLE HumanResources.TerminationReason(
   TerminationReasonID smallint IDENTITY(1,1) NOT NULL,
   TerminationReason varchar(50) NOT NULL,
   DepartmentID smallint NOT NULL,
   INDEX NCI_TerminationReason_DepartmentID NONCLUSTERED (DepartmentID),
   CONSTRAINT FK_TerminationReason_DepartmentID FOREIGN KEY (DepartmentID)
REFERENCES HumanResources.Department(DepartmentID)
        );

/* Create a Primary Key and Clustered Index */
USE AdventureWorks2014;
GO
ALTER TABLE HumanResources.TerminationReason
ADD CONSTRAINT PK_TerminationReason PRIMARY KEY CLUSTERED (TerminationReasonID);
```

How It Works

In this exercise, the TerminationReason table was created without a primary key defined, just like the previous exercise. The difference here is that the table was created with indexes at the same time. The index in this example was created as follows:

```
INDEX NCI_TerminationReason_DepartmentID NONCLUSTERED (DepartmentID),
```

16-3. Enforcing Uniqueness on Non-key Columns

Problem

You need to enforce uniqueness on a non-key column in a table.

Solution

Using the table created in the previous recipe (HumanResources.TerminationReason), I will execute the following script to create a unique index:

```
USE AdventureWorks2014;
GO
CREATE UNIQUE NONCLUSTERED INDEX UNI_TerminationReason ON HumanResources.TerminationReason
(TerminationReason);
```

Now, I will insert two new rows into the table with success:

```
USE AdventureWorks2014;
GO
INSERT INTO HumanResources.TerminationReason (DepartmentID, TerminationReason)
  VALUES (1, 'Bad Engineering Skills')
 ,(2, 'Breaks Expensive Tools');
```

If I attempt to insert a row with a duplicate TerminationReason value, an error will be raised:

```
USE AdventureWorks2014;
GO
INSERT INTO HumanResources.TerminationReason (DepartmentID, TerminationReason)
      VALUES (2, 'Bad Engineering Skills');
```

This query returns the following (results pivoted for formatting):

```
Msg 2601, Level 14, State 1, Line 9
Cannot insert duplicate key row in object 'HumanResources.TerminationReason'
with unique index 'UNI_TerminationReason'.
The duplicate key value is (Bad Engineering Skills).
The statement has been terminated.
```

Selecting the current rows from the table shows that only the first two rows were inserted:

```
USE AdventureWorks2014;
GO
SELECT TerminationReasonID, TerminationReason, DepartmentID
      FROM HumanResources.TerminationReason;
```

This query returns the following (results pivoted for formatting):

```
TerminationReasonID  TerminationReason            DepartmentID
1                    Bad Engineering Skills 1
2                    Breaks Expensive Tools 2
```

How It Works

A unique index was created on the TerminationReason column, which means that each row must have a unique value. You can choose multiple unique constraints for a single table. NULL values are permitted in a unique index and may not be duplicated, much like non-NULL values. Like a primary key, unique indexes enforce entity integrity by ensuring that rows can be uniquely identified.

16-4. Creating an Index on Multiple Columns

Problem

You need to create a composite index to support queries that utilize multiple columns in a search predicate or result set.

Solution

In previous recipes, I showed you how to create an index on a single column; however, many times you will want more than one column to be used in a single index. Use composite indexes when two or more columns are often searched within the same query or are often used in conjunction with one another.

In this example, I have determined that TerminationReason and DepartmentID will often be used in the same WHERE clause of a SELECT query. With that in mind, I will create the following multi-column NONCLUSTERED INDEX:

```
USE AdventureWorks2014;
GO
CREATE NONCLUSTERED INDEX NI_TerminationReason_TerminationReason_DepartmentID
  ON HumanResources.TerminationReason(TerminationReason, DepartmentID);
```

How It Works

Choosing which columns to index is a bit of an art. You'll want to add indexes to columns that you know will be commonly queried; however, you must always keep a column's selectivity in mind. If a column has poor selectivity (containing a few unique values across thousands of rows), it is unlikely that SQL Server will take advantage of that index when creating the query execution plan.

One general rule of thumb when creating a composite index is to put the most selective columns at the beginning, followed by the other, less selective columns. In this recipe's example, the TerminationReason was chosen as the first column, followed by DepartmentID. Both are guaranteed to be totally unique in the table and are, therefore, equally selective.

16-5. Defining Index Column Sort Direction

Problem

You need to create an index to support the sort order expected by the application and business requirements.

Solution

The default sort for an indexed column is ascending order. You can explicitly set the ordering using ASC or DESC in the column definition of CREATE INDEX:

```
( column [ ASC | DESC ] [ ,...n ] )
```

In this example, I add a new column to a table and then index the column using a descending order:

```
USE AdventureWorks2014;
GO
ALTER TABLE HumanResources.TerminationReason
ADD ViolationSeverityLevel smallint;
GO
CREATE NONCLUSTERED INDEX NI_TerminationReason_ViolationSeverityLevel
  ON HumanResources.TerminationReason (ViolationSeverityLevel DESC);
```

How It Works

In this recipe's example, a new column, ViolationSeverityLevel, was added to the TerminationReason table:

```
USE AdventureWorks2014;
GO
ALTER TABLE HumanResources.TerminationReason
ADD ViolationSeverityLevel smallint;
GO
```

Query authors may want to most commonly sort on this value, showing ViolationSeverityLevel from highest to lowest. Matching index order to how you think users will use ORDER BY in the query can improve query performance, because SQL Server isn't then required to re-sort the data when the query is processed. In my example, the index was created with the DESC instruction after the column name: (ViolationSeverityLevel DESC)

If you have multiple key columns in your index, each can have its own sort order.

16-6. Viewing Index Metadata

Problem

You have created indexes in your database. Now, you need some mechanism for tracking where they have been created and what the names, types, and columns are that define them.

Solution

Use the sp_helpindex system stored procedure to view the index names, descriptions, and keys for indexes on a specific table. This system stored procedure only takes a single argument, the name of the table whose indexes you want to view.

This example demonstrates viewing all indexes on the Employee table:

```
USE AdventureWorks2014;
GO
EXEC sp_helpindex 'HumanResources.Employee';
```

This returns the following sample results:

index_name	index_description	index_keys
AK_Employee_LoginID	nonclustered, unique located on PRIMARY	LoginID
AK_Employee_NationalIDNumber	nonclustered, unique located on PRIMARY	NationalIDNumber
AK_Employee_rowguid	nonclustered, unique located on PRIMARY	rowguid
IX_Employee_OrganizationLevel_OrganizationNode	nonclustered located on PRIMARY	OrganizationLevel, OrganizationNode
IX_Employee_OrganizationNode	nonclustered located on PRIMARY	OrganizationNode

For a more in-depth analysis of indexes, you can use the sys.indexes system catalog view. For example, the following query shows index options (which are discussed later in this chapter) for the HumanResources.Employee table:

```
USE AdventureWorks2014;
GO
SELECT index_name = SUBSTRING(name, 1,30) ,
            allow_row_locks,
            allow_page_locks,
            is_disabled,
            fill_factor,
            has_filter
    FROM sys.indexes
    WHERE object_id = OBJECT_ID('HumanResources.Employee');
```

This returns the following sample results:

index_name	allow_row_locks	allow_page_locks	is_disabled	fill_factor	has_filter
PK_Employee_BusinessEntityID	1	1	0	0	0
IX_Employee_OrganizationNode	1	1	0	0	0
IX_Employee_OrganizationLevel_	1	1	0	0	0
AK_Employee_LoginID	1	1	0	0	0
AK_Employee_NationalIDNumber	1	1	0	0	0

How It Works

You can use the system stored procedure sp_helpindex to list the indexes on a specific table. The output also returns a description of the indexes, including the type and filegroup location. The key columns defined for the index are also listed.

The sys.indexes system catalog view can also be used to find out more about the configured settings of a specific index.

■ **Tip** For related index keys and included columns, use the sys.index_columns catalog view.

Several of the options shown in this system catalog view haven't been covered yet, but Table 16-2 discusses some that I've discussed.

Table 16-2. *A Subset of the sys.indexes System Catalog Columns*

Column	Description
object_id	This is the object identifier of the table or view to which the index belongs. You can use the OBJECT_NAME function to show the table or view name, or you can use OBJECT_ID to convert a table or view name into its database object identifier.
name	This indicates the index name.
index_id	When index_id is 0, the index is a heap. When index_id is 1, the index is a clustered index. When index_id is greater than 1, it is a nonclustered index.
type	This specifies the index type, which can be 0 for heap, 1 for clustered index, 2 for nonclustered, 3 for an XML index, 4 for spatial, 5 for clustered columnstore index, and 6 for nonclustered columnstore index.
type_desc	This defines the index-type description.
is_unique	When is_unique is 1, the index is a unique index.
is_primary_key	When is_primary_key is 1, the index is the result of a primary key constraint.
is_unique_constraint	When is_unique_constraint is 1, the index is the result of a unique constraint.

16-7. Disabling an Index

Problem

You have had a disk error and would like to defer the creation of an index affected by the error.

Solution

Disable the index. Consider disabling an index as an index troubleshooting technique, or if a disk error has occurred and you would like to defer the index's recreation.

■ **Caution** If you disable a clustered index, keep in mind that the table index data will no longer be accessible. This is because the leaf level of a clustered index is the actual table data itself. Also, reenabling the index means either recreating or rebuilding it (see the "How It Works" section of this recipe for more information).

An index is disabled by using the ALTER INDEX command. The syntax is as follows:

```
ALTER INDEX index_name ON
table_or_view_name DISABLE
```

The command takes two arguments: the name of the index and the name of the table or view on which the index is created. In this example, I will disable the UNI_TerminationReason index on the TerminationReason table:

```
USE AdventureWorks2014;
GO
ALTER INDEX UNI_TerminationReason
  ON HumanResources.TerminationReason DISABLE;
```

How It Works

This recipe demonstrated how to disable an index. If an index is disabled, the index definition remains in the system tables, although the user can no longer use the index. For nonclustered indexes on a table, the index data is actually removed from the database. For a clustered index on a table, the data remains on disk, but because the index is disabled, you can't query it. For both clustered and nonclustered indexes on the view, the index data is removed from the database.

To reenable the index, you can use either the CREATE INDEX with DROP_EXISTING command (see later in this chapter) or ALTER INDEX REBUILD (described in Chapter 24). Rebuilding a disabled nonclustered index reuses the existing space used by the original index.

16-8. Dropping Indexes

Problem

You have determined that an index is no longer used and needs to be removed from the database.

Solution

Drop the index. When you drop an index, it is physically removed from the database. If this is a clustered index, the table's data remains in an unordered (heap) form. You can remove an index entirely from a database by using the DROP INDEX command. The basic syntax is as follows:

```
DROP INDEX <table_or_view_name>.<index_name> [ ,...n ]
```

In this example, I demonstrate dropping a single index from a table:

```
USE AdventureWorks2014;
GO
DROP INDEX UNI_TerminationReason
ON HumanResources.TerminationReason;
GO
;
```

How It Works

You can drop one or more indexes from a table using the DROP INDEX command. Dropping an index frees the space taken up by the index and removes the index definition from the database. You can't use DROP INDEX to remove indexes that result from the creation of a PRIMARY KEY or UNIQUE CONSTRAINT. If you drop a clustered index that has nonclustered indexes on it, those nonclustered indexes will also be rebuilt in order to swap the clustered index key for a row identifier of the desired heap.

16-9. Changing an Existing Index

Problem

You need to alter an existing index to add or remove columns or to reorganize the column order.

Solution

Change the column definition of an existing index by using CREATE INDEX...DROP_EXISTING. This option also has the advantage of dropping and recreating an index within a single command (instead of using both DROP INDEX and CREATE INDEX). Also, using DROP_EXISTING on a clustered index will not cause existing nonclustered indexes to be automatically rebuilt, unless the index column definition has changed.

I will show you how to drop and recreate an index within a single execution, as well as change the key column definition of an existing index. The ALTER INDEX can be used to change index options, rebuild and reorganize indexes (reviewed in Chapter 23), and disable an index, but it is not used to add, delete, or rearrange columns in the index.

The following example demonstrates simply rebuilding an existing nonclustered index (with no change in the column definition):

```
USE AdventureWorks2014;
GO
CREATE NONCLUSTERED INDEX NI_TerminationReason_TerminationReason_DepartmentID
  ON HumanResources.TerminationReason(TerminationReason, DepartmentID)
WITH (DROP_EXISTING = ON);
GO
```

Next, a new column is added to the existing nonclustered index:

```
USE AdventureWorks2014;
GO
CREATE NONCLUSTERED INDEX NI_TerminationReason_TerminationReason_DepartmentID
  ON HumanResources.TerminationReason(TerminationReason, ViolationSeverityLevel,
```

```
DepartmentID DESC)
WITH (DROP_EXISTING = ON);
GO
```

How It Works

In the first example, CREATE INDEX didn't change anything about the existing index definition, but instead just rebuilt it by using the DROP_EXISTING clause. Rebuilding an index can help defragment the data, something that is discussed in more detail in Chapter 24.

In the second statement, a new column was added to the existing index and placed right before the DepartmentID column. The index was recreated with the new index key column. You cannot use DROP_EXISTING to change the name of the index. For that, use DROP INDEX and CREATE INDEX with the new index name.

Controlling Index Build Performance and Concurrency

So far in this chapter, I've reviewed how an index is defined, but note that you can also determine under what circumstances an index is built. For example, when creating an index in SQL Server, you can designate that a parallel plan of execution is used as well so as to improve the performance, instantiating multiple processors to help complete a time-consuming build. In addition to this, you could also direct SQL Server to create the index in tempdb, instead of causing file-growth operations in the index's home database. If you are using Enterprise Edition, you can also allow concurrent user query access to the underlying table during the index creation by using the ONLINE option.

The next three recipes demonstrate methods for improving the performance of the index build, as well as improving user concurrency during the operation.

16-10. Sorting in Tempdb

Problem

You need to mitigate the length of time it takes to create indexes as well as minimize the potential for file-growth operations in the user database.

Solution

If index creation times are taking too long for what you expect, you can try to use the index option SORT_IN_TEMPDB to improve index build performance (for larger tables). This option pushes the intermediate index build results to the tempdb database instead of using the user database where the index is housed.

In this recipe, I will show you how to push index creation processing to the tempdb system database. This database is used to manage user connections, temporary tables, temporary stored procedures, or temporary work tables needed to process queries on the SQL Server instance. Depending on the database activity on your SQL Server instance, you can sometimes reap performance benefits by isolating the tempdb database on its own disk array, separate from other databases.

The syntax for this option, which can be used with both CREATE INDEX and ALTER INDEX, is as follows:

```
WITH (SORT_IN_TEMPDB = { ON | OFF })
```

The default for this option is OFF. In this example, I will create a new nonclustered index with the SORT_IN_TEMPDB option enabled:

```
USE AdventureWorks2014;
GO
CREATE NONCLUSTERED INDEX NI_Address_PostalCode
  ON Person.Address (PostalCode)
  WITH (SORT_IN_TEMPDB = ON);
```

How It Works

The SORT_IN_TEMPDB option enables the use of the tempdb database for intermediate index results. This option may decrease the amount of time it takes to create the index for a large table, but with the trade-off that the tempdb system database will need additional space in order to participate in this operation.

16-11. Controlling Index Creation Parallelism

Problem

You need to limit the number of processors that index creation can utilize.

Solution

If you are using SQL Server Enterprise Edition with a multiprocessor server, you can control or limit the number of processors potentially used in an index-creation operation by using the MAXDOP index option. *Parallelism,* which in this context is the use of two or more processors to fulfill a single query statement, can potentially improve the performance of the index-creation operation.

The syntax for this option, which can be used with both CREATE INDEX and ALTER INDEX, is as follows:

```
MAXDOP = max_degree_of_parallelism
```

The default value for this option is 0, which means that SQL Server can choose any or all of the available processors for the operation. A MAXDOP value of 1 disables parallelism on the index creation.

■ **Tip** Limiting parallelism for index creation may improve concurrency for user activity running during the build, but may also increase the time it takes for the index to be created.

This example demonstrates how to control the number of processors used in parallel-plan execution (parallelism) during index creation:

```
USE AdventureWorks2014;
GO
CREATE NONCLUSTERED INDEX NI_Address_AddressLine1
  ON Person.Address (AddressLine1)
  WITH (MAXDOP = 4);
```

How It Works

In this recipe, the index creation was limited to four processors, as follows:

```
WITH (MAXDOP = 4)
```

Just because you set MAXDOP doesn't guarantee that SQL Server will actually use the number of processors that you designate. It only ensures that SQL Server will not exceed the MAXDOP threshold.

16-12. User Table Access During Index Creation

Problem

Users must have continued access throughout the creation of indexes.

Solution

In this recipe, I will show you how to allow query activity to continue to access the table even while an index creation process is executing. If you are using SQL Server Enterprise Edition, you can allow concurrent user query access to the underlying table during index creation by using the ONLINE option, which is demonstrated in this recipe, as follows:

```
USE AdventureWorks2014;
GO
CREATE NONCLUSTERED INDEX NCI_ProductVendor_MinOrderQty
  ON Purchasing.ProductVendor(MinOrderQty)
  WITH (ONLINE = ON); -- Online option is an Enterprise Edition feature
```

How It Works

With the ONLINE option in the WITH clause of the index creation, long-term table locks are not held during index creation. This can provide better concurrency on larger indexes that contain frequently accessed data. When the ONLINE option is set ON, only intent share locks are held on the source table for the duration of the index creation, instead of the default behavior of a longer-term table lock held for the duration of the index creation.

Index Options

The next three recipes cover options that affect performance, each in its own way. For example, the INCLUDE keyword allows you to add non-key columns to a nonclustered index. This allows you to create a covering index that can be used to return data to the user without having to access the clustered index data.

The second recipe discusses how the PAD_INDEX and FILLFACTOR options determine how to set the initial percentage of rows to fill the index's leaf-level pages and intermediate levels. The recipe discusses how the fill factor can affect the performance of not only queries, but also insert, update, and delete operations.

The third recipe covers how to disable certain locking types for a specific index. As discussed in the recipe, using these options allows you to control both concurrency and resource usage when queries access the index.

16-13. Using an Index INCLUDE

Problem

You need to provide a covering index for a query that requires the use of several non-key columns.

Solution

One solution to this problem is the INCLUDE keyword, which allows you to add up to 1,023 non-key columns to the nonclustered index, helping you to improve query performance by creating a covered index. These non-key columns are not stored at each level of the index, but instead are found only in the leaf level of the nonclustered index.

A *covering query* is a query whose referenced columns are found entirely within a nonclustered index. This scenario often results in better query performance, because SQL Server does not have to retrieve the actual data from the clustered index or heap—it only needs to read the data stored in the nonclustered index. The drawback, however, is that you can only include up to 16 columns, or up to 900 bytes for an index key.

The syntax for using INCLUDE with CREATE NONCLUSTERED INDEX is as follows:

```
CREATE NONCLUSTERED INDEX index_name
ON table_or_view_name ( column [ ASC | DESC ] [ ,...n ] ) INCLUDE ( column [ ,... n ] )
```

The first column list is for key index columns, and the column list after INCLUDE is for non-key columns. In this example, I create a new large-object data-type column in the TerminationReason table. I drop the existing index on DepartmentID and recreate it with the new non-key value in the index. See the following:

```
USE AdventureWorks2014;
GO
ALTER TABLE HumanResources.TerminationReason
  ADD LegalDescription varchar(max);
Go
DROP INDEX HumanResources.TerminationReason.NI_TerminationReason_TerminationReason_
DepartmentID;
Go
CREATE NONCLUSTERED INDEX NI_TerminationReason_TerminationReason_DepartmentID
  ON HumanResources.TerminationReason (TerminationReason, DepartmentID)
  INCLUDE (LegalDescription);
```

How It Works

This recipe demonstrated a technique for enhancing the usefulness of a nonclustered index. The example started with creating a new varchar(max) data-type column. Because of its data type (large object, LOB), it cannot be used as a key value in the index; however, using it within the INCLUDE keyword will allow you to reference the new large-object data type. The existing index on the TerminationReason table was then dropped and recreated using INCLUDE with the new non-key column.

You can use INCLUDE only with a nonclustered index (where it comes in handy for covering queries), and you still can't include the deprecated image, ntext, or text data types. Also, if the index size increases too significantly because of the additional non-key values, you may lose some of the query benefits that a covering index can give you, so be sure to test comparatively before and after performance.

16-14. Using PADINDEX and FILLFACTOR

Problem

You need to create an index that will help minimize page splits due to insert operations.

Solution

I will set the initial percentage of rows to fill the index's leaf-level pages and intermediate levels. The fill-factor percentage of an index refers to how full the leaf level of the index pages should be when the index is first created. The default fill factor, if not explicitly set, is 0, which equates to filling the pages as full as possible. SQL Server does leave some space available, enough for a single index row. Leaving some space available, however, allows new rows to be inserted without resorting to page splits. A page split occurs when a new row is added to a full index page. To make room, half the rows are moved from the existing full page to a new page. Numerous page splits can slow down INSERT operations. However, fully packed data pages allow for faster read activity, because the database engine can retrieve more rows from fewer data pages.

The PAD_INDEX option, used only in conjunction with FILLFACTOR, dictates that the specified percentage of free space be left open on the intermediate level pages of an index. These options are set in the WITH clause of the CREATE INDEX and ALTER INDEX commands. The syntax is as follows:

```
WITH (PADINDEX = { ON | OFF } FILLFACTOR = fillfactor)
```

In this example, an index is dropped and recreated with a 70 percent fill factor and PADINDEX enabled:

```
USE AdventureWorks2014;
GO
DROP INDEX NI_TerminationReason_TerminationReason_DepartmentID
ON HumanResources.TerminationReason;
GO
CREATE NONCLUSTERED INDEX NI_TerminationReason_TerminationReason_DepartmentID
  ON HumanResources.TerminationReason (TerminationReason ASC, DepartmentID ASC)
  WITH (PAD_INDEX=ON, FILLFACTOR=70);
GO
```

How It Works

In this recipe, the fill factor was configured to 70 percent, leaving 30 percent of the index pages free for new rows. PADINDEX was also enabled, so the intermediate index pages will also be left 30 percent free. Both options are used in the WITH clause of the CREATE INDEX syntax:

```
WITH (PAD_INDEX=ON, FILLFACTOR=70)
```

Using FILLFACTOR can be a balancing act between reads and writes. For example, a 100 percent fill factor can improve reads but will slow down write activity, causing frequent page splitting, because the database engine must continually shift row locations in order to make space in the data pages. Having too low of a fill factor can benefit row inserts, but it can also slow down read operations, because more data pages must be accessed in order to retrieve all required rows. If you're looking for a general rule of thumb, use a 100 percent (default) fill factor for tables with almost no data-modification activity, 80 to 90 percent for low activity, and 70 to 80 percent for moderate to high activity on the index key. When setting this value, test your performance extensively before and after the change to ensure it will work as desired.

16-15. Disabling Page and/or Row Index Locking

Problem

While troubleshooting some performance issues, you determined that you need to create indexes in such a way as to eliminate resource locking.

Solution

Change the resource types that can be locked for a specific index. In Chapter 12, I discussed various lock types and resources within SQL Server. Specifically, various resources can be locked by SQL Server, from small (row and key locks) to medium (page locks, extents) to large (table, database). Multiple smaller-grained locks help with query concurrency, assuming there are a significant number of queries simultaneously requesting data from the same table and associated indexes. Numerous locks take up memory, however, and can lower performance for the SQL Server instance as a whole. The trade-off is larger-grained locks, which increase memory resource availability but also reduce query concurrency.

   You can create an index that restricts certain locking types when it is queried. Specifically, you can designate whether page or row locks are allowed.

   In general, you should allow SQL Server to automatically decide which locking type is best; however, there may be a situation in which you want to temporarily restrict certain resource-locking types for troubleshooting or a severe performance issue. The syntax for configuring these options for both CREATE INDEX and ALTER INDEX is as follows:

```
WITH ( ALLOW_ROW_LOCKS = { ON | OFF } ALLOW_PAGE_LOCKS = { ON | OFF })
```

   This recipe will show you how to disable the database engine's ability to place row or page locks on an index, forcing it to use table locking instead:

```
USE AdventureWorks2014;
GO
-- Disable page locks. Table and row locks can still be used.
CREATE INDEX NI_EmployeePayHistory_Rate
  ON HumanResources.EmployeePayHistory (Rate)
  WITH (ALLOW_PAGE_LOCKS=OFF);
-- Disable page and row locks. Only table locks can be used.
ALTER INDEX NI_TerminationReason_TerminationReason_DepartmentID
  ON HumanResources.TerminationReason
  SET (ALLOW_PAGE_LOCKS=OFF,ALLOW_ROW_LOCKS=OFF );
-- Allow page and row locks.
ALTER INDEX NI_TerminationReason_TerminationReason_DepartmentID
  ON HumanResources.TerminationReason
  SET (ALLOW_PAGE_LOCKS=ON,ALLOW_ROW_LOCKS=ON );
```

How It Works

This recipe demonstrated three variations. The first query created a new index on the table, configured so that the database engine couldn't issue page locks against the index:

```
WITH (ALLOW_PAGE_LOCKS=OFF)
```

In the next statement, both page and row locks were turned OFF (the default for an index is for both to be set to ON):

```
ALTER INDEX NI_TerminationReason_TerminationReason_DepartmentID
ON HumanResources.TerminationReason
SET (ALLOW_PAGE_LOCKS=OFF,ALLOW_ROW_LOCKS=OFF );
```

In the last statement, page and row locking is reenabled:

```
SET (ALLOW_PAGE_LOCKS=ON,ALLOW_ROW_LOCKS=ON )
```

Removing locking options should only be done if you have a good reason to do so; for example, you may have activity that causes too many row locks, which can eat up memory resources. Instead of row locks, you may want to have SQL Server use larger-grained page or table locks instead.

Managing Very Large Indexes

This next set of recipes for this chapter cover methods for managing very large indexes; however, the features demonstrated here can be applied to smaller and medium-sized indexes as well. For example, you can designate that an index be created on a separate filegroup. Doing so can provide benefits from both the manageability and performance sides, because you can then perform separate backups by filegroup, as well as improve I/O performance of a query if the filegroup has files that exist on a separate array.

As was reviewed in Chapter 15, in addition to table partitioning you can implement index partitioning. Partitioning allows you to break down the index data set into smaller subsets of data. As discussed in the recipe, if large indexes are separated onto separate partitions, this can positively impact the performance of a query (particularly for very large indexes).

SQL Server provides us with the filtered index feature and the ability to compress data at the page and row levels. The filtered index feature allows you to create an index and associated statistics for a subset of values. If incoming queries hit only a small percentage of values within a column, for example, you can create a filtered index that will target only those common values, thus reducing the overall index size compared to a full-table index, and also improving the accuracy of the underlying statistics.

As for the compression feature, available in the Enterprise and Developer Editions, you can designate row or page compression for an index or specified partitions. This feature for CREATE TABLE and ALTER TABLE was demonstrated in Chapter 15. In this chapter, I will continue this discussion with how to enable compression using CREATE INDEX and ALTER INDEX.

16-16. Creating an Index on a Filegroup

Problem

You have been tasked with creating indexes in a filegroup other than that containing the tables and data.

Solution

I will create an index on a specific filegroup. If not explicitly designated, an index is created on the same filegroup as the underlying table. This is accomplished using the ON clause of the CREATE INDEX command:

```
ON filegroup_name  | default
```

This option can take either an explicit filegroup name or the database's default filegroup. (For more information on filegroups, see Chapter 15.)

This example demonstrates how to explicitly define in which filegroup an index is stored. First, I will create a new filegroup on the AdventureWorks2014 database:

```
Use master;
GO
ALTER DATABASE AdventureWorks2014
  ADD FILEGROUP FG2;
```

Next, I will add a new file to the database and the newly created filegroup in a folder on the root of C called Apress.

```
Use AdventureWorks2014;
GO
ALTER DATABASE AdventureWorks2014
  ADD FILE
--Please ensure the Apress directory exists or change the path in the FILENAME statement
  ( NAME = AW2,FILENAME = 'c:\Apress\aw2.ndf',SIZE = 1MB )
  TO FILEGROUP FG2;
```

Lastly, I create a new index, designating that it be stored on the newly created filegroup:

```
Use AdventureWorks2014;
GO
CREATE INDEX NI_ProductPhoto_ThumnailPhotoFileName
  ON Production.ProductPhoto (ThumbnailPhotoFileName)
  ON [FG2];
```

How It Works

The first part of the recipe created a new filegroup in the AdventureWorks2014 database called FG2 using the ALTER DATABASE command. After that, a new database data file was created on the new filegroup. Lastly, a new index was created on the FG2 filegroup. The ON clause designated the filegroup name for the index in square brackets.

```
ON [FG2]
```

Filegroups can be used to help manage very large databases, both by allowing separate backups by filegroup and by improving I/O performance if the filegroup has files that exist on a separate array.

16-17. Implementing Index Partitioning

Problem

You have a partitioned table that is being queried. The indexes on this table are touching each partition and are performing less than optimally. You need to optimize the index performance.

Solution

Apply partitioning to a nonclustered index. In Chapter 15, table partitioning was demonstrated. Partitioning can provide manageability, scalability, and performance benefits for large tables. This is because partitioning allows you to break down the data set into smaller subsets of data. Depending on the index key(s), an index on a table can also be quite large. Applying the partitioning concept to indexes, if large indexes are separated onto separate partitions, can positively affect the performance of a query. Queries that target data from just one partition will benefit, because SQL Server will only target the selected partition instead of accessing all partitions for the index.

This recipe demonstrates index partitioning using the HitDateRangeScheme partition scheme that was created in Chapter 15 on the Sales.WebSiteHits table. See the following:

```
Use AdventureWorks2014;
GO
CREATE NONCLUSTERED INDEX NI_WebSiteHits_WebSitePage
  ON Sales.WebSiteHits (WebSitePage)
  ON [HitDateRangeScheme] (HitDate);
```

How It Works

The partition scheme was applied using the ON clause:

```
ON [HitDateRangeScheme] (HitDate)
```

Notice that although the HitDate column wasn't a nonclustered index key, it was included in the partition scheme, matching that of the table. When the index and table use the same partition scheme, they are said to be *aligned*.

You can choose to use a different partitioning scheme for the index than the table uses; however, that scheme must use the same data-type argument, number of partitions, and boundary values. Unaligned indexes can be used to take advantage of co-located joins, meaning that if you have two columns from two tables that are frequently joined that also use the same partition function, same data type, same number of partitions, and same boundaries, you can potentially improve query join performance. However, the common approach will most probably be to use aligned partition schemes between the index and table for administration and performance reasons.

16-18. Indexing a Subset of Rows

Problem

You have a query that is performing subpar. The query searches on a column for a range of values that comprise less than 10 percent of the total rows in the table. You need to optimize this index.

Solution

Add a filtered index to support this query. SQL Server 2008 introduced the ability to create filtered nonclustered indexes in support of queries that require only a small percentage of table rows. The CREATE INDEX command includes a filter predicate that can be used to reduce index size by indexing only rows that meet certain conditions. That reduced index size saves on disk space and potentially improves the performance of queries that now need to only read a fraction of the index entries that they would otherwise have had to process.

The filter predicate allows for several comparison operators to be used, including IS, IS NOT, =, <>, >, <, and more. In this recipe, I will demonstrate how to add filtered indexes to one of the larger tables in the AdventureWorks2014 database: Sales.SalesOrderDetail. To set up this example, let's assume that I have the following common query against the UnitPrice column:

```
Use AdventureWorks2014;
GO
SELECT SalesOrderID
  FROM Sales.SalesOrderDetail
  WHERE UnitPrice BETWEEN 150.00 AND 175.00;
```

Let's also assume that the person executing this query is the only one who typically uses the UnitPrice column in the search predicate. When she does query it, she is concerned only with values between $150 and $175. Creating a full index on this column may be considered to be wasteful. If this query is executed often, and a full clustered index scan is performed against the base table each time, this may cause performance issues.

I have just described an ideal scenario for a filtered index on the UnitPrice column. You can create that filtered index as follows:

```
Use AdventureWorks2014;
GO
CREATE NONCLUSTERED INDEX NCI_UnitPrice_SalesOrderDetail
  ON Sales.SalesOrderDetail(UnitPrice)
  WHERE UnitPrice >= 150.00 AND UnitPrice <= 175.00;
```

Queries that search against UnitPrice and that also search in the defined filter predicate range will likely use the filtered index instead of performing a full-index scan or using full-table index alternatives.

In another example, let's assume it is common to query products with two distinct IDs. In this case, I am also querying anything with an order quantity greater than 10. However, filtering on just the product ID is not my desired filtering scenario:

```
Use AdventureWorks2014;
GO
SELECT SalesOrderDetailID
  FROM Sales.SalesOrderDetail
  WHERE ProductID IN (776, 777)
  AND OrderQty > 10;
```

This query performs a clustered index scan. I can improve the performance of the query by adding a filtered index, which will result in an index seek against that nonclustered index instead of using the clustered index scan. Here's how to create that filtered index:

```
Use AdventureWorks2014;
GO
CREATE NONCLUSTERED INDEX NCI_ProductID_SalesOrderDetail
  ON Sales.SalesOrderDetail(ProductID,OrderQty)
  WHERE ProductID IN (776, 777);
```

The result will be less I/O, because the query can operate against the much smaller, filtered index.

How It Works

This recipe demonstrated how to use the filtered index feature to create a fine-tuned index that requires less storage than the full-table index alternative. Filtered indexes require that you understand the nature of incoming queries against the tables in your database. If you have a high percentage of queries that consistently query a small percentage of data in a set of tables, filtered indexes will allow you to improve I/O performance while also minimizing on-disk storage.

The CREATE INDEX statement isn't modified much from its original format. To implement the filter, I used a WHERE clause after the ON clause (if using an INCLUDE, the WHERE should appear after it):

```
Use AdventureWorks2014;
GO
CREATE NONCLUSTERED INDEX NCI_UnitPrice_SalesOrderDetail
  ON Sales.SalesOrderDetail(UnitPrice)
  WHERE UnitPrice >= 150.00 AND UnitPrice <= 175.00;
```

The filter predicate allows for simple logic using operators such as IN, IS, IS NOT, =, <>, >, >=, !>, <, <=, and !<. You should also be aware that filtered indexes have filtered statistics created along with them. These statistics use the same filter predicate and can result in more accurate results, because the sampling is against a smaller row set.

16-19. Reducing Index Size

Problem

You have discovered that your indexes are significantly large. You need to reduce the size of these indexes without altering the definition of the index.

Solution

Implement compression on the indexes in question. As covered in Chapter 15, the SQL Server 2014 Enterprise and Developer editions provide options for page- and row-level compression of tables, indexes, and the associated partitions. In that chapter, I demonstrated how to enable compression using the DATA_ COMPRESSION clause in conjunction with the CREATE TABLE and ALTER TABLE commands. I covered how you compress clustered indexes and heaps. For nonclustered indexes, you use CREATE INDEX and ALTER INDEX to implement compression. The syntax remains the same, designating the DATA_ COMPRESSION option along with a value of NONE, ROW, or PAGE. The following example demonstrates adding a nonclustered index with page-level compression (based on the example table ArchiveHobPosting created in Chapter 15):

```
Use AdventureWorks2014;
GO
CREATE NONCLUSTERED INDEX NCI_SalesOrderDetail_CarrierTrackingNumber
  ON Sales.SalesOrderDetail (CarrierTrackingNumber)
  WITH (DATA_COMPRESSION = PAGE);
```

I will modify the compression level after the fact by using ALTER INDEX. In this example, I use ALTER INDEX to change the compression level to row-level compression:

```
Use AdventureWorks2014;
GO
ALTER INDEX NCI_SalesOrderDetail_CarrierTrackingNumber
  ON Sales.SalesOrderDetail
  REBUILD WITH (DATA_COMPRESSION = ROW);
```

How It Works

This recipe demonstrated enabling row- and page-level compression for a nonclustered index. The process for adding compression is almost identical to that of adding compression for the clustered index or heap, using the DATA_COMPRESSION index option. When creating a new index, the WITH clause follows the index key definition. When modifying an existing index, the WITH clause follows the REBUILD keyword.

16-20. Further Reducing Index Size

Problem

You have some very large tables. You need to reduce the size of the table while improving performance.

Solution

Implement a clustered columnstore index on the table. The clustered columnstore index improves on the compression over the DATA_COMPRESSION option while offering improved performance. The use of a clustered columnstore index allows for the data to be updated. One can implement a clustered columnstore index as follows.

■ **Note**   For clustered columnstore indexes, no other index can exist on the table. The clustered columnstore index does not contain key columns, since all columns from the table are included in the index.

Prior to creating a columnstore index, I will create a table. Then I will remove the index from the table so the columnstore index can be created:

```
USE AdventureWorks2014;
GO
IF EXISTS (Select 1/0 from sys.objects where name = 'TerminationReason' and SCHEMA_
NAME(schema_id) = 'HumanResources')
BEGIN
      DROP TABLE HumanResources.TerminationReason;
END
```

```
CREATE TABLE HumanResources.TerminationReason(
  TerminationReasonID smallint IDENTITY(1,1) NOT NULL,
  TerminationReason varchar(50) NOT NULL,
  DepartmentID smallint NOT NULL,
  INDEX NCI_TerminationReason_DepartmentID NONCLUSTERED (DepartmentID)
      );
GO

DROP INDEX NCI_TerminationReason_DepartmentID ON HumanResources.TerminationReason;
GO
```

With the table in place and the index on that table dropped, I can now create the clustered columnstore index:

```
CREATE CLUSTERED COLUMNSTORE INDEX PK_TerminationReason ON HumanResources.TerminationReason;
GO
```

How It Works

This recipe demonstrated how to create a clustered columnstore index in order to reduce space in a table. The clustered columnstore index requires that any existing indexes on the table be dropped prior to creating the clustered columnstore index. If there are indexes on the table when a clustered columnstore index is being created, an error would be produced.

This recipe built on a few recipes from this chapter by creating an index inline with the table creation, dropping an index and then creating an index by using the columnstore keyword.

CHAPTER 17

■ ■ ■

Stored Procedures

by Jonathan Gennick

A stored procedure groups one or more Transact-SQL statements into a logical unit, stored as an object in a SQL Server database. When a stored procedure is executed for the first time, SQL Server creates an execution plan and stores it in the plan cache. SQL Server can then reuse the plan on subsequent executions of this stored procedure. Plan reuse allows stored procedures to provide fast and reliable performance compared to noncompiled and unprepared ad hoc query equivalents.

■ **Note** Chapter 19 if you're interested in native compilation in support of in-memory tables.

17-1. Creating a Stored Procedure

Problem

You want to create a simple stored procedure. For example, you want to return the results from a SELECT statement.

Solution

Issue a CREATE PROCEDURE statement. The first parameters are the schema and new procedure name. Next is the Transact-SQL body of your stored procedure. The body contains SQL statements implementing one or more tasks that you want to accomplish. The following example demonstrates creating a stored procedure that queries the database and returns a list of customers having known names (that is, who have corresponding entries in Person.Person):

```
CREATE PROCEDURE dbo.ListCustomerNames
AS
      SELECT    CustomerID,
                LastName,
                FirstName
      FROM      Sales.Customer sc
                INNER JOIN Person.Person pp
                    ON sc.CustomerID = pp.BusinessEntityID
      ORDER BY LastName,
                FirstName;
```

Next, the new stored procedure is executed using the EXEC command, which is shorthand for EXECUTE:

```
EXEC dbo.ListCustomerNames;
```

This returns the following results:

CustomerID	LastName	FirstName
285	Abbas	Syed
293	Abel	Catherine
295	Abercrombie	Kim
38	Abercrombie	Kim
211	Abolrous	Hazem

...

How It Works

This recipe demonstrates creating a stored procedure that queries the contents of two tables, returning a result set. This stored procedure works like a view, but it will have a cached query plan when executed for the first time, which will also make its execution time consistent in consecutive executions.

The example started off by creating a stored procedure called ListCustomerNames:

```
CREATE PROCEDURE dbo.ListCustomerNames
AS
```

The procedure was created in the dbo schema. The letters dbo stand for "database owner." The dbo schema is one that is always present in a database, and it can be a convenient repository for stored procedures.

■ **Tip**   Regardless of target schema, it is good practice to specify that schema explicitly when creating a stored procedure. By doing so, you ensure that there is no mistake as to where the procedure is created.

The Transact-SQL query definition then followed the AS keyword:

```
SELECT   CustomerID,
         LastName,
         FirstName
FROM     Sales.Customer sc
         INNER JOIN Person.Person pp
             ON sc.CustomerID = pp.BusinessEntityID
ORDER BY LastName,
         FirstName;
```

After the procedure was created, it was executed using the EXEC command:

```
EXEC dbo.ListCustomerNames;
```

During the stored procedure creation process, SQL Server checks that the SQL syntax is correct, but it doesn't check for the existence of referenced tables. This means you can reference a table name incorrectly, and the incorrect name will not cause an error until runtime. The process of checking names at runtime is called *deferred name resolution*. It is actually helpful in that it allows you to create or reference objects that don't exist yet. It also means that you can drop, alter, or modify the objects referenced in the stored procedure without invalidating the procedure.

■ **Tip** Avoid problems from deferred name resolution by testing queries ad hoc whenever conveniently possible. That way, you can be sure your syntax is correct and that names resolve properly before creating the procedure.

17-2. Passing Parameters

Problem

You want to pass values to a stored procedure to affect either its behavior or the results it returns. For example, you want to pass an account number and get the customer's name in return. You also want to specify whether the name is returned in all uppercase letters.

Solution

Parameterize the stored procedure. Define one or more parameters between the procedure name and the AS keyword when creating the procedure. Enclose your parameter list within parentheses. Preface each parameter name with an @ character.

For example, the following procedure returns the customer name associated with the account number, which is passed as the first parameter. Use the second parameter to control whether the name is forced to uppercase:

```
CREATE PROCEDURE dbo.LookupByAccount
(@AccountNumber VARCHAR(10),
 @UpperFlag CHAR(1))
AS
    SELECT   CASE UPPER(@UpperFlag)
                WHEN 'U' THEN UPPER(FirstName)
                ELSE FirstName
             END AS FirstName,
             CASE UPPER(@UpperFlag)
                WHEN 'U' THEN UPPER(LastName)
                ELSE LastName
             END AS LastName
    FROM     Person.Person
    WHERE    BusinessEntityID IN (SELECT CustomerID
                                  FROM   Sales.Customer
                                  WHERE  AccountNumber = @AccountNumber) ;
```

Invoke this procedure as follows:

```
EXEC LookupByAccount 'AW00000019', 'u';
```

The results from this invocation should be as follows:

```
FirstName   LastName
----------- -----------
MARY        DEMPSEY
```

You can pass the second parameter in either uppercase or lowercase. Pass any letter but 'U' or 'u' to leave the name in mixed case while it is stored in the database. Here's an example:

```
EXEC LookupByAccount 'AW00000019', 'U';
EXEC LookupByAccount 'AW00000019', 'x';
```

```
FirstName   LastName
----------- -----------
MARY        DEMPSEY

FirstName   LastName
----------- -----------
Mary        Dempsey
```

How It Works

Recipe 17-1 demonstrated a nonparameterized stored procedure, meaning that no external parameters were passed to it. The ability to pass parameters is part of why stored procedures are one of the most important database object types in SQL Server. Using parameters, you can pass information into the body of a procedure in order to control how the procedure operates and to pass values that cause queries to return needed results.

The solution example shows a procedure having two input parameters. The first parameter is an account number. The second is a flag controlling whether the results are forced to uppercase. The procedure queries the database to find out the name of the person behind the number.

Developers executing the procedure given in the recipe solution do not need to worry about how the underlying query is written; they can simply accept that they provide an account number and get back a name. You are able to change the implementation when needed without affecting the interface, and thus without having to change any of the code invoking the procedure.

You're able to make parameters optional by giving default values. Recipe 17-3 will show how. You're also able to return values through so-called output parameters, and Recipe 17-5 will show how to do that.

17-3. Making Parameters Optional

Problem

You want to make certain parameters optional. For example, you are tired of having to always pass an 'x' to the LookupByAccount procedure. You want your names back in mixed case, but without ruining it for those who pass a 'U' to force uppercase.

Solution

Re-create the procedure and make the @UpperFlag parameter optional. First, drop the version of the procedure currently in place from Recipe 17-2:

```
DROP PROCEDURE dbo.LookupByAccount;
```

Then, create a new version of the procedure that has a default value specified for @UpperFlag. Do that by appending = 'x' following the parameter's data type. Here's an example:

```
CREATE PROCEDURE dbo.LookupByAccount
(@AccountNumber VARCHAR(10),
 @UpperFlag CHAR(1) = 'x')
AS
       SELECT   CASE UPPER(@UpperFlag)
                    WHEN 'U' THEN UPPER(FirstName)
                    ELSE FirstName
                END AS FirstName,
                CASE UPPER(@UpperFlag)
                    WHEN 'U' THEN UPPER(LastName)
                    ELSE LastName
                END AS LastName
       FROM     Person.Person
       WHERE    BusinessEntityID IN (SELECT CustomerID
                                     FROM   Sales.Customer
                                     WHERE  AccountNumber = @AccountNumber) ;
```

Now you can invoke the procedure without needing to specify that pesky flag:

```
EXEC LookupByAccount 'AW00000019';
```

```
FirstName    LastName
-----------  -----------
Mary         Dempsey
```

But others who want their results forced to uppercase are still free to do that:

```
EXEC LookupByAccount 'AW00000019', 'U';
```

```
FirstName    LastName
-----------  -----------
MARY         DEMPSEY
```

The default value takes effect whenever the parameter is not specified, but can be overridden when needed.

How It Works

The solution example makes a parameter optional by specifying a default value as follows:

```
@UpperFlag VARCHAR(1) = 'x'
```

It's now possible to invoke the procedure by passing only an account number. The default value takes effect in that case, and the person's name is returned unchanged, without being forced to uppercase.

It's common to specify default parameters at the end of the parameter list. Doing so makes it easier to invoke a procedure in an ad hoc manner from SQL Management Studio. Also, many people are used to this convention. However, you can define optional parameters earlier in the list, and the next recipe shows how.

17-4. Making Early Parameters Optional

Problem

The parameter you want to make optional precedes one that is mandatory. You are thus unable to skip that parameter, even though you've specified a default value for it.

Solution

Invoke your procedure using named notation rather than positional notation. In doing so, you can name the parameter that you do want to pass, and it won't matter where in the list that parameter occurs.

For example, begin with the following version of the procedure from Recipe 17-3. In this version, the UpperFlag parameter comes first:

```
CREATE PROCEDURE dbo.LookupByAccount2
(@UpperFlag CHAR(1) = 'x',
@AccountNumber VARCHAR(10))
AS
      SELECT    CASE UPPER(@UpperFlag)
                   WHEN 'U' THEN UPPER(FirstName)
                   ELSE FirstName
                END AS FirstName,
                CASE UPPER(@UpperFlag)
                   WHEN 'U' THEN UPPER(LastName)
                   ELSE LastName
                END AS LastName
      FROM      Person.Person
      WHERE     BusinessEntityID IN (SELECT CustomerID
                                     FROM   Sales.Customer
                                     WHERE  AccountNumber = @AccountNumber) ;
```

Using named notation, you can pass just the account number, as follows:

```
EXEC LookupByAccount2 @AccountNumber = 'AW00000019';
```

You can use the DEFAULT keyword to make it explicit that you are accepting a default parameter value for @UpperFlag:

```
EXEC LookupByAccount2 @AccountNumber = 'AW00000019', @UpperFlag = DEFAULT;
```

Using named notation, you can specify the parameter values in any order.

How It Works

It's common to pass parameters using positional notation. Named notation takes some extra typing, but in return it can be a bit more self-documenting. That's because each procedure invocation names all the parameters, helping you later remember what the associated parameter values represent.

Named notation also allows you to specify parameters in any order. That ability allows you to skip parameters having default values, no matter where those parameters occur in the list. Don't try to mix the two notations, however. SQL Server requires that you choose one or the other. Specify all parameters by name or all by position—don't try to mix the two approaches.

17-5. Returning Output

Problem

You are writing a stored procedure. You want to return values to the code calling the procedure.

Solution

Specify some parameters as OUTPUT parameters. The following example creates a stored procedure that returns the list of departments for a specific group. In addition to returning the list of departments, an OUTPUT parameter is defined to return the number of departments found for the specific group:

```
CREATE PROCEDURE dbo.SEL_Department
        @GroupName NVARCHAR(50),
        @DeptCount INT OUTPUT
AS
        SELECT    Name
        FROM      HumanResources.Department
        WHERE     GroupName = @GroupName
        ORDER BY Name;
        SELECT    @DeptCount = @@ROWCOUNT;
```

Now you can define a local variable to hold the output and invoke the procedure. Here's an example:

```
DECLARE @DeptCount INT;
EXEC dbo.SEL_Department 'Executive General and Administration',
    @DeptCount OUTPUT;
PRINT @DeptCount;
```

The query in the procedure generates the row set. The PRINT command displays the row count value passed back through the @DeptCount variable. The query in this example returns the following five rows:

```
Name
---------------------------------------------------
Executive
Facilities and Maintenance
Finance
Human Resources
Information Services
```

Next, the stored procedure uses the PRINT statement to return the count of rows. If you're executing the query ad hoc using Management Studio, you will see the value 5 on the Messages tab if you are viewing results as a grid, and at the bottom of the Results tab if you are viewing results as text.

How It Works

The solution began by creating a stored procedure with a defined parameter called @DeptCount, followed by the data type and OUTPUT keyword:

```
@DeptCount INT OUTPUT
```

The stored procedure executed the query and then stored the row count in the parameter:

```
SELECT @DeptCount = @@ROWCOUNT
```

The invoking code created the following variable to pass as the output parameter:

```
DECLARE @DeptCount INT
```

The EXEC statement must also specify that a parameter is an output parameter. That was done by following the passed value with the OUTPUT keyword, as in the following:

```
EXEC dbo.SEL_Department 'Executive General and Administration',
    @DeptCount OUTPUT;
```

You can use OUTPUT parameters as an alternative or additional method for returning information back to the caller of the stored procedure. If you're using OUTPUT only to communicate information back to the calling application, it's usually just as easy to create a second result set containing the information you need. This is because .NET applications, for example, can easily consume the multiple result sets that are returned from a stored procedure. The technique of using OUTPUT parameters versus using an additional result set to return information is often just a matter of preference.

17-6. Modifying a Stored Procedure

Problem

You have an existing stored procedure and want to change its behavior.

Solution

Redefine the procedure using the ALTER PROCEDURE command. You can change everything but the original stored procedure name. The syntax is almost identical to CREATE PROCEDURE.

The following example modifies the stored procedure created in the previous recipe in order to return the number of departments returned by the query as a separate result set instead of via an OUTPUT parameter:

```
ALTER PROCEDURE dbo.SEL_Department
      @GroupName NVARCHAR(50)
AS
      SELECT    Name
      FROM      HumanResources.Department
      WHERE     GroupName = @GroupName
      ORDER BY  Name;
      SELECT    @@ROWCOUNT AS DepartmentCount;
```

You may now execute the stored procedure as follows, and two result sets are returned:

```
EXEC dbo.SEL_Department 'Research and Development';
```

```
Name
--------------------------------------------------
Engineering
Research and Development
Tool Design

DepartmentCount
---------------
              3
```

How It Works

ALTER PROCEDURE is used to modify the definition of an existing stored procedure, in this case both removing a parameter and adding a second result set. You can change everything but the procedure name. Using ALTER PROCEDURE also preserves any existing permissions on the stored procedure. If you drop and re-create the procedure, you'll need to re-grant permissions. Using ALTER PROCEDURE avoids the need for that tedium.

17-7. Removing a Stored Procedure

Problem

You are no longer using a stored procedure and want to remove it from your database.

Solution

Drop the stored procedure from the database using the DROP PROCEDURE command. Here's an example:

```
DROP PROCEDURE dbo.SEL_Department;
```

How It Works

Once a stored procedure is dropped, its definition is removed from the database's system tables. Any cached query execution plans are also removed for that stored procedure. Code references to the stored procedure by other procedures or triggers will fail upon execution once the stored procedure has been dropped.

17-8. Automatically Run a Stored Procedure at Start-Up

Problem

You want to execute some code every time a particular instance is started. For example, you might want to document start-up times or clear out work tables on each restart.

Solution

Invoke the sp_procoption system-stored procedure to designate that a procedure you wrote should be executed automatically upon instance start-up. In the example to follow, a stored procedure is set to execute automatically whenever SQL Server is started. First, set the database context to the master database (which is the only place that start-up stored procedures can be placed).

```
USE master;
```

Next, create a start-up logging table. Do this because the procedure this recipe creates as an example writes to this table. Here is the creation statement:

```
CREATE TABLE dbo.SQLStartupLog
     (
      SQLStartupLogID INT IDENTITY(1, 1)
                      NOT NULL
                      PRIMARY KEY,
      StartupDateTime DATETIME NOT NULL
     );
```

Then create a stored procedure to insert a value into the new table:

```
CREATE PROCEDURE dbo.INS_TrackSQLStartups
AS
        INSERT    dbo.SQLStartupLog
                  (StartupDateTime)
        VALUES    (GETDATE());
```

Finally, invoke sp_procoption to set this new procedure to execute when the SQL Server service restarts:

```
EXEC sp_procoption @ProcName = 'INS_TrackSQLStartups',
    @OptionName = 'startup', @OptionValue = 'true';
```

From now on, starting the instance triggers execution of the stored procedure, which in turn inserts a row into the table to log the start-up event.

How It Works

This recipe creates a new table in the master database to track SQL Server start-ups. A stored procedure is also created in the master database to insert a row into the table with the current date and time of execution.

■ **Caution**   We are not espousing the creation of objects in the system databases, because it generally isn't a good idea to create them there. However, if you must use auto-execution functionality as discussed in this recipe, you have no choice but to create your objects in the system database.

The stored procedure must be created in the master database; otherwise, you'll see the following error message when trying to use sp_procoption:

```
Msg 15398, Level 11, State 1, Procedure sp_procoption, Line 73 Only objects in the master
database owned by dbo can have the startup setting changed.
```

To disable the stored procedure, execute the following command:

```
EXEC sp_procoption @ProcName = 'INS_TrackSQLStartups',
    @OptionName = 'startup', @OptionValue = 'false'
```

Setting @OptionValue to false disables the start-up procedure.

■ **Note**   If you're going to test further recipes in this chapter, be sure to execute USE AdventureWorks2012 to change your database back to the example database generally being used in this chapter.

17-9. Viewing a Stored Procedure's Definition

Problem

You want to view the definition for a stored procedure so that you can ascertain exactly how that procedure operates.

Solution

From an ad hoc session, it's often easiest to execute sp_helptext. Here's an example:

```
EXEC sp_helptext 'LookupByAccount';
```

Your results will be in the form of a CREATE PROCEDURE statement:

```
Text
---------------------------------------------------------------------------
CREATE PROCEDURE dbo.LookupByAccount
(@AccountNumber VARCHAR(10),
 @UpperFlag VARCHAR(1) = 'x')
AS
      SELECT    CASE UPPER(@UpperFlag)
                   WHEN 'U' THEN UPPER(FirstName)
                   ELSE FirstName
                END AS FirstName,
                CASE UPPER(@UpperFlag)
                   WHEN 'U' THEN UPPER(LastName)
                   ELSE LastName
                END AS LastName
      FROM      Person.Person
      WHERE     BusinessEntityID IN (SELECT CustomerID
                                     FROM   Sales.Customer
                                     WHERE  AccountNumber = @AccountNumber) ;
```

From code, you may prefer to query sys.sql_modules and related catalog views. Doing so allows access to a great wealth of information from code, information that you can use in writing helpful utilities to manage objects in your database. For example, execute the following query to retrieve the definition for the stored procedure created in Recipe 17-2:

```
SELECT  definition
FROM    sys.sql_modules m
        INNER JOIN sys.objects o
           ON m.object_id = o.object_id
WHERE   o.type = 'P'
        AND o.name = 'LookupByAccount';
```

Your results will be the following output, which shows the definition in the form of a CREATE PROCEDURE statement. (If outputting as text, be sure to set the maximum number of characters displayed in each column to something higher than the default of just 256.)

```
definition
-------------------------------------------------------------------------------
CREATE PROCEDURE dbo.LookupByAccount
(@AccountNumber VARCHAR(10),
 @UpperFlag CHAR(1) = 'x')
AS
        SELECT    CASE UPPER(@UpperFlag)
                     WHEN 'U' THEN UPPER(FirstName)
                     ELSE FirstName
                  END AS FirstName,
                  CASE UPPER(@UpperFlag)
                     WHEN 'U' THEN UPPER(LastName)
                     ELSE LastName
                  END AS LastName
        FROM      Person.Person
        WHERE     BusinessEntityID IN (SELECT CustomerID
                                       FROM   Sales.Customer
                                       WHERE  AccountNumber = @AccountNumber ) ;
```

You can save these results and execute them to re-create the procedure at some future time or on another database server.

How It Works

Invoke sp_helptext whenever you want to see the definition for a stored procedure or other user-defined object. You'll get the result back in the form of a single text value.

Query the view sys.sql_modules to retrieve the definitions of stored procedures, triggers, views, and other SQL-defined objects. Join sys.sql_modules to sys.objects to gain access to object names and types. For example, the solution query specifically requested o.type = 'P'. That is the type code used to indicate stored procedures.

The two system views expose several other columns that give useful information or that you can use to restrict query results to only procedures and other objects of interest. It's worth reviewing the view definitions (by visiting the SQL Server Books Online manual set) to become familiar with the values available.

17-10. Documenting Stored Procedures

Problem

You are writing a stored procedure and want to leave some notes for the next person (perhaps it will be yourself!) who must maintain that procedure.

Solution

Define a format for stored procedure headers that includes room for commentary and for a history of change over time. The following is an example of a standard stored procedure header:

```
CREATE PROCEDURE dbo.IMP_DWP_FactOrder AS
-- Purpose: Populates the data warehouse, Called by Job
-- Maintenance Log
-- Update By    Update Date
Description
-- Joe Sack     8/15/2008    Created
-- Joe Sack     8/16/2008    A new column was added to
--the base table, so it was added here as well.
... Transact-SQL code here
```

For brevity, the stored procedure examples in this chapter have not included extensive comments or headers. However, in your production database, you should at the very least define headers for each stored procedure created in a production database.

How It Works

This recipe is more of a best practice rather than a review of a command or function. It is important to comment your stored procedure code very well so that future support staff, authors, and editors will understand the business rules and intents behind your Transact-SQL code. Although some code may seem self-evident at the time of authoring, the original logic may not seem so clear a few months after it was written. Business logic is often transient and difficult to understand over time, so including a written description of that logic in the body of the code can save hours of troubleshooting and investigation.

■ **Caution**   One drawback of making your code self-documenting is that other developers who edit your code may not include documentation of their own changes. You may end up being blamed for code you didn't write, just because you were the last person to log a change. This is where your company should strongly consider a source control system to track all check-in and check-out activities, as well as to be able to compare changes between procedure versions.

No doubt you'll see other procedure headers out in the field with much more information included. Don't demand too much documentation, however. Include enough to bring clarity, but not so much that you introduce redundancy. For example, if you include the stored procedure name in the header, in addition to within the actual CREATE PROCEDURE statement, you'll soon start seeing code in which the header name doesn't match the stored procedure name. Why not just document the information that isn't already included in the stored procedure definition? That is the approach we recommend so as to be clear but concise.

17-11. Determining the Current Nesting Level

Problem

You are developing a stored procedure that invokes itself, or a set of procedures that invoke each other. You want to detect programmatically how deeply nested you are in the call stack.

Solution

Execute a query to retrieve the @@NESTLEVEL value. This value begins at zero and is incremented by one for each procedure call. The following are two CREATE PROCEDURE statements to set up the solution example:

```
-- First procedure
CREATE PROCEDURE dbo.QuickAndDirty
AS
SELECT @@NESTLEVEL;
GO
-- Second procedure
CREATE PROCEDURE dbo.Call_QuickAndDirty
AS
SELECT @@NESTLEVEL
EXEC dbo.QuickAndDirty;
GO
```

After creating these two stored procedures, execute the following set of statements to demonstrate the operation of @@NESTLEVEL:

```
SELECT @@NESTLEVEL;
EXEC dbo.Call_QuickAndDirty;
```

Your results should be as follows:

```
-----------
          0
...
-----------
          1
...
-----------
          2
```

How It Works

@@NESTLEVEL returns the current nesting level for the stored procedure context. A stored procedure nesting level indicates how many times a stored procedure has called another stored procedure. SQL Server allows stored procedures to make up to a maximum of 32 nested (incomplete) calls.

The solution example began by creating two stored procedures. One of those procedures invoked the other. The final query and procedure execution showed that @@NESTLEVEL began at zero. It was incremented and reported as 1 by the Call_QuickAndDirty procedure when that procedure was invoked by the EXEC statement. Then @@NESTLEVEL was incremented one more time when the first-invoked stored procedure executed QuickAndDirty.

17-12. Encrypting a Stored Procedure

Problem

You want to encrypt a stored procedure to prevent others from querying the system catalog views to view your code.

Solution

Create the procedure using the WITH ENCRYPTION option. Specify the option after the name of the new stored procedure, as the next example demonstrates:

```
CREATE PROCEDURE dbo.SEL_EmployeePayHistory
      WITH ENCRYPTION
AS
      SELECT    BusinessEntityID,
                RateChangeDate,
                Rate,
                PayFrequency,
                ModifiedDate
      FROM      HumanResources.EmployeePayHistory;
```

Once you've created WITH ENCRYPTION, you'll be unable to view the procedure's text definition. You can try to query for the definition:

```
EXEC sp_helptext SEL_EmployeePayHistory;
```

However, you will receive only the following message:

```
The text for object 'SEL_EmployeePayHistory' is encrypted.
```

Even querying the system catalog directly won't be of help. For example, you can try this:

```
SELECT   definition
FROM     sys.sql_modules m
         INNER JOIN sys.objects o
            ON m.object_id = o.object_id
WHERE    o.type = 'P'
         AND o.name = 'SEL_EmployeePayHistory';
```

and you will be rewarded with only an empty result:

```
definition
----------
NULL
```

The procedure's definition is encrypted, and there is nothing you can do to retrieve that definition. So, be sure to keep a copy outside the database.

How It Works

Stored procedure definitions can have their contents encrypted in the database, thus removing the ability to read a procedure's definition later. Software vendors who use SQL Server in their back end often encrypt stored procedures in order to prevent tampering or reverse engineering from clients or competitors. If you use encryption, be sure to save the original T-SQL definition, because it can't easily be decoded later (legally and reliably, anyhow). Also, perform your encryption only prior to a push to production.

■ **Caution**   Be sure to save your source code, because the encrypted text cannot be decrypted easily.

17-13. Specifying a Security Context

Problem

You want to specify the source for the rights and privileges under which a stored procedure executes. For example, you might want a caller to be able to execute a procedure but also to not have the privileges needed to execute the SELECT statements that the procedure executes internally.

Solution

Create or alter the procedure and specify the EXECUTE AS clause to define the security context under which a stored procedure is executed, regardless of the caller. The options for EXECUTE AS in a stored procedure are as follows:

```
EXECUTE AS { CALLER | SELF | OWNER | 'user_name' }
```

The default behavior for EXECUTE AS is the CALLER option, which means that the permissions of the executing user are used (and if the user doesn't have proper access, that execution will fail). If the SELF option is used, the execution context of the stored procedure will be that of the user who created or last altered the stored procedure. When the OWNER option is designated, the schema of the owner of the stored procedure is used. The user_name option is an explicit reference to a database user under whose security context the stored procedure will be executed.

The following example creates a version of SEL_Department that is owned by HumanResources. The clause EXECUTE AS OWNER specifies that invocations of the procedure will run under the rights and privileges granted to the schema owner:

```
CREATE PROCEDURE HumanResources.SEL_Department
    @GroupName NVARCHAR(50)
WITH EXECUTE AS OWNER
AS
    SELECT    Name
    FROM      HumanResources.Department
    WHERE     GroupName = @GroupName
    ORDER BY  Name;
    SELECT    @@ROWCOUNT AS DepartmentCount;
```

How It Works

SQL Server implements a concept termed *ownership chaining* that comes into play when a stored procedure is created and used to perform an INSERT, UPDATE, DELETE, or SELECT against another database object. If the schema of the stored procedure object is the same as the schema of the object referenced within, SQL Server checks only that the stored procedure caller has EXECUTE permissions to the stored procedure.

Ownership chaining applies only to the INSERT, UPDATE, DELETE, or SELECT commands. This is why stored procedures are excellent for securing the database, because you can grant a user access to execute a stored procedure without giving the user access to the underlying tables.

An issue arises, however, when you are looking to execute commands that are not INSERT, UPDATE, DELETE, or SELECT. In those situations, even if a caller has EXECUTE permissions to a stored procedure that, for example, truncates a table using the TRUNCATE TABLE command, she must still have permissions to use the TRUNCATE TABLE command in the first place. You may not want to grant such broad permission.

Using EXECUTE AS, you can create the procedure to run as the schema owner or as a user that you specify. You need not grant permission for TRUNCATE TABLE to all users who might invoke the procedure, but rather only to the user you specify in the security context.

The same "gotcha" goes for dynamic SQL within a stored procedure. SQL Server will ensure that the caller has both EXECUTE permission and the appropriate permissions in order to perform the task the dynamic SQL is attempting to perform, even if that dynamic SQL is performing an INSERT, UPDATE, DELETE, or SELECT. Specifying a security context lets you avoid granting those privileges broadly to all users who might need to invoke the procedure.

17-14. Avoiding Cached Query Plans

Problem

Your procedure produces wildly different query results based on the application calling it because of the varying selectivity of qualified columns, so much so that the retained execution plan causes performance issues when varying input parameters are used.

Solution

Force a recompilation upon each invocation of the procedure. Do that by including the WITH RECOMPILE clause when creating (or altering) the procedure. Here's an example:

```
ALTER PROCEDURE dbo.LookupByAccount2
    (
    @UpperFlag VARCHAR(1) = 'x',
    @AccountNumber VARCHAR(10)
    )
    WITH RECOMPILE
AS
    SELECT    CASE UPPER(@UpperFlag)
                WHEN 'U' THEN UPPER(FirstName)
                ELSE FirstName
              END AS FirstName,
              CASE UPPER(@UpperFlag)
                WHEN 'U' THEN UPPER(LastName)
                ELSE LastName
              END AS LastName
```

```
FROM        Person.Person
WHERE       BusinessEntityID IN (SELECT CustomerID
                                 FROM   Sales.Customer
                                 WHERE  AccountNumber = @AccountNumber);
```

Now, whenever this procedure is called, a new execution plan will be created by SQL Server.

How It Works

Recompilations occur automatically when underlying table or other object changes occur to objects that are referenced within a stored procedure. They can also occur with changes to indexes used by the plan or after a large number of updates to table keys referenced by the stored procedure. The goal of an automatic recompilation is to make sure the SQL Server execution plan is using the most current information and not using out-of-date assumptions about the schema and data.

SQL Server is able to perform statement-level recompiles within a stored procedure, rather than recompiling the entire stored procedure. Because recompiles cause extra overhead in generating new plans, statement-level recompiles help decrease this overhead by correcting only what needs to be corrected.

After every recompile, SQL Server caches the execution plan for use until the next time a change to an underlying object triggers another recompile. Cached query plans are a good thing, but sometimes they can cause inefficient plans to be chosen. Parameter sniffing, for example, is the process of deferring the generation of an execution plan until the first invocation of a query or procedure, at which time parameter values are examined and a plan is chosen based upon those values passed that very first time. The problem sometimes arises that a plan good for one set of values is actually terrible with another set. The problem can sometimes be bad enough that it is best to recompile at each execution. That is what the solution example accomplishes.

The solution example specifies WITH RECOMPILE to ensure that a query plan is not cached for the procedure during creation or execution. It is rare to need the option, because generally the cached plan chosen by SQL Server will suffice. Use this option if you want to take advantage of a stored procedure's other benefits, such as security and modularization, but don't want SQL Server to store an inefficient plan (such as from a "parameter sniff") based on wildly varying result sets.

17-15. Flushing the Procedure Cache

Problem

You want to remove all cached query plans from the plan cache. For example, you might want to test procedure performance against a so-called cold cache, reproducing the cache as though SQL Server had just been restarted.

■ **Caution**   Think very carefully before unleashing this recipe in a production environment, because you could be knocking out several cached query plans that are perfectly fine.

Solution

Execute the DBCC FREEPROCCACHE command to clear existing cached plans. If you like, you can query the number of cached query plans first. Here's an example:

```
SELECT  COUNT(*) 'CachedPlansBefore'
FROM    sys.dm_exec_cached_plans;
```

```
CachedPlansBefore
-----------------
               20
```

This example shows 20 cached plans. Your results may vary, depending upon the number of procedures you have executed. Clear the cached plans by executing DBCC FREEPROCCACHE as follows, and retrieve the number of cached plans again. Here's an example:

```
DBCC FREEPROCCACHE;
SELECT  COUNT(*) 'CachedPlansAfter'
FROM    sys.dm_exec_cached_plans;
```

You should see output similar to the following:

```
DBCC execution completed. If DBCC printed error messages, contact your system
administrator.
CachedPlansAfter
----------------
               0
```

How It Works

DBCC FREEPROCCACHE clears the procedure cache. The count of cached plans both before and after will vary based on the activity on your SQL Server instance. The query against sys.dm_exec_cached_plans showed one way to retrieve the count of plans currently in the cache. Background processes and jobs that may be running before and after the clearing of the cache can affect the results, and you may not necessarily see a zero for the number of cached plans after you've cleared the cache.

■ ■ ■

User-Defined Functions and Types

by Jason Brimhall

In this chapter, I'll present recipes for user-defined functions and types. User-defined *functions* (UDFs) allow you to encapsulate both logic and subroutines into a single function that can then be used within your Transact-SQL queries and programmatic objects. User-defined *types* (UDTs) allow you to create an alias type based on an underlying system data type and enforce a specific data type, length, and nullability.

In this chapter, I'll also cover the SQL Server user-defined table type, which can be used as a user-defined table parameter for passing table result sets within your T-SQL code.

UDF Basics

Transact-SQL user-defined functions fall into three categories: *scalar, inline table-valued,* and *multi-statement table-valued.*

A scalar user-defined function is used to return a single value based on zero or more parameters. For example, you could create a scalar UDF that accepts a CountryID as a parameter and returns the CountryNM.

■ **Caution**   If you use a scalar user-defined function in the SELECT clause, the function will be executed for each row in the FROM clause, potentially resulting in poor performance, depending on the design of your function.

An inline table-valued UDF returns a table data type based on a single SELECT statement which is used to define the returned rows and columns. Unlike a stored procedure, an inline UDF can be referenced in the FROM clause of a query, as well as be joined to other tables. Unlike a view, an inline UDF can accept parameters.

A multi-statement table-valued UDF also returns a tabular result set and is referenced in the FROM clause. Unlike inline table-valued UDFs, multi-statement UDFs aren't constrained to using a single SELECT statement within the function definition and, instead, allow multiple Transact-SQL statements in the body of the UDF definition in order to define a single, final result set to be returned.

UDFs can also be used in places where a stored procedure can't, like in the FROM and SELECT clauses of a query. UDFs also encourage code reusability. For example, if you create a scalar UDF that returns the CountryNM based on a CountryID, and the same function is needed across several different stored procedures, rather than repeat the 20 lines of code needed to perform the lookup, you can call the UDF function instead.

In the next few recipes, I'll demonstrate how to create, drop, modify, and view metadata for each of these UDF types.

18-1. Creating Scalar Functions

Problem

You need to create a function to check or alter the values in the parameters passed into the function (such as you might do when checking for SQL Injection).

Solution

Create a scalar user-defined function. A scalar user-defined function accepts zero or more parameters and returns a single value. Scalar UDFs are often used for converting or translating a current value to a new value or performing other sophisticated lookups based on specific parameters. Scalar functions can be used within search, column, and join expressions.

The simplified syntax for a scalar UDF is as follows:

```
CREATE FUNCTION [ schema_name. ] function_name
( [ { @parameter_name [ AS ] [ type_schema_name. ] parameter_data_type [ = default ] [
READONLY ] } [ ,...n ] ] ) RETURNS return_data_type
[ WITH <function_option> [ ,...n ] ]
[ AS ]
BEGIN
function_body RETURN scalar_expression END
```

■ **Note**   The full syntax for CREATE FUNCTION can be found in SQL Server Books Online.

Table 18-1 briefly describes each argument's intended use.

Table 18-1. *Scalar UDF Arguments*

Argument	Description
[schema_name.] function_name	This argument defines the optional schema name and required function name of the new scalar UDF.
@parameter_name	This is the name of the parameter to pass to the UDF, and it must be prefixed with an @ sign.
[type_schema_name.] scalar_parameter_data_type	This is the parameter data type and its associated (optional) schema.
[,...n]	Although not an actual argument, this syntax element indicates that one or more parameters can be defined (up to 1,024).
return_data_type	This specifies the data type the user-defined function will return.
function_body	The function body contains one or more of the Transact-SQL statements that are used to produce and evaluate a scalar value.
scalar_expression	This is the actual value that will be returned by the scalar function (notice that it is defined after the function body).

This example creates a scalar UDF that accepts a varchar(max) data type parameter. It returns a bit value (1 or 0) based on whether the passed parameter contains suspicious values (as defined by the function). So, if the input parameter contains a call to a command such as DELETE or SHUTDOWN, the flag is set to 1:

```
Use AdventureWorks2014;
GO

Create Function dbo.udf_CheckForSQLInjection (@TSQLString varchar(max))
Returns bit

AS

BEGIN

DECLARE  @IsSuspect  bit;

-- UDF assumes string will be left padded with a single space
SET @TSQLString = ' ' + @TSQLString;

IF       (PATINDEX('% xp_%'  , @TSQLString ) <> 0 OR
     PATINDEX('% sp_%'  , @TSQLString ) <> 0      OR
     PATINDEX('% DROP %' , @TSQLString ) <> 0    OR
     PATINDEX('% GO %'  , @TSQLString ) <> 0 OR
     PATINDEX('% INSERT %' , @TSQLString ) <> 0 OR
     PATINDEX('% UPDATE %' , @TSQLString ) <> 0 OR
     PATINDEX('% DBCC %' , @TSQLString ) <> 0    OR
     PATINDEX('% SHUTDOWN %' , @TSQLString )<> 0 OR
     PATINDEX('% ALTER %' , @TSQLString )<> 0    OR
     PATINDEX('% CREATE %' , @TSQLString ) <> 0 OR
     PATINDEX('%;%'  , @TSQLString )<> 0  OR
     PATINDEX('% EXECUTE %' , @TSQLString )<> 0  OR
     PATINDEX('% BREAK %' , @TSQLString )<> 0    OR
     PATINDEX('% BEGIN %' , @TSQLString )<> 0    OR
     PATINDEX('% CHECKPOINT %' , @TSQLString )<> 0  OR
     PATINDEX('% BREAK %' , @TSQLString )<> 0    OR
     PATINDEX('% COMMIT %' , @TSQLString )<> 0   OR
     PATINDEX('% TRANSACTION %' , @TSQLString )<> 0 OR
     PATINDEX('% CURSOR %' , @TSQLString )<> 0   OR
     PATINDEX('% GRANT %' , @TSQLString )<> 0    OR
     PATINDEX('% DENY %' , @TSQLString )<> 0     OR
     PATINDEX('% ESCAPE %' , @TSQLString )<> 0   OR
     PATINDEX('% WHILE %' , @TSQLString )<> 0    OR
     PATINDEX('% OPENDATASOURCE %' , @TSQLString )<> 0 OR
     PATINDEX('% OPENQUERY %' , @TSQLString )<> 0 OR
     PATINDEX('% OPENROWSET %' , @TSQLString )<> 0    OR
     PATINDEX('% EXEC %' , @TSQLString )<> 0)

BEGIN
     SELECT @IsSuspect =     1;
END
ELSE
```

```
BEGIN
    SELECT  @IsSuspect  =      0;
END
    RETURN  (@IsSuspect);
END

GO
```

Next, you should test the function by evaluating three different string input values. The first contains a SELECT statement:

```
Use AdventureWorks2014;
GO
SELECT dbo.udf_CheckForSQLInjection ('SELECT * FROM HumanResources.Department');
```

This query returns the following:

0

The next string contains the SHUTDOWN command:

```
Use AdventureWorks2014;
GO
SELECT dbo.udf_CheckForSQLInjection (';SHUTDOWN');
```

This query returns the following:

1

The last string tested contains the DROP command:

```
Use AdventureWorks2014;
GO
SELECT dbo.udf_CheckForSQLInjection ('DROP HumanResources.Department');
```

This query returns the following:

1

In the next example, I create a user-defined function that can be used to set a string to the proper case:

```
Use AdventureWorks2014;
GO
CREATE FUNCTION dbo.udf_ProperCase(@UnCased varchar(max))
RETURNS varchar(max)
AS
BEGIN
```

```
SET @UnCased = LOWER(@UnCased)
DECLARE @C int
SET @C = ASCII('a')
WHILE @C <= ASCII('z') BEGIN
SET @UnCased = REPLACE( @UnCased, ' ' + CHAR(@C), ' ' + CHAR(@C-32)) SET @C = @C + 1
END
SET @UnCased = CHAR(ASCII(LEFT(@UnCased, 1))-32) + RIGHT(@UnCased, LEN(@UnCased)-1)

RETURN @UnCased END
GO
```

Once the user-defined function is created, the string to modify (to proper case) can be used as the function parameter:

```
SELECT dbo.udf_ProperCase(DocumentSummary)
FROM Production.Document
WHERE FileName = 'Installing Replacement Pedals.doc'
```

This query returns the following:

```
Detailed Instructions For Replacing Pedals With Adventure Works Cycles Replacement Pedals.
Instructions Are Applicable To All Adventure Works Cycles Bicycle Models And Replacement
Pedals. Use Only Adventure Works Cycles Parts When Replacing Worn Or Broken Components.
```

How It Works

This recipe demonstrated a scalar UDF, which in this case accepted one parameter and returned a single value. Some of the areas where you can use a scalar function in your Transact-SQL code include the following:

- A column expression in a SELECT or GROUP BY clause

- A search condition for a JOIN in a FROM clause

- A search condition of a WHERE or HAVING clause

The recipe began by defining the UDF name and parameter:

```
CREATE FUNCTION dbo.udf_CheckForSQLInjection (@TSQLString varchar(max))
```

The @TSQLString parameter held the varchar(max) string to be evaluated. In the next line of code, the scalar_return_data_type was defined as bit. This means that the single value returned by the function will be the bit data type:

```
RETURNS BIT AS
```

The BEGIN marked the start of the function_body, where the logic to return the bit value was formulated:

```
BEGIN
```

A local variable was created to hold the bit value. Ultimately, this is the parameter that will be passed as the function's output:

```
DECLARE @IsSuspect bit
```

Next, the string passed to the UDF had a space concatenated to the front of it:

```
-- UDF assumes string will be left padded with a single space SET @TSQLString = ' '
+ @TSQLString
```

The @TSQLString was padded with an extra space in order to make the search of suspicious words or patterns easier to do. For example, if the suspicious word is at the beginning of the @TSQLString and you were searching for the word *drop*, you would have to use PATINDEX to search for both '%DROP %' and '% DROP %'. Of course, searching '%DROP %' could give you false positives, such as the word *gumdrop*, so you should prevent this confusion by padding the beginning of the string with a space.

In the IF statement, @TSQLString was evaluated using PATINDEX. For each evaluation, if a match were found, the condition would evaluate to TRUE.

```
IF   (PATINDEX('% xp_%' , @TSQLString ) <> 0 OR PATINDEX('% sp_%' , @TSQLString ) <> 0
OR PATINDEX('% DROP %' , @TSQLString ) <> 0 OR PATINDEX('% GO %' , @TSQLString ) <> 0 OR
PATINDEX('% BREAK %' , @TSQLString )<> 0 OR
```

If any of the conditions evaluate to TRUE, the @IsSuspect bit flag would be set to 1:

```
BEGIN
     SELECT  @IsSuspect  =     1;
END
ELSE
BEGIN
     SELECT  @IsSuspect  =     0;
END
```

The RETURN keyword was used to pass the scalar value of the @IsSuspect variable back to the caller:

```
RETURN (@IsSuspect)
```

The END keyword was then used to close the UDF, and GO was used to end the batch:

```
END
GO
```

The new scalar UDF created in this recipe was then used to check three different string values. The first string, SELECT * FROM HumanResources.Department, came up clean, but the second and third strings, SHUTDOWN and DROP HumanResources.Department, both returned a bit value of 1 because they matched the suspicious word searches in the function's IF clause.

SQL Server doesn't provide a built-in proper case function, so in my second example, I demonstrate creating a user-defined function that performs this action. The first line of the CREATE FUNCTION definition defines the name and parameter expected—in this case, a varchar(max) data type parameter:

```
CREATE FUNCTION dbo.udf_ProperCase(@UnCased varchar(max))
```

The RETURNS keyword defines what data type would be returned by the function after the logic has been applied:

```
RETURNS varchar(max)
AS
BEGIN
```

Next, the variable passed to the function was first modified to lowercase using the LOWER function:

```
SET @UnCased = LOWER(@UnCased)
```

A new integer local variable, @C, was set to the ASCII value of the letter *a*:

```
DECLARE @C int
SET @C = ASCII('a')
```

A WHILE loop was initiated to go through every letter in the alphabet and, for each, search for a space preceding that letter and then replace each occurrence of a letter preceded by a space with the uppercase version of the character:

```
WHILE @C <= ASCII('z') BEGIN
SET @UnCased = REPLACE( @UnCased, ' ' + CHAR(@C), ' ' + CHAR(@C-32)) SET @C = @C + 1
END
```

The conversion to uppercase is performed by subtracting 32 from the ASCII integer value of the lowercase character. For example, the ASCII value for a lowercase *a* is 97, while the uppercase *A* is 65:

```
SET @UnCased = CHAR(ASCII(LEFT(@UnCased, 1))-32) + RIGHT(@UnCased, LEN(@UnCased)-1)
```

The final proper case string value of @UnCased is then returned from the function:

```
RETURN @UnCased END GO
```

Next, I used the new scalar UDF in the SELECT clause of a query to convert the DocumentSummary text to the proper case:

```
SELECT dbo.udf_ProperCase(DocumentSummary)
```

18-2. Creating Inline Functions

Problem

You need to create a reusable query that can return data in a table form and potentially be joined to tables in queries found throughout views and stored procedures in your database.

Solution

Create an inline user-defined function. An inline UDF returns a table data type. In the UDF definition, you do not explicitly define the returned table but instead use a single SELECT statement for defining the returned rows and columns. An inline UDF uses one or more parameters and returns data using a single SELECT statement. Inline UDFs are very similar to views, in that they are referenced in the FROM clause. However, unlike views, UDFs can accept parameters that can then be used in the function's SELECT statement. The basic syntax is as follows:

```
CREATE FUNCTION [ schema_name. ] function_name
( [ { @parameter_name [ AS ] [ type_schema_name. ] scalar_parameter_data_type [ = default ]
} [ ,...n ] ]
) RETURNS TABLE [ AS ] RETURN [ ( ] select_stmt [ ) ]
```

■ **Note**   The full syntax for CREATE FUNCTION can be found in SQL Server Books Online.

Table 18-2 details the arguments of this command.

Table 18-2. *Inline UDF Arguments*

Argument	Description
[schema_name.] function_name	This defines the optional schema name and required function name of the new inline UDF.
@parameter_name	This is the name of the parameter to pass to the UDF. It must be prefixed with an @ sign.
[type_schema_name.] scalar_parameter_data_type	This is the @parameter_name data type and the optional scalar_parameter_data_type owning schema (used if you are employing a user-defined type).
[,...n]	Although not an actual argument, this syntax element indicates that one or more parameters can be defined (up to 1,024).
select_stmt	This is the single SELECT statement that will be returned by the inline UDF.

The following example demonstrates creating an inline table UDF that accepts an integer parameter and returns the associated addresses of a business entity:

```
Use AdventureWorks2014;
GO
CREATE FUNCTION dbo.udf_ReturnAddress
(@BusinessEntityID int)
RETURNS TABLE
AS RETURN (
SELECT t.Name AddressTypeNM, a.AddressLine1, a.City,
a.StateProvinceID, a.PostalCode
FROM Person.Address a
INNER JOIN Person.BusinessEntityAddress e
ON a.AddressID = e.AddressID
INNER JOIN Person.AddressType t
ON e.AddressTypeID = t.AddressTypeID
WHERE e.BusinessEntityID = @BusinessEntityID )
;
GO
```

Next, the new function is tested in a query, referenced in the FROM clause for business entity 332:

```
Use AdventureWorks2014;
GO
SELECT AddressTypeNM, AddressLine1, City, PostalCode
FROM dbo.udf_ReturnAddress(332);
GO
```

This query returns the following:

AddressTypeNM	AddressLine1	City	PostalCode
Shipping	26910 Indela Road	Montreal	H1Y 2H5
Main Office	25981 College Street	Montreal	H1Y 2H5

How It Works

In this recipe, I created an inline table UDF to retrieve the addresses of a business entity based on the @BusinessEntityID value passed. The UDF started off just like a scalar UDF, but the RETURNS command used a TABLE data type (which is what distinguishes it from a scalar UDF):

```
CREATE FUNCTION dbo.udf_ReturnAddress
(@BusinessEntityID int)
RETURNS TABLE
AS
```

After the AS keyword, the RETURN statement was issued with a single SELECT statement in parentheses:

```
RETURN (
SELECT t.Name AddressTypeNM, a.AddressLine1, a.City,
a.StateProvinceID, a.PostalCode
FROM Person.Address a
INNER JOIN Person.BusinessEntityAddress e
ON a.AddressID = e.AddressID
INNER JOIN Person.AddressType t
ON e.AddressTypeID = t.AddressTypeID
WHERE e.BusinessEntityID = @BusinessEntityID )
;
GO
```

After it was created, the new inline UDF was then used in the FROM clause of a SELECT query. The @BusinessEntityID value of 332 was passed into the function in parentheses:

```
SELECT AddressTypeNM, AddressLine1, City, PostalCode
FROM dbo.udf_ReturnAddress(332);
GO
```

This function then returned a result set, just like when you are querying a view or a table. Also, just like a view or stored procedure, the query you create to define this function must be tuned as you would a regular SELECT statement. Using an inline UDF offers no inherent performance benefits over using a view or stored procedure.

18-3. Creating Multi-Statement User-Defined Functions

Problem

You need to create a function that can accept multiple parameters and that will be able to execute multiple SELECT statements.

Solution

Create a multi-statement table user-defined function. Multi-statement table UDFs are referenced in the FROM clause just like inline UDFs, but unlike inline UDFs, they are not constrained to using a single SELECT statement within the function definition. Instead, multi-statement UDFs can use multiple Transact-SQL statements in the body of the UDF definition in order to define that a single, final result set be returned. The basic syntax of a multi-statement table UDF is as follows:

```
CREATE FUNCTION [ schema_name. ] function_name
( [ { @parameter_name [ AS ] [ type_schema_name. ] parameter_data_type [ = default ]
[READONLY] } [ ,...n ] ] )
RETURNS @return_variable TABLE <table_type_definition> [ WITH <function_option> [ ,...n ] ]
[ AS ] BEGIN
function_body RETURN END
```

Table 18-3 describes the arguments of this command.

Table 18-3. *Multi-Statement UDF Arguments*

Argument	Description
[schema_name.] function_name	This specifies the optional schema name and required function name of the new inline UDF.
@parameter_name	This is the name of the parameter to pass to the UDF. It must be prefixed with an @ sign.
[type_schema_name.] scalar_parameter_data_type	This is the data type of the @parameter_name and the scalar_parameter_data_type optional owning schema (used if you are using a user-defined type).
[,...n]	Although not an actual argument, this syntax element indicates that one or more parameters can be defined (up to 1,024).
@return_variable	This is the user-defined name of the table variable that will hold the results to be returned by the UDF.
< table_type_definition >	This argument contains one or more column definitions for the table variable. Each column definition contains the name and data type and can optionally define a PRIMARY KEY, UNIQUE, NULL, or CHECK constraint.
function_body	The function body contains one or more Transact-SQL statements that are used to populate and modify the table variable that will be returned by the UDF.

Notice the RETURNS keyword, which defines a *table variable* definition. Also notice the RETURN keyword at the end of the function, which doesn't have any parameter or query after it, because it is assumed that the defined table variable will be returned.

In this example, a multi-statement UDF will be created that accepts two parameters: one to hold a string and the other to define how that string will be delimited. The string is then broken apart into a result set based on the defined delimiter:

```
-- Creates a UDF that returns a string array as a table result set
Use AdventureWorks2014;
GO
CREATE FUNCTION dbo.udf_ParseArray
( @StringArray varchar(max), @Delimiter char(1) ) RETURNS @StringArrayTable TABLE (Val
varchar(50))
AS
BEGIN
DECLARE @Delimiter_position int
IF RIGHT(@StringArray,1) != @Delimiter
      SET @StringArray = @StringArray + @Delimiter
WHILE CHARINDEX(@Delimiter, @StringArray) <> 0
BEGIN
SELECT @Delimiter_position = CHARINDEX(@Delimiter, @StringArray)
INSERT INTO @StringArrayTable (Val)
      VALUES (LEFT(@StringArray, @Delimiter_position - 1));

SELECT @StringArray = STUFF(@StringArray, 1, @Delimiter_position, '') ;
END

RETURN
END
GO
```

Now it will be used to break apart a comma-delimited array of values:

```
SELECT Val
FROM dbo.udf_ParseArray('A,B,C,D,E,F,G', ',');
GO
```

This returns the following results:

Val
A
B
C
D
E
F
G

How It Works

The multi-statement table UDF in this recipe was created using two parameters, the first to hold a string and the second to define the character that delimits the string:

```
CREATE FUNCTION dbo.udf_ParseArray
( @StringArray varchar(max), @Delimiter char(1) )
```

Next, a table variable was defined after the RETURNS token. The @StringArrayTable was used to hold the values of the string array after being shredded into the individual values:

```
RETURNS @StringArrayTable TABLE (Val varchar(50))
```

The function body started after AS and BEGIN:

```
AS
BEGIN
```

A local variable was created to hold the delimiter position in the string:

```
DECLARE @Delimiter_position int
```

If the last character of the string array wasn't the delimiter value, then the delimiter value was concatenated to the end of the string array:

```
IF RIGHT(@StringArray,1) != @Delimiter
SET @StringArray = @StringArray + @Delimiter
```

A WHILE loop was created, looping until there were no remaining delimiters in the string array:

```
WHILE CHARINDEX(@Delimiter, @StringArray) <> 0
BEGIN
```

Within the loop, the position of the delimiter was identified using CHARINDEX:

```
SELECT @Delimiter_position = CHARINDEX(@Delimiter, @StringArray)
```

The LEFT function was used with the delimiter position to extract the individual-delimited string part into the table variable:

```
INSERT INTO @StringArrayTable (Val)
    VALUES (LEFT(@StringArray, @Delimiter_position - 1));
```

The inserted chunk was then removed from the string array using the STUFF function:

```
SELECT @StringArray = STUFF(@StringArray, 1, @Delimiter_position, '') ;
```

STUFF is used to delete a chunk of characters and insert another character string in its place. The first parameter of the STUFF function is the character expression, which in this example is the string array. The second parameter is the starting position of the deleted and inserted text, and in this case I am removing text from the string starting at the first position and stopping at the first delimiter. The third parameter is the length of the characters to be deleted, which for this example is the delimiter-position variable value. The last argument is the string to be inserted, which in this case was a blank string represented by two single quotes. The net effect is that the first comma-separated entry was replaced by an empty string—the same result as if the first entry had been deleted.

This process of inserting values continued until there were no longer delimiters in the string array. After this, the WHILE loop ended, and RETURN was called to return the table variable result set:

```
END RETURN END GO
```

The new UDF was then referenced in the FROM clause. The first parameter of the UDF was a comma-delimited list of letters. The second parameter was the delimiting parameter (a comma):

```
-- Now use it to break apart a comma-delimited array
SELECT Val
FROM dbo.udf_ParseArray('A,B,C,D,E,F,G', ',');
GO
```

The list was then broken into a result set, with each individual letter as its own row. As you can see, multi-statement table UDFs allow for much more sophisticated programmability than an inline table-valued UDF, which can use only a single SELECT statement.

18-4. Modifying User-Defined Functions

Problem

You have determined that a user-defined function is not producing the desired results. You need to modify this function.

Solution

A function can be modified by using the ALTER FUNCTION command, as I demonstrate in this next recipe:

```
Use AdventureWorks2014;
GO
ALTER FUNCTION dbo.udf_ParseArray ( @StringArray varchar(max),
@Delimiter char(1),
@MinRowSelect int,
@MaxRowSelect int)
RETURNS @StringArrayTable TABLE (RowNum int IDENTITY(1,1), Val varchar(50))
AS
BEGIN

DECLARE @Delimiter_position int
IF RIGHT(@StringArray,1) != @Delimiter
    SET @StringArray = @StringArray + @Delimiter;
WHILE CHARINDEX(@Delimiter, @StringArray) <> 0
BEGIN
SELECT @Delimiter_position = CHARINDEX(@Delimiter, @StringArray);
```

```
INSERT INTO @StringArrayTable (Val)
    VALUES (LEFT(@StringArray, @Delimiter_position - 1));

SELECT @StringArray = STUFF(@StringArray, 1, @Delimiter_position, '');
END
DELETE @StringArrayTable
    WHERE RowNum < @MinRowSelect OR RowNum > @MaxRowSelect;
RETURN
END
GO

/* Now use it to break apart a comma delimited array */
Use AdventureWorks2014;
GO
SELECT RowNum,Val
FROM dbo.udf_ParseArray('A,B,C,D,E,F,G', ',',3,5);
GO
```

This query returns the following:

RowNum	Val
3	C
4	D
5	E

How It Works

ALTER FUNCTION allows you to modify an existing UDF by using syntax that is almost identical to that of CREATE FUNCTION, with some limitations:

- You can't change the name of the function using ALTER FUNCTION. What you're doing is replacing the code of an *existing* function—therefore, the function needs to exist first.

- You can't convert a scalar UDF to a table UDF (either inline or multi-statement), and you cannot convert a table UDF to a scalar UDF.

In this recipe, the udf_ParseArray from the previous recipe was modified to add two new parameters, @MinRowSelect and @MaxRowSelect:

```
ALTER FUNCTION dbo.udf_ParseArray ( @StringArray varchar(max),
@Delimiter char(1) ,
@MinRowSelect int,
@MaxRowSelect int)
```

The @StringArrayTable table variable also had a new column added to it called RowNum, which was given the IDENTITY property (meaning that it will increment an integer value for each row in the result set):

```
RETURNS @StringArrayTable TABLE (RowNum int IDENTITY(1,1), Val varchar(50))
```

The other modification came after the WHILE loop was finished. Any RowNum values less than the minimum or maximum values were deleted from the @StringArrayTable table array:

```
DELETE @StringArrayTable
    WHERE RowNum < @MinRowSelect OR RowNum > @MaxRowSelect;
```

After altering the function, the function was called using the two new parameters to define the row range to view (in this case, rows 3 through 5):

```
Use AdventureWorks2014;
GO
SELECT RowNum,Val
FROM dbo.udf_ParseArray('A,B,C,D,E,F,G', ',',3,5);
GO
```

This returned the third, fourth, and fifth characters from the string array passed to the UDF.

18-5. Viewing UDF Metadata

Problem

You want to view a list which includes the definitions of all user-defined functions in your database.

Solution

Query the catalog view sys.sql_modules. You can use the sys.sql_modules catalog view to view information regarding all user-defined functions within a database. In this recipe, I will demonstrate how to view the name and the definition of each function.

```
Use AdventureWorks2014;
GO
SELECT name, o.type_desc
    , (Select definition as [processing-instruction(definition)]
        FROM sys.sql_modules
        Where object_id = s.object_id
        FOR XML PATH(''), TYPE
    )
FROM sys.sql_modules s
INNER JOIN sys.objects o
    ON s.object_id = o.object_id
WHERE o.type IN ('IF', -- Inline Table UDF
    'TF', -- Multistatement Table UDF
    'FN') -- Scalar UDF
;
```

How It Works

The sys.sql_modules and sys.objects system views are used to return the UDF name, type description, and SQL definition in a query result set:

```
FROM sys.sql_modules s
INNER JOIN sys.objects o
        ON s.object_id = o.object_id
```

The SQL definition is maintained in sys.sql_modules. In this example, I have shown how to return the result in a clickable format, which will render the function formatted as it is stored in the database (and for readability). This is done through the FOR XML PATH command using the processing-instruction directive:

```
, (Select definition as [processing-instruction(definition)]
     FROM sys.sql_modules
     Where object_id = s.object_id
     FOR XML PATH(''), TYPE
  )
```

Because sys.sql_modules contains rows for other object types, sys.objects must also be qualified to return only UDF rows:

```
WHERE o.type IN ('IF', -- Inline Table UDF
       'TF', -- Multistatement Table UDF
       'FN') -- Scalar UDF
;
```

Benefitting from UDFs

User-defined functions are useful for both the performance enhancements they provide because of their cached execution plans and their ability to encapsulate reusable code. In this next section, I'll discuss some of the benefits of UDFs. For example, scalar functions in particular can be used to help make code more readable and allow you to apply lookup rules consistently across an application rather than repeating the same code multiple times throughout different stored procedures or views.

Table-valued functions are also useful for allowing you to apply parameters to results; for example, using a parameter to define row-level security for a data set (demonstrated later in the chapter).

■ **Caution** When designing user-defined functions, consider the multiplier effect. For example, if you create a scalar user-defined function that performs a lookup against a million-row table in order to return a single value, and if a single lookup with proper indexing takes 30 seconds, chances are you are going to see a significant performance hit if you use this UDF to return values based on each row of another large table. If scalar user-defined functions reference other tables, make sure that the query you use to access the table information performs well and doesn't return a result set that is too large.

The next few recipes will demonstrate some of the more common and beneficial ways in which user-defined functions are used in the field.

18-6. Maintaining Reusable Code

Problem

You have discovered that a code segment has been duplicated numerous times throughout your database. You want to reduce the amount of code bloat in the database.

Solution

Create an appropriate UDF. For instance, scalar UDFs allow you to reduce code bloat by encapsulating logic within a single function, rather than repeating the logic multiple times wherever it happens to be needed.

The following scalar, user-defined function is used to determine the kind of personal computer that an employee will receive. There are several lines of code that evaluate different input parameters, including the employee's title, hire date, and salaried status. Rather than include this logic in multiple areas across your database application, you can encapsulate the logic in a single function.

```
Use AdventureWorks2014;
GO
CREATE FUNCTION dbo.udf_GET_AssignedEquipment (@Title nvarchar(50), @HireDate datetime,
@SalariedFlag bit)
RETURNS nvarchar(50)
AS
BEGIN
DECLARE @EquipmentType nvarchar(50)
IF @Title LIKE 'Chief%' OR
      @Title LIKE 'Vice%' OR
      @Title = 'Database Administrator'
BEGIN
      SET @EquipmentType = 'PC Build A' ;
END
IF @EquipmentType IS NULL AND @SalariedFlag = 1
BEGIN
      SET @EquipmentType = 'PC Build B' ;
END
IF @EquipmentType IS NULL AND @HireDate < '1/1/2002'
BEGIN
      SET @EquipmentType = 'PC Build C' ;
END
IF @EquipmentType IS NULL
BEGIN
      SET @EquipmentType = 'PC Build D' ;
END
RETURN @EquipmentType ;
END
GO
```

Once you've created it, you can use this scalar function in many areas of your Transact-SQL code without having to recode the logic within. In the following example, the new scalar function is used in the SELECT, GROUP BY, and ORDER BY clauses of a query:

```
Use AdventureWorks2014;
GO
SELECT PC_Build = dbo.udf_GET_AssignedEquipment(JobTitle, HireDate, SalariedFlag)
    , Employee_Count = COUNT(*)
FROM HumanResources.Employee
GROUP BY dbo.udf_GET_AssignedEquipment(JobTitle, HireDate, SalariedFlag)
ORDER BY dbo.udf_GET_AssignedEquipment(JobTitle, HireDate, SalariedFlag);
```

This query returns the following:

PC_Build	Employee_Count
PC Build A	7
PC Build B	45
PC Build D	238

This second query uses the scalar function in both the SELECT and WHERE clauses, too:

```
Use AdventureWorks2014;
GO
SELECT JobTitle,BusinessEntityID
    ,PC_Build = dbo.udf_GET_AssignedEquipment(JobTitle, HireDate, SalariedFlag)
FROM HumanResources.Employee
WHERE dbo.udf_GET_AssignedEquipment(JobTitle, HireDate, SalariedFlag)
    IN ('PC Build A', 'PC Build B');
```

This returns the following (abridged) results:

JobTitle	BusinessEntityID	PC_Build
Chief Executive Officer	1	PC Build A
Vice President of Engineering	2	PC Build A
Engineering Manager	3	PC Build B
Design Engineer	5	PC Build B
Design Engineer	6	PC Build B
...		

How It Works

Scalar user-defined functions can help you encapsulate business logic so that it isn't repeated across your code, providing a centralized location for you to make a single modification to a single function when necessary. This also provides consistency so that you and other database developers are using and writing the same logic in the same way. One other benefit is code readability, particularly with large queries that perform multiple lookups or evaluations.

18-7. Cross-Referencing Natural Key Values

A *surrogate key* is an artificial primary key, as opposed to a *natural key*, which represents a unique descriptor of data (for example, a Social Security number is an example of a natural key, but an IDENTITY property column is a surrogate key). IDENTITY values are often used as surrogate primary keys, but are also referenced as foreign keys.

In my own OLTP and star schema database designs, I assign each table a surrogate key by default, unless there is a significant reason not to do so. Doing this helps you abstract your own unique key from any external legacy natural keys. If you are using, for example, an EmployeeNumber that comes from the HR system as your primary key instead, you could run into trouble later if that HR system decides to change its data type (forcing you to change the primary key, any foreign key references, and composite primary keys). Surrogate keys help protect you from changes like this because they are under your control, and thus make good primary keys. You can keep your natural keys' unique constraints without worrying about external changes impacting your primary or foreign keys.

When importing data from legacy systems into production tables, you'll often still need to reference the natural key in order to determine which rows get inserted, updated, or deleted. This isn't very tricky if you're just dealing with a single column (for example, EmployeeID, CreditCardNumber, SSN, UPC). However, if the natural key is made up of multiple columns, the cross-referencing to the production tables may not be quite so easy.

Problem

You are using natural keys and surrogate keys within your database. You need to verify that a natural key exists prior to performing certain actions.

Solution

You can create a scalar user-defined function that can be used to perform natural key lookups.

The following demonstrates a scalar user-defined function that can be used to simplify natural key lookups by checking for their existence prior to performing an action. To set up the example, I'll create a few objects and execute a few commands.

First, I'll create a new table that uses its own surrogate keys, along with three columns that make up the composite natural key (these three columns form the unique value that was received from the legacy system):

```
Use AdventureWorks2014;
GO
CREATE TABLE dbo.DimProductSalesperson
(DimProductSalespersonID int IDENTITY(1,1) NOT NULL PRIMARY KEY,
ProductCD char(10) NOT NULL,
CompanyNBR int NOT NULL,
SalespersonNBR int NOT NULL );
GO
```

■ **Caution**   This recipe doesn't add indexes to the tables (beyond the default clustered index that is created on dbo.DimProductSalesperson); however, in a real-life scenario, you'll want to add indexes for key columns used for join operations or qualified in the WHERE clause of a query.

Next, I'll create a staging table that holds rows from the external legacy data file. For example, this table could be populated from an external text file that is dumped out of the legacy system. This table doesn't have a primary key, because it is just used to hold data prior to being moved to the dbo.DimProductSalesperson table:

```
Use AdventureWorks2014;
GO
CREATE TABLE dbo.Staging_PRODSLSP ( ProductCD char(10) NOT NULL,
CompanyNBR int NOT NULL,
SalespersonNBR int NOT NULL );
GO
```

Next, I'll insert two rows into the staging table:

```
Use AdventureWorks2014;
GO
INSERT dbo.Staging_PRODSLSP (ProductCD, CompanyNBR, SalespersonNBR)
     VALUES ('2391A23904', 1, 24);
INSERT dbo.Staging_PRODSLSP (ProductCD, CompanyNBR, SalespersonNBR)
     VALUES ('X129483203', 1, 34);
GO
```

Now these two rows can be inserted into the DimProductSalesperson table using the following query, which *doesn't* use a scalar UDF:

```
Use AdventureWorks2014;
GO
INSERT Into dbo.DimProductSalesperson (ProductCD, CompanyNBR, SalespersonNBR)
     SELECT s.ProductCD, s.CompanyNBR, s.SalespersonNBR
           FROM dbo.Staging_PRODSLSP s
           LEFT OUTER JOIN dbo.DimProductSalesperson d
                ON s.ProductCD = d.ProductCD
                AND s.CompanyNBR = d.CompanyNBR
                AND s.SalespersonNBR = d.SalespersonNBR
     WHERE d.DimProductSalespersonID IS NULL;
GO
```

Because each column forms the natural key, I must LEFT JOIN each column from the inserted table against the staging table and then check to see whether the row does not already exist in the destination table using IS NULL.

An alternative to this, allowing you to reduce the code in each INSERT/UPDATE/DELETE, is to create a scalar UDF like the following:

```
Use AdventureWorks2014;
GO
CREATE FUNCTION dbo.udf_GET_Check_NK_DimProductSalesperson (@ProductCD char(10), @CompanyNBR
int, @SalespersonNBR int )
RETURNS bit
AS
BEGIN
DECLARE @Exists bit
```

```
IF EXISTS (SELECT DimProductSalespersonID
            FROM dbo.DimProductSalesperson
            WHERE @ProductCD = @ProductCD
            AND @CompanyNBR = @CompanyNBR
            AND @SalespersonNBR = @SalespersonNBR)
BEGIN
     SET @Exists = 1;
END
ELSE
BEGIN
     SET @Exists = 0;
END
RETURN @Exists
END
GO
```

The UDF certainly looks like more code up front, but you'll realize its benefits later during the data-import process. For example, now you can rewrite the INSERT operation demonstrated earlier, as follows:

```
Use AdventureWorks2014;
GO
INSERT INTO dbo.DimProductSalesperson(ProductCD, CompanyNBR, SalespersonNBR)
     SELECT ProductCD, CompanyNBR, SalespersonNBR
     FROM dbo.Staging_PRODSLSP
     WHERE dbo.udf_GET_Check_NK_DimProductSalesperson
      (ProductCD, CompanyNBR, SalespersonNBR) = 0;
GO
```

How It Works

In this recipe, I demonstrated how to create a scalar UDF that returned a bit value based on three parameters. If the three values already existed for a row in the production table, a 1 was returned; otherwise, a 0 was returned. Using this function simplifies the INSERT/UPDATE/DELETE code that you must write in situations where a natural key spans multiple columns.

Walking through the UDF code, the first lines defined the UDF name and parameters. Each of these parameters was for the composite natural key in the staging and production tables:

```
CREATE FUNCTION dbo.udf_GET_Check_NK_DimProductSalesperson (@ProductCD char(10), @CompanyNBR
int, @SalespersonNBR int )
```

Next, a bit data type was defined to be returned by the function:

```
RETURNS bit
AS
BEGIN
```

A local variable was created to hold the bit value:

```
DECLARE @IfExists bit
```

457

An IF statement was used to check for the existence of a row matching all three parameters for the natural composite key. If there is a match, the local variable is set to 1. If not, it is set to 0.

```
IF EXISTS (SELECT DimProductSalespersonID
                   FROM dbo.DimProductSalesperson
                   WHERE @ProductCD = @ProductCD
                   AND @CompanyNBR = @CompanyNBR
                   AND @SalespersonNBR = @SalespersonNBR)
BEGIN
     SET @Exists = 1;
END
ELSE
BEGIN
     SET @Exists = 0;
END
```

The local variable was then passed back to the caller:

```
RETURN @IfExists END
GO
```

The function was then used in the WHERE clause, extracting from the staging table those rows that returned a 0 from the scalar UDF and therefore do not exist in the DimProductSalesperson table:

```
WHERE dbo.udf_GET_Check_NK_DimProductSalesperson (ProductCD, CompanyNBR, SalespersonNBR) = 0
```

18-8. Replacing a View with a Function

Problem

You have a view in your database that you need to parameterize.

Solution

Create a multi-statement UDF to replace the view. Multi-statement UDFs allow you to return data in the same way you would from a view, only with the ability to manipulate data like a stored procedure.

In this example, a multi-statement UDF is created to apply row-based security based on the caller of the function. Only rows for the specified salesperson will be returned. In addition to this, the second parameter is a bit flag that controls whether rows from the SalesPersonQuotaHistory table will be returned in the results.

```
Use AdventureWorks2014;
GO
CREATE FUNCTION dbo.udf_SEL_SalesQuota ( @BusinessEntityID int, @ShowHistory bit )
RETURNS @SalesQuota TABLE (BusinessEntityID int, QuotaDate datetime, SalesQuota money)

AS
BEGIN
INSERT Into @SalesQuota(BusinessEntityID, QuotaDate, SalesQuota)
     SELECT BusinessEntityID, ModifiedDate, SalesQuota
     FROM Sales.SalesPerson
     WHERE BusinessEntityID = @BusinessEntityID;
```

```
IF @ShowHistory = 1
BEGIN
INSERT Into @SalesQuota(BusinessEntityID, QuotaDate, SalesQuota)
    SELECT BusinessEntityID, QuotaDate, SalesQuota
    FROM Sales.SalesPersonQuotaHistory
    WHERE BusinessEntityID = @BusinessEntityID;
END
RETURN
END
GO
```

After the UDF is created, the following query is executed to show sales-quota data for a specific salesperson from the Salesperson table:

```
Use AdventureWorks2014;
GO

SELECT BusinessEntityID, QuotaDate, SalesQuota
    FROM dbo.udf_SEL_SalesQuota (275,0);
```

This query returns the following:

BusinessEntItyID	QuotaDate	SalesQuota
275	2011-05-24 00:00:00.000	300000.00

Next, the second parameter is switched from a 0 to a 1 in order to display additional rows for Salespersons 275 from the SalesPersonQuotaHistory table:

```
Use AdventureWorks2014;
GO

SELECT BusinessEntityID, QuotaDate, SalesQuota
    FROM dbo.udf_SEL_SalesQuota (275,1);
```

This returns the following (abridged) results:

BusinessEntityID	QuotaDate	SalesQuota
275	2011-05-24 00:00:00.000	300000.00
275	2011-05-31 00:00:00.000	367000.00
275	2011-08-31 00:00:00.000	556000.00
275	2011-12-01 00:00:00.000	502000.00
275	2012-02-29 00:00:00.000	550000.00
275	2012-05-30 00:00:00.000	1429000.00
275	2012-08-30 00:00:00.000	1324000.00
...		

How It Works

This recipe demonstrated a multi-statement table-valued UDF to return sales-quota data based on the BusinessEntityID value that was passed. It also included a second bit flag that controlled whether history was also returned.

Walking through the function, you'll notice that the first few lines defined the input parameters (something that a view doesn't allow):

```
CREATE FUNCTION dbo.udf_SEL_SalesQuota ( @BusinessEntityID int, @ShowHistory bit )
```

After this, the table columns that are to be returned by the function were defined:

```
RETURNS @SalesQuota TABLE (BusinessEntityID int, QuotaDate datetime, SalesQuota money)
```

The function body included two separate batch statements, the first being an INSERT into the table variable of rows for the specific salesperson:

```
AS
BEGIN
INSERT Into @SalesQuota(BusinessEntityID, QuotaDate, SalesQuota)
    SELECT BusinessEntityID, ModifiedDate, SalesQuota
    FROM Sales.SalesPerson
    WHERE BusinessEntityID = @BusinessEntityID;
```

Next, an IF statement (another construct not allowed in views) evaluated the bit parameter. If equal to 1, quota history will also be inserted into the table variable:

```
IF @ShowHistory = 1
BEGIN
INSERT Into @SalesQuota(BusinessEntityID, QuotaDate, SalesQuota)
    SELECT BusinessEntityID, QuotaDate, SalesQuota
    FROM Sales.SalesPersonQuotaHistory
    WHERE BusinessEntityID = @BusinessEntityID;
END
```

Lastly, the RETURN keyword signaled the end of the function (and, unlike a scalar function, no local variable is designated after it):

```
RETURN END
GO
```

Although the UDF contained Transact-SQL not allowed in a view, it was still able to be referenced in the FROM clause:

```
Use AdventureWorks2014;
GO

SELECT BusinessEntityID, QuotaDate, SalesQuota
    FROM dbo.udf_SEL_SalesQuota (275,0);
```

The results could be returned in a view using a UNION statement, but with that you wouldn't be able to have the control logic to either show or not show history in a single view.

In this recipe, I demonstrated a method to create your own parameter-based result sets. This can be used to implement row-based security, which is not built natively into the SQL Server security model. You can use functions to return only the rows that are allowed to be viewed by designating input parameters to filter the data.

18-9. Dropping a Function

Problem

You no longer need a user-defined function in your database. You have confirmed that it is not used anywhere else, and you need to remove it from the database.

Solution

You can use DROP FUNCTION to remove a function. The syntax, like other DROP commands, is very straightforward.

```
DROP FUNCTION { [ schema_name. ] function_name } [ ,...n ]
```

Table 18-4 details the arguments of this command.

Table 18-4. DROP FUNCTION *Arguments*

Argument	Description
[schema_name.] function_name	This defines the optional schema name and required function name of the user-defined function.
[,...n]	Although not an actual argument, this syntax element indicates that one or more user-defined functions can be dropped in a single statement.

This recipe demonstrates how to drop the dbo.udf_ParseArray function created in an earlier recipe.

```
Use AdventureWorks2014;
GO
DROP FUNCTION dbo.udf_ParseArray;
```

How It Works

Although there are three different types of user-defined functions (scalar, inline, and multi-statement), you need only drop them using the single DROP FUNCTION command. You can also drop more than one UDF in a single statement; for example:

```
Use AdventureWorks2014;
GO
DROP FUNCTION dbo.udf_ParseArray, dbo.udf_ReturnAddress,
dbo.udf_CheckForSQLInjection;
```

UDT Basics

User-defined types are useful for defining a consistent data type that is named after a known business or application-centric attribute, such as PIN, PhoneNBR, or EmailAddress. Once a user-defined type is created in the database, it can be used within columns, parameters, and variable definitions, providing a consistent underlying data type. The next two recipes will show you how to create and drop user-defined types. Note that unlike some other database objects, there isn't a way to modify an existing type using an ALTER command.

18-10. Creating and Using User-Defined Types

Problem

You have a frequently used account-number field throughout the database. You want to try to enforce a consistent definition for this field while providing convenience to the database developers.

Solution

Create a user-defined type (also called an *alias data type),* which is a specific configuration of a data type that is given a user-specified name, data type, length, and nullability. You can use all base data types except the xml data type.

■ **Caution**   One drawback when using user-defined data types is their inability to be changed without cascading effects, as you'll see in the last recipe of this chapter.

The basic syntax for creating a user-defined type is as follows:

```
CREATE TYPE [ schema_name. ] type_name {
FROM base_type
[ (precision [ ,scale ] ) ]
[ NULL | NOT NULL ] }
```

Table 18-5 details the arguments of these commands.

Table 18-5. CREATE TYPE *Arguments*

Argument	Description
[schema_name.] type_name	This specifies the optional schema name and required type name of the new user-defined type.
base_type	This is the base data type used to define the new user-defined type. You are allowed to use all base system data types except the xml data type.
(precision [,scale])	If using a numeric base type, precision is the maximum number of digits that can be stored both left and right of the decimal point. Scale is the maximum number of digits to be stored right of the decimal point.
NULL	NOT NULL	This defines whether your new user-defined type allows NULL values.

In this recipe, I'll create a new type based on a 14-character string:

```
Use AdventureWorks2014;
GO
/*
-- In this example, we assume the company's Account number will
-- be used in multiple tables, and that it will always have a fixed
-- 14 character length and will never allow NULL values
*/

CREATE TYPE dbo.AccountNBR FROM char(14) NOT NULL;
GO
```

Next, I'll use the new type in the column definition of two tables:

```
Use AdventureWorks2014;
GO
-- The new data type is now used in two different tables
CREATE TABLE dbo.InventoryAccount
(InventoryAccountID int NOT NULL,
InventoryID int NOT NULL,
InventoryAccountNBR AccountNBR);
GO
CREATE TABLE dbo.CustomerAccount
(CustomerAccountID int NOT NULL,
CustomerID int NOT NULL,
CustomerAccountNBR AccountNBR);
GO
```

This type can also be used in the definition of a local variable or input parameter. For example, the following stored procedure uses the new data type to define the input parameter for a stored procedure:

```
Use AdventureWorks2014;
GO
CREATE PROCEDURE dbo.usp_SEL_CustomerAccount
@CustomerAccountNBR AccountNBR

AS
SELECT CustomerAccountID, CustomerID, CustomerAccountNBR
FROM dbo.CustomerAccount
WHERE CustomerAccountNBR = CustomerAccountNBR;
GO
```

Next, a local variable is created using the new data type and is passed to the stored procedure:

```
Use AdventureWorks2014;
GO
DECLARE @CustomerAccountNBR AccountNBR
SET @CustomerAccountNBR = '1294839482';
EXECUTE dbo.usp_SEL_CustomerAccount @CustomerAccountNBR;
GO
```

To view the underlying base type of the user-defined type, you can use the sp_help system stored procedure:

```
Use AdventureWorks2014;
GO
EXECUTE sp_help 'dbo.AccountNBR';
GO
```

This returns the following results (only a few columns are displayed for presentation purposes):

Type_name	Storage_type	Length	Nullable
AccountNbr	char	14	no

How It Works

In this recipe, a new user-defined type called dbo.AccountNBR was created with a char(14) data type and NOT NULL. Once the user-defined type was created, it was then used in the column definition of two different tables:

```
CREATE TABLE dbo.InventoryAccount
(InventoryAccountID int NOT NULL,
InventoryID int NOT NULL,
InventoryAccountNBR AccountNBR);
GO
CREATE TABLE dbo.CustomerAccount
(CustomerAccountID int NOT NULL,
CustomerID int NOT NULL,
CustomerAccountNBR AccountNBR);
GO
```

Because NOT NULL was already inherent in the data type, it wasn't necessary to explicitly define it in the column definition.

After creating the tables, a stored procedure was created that used the new data type in the input parameter definition. The procedure was then called using a local variable that also used the new type.

Although Transact-SQL types may be an excellent convenience for some developers, creating your application's data dictionary and abiding by the data types may suit the same purpose. For example, if an AccountNBR is always 14 characters, as a DBA/developer, you can communicate and check to make sure that new objects are using a consistent name and data type.

18-11. Identifying Dependencies on User-Defined Types

Problem

You want to list all of the columns and parameters that have a dependency on a user-defined data type within your database.

Solution

Query the sys.types catalog view. Before showing you how to remove a user-defined data type, you'll need to know how to identify all database objects that depend on that type. As you'll see later, removing a UDT doesn't automatically cascade changes to the dependent table.

This example shows you how to identify which database objects are using the specified user-defined type. The first query in the recipe displays all columns that use the AccountNBR user-defined type:

```
Use AdventureWorks2014;
GO
SELECT Table_Name = OBJECT_NAME(c.object_id) , Column_name = c.name
FROM sys.columns c
      INNER JOIN sys.types t
            ON c.user_type_id = t.user_type_id
WHERE t.name = 'AccountNBR';
```

This query returns the following:

Table_Name	Column_Name
InventoryAccount	InventoryAccountNBR
CustomerAccount	CustomerAccountNBR

This next query shows any procedures or functions that have parameters defined using the AccountNBR user-defined type:

```
Use AdventureWorks2014;
GO
/*
-- Now see which parameters reference the AccountNBR data type
*/
SELECT ProcFunc_Name = OBJECT_NAME(p.object_id) , Parameter_Name = p.name
FROM sys.parameters p
      INNER JOIN sys.types t
            ON p.user_type_id = t.user_type_id
WHERE t.name = 'AccountNBR';
```

This query returns the following:

ProcFunc_Name	Parameter_Name
usp_SEL_CustomerAccount	@CustomerAccountNBR

465

How It Works

To report which table columns use the user-defined type, the system catalog views sys.columns and sys.types are used:

```
FROM sys.columns c
    INNER JOIN sys.types t
    ON c.user_type_id = t.user_type_id
```

The sys.columns view contains a row for each column defined for a table-valued function, table, and view in the database. The sys.types view contains a row for each user and system data type.

To identify which function or procedure parameters reference the user-defined type, the system catalog views sys.parameters and sys.types are used:

```
FROM sys.parameters p
    INNER JOIN sys.types t
    ON p.user_type_id = t.user_type_id
```

The sys.parameters view contains a row for each database object that can accept a parameter, including stored procedures, for example.

Identifying which objects reference a user-defined type is necessary if you plan on dropping the user-defined type, as the next recipe demonstrates.

18-12. Passing Table-Valued Parameters

Problem

You have an application that calls a stored procedure repetitively to insert singleton records. You would like to alter this process to reduce the number of calls to this stored procedure.

Solution

Table-valued parameters can be used to pass rowsets to stored procedures and user-defined functions. This functionality allows you to encapsulate multi-rowset capabilities within stored procedures and functions without having to make multiple row-by-row calls to data-modification procedures or create multiple input parameters that inelegantly translate to multiple rows.

For example, the following stored procedure has several input parameters that are used to insert rows into the Department table:

```
Use AdventureWorks2014;
GO
CREATE PROCEDURE dbo.usp_INS_Department_Oldstyle
@Name_1 nvarchar(50),
@GroupName_1 nvarchar(50),
@Name_2 nvarchar(50),
@GroupName_2 nvarchar(50),
@Name_3 nvarchar(50),
@GroupName_3 nvarchar(50),
@Name_4 nvarchar(50),
```

```
@GroupName_4 nvarchar(50),
@Name_5 nvarchar(50),
@GroupName_5 nvarchar(50)

AS
INSERT INTO HumanResources.Department(Name, GroupName)
     VALUES (@Name_1, @GroupName_1)
INSERT INTO HumanResources.Department(Name, GroupName)
     VALUES (@Name_2, @GroupName_2);
INSERT INTO HumanResources.Department(Name, GroupName)
     VALUES (@Name_3, @GroupName_3);
INSERT INTO HumanResources.Department (Name, GroupName)
     VALUES (@Name_4, @GroupName_4);
INSERT INTO HumanResources.Department (Name, GroupName)
     VALUES (@Name_5, @GroupName_5);
GO
```

This previous example procedure has several limitations. First, it assumes that each call will contain five rows. If you have ten rows, you must call the procedure twice. If you have three rows, you need to modify the procedure to test for NULL values in the parameters and skip inserts accordingly. If NULL values are allowed in the underlying table, you would also need a method to indicate when a NULL should be stored and when a NULL represents a value not to be stored.

A more common technique is to create a singleton insert procedure, as follows:

```
Use AdventureWorks2014;
GO
CREATE PROCEDURE dbo.usp_INS_Department_Oldstyle_V2
@Name nvarchar(50),
@GroupName nvarchar(50)
AS
INSERT INTO HumanResources.Department (Name, GroupName)
     VALUES (@Name, @GroupName);
GO
```

If you have five rows to be inserted, you would call this procedure five times. This may be acceptable in many circumstances. However, if you will always be inserting multiple rows in a single batch, SQL Server provides a better alternative. Instead of performing singleton calls, you can pass the values to be inserted into a single parameter that represents a table of values. Such a parameter is called a *table-valued parameter*.

To use a table-valued parameter, the first step is to define a user-defined table data type, as I demonstrate here:

```
Use AdventureWorks2014;
GO
CREATE TYPE Department_TT AS TABLE (Name nvarchar(50), GroupName nvarchar(50));
GO
```

Once the new table type is created in the database, it can be referenced in module definitions and within the code:

```
Use AdventureWorks2014;
GO
CREATE PROCEDURE dbo.usp_INS_Department_NewStyle
     @DepartmentTable as Department_TT
READONLY
AS

INSERT INTO HumanResources.Department (Name, GroupName)
     SELECT Name, GroupName
          FROM @DepartmentTable;
GO
```

Let's assume that an external process is used to populate a list of values, which I will then pass to the procedure. In your own applications, the data source that you pass in can be generated from a populated staging table, directly from an application rowset, or from a constructed rowset, as demonstrated next:

```
Use AdventureWorks2014;
GO
/*
-- I can declare our new type for use within a T-SQL batch
-- Insert multiple rows into this table-type variable
*/

DECLARE @StagingDepartmentTable as Department_TT
INSERT INTO @StagingDepartmentTable(Name, GroupName)
     VALUES ('Archivists', 'Accounting');
INSERT INTO @StagingDepartmentTable(Name, GroupName)
     VALUES ('Public Media', 'Legal');
INSERT @StagingDepartmentTable(Name, GroupName)
     VALUES ('Internal Admin', 'Office Administration');
/*
-- Pass this table-type variable to the procedure in a single call
*/
EXECUTE dbo.usp_INS_Department_NewStyle @StagingDepartmentTable;
GO
```

How It Works

To pass result sets to modules, I must first define a user-defined table type within the database. I used the CREATE TYPE command and defined it AS TABLE:

```
CREATE TYPE Department_TT AS TABLE
```

Next, I defined the two columns that made up the table, just as one would for a regular table:

```
(Name nvarchar(50), GroupName nvarchar(50)) GO
```

I could have also defined the table type with PRIMARY KEY, UNIQUE, and CHECK constraints. I could also have designated nullability as well as defined whether the column was computed.

Next, I created a new procedure that used the newly created table type. In the input parameter argument list, I created an input parameter with a type of Department_TT:

```
CREATE PROCEDURE dbo.usp_INS_Department_NewStyle
    @DepartmentTable as Department_TT
READONLY
AS
```

Notice the READONLY keyword after the data type designation. This is a requirement for stored procedure and user-defined function input parameters, because you are not allowed to modify the table-valued result set in this version of SQL Server.

The next block of code handled the INSERT to the table, using the input parameter as the data source of the multiple rows:

```
INSERT INTO HumanResources.Department (Name, GroupName)
    SELECT Name, GroupName
        FROM @DepartmentTable;
GO
```

After that, I demonstrated declaring a local variable that would contain multiple rows that would be passed to the procedure. The DECLARE statement defines the variable name, followed by the name of the table user-defined type defined earlier in the recipe:

```
DECLARE @StagingDepartmentTable as Department_TT
```

Once declared, I inserted multiple rows into this table and then passed it as a parameter to the stored procedure call:

```
INSERT INTO @StagingDepartmentTable(Name, GroupName)
    VALUES ('Archivists', 'Accounting');
INSERT INTO @StagingDepartmentTable(Name, GroupName)
    VALUES ('Public Media', 'Legal');
INSERT @StagingDepartmentTable(Name, GroupName)
    VALUES ('Internal Admin', 'Office Administration');
EXECUTE dbo.usp_INS_Department_NewStyle @StagingDepartmentTable;
GO
```

The benefits of this new functionality come into play when you consider procedures that handle business processes. For example, if you have a web site that handles product orders, you can now pass result sets to a single procedure that includes the general header information along with multiple rows representing the products that were ordered. This application process can be constructed as a single call versus having to issue several calls for each unique product line item ordered. For extremely busy systems, using table-valued parameters allows you to reduce the chatter between the application and the database server, resulting in increased network bandwidth and more efficient batching of transactions on the SQL Server side.

18-13. Dropping User-Defined Types

Problem

You suspect there are unused user-defined types within your database. You would like to remove these types from the database.

Solution

To remove a user-defined type (also called an *alias* data type) from the database, use the DROP TYPE command. As with most DROP commands, the syntax for removing a user-defined type is very straightforward:

```
DROP TYPE [ schema_name. ] type_name
```

The DROP TYPE command uses the schema and type name, as this recipe will demonstrate. First, however, any references to the user-defined type need to be removed beforehand. In this example, the AccountNBR type is changed to the base equivalent for two tables and a stored procedure:

```
Use AdventureWorks2014;
GO
ALTER TABLE dbo.InventoryAccount
ALTER COLUMN InventoryAccountNBR char(14);
GO
ALTER TABLE dbo.CustomerAccount
ALTER COLUMN CustomerAccountNBR char(14);
GO

ALTER PROCEDURE dbo.usp_SEL_CustomerAccount
@CustomerAccountNBR char(14)

AS

SELECT CustomerAccountID, CustomerID, CustomerAccountNBR
FROM dbo.CustomerAccount
WHERE CustomerAccountNBR = @CustomerAccountNBR;
GO
```

With the referencing objects now converted, it is OK to go ahead and drop the type:

```
Use AdventureWorks2014;
GO
DROP TYPE dbo.AccountNBR;
```

How It Works

To remove a type, you must first change or remove any references to the type in a database table. If you are going to change the definition of a UDT, you need to remove *all* references to that UDT everywhere in *all* database objects that use that UDT. That means changing tables, views, stored procedures, and so on before dropping the type. This can be very cumbersome if your database objects depend very heavily on them. Also, if any schema-bound stored procedures, functions, or triggers use the data type as parameters or variables, these references must be changed or removed. In this recipe, ALTER TABLE...ALTER COLUMN was used to change the data type to the system data type.

```
ALTER TABLE dbo.InventoryAccount
ALTER COLUMN InventoryAccountNBR char(14)
```

A stored procedure parameter was also modified using ALTER PROCEDURE:

```
ALTER PROCEDURE usp_SEL_CustomerAccount (@CustomerAccountNBR char(14))
```

CHAPTER 19

■ ■ ■

In-Memory OLTP

by Wayne Sheffield

Perhaps the most anticipated new feature in SQL Server 2014 is the In-Memory OLTP database engine component. As its name implies, this new component works with memory-resident data. Current OLTP workloads, which read the pages from disk, need to take and release locks and latches, and they need to wait for log writes to be performed. In-Memory OLTP was designed for high concurrency with no blocking, which leads to In-Memory OLTP having tremendous performance improvements. This is accomplished by a new optimistic concurrency control model and latch-free data structures that remove locking and blocking contention. Log-write waits are greatly reduced by generating less log data and by needing fewer log writes. When working with In-Memory OLTP, tables (including table variables) can be created to be memory optimized. Stored procedures that only reference memory-optimized tables can be natively compiled, resulting in additional performance improvements. By utilizing In-Memory OLTP, it is possible to achieve performance improvement of up to 20 times. In-Memory OLTP is designed for tables with a high number of concurrent data-manipulation transactions where blocking is causing performance issues.

There are a few requirements in order to use In-Memory OLTP:

1. You need a 64-bit Enterprise, Developer, or Evaluation edition of SQL Server 2014.

2. You need a modern CPU on the server that supports the cmpxchg16b instruction.

3. The server needs to have free disk space that is two times the size of the memory-optimized tables, and it needs enough memory to hold the memory-optimized tables in memory plus row versions (plan on two times the size).

4. The server needs enough memory to also handle the buffer pool and query processing on normal tables.

■ **Note**   The CMPXCHG16B instruction allows for atomic operations on 128-bit memory exchanges. This is useful for performing parallel operations when working with data that is larger than a pointer. This instruction set is present on most Intel processors since the 80486; however, early AMD64 processors lacked this instruction. If you have a modern processor, you have this instruction. Some virtual machines may need to be configured to have this instruction enabled on the VM guest.

19-1. Configuring a Database So That It Can Utilize In-Memory OLTP

Problem

You wish to configure your database so that it can utilize In-Memory OLTP.

Solution #1

Create a new database that includes a filegroup for holding the In-Memory data objects and a file in that filegroup:

```
CREATE DATABASE InMemory
ON
PRIMARY (NAME=[InMemory_data],
        FILENAME = 'C:\APRESS\MSSQL\DATA\InMemory_data.mdf',
        SIZE = 50MB),
FILEGROUP InMemory_mod CONTAINS MEMORY_OPTIMIZED_DATA (
        NAME = [InMemory_dir],
        FILENAME = 'C:\APRESS\MSSQL\DATA\InMemory_dir')
LOG ON (NAME = [InMemory_log],
        FILENAME = 'C:\APRESS\MSSQL\DATA\InMemory_log.ldf',
        SIZE=5MB)
COLLATE LATIN1_GENERAL_BIN2;
```

Solution #2

Create a new filegroup on your existing database for holding In-Memory data objects, with a file in that filegroup:

```
CREATE DATABASE InMemory
ON
PRIMARY (NAME=[InMemory_data],
        FILENAME = 'C:\APRESS\MSSQL\DATA\InMemory_data.mdf',
        SIZE = 50MB)
LOG ON (NAME = [InMemory_log],
        FILENAME = 'C:\APRESS\MSSQL\DATA\InMemory_log.ldf',
        SIZE=5MB)
COLLATE LATIN1_GENERAL_BIN2;

-- now modify the database to utilize In-Memory OLTP
ALTER DATABASE InMemory ADD FILEGROUP InMemory_mod CONTAINS MEMORY_OPTIMIZED_DATA;
ALTER DATABASE InMemory
ADD FILE (
        NAME = [InMemory_dir],
        FILENAME = 'C:\APRESS\MSSQL\DATA\InMemory_dir')
TO FILEGROUP [InMemory_mod];
```

How It Works

In order to utilize In-Memory OLTP on a database, you need to add a filegroup to the database that is specifically for holding memory-optimized data, and the filegroup needs a file specified. The filegroup is necessary in order to make the data in the memory-optimized tables durable. In these two examples, the filegroup is named InMemory_mod. The first solution creates a new database with the filegroup all in one step. The second solution creates the database first, and then alters the database to add the filegroup.

The option CONTAINS MEMORY_OPTIMIZED_DATA specifies that the filegroup will be storing memory-optimized data in the file system. In the file specification for the file being added to the filegroup, the logical name of the memory-optimized filegroup container is specified, as well as the physical path for it.

A memory-optimized filegroup is based on a FileStream filegroup. Despite this, you do not need to enable FileStream to create a memory-optimized filegroup—this is all handled by the In-Memory OLTP engine.

A database can have only one filegroup that contains memory-optimized data. This filegroup cannot be removed from the database; the only way to remove this filegroup is to drop the database. The filegroup needs to have one or more containers.

The filegroup containers will contain two types of files: data files and delta files. Each data file is paired with a delta file, and together this pair is known as a checkpoint file pair (CFP).

The data files are sized based upon the system memory: 16MB for systems with up to 16GB of memory, and 128MB for systems with greater than 16GB of memory. Rows being affected by a single transaction must be in one CFP; therefore, it is possible for the data file to grow beyond this initial size. The data file will hold data inserted into memory-optimized tables (from INSERT or UPDATE statements). However, unlike in a disk-based table, rows can be intermixed between tables—a row from memory-optimized table T1 can be followed by a row from memory-optimized table T2. The rows within the data file are stored in transaction log order. Rows in the data file are accessed sequentially. Since these files are stored and read sequentially, it would be best to have these files on their own drives where the I/O patterns can be truly sequential. Note that the file locations used in this recipe are for demonstration purposes only.

Each data file is paired with a delta file, which contains the reference information for rows deleted by any transactions found in the transaction range of the data file. Like the data file, the delta file is accessed sequentially.

Over the course of time, as data-manipulation operations update and delete rows in the memory-optimized tables, the CFPs will start containing an increasing number of deleted rows. These deleted rows end up contributing to several inefficiencies, as follows:

1. The deleted rows are taking up space in the durable storage of the tables.

2. The deleted rows contribute to an increasing number of CFPs that need to be tracked in the storage array.

3. Operations in the storage array have an increased cost as the number of CFPs increase.

To minimize these issues, the closed CFPs undergo an automatic merge process. The merge process will take adjacent CFPs and, utilizing the delta files to filter the data files, consolidate the active rows into a new CFP.

The .merge process has a merge policy which will consider whether two or more adjacent CFPs have active (non-deleted) rows that can be stored in one new CFP of ideal size. This ideal size is the same as previously mentioned: if the server has up to 16GB of memory, then the data file's ideal size is 16MB and the delta file is 1MB. For systems over 16GB, the ideal data file size is 128MB and the delta file's ideal size is 16MB. Additionally, if a single CFP has a data file greater than 256MB and more than half of the rows are deleted, then this CFP can be self-merged.

19-2. Making a Memory-Optimized Table

Problem

You wish to make a memory-optimized table.

Solution

Create a table, specifying that it is memory optimized:

```
CREATE TABLE dbo.T1 (
        c1 INTEGER NOT NULL PRIMARY KEY NONCLUSTERED,
        c2 NCHAR(48) NOT NULL,
        INDEX ix_T1 HASH(c2) WITH (BUCKET_COUNT=8)
) WITH (MEMORY_OPTIMIZED=ON, DURABILITY=SCHEMA_AND_DATA);
```

How It Works

The CREATE TABLE statement is utilized to create memory-optimized tables. When doing so, you need to utilize the table-option clause to specify that this is a memory-optimized table and what the durability is for this table. In the example above, this table is specified to be memory-optimized with the "MEMORY_OPTIMIZED=ON" clause. (Specifying "OFF" would make this a disk-based table, which is the default.)

There are two levels of durability for a memory-optimized table—SCHEMA_ONLY or SCHEMA_AND_DATA. If you specify SCHEMA_ONLY, data transactions are not put into the transaction log, and they are not persisted to disk to be made durable. In the solution above, this table is specifying to keep both the schema and data durable.

Each memory-optimized table requires at least one index, and also requires a primary key. (Indexes on a memory-optimized table are known as memory-optimized indexes.) Memory-optimized tables only support nonclustered indexes, and the indexes cannot be added or dropped after the table has been created—which means that they must be included as part of the CREATE TABLE statement. In the above solution, a nonclustered index is explicitly created with the primary key on the column c1. Since a primary key creates a clustered index by default, you must specify that this is to be nonclustered.

There are two types of memory-optimized indexes that can be used: a "regular" nonclustered index and a nonclustered hash index (which can only be used on a memory-optimized table). All memory-optimized indexes contain a memory pointer to the actual row in the table, making all memory-optimized indexes inherently covering. Therefore, memory-optimized tables will not incur any bookmark lookups.

Hash indexes are made for point lookups; as such, they only work for index seeks on equality predicates or full index scans. In the above solution, a hash index is also created on column c2. When creating a hash index, a BUCKET_COUNT must also be specified, which indicates the number of buckets that should be created in the hash index. In most cases, this should be between 1 and 2 times the number of distinct values in the index key. Consult the Books Online article "Determining the Correct Bucket Count for Hash Indexes" at http://msdn.microsoft.com/en-us/library/dn494956(v=sql.120).aspx for more detailed information.

Let's discuss some memory-optimized-index limitations:

1. Memory-optimized tables do not support unique or filtered indexes.

2. All key columns of indexes must be declared with NOT NULL.

3. Since all columns of a memory-optimized table are inherently covering, the INCLUDE clause is not allowed.

4. Character columns in an index key must use a BIN2 collation.

5. A hash index does not have an order, so the index cannot specify the ASC/DESC keywords.

6. Memory-optimized tables do not support auto_update_statistics—you must recompute the statistics manually after the table has been populated with data, as follows:

```
UPDATE STATISTICS dbo.T1 WITH FULLSCAN, NORECOMPUTE;
```

19-3. Creating a Memory-Optimized Table Variable

Problem

You wish to utilize a table variable as a memory-optimized table.

Solution

First create a memory-optimized table type, then declare a table variable using this table type:

```
CREATE TYPE dbo.imTV AS TABLE (
        Col1 INTEGER NOT NULL,
        INDEX ix_imTV1 HASH(Col1) WITH (BUCKET_COUNT=8)
) WITH (MEMORY_OPTIMIZED=ON);
GO
DECLARE @imTV dbo.imTV;
```

How It Works

You cannot directly create a table variable as a memory-optimized table. However, you can still create a memory-optimized table variable by creating a memory-optimized table type and then declaring the table variable using that table type.

In this example, the table type is created with a hash index and the memory optimized specification. Notice that the durability is not specified; for memory-optimized table types, the durability is SCHEMA_ONLY. The table variable is then declared using the table type.

19-4. Creating a Natively Compiled Stored Procedure

Problem

You wish to further increase the performance of your data-manipulation operations by utilizing a natively compiled procedure.

Solution

Create a stored procedure, utilizing the new clauses to natively compile it:

```
CREATE PROCEDURE dbo.imProc
WITH NATIVE_COMPILATION, SCHEMABINDING, EXECUTE AS OWNER
AS
BEGIN ATOMIC WITH (TRANSACTION ISOLATION LEVEL = SNAPSHOT, LANGUAGE = N'us_english')
    DECLARE @TV dbo.imTV;
    INSERT INTO @TV VALUES (4);
    INSERT INTO @TV VALUES (5);
    INSERT INTO @TV VALUES (6);
    SELECT Col1 FROM @TV;
END;
```

How It Works

As we start off creating the stored procedure, we immediately run into the first of the changes that are required for creating a natively compiled stored procedure—the WITH clause has three required elements:

1. NATIVE_COMPILATION: This element is used to indicate that this T-SQL stored procedure is to be a natively compiled stored procedure.

2. SCHEMABINDING: Natively compiled stored procedures are required to be schema bound to the objects that the procedure references. (An object that was built with the SCHEMABINDING option prevents the referenced object from being changed.)

3. EXECUTE AS: Natively compiled stored procedures do not support the default execution context EXECUTE AS CALLER. Therefore, you must use EXECUTE AS OWNER, EXECUTE AS SELF or EXECUTE AS USER. (See the "Stored Procedures" chapter for more information about using EXECUTE AS.)

The next required element that is encountered is the BEGIN ATOMIC block. Each natively compiled stored procedure is required to have exactly one atomic block, which guarantees the atomic execution of the stored procedure. There are two required options and three optional options for atomic blocks in natively compiled stored procedures. The required options are:

1. TRANSACTION ISOLATION LEVEL: For memory-optimized tables, this can be SNAPSHOT, REPEATABLE READ or SERIALIZABLE.

2. LANGUAGE: This must be set to one of the available languages (or language aliases).

The optional options are:

1. DATEFORMAT: All SQL date formats are allowed and override the default for the LANGUAGE.

2. DATEFIRST: overrides the default datefirst setting for LANGUAGE

3. DELAYED_DURABILITY: Can be ON or OFF. When ON, transaction log records are kept in a buffer and written to disk when the buffer is full or a buffer-flushing event takes place.

There are many restrictions when using a natively compiled stored procedure. Consult the Books Online topic "Transact-SQL Constructs Not Supported by In-Memory OLTP" at `http://msdn.microsoft.com/en-us/library/dn246937.aspx` for the full list.

For performance purposes, there are two parameter-related items to be aware of:

1. Ensure that the data type of the parameter being passed to the procedure is of the type declared in the procedure.

2. Do not use named parameters when calling the procedure.

Not following these rules will require the server to map parameter names or to convert types.

If one (or more) of these restrictions prevents you from being able to use a natively compiled procedure, you can still use a normal (interpreted) T-SQL stored procedure to access the memory-optimized table. Interpreted T-SQL (batches or non-natively compiled stored procedures) that accesses memory-optimized tables (called interop access) can perform almost any T-SQL query or data-manipulation operation. You might want to have interpreted T-SQL stored procedures when the logic requires a statement or construct that is invalid in natively compiled stored procedures, or to minimize code changes when migrating tables to being memory-optimized tables.

There are a few limitations when referencing memory-optimized tables from interpreted T-SQL. Refer to the Books Online topic "Accessing Memory-Optimized Tables Using Interpreted Transact-SQL" at `http://msdn.microsoft.com/en-us/library/dn133177(v=sql.120).aspx` for this list.

19-5. Determining Which Database Objects Are Configured to Use In-Memory OLTP

Problem

You want to determine which database objects are using In-Memory OLTP.

Solution

Query the `is_memory_optimized` column for tables and table types, or the `uses_native_compilation` column for procedures for objects in the current database:

```
SELECT  object_type_desc = 'Table',
        schema_name = OBJECT_SCHEMA_NAME(object_id),
        object_name = name
FROM    sys.tables
WHERE   is_memory_optimized = 1 UNION ALL
SELECT  'Table Type',
        SCHEMA_NAME(schema_id), name
FROM    sys.table_types
WHERE   is_memory_optimized = 1 UNION ALL
SELECT  so.type_desc,
        OBJECT_SCHEMA_NAME(sasm.object_id),
        OBJECT_NAME(sasm.object_id)
FROM    sys.all_sql_modules sasm
        JOIN sys.objects so ON so.object_id = sasm.object_id
WHERE   uses_native_compilation = 1;
```

This solution returns the following result set:

object_type_desc	schema_name	object_name
Table	dbo	T1
Table Type	dbo	imTV
SQL_STORED_PROCEDURE	dbo	imProc

How It Works

In this recipe, the database's catalog views are directly queried to return all of the objects that utilize In-Memory OLTP in the current database.

19-6. Determining Which Objects Are Actively Using In-Memory OLTP on the Server

Problem

You want to determine which objects from all of the databases on the server are using In-Memory OLTP.

Solution

Query sys.dm_os_loaded_modules to get all objects currently utilizing In-Memory OLTP:

```
SELECT  ca2.database_id,
        database_name = DB_NAME(ca2.database_id),
        dt1.object_type_desc,
        ca2.object_id,
        object_name = OBJECT_SCHEMA_NAME(ca2.object_id, ca2.database_id) + '.' +
                      OBJECT_NAME(ca2.object_id, ca2.database_id)
FROM    sys.dm_os_loaded_modules
        CROSS APPLY (SELECT REPLACE(REPLACE(SUBSTRING(name, CHARINDEX('xtp_', name), 8000),
        '.dll', ''), '_', '.')) ca1(filename)
        CROSS APPLY (SELECT    CONVERT(CHAR(1), PARSENAME(ca1.filename, 3)),
                              CONVERT(INTEGER, PARSENAME(ca1.filename, 2)),
                              CONVERT(INTEGER, PARSENAME(ca1.filename, 1))
                ) ca2(object_type, database_id, object_id)
        JOIN (VALUES ('t', 'Table'), ('v', 'Table Type'), ('p', 'Procedure'))
                dt1(object_type, object_type_desc) ON dt1.object_type = ca2.object_type
WHERE   description = 'XTP Native DLL'
ORDER BY database_name;
```

This solution returns the following result set (your results will vary):

database_id	database_name	object_type_desc	object_id	object_name
5	InMemory	Table	277576027	T1
5	InMemory	Procedure	437576597	imProc
5	InMemory	Table Type	309576141	TT_imTV_1273C1CD

How It Works

In this recipe, the server-wide dynamic-management view sys.dm_os_loaded_modules is queried so as to return all of the XTP dlls that have been compiled and loaded on the instance. The filename of the dll is of the format "xtp_Z_Y_X.dll", where Z is the type of object (t, v, p for table, table variable/table type, and procedure), Y is the database ID of the database, and X is the object ID. It then uses two CROSS APPLY operators; the first extracts the filename (without its extension) and converts the underscores to periods. The second utilizes the PARSENAME function to extract from the filename the various pieces that we are interested in. Next, the derived object_type is joined to a derived table (utilizing the VALUES constrictor) to get the object type name. Finally, the columns being returned utilize the system functions DB_NAME and OBJECT_NAME to get the names of the database and objects. This solution will be useful if the instance has multiple databases utilizing In-Memory OLTP.

The catalog view only shows the objects that are loaded into memory. If the server has been restarted, this solution will only show the memory-optimized tables. The table types and procedures will be reflected the first time that that are used, which will cause the dll for that object to be loaded at that time.

19-7. Detecting Performance Issues with Natively Compiled Stored Procedure Parameters

Problem

You want to detect when parameters are being passed to natively compiled stored procedures in a manner that reduces performance.

Solution

Use an Extended Event (XEvent) session to track the XEvent natively_compiled_proc_slow_parameter_passing:

```
CREATE EVENT SESSION [In-Memory Slow Parameter Passing] ON SERVER
ADD EVENT sqlserver.natively_compiled_proc_slow_parameter_passing(
    ACTION(sqlserver.database_id,sqlserver.database_name,sqlserver.sql_text))
ADD TARGET package0.ring_buffer
WITH (STARTUP_STATE=OFF);
GO

ALTER EVENT SESSION [In-Memory Slow Parameter Passing]
ON SERVER
STATE = start;
```

How It Works

One of the reasons to use a natively compiled stored procedure is to obtain extra performance, so it stands to reason that you want to avoid doing things that will slow it down. One of the things that can slow down a natively compiled stored procedure is how parameters are passed to the procedure. There are two actions that will cause extra work when dealing with parameters:

1. calling the procedure with named parameters, and

2. passing parameters of a different type than what the procedure specifies.

These can be tracked with an XEvent session, using the XEvent `natively_compiled_proc_slow_ parameter_passing` and by examining the reason for why the event was raised. The values for the reason will be `named_parameters` or `parameter_conversion`. In the solution, an XEvent is created and started in order to capture this information and send it to the ring buffer.

To test this XEvent, we need to build a procedure with parameters:

```
CREATE PROCEDURE dbo.imProcWithParams
@Rows INTEGER = 1
WITH NATIVE_COMPILATION, SCHEMABINDING, EXECUTE AS OWNER
AS
BEGIN ATOMIC WITH (TRANSACTION ISOLATION LEVEL = SNAPSHOT, LANGUAGE = N'us_english')
        DECLARE @TV dbo.imTV;
        WHILE @Rows > 0
        BEGIN
                INSERT INTO @TV VALUES (@Rows);
                SET @Rows -= 1;
        END;
        SELECT Col1 FROM @TV;
END;
GO
```

This procedure has a parameter for the number of rows to return. It builds a table variable (using the table type created in Recipe 19-6), and inserts that number of rows into the table variable. Finally, it returns the rows inserted.

Now we need to execute it a few times to cause the XEvent to capture conversion issues:

```
EXECUTE dbo.imProcWithParams 5; -- no issues
GO
EXECUTE dbo.imProcWithParams '5'; -- data-type conversion
GO
EXECUTE dbo.imProcWithParams @Rows = 5; -- named parameter
GO
EXECUTE dbo.imProcWithParams @Rows = '5'; -- named parameter and data-type conversion
GO
```

Now that we have some examples, we can query the ring buffer for the events that have been captured:

```
SELECT  n.value('(event/action[@name="database_name"]/value)[1]', 'sysname') as
[database_name],
        n.value('(event/data[@name="reason"]/text)[1]', 'varchar(100)') as [reason],
        n.value('(event/data[@name="parameter_name"]/value)[1]', 'sysname') as
        [parameter_name],
        n.value('(event/action[@name="sql_text"]/value)[1]', 'varchar(max)') as [sql_text]
```

```
FROM
(    SELECT td.query('.') as n
    FROM
    (    SELECT CAST(target_data AS XML) as target_data
        FROM sys.dm_xe_sessions AS s
        JOIN sys.dm_xe_session_targets AS t
            ON s.address = t.event_session_address
        WHERE s.name = 'In-Memory Slow Parameter Passing'
            AND t.target_name = 'ring_buffer'
    ) AS sub
    CROSS APPLY target_data.nodes('RingBufferTarget/event') AS q(td)
) AS tab;
```

This query returns the following results:

```
database_name reason               parameter_name sql_text
------------- -------------------- -------------- ----------------------------------------
InMemory      parameter_conversion                EXECUTE dbo.imProcWithParams '5';
InMemory      named_parameters     @Rows          EXECUTE dbo.imProcWithParams @Rows = 5;
InMemory      named_parameters     @Rows          EXECUTE dbo.imProcWithParams @Rows = '5';
```

As expected, the three rows with conversion issues are in the results.

19-8. Viewing CFP Metadata

Problem

You wish to see which transactions are associated with the CFPs in a database.

Solution

Select the appropriate data from the sys.dm_db_xtp_checkpoint_files catalog view.

How It Works

The sys.dm_db_xtp_checkpoint_files catalog view displays information about each data and delta file that exists in the database. Some of the data returned is:

- Type of file (data/delta)

- File size

- Used file size

- State

- Inserted row count (for data files)

- Deleted row count (for delta files)

- Lower-bound tsn (the first transaction number in this file)

- Upper-bound tsn (the last transaction number in this file)

19-9. Disabling or Enabling Automatic Merging

Problem

You wish to disable the automatic merging of CFPs so that you can observe the automatic merging process in further detail.

Solution

Use the following respectively to disable and enable automatic merging of CFPs. Note that the statements are a bit counterintuitive in that you issue a TRACEON call to disable, and a TRACEOFF call to enable.

```
DBCC TRACEON (9851, -1); -- disables automatic merging of CFPs
DBCC TRACEOFF (9851, -1);  -- enables automatic merging of CFPs
```

How It Works

The automatic merging of the CFPs can be disabled by enabling trace flag 9851; conversely, disabling this trace flag will enable the automatic merging of CFPs. It is not recommended that you disable the CFP automatic merging on a production system.

19-10. Manually Merging Checkpoint File Pairs

Problem

Your database has several checkpoint file pairs (CFPs) with numerous deleted rows, but not so many as to allow the automatic merge process to merge the adjacent CFPs. You want to manually merge these CFPs.

Solution

Utilize the system-stored procedure sys.sp_xtp_merge_checkpoint_files to manually merge all of the checkpoint file pairs within a specified transaction range.

How It Works

Because of the need to merge adjacent CFPs into a new CFP of ideal size, not all CFPs with available space can be merged. If the adjacent CFPs have enough active rows such that together they cannot fit into one CFP, then those CFPs cannot be merged. The system-stored procedure sys.sp_xtp_merge_checkpoint_files can be utilized to force a merge of all of the CFPs for transactions within a specified range. This procedure has three parameters:

1. @database_name: the name of the database to perform the merge operation in

2. @transaction_lower_bound: the lower-bound transaction number of the starting CFP to be merged

3. @transaction_upper_bound: the upper-bound transaction number of the ending CFP to be merged

When CFPs are being merged and space deallocated, it can take up to five checkpoint operations (and subsequent transaction log backups if the database is not in the simple recovery model) before the space is finally deallocated. During this time, the CFPs will be transitioning through several states. The states that a CFP can be in are:

1. PRECREATED: A small set of CFPs are kept precreated in order to minimize or eliminate waits when allocating new files. These CPFs will be sized at the ideal size mentioned earlier.

2. UNDER CONSTRUCTION: When a CFP is needed, it transitions into this state where newly inserted (and possibly deleted) rows can be stored.

3. ACTIVE: After a checkpoint occurs, all closed CFPs will transition into this state. At this point, inserts are not allowed into this CFP; however, rows can still be deleted. Assuming that merge operations are current with the workload, CFPs in this state will be approximately twice the size of the in-memory size of the memory-optimized tables.

4. MERGE TARGET: This is the first state that a CFP will transition into when involved in a merge operation. The CFP with the MERGE TARGET state will hold the rows from the consolidated (merged) CFPs. Once the merge process completes, the CFP in the MERGE TARGET state will transition into the ACTIVE state.

5. MERGE SOURCE: Once the merge process completes, the CFPs that were the source of the merge will transition into the MERGE SOURCE state.

6. REQUIRED FOR BACKUP/HA: When the merge process has completed, and the new MERGE TARGET CFP has been made part of a durable checkpoint, the CFPs in the MERGE SOURCE state will transition into this state. CFPs in this state are required for the operational correctness of the database for memory-optimized data. Once the log truncation point moves beyond the CFP's transaction range, it can be marked for garbage collection.

7. IN TRANSITION TO TOMBSTONE: CFPs in this state are no longer needed by the In-Memory OLTP engine, and are simply waiting for a background thread to move them along to the next state.

8. TOMBSTONE: CFPs in this final state are waiting for the FileStream garbage-collection process to remove them.

At this point, let's go through a demonstration that will show CFP creation and merging and eventual deallocation of the CFPs. We start off by creating a database for use by the In-Memory OLTP engine, ensuring that it is in the full recovery model. So that we can see the state of the merging throughout this demo, we also turn on the trace flag that turns off automatic merging. Note that on the virtual machine that I used for this, there is 4GB of memory allocated to the server, so the ideal size for the CFPs is 16MB for the data file, and 1MB for the delta file. See the following:

```
USE master;
GO

-- ensure directory exists
EXECUTE xp_create_subdir 'C:\APRESS\MSSQL\DATA\';
GO
```

```
IF DB_ID('InMemory') IS NOT NULL DROP DATABASE [InMemory];
GO

-- create database
CREATE DATABASE InMemory
ON
PRIMARY (NAME=[InMemory_data],
        FILENAME = 'C:\APRESS\MSSQL\DATA\InMemory_data.mdf',
        SIZE = 50MB),
FILEGROUP InMemory_mod CONTAINS MEMORY_OPTIMIZED_DATA (
        NAME = [InMemory_dir],
        FILENAME = 'C:\APRESS\MSSQL\DATA\InMemory_dir')
LOG ON (NAME = [InMemory_log],
        FILENAME = 'C:\APRESS\MSSQL\DATA\InMemory_log.ldf',
        SIZE=5MB)
COLLATE LATIN1_GENERAL_BIN2;
GO

-- ensure database is in the full recovery model
ALTER DATABASE [InMemory] SET RECOVERY FULL;
GO
USE [InMemory];
GO
-- turn off automatic merging so we can control the process for this demo
DBCC TRACEON (9851,-1);
GO
```

At this point, executing SELECT * FROM sys.dm_db_xtp_checkpoint_files will show that there are no CFPs created yet. Let's create a table and then check for CFPs:

```
-- make a memory-optimized table
CREATE TABLE dbo.memTest (
        col1 INTEGER NOT NULL,
        col2 CHAR(4) NOT NULL,
        col3 CHAR(8000) NOT NULL,
        CONSTRAINT PK_memTest PRIMARY KEY NONCLUSTERED HASH (col1)
                WITH (BUCKET_COUNT = 100000)
)
WITH (MEMORY_OPTIMIZED = ON, DURABILITY = SCHEMA_AND_DATA);
GO
-- wait a few seconds, and then check the CFPs on the system
SELECT  file_type_desc, state_desc
FROM    sys.dm_db_xtp_checkpoint_files
ORDER BY container_id, file_type_desc, upper_bound_tsn;
GO
```

This query produces the following result set:

```
file_type_desc state_desc
-------------- -------------------
DATA            PRECREATED
DATA            PRECREATED
DATA            PRECREATED
DATA            PRECREATED
DATA            PRECREATED
DATA            PRECREATED
DATA            PRECREATED
DATA            PRECREATED
DATA            UNDER CONSTRUCTION
DELTA           PRECREATED
DELTA           PRECREATED
DELTA           UNDER CONSTRUCTION
DELTA           PRECREATED
DELTA           PRECREATED
DELTA           PRECREATED
DELTA           PRECREATED
DELTA           PRECREATED
DELTA           PRECREATED
```

At this point, nine checkpoint file pairs have been created, eight of which are in the PRECREATED state, and one is UNDER CONSTRUCTION; this CFP is the one that will have rows added to it. At this point, let's back up the database to start transaction logging, and then insert 8,000 rows into the table and review the CFPs again:

```
-- back up the database to start transaction logging
BACKUP DATABASE InMemory TO DISK='C:\APRESS\MSSQL\ DATA\InMemory.bak';
-- load 8000 rows
WITH cte AS
(
SELECT ROW_NUMBER() OVER (ORDER BY (SELECT NULL)) AS RN
FROM sys.all_columns
)
INSERT INTO dbo.memTest (col1, col2, col3)
-- REPLICATE makes a larger example to force a larger CFP size.
SELECT  TOP (8000) RN, '2', REPLICATE('3', 8000)
FROM    cte;
GO
-- wait a few seconds and look at the CFPs again
SELECT  file_type_desc, state_desc, file_size_in_bytes, inserted_row_count,
        deleted_row_count
FROM    sys.dm_db_xtp_checkpoint_files
ORDER BY container_id, file_type_desc, upper_bound_tsn;
GO
```

file_type_desc	state_desc	file_size_in_bytes	inserted_row_count	deleted_row_count
DATA	PRECREATED	16777216	0	NULL
DATA	PRECREATED	16777216	0	NULL
DATA	PRECREATED	16777216	0	NULL
DATA	PRECREATED	16777216	0	NULL
DATA	PRECREATED	16777216	0	NULL
DATA	PRECREATED	16777216	0	NULL
DATA	PRECREATED	16777216	0	NULL
DATA	PRECREATED	16777216	0	NULL
DATA	ACTIVE	67108864	8000	NULL
DELTA	PRECREATED	1048576	NULL	0
DELTA	PRECREATED	1048576	NULL	0
DELTA	PRECREATED	1048576	NULL	0
DELTA	PRECREATED	1048576	NULL	0
DELTA	PRECREATED	1048576	NULL	0
DELTA	PRECREATED	1048576	NULL	0
DELTA	PRECREATED	1048576	NULL	0
DELTA	PRECREATED	1048576	NULL	0
DELTA	ACTIVE	1048576	NULL	0

Since the 8,000 rows were added as a single transaction, and since a transaction must be contained within a single CFP, that CFP grew to accommodate all of the 8,000 rows. Let's now add another 8,000 rows, with each row being an individual transaction:

```
-- now let's insert some data with singleton transactions
DECLARE @i INT = 8001;
WHILE @i <= 16000
BEGIN
  INSERT INTO dbo.memTest (col1, col2, col3)
  VALUES (@i, '4', REPLICATE('5', 8000));
  SET @i += 1;
END;
GO
-- look at the CFPs again
SELECT  file_type_desc, state_desc, file_size_in_bytes, inserted_row_count,
        deleted_row_count, lower_bound_tsn, upper_bound_tsn
FROM    sys.dm_db_xtp_checkpoint_files
ORDER BY container_id, file_type_desc, upper_bound_tsn;
GO
```

file_type_desc	state_desc	file_size_in_bytes	inserted_row_count	deleted_row_count
DATA	PRECREATED	16777216	0	NULL
DATA	PRECREATED	16777216	0	NULL
DATA	PRECREATED	16777216	0	NULL
DATA	PRECREATED	16777216	0	NULL
DATA	PRECREATED	16777216	0	NULL
DATA	PRECREATED	16777216	0	NULL
DATA	UNDER CONSTRUCTION	16777216	464	NULL
DATA	PRECREATED	16777216	0	NULL

DATA	PRECREATED	16777216	0	NULL
DATA	ACTIVE	67108864	8000	NULL
DATA	UNDER CONSTRUCTION	16777216	1884	NULL
DATA	UNDER CONSTRUCTION	16777216	1884	NULL
DATA	UNDER CONSTRUCTION	16777216	1884	NULL
DATA	UNDER CONSTRUCTION	16777216	1884	NULL
DELTA	PRECREATED	1048576	NULL	0
DELTA	PRECREATED	1048576	NULL	0
DELTA	PRECREATED	1048576	NULL	0
DELTA	PRECREATED	1048576	NULL	0
DELTA	PRECREATED	1048576	NULL	0
DELTA	UNDER CONSTRUCTION	1048576	NULL	0
DELTA	PRECREATED	1048576	NULL	0
DELTA	PRECREATED	1048576	NULL	0
DELTA	PRECREATED	1048576	NULL	0
DELTA	ACTIVE	1048576	NULL	0
DELTA	UNDER CONSTRUCTION	1048576	NULL	0
DELTA	UNDER CONSTRUCTION	1048576	NULL	0
DELTA	UNDER CONSTRUCTION	1048576	NULL	0
DELTA	UNDER CONSTRUCTION	1048576	NULL	0

The above results have the lower_bound_tsn and upper_bound_tsn omitted; you can review those to see which transactions went into each of the CFPs. At this point, all of the CFPs that are holding rows are still in the UNDER CONSTRUCTION state. When a checkpoint occurs, these will transition into the ACTIVE state:

```
CHECKPOINT;
-- look at the CFPs again
SELECT  file_type_desc, state_desc, file_size_in_bytes, inserted_row_count,
        deleted_row_count, lower_bound_tsn, upper_bound_tsn
FROM    sys.dm_db_xtp_checkpoint_files
ORDER BY container_id, file_type_desc, upper_bound_tsn;
```

At this point, all of the CFPs are closed (state = ACTIVE). The data files show the number of rows that are in each CFP, while the delta file shows that there are zero deleted rows. In order to perform automatic merging, there needs to be deleted records in adjacent CFPs, so let's delete half of these records. These will be performed in two batches; the first batch deletes half of the 8,000 that were inserted as a single transaction, and the second batch deletes half of the remaining records. After these batches have run, perform a manual checkpoint. The query results show that the records have been deleted by inserting a row into the delta file for each row being deleted in the data file. Note that from this point on, I'm excluding the PRECREATED CFPs from the results.

```
-- Delete all of the even rows with a value <= 8000
DELETE dbo.memTest
WHERE col1 % 2 = 0
AND col1 <= 8000;
GO
-- the second batch will delete from the 8000 rows inserted one by one
DECLARE @i INT = 8001;
WHILE @i <= 16000
```

```
BEGIN
  DELETE dbo.memTest WHERE col1 = @i;
  SET @i += 2;
END;
GO
CHECKPOINT;
-- look at the CFPs again
SELECT  file_type_desc, state_desc, file_size_in_bytes, inserted_row_count,
        deleted_row_count, lower_bound_tsn, upper_bound_tsn
FROM    sys.dm_db_xtp_checkpoint_files
WHERE   state_desc <> 'PRECREATED'
ORDER BY container_id, file_type_desc, upper_bound_tsn;
GO
```

file_type_desc	state_desc	file_size_in_bytes	inserted_row_count	deleted_row_count
DATA	ACTIVE	67108864	8000	NULL
DATA	ACTIVE	16777216	1884	NULL
DATA	ACTIVE	16777216	1884	NULL
DATA	ACTIVE	16777216	1884	NULL
DATA	ACTIVE	16777216	1884	NULL
DATA	ACTIVE	16777216	464	NULL
DATA	ACTIVE	16777216	0	NULL
DELTA	ACTIVE	1048576	NULL	4000
DELTA	ACTIVE	1048576	NULL	942
DELTA	ACTIVE	1048576	NULL	942
DELTA	ACTIVE	1048576	NULL	942
DELTA	ACTIVE	1048576	NULL	942
DELTA	ACTIVE	1048576	NULL	232
DELTA	ACTIVE	1048576	NULL	0

Notice also that there is a CFP in the ACTIVE state with zero rows. This is due to the checkpoint, which closes the current CFP and makes a new CFP active. At this point, we now have a situation where we can merge the CFPs. Remember that automatic merging has been disabled with the trace flag, so we need to perform a manual merge. The following command will merge just the CFPs where the rows were inserted as individual transactions:

```
EXECUTE sys.sp_xtp_merge_checkpoint_files 'InMemory', 4, 8004;
GO

SELECT  file_type_desc, state_desc
FROM    sys.dm_db_xtp_checkpoint_files
WHERE   state_desc <> 'PRECREATED'
ORDER BY container_id, file_type_desc, upper_bound_tsn;
GO
```

file_type_desc	state_desc
DATA	MERGE TARGET
DATA	ACTIVE
DATA	ACTIVE
DATA	ACTIVE

```
DATA           ACTIVE
DATA           ACTIVE
DATA           ACTIVE
DATA           ACTIVE
DELTA          MERGE TARGET
DELTA          ACTIVE
DELTA          ACTIVE
DELTA          ACTIVE
DELTA          ACTIVE
DELTA          ACTIVE
DELTA          ACTIVE
DELTA          ACTIVE
```

The query results show that there is now one CFP with a status of MERGE TARGET. Remember that a manual merge was performed, which ignores the merge policy and puts all of the non-deleted rows into a single CFP, which ends up being larger than the ideal size. The CFPs will remain in this state until another checkpoint is performed, and a transaction log backup is performed. The following code will perform these actions, and the query results show that the CFP in the MERGE TARGET state has gone active, and that the CFPs that were merged have transitioned into the MERGED SOURCE state:

```
CHECKPOINT
GO
BACKUP LOG [InMemory] TO  DISK = N'C:\MSSQL\MSSQL12.MSSQLSERVER\MSSQL\DATA\InMemory_Log_1.bak';
GO
SELECT  file_type_desc, state_desc
FROM    sys.dm_db_xtp_checkpoint_files
WHERE   state_desc <> 'PRECREATED'
ORDER BY container_id, file_type_desc, upper_bound_tsn;
GO


file_type_desc state_desc
-------------- -------------
DATA           ACTIVE
DATA           MERGED SOURCE
DATA           MERGED SOURCE
DATA           MERGED SOURCE
DATA           MERGED SOURCE
DATA           MERGED SOURCE
DATA           ACTIVE
DATA           ACTIVE
DATA           ACTIVE
DELTA          ACTIVE
DELTA          MERGED SOURCE
DELTA          MERGED SOURCE
DELTA          MERGED SOURCE
DELTA          MERGED SOURCE
DELTA          ACTIVE
DELTA          MERGED SOURCE
DELTA          ACTIVE
DELTA          ACTIVE
```

At this point, a series of checkpoints and transaction log backups are required in order to transition the CFPs through the other states until they are garbage-collected and removed. Rerun the above code that performs the checkpoint and transaction log backup (change the backup file name) multiple times in order to transition the CFPs through the various states. The following query results show that the CFPs transitioned into the REQUIRED FOR BACKUP/HA state, then into the IN TRANSITION TO TOMBSTONE state, and finally into the TOMBSTONE state:

```
file_type_desc state_desc
-------------- ----------------------
DATA           REQUIRED FOR BACKUP/HA
DATA           REQUIRED FOR BACKUP/HA
DATA           REQUIRED FOR BACKUP/HA
DATA           REQUIRED FOR BACKUP/HA
DATA           REQUIRED FOR BACKUP/HA
DATA           ACTIVE
DATA           ACTIVE
DATA           ACTIVE
DATA           ACTIVE
DATA           ACTIVE
DELTA          REQUIRED FOR BACKUP/HA
DELTA          REQUIRED FOR BACKUP/HA
DELTA          REQUIRED FOR BACKUP/HA
DELTA          REQUIRED FOR BACKUP/HA
DELTA          REQUIRED FOR BACKUP/HA
DELTA          ACTIVE
DELTA          ACTIVE
DELTA          ACTIVE
DELTA          ACTIVE
DELTA          ACTIVE


file_type_desc state_desc
-------------- --------------------------
NULL           IN TRANSITION TO TOMBSTONE
NULL           IN TRANSITION TO TOMBSTONE
NULL           IN TRANSITION TO TOMBSTONE
NULL           IN TRANSITION TO TOMBSTONE
NULL           IN TRANSITION TO TOMBSTONE
NULL           IN TRANSITION TO TOMBSTONE
NULL           IN TRANSITION TO TOMBSTONE
NULL           IN TRANSITION TO TOMBSTONE
NULL           IN TRANSITION TO TOMBSTONE
NULL           IN TRANSITION TO TOMBSTONE
DATA           ACTIVE
DATA           ACTIVE
DATA           ACTIVE
DATA           ACTIVE
DATA           ACTIVE
DATA           ACTIVE
DATA           ACTIVE
```

```
DELTA          ACTIVE
DELTA          ACTIVE
DELTA          ACTIVE
DELTA          ACTIVE
DELTA          ACTIVE
DELTA          ACTIVE
DELTA          ACTIVE

file_type_desc state_desc
-------------- ----------
NULL           TOMBSTONE
NULL           TOMBSTONE
NULL           TOMBSTONE
NULL           TOMBSTONE
NULL           TOMBSTONE
NULL           TOMBSTONE
NULL           TOMBSTONE
NULL           TOMBSTONE
NULL           TOMBSTONE
NULL           TOMBSTONE
DATA           ACTIVE
DATA           ACTIVE
DATA           ACTIVE
DATA           ACTIVE
DATA           ACTIVE
DATA           ACTIVE
DATA           ACTIVE
DELTA          ACTIVE
DELTA          ACTIVE
DELTA          ACTIVE
DELTA          ACTIVE
DELTA          ACTIVE
DELTA          ACTIVE
DELTA          ACTIVE
```

When the CFP transitions to the IN TRANSITION TO TOMBSTONE state, it is no longer needed for database-consistency purposes, so it will not be included in a full database backup; however, it is still taking up storage space. Once the CFP is in the TOMBSTATE state, garbage collection occurs to remove the CFP.

If necessary, garbage collection can be run manually with the following statements (note that they will need to be run at least twice):

```
EXECUTE sp_xtp_checkpoint_force_garbage_collection;
GO
CHECKPOINT;
GO
```

After this garbage cleanup has occurred, the CFPs may or may not be visible in the sys.dm_db_xtp_checkpoint_files catalog view. If visible, they will at some time be removed from the view. It should be noted that these are just what are visible within the database engine—the actual on-disk files are still visible.

These go through a separate garbage collection by executing the following commands. As above, they may need to be executed at least twice:

```
BACKUP LOG [InMemory] TO DISK = N'C:\MSSQL\MSSQL12.MSSQLSERVER\MSSQL\DATA\InMemory_Log_1.bak';
GO
EXECUTE sp_filestream_force_garbage_collection;
GO
```

After this garbage-collection process has finished, the CFPs have been entirely removed from both the database engine and the operating system.

At this point, we have gone through an entire merge process where selected CFPs were merged, then put through a series of checkpoints and transaction log backups, and eventually removed entirely from the system. Notice also just how many of the checkpoints and transaction log backups were required. For me, it took five to get to the tombstone state, and then I had to wait while the background garbage-collection thread removed them entirely.

However, all of these checkpoints have created several empty CFPs. Under normal circumstances, where automatic merging is enabled and there is a workload, the normal transaction log checkpoints and backups would clean these up. Let's prove this by enabling the automatic merging with the command DBCC TRACEOFF(9851,-1).

After the garbage collection has occurred, you can run this query to show the CFPs, and you can see that they have been all merged into a new single CFP. Additionally, the CFP that had the 8,000 rows that were inserted as a single transaction has undergone a self-merge, and it is on its path to being removed.

CHAPTER 20

Triggers

by Jason Brimhall

This chapter presents recipes for creating and using Data Manipulation Language (DML) and Data Definition Language (DDL) triggers. *DML triggers* respond to INSERT, UPDATE, and DELETE operations against tables and views. *DDL triggers* respond to server and database events such as CREATE TABLE and DROP TABLE statements.

Triggers, when used properly, can provide a convenient automatic response to specific actions. They are appropriate for situations in which you must create a business-level response to an action. However, they should not be used in place of constraints, such as primary key, foreign key, and check and unique constraints, because constraints will outperform triggers and are better suited to these operations.

Remember that the code inside a trigger executes in response to an action. A user may be attempting to update a table, and the trigger code executes–in many cases, unknown to the user who executed the update. If trigger code is not optimized properly, the triggers may have a severe impact on system performance. Use DML triggers sparingly, and take care to ensure that they are optimized and bug-free.

DDL triggers open a realm of new functionality for monitoring and auditing server activity that cannot be easily replaced by other database object types.

This chapter will cover the following topics:

- How to create an AFTER DML trigger

- How to create an INSTEAD OF DML trigger

- How to create a DDL trigger

- How to modify or drop an existing trigger

- How to enable or disable triggers

- How to limit trigger nesting, set the firing order, and control recursion

- How to view trigger metadata

- How to use triggers to respond to logon events

First, however, I'll start with a background discussion of DML triggers.

20-1. Creating an AFTER DML Trigger

Problem

You want to track the inserts and deletes from your production inventory table. A number of applications access this table, and you cannot dictate that these applications use a common set of stored procedures to access the table.

Solution

DML triggers respond to INSERT, UPDATE, or DELETE operations against a table or a view. When a data modification event occurs, the trigger performs a set of actions defined by that trigger. Similar to stored procedures, triggers are defined as a batch of Transact-SQL statements.

A DML trigger may be declared specifically as FOR UPDATE, FOR INSERT, FOR DELETE, or any combination of the three. UPDATE triggers respond to data modified in one or more columns within the table, INSERT triggers respond to new data being added to a table, and DELETE triggers respond to data being deleted from a table. There are two types of DML triggers: AFTER and INSTEAD OF.

AFTER triggers are allowed only for tables, and they execute *after* the data modification has been completed against the table. INSTEAD OF triggers execute *instead of* the original data modification and can be created for both tables and views.

DML triggers perform actions in response to data modifications. For example, a trigger could populate an audit table based on an operation performed. Or perhaps a trigger could be used to decrement the value of an inventory quantity in response to a sales transaction. Though the ability to trigger actions automatically is a powerful feature, there are a few things to keep in mind when deciding to use a trigger to perform application or business logic.

- Triggers are often forgotten about and therefore become a hidden problem. When troubleshooting performance or logical issues, DBAs and developers often forget that triggers are executing in the background. Make sure that the use of triggers is "visible" in data and application documentation.

- If all data modifications flow through a stored procedure, a set of stored procedures, or even a common data-access layer, then perform all activities within the stored-procedure layer or data-access layer rather than use a trigger. For example, if an inventory quantity should be updated after inserting a sales record, attempt to put the logic within the stored procedure.

- Always keep performance in mind: Write triggers that execute quickly. Long-running triggers can significantly impact data-modification operations. Take particular care in putting triggers onto tables that are subject to either a high rate of data modification or data modifications that affect a large number of rows.

- Nonlogged updates do not cause a DML trigger to fire (for example, WRITETEXT, TRUNCATE TABLE, and bulk insert operations).

- Constraints usually run faster than a DML trigger, so if business requirements can be modeled using constraints, then use constraints instead of triggers.

- AFTER triggers run *after* the data modification has occurred, so they cannot be used to alter data modification to prevent constraint violations.

- Don't allow result sets from a SELECT statement to be returned within your trigger. Most applications cannot consume results from a trigger, and embedded queries may hurt the trigger's performance.

■ **Caution** The ability to return results from triggers was deprecated in SQL Server 2012 and will be removed in a future version of SQL Server. To disable this feature today, use the SQL Server configuration option disable results from triggers.

As long as you keep these general guidelines in mind and use them properly, triggers are an excellent means of enforcing business rules in your database.

■ **Caution** Some of the triggers demonstrated in this chapter may interfere with existing triggers on the SQL instance and database. If you are following along with the code, be sure to test this functionality only on a development SQL Server environment.

An AFTER DML trigger can track the changes to the ProductionInventory table. This recipe creates an AFTER DML trigger that executes when INSERT and DELETE statements are executed against the table.

An AFTER DML trigger executes after an INSERT, UPDATE, and/or DELETE modification has been completed successfully against a table. The specific syntax for an AFTER DML trigger is as follows:

```
CREATE TRIGGER [schema_name.]trigger_name
ON table
[WITH <dml_trigger_option> [...,n]]
AFTER
{[INSERT][,] [UPDATE] [,][DELETE]}
[NOT FOR REPLICATION]
AS {sql_statement[...n]}
```

Table 20-1 details the arguments of this command.

Table 20-1. *CREATE TRIGGER Arguments*

Argument	Description
[schema_name.]trigger_name	Defines the optional schema owner and required user-defined name of the new trigger.
table	Defines the table name that the trigger applies to.
<dml_trigger_option> [...,n]	Allows specification of ENCRYPTION and/or the EXECUTE AS clause. ENCRYPTION encrypts the Transact-SQL definition of the trigger, making it unreadable within the system tables. EXECUTE AS allows the developer to define a security context under which the trigger executes.
[INSERT][,][UPDATE][,][DELETE]	Defines which DML event or events the trigger reacts to, including INSERT, UPDATE, and DELETE. A single trigger can react to one or more of these actions against the table.
NOT FOR REPLICATION	In some cases, the table on which the trigger is defined is updated through the SQL Server replication process. In many cases, the published database has already accounted for any business logic that would normally be executed in the trigger. The NOT FOR REPLICATION option instructs SQL Server not to execute the trigger when the data modification is made as part of a replication process.
sql_statement[...n]	Allows one or more Transact-SQL statements that are used to carry out actions such as performing validations against the DML changes or performing other table DML actions.

Before proceeding to the recipe, it is important to note that SQL Server creates two "virtual" tables that are available specifically for triggers, called the *inserted* and *deleted* tables. These two tables capture the before and after pictures of the modified rows. Table 20-2 shows the tables that each DML operation impacts.

Table 20-2. *Inserted and Deleted Virtual Tables*

DML Operation	Inserted Table Holds...	Deleted Table Holds...
INSERT	Rows to be inserted	Empty
UPDATE	New (proposed) version of rows modified by the update	Existing (pre-update) version of rows modified by the update
DELETE	Empty	Rows to be deleted

The inserted and deleted tables can be used within your trigger to access the versions of data both before and after the data modifications. These tables store data for both single and multi-row updates. Triggers should be coded with both types of updates (single and multi-row) in mind. For example, a DELETE statement may impact either a single row or many, say 50, rows, And the trigger must handle both cases appropriately.

This recipe demonstrates how to use a trigger to track row inserts or deletes from the Production.ProductInventory table:

```
-- Create a table to Track all Inserts and Deletes
USE AdventureWorks2014;
GO

CREATE TABLE Production.ProductInventoryAudit
        (
        ProductID INT NOT NULL,
        LocationID SMALLINT NOT NULL,
        Shelf NVARCHAR(10) NOT NULL,
        Bin TINYINT NOT NULL,
        Quantity SMALLINT NOT NULL,
        rowguid UNIQUEIDENTIFIER NOT NULL,
        ModifiedDate DATETIME NOT NULL,
        InsertOrDelete CHAR(1) NOT NULL
        );
GO
-- Create trigger to populate Production.ProductInventoryAudit table
CREATE TRIGGER Production.trg_id_ProductInventoryAudit ON Production.ProductInventory
        AFTER INSERT, DELETE
AS
BEGIN
        SET NOCOUNT ON;
-- Inserted rows
        INSERT INTO Production.ProductInventoryAudit
                (ProductID,
                LocationID,
                Shelf,
                Bin,
                Quantity,
```

```
                rowguid,
                ModifiedDate,
                InsertOrDelete)
            SELECT
                    i.ProductID,
                    i.LocationID,
                    i.Shelf,
                    i.Bin,
                    i.Quantity,
                    i.rowguid,
                    GETDATE(),
                    'I'
            FROM    inserted i
            UNION ALL
            SELECT  d.ProductID,
                    d.LocationID,
                    d.Shelf,
                    d.Bin,
                    d.Quantity,
                    d.rowguid,
                    GETDATE(),
                    'D'
            FROM    deleted d;

END
GO

-- Insert a new row
INSERT INTO Production.ProductInventory
        (ProductID,
         LocationID,
         Shelf,
         Bin,
         Quantity)
VALUES  (316,
         6,
         'A',
         4,
         22);

-- Delete a row
DELETE
FROM Production.ProductInventory
WHERE   ProductID = 316
        AND LocationID = 6;

-- Check the audit table
SELECT  ProductID,
        LocationID,
        InsertOrDelete
FROM    Production.ProductInventoryAudit;
```

This returns the following:

ProductID	LocationID	InsertOrDelete
316	6	I
316	6	D

How It Works

This recipe started by creating a new table for tracking rows inserted into or deleted from the Production.ProductInventory table. The new table's schema matches the original table, but the table has added a new column named InsertOrUpdate to indicate whether the change was because of an INSERT or DELETE operation. See the following:

```
CREATE TABLE Production.ProductInventoryAudit
        (
        ProductID INT NOT NULL,
        LocationID SMALLINT NOT NULL,
        Shelf NVARCHAR(10) NOT NULL,
        Bin TINYINT NOT NULL,
        Quantity SMALLINT NOT NULL,
        rowguid UNIQUEIDENTIFIER NOT NULL,
        ModifiedDate DATETIME NOT NULL,
        InsertOrDelete CHAR(1) NOT NULL
        );
GO
```

Next, an AFTER DML trigger was created using CREATE TRIGGER. The schema and name of the new trigger were designated in the first line of the statement:

```
CREATE TRIGGER Production.trg_id_ProductInventoryAudit
```

The table (which when updated will cause the trigger to fire) was designated in the ON clause:

```
ON Production.ProductInventory
```

Two types of DML activity were set to be monitored: inserts and deletes:

```
AFTER INSERT, DELETE
```

The body of the trigger began after the AS keyword:

```
AS
BEGIN
```

The SET NOCOUNT was set ON in order to suppress the "rows affected" messages from being returned to the calling application whenever the trigger is fired:

```
        SET NOCOUNT ON;
```

The trigger contained one INSERT statement of the form INSERT INTO ... SELECT, where the SELECT statement was a UNION of two selects. The first SELECT in the UNION returned the rows from the INSERTED table, and the second SELECT in the union returned rows from the DELETED table.

First, we set up the INSERT statement and specified the table into which the statement was to insert rows, as well as the columns that should be specified for each row that was being inserted:

```
INSERT INTO Production.ProductInventoryAudit
        (ProductID,
         LocationID,
         Shelf,
         Bin,
         Quantity,
         rowguid,
         ModifiedDate,
         InsertOrDelete)
```

Next, we selected rows from the INSERTED table (this is a list of rows that were inserted into the ProductInventory table) and specified the columns that were to be mapped to the INSERT clause:

```
SELECT i.ProductID,
       i.LocationID,
       i.Shelf,
       i.Bin,
       i.Quantity,
       i.rowguid,
       GETDATE(),
       'I'
FROM   inserted i
```

The second select returned rows from the DELETED table and concatenated the results with a UNION ALL. The DELETED table contains a list of rows that were deleted from the ProductInventory table:

```
UNION ALL
SELECT  d.ProductID,
        d.LocationID,
        d.Shelf,
        d.Bin,
        d.Quantity,
        d.rowguid,
        GETDATE(),
        'D'
FROM    deleted d;
    END
GO
```

After creating the trigger, in order to test it, a new row was inserted into and then deleted from Production.ProductInventory:

```
INSERT INTO Production.ProductInventory
        (ProductID,
         LocationID,
         Shelf,
         Bin,
         Quantity)
```

501

```
VALUES  (316,
         6,
         'A',
         4,
         22);

-- Delete a row
DELETE
FROM Production.ProductInventory
WHERE   ProductID = 316
        AND LocationID = 6;
```

A query executed against the audit table shows two rows tracking the insert and delete activities against the `Production.ProductInventory` table:

```
SELECT  ProductID,
        LocationID,
        InsertOrDelete
FROM    Production.ProductInventoryAudit;
```

20-2. Creating an INSTEAD OF DML Trigger

Problem

You have a table that contains a list of departments for your human resources group. An application needs to insert new departments. However, new departments should be routed to a separate table that holds these departments "pending approval" by a separate application function. You want to create a view that concatenates the "approved" and "pending approval" departments. You also want to allow the application to insert into this view any new departments that are added to the "pending approval" table.

Solution

An INSTEAD OF DML trigger allows data to be updated in a view that would otherwise not be updateable. The code inside the INSTEAD OF DML trigger executes *instead of* the original data modification statement. These triggers are allowed on both tables and views and are often used to handle data modifications to views that do not usually allow data modifications (see Chapter 14 for a review of what rules a view must follow in order to be updateable). INSTEAD OF DML triggers use the following syntax:

```
CREATE TRIGGER [ schema_name . ]trigger_name ON { table | view }
[ WITH <dml_trigger_option> [ ...,n ] ] INSTEAD OF

{ [ INSERT ] [ , ] [ UPDATE ] [ , ] [ DELETE ] }
[ NOT FOR REPLICATION ]
AS { sql_statement [ ...n ] }
```

Table 20-3 details the arguments of this command.

Table 20-3. *INSTEAD OF Trigger Arguments*

Argument	Description
[schema_name .]trigger_name	Defines the optional schema owner and required user-defined name of the new trigger
table | view	Defines the table name that the trigger applies to
<dml_trigger_option> [...,n]	Allows specification of ENCRYPTION and/or the EXECUTE AS clause. ENCRYPTION encrypts the Transact-SQL definition of the trigger, making it unreadable within the system tables. EXECUTE AS allows the developer to define a security context under which the trigger executes.
[INSERT] [,] [UPDATE] [,] [DELETE]	Defines which DML event or events the trigger reacts to, including INSERT, UPDATE, and DELETE. A single trigger can react to one or more of these actions performed against the table.
NOT FOR REPLICATION	In some cases, the table on which the trigger is defined is updated through SQL Server replication processes. In many cases, the published database has already accounted for any business logic that would normally be executed in the trigger. The NOT FOR REPLICATION option instructs SQL Server not to execute the trigger when the data modification is made as part of a replication process.
sql_statement [...n]	Allows one or more Transact-SQL statements that are used to carry out actions, such as performing validations against the DML changes or performing other table DML actions

This recipe creates a new table that holds "pending approval" rows for the HumanResources.Department table. These are new departments that require manager approval before being added to the actual table. A view is created to display all "approved" and "pending approval" departments from the two tables, and an INSTEAD OF trigger is created for inserts on the view. This INSTEAD OF trigger allows the developer to define an action to take *instead of* the INSERT statement. In this case, the trigger will insert the data into one of the base tables of the view–HumanResources.Department. See the following:

```
USE AdventureWorks2014;
GO

-- Create Department "Approval" table
CREATE TABLE HumanResources.DepartmentApproval
     (
      Name NVARCHAR(50) NOT NULL
                       UNIQUE,
      GroupName NVARCHAR(50) NOT NULL,
      ModifiedDate DATETIME NOT NULL
                       DEFAULT GETDATE()
     ) ;
GO
```

```
-- Create view to see both approved and pending approval departments
CREATE VIEW HumanResources.vw_Department
AS
        SELECT    Name,
                  GroupName,
                  ModifiedDate,
                  'Approved' Status
        FROM      HumanResources.Department
        UNION
        SELECT    Name,
                  GroupName,
                  ModifiedDate,
                  'Pending Approval' Status
        FROM      HumanResources.DepartmentApproval ;
GO


-- Create an INSTEAD OF trigger on the new view
CREATE TRIGGER HumanResources.trg_vw_Department ON HumanResources.vw_Department
        INSTEAD OF INSERT
AS
        SET NOCOUNT ON
        INSERT INTO HumanResources.DepartmentApproval
                (Name,
                 GroupName)
                SELECT  i.Name,
                        i.GroupName
                FROM    inserted i
                WHERE   i.Name NOT IN (
                        SELECT  Name
                        FROM    HumanResources.DepartmentApproval) ;
GO


-- Insert into the new view, even though view is a UNION
-- of two different tables
INSERT INTO HumanResources.vw_Department
        (Name,
         GroupName)
VALUES  ('Print Production',
         'Manufacturing') ;


-- Check the view's contents
SELECT  Status,
        Name
FROM    HumanResources.vw_Department
WHERE   GroupName = 'Manufacturing' ;
```

This returns the following result set:

Status	Name
Approved	Production
Approved	Production Control
Pending Approval	Print Production

How It Works

The recipe began by creating a separate table to hold "pending approval" department rows:

```
CREATE TABLE HumanResources.DepartmentApproval
    (
    Name NVARCHAR(50) NOT NULL
                        UNIQUE,
    GroupName NVARCHAR(50) NOT NULL,
    ModifiedDate DATETIME NOT NULL
                        DEFAULT GETDATE()
    ) ;
GO
```

Next, a view was created to display both "approved" and "pending approval" departments:

```
CREATE VIEW HumanResources.vw_Department
AS
    SELECT    Name,
              GroupName,
              ModifiedDate,
              'Approved' Status
    FROM      HumanResources.Department
    UNION
    SELECT    Name,
              GroupName,
              ModifiedDate,
              'Pending Approval' Status
    FROM      HumanResources.DepartmentApproval ;
GO
```

The UNION in the CREATE VIEW prevented this view from being updateable. INSTEAD OF triggers allowed data modifications against nonupdateable views.

A trigger was created to react to INSERTs against the view, and it inserted the specified data into the approval table as long as the department name did not already exist in the HumanResources.DepartmentApproval table:

```
CREATE TRIGGER HumanResources.trg_vw_Department ON HumanResources.vw_Department
      INSTEAD OF INSERT
AS
      SET NOCOUNT ON;
      INSERT INTO HumanResources.DepartmentApproval
              (Name,
               GroupName)
              SELECT  i.Name,
                      i.GroupName
              FROM    inserted i
              WHERE   i.Name NOT IN (
                      SELECT  Name
                      FROM    HumanResources.DepartmentApproval) ;
GO
```

A new INSERT was tested against the view to see whether it was inserted in the approval table:

```
INSERT INTO HumanResources.vw_Department
        (Name,
         GroupName)
VALUES  ('Print Production',
         'Manufacturing') ;m
```

We then queried the view to show that the row was inserted and displayed a "pending approval" status:

```
SELECT  Status,
        Name
FROM    HumanResources.vw_Department
WHERE   GroupName = 'Manufacturing';
```

20-3. Handling Transactions in Triggers

Problem

You have been viewing the ProductInventory changes that are tracked in your ProductInventoryAudit table. You notice that some applications are violating business rules, and this breaks other applications that are using the ProductInventory table. You want to prevent these changes and roll back the transaction that violates the business rules.

Solution

When a trigger is fired, SQL Server always creates a transaction around it. This allows any changes made by the firing trigger, or the caller, to be rolled back to the previous state. In this example, the trg_uid_ ProductInventoryAudit trigger has been rewritten to fail if certain Shelf or Quantity values are encountered. If they are, ROLLBACK is used to cancel the trigger and reverse any changes.

■ **Note** These examples work with the objects created in Recipe 20-1 and assume that the `Production.ProductInventoryAudit` table and `Production.trg_uid_ProductInventoryAudit` trigger have been created.

```
USE AdventureWorks2014;
GO

ALTER TRIGGER Production.trg_id_ProductInventoryAudit ON Production.ProductInventory
     AFTER INSERT, DELETE
AS
     SET NOCOUNT ON ;
     IF EXISTS ( SELECT    Shelf
                 FROM      inserted
                 WHERE     Shelf = 'A' )
         BEGIN
             PRINT 'Shelf ''A'' is closed for new inventory.' ;
             ROLLBACK ;
         END
-- Inserted rows
     INSERT INTO Production.ProductInventoryAudit
             (ProductID,
              LocationID,
              Shelf,
              Bin,
              Quantity,
              rowguid,
              ModifiedDate,
              InsertOrDelete)
             SELECT DISTINCT
                     i.ProductID,
                     i.LocationID,
                     i.Shelf,
                     i.Bin,
                     i.Quantity,
                     i.rowguid,
                     GETDATE(),
                     'I'
             FROM    inserted i ;
-- Deleted rows
     INSERT INTO Production.ProductInventoryAudit
             (ProductID,
              LocationID,
              Shelf,
              Bin,
              Quantity,
              rowguid,
              ModifiedDate,
              InsertOrDelete)
```

```
            SELECT  d.ProductID,
                    d.LocationID,
                    d.Shelf,
                    d.Bin,
                    d.Quantity,
                    d.rowguid,
                    GETDATE(),
                    'D'
            FROM    deleted d ;
    IF EXISTS ( SELECT    Quantity
                FROM      deleted
                WHERE     Quantity > 0 )
        BEGIN
            PRINT 'You cannot remove positive quantity rows!' ;
            ROLLBACK ;
        END
GO


/* Attempt an insert of a row using Shelf A */

INSERT INTO Production.ProductInventory
        (ProductID,
         LocationID,
         Shelf,
         Bin,
         Quantity)
VALUES  (316,
         6,
         'A',
         4,
         22) ;
```

Because this is not allowed based on the trigger logic, the trigger neither inserts a row into the ProductInventoryAudit table nor allows the INSERT into the ProductInventory table. The following is returned as a result of the INSERT statement:

```
Shelf 'A' is closed for new inventory.
Msg 3609, Level 16, State 1, Line 2
The transaction ended in the trigger. The batch has been aborted.
```

In this example, the INSERT that caused the trigger to fire didn't use an explicit transaction; however, the operation was still rolled back. This next example demonstrates two deletions: one that is allowed (according to the rules of the trigger) and another that is not allowed. Both inserts are embedded in an explicit transaction:

```
BEGIN TRANSACTION ;
-- Deleting a row with a zero quantity
DELETE
FROM Production.ProductInventory
WHERE   ProductID = 853
        AND LocationID = 7 ;
```

```
-- Deleting a row with a non-zero quantity
DELETE
FROM Production.ProductInventory
WHERE    ProductID = 999
          AND LocationID = 60 ;
COMMIT TRANSACTION ;
```

This returns the following:

```
(1 row(s) affected)
You cannot remove positive quantity rows!
Msg 3609, Level 16, State 1, Line 9
The transaction ended in the trigger. The batch has been aborted.
```

Because the trigger issued a rollback, the transaction that caused the trigger to fire is rolled back. Even though the first row would have been a valid deletion, neither row is deleted because they were in the same calling transaction.

```
SELECT  ProductID,
        LocationID
FROM    Production.ProductInventory
WHERE   (ProductID = 853
          AND LocationID = 7)
        OR (ProductID = 999
            AND LocationID = 60) ;
```

This returns the following:

ProductID	LocationID
853	7
999	60

How It Works

This recipe demonstrated the interaction between triggers and transactions. If a trigger issues a ROLLBACK, any data modifications ☺ performed by the trigger or the statements in the calling transaction are undone. The Transact-SQL query or batch that invoked the trigger is canceled and rolled back. If you use explicit transactions within a trigger, SQL Server will treat it as a nested transaction. As discussed in Chapter 12, a ROLLBACK rolls back all transactions, no matter how many levels deep they may be nested.

20-4. Linking Trigger Execution to Modified Columns

Problem

You want to prevent updates to one column in a specific table.

Solution

When a trigger is fired, you can determine which columns have been modified by using the UPDATE function.

UPDATE, not to be confused with the DML command, returns a TRUE value if an INSERT or DML UPDATE references a column. For example, the following DML UPDATE trigger checks to see whether a specific column has been modified and, if so, returns an error and rolls back the modification:

```
USE AdventureWorks2014;
GO
CREATE TRIGGER HumanResources.trg_U_Department ON HumanResources.Department
    AFTER UPDATE
AS
    IF UPDATE(GroupName)
        BEGIN
            PRINT 'Updates to GroupName require DBA involvement.' ;
            ROLLBACK  ;
        END
GO
```

An attempt is made to update a GroupName value in the following query:

```
UPDATE  HumanResources.Department
SET     GroupName = 'Research and Development'
WHERE   DepartmentID = 10 ;
```

This returns a warning message and error telling us that the batch has been aborted (no updates made).

```
Updates to GroupName require DBA involvement.
Msg 3609, Level 16, State 1, Line 1
The transaction ended in the trigger. The batch has been aborted.
```

How It Works

When trigger logic is aimed at more-granular, column-based changes, use the UPDATE function and conditional processing to ensure that the code is executed only against specific columns. Embedding the logic in conditional processing can help reduce the overhead each time the trigger fires.

20-5. Viewing DML Trigger Metadata

Problem

You have a number of DML triggers defined in your database, and you want to list these triggers and the objects on which they are defined.

Solution

This recipe demonstrates how to view information about the triggers in the current database.

The first example queries the sys.triggers catalog view and returns the name of the view or table, the trigger name, whether the trigger is an INSTEAD OF trigger, and whether the trigger is disabled:

```
-- Show the DML triggers in the current database
USE AdventureWorks2014;
GO

SELECT  OBJECT_NAME(parent_id) AS ParentObjName,
        name AS TriggerName,
        is_instead_of_trigger,
        is_disabled
FROM    sys.triggers t
WHERE   parent_class_desc = 'OBJECT_OR_COLUMN'
ORDER BY OBJECT_NAME(parent_id),Name ;
```

This returns the following results (your results may vary slightly depending on what triggers you have defined):

ParentObjName	TriggerName	is_instead_of_trigger	is_disabled
Department	trg_U_Department	0	0
Employee	dEmployee	1	0
Person	iuPerson	0	0
ProductInventory	trg_uid_ProductInventoryAudit	0	0
PurchaseOrderDetail	iPurchaseOrderDetail	0	0
PurchaseOrderDetail	uPurchaseOrderDetail	0	0
PurchaseOrderHeader	uPurchaseOrderHeader	0	0
SalesOrderDetail	iduSalesOrderDetail	0	0
SalesOrderHeader	uSalesOrderHeader	0	0
Vendor	dVendor	1	0
vw_Department	trg_vw_Department	1	0
WorkOrder	iWorkOrder	0	0
WorkOrder	uWorkOrder	0	0

To display a specific trigger's Transact-SQL definition, you can query the `sys.sql_modules` system catalog view:

```
-- Displays the trigger SQL definition --(if the trigger is not encrypted)
USE AdventureWorks2014;
GO

SELECT  o.name
        , (SELECT definition AS [processing-instruction(definition)]
            FROM sys.sql_modules
            WHERE object_id = m.object_id
            FOR XML PATH(''), TYPE
        ) AS TrigDefinition
FROM    sys.sql_modules m
        INNER JOIN sys.objects o
            ON m.object_id = o.object_id
WHERE   o.type = 'TR'
AND o.name = 'trg_id_ProductInventoryAudit';
```

How It Works

The first query in this recipe queried the `sys.triggers` catalog view to show all the DML triggers in the current database. There were DDL triggers in the `sys.triggers` catalog view as well. To prevent DDL triggers from being displayed in the results, the query filtered on the `type` column from the `sys.objects` catalog view, looking for the value 'T.R.' DDL triggers have a different parent class, as we will discuss in Recipe 20-8.

The second query showed the actual Transact-SQL trigger name and definition of each trigger in the database. If the trigger were encrypted (similar to an encrypted view or stored procedure, for example), the trigger definition would be displayed as `NULL`.

20-6. Creating a DDL Trigger

Problem

You are testing index changes in a system and want to log any such changes so that you can correlate the index change with performance data that you are capturing on the server.

Solution

DDL triggers respond to server or database events rather than to table data modifications. For example, a DDL trigger could write to an audit table whenever a database user issues a `CREATE TABLE` or `DROP TABLE` statement. Or, at the server level, a DDL trigger could respond to the creation of a new login and prevent that login from being created, or simply log the activity.

■ **Tip**   System-stored procedures that perform DDL operations will fire DDL triggers. For example, `sp_create_plan_guide` and `sp_control_plan_guide` will fire the `CREATE_PLAN_GUIDE` event and execute any triggers defined on that event type.

DDL triggers may be defined as database; or server triggers. Database DDL triggers are stored as objects within the database in which they were created, and server DDL triggers are stored in the master database. The syntax for a DDL trigger is as follows:

```
CREATE TRIGGER trigger_name
ON { ALL SERVER | DATABASE }
[ WITH <ddl_trigger_option> [ ...,n ] ]
FOR { event_type | event_group } [ ,...n ]
AS { sql_statement [ ...n ]}
```

Table 20-4 details the arguments of this command.

Table 20-4. CREATE TRIGGER (DDL) Arguments

Argument	Description
trigger_name	This argument is the user-defined name of the new DDL trigger (notice that a DDL trigger does not have an owning schema, since it isn't related to an actual database table or view).
ALL SERVER | DATABASE	This argument designates whether the DDL trigger will respond to server-scoped (ALL SERVER) or DATABASE-scoped events.
<ddl_trigger_option> [...,n]	This argument allows you to specify the ENCRYPTION and/or the EXECUTE AS clause. ENCRYPTION will encrypt the Transact-SQL definition of the trigger. EXECUTE AS allows you to define the security context under which the trigger will be executed.
{ event_type | event_group } [,...n]	The event_type indicates a DDL event that the trigger subscribes to; for example, CREATE_TABLE, ALTER_TABLE, and DROP_INDEX. An event_group is a logical grouping of event_type events. A single DDL trigger can subscribe to one or more event types or groups. For example, the DDL_PARTITION_FUNCTION_EVENTS group is comprised of the following events: CREATE_PARTITION_FUNCTION, ALTER_PARTITION_FUNCTION, and DROP_PARTITION_FUNCTION. You can find the complete list of trigger event types in the SQL Server Books Online topic "DDL Events" (http://msdn.microsoft.com/en-us/library/bb522542.aspx) and a complete list of trigger event groups in the SQL Server Books Online topic "DDL Event Groups" (http://msdn.microsoft.com/en-us/library/bb510452.aspx).
sql_statement [...n]	This argument defines one or more Transact-SQL statements that can be used to carry out actions in response to the DDL database or server event.

This recipe demonstrates how to create an audit table that can contain information on any CREATE INDEX, ALTER INDEX, or DROP INDEX statements in the AdventureWorks2014 database.

First, create an audit table to hold the results:

```
USE AdventureWorks2014;
GO

CREATE TABLE dbo.DDLAudit
            (
            EventData XML NOT NULL,
            AttemptDate DATETIME NOT NULL
                        DEFAULT GETDATE(),
            DBUser sysname NOT NULL
            ) ;
GO
```

Next, create a database DDL trigger to track index operations and insert the event data into the audit table:

```
CREATE TRIGGER db_trg_INDEXChanges ON DATABASE
      FOR CREATE_INDEX, ALTER_INDEX, DROP_INDEX
AS
      SET NOCOUNT ON ;
      INSERT INTO dbo.DDLAudit
              (EventData, DBUser)
      VALUES  (EVENTDATA(), USER) ;
GO
```

Next, attempt an index creation in the database:

```
CREATE NONCLUSTERED INDEX ni_DDLAudit_DBUser
      ON dbo.DDLAudit(DBUser) ;
GO
```

Next, I'll query the DDLAudit audit table to see whether the new index-creation event was captured by the trigger:

```
SELECT  EventData
FROM    dbo.DDLAudit
```

This returns the actual event information, stored in XML format (see Chapter 26 for more information on XML in SQL Server).

```
EventData
-----------------------------------------------------------------

<EVENT_INSTANCE>
  <EventType>CREATE_INDEX</EventType>
  <PostTime>2015-02-08T15:29:57.153</PostTime>
  <SPID>59</SPID>
  <ServerName>ROMEForever</ServerName>
  <LoginName>ROMEForever\jason</LoginName>
  <UserName>dbo</UserName>
  <DatabaseName>AdventureWorks2014</DatabaseName>
  <SchemaName>dbo</SchemaName>
  <ObjectName>ni_DDLAudit_DBUser</ObjectName>
  <ObjectType>INDEX</ObjectType>
  <TargetObjectName>DDLAudit</TargetObjectName>
  <TargetObjectType>TABLE</TargetObjectType>
  <TSQLCommand>
    <SetOptions ANSI_NULLS="ON" ANSI_NULL_DEFAULT="ON" ANSI_PADDING="ON"
    QUOTED_IDENTIFIER="ON" ENCRYPTED="FALSE" />
    <CommandText>CREATE NONCLUSTERED INDEX ni_DDLAudit_DBUser
        ON dbo.DDLAudit(DBUser)</CommandText>
  </TSQLCommand>
</EVENT_INSTANCE>
```

How It Works

The recipe began by creating a table that could contain audit information on index modifications. The EventData column used SQL Server's xml data type, which was populated by the new EVENTDATA function (described later in this recipe). See the following:

```
CREATE TABLE dbo.DDLAudit
        (
        EventData XML NOT NULL,
        AttemptDate DATETIME NOT NULL
                        DEFAULT GETDATE(),
        DBUser CHAR(50) NOT NULL
        ) ;
GO
```

The DDL trigger was created to subscribe to CREATE INDEX, ALTER INDEX, or DROP INDEX statements:

```
CREATE TRIGGER db_trg_INDEXChanges ON DATABASE
    FOR CREATE_INDEX, ALTER_INDEX, DROP_INDEX
AS
```

The SET NOCOUNT statement was used in the trigger to suppress the number of row-affected messages from SQL Server (otherwise, every time you made an index modification, you'd see a "1 row affected" message):

```
SET NOCOUNT ON ;
```

A row was inserted into the audit table containing the event data and info on the user who performed the statement that fired the event:

```
INSERT INTO dbo.ChangeAttempt
        (EventData, DBUser)
VALUES  (EVENTDATA(), USER) ;
GO
```

The EVENTDATA function returned server and data event information in XML format. The XML data returned from the EVENTDATA function included useful information such as the event statement text, the login name that attempted the statement, the target object name, and the time the event occurred. For more information about the EVENTDATA function, please refer to SQL Server Books Online (http://msdn.microsoft.com/en-us/library/ms187909.aspx).

20-7. Creating a Logon Trigger

Problem

You want to restrict the times at which certain users can log in to your database server. If an attempt is made to log in during incorrect hours, you want to log that attempt to an audit table.

Solution

Logon triggers fire synchronously in response to a logon event to the SQL Server instance. You can use logon triggers to create reactions to specific logon events, or simply to track information about a logon event.

■ **Caution** Be very careful about how you design your logon trigger. Test it in a development environment first before deploying it to production. If you are using a logon trigger to restrict entry to the SQL Server instance, be careful that you do not restrict all access!

This recipe demonstrates how to create a logon trigger that restricts a login from accessing SQL Server during certain time periods. The example will also log any invalid logon attempts to a table.

First, create the new login:

```
CREATE LOGIN nightworker WITH PASSWORD = 'pass@word1' ;
GO
```

■ **Note** This example assumes that your SQL Server instance is set to Mixed Mode authentication.

Next, create an audit database and a table to track the logon attempts:

```
CREATE DATABASE ExampleAuditDB ;
GO
USE ExampleAuditDB ;
GO
CREATE TABLE dbo.RestrictedLogonAttempt
        (
         LoginName SYSNAME NOT NULL,
         AttemptDate DATETIME NOT NULL
        ) ;
GO
```

Create the logon trigger to restrict the new login from logging into the server from 7 a.m. to 6 p.m.:

■ **Note**   You may need to adjust the times used in this example based on what time you are testing the trigger.

```
USE master ;
GO
CREATE TRIGGER trg_logon_attempt ON ALL SERVER
 WITH EXECUTE AS 'sa'
        FOR LOGON
AS
        BEGIN
                IF ORIGINAL_LOGIN() = 'nightworker'
                    AND DATEPART(hh, GETDATE()) BETWEEN 7 AND 18
                    BEGIN
                            ROLLBACK ;
                            INSERT    ExampleAuditDB.dbo.RestrictedLogonAttempt
                                      (LoginName, AttemptDate)
                            VALUES    (ORIGINAL_LOGIN(), GETDATE()) ;
                    END
        END
GO
```

Now, attempt to log on as the nightworker login with the password pass@word1 during the specified time range. The login attempt should yield the following error message:

```
Logon failed for login 'nightworker' due to trigger execution.
```

After the attempt, query the audit table to see whether the logon was tracked:

```
SELECT  LoginName, AttemptDate
FROM    ExampleAuditDB.dbo.RestrictedLogonAttempt;
```

This returns the following result set (results will vary based on when you execute this recipe).

LoginNM	AttemptDT
nightworker	2015-01-01 03:20:19.577

How It Works

Logon triggers allow you to restrict and track logon activity after authentication to the SQL Server instance but before an actual session is generated. If you want to apply custom business rules to logons above and beyond what is offered within the SQL Server feature set, you can implement them using the logon trigger.

This recipe created a test login, a new auditing database, and an auditing table to track attempts. The logon trigger was created in the master database. Stepping through the code, note that ALL SERVER was used to set the scope of the trigger execution; this is a server DDL trigger as opposed to a database DDL trigger:

```
CREATE TRIGGER trg_logon_attempt ON ALL SERVER
```

The EXECUTE AS clause was used to define the permissions under which the trigger will execute. The recipe could have used a lower-privileged login—any login with permission to write to the login table would suffice:

```
WITH EXECUTE AS 'sa'
```

FOR LOGON designated the event that this trigger subscribes to:

```
    FOR LOGON
AS
```

The body of the trigger logic then started at the BEGIN keyword:

```
BEGIN
```

The original security context of the logon attempt was then evaluated. In this case, the trigger is interested in enforcing logic only if the login is for nightworker:

```
    IF ORIGINAL_LOGIN() = 'nightworker'
```

Included in this logic was an evaluation of the hour of the day. If the current time were between 7 a.m. and 6 p.m., two actions would be performed:

```
        AND DATEPART(hh, GETDATE()) BETWEEN 7 AND 18
        BEGIN
```

The first action would be to roll back the logon attempt:

```
        ROLLBACK ;
```

The second action would be to track the attempt to the audit table:

```
           INSERT    ExampleAuditDB.dbo.RestrictedLogonAttempt
                     (LoginName, AttemptDate)
           VALUES    (ORIGINAL_LOGIN(), GETDATE()) ;
       END
    END
GO
```

Again, it is worthwhile to remind you that how you code the logic of a logon trigger is very important. Improper logging (e.g., logging before a rollback occurs, bad trigger logic, or poor-performing trigger code) can cause unexpected results. Also, if your logon trigger isn't performing the actions you expect, be sure to check your latest SQL log for clues. Logon trigger attempts that are rolled back also get written to the SQL log. If something was miscoded in the trigger–for example, if I hadn't designated the proper, fully qualified table name for `RestrictedLogonAttempt`–the SQL log would have shown the error message "Invalid object name 'dbo.RestrictedLogonAttempt.'"

■ **Note**   Don't forget about disabling this recipe's trigger when you are finished testing it. To disable it, execute `DISABLE TRIGGER trg_logon_attempt ON ALL SERVER` in the master database.

20-8. Viewing DDL Trigger Metadata

Problem

You want to list the server and database DDL triggers that are defined on your server.

Solution

This recipe demonstrates the retrieval of DDL trigger metadata.

The first example queries the `sys.triggers` catalog view, returning the associated *database-scoped* trigger name and the trigger's enabled/disabled status:

```
USE AdventureWorks2014;
GO

-- Show the DML triggers in the current database
SELECT   name AS TriggerName,
         is_disabled
FROM     sys.triggers
WHERE    parent_class_desc = 'DATABASE'
ORDER BY Name;
```

This returns the following results:

TriggerNM	is_disabled
ddlDatabaseTriggerLog	1

This next example queries the sys.server_triggers and sys.server_trigger_events system catalog views to retrieve a list of server-scoped DDL triggers. This returns the name of the DDL trigger, the type of trigger (Transact-SQL or CLR), the disabled state of the trigger, and the events the trigger subscribed to:

```
SELECT   name AS TriggerName,
         s.type_desc AS TriggerType,
         is_disabled,
         e.type_desc AS FiringEvents
FROM     sys.server_triggers s
         INNER JOIN sys.server_trigger_events e
             ON s.object_id = e.object_id;
```

This returns data based on the server-level trigger created previously.

name	SOL_or_CLR	is_disabled	FiringEvents
trg_logon_attempt	SQL_TRIGGER	1	LOGON

To display *database-scoped* DDL trigger Transact-SQL definitions, you can query the sys.sql_modules system catalog view:

```
USE AdventureWorks2014;
GO

SELECT   t.name AS TriggerName
       , (SELECT definition AS [processing-instruction(definition)]
             FROM sys.sql_modules
             WHERE object_id = t.object_id
             FOR XML PATH(''), TYPE
       ) AS TrigDefinition
FROM     sys.triggers AS t
WHERE    t.parent_class_desc = 'DATABASE';
```

To display *server-scoped* DDL triggers, you can query the sys.server_sql_modules and sys.server_triggers system catalog views:

```
USE master;
GO
SELECT   t.name
       , (SELECT definition AS [processing-instruction(definition)]
             FROM sys.server_sql_modules
             WHERE object_id = t.object_id
             FOR XML PATH(''), TYPE
       ) AS TrigDefinition
FROM     sys.server_triggers t;
```

How It Works

The first query in this recipe returned a list of database-scoped triggers using the sys.triggers system catalog view. To display only DDL database-scoped triggers, the query filtered the parent_class_desc value to DATABASE. The second query returned a list of server-scoped triggers and their associated triggering events. These triggers were accessed through the sys.server_triggers and sys.server_trigger_events system catalog views.

The third query returned the Transact-SQL definitions of database-scoped triggers through the sys.triggers and sys.sql_modules catalog views. In the final query, the sys.server_sql_modules and sys.server_triggers system catalog views were joined to return a server-scoped trigger's Transact-SQL definitions.

20-9. Modifying a Trigger

Problem

You have an existing trigger and need to modify the trigger definition.

Solution

To modify an existing DDL or DML trigger, use the ALTER TRIGGER command. ALTER TRIGGER takes the same arguments as the associated DML or DDL CREATE TRIGGER syntax.

This example will modify the login trigger that was created in Recipe 20-7. The login trigger should no longer restrict users from logging in, but instead should allow the login and write the login only to the audit table.

■ **Note** If you have cleaned up the objects that were created in Recipe 20-7, you will need to recreate them for this recipe.

The following statement modifies the login trigger. Note the rollback has been commented out:

```
USE master;
GO

ALTER TRIGGER trg_logon_attempt ON ALL SERVER
 WITH EXECUTE AS 'sa'
      FOR LOGON
AS
      BEGIN
           IF ORIGINAL_LOGIN() = 'nightworker'
              AND DATEPART(hh, GETDATE()) BETWEEN 7 AND 18
              BEGIN
                  --ROLLBACK ;
                  INSERT    ExampleAuditDB.dbo.RestrictedLogonAttempt
                            (LoginName, AttemptDate)
                  VALUES    (ORIGINAL_LOGIN(), GETDATE()) ;
              END
      END
GO
```

An attempt to log in to the server with the login nightworker and password pass@word1 should now be allowed, and you should see the login attempt recorded in the audit table:

```
SELECT  LoginName,
        AttemptDate
FROM    ExampleAuditDB.dbo.RestrictedLogonAttempt;
```

The preceding select statement returns the following:

LoginNM	AttemptDT
nightworker	2014-01-01 012:20:19.577
nightworker	2014-01-02 14:20:33.577

How It Works

ALTER TRIGGER allows you to modify existing DDL or DML triggers. The arguments for ALTER TRIGGER are the same as for CREATE TRIGGER.

20-10. Enabling and Disabling a Trigger

Problem

You have a trigger defined for a table that you would like to disable temporarily, but you still want to keep the definition in the database so that you can easily reenable the trigger.

Solution

Sometimes triggers must be disabled if they are causing problems that you need to troubleshoot, or if you need to import or recover data that shouldn't fire the trigger but might. In this recipe, I demonstrate how to disable a trigger from firing using the DISABLE TRIGGER command, as well as how to reenable a trigger using ENABLE TRIGGER.

The syntax for DISABLE TRIGGER is as follows:

```
DISABLE TRIGGER [ schema . ] trigger_name ON { object_name | DATABASE | ALL SERVER }
```

The syntax for enabling a trigger is as follows:

```
ENABLE TRIGGER [ schema_name . ] trigger_name ON { object_name | DATABASE | ALL SERVER }
```

Table 20-5 details the arguments of this command.

Table 20-5. ENABLE and DISABLE Trigger Arguments

Argument	Description
[schema_name .]trigger_name	The optional schema owner and required user-defined name of the trigger you want to disable
Object_name | DATABASE | ALL SERVER	object_name is the table or view that the trigger was bound to (if it's a DML trigger). Use DATABASE if the trigger was a DDL database-scoped trigger and SERVER if the trigger was a DDL server-scoped trigger.

This example starts by creating a trigger (which is enabled by default) that prints a message that an INSERT has been performed against the HumanResources.Department table:

■ **Note**   The previous few examples use the master database. The next few examples are back in the AdventureWorks2014 database.

```
USE AdventureWorks2014;
GO

CREATE TRIGGER HumanResources.trg_Department ON HumanResources.Department
     AFTER INSERT
AS
     PRINT 'The trg_Department trigger was fired' ;
GO
```

■ **Note**   At the beginning of this chapter, I mentioned that you should not return result sets from triggers. The PRINT statement is a way to return information to a calling application without a result set. Be careful with the use of PRINT statements, because some client APIs interpret PRINT statements as error messages. For the purposes of debugging execution within SQL Server Management Studio or the SQLCMD application, PRINT can be very helpful. For further information on PRINT, see SQL Server Books Online (https://msdn.microsoft.com/en-US/library/ms176047(v=sql.120).aspx).

Disable the trigger using the DISABLE TRIGGER command:

```
USE AdventureWorks2014;
GO

DISABLE TRIGGER HumanResources.trg_Department
ON HumanResources.Department;
```

Because the trigger was disabled, no printed message will be returned when the following INSERT is executed:

```
INSERT   HumanResources.Department
         (Name,
          GroupName)
VALUES   ('Construction',
          'Building Services');
```

This returns the following:

```
(1 row(s) affected)
```

Next, the trigger is enabled using the ENABLE TRIGGER command:

```
USE AdventureWorks2014;
GO

ENABLE TRIGGER HumanResources.trg_Department
        ON HumanResources.Department;
```

Now, when another INSERT is attempted, the trigger will fire, returning a message to the connection:

```
INSERT   HumanResources.Department
         (Name, GroupName)
VALUES   ('Cleaning', 'Building Services');
```

This returns the following:

```
The trg_Department trigger was fired
(1 row(s) affected)
```

How It Works

This recipe started by creating a new trigger that printed a statement whenever a new row was inserted into the HumanResources.Department table.

After creating the trigger, the DISABLE TRIGGER command was used to keep it from firing (although the trigger's definition still stayed in the database):

```
DISABLE TRIGGER HumanResources.trg_Department
ON HumanResources.Department;
```

An insert was performed that did not fire the trigger. The ENABLE TRIGGER command was then executed, and then another insert was attempted; this time, the INSERT fired the trigger.

20-11. Nesting Triggers

Problem

Your trigger inserts data into another table that has triggers defined. You want to control whether the data modifications performed in a trigger will cause additional triggers to fire.

Solution

Trigger nesting occurs when a trigger is fired, that trigger performs some DML, and that DML in turn fires another trigger. Depending on a given database schema and a group's coding standards, this may or may not be a desirable behavior.

The SQL Server instance may be configured to either allow or disallow trigger nesting. Disabling the nested triggers option prevents any AFTER trigger from causing the firing of another trigger.

This example demonstrates how to disable or enable this behavior:

```
USE master ;
GO
-- Disable nesting
EXEC sp_configure 'nested triggers', 0 ;
RECONFIGURE WITH OVERRIDE ;
GO
-- Enable nesting
EXEC sp_configure 'nested triggers', 1 ;
RECONFIGURE WITH OVERRIDE ;
GO
```

This returns the following:

```
Configuration option 'nested triggers' changed from 1 to 0. Run the RECONFIGURE statement
to install.
Configuration option 'nested triggers' changed from 0 to 1. Run the RECONFIGURE statement
to install.
```

How It Works

This recipe used the sp_configure system-stored procedure to change the nested trigger behavior at the server level. To disable nesting altogether, sp_configure was executed for the nested trigger server option, followed by the parameter 0, which disabled nesting:

```
EXEC sp_configure 'nested triggers', 0
RECONFIGURE WITH OVERRIDE;
GO
```

Because server options contain both a current configuration as well as an actual runtime configuration value, the RECONFIGURE WITH OVERRIDE command was used to update the runtime value so that it took effect right away.

To enable nesting again, this server option was set back to 1 in the second batch of the recipe.

> ■ **Note** There is a limit of 32 levels to trigger nesting. The function `TRIGGER_NESTLEVEL` will tell you how many levels into trigger nesting you are. See SQL Server Books Online for more information on the `TRIGGER_NESTLEVEL` function (`https://msdn.microsoft.com/en-us/library/ms182737(v=sql.120).aspx`).

20-12. Controlling Recursion

Problem

You have a table in which a data modification causes a trigger to execute and update the table on which that trigger is defined.

Solution

A specific case of trigger nesting is trigger recursion. Trigger nesting is considered to be recursive if the action performed when a trigger fires causes the *same* trigger to fire again. This may happen directly; for instance, a trigger is defined on a table, and that trigger executes DML back to the table on which it is defined. Or it may be indirect; for example, a trigger updates another table, and a trigger on that other table updates the original table.

Recursion may be either allowed or disallowed by configuring the `RECURSIVE_TRIGGERS` database option. If recursion is allowed, AFTER triggers are still limited by the 32-level nesting limit to prevent an infinite loop.

This example demonstrates enabling and disabling this option:

```
-- Allow recursion
ALTER DATABASE AdventureWorks2014
SET RECURSIVE_TRIGGERS ON ;

-- View the db setting
SELECT  is_recursive_triggers_on
FROM    sys.databases
WHERE   name = 'AdventureWorks2014' ;

-- Prevents recursion
ALTER DATABASE AdventureWorks2014
SET RECURSIVE_TRIGGERS OFF ;

-- View the db setting
SELECT  is_recursive_triggers_on
FROM    sys.databases
WHERE   name = 'AdventureWorks2014';
```

This returns the following:

```
is_recursive_triggers_on 1
is_recursive_triggers_on 0
```

How It Works

ALTER DATABASE was used to configure database-level options, including whether triggers were allowed to fire recursively within the database. The option was enabled by setting RECURSIVE_TRIGGERS ON:

```
ALTER DATABASE AdventureWorks2014
SET RECURSIVE_TRIGGERS ON ;
```

The option was then queried by using the sys.databases system catalog view, which showed the current database option in the is_recursive_triggers_on column (1 for on, 0 for off):

```
SELECT  is_recursive_triggers_on
FROM    sys.databases
WHERE   name = 'AdventureWorks2014' ;
```

The recipe then disabled trigger recursion by setting the option to be OFF, and confirmed this by selecting from the sys.databases view.

20-13. Specifying the Firing Order

Problem

Over time you have accumulated multiple triggers on the same table. You are concerned that the order in which the triggers execute is nondeterministic, and you are seeing inconsistent results from simple insert, update, and delete activity.

Solution

In general, triggers that react to the same event (or events) should be consolidated by placing all their business logic into just one trigger. This improves the manageability and supportability of the triggers. Also, this issue of determining and specifying trigger order is avoidable if the trigger logic is consolidated.

That said, situations arise in which multiple triggers may fire in response to the same DML or DDL action, and often the order in which they are fired is important. The system-stored procedure sp_settriggerorder allows you to specify trigger order.

The syntax for sp_settriggerorder is as follows:

```
sp_settriggerorder [ (@triggername = ] '[ triggerschema.]triggername' , [ (@order = ]
'value' , [ (@stmttype = ] 'statement_type' [ , [ (@namespace = ] { 'DATABASE' | 'SERVER' |
NULL } ]
```

Table 20-6 details the arguments of this command.

Table 20-6. sp_settriggerorder *Arguments*

Argument	Description
'[triggerschema.]triggername'	This defines the optional schema owner and required user-defined name of the trigger to be ordered.
[@order =] 'value'	This can be either First, None, or Last. Any triggers in between these will be fired in a random order after the first and last firings.
[@stmttype =] 'statement_type'	This designates the type of trigger to be ordered; for example, INSERT, UPDATE, DELETE, CREATE_INDEX, ALTER_INDEX, and so forth.
[@namespace =] { 'DATABASE' | 'SERVER' | NULL}	This designates whether this is a DDL trigger and, if so, whether it is database- or server-scoped.

This recipe creates a test table and adds three DML INSERT triggers to it. sp_settriggerorder will then be used to define the execution order of the triggers. See the following:

```
USE AdventureWorks2014;
GO

CREATE TABLE dbo.TestTriggerOrder (TestID INT NOT NULL) ;
GO

CREATE TRIGGER dbo.trg_i_TestTriggerOrder ON dbo.TestTriggerOrder
        AFTER INSERT
AS
        PRINT 'I will be fired first.' ;
GO

CREATE TRIGGER dbo.trg_i_TestTriggerOrder2 ON dbo.TestTriggerOrder
        AFTER INSERT
AS
        PRINT 'I will be fired last.' ;
GO

CREATE TRIGGER dbo.trg_i_TestTriggerOrder3 ON dbo.TestTriggerOrder
        AFTER INSERT
AS
        PRINT 'I will be somewhere in the middle.' ;
GO

EXEC sp_settriggerorder 'trg_i_TestTriggerOrder', 'First', 'INSERT' ;
EXEC sp_settriggerorder 'trg_i_TestTriggerOrder2', 'Last', 'INSERT' ;

INSERT INTO dbo.TestTriggerOrder
        (TestID)
VALUES  (1);
```

This returns the following:

```
I will be fired first.
I will be somewhere in the middle.
I will be fired last.
```

How It Works

This recipe started by creating a single-column test table, and three DML INSERT triggers were added to it. Using sp_settriggerorder, the first and last triggers to fire were defined:

```
EXEC sp_settriggerorder 'trg_i_TestTriggerOrder', 'First', 'INSERT' ;
EXEC sp_settriggerorder 'trg_i_TestTriggerOrder2', 'Last', 'INSERT' ;
```

An INSERT was then executed against the table, and the trigger messages were returned in the expected order.

To reiterate this point, use a single trigger on a table when you can. If you must create multiple triggers of the same type, and one of your triggers contains ROLLBACK functionality if an error occurs, be sure to set the trigger that has the most likely chance of failing as the first trigger to execute. This way, only the first-fired trigger needs to be executed, preventing the other triggers from having to fire and then roll back transactions unnecessarily.

20-14. Dropping a Trigger

Problem

You are deploying a new version of your database schema, and DML is now executed through stored procedures. You have consolidated the business logic that was enforced by your triggers into these stored procedures; it is now time to drop the triggers.

Solution

The syntax for dropping a trigger differs by trigger type (DML or DDL). The syntax for dropping a DML trigger is as follows:

```
DROP TRIGGER schema_name.trigger_name [ ,...n ]
```

Table 20-7 details the argument of this command.

Table 20-7. DROP TRIGGER Argument (DML)

Argument	Description
schema_name.trigger_name	The owning schema name of the trigger and the DML trigger name to be removed from the database

The syntax for dropping a DDL trigger is as follows:

```
DROP TRIGGER trigger_name [ ,...n ]
ON { DATABASE | ALL SERVER }
```

Table 20-8 details the arguments of this command.

Table 20-8. *DROP TRIGGER Arguments (DDL)*

Argument	Description
trigger_name	Defines the DDL trigger name to be removed from the database (for a database-level DDL trigger) or from the SQL Server instance (for a server-scoped trigger)
DATABASE | ALL SERVER	Defines whether you are removing a DATABASE-scoped DDL trigger or a server-scoped trigger (ALL SERVER)

In the case of both DDL and DML syntax statements, the [,... n] syntax block indicates that more than one trigger can be dropped at the same time.

The following example demonstrates dropping both a DML and a DDL trigger:

■ **Note**   The triggers dropped in this recipe were created in previous recipes in this chapter.

```
-- Switch context back to the AdventureWorks2014 database
USE AdventureWorks2014 ;
GO
-- Drop a DML trigger
DROP TRIGGER dbo.trg_i_TestTriggerOrder ;
-- Drop multiple DML triggers
DROP TRIGGER dbo.trg_i_TestTriggerOrder2, dbo.trg_i_TestTriggerOrder3 ;
-- Drop a DDL trigger
DROP TRIGGER db_trg_INDEXChanges
ON DATABASE;
```

How It Works

In this recipe, DML and DDL triggers were explicitly dropped using the DROP TRIGGER command. You will also drop all DML triggers when you drop the table or view that they are bound to. You can also remove multiple triggers in the same DROP command if each of the triggers was created using the same ON clause.

Error Handling

by Jason Brimhall

In this chapter you'll learn several error handling methods in T-SQL including structured error handling.

21-1. Handling Batch Errors

Problem

You have a script containing numerous Data Definition Language (DDL) and Data Manipulation Language (DML) statements that completely fail to run. You need to ensure that if part of the script fails due to an error the remaining script will complete, if there are no other errors.

Solution

A single script can contain multiple statements, and if run as a single batch the entire script will fail. When using SSMS or SQLCMD, batches can be separated with the GO command, but when implemented in an application using an OLEDB or ODBC API, an error will be returned. The following script contains both DDL and DML statements, and when executed as a whole will fail within SSMS:

```
USE master;
GO

IF EXISTS(SELECT 1/0 FROM sys.databases WHERE name = 'Errors')
BEGIN
        DROP DATABASE Errors;
        CREATE DATABASE Errors;
END
ELSE
BEGIN
        CREATE DATABASE Errors;
END

USE Errors;
GO
```

```
CREATE TABLE Works(
number  INT);

INSERT INTO Works
VALUES(1),
       ('A'),
       (3);

SELECT *
FROM Works;
```

The script returns immediately with an error indicating that the Errors database does not exist.

```
Msg 911, Level 16, State 1, Line 11
Database 'Errors' does not exist. Make sure that the name is entered correctly.
```

Reviewing the initial DDL statement shows the use of an IF statement block that will create the Errors database if it does not exist, so this may seem a bit confusing. The fact is that SQL Server evaluates the entire script as a single batch and returns the error since the USE statement references a database that does not exist.

This type of error can be easily overcome by separating each statement with a batch directive. The following code demonstrates how to use the GO keyword to ensure that each statement is executed and evaluated separately:

```
USE master;
GO

IF EXISTS(SELECT 1/0 FROM sys.databases WHERE name = 'Errors')
BEGIN
       DROP DATABASE Errors;
       CREATE DATABASE Errors;
END
ELSE
BEGIN
       CREATE DATABASE Errors;
END
GO

USE Errors;
GO

CREATE TABLE Works(number INT);
GO

INSERT INTO Works
VALUES(1),
       ('A'),
       (3);
GO
```

```
INSERT INTO Works
VALUES(1),
       (2),
       (3);
GO

SELECT *
FROM Works;
```

An error message is still returned showing a data type mismatch that is trying to insert the character "A" into the Errors table; however, all other statements complete, as is shown with the results of the select statement.

```
Msg 245, Level 16, State 1, Line 2
Conversion failed when converting the varchar value 'A' to data type int.

number
-----------
    1
    2
    3
```

How It Works

The GO statement is the default batch directive from Microsoft. SQL Server can accept multiple T-SQL statements for execution as a batch. The statements in the batch are parsed, bound, and compiled into a single execution. If any of the batch fails to parse or bind, then the query fails. Using the GO directive to separate statements ensures that one batch containing an error will not cause the other statements to fail.

The GO directive is one of only a few statements that must be on its own line of code. For example the following statement would fail:

```
SELECT *
FROM Works;
GO
```

```
A fatal scripting error occurred.
Incorrect syntax was encountered while parsing GO.
```

■ **Tip** A semicolon, ";", is not a batch directive, but rather an ANSI standard. The semicolon is a statement terminator and is currently not required for most statements in T-SQL, but it will be required in future versions. See http://msdn.microsoft.com/en-us/library/ms177563.aspx.

21-2. What Are the Error Numbers and Messages Within SQL?

Problem

You need to view the error numbers and messages that are contained within an instance of SQL Server.

Solution

SQL Server contains a catalog view that can be used to query the error messages contained within that specific instance. The view contains all messages for a number of languages, so it is best to filter the query based on the language_id. The following query will return all United States English messages:

```
USE master;
GO
SELECT sl.alias as LangAlias,
        message_id,
        severity,
        text
FROM sys.messages m
      INNER JOIN sys.syslanguages sl
            ON m.language_id = sl.msglangid
WHERE sl.name = 'us_english'
ORDER BY sl.name;
GO
```

This example returns the following abridged results:

LangAlias	message_id		severity	text
English	101	15		Query not allowed in Waitfor.
English	102	15		Incorrect syntax near '%.*ls'.
English	103	15		The %S_MSG that starts with '%.*ls' is too long. Maximum length is %d.

How It Works

The catalog view maintains a list of all system- and user-defined error and information messages. The view contains the message ID, language ID, error severity, if the error was written to the application log, and the message text. The error severity column from the sys.messages catalog view can be very insightful in finding user and system errors. The severity level of system- and user-defined messages are displayed in Table 21-1.

Table 21-1. *Severity Level of System- and User-Defined Messages*

Severity level	Description
0-9	Informational messages status only and are not logged
10	Informational messages status information; not logged
11-16	Error can be corrected by the user; not logged
17-19	Software errors that cannot be corrected by the user. Errors will be logged.
20-24	System problem, and are fatal errors. Errors can affect all processes accessing data in the same database. Errors will be logged.

Based on the severity level, targeting and debugging a query or process can be made easier, since it can be ascertained if the error is user or system based.

21-3. How Can I Implement Structured Error Handling in My Queries?

Problem

You are required to write T-SQL statements that have structured error handling so that the application will not incur a runtime error.

Solution

SQL Server has implemented structured error handling using a BEGIN TRY...BEGIN CATCH block. Structured error handling can be easily implemented within a query by placing the query within the BEGIN TRY block immediately followed by the BEGIN CATCH block:

```
USE tempdb;
GO

BEGIN TRY
 SELECT 1/0  --This will raise a divide by zero error if not handled
END TRY
BEGIN CATCH
END CATCH;
GO
```

The outcome is that no error or results are returned.

```
(0 row(s) affected)
```

How It Works

A query error is handled within the try and catch block, ensuring that, rather than an error being returned, an empty result set is returned. There are several functions that can be called within the scope of a catch block so as to return error information. These functions can be used with a SELECT statement. So, rather than returning an error, a result set can be returned with the desired information, as demonstrated in the following code:

```
BEGIN TRY
  SELECT 1/0 --This will raise a divide-by-zero error if not handled
END TRY
BEGIN CATCH
  SELECT ERROR_LINE() AS 'Line',
                ERROR_MESSAGE() AS 'Message',
                ERROR_NUMBER() AS 'Number',
                ERROR_PROCEDURE() AS 'Procedure',
                ERROR_SEVERITY() AS 'Severity',
                ERROR_STATE() AS 'State'
END CATCH;
```

The results are displayed below, showing that an error is not encountered, and the details are returned as a result set.

Line	Message	Number	Procedure	Severity	State
2	Divide by zero error encountered.	8134	NULL	16	1

ERROR_LINE() returns the approximate line number at which the error occurred. The ERROR_MESSAGE() function returns the text message of the error that is caught in the CATCH block. The ERROR_NUMBER() function returns the error number that caused the error. The ERROR_PROCEDURE() will return the name of the stored procedure or trigger that raised the error. ERROR_SEVERITY() returns the severity, irrespective of how many times it is run or where it is caught within the scope of the CATCH block. The ERROR_STATE() returns the state number of the error message that caused the CATCH block to be run, and it will return NULL if called outside the scope of a CATCH block.

T-SQL's structured error handling is very useful, but it does have its limitations. Unfortunately, not all errors can be captured within a try catch block. For example, compilation errors will not be caught. This is easily demonstrated by placing syntactically incorrect statements within a try catch block, as demonstrated here:

```
USE tempdb;
GO

BEGIN TRY
  SELCT
END TRY
BEGIN CATCH
END CATCH;
```

```
GOMsg 102, Level 15, State 1, Line 2
Incorrect syntax near 'SELCT'.
```

Since SELECT was misspelled, the query could not be compiled. Binding errors will also not be caught within a try catch block, as is demonstrated here:

```
USE tempdb;
GO

BEGIN TRY
  SELECT NoSuchTable
END TRY
BEGIN CATCH
END CATCH;
GO
```

```
Msg 207, Level 16, State 1, Line 3
Invalid column name 'NoSuchTable'.
```

Error messages with a severity of 20 or higher, statements that span batches, and recompilation errors will not be caught within try catch. Errors or messages with a severity of 10 or less will not be caught within the catch block, as these are informational messages. The following code demonstrates using RAISERROR to throw an informational message within a try catch block:

```
BEGIN TRY
  RAISERROR('Information ONLY', 10, 1)
END TRY
BEGIN CATCH
END CATCH;
GO
```

The messages tab of SSMS returns the following message.

```
Information ONLY
```

21-4. How Can I Use Structured Error Handling, but Still Return an Error?

Problem

You are required to write T-SQL statements that have structured error handling, but will also need to return the system- or user-defined error to ensure that the execution failures return the appropriate error message.

Solution

SQL Server 2012 introduced the THROW statement, which can be included in a try and catch block.
The following code demonstrates how using THROW in the catch block will still return a divide-by-zero error:

```
USE tempdb;
GO

BEGIN TRY
    SELECT 1/0
END TRY
BEGIN CATCH
    PRINT 'In catch block.';
    THROW;
END CATCH;
```

```
(0 row(s) affected)
In catch block.
Msg 8134, Level 16, State 1, Line 2
Divide by zero error encountered.
```

How It Works

The try and catch block works as outlined in the solution above, with the only difference being that the THROW statement is contained in the catch block. The result is that the message "In catch block" is printed in the messages tab, followed by the resulting error being raised by the THROW statement.

The severity of any error passed in the THROW statement is set to 16. THROWing the error will then cause the batch to fail. In this example, the throw is being used without any parameters (commonly referred to as rethrowing the error), which can only be done within a catch block, so all error information is thus from the error that is being handled within the try catch block.

A custom error can be thrown based on the error that is raised. The following code demonstrates how to throw an error based upon the error number that is returned:

```
USE tempdb;
GO

BEGIN TRY
    SELECT 1/0
END TRY
BEGIN CATCH
        IF (SELECT @@ERROR) = 8134
        BEGIN;
        THROW 51000, 'Divide by zero error occurred', 10;
          END
          ELSE
        THROW 52000, 'Unknown error occurred', 10;
```

```
END CATCH; (0 row(s) affected)
Msg 51000, Level 16, State 10, Line 7
Divide by zero error occurred
```

21-5. Nested Error Handling

Problem

There may be times when you will be required to use structured error handling, but you will need to ensure that errors are handled in either the try or catch block.

Solution

Try and catch blocks can be nested within either the TRY or the CATCH blocks. The following example displays nesting inside the TRY block:

```
USE tempdb;
GO

BEGIN TRY
  SELECT 1/0 --This will raise a divide-by-zero error if not handled
        BEGIN TRY
                PRINT 'Inner Try'
        END TRY
        BEGIN CATCH
                PRINT CONVERT(CHAR(5), ERROR_NUMBER()) + 'Inner Catch'
        END CATCH
END TRY
BEGIN CATCH
  PRINT CONVERT(CHAR(5), ERROR_NUMBER()) + 'Outer Catch'
END CATCH;
GO
```

```
(0 row(s) affected)
8134 Outer Catch
```

How It Works

The outer try block began and raised a divide-by-zero error. Immediately after the initial outer catch tried raising an error, it bypassed both the inner try and catch blocks and went immediately to the outer catch block to handle the divide-by-zero error. The outer catch block printed the error number and the message "Outer Catch."

To better understand how this works, examine the code below that reverses the code between the outer and inner try, causing the error to be raised within the inner catch nested within the outer try block:

```
USE tempdb;
GO

BEGIN TRY
  PRINT 'Outer Try'
    BEGIN TRY
                SELECT 1/0 --This will raise a divide-by-zero error if not handled
    END TRY
```

```
        BEGIN CATCH
                    PRINT CONVERT(CHAR(5), ERROR_NUMBER()) + 'Inner Catch'
        END CATCH
END TRY
BEGIN CATCH
  PRINT CONVERT(CHAR(5), ERROR_NUMBER()) + 'Outer Catch'
END CATCH;
GO
```

The results show that the outer try executed without an error, then proceeded to the inner try code. Once an error was raised in the inner try, the inner catch block handled the error.

```
Outer Try
(0 row(s) affected)
8134 Inner Catch
```

This demonstrates the order in which a nested TRY...CATCH will occur when nested in the try block.

1. Outer TRY block

2. Outer CATCH block if an error occurs

3. Inner TRY block

4. Inner CATCH if an error occurs

A more complex nested TRY...CATCH demonstrates how the code can dynamically handle errors based on the error number:

```
USE tempdb;
GO

BEGIN TRY
  PRINT 'Outer Try'
    BEGIN TRY
                PRINT ERROR_NUMBER() + ' Inner try'
    END TRY
    BEGIN CATCH
        IF ERROR_NUMBER() = 8134
                PRINT CONVERT(CHAR(5), ERROR_NUMBER()) + ' Inner Catch Divide by zero'
        ELSE
            BEGIN
            PRINT CONVERT(CHAR(6), ERROR_NUMBER()) + ' '
                    + ERROR_MESSAGE() +
              CONVERT(CHAR(2), ERROR_SEVERITY()) + ' ' +
              CONVERT(CHAR(2), ERROR_STATE()) + ' INITIAL Catch';
            END
    END CATCH;
END TRY
BEGIN CATCH
    IF ERROR_NUMBER() = 8134
        PRINT CONVERT(CHAR(5), ERROR_NUMBER()) + ' Outer Catch Divide by zero'
    ELSE
```

```
         BEGIN
         PRINT CONVERT(CHAR(6), ERROR_NUMBER()) + ' ' + ERROR_MESSAGE() +
               CONVERT(CHAR(2), ERROR_SEVERITY()) + ' ' +
               CONVERT(CHAR(2), ERROR_STATE()) + ' OUTER Catch';
         THROW
         END
END CATCH;
```

The results show that the outer try executed without error, then went to the inner try code. Once an error was raised in the inner try, the inner catch block handled the error.

```
Outer Try
245    Conversion failed when converting the varchar value ' Inner try' to data type
int.161 INITIAL Catch
```

These results are drastically changed by adding a THROW in the first catch block, as shown in this code:

```
USE tempdb;
GO

BEGIN TRY
  PRINT 'Outer Try'
    BEGIN TRY
                PRINT ERROR_NUMBER() + ' Inner try'
    END TRY
    BEGIN CATCH
        IF ERROR_NUMBER() = 8134
                PRINT CONVERT(CHAR(5), ERROR_NUMBER()) + ' Inner Catch Divide by zero'
        ELSE
            BEGIN
            PRINT CONVERT(CHAR(6), ERROR_NUMBER()) + ' '
                        + ERROR_MESSAGE() +
              CONVERT(CHAR(2), ERROR_SEVERITY()) + ' ' +
              CONVERT(CHAR(2), ERROR_STATE()) + ' INITIAL Catch';
          THROW --This THROW is added in the initial CATCH
            END
    END CATCH;
END TRY
BEGIN CATCH
    IF ERROR_NUMBER() = 8134
        PRINT CONVERT(CHAR(5), ERROR_NUMBER()) + ' Outer Catch Divide by zero'
    ELSE
        BEGIN
        PRINT CONVERT(CHAR(6), ERROR_NUMBER()) + ' ' + ERROR_MESSAGE() +
              CONVERT(CHAR(2), ERROR_SEVERITY()) + ' ' +
              CONVERT(CHAR(2), ERROR_STATE()) + ' OUTER Catch';
        THROW
        END
END CATCH;
```

The results now show that the outer try executed without error and proceeded to the inner try code. Once an error was raised in the inner try, the inner catch block handled the error and printed to the messages tab the concatenated string of the error number, message, severity, and state, as well as where the error was handled. The execution went immediately to the outer catch block, where the error string was printed out again, and then the conversion error was raised.

```
Outer Try
245     Conversion failed when converting the varchar value ' Inner try' to data type
int.16 1 INITIAL Catch
245     Conversion failed when converting the varchar value ' Inner try' to data type
int.16 1 OUTER Catch
Msg 245, Level 16, State 1, Line 5
Conversion failed when converting the varchar value ' Inner try' to data type int.
```

The confusing part of the execution is why both catch blocks were entered and why the error was raised. The reason is the THROW statement in the inner and outer catch blocks. Once the error was encountered the inner catch handled the error, but then rethrew the error. Since the error was rethrown once leaving the inner catch block, the code went immediately to the outer catch, again raising the error message that was rethrown. The outer catch handled the error with the PRINT statement and finally rethrew the error.

21-6. Throwing an Error

Problem

Certain instances require that a user-defined error be thrown.

Solution #1: Use RAISERROR to throw an error

Throwing an error within a block of code is as simple as using the RAISERROR statement:

```
RAISERROR ('User-defined error', -- Message text.
           16, -- Severity.
           1 -- State.
           );
```

This example throws a user-defined error with the message "User-defined error" and with a severity of 16 and state of 1:

```
Msg 50000, Level 16, State 1, Line 1
User-defined error
```

How It Works

User-defined errors must have an error number that is equal to or greater than 50000, so if a number isn't defined in the RAISERROR statement the default error number will be 50000.

A more practical example can be given by using RAISERROR in a DELETE trigger on a table that does not allow the deletion of records. Using RAISERROR can stop the transaction from occurring by raising a user-defined error that specifies that deletions are not permitted.

The following code creates a table in the tempdb database called Creditor and then creates an after delete trigger that raises an error. The result is that any attempt to delete a record will return an error with a message explaining that deletions are not permitted:

```
USE tempdb;
GO

CREATE TABLE Creditor(
CreditorID              INT IDENTITY PRIMARY KEY,
CreditorName     VARCHAR(50)
);
GO

INSERT INTO Creditor
VALUES('You Owe Me'),
       ('You Owe Me More');
GO

SELECT *
FROM Creditor;
GO
```

Executing the above query shows that the table is created and populated with two rows.

CreditorID,	CreditorName,
1	You Owe Me
2	You Owe Me More

```
USE tempdb;
GO

CREATE TRIGGER Deny_Delete
ON Creditor
FOR DELETE
AS
RAISERROR('Deletions are not permitted',
       16,
                1)
ROLLBACK TRANSACTION;
GO

DELETE
FROM Creditor
WHERE CreditorID = 1;
GO
```

Once the trigger is created and a deletion is attempted, the transaction fails with two errors. The first error is the error thrown using RAISERROR, and the second is thrown from the ROLLBACK command that is within the trigger.

```
Msg 50000, Level 16, State 1, Procedure Deny_Delete, Line 6
Deletions are not permitted
Msg 3609, Level 16, State 1, Line 1
The transaction ended in the trigger. The batch has been aborted.
```

```
SELECT *
FROM Creditor;
GO
```

The results of selecting all the records from the Creditor table shows that both rows are still in the table.

CreditorID	CreditorName
1	You Owe Me
2	You Owe Me More

Solution #2: Use THROW to throw an error

SQL 2012 introduced the THROW statement, which can also be used to throw an error. The following example demonstrates using the THROW statement:

```
THROW 50000, 'User-defined error', 1;
```

The preceding statement produces the following error.

```
Msg 50000, Level 16, State 1, Line 1
User-defined error
```

How It Works

The THROW statement is very similar to RAISERROR, but each has its own nuances. The most notable difference is in how each is handled within a TRY...CATCH block. For example, THROW stops the batch if not trapped in the CATCH. In Recipe 21-5, I demonstrated how THROW can be used without parameters in a TRY...CATCH block to rethrow the original error. RAISERROR requires that the associated error parameters be passed. Rewriting the example from 21-5, using RAISERROR, without parameters, in place of THROW will return an error as demonstrated here:

```
USE tempdb;
GO

BEGIN TRY
  PRINT 'Outer Try'
```

```
    BEGIN TRY
                PRINT ERROR_NUMBER() + ' Inner try'
    END TRY
    BEGIN CATCH
        IF ERROR_NUMBER() = 8134
                    PRINT CONVERT(CHAR(5), ERROR_NUMBER()) + ' Inner Catch Divide by zero'
        ELSE
            BEGIN
            PRINT CONVERT(CHAR(6), ERROR_NUMBER()) + ' '
                        + ERROR_MESSAGE() +
               CONVERT(CHAR(2), ERROR_SEVERITY()) + ' ' +
               CONVERT(CHAR(2), ERROR_STATE()) + ' INITIAL Catch';
            RAISERROR
            END
    END CATCH;
END TRY
BEGIN CATCH
    IF ERROR_NUMBER() = 8134
        PRINT CONVERT(CHAR(5), ERROR_NUMBER()) + ' Outer Catch Divide by zero'
    ELSE
        BEGIN
        PRINT CONVERT(CHAR(6), ERROR_NUMBER()) + ' ' + ERROR_MESSAGE() +
              CONVERT(CHAR(2), ERROR_SEVERITY()) + ' ' +
              CONVERT(CHAR(2), ERROR_STATE()) + ' OUTER Catch';
        RAISERROR
        END
END CATCH;
```

```
Msg 156, Level 15, State 1, Line 15
Incorrect syntax near the keyword 'END'.
Msg 156, Level 15, State 1, Line 27
Incorrect syntax near the keyword 'END'
```

Although RAISERROR can be used in place of THROW in such a case, it requires substantially more code, and the end result still provides a different error number:

```
BEGIN TRY
  PRINT 'Outer Try'
    BEGIN TRY
                PRINT ERROR_NUMBER() + ' Inner try'
    END TRY
    BEGIN CATCH
        DECLARE @error_message AS VARCHAR(500) = ERROR_MESSAGE()
        DECLARE @error_severity AS INT = ERROR_SEVERITY()
        DECLARE @error_state AS INT = ERROR_STATE()

        IF ERROR_NUMBER() = 8134
                    PRINT CONVERT(CHAR(5), ERROR_NUMBER()) + ' Inner Catch Divide by zero'
        ELSE
            BEGIN
```

```
                    PRINT CONVERT(CHAR(6), ERROR_NUMBER()) + ' '
                            + ERROR_MESSAGE() +
                CONVERT(CHAR(2), ERROR_SEVERITY()) + ' ' +
                CONVERT(CHAR(2), ERROR_STATE()) + ' INITIAL Catch';
            RAISERROR(@error_message,@error_severity,@error_state);
            END
    END CATCH;
END TRY
BEGIN CATCH
    IF ERROR_NUMBER() = 8134
        PRINT CONVERT(CHAR(5), ERROR_NUMBER()) + ' Outer Catch Divide by zero'
    ELSE
        BEGIN
        PRINT CONVERT(CHAR(6), ERROR_NUMBER()) + ' ' + ERROR_MESSAGE() +
                CONVERT(CHAR(2), ERROR_SEVERITY()) + ' ' +
                CONVERT(CHAR(2), ERROR_STATE()) + ' OUTER Catch';
        RAISERROR(@error_message,@error_severity,@error_state);

        END
END CATCH;
```

The results appear almost identical to the example from 21-5 using THROW, except for the error number.

```
Outer Try
245    Conversion failed when converting the varchar value ' Inner try' to data type
int.16 1 INITIAL Catch
50000  Conversion failed when converting the varchar value ' Inner try' to data type
int.16 1 OUTER Catch
Msg 50000, Level 16, State 1, Line 33
Conversion failed when converting the varchar value ' Inner try' to data type int.
```

21-7. Creating a User-Defined Error

Problem

A user-defined error message needs to be created to be used from RAISERROR.

Solution

Messages can be added to an instance of SQL Server using the system-stored procedure sp_addmessage. User-defined messages are added to an instance and can be viewed from the sys.messages system catalog view and called from either THROW or the RAISERROR command. The following query creates a user-defined message:

```
USE master
GO
EXEC sp_addmessage 50001, 16,
   N'This is a user-defined error that can be corrected by the user';
GO
```

This message will then be made available within an instance of SQL Server and can be viewed within the sys.messages catalog view:

```
SELECT message_id,
       text
FROM sys.messages
WHERE message_id = 50001;
GO
```

```
message_id                  text
-----------------           ------
50001                       This is a user-defined error that can be corrected by the user
```

Once the message is created in the instance of SQL Server, it can be called from the RAISERROR statement:

```
RAISERROR (50001,16,1);
GO
```

```
Msg 50001, Level 16, State 1, Line 1
This is a user-defined error that can be corrected by the user
```

How It Works

The system-stored procedure adds the user-defined message to the master database, where it can be called by using the RAISERROR command. The error number must be 50000 or greater, but the message, severity, and whether the message is logged to the application log can be specified when adding the message to the master database.

The next example adds a message of severity 16, user caused, to the master database, but will be logged to the application log:

```
USE master
GO
sp_addmessage @msgnum = 50002 ,
        @severity = 16 ,
        @msgtext = 'User error that IS logged',
        @with_log = 'TRUE';
GO

RAISERROR (50002,16,1);
GO
```

```
Msg 50002, Level 16, State 1, Line 1
User error that IS logged
```

Despite the severity of this error being set to 16, user defined, the error will still be logged to the Windows application log, because the "with_log" parameter was set to TRUE. This can be verified by viewing the application log as displayed in Figure 21-1 (or even from within the SQL Server Error Log):

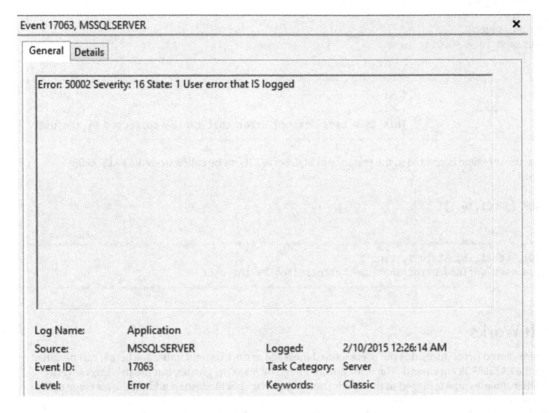

Figure 21-1. Whenever raised, the message is recorded in the application log

Any time the alert is called it will still be recorded in the application log, which provides a great deal of functionality in administration, as it can be used to fire off events from SQL alerts. This demonstrates how user-defined errors can be created and leveraged for both development and administrative purposes.

21-8. Removing a User-Defined Error

Problem

A user-defined error has been created and needs to be removed.

Solution

Messages can be removed from an instance of SQL Server by using the system-stored procedure sp_dropmessage. Once dropped, the message will be removed from the master database and will no longer be available within the instance. This example first verifies that an error with message_id 50001 exists by querying the sys.messages catalog view and then drops the message using sp_dropmessage:

```
USE master
GO

IF EXISTS ( SELECT 1/0 FROM sys.messages WHERE message_id = 50001)
BEGIN
  EXEC sp_dropmessage 50001;
END
GO

/* Confirm the error has been deleted */
SELECT message_id,
       text
FROM sys.messages
WHERE message_id = 50001;
GO
```

The results of the query show that the error has indeed been deleted.

message_id	text

How It Works

The system-stored procedure drops the user-defined message from the master database, thus removing it from the entire instance of SQL Server. Any future attempts to call the error with either RAISERROR or THROW will result in an error indicating that the message does not exist:

```
RAISERROR(50001,16,1);
GO
```

```
Msg 18054, Level 16, State 1, Line 1
Error 50001, severity 16, state 1 was raised, but no message with that error number was
found in sys.messages. If error is larger than 50000, make sure the user-defined message
is added using sp_addmessage.
```

CHAPTER 22

■ ■ ■

Query Performance Tuning

by Jason Brimhall

SQL Server query performance tuning and optimization requires a multilayered approach. The following are a few key factors that impact SQL Server query performance:

- *Database design*: Probably one of the most important factors influencing both query performance and data integrity, design decisions impact both read and modification performance. Standard designs include OLTP-normalized databases, which focus on data integrity, removal of redundancy, and the establishment of relationships between multiple entities. This is a design most appropriate for quick transaction processing. You'll usually see more tables in a normalized OLTP design, which means more table joins in your queries. Data-warehouse designs, on the other hand, often use a more denormalized star or snowflake design. These designs use a central fact table, which is joined to two or more description dimension tables. For snowflake designs, the dimension tables can also have related tables associated with them. The focus of this design is on query speed, not on fast updates to transactions.

- *Configurations*: This category includes databases, the SQL instance, and operating system configurations. Poor choices in configurations (such as enabling automatic shrinking or automatic closing of a database) can lead to performance issues for a busy application.

- *Hardware*: I once spent a day trying to get a three-second query down to one second. No matter which indexes I tried to add or query modifications I made, I couldn't get its duration lowered. This was because there were simply too many rows required in the result set. The limiting factor was I/O. A few months later, I migrated the database to a higher-powered production server. After that, the query executed consistently in less than one second. This underscores the fact that well-chosen hardware *does* matter. Your choice of processor architecture, available memory, and disk subsystem can have a significant impact on query performance.

- *Network throughput*: The time it takes to obtain query results can be impacted by a slow or unstable network connection. This doesn't mean you should be quick to blame the network engineers whenever a query executes slowly, but do keep this potential cause on your list of areas to investigate.

In this chapter, I'll demonstrate the T-SQL commands and techniques you can use to help evaluate and troubleshoot your query performance. I will follow that up in Chapter 24 when I discuss the related topics of fragmented indexes, out-of-date statistics, and the usage of indexes in the database.

■ **Note**   Since this is a T-SQL book, I will not be reviewing the graphical interface tools that also assist with performance tuning, such as SQL Server Profiler, graphical execution plans, System Monitor, and the Database Engine Tuning Advisor. These are all extremely useful tools, so I still encourage you to use them as part of your overall performance-tuning strategy in addition to the T-SQL commands and techniques you'll learn about in this chapter.

In this chapter, I'll demonstrate how to do the following:

- Control workloads and associated CPU and memory resources using Resource Governor

- Create statistics on a subset of data using the new filtered statistics improvement

- Display query statistics aggregated across near-identical queries (queries that are identical with the exception of nonparameterized literal values) or queries with identical query execution plans

- Create plan guides based on *existing* query plans in the query plan cache using the sp_create_plan_guide_from_handle system stored procedure

I will also demonstrate some changes made in SQL Server 2014 relevant to the sys.dm_exec_query_stats Dynamic Management View.

This chapter will also review a few miscellaneous query performance topics, including how to use sp_executesql as an alternative to dynamic SQL, how to apply query hints to a query without changing the query itself, and how to force a query to use a specific query execution plan.

Query Performance Tips

Before I start discussing the commands and tools you can use to evaluate query performance, I will first briefly review a few basic query performance-tuning guidelines. Query performance is a vast topic, and in many of the chapters I've tried to include small tips along with the various content areas. Since this is a chapter that discusses query performance independently of specific objects, the following list details a few query performance best practices to be aware of when constructing SQL Server queries (note that indexing tips are reviewed in Chapter 24):

- In your SELECT query, return only the columns you need. Having fewer columns in your query translates to less I/O and network bandwidth.

- Along with fewer columns, you should also be thinking about fewer rows. Use a WHERE clause to help reduce the number of rows returned by your query. Don't let the application return 20,000 rows when you need to display only the first 10.

- Keep the FROM clause under control. Each table you JOIN to in a single query can add overhead. I can't give you an exact number to watch out for, because it depends on your database's design and size, and the columns used to join a query. However, over the years, I've seen enormous queries that are functionally correct but take far too long to execute. Although it is convenient to use a single query to perform a complex operation, don't underestimate the power of smaller queries. If I have a very large query in a stored procedure that is taking too long to execute, I'll usually try breaking that query down into smaller intermediate result sets. This usually results in a significantly faster generation of the final desired result set.

- Use ORDER BY only if you *need* ordered results. Sorting operations in larger result sets can incur additional overhead. If it isn't necessary for your query, remove it.

- Avoid implicit data-type conversions in your JOIN, FROM, WHERE, and HAVING clauses. Implicit data-type conversions happen when the underlying data types in your predicates don't match and are automatically converted by SQL Server. One example is a Java application sending Unicode text to a non-Unicode column. For applications processing hundreds of transactions per second, these implicit conversions can really add up.

- Don't use DISTINCT or UNION (instead of UNION ALL) if having unique rows is not a necessity.

- Beware of testing in a vacuum. When developing your database on a test SQL Server instance, it is very important that you populate the tables with a representative data set. This means you should populate the table with the estimated number of rows you would actually see in production, as well as with a representative set of values. Don't use dummy data in your development database and then expect the query to execute with similar performance in production. SQL Server performance is highly dependent on indexes and statistics, and SQL Server will make decisions based on the actual values contained within a table. If your test data isn't representative of "real-life" data, you'll be in for a surprise when queries in production don't perform as you saw them perform on the test database.

- When choosing between cursors and set-based approaches, always favor the latter. If you must use cursors, be sure to close and deallocate them as soon as possible.

- Query hints can sometimes be necessary in more complex database-driven applications; however, they often outlast their usefulness once the underlying data volume or distribution changes. Avoid overriding SQL Server's decision process by using hints sparingly.

- Avoid nesting views. I've often seen views created that reference other views, which in turn reference objects that are already referenced in the calling view! This overlap and redundancy can often result in nonoptimal query plans because of the resulting query complexity.

- I pushed this point hard in Chapter 18, and I think it is worth repeating here: stored procedures often yield excellent performance gains over regular ad hoc query calls. Stored procedures also promote query execution stability (reusing existing query execution plans). If you have a query that executes with unpredictable durations, consider encapsulating the query in a stored procedure.

When reading about SQL Server performance tuning (like you are now), be careful about saying "never" and "always." Instead, get comfortable with the answer "it depends." When it comes to query tuning, results may vary. Keep your options open and feel free to experiment (in a test environment, of course). Ask questions, and don't accept conventional wisdom at face value.

Capturing and Evaluating Query Performance

In this next set of recipes, I'll demonstrate how to capture and evaluate query performance and activity. I'll also demonstrate several other Transact-SQL commands, which can be used to return detailed information about the query execution plan.

22-1. Capturing Executing Queries

Problem

You need to find the currently executing queries in your database while incurring minimal performance impact.

Solution #1

Use sys.dm_exec_requests. In addition to capturing queries in SQL Server Profiler, you can also capture the SQL for currently executing queries by querying the sys.dm_exec_requests dynamic management view (DMV), as this recipe demonstrates:

```
USE AdventureWorks2014;
GO

SELECT r.session_id, r.status, r.start_time, r.command, s.text
FROM sys.dm_exec_requests r
CROSS APPLY sys.dm_exec_sql_text(r.sql_handle) s
WHERE r.status = 'running';
```

This captures any queries that are currently being executed, even the current query being used to capture those very queries:

session_id	status	start_time	command	text
55	running	2012-04-05 13:53:52.670	SELECT	SELECT r.session_id, r.status, r.start_time, r.command, s.text FROM sys.dm_exec_requests r CROSS APPLY sys.dm_exec_sql_text(r.sql_handl e) s WHERE r.status = 'running'

How It Works

The sys.dm_exec_requests DMV returns information about all requests executing on a SQL Server instance.

The first line of the query selected the session ID, status of the query, start time, command type (for example, SELECT, INSERT, UPDATE, DELETE), and actual SQL text:

```
SELECT r.session_id, r.status, r.start_time, r.command, s.text
```

In the FROM clause, the sys.dm_exec_requests DMV was cross-applied against the sys.dm_exec_sql_text dynamic management function. This function takes the sql_handle from the sys.dm_exec_requests DMV and returns the associated SQL text.

```
FROM sys.dm_exec_requests r
CROSS APPLY sys.dm_exec_sql_text(r.sql_handle) s
```

The WHERE clause then designates that currently running processes be returned.

```
WHERE r.status = 'running'
```

Solution #2

Create an Extended Event session to trap the queries as they are executed. Extended Events offer a lightweight means, compared to Profiler, to trap the incoming queries. This recipe will demonstrate how to implement an Extended Event session and read the captured data:

```
USE master;
GO
-- Create the Event Session
IF EXISTS(SELECT *
            FROM sys.server_event_sessions
            WHERE name='TraceIncomingQueries')
    DROP EVENT SESSION TraceIncomingQueries
    ON SERVER;
GO
CREATE EVENT SESSION TraceIncomingQueries
ON SERVER
ADD EVENT sqlserver.sql_statement_starting(
    ACTION(sqlserver.database_name,sqlserver.nt_username,sqlserver.session_id,sqlserver.
    client_hostname,sqlserver.client_app_name)
WHERE sqlserver.database_name='AdventureWorks2014'
        AND sqlserver.client_app_name <> 'Microsoft SQL Server Management Studio -
        Transact-SQL IntelliSense'
        )
ADD TARGET package0.event_file(SET filename=N'C:\Database\XE\TraceIncomingQueries.xel')

/* start the session */
ALTER EVENT SESSION TraceIncomingQueries
ON SERVER
STATE = START;
GO
```

With the Extended Event (XE) session in place, I will execute a query:

```
USE AdventureWorks2014;
GO

SELECT r.session_id, r.status, r.start_time, r.command, s.text
FROM sys.dm_exec_requests r
CROSS APPLY sys.dm_exec_sql_text(r.sql_handle) s
WHERE r.status = 'running';
```

To confirm that data was captured, I then need to parse the session data from the XE session:

```
use master;
GO

SELECT
event_data.value('(event/@name)[1]', 'varchar(50)') AS event_name,
    event_data.value('(event/@timestamp)[1]', 'varchar(50)') AS [TIMESTAMP],
        event_data.value('(event/action[@name="database_name"]/value)[1]', 'varchar(max)')
        AS DBName
```

```
            ,event_data.value('(event/data[@name="statement"]/value)[1]', 'varchar(max)')
            AS SQLText
            ,event_data.value('(event/action[@name="session_id"]/value)[1]', 'varchar(max)')
            AS SessionID
            ,event_data.value('(event/action[@name="nt_username"]/value)[1]', 'varchar(max)')
            AS ExecUser
            ,event_data.value('(event/action[@name="client_hostname"]/value)[1]', 'varchar(max)')
            AS Client_HostName,
            event_data.value('(event/action[@name="client_app_name"]/value)[1]', 'varchar(max)')
            AS Client_AppName
FROM(
SELECT CONVERT(XML, t2.event_data) AS event_data
 FROM (
  SELECT target_data = convert(XML, target_data)
   FROM sys.dm_xe_session_targets t
    INNER JOIN sys.dm_xe_sessions s
        ON t.event_session_address = s.address
   WHERE t.target_name = 'event_file'
   AND s.name = 'TraceIncomingQueries') cte1
   CROSS APPLY cte1.target_data.nodes('//EventFileTarget/File') FileEvent(FileTarget)
   CROSS APPLY  sys.fn_xe_file_target_read_file(FileEvent.FileTarget.value('@name',
   'varchar(1000)'), NULL, NULL, NULL) t2)
    AS evts(event_data);
```

How It Works

Extended events are a lightweight tracing engine that allows events to be trapped, similar to Profiler. This
script first checks to see if the session exists. If the session exists, it is dropped and then recreated. The
session is defined to write the session data out to a file if the criteria matches. The session checks that the
query is running in a connection to the AdventureWorks2014 database, and that the source application is
not Intellisense. To read the data from the session, we convert the data from the file target to XML and then
use XML methods to parse the data to a desired output.

22-2. Viewing Estimated Query Execution Plans

Problem

You are troubleshooting a query and need to see how SQL Server is executing that query.

Solution

Use the following Transact-SQL commands: SET SHOWPLAN_ALL, SET SHOWPLAN_TEXT, and SET SHOWPLAN_XML.
    Knowing how SQL Server executes a query can help you determine how best to fix a poorly performing
query. Details you can identify by viewing a query's execution plan (either graphical or command-based)
include the following:

- Highest-cost queries within a batch and highest-cost operators within a query

- Index or table scans (accessing all the pages in a heap or index) versus using seeks
  (accessing only selected rows)

- Missing statistics or other warnings

- Costly sort or calculation activities

- Lookup operations where a nonclustered index is used to access a row but then needs to access the clustered index to retrieve columns not covered by the nonclustered index

- High row counts being passed from operator to operator

- Discrepancies between the estimated and actual row counts

- Implicit data-type conversions (identified in an XML plan where the Implicit attribute of the Convert element is equal to 1)

In SQL Server, three commands can be used to view detailed information about a query execution plan for a SQL statement or batch: SET SHOWPLAN_ALL, SET SHOWPLAN_TEXT, and SET SHOWPLAN_XML. The output of these commands helps you understand how SQL Server plans to process and execute your query, identifying information such as table join types used and the indexes accessed. For example, using the output from these commands, you can see whether SQL Server is using a specific index in a query and, if so, whether it is retrieving the data using an index seek (a nonclustered index is used to retrieve selected rows for the operation) or an index scan (all index rows are retrieved for the operation).

When enabled, the SET SHOWPLAN_ALL, SET SHOWPLAN_TEXT, and SET SHOWPLAN_XML commands provide you with the plan information without executing the query, allowing you to adjust the query or indexes on the referenced tables before actually executing it.

Each of these commands returns information in a different way. SET SHOWPLAN_ALL returns the estimated query plan in a tabular format, with multiple columns and rows. The output includes information such as the estimated I/O or CPU of each operation, estimated rows involved in the operation, operation cost (relative to itself and variations of the query), and the physical and logical operators used.

■ **Note** Logical operators describe the conceptual operation SQL Server must perform in the query execution. Physical operators are the actual implementation of that logical operation. For example, a logical operation in a query, INNER JOIN, could be translated into the physical operation of a nested loop in the actual query execution.

The SET SHOWPLAN_TEXT command returns the data in a single column, with multiple rows for each operation. You can also return a query execution plan in XML format using the SET SHOWPLAN_XML command.

The syntax for each of these commands is very similar. Each command is enabled when set to ON and disabled when set to OFF:

```
SET SHOWPLAN_ALL { ON | OFF }
SET SHOWPLAN_TEXT { ON | OFF}
SET SHOWPLAN_XML { ON | OFF }
```

This recipe's example demonstrates returning the estimated query execution plan of a query in the AdventureWorks2014 database using SET SHOWPLAN_TEXT and then SET SHOWPLAN_XML:

```
USE AdventureWorks2014;
GO
SET SHOWPLAN_TEXT ON;
GO
SELECT p.Name, p.ProductNumber, r.ReviewerName
```

```
FROM Production.Product p
INNER JOIN Production.ProductReview r
ON p.ProductID = r.ProductID
WHERE r.Rating > 2;
GO
SET SHOWPLAN_TEXT OFF;
GO
```

This returns the following estimated query execution plan output:

```
StmtText
SELECT p.Name, p.ProductNumber, r.ReviewerName
FROM Production.Product p
INNER JOIN Production.ProductReview r
ON p.ProductID = r.ProductID
WHERE r.Rating > 2;

(1 row(s) affected)

StmtText
  |--Nested Loops(Inner Join, OUTER REFERENCES:([r].[ProductID]))
       |--Clustered Index Scan(OBJECT:([AdventureWorks2014].[Production].[ProductReview].
[PK_ProductReview_ProductReviewID] AS [r]), WHERE:([AdventureWorks2014].[Production].
[ProductReview].[Rating] as [r].[Rating]>(2)))
       |--Clustered Index Seek(OBJECT:([AdventureWorks2014].[Production].[Product].
[PK_Product_ProductID] AS [p]), SEEK:([p].[ProductID]=[AdventureWorks2014].[Production].
[ProductReview].[ProductID] as [r].[ProductID]) ORDERED FORWARD)

(3 row(s) affected)
```

The next example returns estimated query plan results in XML format:

```
USE AdventureWorks2014;
GO
SET SHOWPLAN_XML ON;
GO
SELECT p.Name, p.ProductNumber, r.ReviewerName
FROM Production.Product p
INNER JOIN Production.ProductReview r
ON p.ProductID = r.ProductID
WHERE r.Rating > 2;
GO
SET SHOWPLAN_XML OFF;
GO
```

This returns the following (this is an abridged snippet, because the actual output is more than a page long):

```
<ShowPlanXML xmlns="http://schemas.microsoft.com/sqlserver/2004/07/showplan" Version="1.2"
Build="12.0.2000.8">  <BatchSequence>
    <Batch>
      <Statements>
...
        <RelOp NodeId="0" PhysicalOp="Nested Loops" LogicalOp="Inner Join"
        EstimateRows="3" EstimateIO="0" EstimateCPU="1.254e-005" AvgRowSize="140"
        EstimatedTotalSubtreeCost="0.0099657" Parallel="0" EstimateRebinds="0"
        EstimateRewinds="0" EstimatedExecutionMode="Row">
            <OutputList>
              <ColumnReference Database="[AdventureWorks2014]" Schema="[Production]"
              Table="[Product]" Alias="[p]" Column="Name" />
              <ColumnReference Database="[AdventureWorks2014]" Schema="[Production]"
              Table="[Product]" Alias="[p]" Column="ProductNumber" />
              <ColumnReference Database="[AdventureWorks2014]" Schema="[Production]"
              Table="[ProductReview]" Alias="[r]" Column="ReviewerName" />
            </OutputList>...
```

How It Works

You can use SHOWPLAN_ALL, SHOWPLAN_TEXT, or SHOWPLAN_XML to tune your Transact-SQL queries and batches. These commands show you the estimated execution plan without actually executing the query. You can use the information returned in the command output to take action toward improving the query performance (for example, adding indexes to columns being used in search or join conditions). Looking at the output, you can determine whether SQL Server is using the expected indexes and, if so, whether SQL Server is using an index seek, index scan, or table scan operation. In this recipe, the SET SHOWPLAN for both TEXT and XML was set to ON and then followed by GO.

```
SET SHOWPLAN_TEXT ON;
GO
```

A query referencing Production.Product and Production.ProductReview was then evaluated. The two tables were joined using an INNER join on the ProductID column, and only those products with a product rating of 2 or higher would be returned:

```
SELECT p.Name, p.ProductNumber, r.ReviewerName
FROM Production.Product p
INNER JOIN Production.ProductReview r
ON p.ProductID = r.ProductID
WHERE r.Rating > 2;
```

The SHOWPLAN was set OFF at the end of the query, so as not to keep executing SHOWPLAN for subsequent queries for that connection.

Looking at snippets from the output, you can see that a nested loop join (physical operation) was used to perform the INNER JOIN (logical operation).

```
--Nested Loops(Inner Join, OUTER REFERENCES:([r].[ProductID]))
```

You can also see from this output that a clustered index scan was performed using the PK_ProductReview_ProductReviewID primary key clustered index to retrieve data from the ProductReview table.

```
|--Clustered Index Scan (OBJECT:([AdventureWorks2014].[Production].[ProductReview].
[PK_ProductReview_ProductReviewID] AS [r]),
```

A clustered index *seek*, however, was used to retrieve data from the Product table.

```
|--Clustered Index Seek(OBJECT:([AdventureWorks2014].[Production].[Product].
[PK_Product_ProductID] AS [p]),
```

The SET SHOWPLAN_XML command returned the estimated query plan in an XML document format, displaying similar data as SHOWPLAN_TEXT. The XML data is formatted using attributes and elements.

For example, the attributes of the RelOp element show a physical operation of nested loops and a logical operation of Inner Join—along with other statistics such as estimated rows impacted by the operation.

```
<RelOp NodeId="0" PhysicalOp="Nested Loops" LogicalOp="Inner Join"
EstimateRows="3" EstimateIO="0" EstimateCPU="1.254e-005" AvgRowSize="140"
EstimatedTotalSubtreeCost="0.0099657" Parallel="0" EstimateRebinds="0" EstimateRewinds="0"
EstimatedExecutionMode="Row">
```

The XML document follows a specific schema definition format that defines the returned XML elements, attributes, and data types. This schema can be viewed at the following URL: http://schemas.microsoft.com/sqlserver/2004/07/showplan/showplanxml.xsd.

22-3. Viewing Execution Runtime Information

Problem

You want to evaluate various execution statistics for a query that you are attempting to tune for better performance.

Solution

SQL Server provides four commands that are used to return query- and batch-execution statistics and information: SET STATISTICS IO, SET STATISTICS TIME, SET STATISTICS PROFILE, and SET STATISTICS XML.

Unlike the SHOWPLAN commands, STATISTICS commands return information for queries that have actually been executed in SQL Server. The SET STATISTICS IO command is used to return disk activity (hence I/O) generated by the executed statement. The SET STATISTICS TIME command returns the number of milliseconds taken to parse, compile, and execute each statement executed in the batch.

SET STATISTICS PROFILE and SET STATISTICS XML are the equivalents of SET SHOWPLAN_ALL and SET SHOWPLAN_XML, only the actual (*not* estimated) execution plan information is returned along with the actual results of the query.

The syntax of each of these commands is similar, with ON enabling the statistics and OFF disabling them:

```
SET STATISTICS IO  { ON | OFF }
SET STATISTICS TIME { ON | OFF }
SET STATISTICS PROFILE { ON | OFF }
SET STATISTICS XML { ON | OFF }
```

In the first example, STATISTICS IO is enabled prior to executing a query that totals the amount due by territory from the Sales.SalesOrderHeader and Sales.SalesTerritory tables. See the following:

```
USE AdventureWorks2014;
GO
SET STATISTICS IO ON;
GO
SELECT t.Name TerritoryNM,
SUM(TotalDue) TotalDue
FROM Sales.SalesOrderHeader h
INNER JOIN Sales.SalesTerritory t
ON h.TerritoryID = t.TerritoryID
WHERE OrderDate BETWEEN '1/1/2014' AND '12/31/2014'
GROUP BY t.Name
ORDER BY t.Name
SET STATISTICS IO OFF;
GO
```

This returns the following (abridged) results:

TerritoryNM	TotalDue
Australia	3071053.8419
Canada	2681602.5941
...	
Southwest	4437517.8076
United Kingdom	2335108.8971

```
Table 'Worktable'. Scan count 1, logical reads 39, physical reads 0, read-ahead reads 0,
lob logical reads 0, lob physical reads 0, lob read-ahead reads 0.
Table 'Workfile'. Scan count 0, logical reads 0, physical reads 0, read-ahead reads 0,
lob logical reads 0, lob physical reads 0, lob read-ahead reads 0.
Table 'SalesOrderHeader'. Scan count 1, logical reads 689, physical reads 0, read-ahead
reads 0, lob logical reads 0, lob physical reads 0, lob read-ahead reads 0.
Table 'SalesTerritory'. Scan count 1, logical reads 2, physical reads 0, read-ahead reads
0, lob logical reads 0, lob physical reads 0, lob read-ahead reads 0.
```

Substituting SET STATISTICS IO with SET STATISTICS TIME would have returned the following (abridged) results for that same query:

TerritoryNM	TotalDue
Australia	3071053.8419
...	
Southeast	985940.2109
Southwest	4437517.8076
United Kingdom	2335108.8971

```
SQL Server parse and compile time:
   CPU time = 0 ms, elapsed time = 4 ms.

(10 row(s) affected)

 SQL Server Execution Times:
   CPU time = 0 ms,  elapsed time = 6 ms.
```

How It Works

The SET STATISTICS commands return information about the actual execution of a query or batch of queries. In this recipe, SET STATISTICS IO returned information about logical, physical, and large object read events for tables referenced in the query. For a query that is having performance issues (based on your business requirements and definition of *issues*), you can use SET STATISTICS IO to see where the I/O hot spots are occurring. For example, in this recipe's result set, you can see that SalesOrderHeader had the highest number of logical reads.

```
...
Table 'SalesOrderHeader'. Scan count 1, logical reads 689, physical reads 0,
read-ahead reads 0, lob logical reads 0, lob physical reads 0, lob read-ahead
  reads 0.
...
```

Pay attention to high physical (reads from disk) or logical (reads from the data cache) read values, even if the physical read is zero and the logical read is a high value. Also look for worktables (which were also seen in this recipe), as follows:

```
Table 'Worktable'. Scan count 1, logical reads 39, physical reads 0, read-ahead reads 0,
lob logical reads 0, lob physical reads 0, lob read-ahead reads 0.
```

Worktables are usually seen in conjunction with GROUP BY, ORDER BY, hash joins, and UNION operations in the query. Worktables are created in tempdb for the duration of the query and are removed automatically when SQL Server has finished the operation.

In the second example in this recipe, SET STATISTICS TIME was used to show the parse and compile time of the query (shown before the actual query results) and then the actual execution time (displayed after the query results). This command is useful for measuring the amount of time a query takes to execute from end to end, allowing you to see whether precompiling is taking longer than you realized or whether the slowdown occurs during the actual query execution.

The two other STATISTICS commands, SET STATISTICS PROFILE and SET STATISTICS XML, return information similar to that returned by SET SHOWPLAN_ALL and SET SHOWPLAN_XML, only the results are based on the *actual*, rather than the estimated, execution plan.

22-4. Viewing Statistics for Cached Plans

Problem

You need to determine the number of reads or writes that occur when a query is executed.

Solution

Query the sys.dm_exec_query_stats DMV to view performance statistics for cached query plans.

■ **Tip** SQL Server 2008 introduced various improvements for managed collection and analysis of performance statistics. For example, the Data Collector uses stored procedures, SQL Server Integration Services, and SQL Server Agent jobs to collect data and load it into the Management Data Warehouse (MDW). These features are available in SQL Server 2014 as well.

In this example, a simple query that returns all rows from the Sales.Salesperson table is executed against the AdventureWorks2014 database. Prior to executing it, you'll clear the procedure cache so that you can identify the query more easily in this demonstration (remember that you should clear out the procedure cache only on test SQL Server instances):

```
DBCC FREEPROCCACHE;
GO
USE AdventureWorks2014;
GO
SELECT BusinessEntityID, TerritoryID, SalesQuota
FROM Sales.SalesPerson;
```

Now, I'll query the sys.dm_exec_query_stats DMV, which contains statistical information regarding queries cached on the SQL Server instance. This view contains a sql_handle, which I'll use as an input to the sys.dm_exec_sql_text dynamic management function. This function is used to return the text of a Transact-SQL statement:

```
USE AdventureWorks2014;
GO
SELECT  t.text,
st.total_logical_reads,
st.total_physical_reads,
```

```
st.total_elapsed_time/1000000 Total_Time_Secs,
st.total_logical_writes
FROM sys.dm_exec_query_stats st
CROSS APPLY sys.dm_exec_sql_text(st.sql_handle) t;
```

This returns the following abridged results:

text	total_logical_	total_physical_	Total_Time_	total_logical_
	reads	reads	Secs	writes
SELECT BusinessEntityID...	2	8	0	0

How It Works

This recipe demonstrated clearing the procedure cache and then executing a query that took a few seconds to finish executing. After that, the sys.dm_exec_query_stats DMV was queried to return statistics about the cached execution plan.

The SELECT clause retrieved information on the Transact-SQL text of the query—the number of logical and physical reads, the total time elapsed in seconds, and the logical writes (if any).

```
SELECT  t.text,
st.total_logical_reads, st.total_physical_reads,
st.total_elapsed_time/1000000 Total_Time_Secs, st.total_logical_writes
```

The total elapsed time column was in microseconds, so it was divided by 1,000,000 in order to return the number of full seconds.

In the FROM clause, the sys.dm_exec_query_stats DMV was cross-applied against the sys.dm_exec_sql_text dynamic management function in order to retrieve the SQL text of the cached query:

```
FROM sys.dm_exec_query_stats st
CROSS APPLY sys.dm_exec_sql_text(st.sql_handle) t
```

This information is useful for identifying read-intensive and/or write-intensive queries, helping you determine which queries should be optimized. Keep in mind that this recipe's query can retrieve information only on queries still in the cache. This query returned the totals, but sys.dm_ exec_query_ stats also includes columns that track the minimum, maximum, and last measurements for reads and writes. Also note that sys.dm_exec_query_stats has other useful columns that can measure CPU time (total_worker_time, last_worker_time, min_worker_time, and max_worker_time) and .NET CLR object execution time (total_clr_time, last_clr_time, min_clr_time, max_clr_time).

22-5. Viewing Record Counts for Cached Plans

Problem

A query suddenly started taking twice as long to complete as it did in prior executions. You suspect that the decrease in performance is related to the number of records being returned. You need to find out whether there has been a variance in the number of records returned by this query.

Solution

Query the sys.dm_exec_query_stats DMV to view performance statistics for cached query plans.

In this example, we will reuse the query from the previous example to query Sales.SalesPerson.

```
USE AdventureWorks2014;
GO
SELECT BusinessEntityID, TerritoryID, SalesQuota
FROM Sales.SalesPerson;
```

Now, I'll query the sys.dm_exec_query_stats DMV, which contains two new columns introduced in SQL Server 2014 (currently reserved for future use). This DMV contains statistical information regarding queries cached on the SQL Server instance. This view contains a sql_handle, which I'll use as an input to the sys.dm_exec_sql_text dynamic management function. This function is used to return the text of a Transact-SQL statement:

```
USE AdventureWorks2014;
GO
SELECT  t.text,
st.total_rows,
st.last_rows,
st.min_rows,
st.max_rows
FROM sys.dm_exec_query_stats st
CROSS APPLY sys.dm_exec_sql_text(st.sql_handle) t
WHERE t.text like '%FROM Sales.SalesPerson%';
```

This returns the following (abridged) results:

text	total_rows	last_rows	min_rows	max_rows
SELECT BusinessEntityID...	17	17	17	17

How It Works

The sys.dm_exec_query_stats DMV was queried to return statistics about the cached execution plan.

The SELECT clause retrieved information on the Transact-SQL text of the query—minimum and maximum number of rows returned by the query, total rows returned by the query, and number of rows returned by the query on its last execution:

```
SELECT  t.text,
st.total_rows,
st.last_rows,
st.min_rows,
st.max_rows
FROM sys.dm_exec_query_stats st
```

Like the last query, we cross-applied to the sys.dm_exec_sql_text dynamic management function using sql_handle from sys.dm_exec_query_stats.

This information is useful in determining variances in the number of rows returned by a query. If the number of records to be returned has suddenly grown, the query to return those records may also increase in duration. By querying sys.dm_exec_query_stats, you can determine whether the query in question is returning a different number of records. Remember, though, that this query will return values only for queries that are presently in the cache.

22-6. Viewing Aggregated Performance Statistics Based on Query or Plan Patterns

Problem

You have an application that utilizes ad hoc queries. You need to aggregate performance statistics for similar ad hoc queries.

Solution

Query the sys.dm_exec_query_stats DMV. The previous recipe demonstrated viewing query statistics using the sys.dm_exec_query_stats DMV. Statistics in this DMV are displayed as long as the query plan remains in the cache. For applications that use stored procedures or prepared plans, sys.dm_exec_query_stats can give an accurate picture of overall aggregated statistics and resource utilization. However, if the application sends unprepared query text and does not properly parameterize literal values, individual statistic rows will be generated for each variation of an almost identical query, making the statistics difficult to correlate and aggregate.

For example, assume that the application sends the following three individual SELECT statements:

```
USE AdventureWorks2014;
GO
SELECT BusinessEntityID
FROM Purchasing.vVendorWithContacts
WHERE EmailAddress = 'cheryl1@adventure-works.com';
GO
SELECT BusinessEntityID
FROM Purchasing.vVendorWithContacts
WHERE EmailAddress = 'stuart2@adventure-works.com';
GO
SELECT BusinessEntityID
FROM Purchasing.vVendorWithContacts
WHERE EmailAddress = 'suzanne0@adventure-works.com';
GO
```

After executing this set of queries, the following query is executed:

```
USE AdventureWorks2014;
GO
SELECT  t.text,
st.total_logical_reads
FROM sys.dm_exec_query_stats st
CROSS APPLY sys.dm_exec_sql_text(st.sql_handle) t
WHERE t.text LIKE '%Purchasing.vVendorWithContacts%';
```

This query returns the following:

Text	total_logical_reads
SELECT BusinessEntityID FROM Purchasing.vVendorWithContacts WHERE EmailAddress = 'stuart2@adventure-works.com'	12
SELECT BusinessEntityID FROM Purchasing.vVendorWithContacts WHERE EmailAddress = 'cheryl1@adventure-works.com'	12
SELECT BusinessEntityID FROM Purchasing.vVendorWithContacts WHERE EmailAddress = 'suzanne0@adventure-works.com'	12

Notice that a statistics row was created for each query, even though each query against Purchasing.vVendorWithContacts was identical, with the exception of the EmailAddress literal value. This is an issue you'll see for applications that do not prepare the query text.

To address this issue, there are two helpful columns in the sys.dm_exec_ query_stats DMV: query_hash and query_plan_hash. Each of these columns contain a binary hash value. The query_hash binary value is the same for those queries that are identical with the exception of literal values (in this example, differing e-mail addresses). The generated query_plan_hash binary value is the same for those queries that use identical query plans. These two columns add the ability to aggregate overall statistics across identical queries or query execution plans. Here's an example:

```
USE AdventureWorks2014;
GO
SELECT
MAX(t.text) as query_text,
COUNT(t.text) query_count,
SUM(st.total_logical_reads) total_logical_reads
FROM sys.dm_exec_query_stats st
CROSS APPLY sys.dm_exec_sql_text(st.sql_handle) t
WHERE text LIKE '%Purchasing.vVendorWithContacts%'
GROUP BY st.query_hash;
```

This query returns the following:

query_ text	query_count	total_logical_reads
SELECT BusinessEntityID	3	36

How It Works

I started the recipe by executing three queries that were identical with the exception of the literal values defined for the EmailAddress column in the WHERE clause. After that, I demonstrated querying the sys.dm_exec_query_stats DMV to view the logical read statistics for each query. Three separate rows were generated for each query against Purchasing.vVendorWithContacts, instead of showing an aggregated single row. This can be problematic if you are trying to capture the TOP X number of high-resource-usage queries, because your result may not reflect the numerous variations of the same query that exist in the query plan cache.

To address this problem, I demonstrated using the query_hash column that was introduced to the sys.dm_exec_query_stats DMV back in SQL Server 2008.

Walking through the query, the SELECT clause of the query referenced the text column and produced a COUNT of the distinct queries using different literal values and a SUM of the logical reads across these queries:

```
SELECT MAX(t.text) as query_text,
COUNT(t.text) query_count, SUM(st.total_logical_reads) total_logical_reads
```

The FROM clause referenced the sys.dm_exec_query_stats DMV and used CROSS APPLY to access the query text based on the sql_handle:

```
FROM sys.dm_exec_query_stats st
CROSS APPLY sys.dm_exec_sql_text(st.sqljandle) t
```

I narrowed down the result set to those queries referencing the Purchasing.vVendorWithContacts view:

```
WHERE text LIKE '%Purchasing.vVendorWithContacts%'
```

Lastly, since I was aggregating the statistics by the query_hash, I used a GROUP BY clause with the query_hash column:

```
GROUP BY st.query_hash
```

The query_hash value of 0x5C4B94191341266A was identical across all three queries, allowing me to aggregate each of the individual rows into a single row and properly sum the statistic columns I was interested in. Aggregating by the query_hash or query_plan_hash improves visibility for specific query or plan patterns and their associated resource costs.

22-7. Identifying the Top Bottleneck

Problem

Have you ever been approached by a customer or coworker who reports that "SQL Server is running slow"? When you ask for more details, that person may not be able to properly articulate the performance issue, or may attribute the issue to some random change or event without having any real evidence to back it up.

Solution

In this situation, your number one tool for identifying and narrowing down the field of possible explanations is the sys.dm_os_wait_stats DMV. This DMV provides a running total of all waits encountered by executing threads in the SQL Server instance. Each time SQL Server is restarted, or if you manually clear the statistics, the data is reset to zero and accumulates over the uptime of the SQL Server instance.

SQL Server categorizes these waits across several different types. Some of these types only indicate quiet periods on the instance where threads lay in waiting, whereas other wait types indicate external or internal contention on specific resources.

■ **Tip** The technique described here is part of the Waits and Queues methodology. An in-depth discussion of this methodology can be found under the Technical White Papers section at http://technet.microsoft.com/en-us/sqlserver/bb671430.

The following recipe shows the top two wait types that have accumulated for the SQL Server instance since it was last cleared or since the instance started (the waits in the exclusion list are not comprehensive, and rather are just an example of what can be excluded). See the following:

```
USE AdventureWorks2014;
GO
SELECT  TOP 2
wait_type, wait_time_ms FROM sys.dm_os_wait_stats WHERE wait_type NOT IN
('LAZYWRITER_SLEEP', 'SQLTRACE_BUFFER_FLUSH', 'REQUEST_FOR_DEADLOCK_SEARCH', 'LOGMGR_QUEUE'
, 'CHECKPOINT_QUEUE', 'CLR_AUTO_EVENT','WAITFOR', 'BROKER_TASK_STOP', 'SLEEP_TASK',
'BROKER_TO_FLUSH'
,'HADR_FILESTREAM_IOMGR_IOCOMPLETION','SQLTRACE_INCREMENTAL_FLUSH_SLEEP',
'QDS_CLEANUP_STALE_QUERIES_TASK_MAIN_LOOP_SLEEP'
,'DIRTY_PAGE_POLL','XE_TIMER_EVENT','QDS_PERSIST_TASK_MAIN_LOOP_SLEEP')
ORDER BY wait_time_ms DESC;
```

This returns the following (your results will vary based on your SQL Server activity):

wait_type	wait_time_ms
LCK_M_U	31989
LCK_M_S	12133

In this case, the top two waits for the SQL Server instance are related to requests waiting to acquire update and shared locks. You can interpret these wait types by looking them up in SQL Server Books Online or in the Waits and Queues white papers published by Microsoft. In this recipe's case, the top two wait types are often associated with long-running blocks. This result is an indication that if an application is having performance issues, you would be wise to start looking for additional evidence of long-running blocks using more granular tools (DMVs, SQL Profiler). The key purpose of looking at sys.dm_os_wait_stats is that you troubleshoot the predominant issue, not just the root cause of an unrelated issue or something that is a lower-priority issue.

If you want to clear the currently accumulated wait-type statistics, you can then run the following query:

```
DBCC SQLPERF ('sys.dm_os_wait_stats', CLEAR);
```

Clearing the wait-type statistics allows you to later provide a delta of accumulated wait statistics based on a defined period of time.

How It Works

This recipe demonstrated using the sys.dm_os_wait_stats DMV to help determine what the predominant wait stats were for the SQL Server instance.

The SELECT clause chose the wait type and wait time (in milliseconds) columns:

```
SELECT  TOP 2
wait_type, wait_time_ms FROM sys.dm_os_wait_stats
```

Since not all wait types are necessarily indicators of real issues, the WHERE clause was used to filter out nonexternal or nonresource waits (although this isn't a definitive list of those wait types you would need to filter out). See the following:

```
WHERE wait_type NOT IN
('LAZYWRITER_SLEEP', 'SQLTRACE_BUFFER_FLUSH', 'REQUEST_FOR_DEADLOCK_SEARCH', 'LOGMGR_QUEUE'
, 'CHECKPOINT_QUEUE', 'CLR_AUTO_EVENT','WAITFOR', 'BROKER_TASK_STOP', 'SLEEP_TASK',
'BROKER_TO_FLUSH'
,'HADR_FILESTREAM_IOMGR_IOCOMPLETION','SQLTRACE_INCREMENTAL_FLUSH_SLEEP',
'QDS_CLEANUP_STALE_QUERIES_TASK_MAIN_LOOP_SLEEP'
,'DIRTY_PAGE_POLL','XE_TIMER_EVENT','QDS_PERSIST_TASK_MAIN_LOOP_SLEEP')
ORDER BY wait_time_ms DESC;
```

The DMV's data is grouped at the instance level, not at the database level, so it is a good first step in your performance troubleshooting mission. It is *not* your end-all be-all solution, but rather a very useful tool for helping point you in the right direction when troubleshooting a poorly defined performance issue. This DMV also comes in handy for establishing trends over time. If a new wait type arises, it may be a leading indicator of a new performance issue.

22-8. Identifying I/O Contention by Database and File

Problem

Assume for a moment that you queried sys.dm_os_wait_stats and found that most of your waits are attributed to I/O. Since the wait stats are scoped at the SQL Server instance level, you now need to identify which databases are experiencing the highest amount of I/O contention.

Solution

One method you can use to determine which databases have the highest number of read, write, and I/O stall behaviors is the sys.dm_io_virtual_file_stats DMV (this DMV shows data that is equivalent to the fn_virtualfilestats function).

This recipe demonstrates viewing database I/O statistics, ordered by I/O stalls. I/O stalls are measured in milliseconds and represent the total time users had to wait for read or write I/O operations to complete on a file since the instance was last restarted or the database was created:

```
USE master;
GO
SELECT DB_NAME(ifs.database_id) AS DBName,
ifs.file_id AS FileID,
mf.type_desc AS FileType,
io_stall AS IOStallsMs,
size_on_disk_bytes AS FileBytes,
num_of_bytes_written AS BytesWritten,
num_of_bytes_read AS BytesRead,
```

```
io_stall_queued_read_ms AS RGStallReadMS,
io_stall_queued_write_ms AS RGStallWriteMS
FROM sys.dm_io_virtual_file_stats(NULL, NULL) ifs
    Inner Join sys.master_files mf
        On ifs.database_id = mf.database_id
        And ifs.file_id = mf.file_id
ORDER BY io_stall DESC;
```

This query returns (your results will vary):

DBName	FileID	FileType	IOStallsMs	FileBytes	BytesWritten
AdventureWorks2014	1	ROWS	179475	209453056	25501696
msdb	1	ROWS	90742	14417920	1048576
master	1	ROWS	62727	4194304	2785280
tempdb	1	ROWS	37860	8388608	10854400
model	1	ROWS	19647	3211264	720896
AdventureWorks2014	2	LOG	5190	12648448	18268160
tempdb	2	LOG	1245	1310720	5873664
AdventureWorks2014	3	ROWS	626	1048576	139264
msdb	2	LOG	266	786432	561152
model	2	LOG	234	786432	512000
master	2	LOG	224	786432	1028096

How It Works

This recipe demonstrated using the sys.dm_io_virtual_file_stats DMV to return statistics about each database and file on the SQL Server instance. This DMV takes two input parameters: the first is the database ID, and the second is the file ID. Designating NULL for the database ID shows results for all databases. Designating NULL for the file ID results in showing all files for the database.

In this recipe, I designated that all databases and associated files be returned:

```
FROM sys.dm_io_virtual_file_stats(NULL, NULL)
```

I also ordered the I/O stalls in descending order so as to see the files with the most I/O delay activity first:

```
ORDER BY io_stall DESC
```

These results showed that the highest number of stalls were seen on file ID 1 for the AdventureWorks2014 database, which in this example is one of the data files. If you have identified that I/O is the predominant performance issue, using sys.dm_io_virtual_file_stats is an efficient method for narrowing down which databases and files should be the focus of your troubleshooting efforts.

This recipe also introduced two new fields that are new as of SQL Server 2014: io_stall_queued_read_ms and io_stall_queued_write_ms. These fields will help determine the latency that is attributed to the use of Resource Governor. Resource governor will be discussed in more detail later in this chapter in other recipes.

Miscellaneous Techniques

The next several recipes detail techniques that don't cleanly fall under any of the previous sections in this chapter. These recipes will demonstrate how to do the following:

- Employ an alternative to dynamic SQL and stored procedures using the sp_executesql system stored procedure

- Force a query to use a specified query plan

- Apply query hints to an existing query without having to actually modify the application's SQL code using plan guides

- Create a plan guide based on a pointer to the cached plan

- Check the validity of a plan guide (in case reference objects have rendered the plan invalid)

- Force parameterization of a nonparameterized query

- Use the Resource Governor feature to limit query resource consumption (for both CPU and memory)

I'll start this section by describing an alternative to using dynamic SQL.

22-9. Parameterizing Ad Hoc Queries

Problem

You have an application that performs queries using dynamic SQL and ad hoc queries. You are required to provide a means of preventing SQL injection for use by this application.

Solution

If stored procedures are not an option for your application, an alternative, the sp_executesql system stored procedure, addresses the dynamic SQL performance issue by allowing you to create and use a reusable query execution plan where the only items that change are the query parameters. Parameters are also type safe, meaning you cannot use them to hold unintended data types. This is a worthy solution when given a choice between ad hoc statements and stored procedures.

Using the EXECUTE command, you can execute the contents of a character string within a batch, procedure, or function. You can also abbreviate EXECUTE to EXEC.

For example, the following statement performs a SELECT from the Sales.Currency table:

```
EXEC ('SELECT CurrencyCode FROM Sales.Currency')
```

Although this technique allows you to dynamically formulate strings that can then be executed, this technique has some major hazards. The first and most concerning hazard is the risk of SQL injection. SQL injection occurs when harmful code is inserted into an existing SQL string prior to it being executed on the SQL Server instance. Allowing user input into variables that are concatenated to a SQL string and then executed can cause all sorts of damage to your database (not to mention the potential privacy issues). The malicious code, if executed under a context with sufficient permissions, can drop tables, read sensitive data, or even shut down the SQL Server process.

The second issue with character-string execution techniques concerns their performance. Although the performance of dynamically generated SQL may sometimes be fast, the query performance can also be unreliable. Unlike with stored procedures, dynamically generated and regular ad hoc SQL batches and statements will cause SQL Server to generate a new execution plan each time they are run.

▪ **Caution**   sp_executesql addresses some performance issues but does not entirely address the SQL injection issue. Beware of allowing user-passed parameters that are concatenated into a SQL string! Stick with the parameter functionality described next.

The syntax for sp_executesql is as follows:

```
sp_executesql [ @stmt = ] stmt
[
        {, [@params=] N'@parameter_name data_type [ OUT | OUTPUT ][,...n]' }
        {, [ @param1 = ] 'value1' [ ,...n ] }
]

 sp_executesql [ (@stmt = ] stmt [
{, [|@params=] N'@parameter_name data_type [ OUT | OUTPUT ][,...n]' } {, [ (@param1 = ]
'value1' [ ,...n ] } ]
```

Table 22-1 describes the arguments of this command.

Table 22-1. sp_executesql *Arguments*

Argument	Description
stmt	The string to be executed
@parameter_name data_type [[OUTPUT][,...n]	One or more parameters that are embedded in the string statement. OUTPUT is used similarly to a stored procedure OUTPUT parameter.
'value1' [,...n]	The actual values passed to the parameters

In this example, the Production.TransactionHistoryArchive table is queried based on a specific ProductID, TransactionType, and minimum Quantity values:

```
USE AdventureWorks2014;
GO
EXECUTE sp_executesql N'SELECT TransactionID, ProductID, TransactionType, Quantity FROM
Production.TransactionHistoryArchive WHERE    ProductID = @ProductID AND
TransactionType = @TransactionType AND Quantity > @Quantity', N'@ProductID int,
@TransactionType char(1), @Quantity int', @ProductID =813, @TransactionType = 'S',
@Quantity = 5
;
```

This returns the following results (your results will vary):

TransactionID	ProductID	TransactionType	Quantity
28345	813	S	7
31177	813	S	9
35796	813	S	6
36112	813	S	7
40765	813	S	6
47843	813	S	7
69114	813	S	6
73432	813	S	6

How It Works

The sp_executesql procedure allows you to execute a dynamically generated Unicode string. This system stored procedure allows parameters, which in turn allow SQL Server to reuse the query execution plan generated by its execution.

Notice in the recipe that the first parameter was preceded with the N' Unicode prefix, because sp_executesql requires a Unicode statement string. The first parameter also included the SELECT query itself, as well as the parameters embedded in the WHERE clause:

```
USE AdventureWorks2014;
GO
EXECUTE sp_executesql N'SELECT TransactionID, ProductID, TransactionType, Quantity FROM
Production.TransactionHistoryArchive WHERE ProductID = @ProductID AND
TransactionType = @TransactionType AND Quantity > @Quantity',
```

The second argument further defined the data type of each parameter that was embedded in the first parameter's SQL statement. Each parameter is separated by a comma:

```
N'@ProductID int,
@TransactionType char(1),
@Quantity int',
```

The last argument assigned each embedded parameter a value, which was put into the query dynamically during execution:

```
@ProductID =813,
@TransactionType = 'S',
@Quantity = 5
```

The query returned eight rows based on the three parameters provided. If the query is executed again, but with different parameter values, it is likely that the original query execution plan will be used by SQL Server (instead of a new execution plan being created).

22-10. Forcing the Use of a Query Plan

Problem

You suspect that a less than optimal query plan is being used for a poorly performing query. You want to test the query by using different query plans.

Solution

The USE PLAN command allows you to force the query optimizer to use an existing, specific query plan for a SELECT query. You can use this functionality to override SQL Server's choice in those rare circumstances when SQL Server chooses a less efficient query plan over one that is more efficient. Like plan guides (covered later), this option should be used only by an experienced SQL Server professional, because SQL Server's query optimizer usually makes good decisions when deciding whether to reuse or create new query execution plans. The syntax for USE PLAN is as follows:

```
USE PLAN N'xml_plan'
```

The xml_plan parameter is the XML data-type representation of the stored query execution plan. The specific XML query plan can be derived using several methods, including SET SHOWPLAN_XML, SET STATISTICS XML, the sys.dm_exec_query_plan DMV, sys.dm_exec_text_query_plan, and via SQL Server Profiler's Showplan XML events.

In this example, SET STATISTICS XML is used to extract the XML-formatted query plan for use in the USE PLAN command:

```
SET STATISTICS XML ON;
GO
USE AdventureWorks2014;
GO
SELECT TOP 10 Rate
FROM HumanResources.EmployeePayHistory
ORDER BY Rate DESC
SET STATISTICS XML OFF;
```

The XML document results returned from SET STATISTICS XML are then copied to the next query. Note that all the single quotes (') in the XML document have to be escaped with an additional single quote (except for the quotes used for USE PLAN):

```
USE AdventureWorks2014;
GO
SELECT TOP 10 Rate
FROM HumanResources.EmployeePayHistory
ORDER BY Rate DESC
OPTION (USE PLAN
'<ShowPlanXML xmlns="http://schemas.microsoft.com/sqlserver/2004/07/showplan" Version="1.2"
Build="12.0.2000.8">
```

```xml
<BatchSequence>
  <Batch>
    <Statements>
      <StmtSimple StatementText="SELECT TOP 10 Rate&#xD;&#xA;FROM HumanResources.Empl
      oyeePayHistory&#xD;&#xA;ORDER BY Rate DESC" StatementId="1" StatementCompId="1"
      StatementType="SELECT" RetrievedFromCache="true" StatementSubTreeCost="0.019825"
      StatementEstRows="10" StatementOptmLevel="TRIVIAL" QueryHash="0xF837F06798E85035"
      QueryPlanHash="0x65B8DEE1A2B5457C" CardinalityEstimationModelVersion="120">
        <StatementSetOptions QUOTED_IDENTIFIER="true" ARITHABORT="true"
        CONCAT_NULL_YIELDS_NULL="true" ANSI_NULLS="true" ANSI_PADDING="true"
        ANSI_WARNINGS="true" NUMERIC_ROUNDABORT="false" />
        <QueryPlan DegreeOfParallelism="1" MemoryGrant="1024" CachedPlanSize="16"
        CompileTime="0" CompileCPU="0" CompileMemory="96">
          <MemoryGrantInfo SerialRequiredMemory="16" SerialDesiredMemory="24"
          RequiredMemory="16" DesiredMemory="24" RequestedMemory="1024" GrantWaitTime="0"
          GrantedMemory="1024" MaxUsedMemory="16" />
          <OptimizerHardwareDependentProperties EstimatedAvailableMemoryGrant="30720"
          EstimatedPagesCached="15360" EstimatedAvailableDegreeOfParallelism="4" />
          <RelOp NodeId="0" PhysicalOp="Sort" LogicalOp="TopN Sort" EstimateRows="10"
          EstimateIO="0.0112613" EstimateCPU="0.00419345" AvgRowSize="15"
          EstimatedTotalSubtreeCost="0.019825" Parallel="0" EstimateRebinds="0"
          EstimateRewinds="0" EstimatedExecutionMode="Row">
            <OutputList>
              <ColumnReference Database="[AdventureWorks2014]" Schema="[HumanResources]"
              Table="[EmployeePayHistory]" Column="Rate" />
            </OutputList>
            <MemoryFractions Input="1" Output="1" />
            <RunTimeInformation>
              <RunTimeCountersPerThread Thread="0" ActualRows="10" ActualRebinds="1"
              ActualRewinds="0" ActualEndOfScans="1" ActualExecutions="1" />
            </RunTimeInformation>
            <TopSort Distinct="0" Rows="10">
              <OrderBy>
                <OrderByColumn Ascending="0">
                  <ColumnReference Database="[AdventureWorks2014]"
                  Schema="[HumanResources]" Table="[EmployeePayHistory]" Column="Rate" />
                </OrderByColumn>
              </OrderBy>
              <RelOp NodeId="1" PhysicalOp="Clustered Index Scan"
              LogicalOp="Clustered Index Scan" EstimateRows="316"
              EstimateIO="0.00386574" EstimateCPU="0.0005046" AvgRowSize="15"
              EstimatedTotalSubtreeCost="0.00437034" TableCardinality="316" Parallel="0"
              EstimateRebinds="0" EstimateRewinds="0" EstimatedExecutionMode="Row">
                <OutputList>
                  <ColumnReference Database="[AdventureWorks2014]"
                  Schema="[HumanResources]" Table="[EmployeePayHistory]" Column="Rate" />
                </OutputList>
                <RunTimeInformation>
                  <RunTimeCountersPerThread Thread="0" ActualRows="316"
                  ActualEndOfScans="1" ActualExecutions="1" />
                </RunTimeInformation>
```

```
            <IndexScan Ordered="0" ForcedIndex="0" ForceScan="0" NoExpandHint="0"
            Storage="RowStore">
              <DefinedValues>
                <DefinedValue>
                  <ColumnReference Database="[AdventureWorks2014]"
                  Schema="[HumanResources]" Table="[EmployeePayHistory]" Column="Rate" />
                </DefinedValue>
              </DefinedValues>
              <Object Database="[AdventureWorks2014]" Schema="[HumanResources]"
              Table="[EmployeePayHistory]" Index="[PK_EmployeePayHistory_
              BusinessEntityID_RateChangeDate]" IndexKind="Clustered"
              Storage="RowStore" />
            </IndexScan>
          </RelOp>
        </TopSort>
      </RelOp>
    </QueryPlan>
  </StmtSimple>
 </Statements>
 </Batch>
 </BatchSequence>
</ShowPlanXML>');
```

How It Works

USE PLAN allows you to capture the XML format of a query's execution plan and then force the query to use it on subsequent executions. In this recipe, I used SET STATISTICS XML ON to capture the query's XML execution plan definition. That definition was then copied into the OPTION clause. The USE PLAN hint requires a Unicode format, so the XML document text was prefixed with an N'.

Both USE PLAN and plan guides should be used only as a *last resort* after you have thoroughly explored other possibilities, such as query design, indexing, database design, index fragmentation, and out-of-date statistics. USE PLAN may have short-term effectiveness, but as data changes, so too will the needs of the query execution plan. In the end, the odds are that, over time, SQL Server will be better able, than you, to dynamically decide on the correct SQL plan. Nevertheless, Microsoft provided this option for those advanced troubleshooting cases when SQL Server doesn't choose a query execution plan that's good enough.

22-11. Applying Hints Without Modifying a SQL Statement

Problem

You are experiencing performance issues in a database in which you are not permitted to make code changes.

Solution

As was discussed at the beginning of this chapter, troubleshooting poor query performance involves reviewing many areas, such as database design, indexing, and query construction. You can make modifications to your code, but what if the problem is with code that you *cannot* change?

If you are encountering issues with a database and/or queries that are not your own to change (in shrink-wrapped software, for example), then your options become more limited. In the case of third-party software, you are usually restricted to adding new indexes or archiving data from large tables. Making changes to the vendor's actual database objects or queries is most likely off-limits.

SQL Server provides a solution to this common issue that uses plan guides. Plan guides allow you to apply hints to a query without having to change the actual query text sent from the application.

■ **Tip** In SQL Server 2014, you can designate both query and table hints within plan guides.

Plan guides can be applied to specific queries that are embedded within database objects (stored procedures, functions, triggers) or to specific stand-alone SQL statements.

A plan guide is created using the sp_create_plan_guide system stored procedure:

```
sp_create_plan_guide [ @name = ] N'plan_guide_name'
    , [ @stmt = ] N'statement_text'
    , [ @type = ] N' { OBJECT | SQL | TEMPLATE }'
    , [ @module_or_batch = ]
        {
        N'[ schema_name.]object_name'
        | N'batch_text'
        | NULL
        }
    , [ @params = ] { N'@parameter_name data_type [,...n ]' | NULL }
    , [ @hints = ] { N'OPTION ( query_hint [,...n ] ) ' | N'XML_showplan' | NULL }
```

Table 22-2 describes the arguments of this command.

Table 22-2. sp_create_plan_guide Arguments

Argument	Description
plan_guide_name	This defines the name of the new plan guide.
statement_text	This specifies the SQL text identified for optimization.
OBJECT | SQL | TEMPLATE	When OBJECT is selected, the plan guide will apply to the statement text found within a specific stored procedure, function, or DML trigger. When SQL is selected, the plan guide will apply to statement text found in a stand-alone statement or batch. The TEMPLATE option is used to either enable or disable parameterization for a SQL statement. Note that the PARAMETERIZATION option, when set to FORCED, increases the chance that a query will become parameterized, allowing it to form a reusable query execution plan. SIMPLE parameterization, however, affects a smaller number of queries (at SQL Server's discretion). The TEMPLATE option is used to override a database's SIMPLE or FORCED parameterization option. If a database is using SIMPLE parameterization, you can force a specific query statement to be parameterized. If a database is using FORCED parameterization, you can force a specific query statement to *not* be parameterized.

(continued)

Table 22-2. (*continued*)

Argument	Description
N'[schema_name.]object_name' | N'batch_text' | NULL	This specifies the name of the object the SQL text will be in, the batch text, or NULL, when TEMPLATE is selected.
N'@parameter_name data_type [,...n]' | NULL N'OPTION (query_hint [,...n])' | N'XML_showplan' | NULL	This defines the name of the parameters to be used for either SQL or TEMPLATE plan guide types. This defines the hint or hints to be applied to the statement, the XML query plan to be applied, or NULL, which is used to indicate that the OPTION clause will not be employed for a query.

■ **Note** In SQL Server 2014, the @hints argument accepts XML Showplan output as direct input.

To remove or disable a plan guide, use the sp_control_plan_guide system stored procedure:

```
sp_control_plan_guide [ @operation = ] N'<control_option>'
    [ , [ @name = ] N'plan_guide_name' ]

<control_option>::=
{
      DROP
    | DROP ALL
    | DISABLE
    | DISABLE ALL
    | ENABLE
    | ENABLE ALL
}
```

Table 22-3 describes the arguments of this command.

Table 22-3. *sp_control_plan_guide Arguments*

Argument	Description
DROP	The DROP operation removes the plan guide from the database.
DROP ALL	DROP ALL drops all plan guides from the database.
DISABLE	DISABLE disables the plan guide but doesn't remove it from the database.
DISABLE ALL	DISABLE ALL disables all plan guides in the database.
ENABLE	ENABLE enables a disabled plan guide.
ENABLE ALL	ENABLE ALL does so for all disabled plan guides in the database.
plan_guide_name	plan_guide_name defines the name of the plan guide on which to perform the operation.

In this recipe's example, I'll create a plan guide in order to change the table join type for a stand-alone query. In this scenario, assume the third-party software package is sending a query that is causing a LOOP join. In this scenario, I want the query to use a MERGE join instead.

■ **Caution** SQL Server should almost always be left to make its own decisions regarding how a query is processed. Only under special circumstances (and only when administered by an experienced SQL Server professional) should plan guides be created in your SQL Server environment.

In this example, the following query is executed using sp_executesql:

```
USE AdventureWorks2014;
GO
EXEC sp_executesql
N'SELECT v.Name ,a.City
FROM Purchasing.Vendor v
INNER JOIN [Person].BusinessEntityAddress bea
ON bea.BusinessEntityID = v.BusinessEntityID
INNER JOIN Person.Address a
ON a.AddressID = bea.AddressID';;
```

Looking at a snippet of this query's execution plan using SET STATISTICS XML ON shows that the Vendor and BusinessEntityAddress tables are joined together through the use of a nested loop operator.

```
<RelOp AvgRowSize="93" EstimateCPU="0.000440767" EstimateIO="0" EstimateRebinds="0"
EstimateRewinds="0" EstimatedExecutionMode="Row" EstimateRows="105.447"
LogicalOp="Inner Join" NodeId="0" Parallel="false" PhysicalOp="Nested Loops"
EstimatedTotalSubtreeCost="0.323111">
```

If, for example, I want SQL Server to use a different join method, but without having to change the actual query sent by the application, I can enforce this change by creating a plan guide. The following plan guide is created to apply a join hint to the query being sent from the application:

```
USE AdventureWorks2014;
GO
EXEC sp_create_plan_guide
@name = N'Vendor_Query_Loop_to_Merge',
@stmt =
N'SELECT v.Name ,a.City
FROM Purchasing.Vendor v
INNER JOIN [Person].BusinessEntityAddress bea
ON bea.BusinessEntityID = v.BusinessEntityID
INNER JOIN Person.Address a
ON a.AddressID = bea.AddressID',
@type = N'SQL', @module_or_batch = NULL, @params = NULL, @hints = N'OPTION (MERGE JOIN)';
```

■ **Tip** Since SQL Server 2008, you can also designate *table* hints in the plan guide @hints parameter.

I can confirm that the plan guide was created (as well as confirm the settings) by querying the sys. plan_guides catalog view:

```
USE AdventureWorks2014;
GO
SELECT name, is_disabled, scope_type_desc, hints
FROM sys.plan_guides;
```

This query returns the following:

name	is_disabled	scope_type_desc	hints
Vendor_Query_Loop_to_Merge	0	SQL	OPTION (MERGE JOIN)

After creating the plan guide, I execute the query again using sp_executesql. Looking at the XML execution plan, I now see that the nested loop joins have changed into merge join operators—all without changing the actual query being sent from the application to SQL Server.

```
<RelOp AvgRowSize="93" EstimateCPU="0.0470214" EstimateIO="0" EstimateRebinds="0"
EstimateRewinds="0" EstimatedExecutionMode="Row" EstimateRows="105.447"
LogicalOp="Inner Join" NodeId="0" Parallel="false" PhysicalOp="Merge Join"
EstimatedTotalSubtreeCost="0.495179">
```

In fact, all joins in the query were converted from loops to merge joins, which may not be a desired effect of designating the hint for a multijoin statement! If it is decided that this merge join is no longer more effective than a nested loop join, you can drop the plan guide using the sp_control_plan_guide system stored procedure, as follows:

```
USE AdventureWorks2014;
GO
EXEC sp_control_plan_guide N'DROP', N'Vendor_Query_Loop_to_Merge';
```

How It Works

Plan guides allow you to add query hints to a query being sent from an application without having to change the application itself. In this example, a particular SQL statement was performing nested loop joins. Without changing the actual query, SQL Server "sees" the plan guide and matches the incoming query to the query in the plan guide. When matched, the hints in the plan guide are applied to the incoming query.

The sp_create_plan_guide stored procedure allows you to create plans for stand-alone SQL statements, SQL statements within objects (procedures, functions, DML triggers), and SQL statements that are either being parameterized or not, because of the database's PARAMETERIZATION setting.

In this recipe, the first parameter sent to sp_create_plan_guide was the name of the new plan guide:

```
USE AdventureWorks2014;
GO
EXEC sp_create_plan_guide
@name = N'Vendor_Query_Loop_to_Merge',
```

The second parameter was the SQL statement to apply the plan guide to (whitespace characters, comments, and semicolons will be ignored):

```
@stmt =
N'SELECT v.Name ,a.City
FROM Purchasing.Vendor v
INNER JOIN [Person].BusinessEntityAddress bea
ON bea.BusinessEntityID = v.BusinessEntityID
INNER JOIN Person.Address a
ON a.AddressID = bea.AddressID',
```

The third parameter was the type of plan guide, which in this case was stand-alone SQL:

```
@type = N'SQL',
```

For the fourth parameter, since it was not for a stored procedure, function, or trigger, the @module_or_batch parameter was NULL:

```
@module_or_batch = NULL,
```

The @params parameter was also sent NULL since this was not a TEMPLATE plan guide:

```
@params = NULL,
```

The last parameter contained the actual hint to apply to the incoming query—in this case forcing all joins in the query to use a MERGE operation:

```
@hints = N'OPTION (MERGE JOIN)'
```

Finally, the sp_control_plan_guide system stored procedure was used to drop the plan guide from the database, designating the operation of DROP in the first parameter and the plan guide name in the second parameter.

22-12. Creating Plan Guides from Cache

Problem

You are planning the migration of a database to a new server. You want to ensure that a particular query continues to perform the same on the new server as it does the current server.

Solution

In SQL Server (since SQL Server 2008), you have the ability to create plan guides based on existing query plans found in the query plan cache. You do this by using the sp_create_plan_guide_from_handle system stored procedure. Consider using this functionality under the following circumstances:

- You need a query plan (or plans) to remain stable after an upgrade or database migration.

- You have a specific query that uses a "bad" plan, and you want it to use a known "good" plan.

- Your application has mission-critical queries that have service-level agreements regarding specific response times, and you want to keep those times stable.

- You need to reproduce the exact query execution plan on another SQL Server instance (test or QA, for example).

- You have a query that needs to execute predictably but not necessarily perform as optimally as it always could.

■ **Caution** You should almost always let SQL Server compile and recompile plans as needed instead of relying on plan guides. SQL Server can adapt to any new changes in the data distribution and objects referenced in the query by recompiling an existing plan when appropriate.

The syntax for the sp_create_plan_guide_from_handle system stored procedure is as follows:

```
sp_create_plan_guide_from_handle [ @name = ] N'plan_guide_name' , [ @plan_handle = ]
plan_handle , [ [ @statement_start_offset = ] { statement_start_offset | NULL } ]
```

Table 22-4 describes the arguments of this command.

Table 22-4. sp_create_plan_guide_from_handle Arguments

Argument	Description
plan_guide_name	This defines the name of the new plan guide.
plan_handle	This designates the plan handle from the sys.dm_exec_query_stats DMV.
statement_start_offset | NULL	The statement start offset designates the starting position within the query batch. If NULL, the query plan for each statement in the batch will have a plan guide created for it.

This functionality allows you to preserve desired query plans for future reuse on the SQL Server instance. In this recipe, I'll demonstrate creating a plan guide from the cache for the following query (which I will execute first in order to get a plan created in cache):

```
USE AdventureWorks2014;
GO
SELECT
p.Title,
p.FirstName,
p.MiddleName,
p.LastName
FROM HumanResources.Employee e
INNER JOIN Person.Person p
ON p.BusinessEntityID = e.BusinessEntityID
WHERE Title = 'Ms.';
GO
```

After executing the query, I can retrieve the plan handle pointing to the query plan in the cache by executing the following query:

```
USE AdventureWorks2014;
GO
SELECT plan_handle
FROM sys.dm_exec_query_stats qs
CROSS APPLY sys.dm_exec_sql_text(plan_handle) t
WHERE t.text LIKE 'SELECT%p.Title%'
AND t.text LIKE '%Ms%';
```

This query returns the following (your results will vary):

```
Plan_handle
0x06000800AEC42626F0F03B020100000001000000000000000000000000000000000000000000000000000000000000
```

Next, I will create a plan guide based on the plan handle (returned in the previous query) using the sp_create_plan_guide_from_handle system stored procedure:

```
EXEC sp_create_plan_guide_from_handle 'PlanGuide_EmployeeContact',
@plan_handle = 0x06000600AEC426269009DAFC020000000100000000000000000000000000000000000000000
00000000000000,
@statement_start_offset = NULL;
```

Querying the sys.plan_handles system catalog view, I can confirm that the plan guide was created properly (results not displayed, because of the query plan and text display issues on the printed page). See here:

```
USE AdventureWorks2014;
GO
SELECT name, query_text, hints
FROM sys.plan_guides;
```

The hints column from sys.plan_guides actually contains the query execution plan in XML format.

■ **Tip** You can confirm whether your plan guide is being successfully used by tracking the SQL Server Profiler events "Plan Guide Successful" and "Plan Guide Unsuccessful."

How It Works

This recipe demonstrated how to preserve an existing cached plan as a plan guide. This is the execution plan that will be used for the query matching the query text of the plan guide. Even after a SQL Server instance restart or the flushing of the procedure cache, the associated plan guide query plan will still be used.

I started off the recipe by executing the SELECT query so that a query plan would be cached on the SQL Server instance. After doing that, I can search for the plan handle of the cached plan by querying sys.dm_exec_query_stats. I also used CROSS APPLY with sys.dm_exec_sql_text so that I could search for text that contained the start and end of my query.

Once I had the plan handle, I executed the sp_create_plan_guide_from_handle system stored procedure. The first parameter was the name of the plan guide:

```
EXEC sp_create_plan_guide_from_handle 'PlanGuide_EmployeeContact',
```

The second parameter contains the plan handle (note that I could have placed the plan handle in a local variable and then fed it to the stored procedure in a single batch with the sys.dm_exec_query_stats query).

Lastly, I designated the statement start offset as NULL. This is because the cached plan contained only a single statement. If this were a multistatement batch, I could have used this parameter to designate the statement start offset number:

```
@statement_start_offset = NULL
```

Once the plan guide is created, any matching SQL that is executed will use the query execution plan designated in the plan guide (look at the hints column of the sys.plan_guides system catalog view to confirm). This allows you to keep a plan stable across several scenarios—for example, after a database migration to a new SQL Server instance, service pack upgrade, or version upgrade. Highly volatile query execution plans (recompiled often with varying execution plan performance impacts) can benefit from the "freezing" of the most efficient or best-performing plan for the associated query.

22-13. Checking the Validity of a Plan Guide

Problem

You want to confirm that existing plan guides are still valid after having made significant object changes in the database.

Solution

Use the system function sys.fn_validate_plan_guide, which allows you to check the validity of existing plan guides. SQL Server typically does a great job of compiling and recompiling query execution plans based on changes to objects referenced within a query. Plan guides, on the other hand, are not automatically modified based on changing circumstances.

The sys.fn_validate_plan_guide is a table-valued function that takes a single argument, the plan_guide_id. In this recipe, I demonstrate validating all plan guides within the database context I am interested in (for example, AdventureWorks2014):

```
USE AdventureWorks2014;
GO
SELECT pg.plan_guide_id, pg.name, v.msgnum,
v.severity, v.state, v.message
FROM sys.plan_guides pg
CROSS APPLY sys.fn_validate_plan_guide(pg.plan_guide_id) v;
```

If this query returns no rows, it means there are no errors with existing plan guides. If rows are generated, you will need to recreate a valid plan guide based on the changed circumstances.

How It Works

This recipe demonstrated how to check the validity of each plan guide in a specific database. The SELECT statement referenced the plan guide ID and name, along with the message number, severity, state, and message if errors exist:

```
SELECT pg.plan_guide_id, pg.name, v.msgnum, v.severity, v.state, v.message
```

The FROM clause included sys.plan_guides, which returns all plan guides for the database context:

```
FROM sys.plan_guides pg
```

Since this is a table-valued function expecting an input argument, I used CROSS APPLY against sys.fn_validate_plan_guide and used the plan guide from sys.plan_guides as input:

```
CROSS APPLY sys.fn_validate_plan_guide(pg.plan_guide_id) v
```

This query returns rows for any plan guides invalidated because of underlying object changes.

22-14. Parameterizing a Nonparameterized Query Using Plan Guides

Problem

You have been monitoring server health and have noticed that there is a very large query cache filled with nearly identical queries.

Solution

When I am evaluating the overall performance of a SQL Server instance, I like to take a look at the sys.dm_exec_cached_plans DMV to see what kind of plans are cached on the SQL Server instance. In particular, I'm interested in the objtype column and seeing whether the applications using the SQL Server instance are using mostly prepared statements, stored procedures, or ad hoc queries.

For applications that make heavy use of ad hoc queries, I'll often see a very large query cache filled with nearly identical queries. For example, the following query shows the object type and associated query text:

```
USE AdventureWorks2014;
GO
SELECT cp.objtype, AdHocText
FROM sys.dm_exec_cached_plans cp
CROSS APPLY (SELECT text AS [processing-instruction(definition)]
            FROM sys.dm_exec_sql_text(cp.plan_handle) st
            WHERE st.text LIKE 'SELECT BusinessEntityID%'
            FOR XML PATH(''), TYPE
    ) AS st(AdHocText)
WHERE st.AdHocText IS NOT NULL;
GO
```

In my database, I see three rows returned.

```
objtype      AdHocText
Adhoc    SELECT BusinessEntityID
         FROMHumanResources.Employee
         WHERE NationalIDNumber = 509647174
Adhoc    SELECT BusinessEntityID
         FROM HumanResources.Employee
         WHERE NationalIDNumber = 245797967
Adhoc    SELECT BusinessEntityID
         FROM HumanResources.Employee
         WHERE NationalIDNumber = 295847284
```

Notice that each row is almost identical, except that the NationallDNumber value is different. Ideally, this form of query should be encapsulated in a stored procedure or be called using sp_executesql in order to prevent identical plans in the cache and to encourage plan reuse.

If you cannot control the form in which queries are called by the execution, one option you have is to use a plan guide to force parameterization of the query, which I will demonstrate in this recipe.

In Recipe 22-11, I introduced the sp_create_plan_guide system stored procedure. The TEMPLATE option in that procedure is used to override a database's SIMPLE or FORCED parameterization option. If a database is using SIMPLE parameterization, you can force a specific query statement to be parameterized. If a database is using FORCED parameterization, you can force a specific query statement to *not* be parameterized.

The sp_get_query_template system stored procedure makes deploying template plan guides a little easier by taking a query and outputting the parameterized form of it for use by sp_create_ plan_guide. The syntax for this procedure is as follows:

```
sp_get_query_template
[ @querytext = ] N'query_text' , @templatetext OUTPUT , @parameters OUTPUT
```

Table 22-5 describes the arguments of this command.

Table 22-5. sp_get_query_template Arguments

Argument	Description
querytext	The query you want to parameterize
templatetext	The output parameter containing the parameterized form of the query
parameters	The output parameter containing the list of parameter names and data types

In this recipe, I'll start by populating the template SQL and parameters using sp_get_query_template and then I will send these values to sp_create_plan_guide (I'll walk through the code step by step in the "How It Works" section). See here:

```
DECLARE @sql  nvarchar(max) DECLARE @parms nvarchar(max)
EXEC sp_get_query_template
N'SELECT BusinessEntityID FROM HumanResources.Employee WHERE NationalIDNumber = 295847284',
@sql OUTPUT,
@parms OUTPUT;

EXEC sp_create_plan_guide N'PG_Employee_Contact_Ouery', @sql,
N'TEMPLATE', NULL, @parms, N'OPTION(PARAMETERIZATION FORCED)';
```

After the plan guide is created, I can execute three different versions of the same query (with three different values for NationalIDNumber—each executed separately and not as part of the same batch). See the following:

```
USE AdventureWorks2014;
GO
SELECT BusinessEntityID
        FROM HumanResources.Employee
        WHERE NationalIDNumber = 509647174;
GO
SELECT BusinessEntityID
        FROM HumanResources.Employee
        WHERE NationalIDNumber = 245797967;
GO
SELECT BusinessEntityID
        FROM HumanResources.Employee
        WHERE NationalIDNumber = 295847284;
GO
```

After executing these queries, I will check the cache to see whether there is a prepared plan for this query:

```
USE AdventureWorks2014;
GO
SELECT usecounts,objtype,PreparedText
FROM sys.dm_exec_cached_plans cp
CROSS APPLY (SELECT text AS [processing-instruction(definition)]
            FROM sys.dm_exec_sql_text(cp.plan_handle) st
            WHERE st.text LIKE '%SELECT BusinessEntityID%'
            FOR XML PATH(''), TYPE
        ) AS st(PreparedText)
WHERE st.PreparedText IS NOT NULL
AND objtype = 'Prepared';
```

This returns the number of times the prepared plan has been used (three times since the plan guide was created), the object type, and the parameterized SQL text.

usecounts	objtype	PreparedText
3	Prepared	(@0 int)Select BusinessEntityID from HumanResources.Employee WHERE NationalIDNumber = @0

How It Works

In this recipe, I demonstrated how to force parameterization for a single query. Near-identical queries such as the one I demonstrated can unnecessarily expand the cache, consuming memory and creating excessive compilation operations. By reducing compilation and encouraging the use of prepared plans, you can improve the performance of the query itself and reduce resource consumption on the SQL Server instance.

I started off by declaring two local variables to be used to hold the template SQL and associated parameters:

```
DECLARE @sql nvarchar(max)
DECLARE @parms nvarchar(max)
```

I then executed a call against the sp_get_query_template system stored procedure:

```
EXEC sp_get_query_template
```

The first parameter of this procedure expects the SQL to be converted to template format:

```
N'SELECT BusinessEntityID
FROM HumanResources.Employee
WHERE NationalIDNumber = 295847284',
```

The second parameter is used for the output parameter that will contain the template SQL:

```
@sql OUTPUT,
```

The third parameter is used for the output parameter containing the parameters used in association with the template SQL:

```
@parms OUTPUT
```

Next, I called sp_create_plan_guide to create a plan guide:

```
EXEC sp_create_plan_guide
```

The first parameter of this procedure took the name of the new plan guide:

```
N'PG_Employee_Contact_Query',
```

The second parameter took the value of the template SQL:

```
@sql,
```

The third parameter designated that this would be a TEMPLATE plan guide:

```
N'TEMPLATE',
```

The @module_or_batch parameter was given a NULL value, which is the required value for TEMPLATE plan guides:

```
NULL,
```

The next parameter contained the definition of all parameters associated with the template SQL:

```
@parms,
```

The last parameter designated the hints to attach to the query. In this case, I asked that the query use forced parameterization:

```
N'OPTION(PARAMETERIZATION FORCED)'
```

Once the plan guide was created, I executed the query in three different forms, each with a different NationalIDNumber literal value. I then checked sys.dm_exec_cached_plans to see whether there was a new row for a prepared plan. I confirmed that the usecounts column had a value of 3 (one for each query execution I had just performed), which helped me confirm that the newly parameterized prepared plan was being reused.

22-15. Limiting Competing Query Resource Consumption

Problem

You have various processes that regularly compete for CPU resources. You need to implement a solution that will limit the resource consumption of some of these processes.

Solution

Utilize the Resource Governor to constrain resource consumption for workloads. Resource Governor allows you to define resource pools that constrain the minimum and maximum CPU task-scheduling bandwidth and memory reserved.

■ **Tip** CPU task scheduling is limited only when there is CPU contention across all available schedulers.

SQL Server provides two resource pools out of the box: *default* and *internal*. The internal resource pool, which cannot be modified, uses unrestricted resources for SQL Server ongoing process activity. The default resource pool is used for connections and requests prior to Resource Governor being configured, and by default it has no limitations on resources (although you can change this later).

You can create your own resource pools by using the CREATE RESOURCE POOL command. The syntax for this command is as follows:

```
CREATE RESOURCE POOL pool_name [ WITH
( [ MIN_CPU_PERCENT = value ]
[ [ , ] MAX_CPU_PERCENT = value ]
[ [ , ] CAP_CPU_PERCENT = value ]
[ [ , ] AFFINITY {SCHEDULER = AUTO | (Scheduler_range_spec)
    | NUMANODE = (NUMA_node_range_spec)} ]
[ [ , ] MIN_MEMORY_PERCENT = value ]
[ [ , ] MAX_MEMORY_PERCENT = value ] )]
[ [ , ] MIN_IOPS_PER_VOLUME = value ]
[ [ , ] MAX_IOPS_PER_VOLUME = value ]
```

Table 22-6 describes the arguments of this command.

Table 22-6. CREATE RESOURCE POOL *Arguments*

Argument	Description
Pool_name	This defines the name of the resource pool.
MIN_CPU_PERCENT = value	When there is query contention, this defines a minimum guaranteed average CPU task-scheduling percentage, ranging from 0 to 100.
MAX_CPU_PERCENT = value	When there is query contention, this defines the maximum CPU task-scheduling percentage for all query requests in the resource pool.
CAP_CPU_PERCENT = value	This is a hard cap for CPU task-scheduling percentage that all requests in the resource pool will receive. This is a new option in SQL Server 2012.
AFFINITY {SCHEDULER = AUTO | (Scheduler_range_spec) | NUMANODE = (NUMA_node_range_spec)}	As of SQL Server 2012, this option allows you to specify schedulers for each resource pool.
MIN_MEMORY_PERCENT = value	This specifies the minimum percentage of reserved memory for the resource pool.
MAX_MEMORY_PERCENT = value	This specifies the maximum percentage of server memory that can be used for query requests in the pool.
MIN_IOPS_PER_VOLUME =value	This specifies the minimum boundary to reserve for IO operations (IOPS) per disk volume. Zero is the default.
MAX_IOPS_PER_VOLUME =value	This specifies the upper boundary to reserve for IO operations (IOPS) per disk volume. Zero is the default and specifies an unlimited threshold.

Once you create one or more resource pools, you can then associate them with workload groups. One or more workload groups can be bound to a single resource pool. Workload groups allow you to define the importance of requests within the pool, maximum memory-grant percentage, maximum CPU time in seconds, maximum memory-grant time out, maximum degree of parallelism, and maximum number of concurrently executing requests. You can create resource pools using the CREATE WORKLOAD GROUP command. The syntax for this command is as follows:

```
CREATE WORKLOAD GROUP group_name
[ WITH
        ( [  IMPORTANCE = { LOW | MEDIUM | HIGH } ]
        [ [  ,  ]      REQUEST_MAX_MEMORY_GRANT_PERCENT = value ]
        [ [  ,  ]  REQUEST_MAX_CPU_TIME_SEC = value ]
        [ [  ,  ]      REQUEST_MEMORY_GRANT_TIMEOUT_SEC = value ]
        [ [  ,  ]  MAX_DOP = value ]
        [ [  ,  ]  GROUP_MAX_REQUESTS = value ] )]
[ USING { pool_name | "default" } ]
```

Table 22-7 describes the arguments of this command.

Table 22-7. CREATE WORKLOAD GROUP Arguments

Argument	Description
group_name	Defines the name of the workload group
IMPORTANCE = {LOW | MEDIUM | HIGH}	Defines the importance of requests within the workload group. If two workloads share the same resource pool, the importance of each workload can determine which requests have a higher priority.
REQUEST_MAX_MEMORY_GRANT_PERCENT = value	Caps maximum memory a request can use from the resource pool
REQUEST_MAX_CPU_TIME_SEC = value	Caps maximum CPU time (seconds) a single request can use from the resource pool
REQUEST_MEMORY_GRANT_TIMEOUT_SEC = value	Caps maximum seconds a request will wait for memory before failing
MAX_DOP = value	Defines maximum degree of parallelism allowed for requests in the workload group
GROUP_MAX_REQUESTS = value	Caps concurrently executing requests in the workload group
USING { pool_name | "default" }	Designates to which pool the workload group will be bound

■ **Note** Multiple workload *groups* can be associated with a single resource *pool*, but a workload group cannot be associated with multiple resource pools.

Just as there are the internal and default resource pools, there are also the internal and default workload groups. The default workload group is used for any requests that are not covered by the classifier user-defined function (a function that determines which pool a workload group's incoming connections are assigned to, demonstrated later in this recipe).

After creating user-defined workload groups and binding them to resource pools, you can then create a single classifier user-defined function that will help determine which workload group an incoming SQL Server connection and request belongs to.

For example, if you have a SQL login named Sue, you can assign that login via the classifier function to belong to a specific workload group that is associated with a specific resource pool.

The classifier user-defined function is created in the master database and returns the workload group name that the incoming SQL Server connection will use. To activate the classifier for incoming connections, the ALTER RESOURCE GOVERNOR command is used, which I'll demonstrate later in this recipe.

Beginning the recipe, let's assume I have a SQL Server instance that is used by an application with two general types of activity. The first type of activity relates to the application. The application uses ongoing automated processes with specific connection qualities and must run reliably. The second type of activity comes from ad hoc query users. These are users who require periodic information about transactional activity, but getting that information must never hamper the performance of the main application. Granted, the best practice would be to separate this activity onto two SQL Server instances; however, if this isn't possible, I can use Resource Governor to constrain resources instead.

I'll start by creating two separate user-defined resource pools for the SQL Server instance. The first pool will be used for the high-priority application. I will make sure that this pool reserves at least 25% of CPU and memory during times of query contention:

```
USE master;
GO
CREATE RESOURCE POOL priority_app_queries WITH ( MIN_CPU_PERCENT = 25,
MAX_CPU_PERCENT = 75,
MIN_MEMORY_PERCENT = 25,
MAX_MEMORY_PERCENT = 75);
GO
```

Next, I will create a second resource pool that will be reserved for ad hoc queries. I will cap the maximum CPU and memory of these pools at 25% during times of high query contention in order to preserve resources for the previously created resource pool. This pool will also take advantage of one of the new options in SQL Server 2014 that will allow you to limit IO on queries during times of high query contention:

```
USE master;
GO
CREATE RESOURCE POOL ad_hoc_queries WITH ( MIN_CPU_PERCENT = 5,
MAX_CPU_PERCENT = 25,
MIN_MEMORY_PERCENT = 5,
MAX_MEMORY_PERCENT = 25,
MAX_IOPS_PER_VOLUME = 50);
GO
```

I can change the values of the resource pools using the ALTER RESOURCE POOL command. For example, I am now going to change the minimum memory for the ad hoc query pool to 10% and maximum memory to 50%:

```
USE master;
GO
ALTER RESOURCE POOL ad_hoc_queries
WITH ( MIN_MEMORY_PERCENT = 10, MAX_MEMORY_PERCENT = 50, MAX_IOPS_PER_VOLUME = 75);
GO
```

Once I have created the pools, I can now confirm the settings by using the sys.resource_ governor_resource_pools catalog view:

```
USE master;
GO
SELECT pool_id,name AS PoolName
,min_cpu_percent,max_cpu_percent
,min_memory_percent,max_memory_percent, max_iops_per_volume
FROM sys.resource_governor_resource_pools rp
WHERE rp.pool_id > 2;
GO
```

This query returns the following:

pool_id	PoolName	min_cpu	max_cpu	min_memory	max_memory	max_iops
258	ad_hoc_queries	5	25	10	50	0
259	priority_app_queries	25	75	25	75	75

Now that I have created the resource pools, I can bind workload groups to them. In this case, I will start by creating a workload group for my highest-priority application connections. I will set this workload group to a high importance and be generous with the maximum memory-grant percentage and other arguments:

```
USE master;
GO
CREATE WORKLOAD GROUP application_alpha WITH
( IMPORTANCE = HIGH,
REQUEST_MAX_MEMORY_GRANT_PERCENT = 75,
REQUEST_MAX_CPU_TIME_SEC = 75,
REQUEST_MEMORY_GRANT_TIMEOUT_SEC = 120,
MAX_DOP = 8,
GROUP_MAX_REQUESTS = 8 ) USING priority_app_queries;
GO
```

Next, I will create another workload group that will share that same resource pool with application_alpha, but with a lower IMPORTANCE level and less generous resource consumption capabilities:

```
USE master;
GO
CREATE WORKLOAD GROUP application_beta WITH
( IMPORTANCE = LOW,
REQUEST_MAX_MEMORY_GRANT_PERCENT = 50,
REQUEST_MAX_CPU_TIME_SEC = 50,
REQUEST_MEMORY_GRANT_TIMEOUT_SEC = 360,
MAX_DOP = 1,
GROUP_MAX_REQUESTS = 4 ) USING priority_app_queries;
GO
```

I can modify the various limits of the workload group by using ALTER WORKLOAD GROUP. Here's an example:

```
USE master;
GO
ALTER WORKLOAD GROUP application_beta WITH ( IMPORTANCE = MEDIUM);
GO
```

The prior two workload groups will share the same resource pool. I will now create one more workload group that will bind to the ad hoc resource pool I created earlier. This workload group will be able to use the maximum memory available to the ad hoc pool:

```
USE master;
GO
CREATE WORKLOAD GROUP adhoc_users WITH
```

```
( IMPORTANCE = LOW,
REQUEST_MAX_MEMORY_GRANT_PERCENT = 100,
REQUEST_MAX_CPU_TIME_SEC = 120,
REQUEST_MEMORY_GRANT_TIMEOUT_SEC = 360,
MAX_DOP = 1,
GROUP_MAX_REQUESTS = 5 ) USING ad_hoc_queries;
GO
```

Once finished, I can confirm the configurations of the workload groups by querying the sys.resource_governor_workload_groups catalog view:

```
USE master;
GO
SELECT name AS GrpName,
Importance AS impt,
request_max_memory_grant_percent AS max_m_g,
request_max_cpu_time_sec AS max_cpu_sec,
request_memory_grant_timeout_sec AS m_g_to,
max_dop,
group_max_requests AS max_req,
pool_id
FROM sys.resource_governor_workload_groups
WHERE pool_id > 2;
```

This query returns the following:

GrpName	impt	max_m_g	max_cpu_sec	m_g_to	max_dop	max_req	pool_id
application_alpha	High	75	75	120	8	8	256
application_beta	Medium	50	50	360	1	4	256
adhoc_users	Low	100	120	360	1	5	257

Now I am ready to create the classifier function. This function will be called for each new connection. The logic of this function will return the workload group where all connection requests will be sent. The classifier function can use several different connection-related functions for use in its logic, including HOST_NAME, APP_NAME, SUSER_NAME, SUSER_SNAME, IS_SRVROLEMEMBER, and IS_MEMBER.

■ **Caution**   Make sure this function is tuned properly and executes quickly.

I create the following function that looks at the SQL Server login name and connection host name in order to determine which workload group the new connection should be assigned to:

```
USE master;
GO
CREATE FUNCTION dbo.RECIPES_classifier()
RETURNS sysname
WITH SCHEMABINDING
AS
```

```
BEGIN
DECLARE @resource_group_name sysname;
IF SUSER_SNAME() IN ('AppLoginl', 'AppLogin2')
    SET @resource_group_name = 'application_alpha';
IF SUSER_SNAME() IN ('AppLogin3', 'AppLogin4')
    SET @resource_group_name = 'application_beta';
IF HOST_NAME() IN ('Workstationl234', 'Workstation4235')
    SET @resource_group_name = 'adhoc_users';
-- If the resource group is still unassigned, use default
IF @resource_group_name IS NULL
    SET @resource_group_name = 'default';
RETURN @resource_group_name;
END
GO
```

Now that I've created the classifier function, I can activate it using ALTER RESOURCE GOVERNOR and the CLASSIFIER_FUNCTION argument:

```
USE master;
GO
-- Assign the classifier function
ALTER RESOURCE GOVERNOR
WITH (CLASSIFIER_FUNCTION = dbo.RECIPES_classifier);
GO
```

To enable the configuration, I must also execute ALTER RESOURCE GOVERNOR with the RECONFIGURE option:

```
USE master;
GO
ALTER RESOURCE GOVERNOR RECONFIGURE;
GO
```

I'll validate the settings using the sys.resource_governor_configuration catalog view:

```
USE master;
GO
SELECT OBJECT_NAME(classifier_function_id,DB_ID('master')) FuncName,
is_enabled
FROM sys.resource_governor_configuration;
```

This query returns the following:

FuncName	is_enabled
RECIPES_classifier	1

Incoming activity for new connections will now be routed to the appropriate workload groups and will use resources from their associated resource pools.

■ Tip You can monitor the incoming request statistics for resource pools and workload groups using the sys.dm_resource_governor_resource_pools and sys.dm_resource_governor_workload_groups DMVs.

To disable the settings, I can execute the ALTER RESOURCE GOVERNOR with the DISABLE argument:

```
USE master;
GO
ALTER RESOURCE GOVERNOR DISABLE;
GO
```

I can remove the user-defined workload groups and resource pools by executing DROP WORKLOAD GROUP and DROP RESOURCE POOL:

```
USE master;
GO
DROP WORKLOAD GROUP application_alpha;
DROP WORKLOAD GROUP application_beta;
DROP WORKLOAD GROUP adhoc_users;
DROP RESOURCE POOL ad_hoc_queries;
DROP RESOURCE POOL priority_app_queries;
```

I can also drop the classifier function once it is no longer being used:

```
USE master;
GO
ALTER RESOURCE GOVERNOR
WITH (CLASSIFIER_FUNCTION = NULL);
DROP FUNCTION dbo.RECIPES_classifier;
GO
```

How It Works

This recipe demonstrated how to use Resource Governor to allocate memory and CPU resources into separate user-defined resource pools. Once the resource pools were defined, I created workload groups, which in turn had associated limits within the confines of their assigned user-defined resource pool. I then created a classifier user-defined function, which was used to assign workload groups to incoming connection requests. This allowed me to limit the resources available to lower-priority requests to free up resources for higher-priority requests.

This functionality allows you to maintain significant control over SQL Server instances that have varying workload requirements and limited system resources. Even on systems with generous system resources, you can use Resource Governor to protect higher-priority workloads from being negatively impacted by lower-priority requests.

CHAPTER 23

Hints

by Jonathan Gennick

SQL Server's query optimization process is responsible for producing a query execution plan when a SELECT query is executed. Typically, SQL Server will choose an efficient plan over an inefficient one. When this doesn't happen, you will want to examine the query execution plan, table statistics, supporting indexes, and other factors that are discussed in more detail in Chapters 22 and 24. Ultimately, after researching the query's performance, you may decide to override the decision-making process of the SQL Server query optimizer by using hints.

■ **Caution**   You should almost always let SQL Server's query optimization process formulate the query execution plan without the aid of hints. Even if a hint works for the short term, keep in mind that there may be more efficient query plans in the future that could be used as the contents of the database change, but they won't be, because you have overridden the optimizer with the specified hint. Also, the validity or effectiveness of a hint may change when new service packs or editions of SQL Server are released.

23-1. Forcing a Join's Execution Approach

Problem

You are joining two tables. The optimizer has made a poor choice on the approach to take in executing the join. You want to override the optimizer and exert control over the mechanism used to perform the join.

Solution

Apply one of the join hints from Table 23-1 in the section "How It Works" later in this chapter For example, the following is a query with no hints that will trigger a nested-loops join operation:

```
SELECT  p.Name,
        r.ReviewerName,
        r.Rating
FROM    Production.Product p
        INNER JOIN Production.ProductReview r
            ON r.ProductID = p.ProductID;
```

Figure 23-1 shows the relevant part of the execution plan. You can see that the optimizer has chosen a nested-loops join.

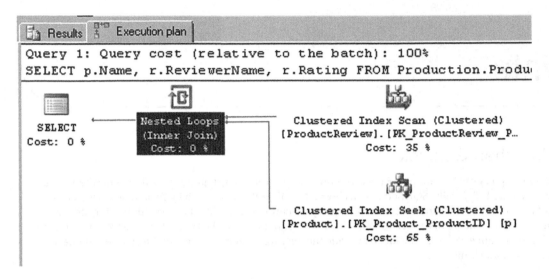

Figure 23-1. *A nested-loops join*

You can force one of the other join types by placing the relevant hint from Table 23-1 between the words INNER and JOIN. The following example uses INNER HASH JOIN to force a hash join:

```
SELECT   p.Name,
         r.ReviewerName,
         r.Rating
FROM     Production.Product p
         INNER HASH JOIN Production.ProductReview r
             ON r.ProductID = p.ProductID;
```

Figure 23-2 shows the new execution plan, this time with a hash join operation.

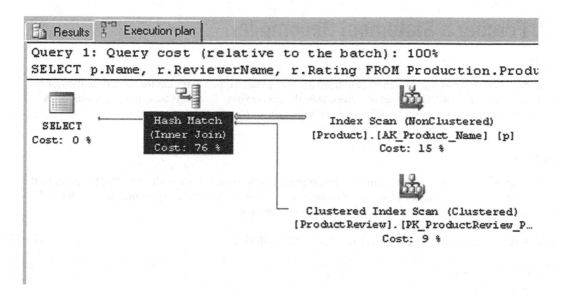

Figure 23-2. *A hash join operation*

How It Works

Table 23-1 shows the join hints at your disposal. The table also provides some general guidance on the situations in which each join method is optimally used. Generally the optimizer will make a reasonable choice. You should think about overriding the optimizer only when you have good reason and no other alternative.

Table 23-1. *Join Hints*

Hint Name	Description
LOOP	Loop joins operate best when one table is small and the other is large, with indexes on the joined columns.
HASH	Hash joins are optimal for large, unsorted tables.
MERGE	Merge joins are optimal for medium or large tables that are sorted on the joined column.
REMOTE	This causes the join to be performed on the server hosting the table that is listed on the right-hand side of the join clause. This hint matters only when a join involves tables sitting on two different servers.

The first solution query generates an execution plan showing a nested-loops join. The second solution query shows the HASH hint from Table 23-1 being used to force a hash join.

Be careful and thoughtful in applying hints. Don't get carried away. Once you apply a hint, you freeze that hint's aspect of the execution plan until such time as you change the hint or remove it. Future improvements to the optimizer and future join methods won't ever get applied, because your hint forces the one approach you've chosen.

23-2. Forcing a Statement Recompile

Problem

Normally, SQL Server saves the execution plan from a query so as to reuse that plan the next time the query is executed, perhaps with a different set of values. Your data is skewed, and plans for one set of values may work poorly for others. You want the optimizer to generate a new plan for each execution.

Solution

Submit your query using the RECOMPILE query hint. Typically, you will want to use this RECOMPILE query hint within a stored procedure—so that you can control which statements automatically recompile—instead of having to recompile the entire stored procedure. Here's an example:

```
DECLARE @CarrierTrackingNumber nvarchar(25) = '5CE9-4D75-8F';

SELECT  SalesOrderID,
        ProductID,
        UnitPrice,
        OrderQty
FROM    Sales.SalesOrderDetail
WHERE   CarrierTrackingNumber = @CarrierTrackingNumber
ORDER BY SalesOrderID,
        ProductID
OPTION (RECOMPILE);
```

This returns the following:

SalesOrderID	ProductID	UnitPrice	OrderQty
47964	760	469.794	1
47964	789	1466.01	1
47964	819	149.031	4
47964	843	15.00	1
47964	844	11.994	6

How It Works

This example uses the RECOMPILE query hint to recompile the query, forcing SQL Server to discard the plan generated for the query after it executes. With the RECOMPILE query hint, a new plan will be generated the next time the same or a similar query is executed. The hint goes in the OPTION clause at the end of the query.

```
OPTION (RECOMPILE)
```

You may decide that you want to take this recipe's approach when faced with a query for which query plans are volatile, in which differing search-condition values for the same plan cause extreme fluctuations in the number of rows returned. In such a scenario, using a compiled query plan may hurt, not help, query performance. The benefit of a cached and reusable query execution plan (the avoided cost of compilation) may occasionally be outweighed by the actual poor performance of the query as it is executed using the saved plan.

■ **Note** It bears repeating that SQL Server should be relied upon most of the time to make the correct decisions when processing a query. Query hints can provide you with more control for those exceptions when you need to override SQL Server's choices.

23-3. Executing a Query Without Locking

Problem

You want to execute a query without being blocked and without blocking others. You are willing to risk seeing uncommitted changes from other transactions.

Solution #1: The NOLOCK Hint

Apply the NOLOCK table hint, as in the following example:

```
SELECT  DocumentNode,
        Title
FROM    Production.Document WITH (NOLOCK)
WHERE   Status = 1;
```

Solution #2: The Isolation Level

Another approach here is to execute a SET TRANSACTION statement to specify an isolation level which has the same effect as the NOLOCK hint. Here's an example:

```
SET TRANSACTION ISOLATION LEVEL READ UNCOMMITTED;
SELECT  DocumentNode,
        Title
FROM    Production.Document
WHERE   Status = 1;
```

How It Works

The crux of this example is the WITH clause, which specifies the NOLOCK table hint in parentheses:

```
WITH (NOLOCK)
```

The example in Solution #1 returns the DocumentID and Title from the Production.Document table where the Status column is equal to 1. The NOLOCK table hint prevents the query from placing shared locks on the Production.Document table. You can then read without being blocked or blocking others (although you are now subject to reading uncommitted and possibly inconsistent data).

The example in Solution #2 accomplishes the same thing by setting the transaction isolation level in a separate statement. Doing that avoids the need for a hint in the query. The command affects all subsequent transactions in the session.

Your transaction isolation level options are as follows:

READ UNCOMMITTED: You can read uncommitted changes from other transactions.

READ COMMITTED: You see only committed changes from other transactions.

REPEATABLE READ: You are not able to read data that has been modified, but not yet committed, by other transactions.

SNAPSHOT: You see all data as it existed at the precise moment the transaction began.

SERIALIZABLE: Transactions are guaranteed to be serializable, meaning they can be played back in sequence. You won't be able to read uncommitted data from other transactions. Other transactions will not be able to modify data that you have read, nor will other transactions be allowed to insert new rows that have key values falling into any of the ranges selected by your transaction.

READ COMMITTED is the default level. If you aren't reasonably familiar with what the various levels mean, take the time to read the Books Online section on "Transaction Statements." The URL for the 2012 version of that section is http://msdn.microsoft.com/en-us/library/ms174377.aspx.

23-4. Forcing an Index Seek

Problem

You are executing a query that you know is best executed via an index seek operation, yet the optimizer persists in choosing to scan the index. You've done your due diligence by updating statistics, but you are still getting the scan operation.

Solution

Specify the FORCESEEK hint, which is available from SQL Server 2008 onward. Here's an example:

```
SELECT DISTINCT
        TransactionID,
        TransactionDate
FROM    Production.TransactionHistory WITH (FORCESEEK)
WHERE   ReferenceOrderID BETWEEN 1000 AND 100000;
```

You also have the option to designate which index should be used. Here's an example:

```
SELECT DISTINCT
        TransactionID,
        TransactionDate
FROM    Production.TransactionHistory WITH (FORCESEEK,
        INDEX (IX_TransactionHistory_ReferenceOrderID_ReferenceOrderLineID))
WHERE   ReferenceOrderID BETWEEN 1000 AND 100000;
```

Your query will now directly seek the index keys needed to resolve the query.

■ **Caution**   This example is for illustrative purposes only. The forced seek in this query is nonoptimal.

How It Works

Bad query plans happen for several reasons. For example, if your table data is highly volatile and your statistics are no longer accurate, a bad plan can be produced. Another example would be a query with a poorly constructed WHERE clause that doesn't provide sufficient or useful information to the query optimization process.

If the intent of your query is to perform a singleton lookup against a specific value, and instead you see that the query scans the entire index before retrieving your single row, the I/O costs of the scan can be significant (particularly for very large tables). You may then want to consider using the new FORCESEEK table hint. FORCESEEK can be used in the FROM clause of a SELECT, UPDATE, or DELETE statement.

The solution example invokes the hint by placing the WITH keyword into the query, followed by the hint name in parentheses:

```
FROM Production.TransactionHistory WITH (FORCESEEK)
```

Using the hint overrides the query's original clustered-index-scan access path.

You can further narrow down the instructions by designating the INDEX hint as well, forcing the seek to occur against the specific index you name. Here's an example:

```
FROM Production.TransactionHistory WITH (FORCESEEK,
   INDEX (IX_TransactionHistory_ReferenceOrderID_ReferenceOrderLineID))
```

The INDEX hint is followed by the name of the index within parentheses. You can also specify the index number.

23-5. Forcing an Index Scan

Problem

The optimizer underestimates the number of rows to be returned from a table and chooses to execute a seek operation against an index on the table. You know from your knowledge of the data that an index scan is the better choice.

Solution

Specify the FORCESCAN hint, which is available from SQL Server 2008 R2 SP1 onward. Here's an example:

```
SELECT DISTINCT
       TransactionID,
       TransactionDate
FROM   Production.TransactionHistory WITH (FORCESCAN)
WHERE  ReferenceOrderID BETWEEN 1000 AND 100000;
```

If you like, you can specify which index to scan:

```
SELECT DISTINCT
       TransactionID,
       TransactionDate
FROM   Production.TransactionHistory WITH (FORCESCAN,
       INDEX (PK_TransactionHistory_TransactionID))
WHERE  ReferenceOrderID BETWEEN 1000 AND 100000;
```

Your query will now scan the specified index to resolve the query.

How It Works

The FORCESCAN hint is the complement of FORCESEEK, described in Recipe 23-4. The hint applies to SELECT, INSERT, and UPDATE statements. With it, you can specify that you want an index seek 6peration to take place when executing a query.

23-6. Optimizing for First Rows

Problem

You want the optimizer to favor execution plans that will return some number of rows very quickly. For example, you are writing a query for an interactive application and would like to display the first screen full of results as soon as possible.

Solution

Place the FAST n hint into the OPTION clause at the end of your query. Specify the number of rows that you would like to be returned quickly. Here's an example:

```
SELECT  ProductID, TransactionID, ReferenceOrderID
FROM    Production.TransactionHistory
ORDER BY ProductID
OPTION (FAST 20);
```

How It Works

Specify FAST n to alert the optimizer to your need for n rows to come back very quickly. In theory, the optimizer then favors execution plans yielding quick initial results at the expense of plans that might be more efficient overall.

An example of a typical trade-off would be when the optimizer chooses a nested-loops join over a hash join or some other operation. Figure 23-3 shows the execution plan for the solution query when that query is executed without the hint. Figure 23-4 shows the plan with the hint included. You can see the nested-loops operation in the second figure.

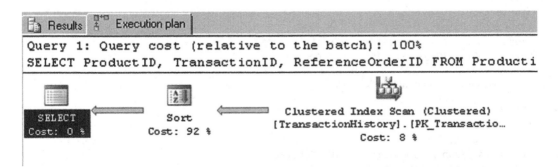

Figure 23-3. *Query plan optimized for overall execution*

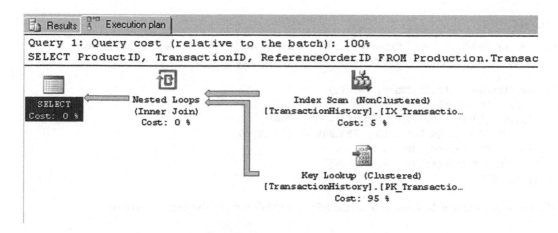

Figure 23-4. *Query plan with FAST 20 in effect*

In the case of the solution query, the hint FAST 20 causes the optimizer to drive the query from an index on the ProductID column. By doing so, the query engine is able to begin immediately returning the rows in sorted order, because the query engine can simply read the index in order. The trade-off, which you can see when you compare the two plans as shown in Figures 23-3 and 23-4, is that each time the one index is accessed it is accompanied by a key lookup Into the table in order to return the other two column values. Figure 23-4's plan is probably more costly, but it does begin to return rows immediately. Figure 23-3's plan might be more efficient, but no rows can be returned until the table has been scanned and the sort operation has been completed.

FAST n is no guarantee that you'll get n rows any faster than before. Results depend upon available indexes and join types and upon the various possibilities that the programmers writing the optimizer happened to think about ahead of time. Check your query's execution plan before and after adding the hint to see whether doing so made a difference.

■ **Caution** There used to be a FASTFIRSTROW hint. It is no longer supported in SQL Server 2012. Specify FAST 1 instead.

23-7. Specifying Join Order

Problem

You are joining two or more tables. You want to force the order in which the tables are accessed while executing the join.

Solution

List the tables in the FROM clause in the order in which you want them to be accessed. Then specify FORCE ORDER in an OPTION clause at the end of the query. Here's an example:

```
SELECT  PP.FirstName, PP.LastName, PA.City
FROM    Person.Person PP
        INNER JOIN Person.BusinessEntityAddress PBA
            ON PP.BusinessEntityID = PBA.BusinessEntityID
        INNER JOIN Person.Address PA
            ON PBA.AddressID = PA.AddressID
OPTION (FORCE ORDER)
```

The join order will now be Person to BusinessEntityID followed by the join to Address.

How It Works

Specifying FORCE ORDER causes tables to be joined in the order listed in the FROM cause. Figures 23-5 and 23-6 show the effect of the hint on the solution query. Without the hint (Figure 23-5), the first two tables to be joined are Address and BusinessEntityAddress. With the hint (Figure 23-6), the first two tables are Person and BusinessEntityAddress, matching the order specified in the FROM clause.

Figure 23-5. *Execution plan without the FORCE ORDER hint*

Figure 23-6. *Execution with the FORCE ORDER hint*

23-8. Forcing the Use of a Specific Index

Problem

You aren't happy with the optimizer's index choice. You want to force the use of a specific index in connection with a given table.

Solution

Specify the INDEX hint at the table level. For example, the following is another rendition of the query first shown in Recipe 23-6. This time, the table reference is followed by a WITH clause containing an INDEX hint:

```
SELECT  ProductID, TransactionID, ReferenceOrderID
FROM    Production.TransactionHistory
        WITH (INDEX (IX_TransactionHistory_ProductID))
ORDER BY ProductID
```

The INDEX hint in this query forces the use of the named index: IX_TransactionHistory_ProductID.

How It Works

Figures 23-7 and 23-8 show an execution plan without and with the INDEX hint, respectively. You can see in Figure 23-8 that the hint forces the use of the index on the ProductID column.

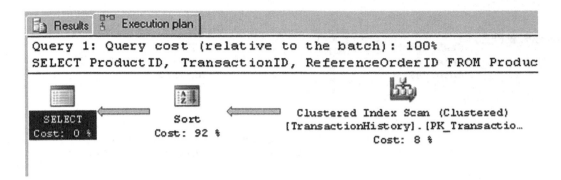

Figure 23-7. Unhinted execution plan

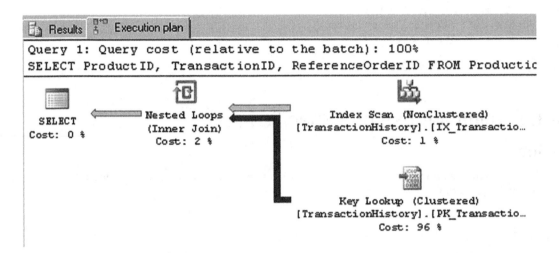

Figure 23-8. Execution plan forcing use of a specific index

Think twice before forcing the use of an index as shown in this recipe. Whenever you lock in an index choice with a hint, that choice remains locked in no matter what optimizer improvements are made. It remains locked in even if the data changes to favor the use of some other index. Before hinting an index, consider whether the statistics are up to date and whether you can do something to trigger the use of the index without having to hard-code that usage in the form of a table hint.

23-9. Optimizing for Specific Parameter Values

Problem

You want to avoid trouble from parameter-sniffing by instructing the optimizer to consider specific values when parsing a query that has bind variables.

Solution

Specify the OPTIMIZE FOR hint. Here's an example:

```
DECLARE @TTYPE NCHAR(1);
SET @TTYPE = 'P';

SELECT  *
FROM    Production.TransactionHistory TH
WHERE   TH.TransactionType = @TTYPE
OPTION (OPTIMIZE FOR (@TTYPE = 'S'));
```

How It Works

The solution example specifies the hint OPTIMIZE FOR (@TTYPE = 'S'). The optimizer will take the value 'S' into account when building a query plan. Hinting like this can sometimes be helpful in cases in which data is badly skewed, especially when the risk is high that the first execution of a given query will be done using a value that results in a plan that will work poorly for subsequent values passed in future executions.

If you execute the solution query and choose to view the actual execution plan in XML form, you'll find the following:

```
<ColumnReference Column="@TTYPE"
    ParameterCompiledValue="N'S'"
    ParameterRuntimeValue="N'P'" />
```

Here you can see that the compiled query took into account the value S. But the query as actually executed used the value P. However, plan actually executed is the one compiled for the S, just as the hint specified.

■ **Tip** You may specify OPTIMIZE FOR UNKNOWN to essentially inhibit parameter sniffing altogether. In doing so, you cause the optimizer to rely upon table and index statistics alone, without regard to the initial value that is ultimately passed to the query.

CHAPTER 24

■ ■ ■

Index Tuning and Statistics

By Jason Brimhall

As discussed in Chapter 22, SQL Server query performance tuning and optimization requires a multilayered approach. This chapter focuses on the index and statistics tuning aspects of that approach. The following are a few key factors that impact SQL Server query performance:

- *Appropriate indexing:* Your table indexes should be based on your high-priority or frequently executed queries. If a query is executed thousands of times a day and completes in two seconds, but could be running in less than one second with the proper index, adding this index could reduce the I/O pressure on your SQL Server instance significantly. You should create indexes as needed and remove indexes that aren't being used (this chapter shows you how to do this). As with most changes, there is a trade-off. Each index on your table adds overhead to data modification operations and can even slow down SELECT queries if SQL Server decides to use the less efficient index. When you're initially designing your database, it is better for you to keep the number of indexes at a minimum (having at least a clustered index and nonclustered indexes for your foreign keys). Add indexes once you have a better idea of the actual queries that will be executed against the database. Indexing requirements are organic, particularly on volatile, frequently updated databases, so your approach to adding and removing indexes should be flexible and iterative.

- *Index fragmentation:* As data modifications are made over time, your indexes will become fragmented. As fragmentation increases, index data will become spread out over more data pages. The more data pages your query needs to retrieve, the higher the I/O and memory requirements are and the slower the query is.

- *Up-to-date statistics:* The AUTO_CREATE_STATISTICS database option enables SQL Server to automatically generate statistical information regarding the distribution of values in a column. The AUTO_UPDATE_STATISTICS database option enables SQL Server to automatically update statistical information regarding the distribution of values in a column. If you disable these options, statistics can get out of date. Since SQL Server depends on statistics to decide how to best execute a query, SQL Server may choose a less-than-optimal plan if it is basing its execution decisions on stale statistics.

In this chapter, I'll demonstrate the T-SQL commands and techniques you can use to help address fragmented indexes and out-of-date statistics and to evaluate the use of indexes in the database.

■ **Note**   Since this is a book about T-SQL, I don't review the graphical interface tools that also assist with performance tuning, such as SQL Server Profiler, graphical execution plans, System Monitor, and the Database Engine Tuning Advisor. These are all extremely useful tools, so I do encourage you to use them as part of your overall performance-tuning strategy in addition to the T-SQL commands and techniques you'll learn in this chapter.

Index Tuning

The first few recipes demonstrate techniques for managing indexes. Specifically, I'll be covering how to do the following:

- Identify index fragmentation so you can figure out which indexes should be rebuilt or reorganized.

- Display index use so you can determine which indexes *aren't* being used by SQL Server.

Before getting into the recipes, let's discuss some general indexing best practices. When considering these best practices, always remember that, as with query tuning, there are few hard and fast "always" or "never" rules. Index use by SQL Server depends on a number of factors, including, but not limited to: the query construction, referenced tables in the query, referenced columns, number of rows in the table, data distribution, and the uniqueness of the index column(s) data. The following are some basic guidelines to keep in mind when building your index strategy:

- Add indexes based on your high-priority and high-execution count queries. Determine ahead of time what acceptable query execution durations might be (based on your business requirements).

- Don't add too many indexes at the same time. Instead, add an index and test the query to verify that the new index is used. If it is not used, remove it. If it is used, test to make sure there are no negative side effects for other queries. Remember that each additional index adds overhead to any data modifications made to the base table.

- Unless you have a very good reason not to do so, always add a clustered index to each table. A table without a clustered index is a heap, meaning that the data is stored in no particular order. Clustered indexes are ordered according to the clustered key, and its data pages are reordered during an index rebuild or reorganization. Heaps, however, are not automatically rebuilt during an index rebuild or reorganization process, and therefore can grow out of control, taking up many more data pages than is necessary.

- Monitor query performance and index use over time. As your data and application activity changes, so too will the performance and effectiveness of your indexes.

- Fragmented indexes can slow down query performance, since more I/O operations are required in order to return results for a query. Keep index fragmentation to a minimum by rebuilding and/or reorganizing your indexes on a scheduled or as-needed basis.

- Select clustered index keys that are rarely modified, are highly unique, and are narrow in data-type width. Width is particularly important, because each nonclustered index also contains within it the clustered index key. Clustered indexes are useful when applied to columns being used in range queries. This includes queries that use the operators BETWEEN, >, >=, <, and <=. Clustered index keys also help reduce execution time for queries that return large result sets or that depend heavily on ORDER BY and GROUP BY clauses. With all these factors in mind, remember that you can have only a single clustered index for your table, so choose one carefully.

- Nonclustered indexes are ideal for small or one-row result sets. Again, columns should be chosen based on their use in a query, specifically in the JOIN or WHERE clauses. Nonclustered indexes should be made on columns containing highly unique data. As discussed in Chapter 16, don't forget to consider using covering queries and the INCLUDE functionality for nonkey columns.

- Use a 100 percent fill factor for those indexes that are located within read-only filegroups or databases. This reduces I/O and can improve query performance, because fewer data pages are required to fulfill a query's result set.

- Try to anticipate which indexes will be needed based on the queries you perform—but also don't be afraid to make frequent use of the Database Engine Tuning Advisor tool. Using the Database Engine Tuning Advisor, SQL Server can evaluate your query or batch of queries and suggest index changes for you to review.

Index Maintenance

In the next two recipes, I'll demonstrate two methods you can use to defragment your indexes.

■ **Tip** It is important that you rebuild only the indexes that require it. The rebuild process is resource intensive.

24-1. Displaying Index Fragmentation

Problem

You suspect that you have indexes that are heavily fragmented. You need to run a query to confirm the fragmentation levels of the indexes in your database.

Solution

Query the sys.dm_db_index_physical_stats dynamic management function.

Fragmentation is the natural byproduct of data modifications to a table. When data is updated in the database, the logical order of indexes (based on the index key) gets out of sync with the actual physical order of the data pages. As data pages become further and further out of order, more I/O operations are required in order to return the results requested by a query. Rebuilding or reorganizing an index allows you to defragment the index by synchronizing the logical index order, reordering the physical data pages to match the logical index order.

■ **Note**   See Chapter 16 for a review of index management, and later in this chapter for a review of index defragmentation and reorganization.

The sys.dm_db_index_physical_stats dynamic management function returns information that allows you to determine the fragmentation level of an index. The syntax for sys.dm_db_index_physical_stats is as follows:

```
sys.dm_db_index_physical_stats (
{       database_id | NULL }
,       { object_id | NULL }
,       { index_id | NULL | 0 }
,       { partition_number | NULL }
,       { mode | NULL | DEFAULT }
)
```

Table 24-1 describes the arguments of this command.

Table 24-1. sys.dm_db_index_physical_stats Arguments

Argument	Description
database_id | NULL	This specifies the database ID of the indexes to evaluate. If NULL, all databases for the SQL Server instance are returned.
object_id | NULL	This specifies the object ID of the table and views (*indexed* views) to evaluate. If NULL, all tables are returned.
index_id | NULL | 0	This gives the specific index ID of the index to evaluate. If NULL, all indexes are returned for the table(s).
partition_number | NULL	This specifies the specific partition number of the partition to evaluate. If NULL, all partitions are returned based on the defined database/table/indexes selected.
LIMITED | SAMPLED | DETAILED | NULL | DEFAULT	These modes impact how the fragmentation data is collected. The LIMITED mode scans all pages of a heap as well as the pages above the leaf level. SAMPLED collects data based on a 1 percent sampling of pages in the heap or index. The DETAILED mode scans all pages (heap or index). DETAILED is the slowest, but most accurate, option. Designating NULL or DEFAULT is the equivalent of choosing the LIMITED mode.

In this example, the sys.dm_db_index_physical_stats dynamic management function is queried for all objects in the AdventureWorks2014 database with an average fragmentation percent greater than 30:

```
USE AdventureWorks2014;
GO
SELECT OBJECT_NAME(object_id) AS ObjectName,
index_id,
index_type_desc,
avg_fragmentation_in_percent
```

```
FROM sys.dm_db_index_physical_stats (DB_ID('AdventureWorks2014'),NULL, NULL, NULL, 'LIMITED')
WHERE avg_fragmentation_in_percent > 30
ORDER BY OBJECT_NAME(object_id);
```

This returns the following (abridged) results:

ObjectName	index_id	index_type_desc	avg_fragmentation_in_percent
BillOfMaterials	2	NONCLUSTERED INDEX	33.3333333333333
BusinessEntityContact	1	CLUSTERED INDEX	50
BusinessEntityContact	2	NONCLUSTERED INDEX	50
BusinessEntityContac t	3	NONCLUSTERED INDEX	50
BusinessEntityContact	4	NONCLUSTERED INDEX	50
CountryRegion	1	CLUSTERED INDEX	50
DatabaseLog	0	HEAP	32.6732673267327

This second example returns fragmentation for a specific database, table, and index:

```
USE AdventureWorks2014;
GO
SELECT OBJECT_NAME(f.object_id) AS ObjectName,
       i.name AS IndexName,
       f.index_type_desc,
       f.avg_fragmentation_in_percent
FROM sys.dm_db_index_physical_stats
       (DB_ID('AdventureWorks2014'), OBJECT_ID('Production.ProductDescription'), 2, NULL,
'LIMITED')  f
INNER JOIN sys.indexes i
       ON i.object_id = f.object_id
       AND i.index_id = f.index_id;
```

This query returns the following:

ObjectName	IndexName	index_type_desc	avg_fragmentation_in_percent
ProductDescription	AK_ProductDescription _rowguid	NONCLUSTERED INDEX	66.6666666666667

How It Works

The first example started by changing the database context to the AdventureWorks2014 database:

```
USE AdventureWorks2014;
GO
```

Since the OBJECT_NAME function is database-context sensitive, changing the database context ensured that we were viewing the proper object name.

Next, the SELECT clause displayed the object name, index ID, description, and average fragmentation percentage:

```
SELECT OBJECT_NAME(object_id) ObjectName, index_id, index_type_desc, avg_fragmentation_in_percent
```

The index_type_desc column tells us if the index is a heap, clustered index, nonclustered index, primary XML index, spatial index, or secondary XML index.

Next, the FROM clause referenced the sys.dm_db_index_physical_stats dynamic management function. The parameters, which were put in parentheses, included the database name and NULL for all other parameters except the scan mode:

```
FROM sys.dm_db_index_physical_stats (DB_ID('AdventureWorks2014'),NULL, NULL, NULL, 'LIMITED')
```

Since sys.dm_db_index_physical_stats is table-valued function, the WHERE clause was used to qualify that only rows with a fragmentation percentage greater than 30 percent be returned in the results:

```
WHERE avg_fragmentation_in_percent > 30
```

The query returned several rows for objects in the AdventureWorks2014 database with a fragmentation level greater than 30 percent. The avg_fragmentation_in_percent column shows logical fragmentation of nonclustered or clustered indexes, returning the percentage of disordered pages at the leaf level of the index. For heaps, avg_fragmentation_in_percent shows extent-level fragmentation. Regarding extents, recall that SQL Server reads and writes data at the page level. Pages are stored in blocks called *extents,* which consist of eight contiguous 8KB pages. Using the avg_fragmentation_in_percent, you can determine whether the specific indexes need to be rebuilt or reorganized using ALTER INDEX.

In the second example, fragmentation was displayed for a specific database, table, and index. The SELECT clause included a reference to the index name (instead of index number):

```
SELECT OBJECT_NAME(f.object_id) ObjectName, i.name IndexName, f.index_type_desc, f.avg_
fragmentation_in_percent
```

The FROM clause included the specific table name, which was converted to an ID using the OBJECT_ID function. The third parameter included the index number of the index to be evaluated for fragmentation:

```
FROM sys.dm_db_index_physical_stats
(DB_ID('AdventureWorks2014'),
OBJECT_ID('Production.ProductDescription'),
2,
NULL,
'LIMITED') f
```

The sys.indexes system catalog view was joined to the sys.dm_db_index_physical_stats function based on the object_id and index_id:

```
INNER JOIN sys.indexes i ON i.object_id = f.object_id AND i.index_id = f.index_id;
```

The query returned the fragmentation results just for that specific index.

24-2. Rebuilding Indexes

Problem

After analyzing fragmentation levels of your indexes, you have determined that many indexes need to be rebuilt.

Solution

Rebuild the indexes using `ALTER INDEX`.

Rebuilding an index serves many purposes, the most popular being the removal of any fragmentation that occurs as data modifications are made to a table over time. As fragmentation increases, query performance can slow. Rebuilding an index removes this fragmentation of the index rows and frees up physical disk space.

Large indexes that are quite fragmented can reduce query speed. The frequency with which you rebuild your indexes depends on your database size, how much data modification occurs, how much activity occurs against your tables, and whether your queries typically perform ordered scans or singleton lookups.

The syntax for `ALTER INDEX` to rebuild an index is as follows:

```
ALTER INDEX   { index_name  |  ALL }
       ON  <object>
       {       REBUILD
       [  [  WITH  ( <rebuild_index_option>  [  ,...n  ]  )  ]
       |  [  PARTITION  =  partition_number
[  WITH  ( <single_partition_rebuild_index_option>
       [  ,...n  ]  )
       ]
       ]
       ]
       }
```

Table 24-2 describes the arguments of this command.

Table 24-2. `ALTER INDEX...REBUILD` Arguments

Argument	Description
`index_name	ALL`	This defines the name of the index to rebuild. If `ALL` is chosen, all indexes for the specified table or view will be rebuilt.
`<object>`	This specifies the name of the table or view that the index is built on.
`<rebuild_index_option>`	One or more index options can be applied during a rebuild, including `FILLFACTOR`, `PAD_INDEX`, `SORT_IN_TEMPDB`, `IGNORE_DUP_KEY`, `STATISTICS_NORECOMPUTE`, `ONLINE`, `ALLOW_ROW_LOCKS`, `ALLOW_PAGE_LOCKS`, `DATA_COMPRESSION`, and `MAXDOP`.
`partition_number`	If using a partitioned index, `partition_number` designates that only one partition of the index is to be rebuilt.
`<single_partition_ rebuild_index_option>`	If designating a partition rebuild, you are limited to using the following index options in the `WITH` clause: `SORT_IN_TEMPDB`, `DATA_COMPRESSION`, `ONLINE`, and `MAXDOP`.

This recipe demonstrates ALTER INDEX REBUILD, which drops and recreates an existing index. It demonstrates a few variations for rebuilding an index in the AdventureWorks2014 database.

```
-- Rebuild a specific index
USE AdventureWorks2014;
GO
ALTER INDEX PK_ShipMethod_ShipMethodID ON Purchasing.ShipMethod REBUILD;

-- Rebuild all indexes on a specific table
USE AdventureWorks2014;
GO
ALTER INDEX ALL
ON Purchasing.PurchaseOrderHeader REBUILD;

-- Rebuild an index, while keeping it available -- for queries (requires Enterprise Edition)
USE AdventureWorks2014;
GO
ALTER INDEX PK_ProductReview_ProductReviewID
ON Production.ProductReview REBUILD WITH (ONLINE = ON);

-- Rebuild an index, using a new fill factor and -- sorting in tempdb
USE AdventureWorks2014;
GO
ALTER INDEX PK_TransactionHistory_TransactionID
ON Production.TransactionHistory REBUILD WITH (FILLFACTOR = 75, SORT_IN_TEMPDB = ON);

-- Rebuild an index with page-level data compression enabled
USE AdventureWorks2014;
GO
ALTER INDEX PK_ShipMethod_ShipMethodID
ON Purchasing.ShipMethod REBUILD WITH (DATA_COMPRESSION = PAGE);

-- Rebuild an index with low priority wait
USE AdventureWorks2014;
GO
ALTER INDEX PK_ShipMethod_ShipMethodID
ON Purchasing.ShipMethod
REBUILD WITH (ONLINE = ON (
    WAIT_AT_LOW_PRIORITY ( MAX_DURATION = 2 MINUTES, ABORT_AFTER_WAIT = SELF )
    ));
```

How It Works

In this recipe, the first ALTER INDEX was used to rebuild the primary key index on the Purchasing.ShipMethod table (rebuilding a clustered index does not cause the rebuild of any nonclustered indexes for the table).

```
ALTER INDEX PK_ShipMethod_ShipMethodID ON Purchasing.ShipMethod REBUILD
```

In the second example, the ALL keyword was used, which means that any indexes, whether nonclustered or clustered (remember, only one clustered index can exist on a table), will be rebuilt:

```
ALTER INDEX ALL
ON Purchasing.PurchaseOrderHeader REBUILD
```

The third example in the recipe rebuilt an index *online,* which means that user queries can continue to access the data of the PK_ProductReview_ProductReviewID index while it's being rebuilt:

```
WITH (ONLINE = ON)
```

The ONLINE option requires SQL Server Enterprise Edition, and it can't be used with XML indexes, disabled indexes, or partitioned indexes. Also, indexes using large object data types or indexes made on temporary tables can't take advantage of this option.

In the fourth example, two index options were modified for an index–the fill factor and a directive to sort the temporary index results in tempdb:

```
WITH (FILLFACTOR = 75, SORT_IN_TEMPDB = ON)
```

In the fifth example, an uncompressed index was rebuilt using page-level data compression:

```
WITH (DATA_COMPRESSION = PAGE)
```

In the final example, an index was rebuilt using the wait_at_low_priority option, with a max duration of two minutes. This option allows for queries holding low-level locks to first complete. If they do not complete, then the online rebuild takes the action-specified abort_after_wait setting.

```
REBUILD WITH (ONLINE = ON (
    WAIT_AT_LOW_PRIORITY ( MAX_DURATION = 2 MINUTES, ABORT_AFTER_WAIT = SELF )
    ));
```

■ **Tip**   You can validate whether an index or partition is compressed by looking at the data_compression_desc column in sys.partitions.

24-3. Defragmenting Indexes

Problem

In addition to the many indexes that need to be rebuilt, you have determined that several need to be defragmented.

Solution

Use ALTER INDEX REORGANIZE to reduce fragmentation on the leaf level of an index (clustered or nonclustered), forcing the physical order of the database pages to match the logical order. During this reorganization process, the indexes are also compacted based on the fill factor, resulting in freed space and a smaller index. ALTER TABLE REORGANIZE is automatically an online operation, meaning that you can continue to query the target data during the reorganization process. The syntax is as follows:

```
ALTER INDEX { indexname | ALL } ON <object> { REORGANIZE
[ PARTITION = partition_number ]
[ WITH ( LOB_COMPACTION = { ON | OFF } ) ] }
```

Table 24-3 describes the arguments of this command.

Table 24-3. *ALTER INDEX...REORGANIZE Arguments*

Argument	Description
index_name	ALL	This defines the name of the index that you want to rebuild. If ALL is chosen, all indexes for the table or view will be rebuilt.
<object>	This specifies the name of the table or view that you want to build the index on.
partition_number	If using a partitioned index, the partition_number designates that partition to be reorganized.
LOB_COMPACTION = { ON	OFF }	When this argument is enabled, large object data types (varchar(max), navarchar(max), varbinary(max), xml, text, ntext, and image data) are compacted.

This recipe demonstrates how to defragment a single index, as well as all indexes on a single table:

```
-- Reorganize a specific index
USE AdventureWorks2014;
GO
ALTER INDEX PK_TransactionHistory_TransactionID
ON Production.TransactionHistory
REORGANIZE;
-- Reorganize all indexes for a table
-- Compact large object data types
USE AdventureWorks2014;
GO
ALTER INDEX ALL
ON HumanResources.JobCandidate
REORGANIZE
WITH (LOB_COMPACTION = ON);
```

How It Works

In the first example of this recipe, the primary-key index of the Production.TransactionHistory table was reorganized (defragmented). The syntax was very similar to that for rebuilding an index, only instead of REBUILD, the REORGANIZE keyword was used.

In the second example, all indexes (using the ALL keyword) were defragmented for the HumanResources.Jobcandidate table. Using the WITH clause, large object data type columns were also compacted.

Use ALTER INDEX REORGANIZE if you cannot afford to take the index offline during an index rebuild (and if you cannot use the ONLINE option in ALTER INDEX REBUILD because you aren't running SQL Server Enterprise Edition). Reorganization is always an online operation, meaning that an ALTER INDEX REORGANIZE operation doesn't block database traffic for significant periods of time, although it may be a slower process than a REBUILD.

24-4. Rebuilding a Heap

Problem

You have a table in the database that does not have a clustered index and is a heap. You have noticed that this table is nearly 90 percent fragmented, littered with forwarding pointers, and you want to defragment the table.

Solution

Since SQL Server 2008, you can rebuild a heap (a table without a clustered index) using the ALTER TABLE command. In previous versions, rebuilding a heap required adding and removing a temporary clustered index or performing a data migration or recreating a table.

In this example, I will create a heap table (using SELECT INTO) and then rebuild it:

```
USE AdventureWorks2014;
GO
-- Create an unindexed table based on another table
SELECT ShiftID, Name, StartTime, EndTime, ModifiedDate
INTO dbo.Heap_Shift
FROM HumanResources.Shift;
```

I can validate whether the new table is a heap by querying the sys.indexes system catalog view:

```
USE AdventureWorks2014;
GO
SELECT type_desc
FROM sys.indexes
WHERE object_id = OBJECT_ID('Heap_Shift');
```

This query returns the following:

```
type_desc
HEAP
```

If I want to rebuild the heap, I can issue the following ALTER TABLE command:

```
USE AdventureWorks2014;
GO
ALTER TABLE dbo.Heap_Shift REBUILD;
```

How It Works

In this recipe, I created a heap table and then rebuilt it using ALTER TABLE...REBUILD. By using ALTER TABLE...REBUILD, you can rebuild a table, even if it does not have a clustered index (and is thus a heap). If the table is partitioned, this command also rebuilds all partitions on that table and rebuilds the clustered index if one exists.

24-5. Displaying Index Usage

Problem

You are concerned you may have some indexes in the database that are more costly than the benefit they provide is worth or that are no longer being used. You want to find out which indexes fit these criteria.

Solution

You can query the sys.dm_db_index_usage_stats dynamic management view (DMV).

Creating useful indexes in your database is a balancing act between read and write performance. Indexes can slow down data modifications while at the same time speed up SELECT queries. You must balance the cost/benefit of index overhead with read activity versus data modification activity. Every additional index added to a table may improve query performance at the expense of data modification speed. On top of this, index effectiveness changes as the data changes, so an index that was useful a few weeks ago may not be useful today. If you are going to have indexes on a table, they should be put to good use on high-priority queries.

To identify unused indexes, you can query the sys.dm_db_index_usage_stats DMV. This view returns statistics on the number of index seeks, scans, updates, or lookups since the SQL Server instance was last restarted. It also returns the last dates the index was referenced.

In this example, the sys.dm_db_index_usage_stats DMV is queried to see whether the indexes on the Sales.Customer table are being used. Prior to referencing sys.dm_db_ index_usage_stats, two queries will be executed against the Sales.Customer table: one query returning all rows and columns and the second returning the AccountNumber column for a specific TerritoryID:

```
USE AdventureWorks2014;
GO
SELECT *
FROM Sales.Customer;

USE AdventureWorks2014;
GO
SELECT AccountNumber
FROM Sales.Customer
WHERE TerritoryID = 4;
```

After executing the queries, the sys.dm_db_index_usage_stats DMV is queried:

```
USE AdventureWorks2014;
GO
SELECT i.name IndexName, user_seeks, user_scans, last_user_seek, last_user_scan
FROM sys.dm_db_index_usage_stats s
INNER JOIN sys.indexes i
```

```
ON s.object_id = i.object_id
AND s.index_id = i.index_id
WHERE database_id = DB_ID('AdventureWorks2014')
AND s.object_id = OBJECT_ID('Sales.Customer');
```

This query returns the following:

IndexName	user_seeks	user_scans	last_user_seek	last_user_scan
IX_Customer_TerritoryID	1	0	2015-02-19 10:07:17.750	NULL
PK_Customer_CustomerID	0	1	NULL	2015-02-19 10:07:17.533

How It Works

The sys.dm_db_index_usage_stats DMV allows you to see what indexes are being used in your SQL Server instance. The statistics are valid back to the last SQL Server restart.

In this recipe, two queries were executed against the Sales.Customer table. After executing the queries, the sys.dm_db_index_usage_stats DMV was queried.

The SELECT clause displayed the name of the index, the number of user seeks and user scans, and the dates of the last user seeks and user scans:

```
SELECT i.name IndexName, user_seeks, user_scans, last_user_seek, last_user_scan
```

The FROM clause joined the sys.dm_db_index_usage_stats DMV to the sys.indexes system catalog view (so the index name could be displayed in the results) on object_id and index_id:

```
FROM sys.dm_db_index_usage_stats s
INNER JOIN sys.indexes i ON
s.object_id = i.object_id AND
s.index_id = i.index_id
```

The WHERE clause qualified that only indexes for the AdventureWorks2014 database should be displayed and, of those indexes, only those for the Sales.Customer table. The DB_ID function was used to get the database system ID, and the OBJECT_ID function was used to get the table's object ID.

```
WHERE database_id = DB_ID('AdventureWorks2014')
AND s.object_id = OBJECT_ID('Sales.Customer');
```

The query returned two rows, showing that the PK_Customer_CustomerID clustered index of the Sales.Customer table had indeed been scanned recently (caused by the first SELECT * query), and the IX_Customer_TerritoryID nonclustered index had been used in the second query (which qualified TerritoryID = 4).

Indexes assist with query performance but also add disk space and data modification overhead. By using the sys.dm_db_index_usage_stats DMV, you can monitor whether indexes are actually being used and, if not, replace them with more effective indexes.

Statistics

The AUTO_CREATE_STATISTICS database option enables SQL Server to automatically generate statistical information regarding the distribution of values in a column. The AUTO_UPDATE_STATISTICS database option automatically updates existing statistics on your table or indexed view. Unless you have a *very* good reason for doing so, these options should never be disabled in your database, because they are critical for good query performance.

Statistics are critical for efficient query processing and performance, allowing SQL Server to choose the correct physical operations when generating an execution plan. Table and indexed view statistics, which can be created manually or generated automatically by SQL Server, collect information that is used by SQL Server to generate efficient query execution plans.

The next few recipes will demonstrate how to work directly with statistics. When reading these recipes, remember to let SQL Server manage the automatic creation and updating of statistics in your databases whenever possible. Save most of these commands for special troubleshooting circumstances or when you've made significant data changes (for example, executing sp_updatestats right after a large data load).

24-6. Manually Creating Statistics

Problem

You have noticed that a high-use query is performing poorly. After some investigation, you have noted that AUTO_CREATE_STATISTICS and AUTO_UPDATE_STATISTICS are enabled. You are certain that new statistics are needed.

Solution

Use the CREATE STATISTICS command and create new statistics.

SQL Server will usually generate the statistics it needs based on query activity. However, if you still want to explicitly create statistics on a column or columns, you can use the CREATE STATISTICS command.

The syntax is as follows:

```
CREATE STATISTICS statistics_name ON { table | view } ( column [ ,...n ] )
[ WHERE <filter_predicate> ]
[ WITH
[ [ FULLSCAN
| SAMPLE number { PERCENT | ROWS } STATS_STREAM = stats_stream ] [ , ] ]

[ NORECOMPUTE ] ]
```

Table 24-4 describes the arguments of this command.

Table 24-4. CREATE STATISTICS Arguments

Argument	Description
statistics_name	This defines the name of the new statistics.
table | view	This specifies the table or indexed view from which the statistics are based.
column [,...n]	This specifies one or more columns to be used for generating statistics.
WHERE <filter_predicate>	Expression for filtering a subset of rows on the statistics object
FULLSCAN| SAMPLE number { PERCENT | ROWS }	FULLSCAN, when specified, reads all rows when generating the statistics. SAMPLE reads either a defined number of rows or a defined percentage of rows.
STATS_STREAM = stats_stream	This is reserved for Microsoft's internal use.
NORECOMPUTE	This option designates that once the statistics are created, they should not be updated–even when data changes occur afterward. This option should rarely, if ever, be used. Fresh statistics allow SQL Server to generate good query plans.
INCREMENTAL	Enabling this option sets the statistics per partition. The default is OFF, which combines stats across all partitions.

In this example, new statistics are created on the Sales.Customer AccountNumber column:

```
USE AdventureWorks2014;
GO
CREATE STATISTICS Stats_Customer_AccountNumber
ON Sales.Customer (AccountNumber) WITH FULLSCAN;
```

How It Works

This recipe demonstrated manually creating statistics on the Sales.Customer table. The first line of code designated the statistics' name:

```
CREATE STATISTICS Stats_Customer_AccountNumber
```

The second line of code designated the table on which to create statistics, followed by the name of the column being used to generate the statistics:

```
ON Sales.Customer (AccountNumber)
```

The last line of code designated that all rows in the table would be read so as to generate the statistics:

```
WITH FULLSCAN
```

Using the FULLSCAN option will typically take longer to generate statistics, but will provide a higher-quality sampling. The default behavior in SQL Server is to use SAMPLE with an automatically determined sample size.

24-7. Creating Statistics on a Subset of Rows

Problem

You have a very large table that is frequently queried. Most of the queries performed are against a range of data that comprises less than 20 percent of the records in the table. You have determined that the indexes are appropriate, but you may be missing a statistic. You want to improve the performance of these queries.

Solution

Create filtered statistics.

In Chapter 16, I demonstrated the ability to create filtered, nonclustered indexes that cover a small percentage of rows. Doing this reduced the index size and improved the performance of queries that needed to read only a fraction of the index entries that they would otherwise have to process. Creating a filtered index also creates associated statistics.

These statistics use the same filter predicate and can result in more-accurate results because the sampling is against a smaller row set.

You can also explicitly create filtered statistics using the CREATE STATISTICS command. Similar to creating a filtered index, filtered statistics support filter predicates for several comparison operators to be used, including IS, IS NOT, =, <>, >, <, and more.

The following query demonstrates creating filtered statistics on a range of values for the UnitPrice column in the Sales.SalesOrderDetail table:

```
USE AdventureWorks2014;
GO
CREATE STATISTICS Stats_SalesOrderDetail_UnitPrice_Filtered ON Sales.SalesOrderDetail
(UnitPrice)
WHERE UnitPrice >= 1000.00 AND UnitPrice <= 1500.00
WITH FULLSCAN;
```

How It Works

This recipe demonstrated creating filtered statistics. Similar to filtered indexes, we just added a WHERE clause within the definition of the CREATE STATISTICS call and defined a range of allowed values for the UnitPrice column. Creating statistics on a column creates a histogram with up to 200 interval values that designates how many rows are at each interval value, as well as how many rows are smaller than the current key but are also less than the previous key. The query optimization process depends on highly accurate statistics. Filtered statistics allow you to specify the key range of values your application focuses on, resulting in more-accurate statistics for that subset of data.

24-8. Updating Statistics

Problem

You have created some statistics on a table in your database and now want to update them immediately.

Solution

You can use the UPDATE STATISTICS command.

The syntax is as follows:

```
UPDATE STATISTICS table | view
       [
       {
       { index | statistics_name }
       | ( { index |statistics_name } [ ,...n ] )
       }
       ]
       [       WITH
       [
       [ FULLSCAN ]
       | SAMPLE number { PERCENT | ROWS }
       | RESAMPLE
       ]
       [ , ] [ ALL | COLUMNS | INDEX ]
       [ [ , ] NORECOMPUTE ]
       ]
```

Table 24-5 shows the arguments of this command.

Table 24-5. UPDATE STATISTICS Arguments

Argument	Description
table | view	This defines the table name or indexed view for which to update statistics.
{ index | statistics_name}|	This specifies the name of the index or named statistics to update.
FULLSCAN| SAMPLE number { PERCENT | ROWS } |RESAMPLE	FULLSCAN, when specified, reads all rows when generating the statistics. SAMPLE reads either a defined number of rows or a percentage. RESAMPLE updates statistics based on the original sampling method.
[ALL | COLUMNS | INDEX]	When ALL is designated, all existing statistics are updated. When COLUMN is designated, only column statistics are updated. When INDEX is designated, only index statistics are updated.
NORECOMPUTE	This option designates that once the statistics are created, they should not be updated–even when data changes occur. Again, this option should rarely, if ever, be used. Fresh statistics allow SQL Server to generate good query plans.
INCREMENTAL	Enabling this option sets the statistics per partition. The default is OFF, which combines stats across all partitions.

This example updates all the statistics for the Sales.Customer table, populating statistics based on the latest data:

```
USE AdventureWorks2014;
GO
UPDATE STATISTICS Sales.Customer
WITH FULLSCAN;
```

This next example illustrates how to update statistics on a partitioned table while taking advantage of the INCREMENTAL option introduced in SQL Server 2014. This example uses the partitioned table created in Chapter 15 (Managing Large Tables):

```
USE MegaCorpData;
GO
UPDATE STATISTICS dbo.WebSiteHits
WITH INCREMENTAL = ON;
```

How It Works

This example updated all the statistics for the Sales.Customer table, refreshing them with the latest data. The first line of code designated the table name containing the statistics to be updated:

```
UPDATE STATISTICS Sales.Customer
```

The last line of code designated that all rows in the table would be read so as to update the statistics:

```
WITH FULLSCAN
```

The second example illustrated the use of INCREMENTAL to update the stats on a partitioned table. This was done through the last line:

```
WITH INCREMENTAL = ON;
```

24-9. Generating Statistics Across All Tables

Problem

You are benchmarking new queries and do not want to wait for the query optimizer to create new single-column statistics.

Solution

Execute sp_createstats to create single-column statistics.

You can automatically generate statistics across all tables in a database for those columns that don't already have statistics associated with them by using the system-stored procedure sp_createstats. The syntax is as follows:

```
sp_createstats [ [ @indexonly = ] 'indexonly' ] [ , [ @fullscan = ] 'fullscan' ] [ ,
[ @norecompute = ] 'norecompute' ]
```

Table 24-6 describes the arguments of this command.

Table 24-6. sp_createstats Arguments

Argument	Description
indexonly	When indexonly is designated, only columns used in indexes will be considered for statistics creation.
fullscan	When fullscan is designated, all rows will be evaluated for the generated statistics. If not designated, the default behavior is to extract statistics via sampling.
norecompute	The norecompute option designates that once the statistics are created, they should not be updated, even when data changes occur. Like with CREATE STATISTICS and UPDATE STATISTICS, this option should rarely, if ever, be used. Fresh statistics allow SQL Server to generate good query plans.
incremental	Enabling this option sets the statistics per partition. The default is OFF, which combines stats across all partitions.

This example demonstrates creating new statistics on columns in the database that don't already have statistics created for them:

```
USE AdventureWorks2014;
GO
EXECUTE sp_createstats;
GO
```

This returns the following (abridged) result set:

```
Table 'AdventureWorks2014.Production.ProductProductPhoto': Creating statistics for the
following columns:
    Primary
    ModifiedDate
Table 'AdventureWorks2014.Production.TransactionHistory': Creating statistics for the
following columns:
    ReferenceOrderLineID
    TransactionDate
    TransactionType
    Quantity
    ActualCost
    ModifiedDate
Table 'AdventureWorks2014.Production.ProductReview': Creating statistics for the following
columns:
    ReviewerName
    ReviewDate
...
```

How It Works

This example created single-column statistics for the tables within the AdventureWorks2014 database, refreshing them with the latest data.

24-10. Updating Statistics Across All Tables

Problem

You want to update statistics across all tables in the current database.

Solution

You can execute the stored procedure sp_updatestats.

If you want to update all statistics in the current database, you can use the system-stored procedure sp_updatestats. This stored procedure updates statistics only when necessary (when data changes have occurred). Statistics on unchanged data will not be updated.

The next example automatically updates all statistics in the current database:

```
USE AdventureWorks2014;
GO
EXECUTE sp_updatestats;
GO
```

This returns the following (abridged) results. Notice the informational message of "update is not necessary." The results you see may differ based on the state of your table statistics.

```
Updating [Production].[ProductProductPhoto]
[PK_ProductProductPhoto_ProductID_ProductPhotoID], update is not necessary...
[AK_ProductProductPhoto_ProductID_ProductPhotoID], update is not necessary...
[_WA_Sys_00000002_01142BA1], update is not necessary...
[Primary], update is not necessary...
[ModifiedDate], update is not necessary...
0 index(es)/statistic(s) have been updated, 5 did not require update.
...
```

How It Works

This example updated statistics for the tables within the AdventureWorks2014 database, updating only the statistics where data modifications had impacted the reliability of the statistics.

24-11. Viewing Statistics Details

Problem

You want to see detailed information about column statistics.

Solution

To view detailed information about column statistics, you can use the DBCC SHOW STATISTICS command.
The syntax is as follows:

```
DBCC SHOW_STATISTICS ( 'tablename' | 'viewname' , target )
[ WITH [ NO_INFOMSGS ]
< STAT_HEADER | DENSITY_VECTOR | HISTOGRAM > [ , n ] ]
```

Table 24-7 shows the arguments of this command.

Table 24-7. DBCC SHOW_STATISTICS *Arguments*

Argument	Description
'table_name'	'view_name'	This defines the table or indexed view to evaluate.
target	This specifies the name of the index or named statistics to evaluate.
NO_INFOMSGS	When designated, NO_INFOMSGS suppresses informational messages.
STAT_HEADER	DENSITY_VECTOR	HISTOGRAM	STATS_STREAM [, n]	Specifying STAT_HEADER, DENSITY_VECTOR,	STATS_STREAM, or HISTOGRAM designates which result sets will be returned by the command (you can display one or more). Not designating any of these means that all three result sets will be returned.

This example demonstrates how to view the statistics information on the Sales.Customer Stats_
Customer_CustomerType statistics:

```
USE AdventureWorks2014;
GO
DBCC SHOW_STATISTICS ( 'Sales.Customer' , Stats_Customer_AccountNumber);
```

This returns the following result sets:

Name	Updated	Rows	Rows Sampled	Steps	Density	Average key length	String Index	Filter Expression	Unfiltered Rows
AK_Customer_ AccountNumber	Feb 19 2015 10:28AM	19820	19820	152	1	10	YES	NULL	19820

All density	Average Length	Columns
5.045409E-05	10	AccountNumber

RANGE_HI_KEY	RANGE_ ROWS	EQ_ROWS	DISTINCT_ RANGE_ROWS	AVG_RANGE_ROWS
AW00000001	0	1	0	1
...				
AW00027042	127	1	127	1
AW00027298	255	1	255	1
AW00027426	127	1	127	1
...				
AW00030118	0	1	0	1

How It Works

This recipe demonstrated how to get more-specific information about column statistics. In the results of this recipe's example, the All density column points to the selectivity of a column. *Selectivity* refers to the percentage of rows that will be returned given a specific column's value. Columns with a low density and high selectivity often make for useful indexes (useful to the query optimization process).

In this recipe's example, the All density value was 5.045409E-05 (float), which equates to a decimal value of 0.00005045409. This is the result of dividing 1 by the number of rows, in this case 19,820.

If you had a column with a high density of similar values and low selectivity (one value is likely to return many rows), you can make an educated assumption that an index on this particular column is unlikely to be very useful to SQL Server in generating a query execution plan.

24-12. Removing Statistics

Problem

You have finished a cycle in your benchmarking and want to remove statistics that were created during that cycle.

Solution

To remove statistics, use the DROP STATISTICS command. The syntax is as follows:

```
DROP STATISTICS table.statistics_name | view.statistics_name [ ,...n ]
```

This command allows you to drop one or more statistics, prefixed with the table or indexed view name.

In this example, the Sales.Customer_Stats_Customer_AccountNumber statistics are dropped from the database:

```
USE AdventureWorks2014;
GO
DROP STATISTICS Sales.SalesOrderDetail.Stats_SalesOrderDetail_UnitPrice_Filtered;
```

How It Works

This recipe dropped user-created statistics using DROP STATISTICS. The statistics were dropped using the three-part name of schema.table.statistics_name.

24-13. Finding When Stats Need to Be Created

Problem

You have an application on which the vendor recommends not having AUTO_CREATE_STATISTICS enabled. You need to determine when to manually create statistics based on workload.

Solution

Extended Events (XEvent) provide a means by which to track when statistics might be missing for columns in a query. When a query is executed and a new plan is generated, if statistics are missing, the event will trigger and data could be captured to help determine if statistics should be created on the column(s) in question.

To demonstrate this, we will disable AUTO_CREATE_STATISTICS in the AdventureWorks2014 database and then create the XEvent session to trap the data associated to the missing statistics:

```
-- Create database and turn auto create statistics off
USE master;
GO

ALTER DATABASE AdventureWorks2014
SET AUTO_CREATE_STATISTICS OFF WITH NO_WAIT
GO
```

```
USE master;
GO
-- Create the Event Session
IF EXISTS(SELECT *
        FROM sys.server_event_sessions
        WHERE name='MissingColumnStats')
    DROP EVENT SESSION MissingColumnStats
    ON SERVER;
GO
-- Create XEvent session
CREATE EVENT SESSION [MissingColumnStats] ON SERVER
ADD EVENT sqlserver.missing_column_statistics(SET collect_column_list=(1)
ACTION(sqlserver.sql_text, sqlserver.database_name))
ADD TARGET package0.event_file(SET filename=N'C:\Database\XE\MissingColumnStats.xel')
GO
--Start XEvent session
ALTER EVENT SESSION [MissingColumnStats]
ON SERVER
STATE = START
GO
```

With the session running in the background on the server, we will now execute a query to generate a missing statistics event:

```
USE AdventureWorks2014;
GO
Select Unitprice
        From Sales.SalesOrderDetail
        WHERE UnitPrice >= 1000.00 AND UnitPrice <= 1500.00;
GO
```

Finally, I will wrap it up by querying the session data so as to determine what statistics may be missing:

```
use master;
GO

SELECT
event_data.value('(event/@name)[1]', 'varchar(50)') AS event_name,
    event_data.value('(event/@timestamp)[1]', 'varchar(50)') AS [TIMESTAMP],
        event_data.value('(event/action[@name="database_name"]/value)[1]', 'varchar(max)')
AS DBName
        ,event_data.value('(event/action[@name="sql_text"]/value)[1]', 'varchar(max)') AS
SQLText
        ,event_data.value('(event/data[@name="column_list"]/value)[1]', 'varchar(max)') AS
AffectedColumn
FROM(
SELECT CONVERT(XML, t2.event_data) AS event_data
 FROM (
  SELECT target_data = convert(XML, target_data)
   FROM sys.dm_xe_session_targets t
    INNER JOIN sys.dm_xe_sessions s
```

```
       ON t.event_session_address = s.address
   WHERE t.target_name = 'event_file'
    AND s.name = 'MissingColumnStats') cte1
   CROSS APPLY cte1.target_data.nodes('//EventFileTarget/File') FileEvent(FileTarget)
   CROSS APPLY  sys.fn_xe_file_target_read_file(FileEvent.FileTarget.value('@name',
'varchar(1000)'), NULL, NULL, NULL) t2)
     AS evts(event_data);
```

How It Works

This recipe showed how to trap data from an Extended Event session to determine when there may be missing statistics. When circumstances forbid the use of AUTO_CREATE_STATISTICS, it may be necessary to monitor for the missing statistics and then to manually create those statistics where appropriate. To demonstrate how this works, the AdventureWorks2014 database had the AUTO_CREATE_STATISTICS setting disabled. Then the XEvent session was created to monitor for missing_column_statistics. Once the session was created, a query was executed and then the XEvent session data was evaluated.

XML

by Wayne Sheffield

In SQL Server 2000, if you wanted to store XML data within the database, you had to store it in a character or binary format. This wasn't too troublesome if you just used SQL Server for XML document storage, but attempts to query or modify the stored document within SQL Server were not so straightforward. Introduced in SQL Server 2005, the SQL Server native XML data type helps address this issue.

Relational-database designers may be concerned about this data type, and rightly so. The normalized database provides performance and data integrity benefits that cause us to question why we would need to store XML documents in the first place. Having an XML data type allows you to have your relational data stored alongside your unstructured data. By providing this data type, Microsoft isn't suggesting that you run your high-speed applications based on XML documents. Rather, you may find XML document storage to be useful when data must be "somewhat" structured. For example, let's say your company's website offers an online contract. This contract is available over the Internet for your customer to fill out and then submit. The submitted data is stored in an XML data type. You might choose to store the submitted data in an XML document because your legal department is always changing the document's fields. Also, since this document is submitted only a few times a day, throughput is not an issue. Another good reason to use the native XML data type is for "state" storage. For example, if your .NET applications use XML configuration files, you can store them in a SQL Server database in order to maintain a history of changes and as a backup or recovery option.

■ **Caution** The elements in an XML document and in XQuery methods are case sensitive, regardless of the case sensitivity of the SQL Server instance.

25-1. Creating an XML Column

Problem

You want to store an XML document in your database.

Solution

Store the document in a column with the XML data type:

```
USE tempdb;
CREATE TABLE dbo.Book
        (
        BookID INT IDENTITY CONSTRAINT PK_Book PRIMARY KEY,
        ISBNNBR CHAR(13) NOT NULL,
        BookNM VARCHAR(250) NOT NULL,
        AuthorID INT NOT NULL,
        ChapterDesc XML NULL
        );
GO
```

How It Works

Native XML data types can be used as the data type for columns in a table. Data stored in the XML data type can contain an XML document or XML fragments. An *XML fragment* is an XML instance without a single top-level element for the contents to nest in. Creating an XML-data-type column is as easy as simply using it in the table definition, as shown earlier.

The XML data type can also be used as a parameter to a procedure. See the following:

```
CREATE PROCEDURE dbo.INS_Book
        @ISBNNBR CHAR(13),
        @BookNM VARCHAR(250),
        @AuthorID INT,
        @ChapterDesc XML
AS
INSERT   dbo.Book
        (ISBNNBR,
         BookNM,
         AuthorID,
         ChapterDesc)
VALUES   (@ISBNNBR,
         @BookNM,
         @AuthorID,
         @ChapterDesc);
GO
```

And it can be used as a variable in a batch:

```
DECLARE @Book XML;
SET @Book =
'
<Book name="SQL Server 2014 T-SQL Recipes">
<Chapters>
<Chapter id="1">Getting Started with SELECT</Chapter>
<Chapter id="2">Elementary Programming</Chapter>
<Chapter id="3">Working with NULLs</Chapter>
<Chapter id="4">Combining Data from Multiple Tables</Chapter>
</Chapters>
</Book>
';
```

In the previous example, the variable was declared and then populated with XML data. The next recipe will show you how to use the XML data in the variable.

25-2. Inserting XML Data

Problem

You want to insert XML data into an XML column in a table.

Solution

Utilize the INSERT statement to insert XML data into a column of the XML data type:

```
INSERT  dbo.Book
        (ISBNNBR,
         BookNM,
         AuthorID,
         ChapterDesc)
VALUES  ('9781430242000',
         'SOL Server T-SQL Recipes',
         55,
'<Book name="SQL Server T-SQL Recipes">
<Chapters>
<Chapter id="1">Getting Started with SELECT</Chapter>
<Chapter id="2">Elementary Programming</Chapter>
<Chapter id="3">Nulls and Other Pitfalls</Chapter>
<Chapter id="4">Combining Data from Multiple Tables</Chapter>
</Chapters>
</Book>');
```

How It Works

In this example, data was inserted directly into the table with the INSERT statement. The XML data was passed as a string, which was implicitly converted to the XML data type.

XML data can also be saved into a variable, and the variable can then be used in the INSERT statement:

```
DECLARE @Book XML;
SET @Book =
CAST('<Book name="SOL Server 2014 Fast Answers">
<Chapters>
<Chapter id="1"> Installation, Upgrades... </Chapter>
<Chapter id="2"> Configuring SQL Server </Chapter>
<Chapter id="3"> Creating and Configuring Databases </Chapter>
<Chapter id="4"> SQL Server Agent and SQL Logs </Chapter>
</Chapters>
</Book>' as XML);
```

```
INSERT   dbo.Book
         (ISBNNBR,
          BookNM,
          AuthorID,
          ChapterDesc)
VALUES   ('1590591615',
          'SOL Server 2014 Fast Answers',
          55,
     @Book);
```

In this example, the XML data was first explicitly converted to the XML data type with the CAST function and then stored in a variable of the XML data type. The variable was then used in the SELECT statement to insert the data into the table.

In either example, when the string XML data was being converted to the XML data type (in the first example when being inserted into the column and in the second when being converted with the CAST function), the XML data was checked to ensure that it was well formed. *Well formed* means that it follows the general rules of an XML document. For example, the following code is not well formed (it is missing the closing </Book> tag):

```
DECLARE @Book XML;
SET @Book =
CAST('<Book name="SOL Server 2000 Fast Answers">
<Chapters>
<Chapter id="l"> Installation, Upgrades... </Chapter>
<Chapter id="2"> Configuring SQL Server </Chapter>
<Chapter id="3"> Creating and Configuring Databases </Chapter>
<Chapter id="4"> SQL Server Agent and SQL Logs </Chapter>
</Chapters>
' as XML);
```

When executing this code, the following error is generated:

```
Msg 9400, Level 16, State 1, Line 2
XML parsing: line 8, character 0, unexpected end of input
```

The XML column in this example was untyped. When an XML column is untyped, it means that the contents inserted into the column are not validated against an XML schema. An XML schema is used to define the allowed elements and attributes for an XML document and is discussed in the next recipe.

25-3. Validating XML Data

Problem

You want to ensure that all the elements and attributes of XML data are verified as being in accordance with an agreed-upon standard.

Solution

Utilize an XML schema collection to validate that the elements, attributes, data types, and allowed values are followed in an XML document, as follows:

```
CREATE XML SCHEMA COLLECTION dbo.BookStoreCollection
AS
N'<xsd:schema  targetNamespace="http://PROD/BookStore"
               xmlns:xsd="http://www.w3.org/2001/XMLSchema"
               xmlns:sqltypes="http://schemas.microsoft.com/sqlserver/2004/sqltypes"
               elementFormDefault="qualified">
    <xsd:import  namespace="http://schemas.microsoft.com/sqlserver/2004/sqltypes"/>
    <xsd:element  name="Book">
        <xsd:complexType>
            <xsd:sequence>
                <xsd:element  name="BookName"  minOccurs="0">
                    <xsd:simpleType>
                        <xsd:restriction          base="sqltypes:varchar">
                            <xsd:maxLength  value="50"    />
                        </xsd:restriction>
                    </xsd:simpleType>
                </xsd:element>
                <xsd:element  name="ChapterID"  type="sqltypes:int" minOccurs="0"/>
                <xsd:element  name="ChapterNM"  minOccurs="0">
                    <xsd:simpleType>
                        <xsd:restriction          base="sqltypes:varchar">
                            <xsd:maxLength  value="50"    />
                        </xsd:restriction>
                    </xsd:simpleType>
                </xsd:element>
            </xsd:sequence>
        </xsd:complexType>
    </xsd:element>
</xsd:schema>';
GO
```

How It Works

This example built an XML schema (which is also referred to as an XML schema definition, or XSD). An XML schema defines the elements, attributes, data types, and allowed values for the XML document. In particular, note the lines that define the elements ChapterID and ChapterNM. Both of these specify that minOccurs=0, which means that the element does not have to exist. This value, if not specified, defaults to 1. Another item that is unspecified in the example is maxOccurs. This value also defaults to 1, and this indicates the maximum number of times that this element can exist.

■ **Tip** For a review of XML schema fundamentals, visit the World Wide Web Consortium (W3C) standards site at www.w3.org/TR/XMLschema-0/.

The syntax for the CREATE XML SCHEMA COLLECTION statement is as follows:

```
CREATE XML SCHEMA COLLECTION [ <relational_schema>. ]sql_identifier AS Expression
```

Table 25-1 describes the arguments.

Table 25-1. *CREATE XML SCHEMA COLLECTION Arguments*

Argument	Description
relational_schema	Identifies the relational schema name. If it's not specified, the default relational schema is assumed.
sql_identifier	The SQL identifier for the XML schema collection
Expression	A string constant or scalar variable of the varchar, varbinary, nvarchar, or XML types

You can now create a variable that requires that the XML document adheres to this definition. See the following:

```
DECLARE @Book XML (DOCUMENT BookStoreCollection);
SET @Book =
CAST('
<Book xmlns="http://PROD/BookStore">
    <BookName>"SQL Server 2014 Fast Answers"</BookName>
    <ChapterID>1</ChapterID>
    <ChapterNM>Installation, Upgrades...</ChapterNM>
</Book>' as XML);
GO
```

Note that the <Book> tag specifies the xmlns for the default namespace of the XML schema collection. Using the keyword DOCUMENT or CONTENT with the schema-collection reference lets you determine whether the allowed XML will permit only a full XML document (DOCUMENT) or will also allow XML fragments (CONTENT).

If you attempt to set this variable to XML data that does not adhere to the XML schema, an error is generated:

```
DECLARE @Book XML (DOCUMENT BookStoreCollection);
SET @Book =
CAST('
<Book xmlns="http://PROD/BookStore">
    <BookName>"SOL Server 2014 Fast Answers"</BookName>
    <ChapterID>1</ChapterID>
    <ChapterID>2</ChapterID>
    <ChapterNM>Installation, Upgrades...</ChapterNM>
    <ChapterNM>Configuring SQL Server</ChapterNM>
</Book>' as XML);
GO
```

This XML data has extra `ChapterID` and `ChapterNM` tags. Executing this code generates the following error:

```
Msg 6965, Level 16, State 1, Line 148
XML Validation: Invalid content. Expected element(s): '{http://PROD/BookStore}
ChapterNM'. Found: element '{http://PROD/BookStore}ChapterID' instead. Location:
/*:Book[1]/*:ChapterID[2].
```

This is because the schema did not specify the maxOccurs, which defaults to 1. If maxOccurs were to be added to the schema, this this script would be able to execute:

```
IF EXISTS (SELECT * FROM sys.xml_schema_collections WHERE name = 'BookStoreCollection')
DROP XML SCHEMA COLLECTION dbo.BookStoreCollection;
GO
CREATE XML SCHEMA COLLECTION dbo.BookStoreCollection
AS
N'<xsd:schema   targetNamespace="http://PROD/BookStore"
               xmlns:xsd="http://www.w3.org/2001/XMLSchema"
               xmlns:sqltypes="http://schemas.microsoft.com/sqlserver/2004/sqltypes"
               elementFormDefault="qualified">
    <xsd:import  namespace="http://schemas.microsoft.com/sqlserver/2004/sqltypes"/>
    <xsd:element  name="Book">
        <xsd:complexType>
            <xsd:sequence>
                <xsd:element  name="BookName"  minOccurs="0">
                    <xsd:simpleType>
                        <xsd:restriction          base="sqltypes:varchar">
                            <xsd:maxLength  value="50"    />
                        </xsd:restriction>
                    </xsd:simpleType>
                </xsd:element>
                <xsd:element  name="ChapterID"  type="sqltypes:int" minOccurs="0"
maxOccurs="5"/>
                <xsd:element  name="ChapterNM"  minOccurs="0" maxOccurs="5">
                    <xsd:simpleType>
                        <xsd:restriction          base="sqltypes:varchar">
                            <xsd:maxLength  value="50"    />
                        </xsd:restriction>
                    </xsd:simpleType>
                </xsd:element>
            </xsd:sequence>
        </xsd:complexType>
    </xsd:element>
</xsd:schema>';
```

645

```
GO
DECLARE @Book XML (DOCUMENT BookStoreCollection);
SET @Book =
CAST('
<Book xmlns="http://PROD/BookStore">
    <BookName>"SQL Server 2014 Fast Answers"</BookName>
    <ChapterID>1</ChapterID>
    <ChapterID>2</ChapterID>
    <ChapterNM>Installation, Upgrades...</ChapterNM>
    <ChapterNM>Configuring SQL Server</ChapterNM>
</Book>' as XML);
GO
```

You can also build a table with a column of the XML data type that is required to adhere to this XML schema:

```
CREATE TABLE dbo.BookInfoExport
    (
     BookID INT IDENTITY PRIMARY KEY,
     ISBNNBR CHAR(10) NOT NULL,
     BookNM VARCHAR(250) NOT NULL,
     AuthorID INT NOT NULL,
     ChapterDesc XML(BookStoreCollection) NULL
    );
```

To add additional XML schemas to an existing XML schema collection, you can use the ALTER XML SCHEMA COLLECTION statement. The syntax is as follows:

```
ALTER XML SCHEMA COLLECTION [ relational_schema. ]sql_identifier ADD 'Schema Component'
```

To remove the entire XML schema collection from the database, use the DROP XML SCHEMA COLLECTION statement. The syntax is as follows:

```
DROP XML SCHEMA COLLECTION [ relational_schema. ]sql_identifier
```

The only argument for dropping an existing XML schema collection is the name of the collection. In order to drop an XML schema collection, it cannot be in use in any table definitions.

25-4. Verifying the Existence of XML Schema Collections

Problem

You need to determine which XML schema collections exist on a database.

Solution

Use the system catalog views XML_schema_collections and XML_schema_namespaces to retrieve information about existing XML schema collections:

```
SELECT  SCHEMA_NAME(schema_id) AS SchemaName, name
FROM    sys.XML_schema_collections
ORDER BY create_date;
```

This query returns the following result set:

SchemaName	name
sys	sys
dbo	BookStoreCollection

How It Works

The system catalog views XML_schema_collections and XML_schema_namespaces contain information about existing XML schema collections, and they can be queried to return this information. In the previous example, all of the XML schema collections for the database were returned by querying the XML_schema_collections system catalog view. The namespaces used by XML schema collections can thus be returned with the following query:

```
SELECT  SCHEMA_NAME(c.schema_id) AS SchemaName, n.name
FROM    sys.XML_schema_namespaces n
        INNER JOIN sys.XML_schema_collections c
            ON c.XML_collection_id = n.XML_collection_id
WHERE   c.name = 'BookStoreCollection';
```

This query returns the following result set:

SchemaName	name
dbo	http://PROD/BookStore

25-5. Retrieving XML Data

Problem

You need to extract data from the XML document.

Solution

To extract data from an XML document, you would utilize one of the various XQuery methods. See the following:

```
CREATE  TABLE dbo.BookInvoice
        (
        BookInvoiceID INT IDENTITY PRIMARY  KEY,
        BookInvoiceXML XML NOT  NULL
        );
GO
```

```
INSERT   dbo.BookInvoice (BookInvoiceXML)
VALUES
('<BookInvoice  invoicenumber="1"  customerid="22"     orderdate="2008-07-01Z">
<OrderItems>
<Item  id="22"  qty="1"  name="SQL Fun in the Sun"/>
<Item  id="24"  qty="1"  name="T-SQL Crossword Puzzles"/>
</OrderItems>
</BookInvoice>'),

('<BookInvoice  invoicenumber="1"  customerid="40"  orderdate="2008-07-11Z">
<OrderItems>
<Item  id="11"  qty="1"  name="MCITP Cliff Notes"/>
</OrderItems>
</BookInvoice>'),

('<BookInvoice  invoicenumber="1"  customerid="9"  orderdate="2008-07-22Z">
<OrderItems>
<Item  id="11"  qty="1"  name="MCITP Cliff Notes"/>
<Item  id="24"  qty="1"  name="T-SQL Crossword Puzzles"/>
</OrderItems>
</BookInvoice>');


SELECT   BookInvoiceID
FROM     dbo.BookInvoice
WHERE    BookInvoiceXML.exist('/BookInvoice/OrderItems/Item[@id=11]') = 1;
```

This query returns the following result set:

```
BookInvoiceID
-------------
2
3
```

How It Works

The XML-data-type column can be queried and the data can be modified using XQuery methods. *XQuery* is a query language that is used to search XML documents. The XQuery methods described in Table 25-2 are integrated into SQL Server and can be used in regular Transact-SQL queries. (Data modifications using XQuery are demonstrated in the next recipe.)

Table 25-2. *XQuery Methods*

Method	Description
exist	Returns 1 for an XQuery expression when it evaluates to TRUE; otherwise, returns 0 for FALSE
modify	Performs updates against XML data (demonstrated after this recipe)
nodes	Shreds XML data to relational data, identifying nodes-to-row mapping
query	Returns XML results based on an XQuery expression
value	Returns a scalar SQL data-type value based on an XQuery expression

■ **Tip** For an in-depth review of XQuery fundamentals, visit the World Wide Web Consortium (W3C) standards site at www.w3.org/TR/xquery/. XQuery supports iteration syntax using the for, let, where, order by, and return clauses (acronym FLWOR). In SQL Server 2005, let was not supported. SQL Server now supports let, starting from SQL Server 2008.

XQuery methods are implemented as a method of the XML column. Thus, they are called in the format (XML Column).(XQuery method). Additionally, as pointed out at the beginning of the chapter, these methods are case sensitive and must be used in lowercase, regardless of the case sensitivity of your SQL Server instance.

In the previous example, the exist method was used to find all rows from the table for purchases of the item with an ID of 11. The next example demonstrates the nodes method, which shreds a document into a relational rowset. A local variable is used to populate a single XML document from the BookInvoice table, which is then referenced using the nodes method. This query retrieves a document and lists the ID element of each BookInvoice/OrderItems/Item node:

```
DECLARE @BookInvoiceXML XML;
SELECT  @BookInvoiceXML = BookInvoiceXML
FROM    dbo.BookInvoice
WHERE   BookInvoiceID = 2;

SELECT  BookID.value('@id', 'integer') BookID
FROM    @BookInvoiceXML.nodes('/BookInvoice/OrderItems/Item') AS BookTable (BookID);
```

This query returns the following result set:

```
BookID
-----------
11
```

The next example demonstrates the query method, which is used to return the two-item elements from a specific XML document:

```
DECLARE @BookInvoiceXML XML;
SELECT  @BookInvoiceXML = BookInvoiceXML
FROM    dbo.BookInvoice
WHERE   BookInvoiceID = 3;
SELECT  @BookInvoiceXML.query('/BookInvoice/OrderItems');
```

This query returns the following result set:

```
<OrderItems><Item id="11" qty="1" name="MCITP Cliff Notes" /><Item id="24" qty="1"
name="T-SQL Crossword Puzzles" /></OrderItems>
```

The final example of this recipe demonstrates the value method, which is used to find the distinct book names from the first and second items within the BookInvoiceXML XML column. See the following:

```
SELECT BookInvoiceXML.value('(/BookInvoice/OrderItems/Item/@name)[1]',
                             'varchar(30)') AS BookTitles
FROM    dbo.BookInvoice
UNION
SELECT BookInvoiceXML.value('(/BookInvoice/OrderItems/Item/@name)[2]',
                             'varchar(30)')
FROM    dbo.BookInvoice;
```

This query returns the following result set:

```
BookTitles
------------------------------
NULL
MCITP Cliff Notes
SQL Fun in the Sun
T-SQL Crossword Puzzles
```

The NULL value in the above results comes from customerid=40–that order only had one book and we were looking for orders with two items. If you run just the second half of the last query, you will see that the second order (for this customer) is returning a NULL value.

The value method has two parameters: the first is a singleton value and the second is the data type to be returned. If the query does not return a singleton value, an error will be returned:

```
SELECT DISTINCT
        BookInvoiceXML.value('(/BookInvoice/OrderItems/Item/@name)',
                             'varchar(30)')
FROM    dbo.BookInvoice;
```

This query generates the following error:

```
Msg 2389, Level 16, State 1, Line 245
XQuery [dbo.BookInvoice.BookInvoiceXML.value()]: 'value()' requires a singleton
(or empty sequence), found operand of type 'xdt:untypedAtomic *'
```

25-6. Modifying XML Data

Problem

You want to modify data stored in a column with the XML data type.

Solution

Utilize the XQuery `modify` method to update XML data:

```
SELECT BookInvoiceXML
FROM dbo.BookInvoice
WHERE BookInvoiceID = 2;

UPDATE dbo.BookInvoice
SET BookInvoiceXML.modify
('insert <Item id="920" qty="1" name="SQL Server 2014 Transact-SQL Recipes"/>
into (/BookInvoice/OrderItems)[1]')
WHERE BookInvoiceID = 2;

SELECT BookInvoiceXML
FROM dbo.BookInvoice
WHERE BookInvoiceID = 2;
```

These queries return the following result sets:

```
BookInvoiceXML
--------------------------------------------------------------------------------
<BookInvoice invoicenumber="1" customerid="40" orderdate="2008-07-11Z"><OrderItems><Item
id="11" qty="1" name="MCDBA Cliff Notes" /></OrderItems></BookInvoice>
```

```
BookInvoiceXML
--------------------------------------------------------------------------------
<BookInvoice invoicenumber="1" customerid="40" orderdate="2008-07-11Z"><OrderItems><Item
id="11" qty="1" name="MCDBA Cliff Notes" /><Item id="920" qty="1" name="SQL Server 2014
Transact-SQL Recipes" /></OrderItems></BookInvoice>
```

How It Works

XML-data-type columns can be modified using the `modify` method in conjunction with the UPDATE statement, allowing you to insert, update, or delete an XML node in the XML-data-type column. In this example, the XQuery `modify` function is used to call an `insert` command to add a new item element into the existing XML document. The `insert` command inside the XQuery modify method is known as the XML DML operator; other XML DML operators are `delete` (which removes a node from the XML) and `replace` (which updates XML data).

25-7. Indexing XML Data

Problem

You want to improve the performance of queries that are selecting data from XML data-typed columns.

Solution

Add an XML index on the XML column:

```
CREATE PRIMARY XML INDEX idx_XML_Primary_Book_ChapterDESC
ON dbo.Book(ChapterDesc);
```

How It Works

XML columns can store up to 2GB per column, per row. Because of this potentially large amount of data, querying against the XML column can cause poor query performance. You can improve the performance of queries against XML-data-type columns by using XML indexes. When you create the primary XML index, the XML data is persisted to a special internal table in tabular form, which allows for more-efficient querying. To create an XML index, the table must first already have a clustered index defined on the primary key of the table.

XML columns can have only *one* primary XML index defined and then up to *three* secondary indexes (of different types, described in a bit). The CREATE INDEX command is used to define XML indexes. The abridged syntax is as follows:

```
CREATE [ PRIMARY ] XML INDEX index_name ON <object> ( xml_column_name ) [ USING XML INDEX
xml_index_name
[ FOR { VALUE | PATH | PROPERTY } ] ] [ WITH ( <xml_index_option> [ ,...n ] ) ][ ; ]
```

Creating an index for an XML column uses several of the same arguments as for creating a regular table index (see the "Managing Indexes" chapter for more information). Table 25-3 describes the XML-specific arguments of this command.

Table 25-3. CREATE XML INDEX *Arguments*

Argument	Description
Object	This specifies the name of the table the index is being added to.
XML_column_name	This defines the name of the XML-data-type column.
XML_index_name	This is the unique name (at the table level) of the XML index.
VALUE | PATH | PROPERTY	These are arguments for secondary indexes only and relate to XQuery optimization. A VALUE secondary index is used for indexing based on imprecise paths. A PATH secondary index is used for indexing via a path and value. A PROPERTY secondary index is used for indexing based on querying node values that are based on a path.

In the first example shown earlier, a primary XML index was created on an XML-data-type column. Now that a primary XML index has been created, secondary XML indexes can also be created. The following example creates a VALUE secondary XML index:

```
CREATE XML INDEX idx_XML_Value_Book_ChapterDESC ON dbo.Book(ChapterDESC)
USING XML INDEX idx_XML_Primary_Book_ChapterDESC FOR VALUE;
```

XML indexes may look a little odd at first, because you are adding secondary indexes to the same XML-data-type column. Adding the different types of secondary indexes helps benefit performance, based on the different types of XQuery queries you plan to execute. All in all, you can have up to four indexes on a single XML-data-type column: one primary and three secondary. A primary XML index must be created prior to being able to create secondary indexes. A PATH secondary index is used to enhance performance for queries that specify a path and value from the XML column using XQuery. A PROPERTY secondary index is used to enhance the performance of queries that retrieve specific node values by specifying a path using XQuery. The VALUE secondary index is used to enhance the performance of queries that retrieve data using an imprecise path (for example, for an XPath expression that employs //, which can be used to find nodes in a document no matter where they exist).

25-8. Formatting Relational Data as XML

Problem

You need to convert relational data stored in your database into an XML document.

Solution

Utilize the FOR XML clause of a SELECT statement to return an XML document from the tables and columns selected:

```
SELECT   ShiftID,
         Name
FROM     AdventureWorks2014.HumanResources.[Shift]
FOR      XML RAW('Shift'),
             ROOT('Shifts'),
             TYPE;
```

This query returns the following result set:

```
<Shifts>
    <Shift ShiftID="1" Name="Day" />
    <Shift ShiftID="2" Name="Evening" />
    <Shift ShiftID="3" Name="Night" />
</Shifts>
```

How It Works

The FOR XML clause is included at the end of a SELECT query in order to return data in an XML format. FOR XML extends a SELECT statement by returning the relational query results in an XML format. FOR XML operates in four different modes: RAW, AUTO, EXPLICIT, and PATH. The AUTO and RAW modes allow for a quick and semi-automated formatting of the results, whereas EXPLICIT and PATH provide more control over the hierarchy of data and the assignment of elements versus attributes. FOR XML PATH, however, is an easier alternative to EXPLICIT mode for those developers who are more familiar with the XPath language.

In RAW mode, a single-row element is generated for each row in the result set, with each column in the result set being converted to an attribute within the single-row element.

In this example, FOR XML RAW is used to return the results of the HumanResources.Shift table in an XML format. The TYPE option is used to return the results in the XML data type, and ROOT is used to define a top-level element where the results will be nested. The FOR XML AUTO mode creates XML elements in the results of a SELECT statement and also automatically nests the data based on the columns in the SELECT clause. AUTO shares the same options as RAW.

In this example, Employee, Shift, and Department information is queried from the AdventureWorks2014 database, with XML AUTO automatically arranging the hierarchy of the results:

```
SELECT TOP 3
        BusinessEntityID,
        Shift.Name,
        Department.Name
FROM    AdventureWorks2014.HumanResources.EmployeeDepartmentHistory Employee
        INNER JOIN AdventureWorks2014.HumanResources.Shift Shift
            ON Employee.ShiftID = Shift.ShiftID
        INNER JOIN AdventureWorks2014.HumanResources.Department Department
            ON Employee.DepartmentID = Department.DepartmentID
ORDER BY BusinessEntityID
FOR     XML AUTO,
            TYPE;
```

This query returns the following result set:

```
<Employee BusinessEntityID="1">
    <Shift Name="Day">
        <Department Name="Executive" />
    </Shift>
</Employee>
<Employee BusinessEntityID="2">
    <Shift Name="Day">
        <Department Name="Engineering" />
    </Shift>
</Employee>
<Employee BusinessEntityID="3">
    <Shift Name="Day">
        <Department Name="Engineering" />
    </Shift>
</Employee>
```

Notice that the second `INNER JOIN` caused the values from the `Department` table to be children of the `Shift` table's values. The `Shift` element was then included as a child of the `Employee` element. Rearranging the order of the columns in the `SELECT` clause, however, impacts how the hierarchy is returned. Here's an example:

```
SELECT TOP 3
        Shift.Name,
        Department.Name,
        BusinessEntityID
FROM    AdventureWorks2014.HumanResources.EmployeeDepartmentHistory Employee
        INNER JOIN AdventureWorks2014.HumanResources.Shift Shift
            ON Employee.ShiftID = Shift.ShiftID
        INNER JOIN AdventureWorks2014.HumanResources.Department Department
            ON Employee.DepartmentID = Department.DepartmentID
ORDER BY Shift.Name,
        Department.Name,
        BusinessEntityID
FOR     XML AUTO,
            TYPE;
```

This query returns the following result set:

```
<Shift Name="Day">
    <Department Name="Document Control">
        <Employee BusinessEntityID="217" />
        <Employee BusinessEntityID="219" />
        <Employee BusinessEntityID="220" />
    </Department>
</Shift>
```

This time, the top of the hierarchy was `Shift`, with a child element of `Department`, and `Employees` were child elements of the `Department` elements.

The `FOR XML EXPLICIT` mode allows you more control over the XML results, letting you define whether columns are assigned to elements or attributes. The `EXPLICIT` parameters have the same use and meaning as those for RAW and AUTO; however, `EXPLICIT` also makes use of *directives*, which are used to define the resulting elements and attributes. For example, the following query displays the `VendorID` and `CreditRating` columns as attributes and displays the `VendorName` column as an element. The column is defined after the column alias using an element name, tag number, attribute, and directive. See the following:

```
SELECT TOP 3
        1 AS Tag,
        NULL AS Parent,
        BusinessEntityID AS [Vendor!1!VendorID],
        Name AS [Vendor!1!VendorName!ELEMENT],
        CreditRating AS [Vendor!1!CreditRating]
FROM    AdventureWorks2014.Purchasing.Vendor
ORDER BY CreditRating
FOR     XML EXPLICIT,
            TYPE;
```

This query returns the following result set:

```
<Vendor VendorID="1496" CreditRating="1">
    <VendorName>Advanced Bicycles</VendorName>
</Vendor>
<Vendor VendorID="1492" CreditRating="1">
    <VendorName>Australia Bike Retailer</VendorName>
</Vendor>
<Vendor VendorID="1500" CreditRating="1">
    <VendorName>Morgan Bike Accessories</VendorName>
</Vendor>
```

The Tag column in the SELECT clause was required in EXPLICIT mode in order to produce the XML document output. Each tag number represents a constructed element. The Parent column alias was also required, providing the hierarchical information about any parent elements. The Parent column referenced the tag of the parent element. If the Parent column were NULL, this would indicate that the element had no parent and was top-level.

The TYPE directive in the FOR XML clause of the previous query was used to return the results as a true SQL Server native XML data type, allowing you to store the results in XML or query them using XQuery.

Next, the FOR XML PATH option defines column names and aliases as XPath expressions. XPath is a language used for searching data within an XML document.

■ **Tip** For information on XPath, visit the World Wide Web Consortium (W3C) standards site at www.w3.org/TR/xpath.

FOR XML PATH uses some of the same arguments and keywords as other FOR XML variations. Where it differs, however, is in the SELECT clause, where XPath syntax is used to define elements, subelements, attributes, and data values. Here's an example:

```
SELECT  Name AS "@Territory",
        CountryRegionCode AS "@Region",
        SalesYTD
FROM    AdventureWorks2014.Sales.SalesTerritory
WHERE   SalesYTD > 6000000
ORDER BY SalesYTD DESC
FOR     XML PATH('TerritorySales'),
        ROOT('CompanySales'),
        TYPE;
```

This query returns the following result set:

```
<CompanySales>
    <TerritorySales Territory="Southwest" Region="US">
        <SalesYTD>10510853.8739</SalesYTD>
    </TerritorySales>
    <TerritorySales Territory="Northwest" Region="US">
        <SalesYTD>7887186.7882</SalesYTD>
    </TerritorySales>
    <TerritorySales Territory="Canada" Region="CA">
        <SalesYTD>6771829.1376</SalesYTD>
    </TerritorySales>
</CompanySales>
```

This query returned results with a root element of CompanySales and a subelement of TerritorySales. The TerritorySales element was then attributed based on the territory and region codes (both prefaced with @ in the SELECT clause). The SalesYTD, which was unmarked with XPath directives, became a subelement to TerritorySales. Using a column alias starting with @ and not containing a / is an example of an *XPath-like name*.

In this next example, the query explicitly specifies the hierarchy of the elements:

```
SELECT  Name AS "Territory",
        CountryRegionCode AS "Territory/Region",
        SalesYTD AS "Territory/Region/YTDSales"
FROM    AdventureWorks2014.Sales.SalesTerritory
WHERE   SalesYTD > 6000000
ORDER BY SalesYTD DESC
FOR     XML PATH('TerritorySales'),
            ROOT('CompanySales'),
            TYPE;
```

This query returns the following result set:

```
<CompanySales>
    <TerritorySales>
        <Territory>Southwest
            <Region>US
                <YTDSales>10510853.8739</YTDSales>
            </Region>
        </Territory>
    </TerritorySales>
    <TerritorySales>
        <Territory>Northwest
            <Region>US
                <YTDSales>7887186.7882</YTDSales>
            </Region>
```

```
        </Territory>
    </TerritorySales>
    <TerritorySales>
        <Territory>Canada
            <Region>CA
                <YTDSales>6771829.1376</YTDSales>
            </Region>
        </Territory>
    </TerritorySales>
</CompanySales>
```

The query specified that the CountryRegionCode should have an element name of Region as a subelement to the Territory element, and also specified that the SalesYTD should have an element name of YTDSales as a subelement to the Region element.

25-9. Formatting XML Data as Relational

Problem

You need to return parts of an XML document as relational data.

Solution

Utilize the OPENXML function to parse a document and return the selected parts as a rowset:

```
DECLARE @XMLdoc XML,
        @iDoc   INTEGER;
SET   @XMLdoc  =
'<Book  name="SQL Server 2000 Fast Answers">
    <Chapters>
        <Chapter  id="1"  name="Installation, Upgrades"/>
        <Chapter  id="2"  name="Configuring SQL Server"/>
        <Chapter  id="3"  name="Creating and Configuring Databases"/>
        <Chapter  id="4"  name="SQL Server Agent and SQL Logs"/>
    </Chapters>
</Book>';

EXECUTE sp_XML_preparedocument @iDoc OUTPUT, @XMLdoc;

SELECT Chapter, ChapterNm
FROM OPENXML(@iDoc, '/Book/Chapters/Chapter', 0)
WITH (Chapter INT '@id', ChapterNm VARCHAR(50) '@name');

EXECUTE sp_xml_removedocument @idoc;
```

This query returns the following result set:

```
Chapter     ChapterNm
----------- --------------------------------------------------------
1           Installation, Upgrades
2           Configuring SQL Server
3           Creating and Configuring Databases
4           SQL Server Agent and SQL Logs
```

How It Works

OPENXML converts XML format to a relational form. To perform this conversion, the sp_XML_preparedocument system-stored procedure is used to create an internal pointer to the XML document, which is then used with OPENXML in order to return the rowset data.

The syntax for the sp_XML_preparedocument system-stored procedure is as follows:

```
sp_xml_preparedocument
hdoc
OUTPUT
[ , xmltext ]
[ , xpath_namespaces ]
```

Table 25-4 describes the arguments for this command.

Table 25-4. sp_XML_preparedocument Arguments

Argument	Description
hdoc	The handle to the newly created document
xmltext	The original XML document. The MSXML parser parses this XML document. xmltext is a text parameter: char, nchar, varchar, nvarchar, text, ntext, or XML. The default value is NULL, in which case an internal representation of an empty XML document is created.
xpath_namespaces	Specifies the namespace declarations that are used in row and column XPath expressions in OPENXML. xpath_namespaces is a text parameter: char, nchar, varchar, nvarchar, text, ntext, or XML.

The syntax for the OPENXML command is as follows:

```
OPENXML(idoc ,rowpattern, flags)
[WITH (SchemaDeclaration | TableName)]
```

Table 25-5 shows the arguments for this command.

Table 25-5. OPENXML Arguments

Argument	Description
idoc	This is the internal representation of the XML document as represented by the sp_XML_preparedocument system-stored procedure.
rowpattern	This defines the XPath pattern used to return nodes from the XML document.
flags	When the flag 0 is used, results default to attribute-centric mappings. When flag 1 is used, attribute-centric mappings are used. If combined with XML_ELEMENTS, then attribute-centric mapping is applied first and then element-centric mapping is applied for columns that are not processed. Flag 2 uses element-centric mapping. If combined with XML_ATTRIBUTES, then attribute-centric mapping is applied first and then element-centric mapping is applied for columns that are not processed. Flag 8 specifies that consumed data should not be copied to the overflow property @mp:xmltext. This flag can be combined with XML_ATTRIBUTES or XML_ELEMENTS, and when specified they are combined with a logical OR.
SchemaDeclaration | TableName	SchemaDeclaration defines the output of the column name (rowset name), column type (valid data type), column pattern (optional XPath pattern), and optional metadata properties (about the XML nodes). If Tablename is used instead, a table must already exist for holding the rowset data.

In this example, the XML document was stored in an XML-data-typed variable. The document was then passed to the sp_XML_preparedocument system-stored procedure, and the document handle was returned.

Next, a SELECT statement called the OPENXML function, passing the XML document handle returned from the sp_XML_preparedocument system-stored procedure for the first parameter and the XPath expression of the node to be queried for the second parameter. For the flags parameter, a 0 was passed in, specifying the use of attribute-centric mappings. The WITH clause defined the actual result output. Two columns were defined: the chapter and the chapter name (Chapter and ChapterNm). For the column definitions, the column name, the data type, and the attribute from the XML document to be used for this column are specified.

Finally, the sp_xml_removedocument system-stored procedure was called, which removed the internal representation of the XML document specified by the document handle and invalidated the document handle.

■ **Note** A parsed XML document is stored in the internal cache of SQL Server, and it uses one-eighth of the total memory available for SQL Server. sp_xml_removedocument should be run to free up the memory used by this parsed XML document.

25-10. Using XML to Return a Delimited String

Problem

You want to return a comma-delimited string from the values of a table's column.

Solution

Utilize the value XML method and the FOR XML clause to have the selected columns from all of the selected rows returned as a comma-delimited string:

```
SELECT STUFF((SELECT TOP (25) ',' + CONVERT(VARCHAR(15), BusinessEntityID)
          FROM AdventureWorks2014.HumanResources.Employee
          ORDER BY BusinessEntityID
          FOR XML PATH(''), TYPE).value('.','varchar(max)'),1,1,'');
```

This query returns the following result set:

```
----------------------------------------------------------------
1,2,3,4,5,6,7,8,9,10,11,12,13,14,15,16,17,18,19,20,21,22,23,24,25
```

How It Works

This recipe created a comma-delimited string of the BusinessEntityID column for the first 25 rows from the HumanResources.Employee table, using a method that has been proven to perform extremely well. Let's examine this query piece by piece:

```
SELECT TOP (25) ',' + CONVERT(VARCHAR(15), BusinessEntityID)
```

This specified the use of the first 25 rows. It created a computed column without a column alias; the computed column consisted of a comma prefixed to the BusinessEntityID (after being converted from an integer to a varchar):

```
FROM AdventureWorks2014.HumanResources.Employee
ORDER BY BusinessEntityID
```

This specified the source of the data and how it should be ordered.

```
FOR XML PATH('') , TYPE
```

This specified that the root of the XML tree should not have a tag name, and to return the results as an XML data type. The combination of the unnamed root element and the calculated column without a column alias returned XML that was just the comma-delimited data.

```
.value('.','varchar(max)')
```

This specified that the XML data returned was to be sent to the XML value method. The '.' instructed the method to use the entire XML tree returned, and to convert it to a specified data type (varchar(max)).

All that remains of this query is the STUFF function. This simply took the result from the query after being converted to a character data type and, starting at the first character (the first comma), replaced one character (that first comma) with an empty string. If you desire to have the values delimited with, say, a comma plus a space, then in the STUFF function you would replace two characters with an empty string, and in the calculated column you would specify the two characters at the beginning of each value.

661

CHAPTER 26

■ ■ ■

Files, Filegroups, and Integrity

by Wayne Sheffield

Every database has a minimum of two files associated with it: the data file and the log file. However, sometimes you may want to add more files (of either type) to the database, increase their size, move them to a different drive, or perform other file-level activities. And once you have all the files on your databases placed and sized appropriately, you will need to perform regular maintenance activities on them to ensure that their integrity does not become compromised. This chapter will show you how to perform these activities.

This chapter simulates having three disk drives by using three subdirectories in the C:\Apress directory. The recipes in this chapter use the following database and are designed to be followed in order. The following code will create these directories and the database:

```
EXECUTE sys.xp_create_subdir 'C:\Apress\Drive1';
EXECUTE sys.xp_create_subdir 'C:\Apress\Drive2';
EXECUTE sys.xp_create_subdir 'C:\Apress\Drive3';

USE master;
GO
IF DB_ID('BookStoreArchive') IS NOT NULL DROP DATABASE BookStoreArchive;
GO

CREATE DATABASE BookStoreArchive
ON PRIMARY
(NAME = 'BookStoreArchive',
 FILENAME = 'C:\Apress\Drive1\BookStoreArchive.MDF',
 SIZE = 4MB,
 MAXSIZE = UNLIMITED,
 FILEGROWTH = 10MB)
LOG ON
(NAME = 'BookStoreArchive_log',
 FILENAME = 'C:\Apress\Drive3\BookStoreArchive_log.LDF',
 SIZE = 512KB,
 MAXSIZE = UNLIMITED,
 FILEGROWTH = 512KB);
```

26-1. Adding a Data File or a Log File

Problem

You need to add a data file and transaction log file to your database.

Solution

Utilize the ALTER DATABASE statement to add new files to a database as follows:

```
ALTER DATABASE BookStoreArchive
ADD FILE
(  NAME = 'BookStoreArchive2',
FILENAME = 'C:\Apress\Drive2\BookStoreArchive2.NDF' ,
SIZE = 1MB ,
MAXSIZE = 10MB,
FILEGROWTH = 1MB )
TO FILEGROUP [PRIMARY];

ALTER DATABASE BookStoreArchive
ADD LOG FILE
(  NAME = 'BookStoreArchive2Log',
FILENAME = 'C:\Apress\Drive3\BookStoreArchive2_log.LDF' ,
SIZE = 1MB ,
MAXSIZE = 5MB,
FILEGROWTH = 1MB)
GO
```

How It Works

Once a database is created, assuming you have available disk space, you can add data files or transaction log files to it as needed. This allows you to expand to new drives if the current physical drive/array is close to filling up or if you are looking to improve performance by spreading I/O across multiple drives. It usually makes sense to add additional data files and log files to a database only if you plan on putting these files on a separate drive/array. Putting multiple files on the same drive/array doesn't improve performance and may benefit you only if you plan on performing separate file or filegroup backups for a very large database.

Adding files doesn't require you to bring the database offline. The syntax for ALTER DATABASE when adding a data file or transaction log file is as follows:

```
ALTER DATABASE database_name {ADD FILE <filespec> [ ,...n ]
[ TO FILEGROUP { filegroup_name | DEFAULT } ] ADD LOG FILE <filespec> [ ,...n ] }
```

Table 26-1 describes the syntax arguments.

Table 26-1. `ALTER DATABASE...ADD FILE` *Arguments*

Argument	Description
database_name	Defines the name of the existing database.
<filespec> [,...n]	Designates one or more explicitly defined data files to add to the database.
filegroup_name | DEFAULT	Designates the logical name of the filegroup. If followed by the DEFAULT keyword, this filegroup will be the default filegroup of the database (meaning all objects will by default be created there).
[LOG ON { <filespec> [,...n] }]	Designates one or more explicitly defined transaction log files for the database.

In this recipe, new data and transaction log files were added to the BookStoreArchive database. To add the data file, the ALTER DATABASE statement was used with the ADD FILE argument, followed by the file specification:

```
ALTER DATABASE BookStoreArchive ADD FILE
```

The filegroup where the new file was added was specified using the TO FILEGROUP clause, followed by the filegroup name in brackets:

```
TO FILEGROUP [PRIMARY]
```

In the second query in the recipe, a new transaction log file was added using the ALTER DATABASE statement and the ADD LOG FILE argument:

```
ALTER DATABASE BookStoreArchive ADD LOG FILE
```

26-2. Retrieving Information about the Files in a Database

Problem

You want to view information about the files that make up a database.

Solution

Query the database's sys.database_files view or the instance's sys.master_files view:

```
SELECT  file_id, type_desc, name, physical_name, state_desc, size, max_size, growth,
is_percent_growth
FROM    BookStoreArchive.sys.database_files;

SELECT  file_id, type_desc, name, physical_name, state_desc, size, max_size, growth,
is_percent_growth
FROM    sys.master_files
WHERE   database_id = DB_ID('BookStoreArchive');
```

Both of these queries produce the following results (results are split into two sections for formatting):

```
file_id type_desc name                  physical_name
------- --------- ------------------    -----------------------------------------
1       ROWS      BookStoreArchive      C:\Apress\Drive1\BookStoreArchive.MDF
2       LOG       BookStoreArchive_log  C:\Apress\Drive3\BookStoreArchive_log.LDF
3       ROWS      BookStoreArchive2     C:\Apress\Drive2\BookStoreArchive2.NDF
4       LOG       BookStoreArchive2Log  C:\Apress\Drive3\BookStoreArchive2_log.LDF

state_desc size max_size    growth is_percent_growth
---------- ---- ----------- ------ -----------------
ONLINE     512  -1          1280   0
ONLINE     64   268435456   64     0
ONLINE     128  1280        128    0
ONLINE     128  640         128    0
```

How It Works

The sys.database_files catalog view stores information about a database's files. This is a database-level view, so it contains information about the files in the current database only.

The sys.master_files catalog view stores information about all of the database files on an instance. In addition to all of the columns that are in the sys.database_files view, sys.master_files also contains the database_id in order to identify the database that each file belongs to.

The queries in this recipe returned the logical and physical name for each file, along with the type of file, the status of the file, the size and max_size of the file, and the growth settings for that file. If the growth is by percent, then the is_percent_growth column will return 1, and the data in the growth column will be the percentage growth. The size, max_size, and growth columns (for fixed-size growths) will show the size in number of 8K pages. A max_size value of -1 indicates that the file will be able to grow until all of the disk space is used.

26-3. Removing a Data File or a Log File

Problem

You need to remove a data file or transaction log file from a database.

Solution

Utilize the ALTER DATABASE statement to remove data files or transaction log files from a database:

```
ALTER DATABASE BookStoreArchive REMOVE FILE BookStoreArchive2;
```

Running this command produces the following message:

```
The file 'BookStoreArchive2' has been removed.
```

How It Works

The ALTER DATABASE statement removed the specified logical file name from the database. You might want to do this if you are relocating a database from one drive to another by creating a new file on one drive and then dropping the old file from the other.

The syntax for dropping a file is as follows:

```
ALTER DATABASE database_name
REMOVE FILE logical_file_name
```

where database_name is the name of an existing database, and logical_file_name is the name of the logical file to be removed from the database.

The logical file being removed must be empty (no data and no active transactions), and it cannot be the primary data file or primary transaction log file. You can use DBCC SHRINKFILE with the EMPTYFILE parameter to empty a file and move any data within it to another file.

26-4. Relocating a Data File or a Log File

Problem

You need to move a data or transaction log file from one physical location to another—for example, from one drive to another.

Solution

Utilize the ALTER DATABASE statement to move data files or transaction log files belonging to a database. The first step is as follows:

```
ALTER DATABASE BookStoreArchive
MODIFY FILE
(NAME = 'BookStoreArchive', FILENAME = 'O:\Apress\BookStoreArchive.mdf')
GO
```

Upon executing this statement, the following message is returned:

```
The file "BookStoreArchive" has been modified in the system catalog. The new path will be
used the next time the database is started.
```

■ **Note** This does not physically move the specified file. Within SQL Server, the location for the file has just been updated. The file will still need to be moved to its proper location using operating system file copy routines.

667

How It Works

The ALTER DATABASE statement updated the specified logical file name to a new file name. As the returned message indicated, this new path will be used when the database is next started. This can occur by stopping and starting the SQL Server instance or by taking the database offline and then bringing it back online. After the SQL Server instance has been shut down or the database has been taken offline, you will still have to move this file to its new location before starting up the SQL Server instance or bringing the database back online. The database can be taken offline, and then be brought back online, with the following commands:

```
USE master;
GO
-- This next statement will close all open connections for users that are not sysadmins
ALTER DATABASE BookStoreArchive SET RESTRICTED_USER WITH ROLLBACK IMMEDIATE;
GO
-- This next statement will close the database
ALTER DATABASE BookStoreArchive SET OFFLINE;
GO
-- Move BookStoreArchive.mdf file from N:\Apress\ to O:\Apress now.
-- On my Windows 7 PC, I had to use Administrator access to move the file.
-- On other operating systems, you may have to modify file/folder permissions
-- to prevent an access denied error.

USE master;
GO
ALTER DATABASE BookStoreArchive SET ONLINE;
GOALTER DATABASE BookStoreArchive SET MULTI_USER WITH ROLLBACK IMMEDIATE;
GO
```

The ALTER DATABASE BookStoreArchive SET RESTRICTED_USER WITH ROLLBACK IMMEDIATE; statement sets the database to where only users that are members of the db_owner database role, or the db_creator or sysadmin server roles, can connect to the database. Any statements currently being run by other connections are canceled and rolled back. The database is then taken offline.

After the database file has been physically moved to its new location, the database is brought back online, and then the database is opened back up to all users.

26-5. Changing a File's Logical Name

Problem

You need to change the logical name of a file in a database.

Solution

Utilize the ALTER DATABASE statement to rename the logical name of a file belonging to a database, as follows:

```
SELECT  name
FROM    BookStoreArchive.sys.database_files;

ALTER DATABASE BookStoreArchive
MODIFY FILE
```

```
(NAME = 'BookStoreArchive',
NEWNAME = 'BookStoreArchive_Data');

SELECT   name
FROM     BookStoreArchive.sys.database_files;
```

This statement returns the following message and result set:

```
name
----------------------------------------------------
BookStoreArchive
BookStoreArchive_log
BookStoreArchive2Log

The file name 'BookStoreArchive_Data' has been set.
name
----------------------------------------------------
BookStoreArchive_Data
BookStoreArchive_log
BookStoreArchive2Log
```

How It Works

The ALTER DATABASE statement allows you to change the logical name of a file belonging to the database without taking the database offline. The logical name of a database doesn't affect the functionality of the database itself, allowing you to change the name for consistency and naming-convention purposes. For example, if you restore a database from a backup using a new database name, you may want the file's logical name to match the new database name.

The syntax of the ALTER DATABASE statement to change the logical name is as follows:

```
ALTER DATABASE database_name
MODIFY FILE
(NAME = logical_file_name, NEWNAME = new_logical_name);
```

where database_name is the name of an existing database, logical_file_name is the logical name of the file to be renamed, and new_logical_name is the new logical file name.

26-6. Increasing the Size of a Database File

Problem

You have a scheduled downtime for your database. During this downtime, you want to increase the database's size to prevent autogrowth operations until your next scheduled downtime.

Solution

Utilize the ALTER DATABASE statement to increase the size of a file belonging to a database:

```
SELECT name, size FROM BookStoreArchive.sys.database_files;

ALTER DATABASE BookStoreArchive
MODIFY FILE
(NAME = 'BookStoreArchive_Data',
 SIZE = 5MB);

SELECT name, size FROM BookStoreArchive.sys.database_files;
```

This statement returns the following result sets:

```
name                   size
---------------------- ----
BookStoreArchive_Data  512
BookStoreArchive_log   64
BookStoreArchive2Log   128

name                   size
---------------------- ----
BookStoreArchive_Data  640
BookStoreArchive_log   64
BookStoreArchive2Log   128
```

How It Works

The MODIFY FILE clause of the ALTER DATABASE statement allows you to increase the size of a file. In the previous example, the size of the BookStoreArchive_Data file was changed from 4MB to 5MB. If you specify the same file size, or lower, you will receive this error message:

```
Msg 5039, Level 16, State 1, Line 1
MODIFY FILE failed. Specified size is less than or equal to current size.
```

▪ **Note** The size column of the sys.databases_files system view reports the quantity of 8KB pages. You will need to convert this number to an appropriate size (MB, GB, etc.)

The syntax of the ALTER DATABASE statement to increase a file size or to modify the file's growth/maxsize settings is as follows:

```
ALTER DATABASE database_name
MODIFY FILE
(
NAME = logical_file_name
[ , SIZE = size [ KB | MB | GB | TB ] ]
[ , MAXSIZE = { max_size [ KB | MB | GB | TB ]
UNLIMITED } ]
[ , FILEGROWTH = growth_increment [ KB | MB | % ] ]
)
```

Table 26-2 shows the arguments of this syntax.

Table 26-2. *ALTER DATABASE...MODIFY FILE Arguments*

Argument	Description
database_name	The name of the existing database
logical_file_name	The logical file name to change size or growth options for
size [KB	MB	GB	TB]	The new size (must be larger than the existing size) of the file based on the sizing attribute of choice (kilobytes, megabytes, gigabytes, terabytes)
{ max_size [KB	MB	GB	TB]	UNLIMITED }]	The new maximum allowable size of the file based on the chosen sizing attributes. If UNLIMITED is chosen, the file can grow to the available space of the physical drive.
growth_increment [KB	MB	%]]	The new amount that the file size increases when space is required. You can designate either the number of kilobytes or megabytes or the percentage of existing file size. If you select 0, file growth will not occur.

These changes are instantaneous. If you are changing the size of a data file, and the local security permission "Perform Volume Maintenance Tasks" (PVMT) has not been granted to the SQL Server service account, or if you are changing the size of a log file, then the newly added space to the file must be zero-initialized. During the time that this is occurring, all other database activity is paused. To minimize the impact of the growth on database operations, it is a best practice to manually grow the files during scheduled maintenance periods. This manual growth should be large enough so that the database will have enough space so that an automatic growth would not be necessary until the next maintenance period. If the PVMT security permission has been granted to the SQL Server service account, data-file growths will be nearly instantaneous (log-file growths always require the zero-initialization process). If the PVMT security permission is being added to the SQL Server service account, the SQL Server instance will need to be restarted in order to pick up this change.

26-7. Adding a Filegroup

Problem

You want to add a new filegroup to your database.

Solution

Utilize the ALTER DATABASE statement to add a filegroup to a database, as follows:

```
ALTER DATABASE BookStoreArchive
ADD FILEGROUP FG2;
GO
```

How It Works

The ALTER DATABASE was utilized to add a filegroup to a database. The syntax is as follows:

```
ALTER DATABASE database_name
ADD FILEGROUP filegroup_name
```

where database_name is the name of an existing database, and filegroup_name is the name of the new filegroup being added.

You might want to add a new filegroup for a multitude of reasons. Some of these include the following:

- Putting read-only tables into a read-only filegroup

- Moving data that must be restored first into a separate file group in order to bring your application back up faster in the event of a disaster. Filegroups can be backed up and restored individually. This may enable your core business functions to get back online faster while the restoration of other filegroups proceeds.

- Relocating the database for disk maintenance.

26-8. Adding a File to a Filegroup

Problem

You want to add a new file to a filegroup.

Solution

Utilize the ALTER DATABASE statement to add a new file to a specified filegroup, as follows:

```
ALTER DATABASE BookStoreArchive
ADD FILE
(  NAME = 'BW2',
FILENAME = 'N:\Apress\FG2_BookStoreArchive.NDF' ,
SIZE = 1MB ,
MAXSIZE = 50MB,
FILEGROWTH = 5MB )
TO FILEGROUP FG2;
```

How It Works

Just like in Recipe 26-1, this added a new file to the database. The difference is the specification of the filegroup that the file should be added to. Without this specification, the file would be added to the default filegroup.

26-9. Setting the Default Filegroup

Problem

You want to change the default filegroup so that new tables will be added to the files in that filegroup.

Solution

Utilize the ALTER DATABASE statement to set a filegroup as the default filegroup for a database, as follows:

```
ALTER DATABASE BookStoreArchive
MODIFY FILEGROUP FG2 DEFAULT;
GO
```

This query returns the following message:

```
The filegroup property 'DEFAULT' has been set.
```

How It Works

The ALTER DATABASE statement was used to set the default filegroup for a database. The default filegroup is the filegroup to which new objects will be added if a filegroup is not specified. Only one filegroup can be the default filegroup at any point in time. The syntax for this statement is as follows:

```
ALTER DATABASE database_name
MODIFY FILEGROUP filegroup_name DEFAULT
```

where database_name is the name of an existing database and filegroup_name is the name of an existing filegroup within the specified database.

26-10. Adding Data to a Specific Filegroup

Problem

You want to add a new table to a specific filegroup.

Solution

In the CREATE TABLE statement, specify the filegroup that the table is to be added to, as follows:

```
CREATE TABLE dbo.Test
        (
         TestID  INT IDENTITY,
         Column1 INT,
         Column2 INT,
         Column3 INT
        )
ON      FG2;
```

How It Works

The ON clause specified the partition scheme or filegroup that the table was to be built in.

■ **Note** If the CREATE TABLE statement also specifies the creation of a clustered index on a different partition or filegroup, the table will be created on the partition or filegroup specified by the clustered index.

26-11. Moving Data to a Different Filegroup

Problem

You need to remove a table from one filegroup and place it in a different filegroup.

Solution #1

If the table does not have a clustered index, add a clustered index or constraint to the table, specifying the new filegroup:

```
ALTER TABLE dbo.Test
  ADD CONSTRAINT PK_Test PRIMARY KEY CLUSTERED (TestId)
  ON [PRIMARY];
```

Solution #2

If the table does have a clustered index that is enforcing a constraint, drop and recreate the clustered constraint, specifying the new filegroup:

```
CREATE TABLE dbo.Test2
        (
         TestID INT IDENTITY
                  CONSTRAINT PK__Test2 PRIMARY KEY CLUSTERED,
         Column1 INT,
```

```
        Column2 INT,
        Column3 INT
        )
ON      FG2;
GO


ALTER TABLE dbo.Test2
DROP CONSTRAINT PK__Test2;

ALTER TABLE dbo.Test2
ADD CONSTRAINT PK__Test2 PRIMARY KEY CLUSTERED (TestId)
ON [PRIMARY];
```

Solution #3

If the table has a clustered index that is not enforcing a constraint, rebuild the index using the DROP
EXISTING clause and specify the filegroup that it should be moved to, as follows:

```
CREATE TABLE dbo.Test3
        (
        TestID INT IDENTITY,
        Column1 INT,
        Column2 INT,
        Column3 INT
        )
ON      FG2;
GO

CREATE CLUSTERED INDEX IX_Test3 ON dbo.Test3 (TestId)
ON FG2;
GO

CREATE CLUSTERED INDEX IX_Test3 ON dbo.Test3 (TestId)
WITH (DROP_EXISTING = ON)
ON [PRIMARY];
GO
```

How It Works

Since a clustered index contains, at the leaf level, all the data for the table, moving the clustered index to
a different filegroup moves the table to the new filegroup as well. In the same manner, adding a clustered
index to a table that doesn't have one will move the data from the table into the clustered index and thus
into the filegroup as specified by the index. If the clustered index is enforcing a constraint, the constraint will
need to be dropped and recreated in order to move the table; you can rebuild an index on a constraint only
if everything about the new index is identical to the current index and the filegroup that the index is on is
being changed. If this is the only method available to you, you should do this during a maintenance period
so that you can ensure that data won't be entered that would violate the constraint.

In the first solution, the dbo.Test table did not have a clustered index, so one was created on it with
the ALTER TABLE statement, specifying the filegroup to put the index on. Creating the clustered index on a
different filegroup moved the table to the other filegroup.

In the second solution, a new table was created on filegroup FG2 with a clustered index on a primary-key constraint. To move this table, the constraint was first dropped with the ALTER TABLE statement, creating a table without any clustered index. The clustered primary-key constraint was then recreated on the desired filegroup, thus moving the table to that filegroup.

In the third solution, a table and a clustered index were created on FG2. Since the clustered index was not enforcing a constraint, this table could be moved to the new filegroup by utilizing the CREATE INDEX statement and by specifying the DROP_EXISTING = ON clause along with the filegroup to put the index on.

■ **Tip**   For more information on utilizing the ALTER TABLE statement, see the "Managing Tables" chapter. For more information on utilizing indexes and the CREATE INDEX statement, see the "Managing Indexes" chapter.

26-12. Removing a Filegroup

Problem

You want to remove an empty filegroup from your database.

Solution

Utilize the ALTER DATABASE statement to remove filegroups from a database:

```
ALTER DATABASE BookStoreArchive
MODIFY FILEGROUP [PRIMARY] DEFAULT;
GO

ALTER DATABASE BookStoreArchive
REMOVE FILE BW2;
GO

ALTER DATABASE BookStoreArchive
REMOVE FILEGROUP FG2;
GO
```

These statements return the following messages:

```
The filegroup property 'DEFAULT' has been set.
The file 'BW2' has been removed.
The filegroup 'FG2' has been removed.
```

How It Works

To remove a filegroup, it cannot contain any files within it. Furthermore, you cannot remove the last file from the default filegroup. Therefore, the first ALTER DATABASE statement was necessary to change the default filegroup back to the PRIMARY filegroup. Since the filegroup name PRIMARY is a keyword, it had to be enclosed in brackets. The second ALTER DATABASE statement removes the empty file from the filegroup (see Recipe 26-3). The third ALTER DATABASE statement removed the filegroup. The syntax is as follows:

```
ALTER DATABASE database_name
REMOVE FILEGROUP filegroup_name
```

where database_name is the name of the existing database and filegroup_name is the name of the existing and empty filegroup to be removed.

26-13. Making a Database or a Filegroup Read-Only

Problem #1

You have historical data in your database that cannot have any modifications made to it. However, the data needs to be available for querying.

Problem #2

Your entire database contains historical data, and it cannot have any modifications made to it. However, the data needs to be available for querying.

Solution #1

Move the historical data to a separate filegroup, and then set that filegroup to be read-only. See the following:

```
ALTER DATABASE BookStoreArchive SET RESTRICTED_USER WITH ROLLBACK IMMEDIATE;
GO

ALTER DATABASE BookStoreArchive
ADD FILEGROUP FG3;
GO

ALTER DATABASE BookStoreArchive
ADD FILE
(  NAME = 'ArchiveData',
FILENAME = 'N:\Apress\BookStoreArchiveData.NDF' ,
SIZE = 1MB ,
MAXSIZE = 10MB,
FILEGROWTH = 1MB )
TO FILEGROUP [FG3];
GO
-- move historical tables to this filegroup

ALTER DATABASE BookStoreArchive
MODIFY FILEGROUP FG3 READ_ONLY;
GO

ALTER DATABASE BookStoreArchive SET MULTI_USER;
GO
```

677

Solution #2

Since the entire database consists of the historical data, you can set the entire database to READ_ONLY with this statement:

```
ALTER DATABASE BookStoreArchive SET READ_ONLY;
GO
```

If you ran this statement, please set the database back to multi-user mode with this statement so that the remaining recipes will work:

```
ALTER DATABASE BookStoreArchive SET READ_WRITE;
GO
```

How It Works

In Solution #1, a new filegroup was created on this database, and a file was added to this filegroup. The archived data was then moved into this filegroup. Finally, the filegroup was set to READ_ONLY. When changing the status of the filegroup, you cannot have other users in the database, so the database is first set so as to only allow restricted users. Once all work has been finished, it is opened back up to all users. The filegroup can be set back to a read-write status by executing this statement (after setting it to allow only restricted users again):

```
ALTER DATABASE BookStoreArchive
MODIFY FILEGROUP FG3 READ_ONLY;
```

In Solution #2, the entire database was set to a READ_ONLY status. You can set it back to a read-write status with this statement:

```
ALTER DATABASE BookStoreArchive SET READ_WRITE;
```

26-14. Viewing Database Space Usage

Problem

You need to know how much space is being used by the objects in the database.

Solution #1

Utilize the sp_spaceused stored procedure to obtain information about space usage within the database and transaction log, as follows:

```
EXECUTE sp_spaceused;
```

Executing the sp_spaceused stored procedure without any parameters returns the following result set:

database_name	database_size	unallocated space	
BookStoreArchive	7.50 MB	3.88 MB	

reserved	data	index_size	unused
2168 KB	824 KB	1128 KB	216 KB

Solution #2

Utilize the sp_spaceused stored procedure to obtain information about space usage for a specific object within a database, as follows:

```
EXECUTE sp_spaceused 'dbo.test';
```

Executing the sp_spaceused stored procedure with an object name returns the following result set:

name	rows	reserved	data	index_size	unused
Test	0	0 KB	0 KB	0 KB	0 KB

Solution #3

Utilize DBCC_SQLPERF to obtain space-used information about all transaction logs on your SQL Server instance, as follows:

```
DBCC SQLPERF(LOGSPACE);
```

Executing this returns the following result set (results will contain a row for each database on your SQL Server instance that this command is being run on):

Database Name	Log Size (MB)	Log Space Used (%)	Status
master	2.242188	32.40418	0
tempdb	0.4921875	86.0119	0
model	0.7421875	84.47369	0
msdb	0.7421875	71.31579	0
AdventureWorks2014	113.9922	3.003564	0
BookStoreArchive	1.484375	30.49342	0

DBCC execution completed. If DBCC printed error messages, contact your system administrator.

Solution #4

Query the system views/dynamic-management views to obtain the allocation information for the database files:

```
SELECT  sdf.physical_name,
        su.allocated_extent_page_count / 128.0 allocated_ mb,
        su.unallocated_extent_page_count / 128.0 unallocated_ mb,
        su.total_page_count / 128.0 total_size_mb
FROM    sys.database_files sdf
        JOIN sys.dm_db_file_space_usage su
            ON sdf.file_id = su.file_id;
```

This query returns the following information:

physical_name	allocated_mb	unallocated_mb	total_size_mb
C:\Apress\Drive2\BookStoreArchive.mdf	2.312500	2.687500	5.000000
C:\Apress\Drive1\BookStoreArchiveData.NDF	0.062500	0.937500	1.000000

How It Works

The sp_spaceused system-stored procedure returns information about the specified object, including the number of rows in the object, how much space the data and indexes are using, and any unused space. If an object isn't specified, the information returned is about the database: the size, unallocated space, data space, index space, and unused space. The syntax for this procedure is as follows:

```
sp_spaceused [[ (@objname = ] 'objname' ]
[,[ (@updateusage = ] 'updateusage' ]
```

Table 26-3 describes the parameters of this procedure.

Table 26-3. sp_spaceused Parameters

Parameter	Description
'objname'	This parameter defines the optional object name (table, for example) to view space usage. If not designated, the entire database's space-usage information is returned.
'updateusage'	This parameter is used with a specific object and accepts either true or false. If true, DBCC UPDATEUSAGE is used to update space-usage information in the system tables.

In Solution #3, DBCC SQLPERF was used to obtain transaction log space-usage statistics for all databases. (It can also be used to reset wait and latch statistics.) The syntax for DBCC SOLPERF is as follows:

```
DBCC SQLPERF
(
    [ LOGSPACE ]
    |
    [ "sys.dm_os_latch_stats" , CLEAR ]
    |
    [ "sys.dm_os_wait_stats" , CLEAR ]
)
    [WITH NO_INFOMSGS ]
```

Table 26-4 briefly describes this DBCC command's arguments.

Table 26-4. DBCC SQLPERF Arguments

Parameter	Description
LOGSPACE	Returns the current size of the transaction log and the percentage of log space used for each database. You can use this information to monitor the amount of space being used in a transaction log.
"sys.dm_os_latch_stats", CLEAR	Resets the last statistics. For more information, see sys.dm_os_latch_stats at https://msdn.microsoft.com/en-us/library/ms175066.aspx.
"sys.dm_os_wait_stats", CLEAR	Resets the wait statistics. For more information, see sys.dm_os_wait_stats at https://msdn.microsoft.com/en-us/library/ms179984.aspx.
WITH NO_INFOMSGS	When included in the command, WITH NO_INFOMSGS suppresses informational messages from the DBCC output that have severity levels from 0 through 10.

In Solution #4, the system and dynamic management views (DMV) were queried to obtain allocation-usage information for the database files in the current database. The sys.dm_db_file_space_usage DMV can additionally return information about which filegroup the file is in, and the used-page counts can be broken down into what is used by the version store, internal objects, and mixed extents, as well as by user objects. This DMV reports the number of pages; since a page is 8KB, the query divides the page count by 128 to convert to MB.

26-15. Shrinking the Database or a Database File

Problem

You need to shrink either one database file or the entire database.

Solution #1

Utilize DBCC SHRINKDATABASE to shrink an entire database. We will first expand some of the files in the database, and then we will use DBCC SHRINKDATABASE to shrink all of the files in the database (we will use sp_spaceused to show the information before and after executing DBCC SHRINKDATABASE). See the following:

```
ALTER DATABASE BookStoreArchive
MODIFY FILE (NAME = 'BookStoreArchive_log', SIZE = 100MB);

ALTER DATABASE BookStoreArchive
MODIFY FILE (NAME = 'BookStoreArchive_Data', SIZE = 200MB);
GO

USE BookStoreArchive;
GO

EXECUTE sp_spaceused;
GO

DBCC SHRINKDATABASE ('BookStoreArchive', 10);
GO

EXECUTE sp_spaceused;
GO
```

These statements produce the following result sets and messages:

database_name	database_size	unallocated space
BookStoreArchive 302.00 MB		198.88 MB

reserved	data	index_size	unused
2296 KB	944 KB	1176 KB	176 KB

DbId	FileId	CurrentSize	MinimumSize	UsedPages	EstimatedPages
8	1	512	512	288	288
8	2	1656	64	1656	64
8	4	128	128	128	128

DBCC execution completed. If DBCC printed error messages, contact your system administrator.

database_name	database_size	unallocated space
BookStoreArchive 17.94 MB		1.88 MB

reserved	data	index_size	unused
2168 KB	824 KB	1128 KB	216 KB

Solution #2

Utilize DBCC SHRINKFILE to shrink one file in the database. Here we will expand one file in the database and then use DBCC SHRINKFILE to shrink that file. Again, we will use sp_spaceused to view the database space information before and after shrinking the file. See the following:

```
ALTER DATABASE BookStoreArchive
MODIFY FILE (NAME = 'BookStoreArchive_Log', SIZE = 200MB);
GO


USE BookStoreArchive;
GO


EXECUTE sp_spaceused;
GO


DBCC SHRINKFILE ('BookStoreArchive_Log', 2);
GO


EXECUTE sp_spaceused;
GO
```

These statements produce the following result sets and messages:

database_name	database_size	unallocated space	
database_name	database_size	unallocated space	
BookStoreArchive	206.00 MB	2.76 MB	

reserved	data	index_size	unused
2296 KB	944 KB	1176 KB	176 KB

DbId	FileId	CurrentSize	MinimumSize	UsedPages	EstimatedPages
8	2	1656	64	1656	64

DBCC execution completed. If DBCC printed error messages, contact your system administrator.

database_name	database_size	unallocated space	
BookStoreArchive	18.94 MB	2.76 MB	

reserved	data	index_size	unused
2296 KB	944 KB	1176 KB	176 KB

How It Works

DBCC SHRINKDATABASE shrinks the data and log files in your database. In the first example, data and log files were both increased to a larger size. After that, the DBCC SHRINKDATABASE command was used to reduce them down to a target free-space size of 10 percent:

```
DBCC SHRINKDATABASE (BookStoreArchive, 10)
```

After execution, the command returned a result set showing the current size (in 8KB pages), minimum size (in 8KB pages), currently used 8KB pages, and estimated 8KB pages that SQL Server could shrink the file down to.

The syntax for DBCC SHRINKDATABASE is as follows:

```
DBCC SHRINKDATABASE
( 'database_name' | database_id | 0
[ ,target_percent ]
[ , { NOTRUNCATE | TRUNCATEONLY } ] ) [ WITH NO_INFOMSGS ]
```

Table 26-5 describes the arguments for this command.

Table 26-5. DBCC SHRINKDATABASE *Arguments*

Argument	Description
'database_name' | database_id | 0	You can designate a specific database name or the database ID of the database to shrink or, if 0 is specified, the current database your query session is connected to will be shrunk.
target_percent	The target percentage designates the free space remaining in the database file after the shrinking event.
NOTRUNCATE | TRUNCATEONLY	NOTRUNCATE performs the data movements needed to create free space but retains the freed space in the file without releasing it to the operating system. If NOTRUNCATE is not designated, the free file space is released to the operating system. TRUNCATEONLY frees up space without relocating data within the files. If not designated, data pages are reallocated within the files to free up space, which can lead to extensive I/O.
WITH NO_INFOMSGS	This argument prevents informational messages from being returned from the DBCC command.

In the second solution, one of the log files was increased to a larger size. This time, the DBCC SHRINKFILE command was used to shrink that individual file down to a specified size (in megabytes):

```
DBCC SHRINKFILE ('BookStoreArchive_Log', 2);
```

The syntax for DBCC SHRINKFILE is as follows:

```
DBCC SHRINKFILE (
{ ' file_name ' | file_id }
{ [ , EMPTYFILE]
| [ [ , target_size ] [ , { NOTRUNCATE | TRUNCATEONLY } ] ]
} ) [ WITH NO_INFOMSGS ]
```

Table 26-6 describes the arguments for this command.

Table 26-6. DBCC SHRINKFILE *Arguments*

Argument	Description
' file_name ' | file_id	This option defines the specific logical file name or file ID to shrink.
EMPTYFILE	This argument moves all data off the file so that it can be dropped using ALTER DATABASE and REMOVE FILE.
target_size	This option specifies the free space to be left in the database file (in megabytes). Leaving this blank instructs SQL Server to free up space equal to the default file size.
NOTRUNCATE | TRUNCATEONLY	NOTRUNCATE relocates allocated pages from within the file to the front of the file but does not free the space to the operating system. Target size is ignored when used with NOTRUNCATE. TRUNCATEONLY causes unused space in the file to be released to the operating system but does so only with free space found at the end of the file. No pages are rearranged or relocated. Target size is also ignored with the TRUNCATEONLY option. Use this option if you must free up space on the database file with minimal impact on database performance (rearranging pages on an actively utilized production database can cause performance issues, such as slow query response time).
WITH NO_INFOMSGS	This argument prevents informational messages from being returned from the DBCC command.

This command shrinks the specified physical file. In this example, we specified a log file. Transaction log files are shrunk by removing inactive virtual log files. The transaction log for any database is managed as a set of *virtual log files (VLFs)*. VLFs are created when the transaction log is created or undergoes expansion, and the quantity and size of the new VLFs are based upon the size of the growth of the transaction log file, with a minimum size of 256KB.

Within the transaction log is the "active" logical portion of the log. This is the area of the transaction log containing active transactions. This active portion does not usually match the physical bounds of the file, but will instead "round-robin" from VLF to VLF. Once a VLF)no longer contains active transactions, it can be marked as reusable through a BACKUP LOG operation or automated system truncation, which makes the VLFs available for new log records.

It needs to be pointed out that when SQL Server talks about truncating the transaction log, the transaction log is not actually truncated; the process will mark zero or more VLFs as reusable. This is an example of misused verbiage in SQL Server documentation.

DBCC SHRINKFILE or DBCC SHRINKDATABASE will make their best effort to remove inactive VLFs from the end of the physical file. SQL Server will also attempt to add "dummy" rows to push the active logical log toward the beginning of the physical file—so sometimes issuing a BACKUP LOG after the first execution of the DBCC SHRINKFILE command and then issuing the DBCC SHRINKFILE command again will allow you to free up the originally requested space.

Database transaction log files should be sized so that they will not need to grow during normal operations. This size needs to be able to encompass the regular data-modification activity on the database, as well as periodic maintenance (specifically index rebuilds).

Database data files, when autogrowth is enabled, can expand because of index rebuilds or data-modification activity. You may have extra space in the database because of those data modifications and index rebuilds. If you don't need to free up the unused space, you should allow the database to keep it reserved. However, if you do need the unused space and want to free it up, use DBCC SHRINKDATABASE or DBCC SHRINKFILE. It is a best practice to manually grow your data files during scheduled maintenance periods, and they should be grown to a size such that they will not need to grow automatically until the next manual growth during the next scheduled maintenance period.

■ **Caution**   When either DBCC SHRINKDATABASE or DBCC SHRINKFILE is run against a data file, pages from the end of the file are moved to unallocated space, starting from the beginning of the file. This action obviously will cause those pages for that data structure to now be fragmented. Additionally, due to the high amount of disk I/O activity, this is an expensive operation. Because of these reasons, shrinking activities should only be performed when absolutely necessary. If you find that the database/database files are being shrunk on a regular basis (or even through a job), then the size of the files needs to be re-evaluated and files properly sized so that the regular shrinking can be stopped. Shrinking should only be performed on rare occurrences, when unplanned or unanticipated activity has caused the files to expand to unacceptable levels such that the space must be reclaimed.

26-16. Checking the Consistency of Allocation Structures

Problem

You want to test a database's disk-space-allocation structures for consistency.

Solution

Utilize DBCC CHECKALLOC to check page usage and allocation within the database:

```
DBCC CHECKALLOC ('BookStoreArchive');
```

This statement produces the following messages. (Since this actually produces more than 500 lines of output, this result set as shown is greatly abridged.)

```
DBCC results for 'BookStoreArchive'.
***************************************************************
Table sys.sysrscols              Object ID 3.
Index ID 1, partition ID 196608, alloc unit ID 196608 (type In-row data). FirstIAM (1:157).
Root (1:158). Dpages 12.
Index ID 1, partition ID 196608, alloc unit ID 196608 (type In-row data). 14 pages used in 1
dedicated extents.
Total number of extents is 1.
***************************************************************
Table sys.sysrowsets             Object ID 5.
Index ID 1, partition ID 327680, alloc unit ID 327680 (type In-row data). FirstIAM (1:131).
Root (1:270). Dpages 1.
Index ID 1, partition ID 327680, alloc unit ID 327680 (type In-row data). 4 pages used in 0
dedicated extents.
Total number of extents is 0.
***************************************************************
...
File 3. The number of extents = 1, used pages = 6, and reserved pages = 8.
          File 3 (number of mixed extents = 0, mixed pages = 0).
    Object ID 99, index ID 0, partition ID 0, alloc unit ID 6488064 (type Unknown), index
extents 1, pages 6, mixed extent pages 0.
The total number of extents = 36, used pages = 257, and reserved pages = 288 in this database.
          (number of mixed extents = 21, mixed pages = 168) in this database.
CHECKALLOC found 0 allocation errors and 0 consistency errors in database
'BookStoreArchive'.
DBCC execution completed. If DBCC printed error messages, contact your system
administrator.
```

How It Works

DBCC CHECKALLOC checks page usage and allocation in the database and will report on any errors that are found (this command is automatically included in the execution of DBCC CHECKDB, so if you are already running CHECKDB periodically, there is no need to also run CHECKALLOC). The syntax is as follows:

```
DBCC CHECKALLOC (
[ 'database_name' | database_id | 0 ] [ , NOINDEX
{ REPAIR_ALLOW_DATA_LOSS | REPAIR_FAST |   REPAIR_REBUILD } ] )
[ WITH { [ ALL_ERRORMSGS ]
[ , NO_INFOMSGS ]
[ , TABLOCK ]
[ , ESTIMATEONLY ]
}
]
```

Table 26-7 describes the arguments of this command.

Table 26-7. DBCC CHECKALLOC *Arguments*

Argument	Description
'database_name' | database_id | 0	This defines the database name or database ID that you want to check for errors. When 0 is selected, the current database is used.
NOINDEX	When NOINDEX used, nonclustered indexes are not included in the checks. This is a backward-compatible option that has no effect on DBCC CHECKALLOC.
REPAIR_ALLOW_DATA_LOSS | REPAIR_FAST | REPAIR_REBUILD	REPAIR_ALLOW_DATA_LOSS attempts a repair of the table or indexed view, with the risk of losing data in the process. REPAIR_FAST and REPAIR_REBUILD are maintained for backward compatibility only.
ALL_ERRORMSGS	When ALL_ERRORMSGS is chosen, every error found will be displayed. If this option isn't designated, a maximum of 200 error messages can be displayed.
NO_INFOMSGS	NO_INFOMSGS represses all informational messages from the DBCC output.
TABLOCK	When TABLOCK is selected, an exclusive table lock is placed on the table instead of using an internal database snapshot, thus potentially decreasing query concurrency in the database.
ESTIMATEONLY	This provides the estimated space needed by the tempdb database to execute the command.

■ **Caution** This DBCC command has several REPAIR options. Microsoft recommends that you solve data-integrity issues by restoring the database from the last good backup rather than resorting to a REPAIR option. If restoring from backup is not an option, the REPAIR option should be used only as a last resort. Depending on the REPAIR option selected, data loss can and will occur, and the problem may still not be resolved.

The output includes information about pages used and extents for each index. The key piece of information is in the next-to-last line, where you can see the reporting of the number of allocation and consistency errors encountered in the database being checked. If it reports anything other than 0 allocation errors and 0 consistency errors, then the errors need to be investigated and the corruption corrected.

When DBCC CHECKALLOC is executed, an internal database snapshot is created to maintain transactional consistency during the operation. If for some reason a database snapshot can't be created or if TABLOCK is specified, an exclusive database lock is acquired during the execution of the command (thus potentially hurting database query concurrency). Unless you have a good reason not to, you should allow SQL Server to issue an internal database snapshot so that concurrency in your database is not impacted.

26-17. Checking Allocation and Structural Integrity

Problem

You want to check the integrity of all objects in a database.

Solution

Use DBCC CHECKDB to check the allocation and structural integrity of all objects in the database, as follows:

```
DBCC CHECKDB ('BookStoreArchive');
```

Executing this command produces the following messages (as in the previous recipe, this output can be quite large, so only abridged results are being displayed):

```
DBCC results for 'BookStoreArchive'.
Service Broker Msg 9675, State 1: Message Types analyzed: 14.
Service Broker Msg 9676, State 1: Service Contracts analyzed: 6.
...
DBCC results for 'sys.sysrscols'.
There are 883 rows in 12 pages for object "sys.sysrscols".
DBCC results for 'sys.sysrowsets'.
There are 127 rows in 2 pages for object "sys.sysrowsets".
...
DBCC results for 'Test'.
There are 0 rows in 0 pages for object "Test".
...
DBCC results for 'sys.queue_messages_1977058079'.
There are 0 rows in 0 pages for object "sys.queue_messages_1977058079".
DBCC results for 'sys.queue_messages_2009058193'.
There are 0 rows in 0 pages for object "sys.queue_messages_2009058193".
DBCC results for 'sys.queue_messages_2041058307'.
There are 0 rows in 0 pages for object "sys.queue_messages_2041058307".
DBCC results for 'sys.filestream_tombstone_2073058421'.
There are 0 rows in 0 pages for object "sys.filestream_tombstone_2073058421".
DBCC results for 'sys.syscommittab'.
There are 0 rows in 0 pages for object "sys.syscommittab".
DBCC results for 'sys.filetable_updates_2105058535'.
There are 0 rows in 0 pages for object "sys.filetable_updates_2105058535".
CHECKDB found 0 allocation errors and 0 consistency errors in database 'BookStoreArchive'.
DBCC execution completed. If DBCC printed error messages, contact your system
administrator.
```

How It Works

The DBCC CHECKDB command checks the integrity of objects in a database. Running DBCC CHECKDB periodically against your databases is a good maintenance practice. Weekly execution is usually sufficient; however, the optimal frequency depends on the activity and size of the database in question. If possible, DBCC CHECKDB should be executed during periods of light or no database activity. Executing DBCC CHECKDB in this manner will allow DBCC CHECKDB to finish faster and keep other processes from being slowed down by its overhead.

When executing DBCC CHECKDB, an internal database snapshot is created to maintain transactional consistency during the operation. If for some reason a database snapshot cannot be created (or the TABLOCK option is specified), shared table locks are held for table checks and exclusive database locks for allocation checks. (One of the reasons a snapshot cannot be created is if there are read-only filegroups; for this reason, the example first changes the FG3 filegroup to be read-write.)

As part of its execution, DBCC CHECKDB executes other DBCC commands that are discussed elsewhere in this chapter, including DBCC CHECKTABLE, DBCC CHECKALLOC, and DBCC CHECKCATALOG. In addition to this, CHECKDB verifies the integrity of Service Broker data indexed views and FILESTREAM link consistency for table and file-system directories.

The syntax for DBCC CHECKDB is as follows:

```
DBCC  CHECKDB
(
        'database_name'  |  database_id  |  0
        [  ,   NOINDEX
        |   {  REPAIR_ALLOW_DATA_LOSS
        |   REPAIR_FAST
        |   REPAIR_REBUILD
        }  ]
)
        [  WITH  {
        [  ALL_ERRORMSGS      ]
        [  ,  [EXTENDED_LOGICAL_CHECKS]  ]
        [  ,  [  NO_INFOMSGS  ]  ]
        [  ,  [  TABLOCK  ]      ]
        [  ,  [  ESTIMATEONLY  ]  ]
        [  ,  {  PHYSICAL_ONLY  |  DATA_PURITY  }  ]
        }
        ]
```

Table 26-8 describes the arguments of this command.

Table 26-8. DBCC CHECKDB Arguments

Argument	Description
`'database_name'` | `database_id` | `0`	This defines the database name or database ID that you want to check for errors. When `0` is selected, the current database is used.
`NOINDEX`	Nonclustered indexes are not included in the integrity checks when this option is selected.
`REPAIR_ALLOW_DATA_LOSS` | `REPAIR_FAST` | `REPAIR_REBUILD`	`REPAIR_ALLOW_DATA_LOSS` attempts a repair of the table or indexed view, with the risk of losing data in the process. `REPAIR_FAST` is maintained for backward compatibility only, and `REPAIR_REBUILD` performs fixes without risk of data loss.
`ALL_ERRORMSGS`	When `ALL_ERRORMSGS` is chosen, every error found will be displayed (instead of just the default 200 error message limit). If you should happen to run `CHECKDB` and receive more than 200 error messages, you should rerun it with this option so that you can ascertain the full extent of errors in the database.
`EXTENDED_LOGICAL_CHECKS`	When `EXTENDED_LOGICAL_CHECKS` is chosen, it enables logical consistency checks on spatial and XML indexes, as well as on indexed views. This option can impact performance significantly and should be used sparingly.
`NO_INFOMSGS`	`NO_INFOMSGS` represses all informational messages from the DBCC output.
`TABLOCK`	When `TABLOCK` is selected, an exclusive database lock is used instead of an internal database snapshot. Using this option decreases concurrency with other queries being executed against objects in the database.
`ESTIMATEONLY`	This argument provides the estimated space needed by the `tempdb` database to execute the command.
`PHYSICAL_ONLY` | `DATA_PURITY`	The `PHYSICAL_ONLY` argument limits the integrity checks to physical issues only, skipping logical checks. `DATA_PURITY` is selected for use on upgraded databases (pre–SQL Server 2005 databases); it instructs DBCC CHECKDB to detect column values that do not conform to the data type (for example, if an integer value has a `bigint`-sized value stored in it). Once all bad values in the upgraded database are cleaned up, SQL Server maintains the column-value integrity moving forward.

■ **Caution** This DBCC command has several REPAIR options. Microsoft recommends that you solve data-integrity issues by restoring the database from the last good backup rather than resorting to a REPAIR option. If restoring from backup is not an option, the REPAIR option should be used only as a last resort. Depending on the REPAIR option selected, data loss can and will occur, and the problem may still not be resolved.

Despite all of these syntax options, the common form of executing this command is also most likely the simplest. The example for this recipe executes DBCC CHECKDB against the BookStoreArchive database. For thorough integrity and data checking of your database, the default is often suitable:

```
DBCC CHECKDB('BookStoreArchive');
```

As with the previous recipe, it is the next-to-last line of output that is the most important, where CHECKDB reports on the number of allocation and consistency errors found.

DBCC CHECKDB performs its validation checks against disk-based tables only. If your database is using In-Memory OLTP, you will need to back up the database and test the restore to ensure that the memory-optimized table structures are not corrupted. If issues arise in a memory-optimized table, you will need to restore from the last good backup.

26-18. Checking the Integrity of Tables in a Filegroup

Problem

You want to perform CHECKDB on a database, but you want to limit it to running against a specific filegroup.

Solution

Utilize DBCC CHECKFILEGROUP to perform CHECKDB operations against a specific filegroup:

```
USE BookStoreArchive;
GO
DBCC CHECKFILEGROUP ('PRIMARY');
GO
```

This returns the following (abridged) results:

```
DBCC results for 'BookStoreArchive'.
DBCC results for 'sys.sysrscols'.
There are 883 rows in 12 pages for object "sys.sysrscols".
DBCC results for 'sys.sysrowsets'.
There are 127 rows in 2 pages for object "sys.sysrowsets".
...
DBCC results for 'sys.syscommittab'.
There are 0 rows in 0 pages for object "sys.syscommittab".
DBCC results for 'sys.filetable_updates_2105058535'.
There are 0 rows in 0 pages for object "sys.filetable_updates_2105058535".
CHECKFILEGROUP found 0 allocation errors and 0 consistency errors in database
'BookStoreArchive'.
DBCC execution completed. If DBCC printed error messages, contact your system
administrator.
```

How It Works

The DBCC CHECKFILEGROUP command is very similar to DBCC CHECKDB, but limits its integrity and allocation checking to objects within a single filegroup. For very large databases (VLDBs), performing a DBCC CHECKDB operation may be time prohibitive. If you use user-defined filegroups in your database, you can employ DBCC CHECKFILEGROUP to perform your weekly (or periodic) checks instead—spreading out filegroup checks across different days.

When this command is executed, an internal database snapshot is created to maintain transactional consistency during the operation. If for some reason a database snapshot can't be created (or the TABLOCK option is specified), shared table locks are created by the command for table checks, as well as an exclusive database lock for the allocation checks.

Again, if errors are found by DBCC CHECKFILEGROUP, Microsoft recommends that you solve any discovered issues by restoring from the last good database backup. Unlike other DBCC commands in this chapter, DBCC CHECKFILEGROUP doesn't have repair options, so you would need to utilize DBCC CHECKDB to resolve them (although repair options are not recommended by Microsoft anyway).

The syntax is as follows:

```
DBCC  CHECKFILEGROUP
(
[ { 'filegroup' | filegroup_id | 0 } ]
[ , NOINDEX ]
)
      [ WITH
      {
      [ ALL_ERRORMSGS | NO_INFOMSGS ]
      [ , [ TABLOCK ] ]
      [ , [ ESTIMATEONLY ] ]
      }
      ]
```

Table 26-9 describes the arguments of this command.

Table 26-9. DBCC CHECKFILEGROUP *Arguments*

Argument	Description
'filegroup' | filegroup_id | 0	This defines the filegroup name or filegroup ID that you want to check. If 0 is designated, the primary filegroup is used.
NOINDEX	When NOINDEX is designated, nonclustered indexes are not included in the integrity checks.
ALL_ERRORMSGS	When ALL_ERRORMSGS is chosen, all errors are displayed in the output, instead of the default 200 message limit.
NO_INFOMSGS	NO_INFOMSGS represses all informational messages from the DBCC output.
TABLOCK	When TABLOCK is selected, an exclusive database lock is used instead of using an internal database snapshot (using this option decreases concurrency with other database queries but speeds up the DBCC command execution).
ESTIMATEONLY	ESTIMATEONLY provides the estimated space needed by the tempdb database to execute the command.

As with the previous recipes, it is the next-to-last line of output that is the most important, where the number of allocation and consistency errors are reported.

26-19. Checking the Integrity of Specific Tables and Indexed Views

Problem

You want to check for integrity issues within a specific table or indexed view.

Solution #1

Utilize DBCC CHECKTABLE to check a specific table or indexed view for integrity issues. (This solution utilizes the AdventureWorks2014 database.) See the following:

```
DBCC CHECKTABLE ('Production.Product');
```

Executing this command produces the following messages:

```
DBCC results for 'Production.Product'.
There are 504 rows in 13 pages for object "Production.Product".
DBCC execution completed. If DBCC printed error messages, contact your system administrator.
```

Solution #2

Utilize DBCC CHECKTABLE with the optional WITH ESTIMATEONLY clause to obtain an estimate of the space required in the tempdb database for checking the specified table.

```
DBCC CHECKTABLE ('Sales.SalesOrderDetail') WITH ESTIMATEONLY;
```

Executing this command produces the following messages:

```
Estimated TEMPDB space (in KB) needed for CHECKTABLE on database AdventureWorks2014 = 1154.
DBCC execution completed. If DBCC printed error messages, contact your system administrator.
```

Solution #3

Utilize DBCC CHECKTABLE to check a specified index:

```
DECLARE @IndexID INTEGER;
SELECT  @IndexID = index_id
FROM    sys.indexes
WHERE   object_id = OBJECT_ID('Sales.SalesOrderDetail')
AND     name = 'IX_SalesOrderDetail_ProductID';

DBCC CHECKTABLE ('Sales.SalesOrderDetail', @IndexID) WITH PHYSICAL_ONLY;
```

Executing this command produces the following messages:

```
DBCC execution completed. If DBCC printed error messages, contact your system administrator.
```

How It Works

To identify issues in a specific table or indexed view, you can use the DBCC CHECKTABLE command. (If you want to run it for all tables and indexed views in the database, use DBCC CHECKDB instead, which performs DBCC CHECKTABLE for each table in your database.)

When DBCC CHECKTABLE is executed, an internal database snapshot is created to maintain transactional consistency during the operation. If for some reason a database snapshot can't be created, a shared table lock is applied to the target table or indexed view instead (thus potentially hurting database query concurrency against the target objects). DBCC CHECKTABLE checks for errors regarding data page linkages, pointers, verification that rows in a partition are actually in the correct partition, and more.

The syntax is as follows:

```
DBCC CHECKTABLE
(
    table_name | view_name
    [ , { NOINDEX | index_id }
    |, { REPAIR_ALLOW_DATA_LOSS | REPAIR_FAST | REPAIR_REBUILD }
    ]
)
    [ WITH
        { ALL_ERRORMSGS ]
          [ , EXTENDED_LOGICAL_CHECKS ]
          [ , NO_INFOMSGS ]
          [ , TABLOCK ]
          [ , ESTIMATEONLY ]
          [ , { PHYSICAL_ONLY | DATA_PURITY } ]
        }
    ]
```

Table 26-10 describes the arguments of this command.

Table 26-10. *DBCC CHECKTABLE Arguments*

Argument	Description
'table_name' | 'view_name'	This defines the table or indexed view you want to check.
NOINDEX	This keyword instructs the command to not check nonclustered indexes.
index_id	This specifies the specific ID of the index to be checked (if you are checking a specific index).
REPAIR_ALLOW_DATA_LOSS | REPAIR_FAST | REPAIR_REBUILD	REPAIR_ALLOW_DATA_LOSS attempts a repair of the table or indexed view, with the risk of losing data in the process. REPAIR_FAST is no longer used and is kept for backward compatibility only. REPAIR_REBUILD does repairs and index rebuilds without any risk of data loss.
ALL_ERRORMSGS	When ALL_ERRORMSGS is chosen, every error found during the command execution will be displayed.
EXTENDED_LOGICAL_CHECKS	EXTENDED_LOGICAL_CHECKS enables logical consistency checks on spatial and XML indexes, as well as on indexed views. This option can impact performance significantly and should be used sparingly.
NO_INFOMSGS	NO_INFOMSGS represses all informational messages from the DBCC output.
TABLOCK	When TABLOCK is selected, a shared table lock is placed on the table instead of using an internal database snapshot. Using this option decreases concurrency with other database queries accessing the table or indexed view.
ESTIMATEONLY	ESTIMATEONLY provides the estimated space needed by the tempdb database to execute the command (but doesn't actually execute the integrity checking).
PHYSICAL_ONLY	PHYSICAL_ONLY limits the integrity checks to physical issues only, skipping logical checks.
DATA_PURITY	This argument is used on upgraded databases (pre–SQL Server 2005 databases); this instructs DBCC CHECKTABLE to detect column values that do not conform to the data type (for example, if an integer value has a bigint-sized value stored in it). Once all bad values in the upgraded database are cleaned up, SQL Server maintains the column-value integrity moving forward.

■ **Caution** This DBCC command has several REPAIR options. Microsoft recommends that you solve data-integrity issues by restoring the database from the last good backup rather than resorting to a REPAIR option. If restoring from backup is not an option, the REPAIR option should be used only as a last resort. Depending on the REPAIR option selected, data loss can and will occur, and the problem may still not be resolved.

In the first example, the integrity of the AdventureWorks2014.Production.Product table was examined for integrity issues.

In the second example, an estimate of `tempdb` space required for a check on the `AdventureWorks2014.Sales.SalesOrderDetail` table was returned. This allows you to know ahead of time if a specific `CHECKTABLE` operation requires more space than you have available.

The third example examined a specific index for physical errors only (not logical errors). To specify an index, you must pass in the `index_id`, so we first have to query the `sys.indexes` system view to obtain this value.

26-20. Checking Constraint Integrity

Problem

You want to check a specific table or constraint for any violations in `CHECK` or `FOREIGN KEY` constraints.

Solution

Utilize `DBCC CHECKCONSTRAINTS` to validate that `CHECK` or `FOREIGN KEY` constraints in a table are valid. (This solution utilizes the `AdventureWorks2014` database.)

In this example, we are going to disable a check constraint, then enter data that violates this constraint. To view the existing constraint definition, the following query can be run:

```
SELECT  definition
FROM    sys.check_constraints
WHERE   name = 'CK_WorkOrder_EndDate';
GO
```

Which returns the following:

```
definition
-----------------------------------------------
([EndDate]>=[StartDate] OR [EndDate] IS NULL)
```

```
-- Disable the constraint
ALTER TABLE Production.WorkOrder NOCHECK CONSTRAINT CK_WorkOrder_EndDate;
GO
-- Set an EndDate to earlier than a StartDate to violate the constraint
UPDATE Production.WorkOrder
SET EndDate = '2001-01-01T00:00:00'
WHERE WorkOrderID = 1;
GO
-- Enable the constraint
ALTER TABLE Production.WorkOrder CHECK CONSTRAINT CK_WorkOrder_EndDate;
GO
DBCC CHECKCONSTRAINTS ('Production.WorkOrder');
GO
```

This code produces the following messages:

```
Table                     Constraint                Where
------------------------   ------------------------  --------------------------------------------
[Production].[WorkOrder]   [CK_WorkOrder_EndDate]    [StartDate] = '2005-07-04 00:00:00.000'
                                                     AND [EndDate] = '2001-01-01 00:00:00.000'

DBCC execution completed. If DBCC printed error messages, contact your system administrator.
```

How It Works

DBCC CHECKCONSTRAINTS alerts you to any CHECK or FOREIGN KEY constraint violations found in a specific table or constraint. This command allows you to return the violating data so that you can correct the constraint violation accordingly (although this command does not catch constraints that have been disabled using NOCHECK unless ALL_CONSTRAINTS is used). The syntax is as follows:

```
DBCC CHECKCONSTRAINTS
[( 'table_name' | table_id | 'constraint_name'
constraint_id )]
[ WITH
{ ALL_CONSTRAINTS | ALL_ERRORMSGS } [ , NO_INFOMSGS ] ]
```

Table 26-11 describes the arguments of this command.

Table 26-11. DBCC CHECKCONSTRAINTS Arguments

Argument	Description
'table_name' | table_id | 'constraint_name' | constraint_id	This defines the table name, table ID, constraint name, or constraint ID that you want to validate. If a specific object isn't designated, all the objects in the database will be evaluated.
ALL_CONSTRAINTS | ALL_ERRORMSGS	When ALL_CONSTRAINTS is selected, all constraints (enabled or disabled) are checked. When ALL_ERRORMSGS is selected, all rows that violate constraints are returned in the result set (instead of the default maximum of 200 rows).
NO_INFOMSGS	NO_INFOMSGS represses all informational messages from the DBCC output.

In this recipe, the check constraint named CK_WorkOrder on the Production.WorkOrder table was disabled, using the ALTER TABLE...NOCHECK CONSTRAINT command:

```
ALTER TABLE Production.WorkOrder NOCHECK CONSTRAINT CK_WorkOrder_EndDate;
```

This disabled constraint restricted values in the EndDate column from being less than the date in the StartDate column. After disabling the constraint, a row was updated to violate this check constraint's rule:

```
UPDATE Production.WorkOrder SET EndDate = '2001-01-01T00:00:00' WHERE WorkOrderID = 1;
```

The constraint was then reenabled:

```
ALTER TABLE Production.WorkOrder CHECK CONSTRAINT CK_WorkOrder_EndDate;
```

The DBCC CHECKCONSTRAINTS command was then executed against the table:

```
DBCC CHECKCONSTRAINTS('Production.WorkOrder');
```

When the command was run, it returned the data that failed the validation. Now that we know that the table has invalid data, the data can be corrected and validated, as follows:

```
UPDATE Production.WorkOrder
SET EndDate = '2011-06-13T00:00:00.000'
WHERE WorkOrderID = 1;
GO

DBCC CHECKCONSTRAINTS ('Production.WorkOrder');
GO
```

This code returned the following message:

```
DBCC execution completed. If DBCC printed error messages, contact your system
administrator.
```

DBCC CHECKCONSTRAINTS will only validate an enabled constraint; however it does not enable a constraint or make it trusted. You can see that the constraint was not marked trusted with the following query (the constraint was previously enabled so that DBCC CHECKCONSTRAINTS would be able to validate it):

```
SELECT  name,
        is_disabled,
        is_not_trusted
FROM    sys.check_constraints
WHERE   name = 'CK_WorkOrder_EndDate';
```

This returns the following result set:

```
name                  is_disabled is_not_trusted
--------------------- ----------- --------------
CK_WorkOrder_EndDate  0           1
```

The constraint can be enabled with the following:

```
ALTER TABLE Production.WorkOrder WITH CHECK CHECK CONSTRAINT CK_WorkOrder_EndDate;
```

This query will now return:

```
name                  is_disabled is_not_trusted
--------------------- ----------- --------------
CK_WorkOrder_EndDate  0           0
```

■ **Note** Unlike several other database integrity DBCC commands, DBCC CHECKCONSTRAINTS is *not* run within DBCC CHECKDB, so you must execute it as a stand-alone process if you need to identify data constraint violations in the database.

26-21. Checking System Table Consistency

Problem

You want to check for consistency in and between system tables in your database.

Solution

Execute DBCC CHECKCATALOG against the database to verify consistency in and between system tables, as follows:

```
DBCC CHECKCATALOG ('BookStoreArchive');
```

Assuming no errors are found, the following message is returned:

```
DBCC execution completed. If DBCC printed error messages, contact your system
administrator.
```

How It Works

DBCC CHECKCATALOG checks for consistency in and between system tables. The syntax is as follows:

```
DBCC CHECKCATALOG
[ ( 'database_name' | database_id | 0)] [ WITH NO_INFOMSGS ]
```

Table 26-12 describes the arguments of this command.

Table 26-12. *DBCC CHECKCATALOG Arguments*

Argument	Description
'database_name'	database_id	0	This defines the database name or database ID to be checked for errors. When 0 is selected, the current database is used.
NO_INFOMSGS	NO_INFOMSGS suppresses all informational messages from the DBCC output.

In this recipe, the system catalog data was checked in the BookStoreArchive database. If any errors were identified, they would be returned in the command output. DBCC CHECKCATALOG doesn't have repair options, so if any errors are found, then a restore from the last good database backup may be your only repair option.

When DBCC CHECKCATALOG is executed, an internal database snapshot is created to maintain transactional consistency during the operation. If for some reason a database snapshot cannot be created, an exclusive database lock is acquired during the execution of the command (thus potentially hurting database query concurrency).

■ **Note** CHECKCATALOG is executed automatically within a DBCC CHECKDB command, so a separate execution is not necessary, unless you want to investigate only system table consistency issues.

Backup

By Jason Brimhall

In this chapter, you'll find recipes covering several methods of backing up a database using T-SQL. This chapter is in no way meant to be a comprehensive source for database backups, but rather provides greater insight into the problems or limitations you may encounter. This chapter will outline the different types of backup methods using T-SQL as well as how to query the msdb database to find information about backup information.

27-1. Backing Up a Database

Problem

You want to do a full backup of the AdventureWorks2014 database to your C:\Apress\ folder using T-SQL.

Solution

Execute a BACKUP DATABASE statement. Specify TO DISK and provide the path and desired file name. There are several options that can be used with the BACKUP DATABASE statement that will be covered in the following recipes. Note that this example will perform a backup of the AdventureWorks2014 database, which does not currently have any differential backups. If differential backups were present, the differential recovery chain would be disrupted. More on differential backups will be discussed later in this chapter.

The following example demonstrates using the BACKUP DATABASE statement and specifying the file location where the backup will be stored:

```
BACKUP DATABASE AdventureWorks2014
TO DISK = 'C:\Apress\AdventureWorks2014.bak';
GO
```

```
Processed 24528 pages for database 'AdventureWorks2014', file 'AdventureWorks2014_Data' on
file 1.
Processed 2 pages for database 'AdventureWorks2014', file 'AdventureWorks2014_Log' on file 1.
BACKUP DATABASE successfully processed 24530 pages in 0.451 seconds (424.922 MB/sec).
```

■ **Tip** Make sure that the `Apress` folder exists on the `C:` drive, or change the path in the previous query.

This command will make a full backup of all data and log files in the `AdventureWorks2014` database, including the `FILESTREAM` file.

How It Works

The `BACKUP DATABASE` command, absent all options, will make a full backup of all data and log files in the specified database to the path or device declared in the statement. The process involves copying the data files as well as the active portion of any log files.

This process is rather straightforward, but the resulting backup can be a bit confusing. Consider a database that has a single 50GB data file and a 10MB log file. One would think the resulting backup should be just more than 50GB, but this is not always the case.

During the backup process, SQL Server does not back up empty data pages, meaning that the backup will contain only partially or fully used data pages found within the data files. Comparing the backups may lead some to believe that proprietary compression is involved in the backup process, but really only "used" space is copied to the backup media.

Do not assume that the size of the backup file will translate bit for bit to the size of the database when restored. People frequently ask: "If I restore the database from a backup that is 50GB, will the database only be 50GB?" The database may or may not be just 50GB after the restore is complete, depending on the used space within the database pages that are in the backup. The data files' size information is contained in the backup media, and that file size is what is used to reserve the space to which the data pages are written. In this example, this would mean that another 50GB data file would be created in the restored path, and the data pages would then be written to the data file.

27-2. Compressing a Backup

Problem

As a database grows, disk space can be a fleeting commodity, and the space needed to store a full backup can be prohibitive. Thus, you want to compress your backup files to reduce disk space requirements.

Solution

Backing up the database using the `WITH COMPRESSION` clause will compress the associated backup. The following example demonstrates creating a full backup of the `AdventureWorks2014` database using compression:

```
USE master;
GO
BACKUP DATABASE AdventureWorks2014
TO DISK = 'C:\Apress\AdventureWorks2014compress.bak'
WITH COMPRESSION;
GO
```

```
Processed 24528 pages for database 'AdventureWorks2014', file 'AdventureWorks2014_Data'
on file 1.
Processed 2 pages for database 'AdventureWorks2014', file 'AdventureWorks2014_Log' on file 1.
BACKUP DATABASE successfully processed 24530 pages in 0.507 seconds (377.974 MB/sec).
```

How It Works

The solution example created a full backup to the C:\Apress\ folder with the file name
AdventureWorks2014compress.bak; it utilized compression to reduce the size of the backup file. Using
compression in your backup sets can provide a few benefits, such as reducing the disk space required for
the backups and reduced disk I/O. This only seems reasonable: because there is less to write to disk, there is
noticeably reduced disk I/O.

The specific compression ratio is dependent on the data that is compressed, which in turn is based on
the following factors:

- The type of data

- The consistency of the data among rows on a page

- Whether the data is encrypted

- Whether the database is compressed

This makes it difficult to ascertain the specific compression ratio and the resulting backup size without
first comparing a compressed file to an uncompressed backup file. Since the exact compressed size is
mostly unknown until completion, the database engine uses a preallocation algorithm to reserve space for
the backup file. The algorithm reserves a predefined percentage of the size of the database for the backup.
During the backup process, if more space is required, the database engine will grow the file as needed. Upon
completing the backup, the database engine will shrink the file size of the backup as needed.

The following script illustrates the difference, as a ratio, between a compressed and an uncompressed
backup file of the AdventureWorks2014 database. This query is dependent on having performed the two
backups earlier in this chapter:

```
USE msdb;
GO
SELECT TOP 2
        bs.database_name
    ,CONVERT(DECIMAL(18,2),backup_size/1024/1024.0) AS backup_mb
    ,CONVERT(DECIMAL(18,2),compressed_backup_size/1024/1024.0) AS compressed_backup_mb
    ,CONVERT(DECIMAL(18,2),backup_size/compressed_backup_size)  AS ratio
        ,(1 - CONVERT(DECIMAL(18,2),compressed_backup_size/backup_size))*100 as
CompressPercent
FROM msdb.dbo.backupset bs
WHERE bs.database_name = 'Adventureworks2014'
        AND bs.type = 'D'
ORDER BY backup_start_date DESC;
GO
```

Results may vary.

```
------------- ----------------
AdventureWorks2014    192.08   45.02   4.27    77.00
AdventureWorks2014    192.08  192.08   1.00     0.00
```

This shows that the compressed backup had a compression ratio of just over 4 to 1, while the uncompressed was obviously 1 to 1. This in turn means the compressed backup achieved a 77% reduction in backup size over the uncompressed backup. This substantially reduced file size can also be evaluated by comparing the physical file size from within Windows Explorer.

So as to not paint a one-sided picture, it is important to note that there are some considerations regarding backup compression, including the inability of previous versions (prior to SQL Server 2008) to read a compressed backup. In addition, a compressed SQL backup cannot coexist on tape with an NTBackup.

After this discussion of the performance benefits in both backup size and disk I/O, you may be convinced to begin changing all of your maintenance plans and scripts to utilize WITH COMPRESSION, but you will need to consider the cost. The reduced file size and disk I/O are replaced with increased CPU usage during the backup process, which can prove to be significant. The increase in CPU can be mitigated by using Resource Governor, an Enterprise Edition feature, but it does need to be weighed against server resources and priorities.

Compressed backups also cannot coexist with uncompressed backups on the same media set, which means that full, differential, and transaction log compressed backups must be stored in separate media sets than those that are uncompressed.

27-3. Ensuring That a Backup Can Be Restored

Problem

Backing up a database is straightforward, but you want to make sure that the backup is not corrupt and can be successfully restored.

Solution

There are several ways to ensure that a backup can be successfully restored, the first of which is to utilize the WITH CHECKSUM option in the backup command:

```
USE master;
GO
BACKUP DATABASE AdventureWorks2014
TO  DISK = 'C:\Apress\AdventureWorks2014check.bak'
WITH CHECKSUM;
```

This can be partnered with the command RESTORE VERIFYONLY to ensure not only that a backup is not corrupted, but also that it can be restored:

```
USE master;
GO
RESTORE VERIFYONLY
FROM  DISK = 'C:\Apress\AdventureWorks2014check.bak'
WITH CHECKSUM;
```

Results from the two preceding statements are as follows (results may vary).

```
Processed 24536 pages for database 'AdventureWorks2014', file 'AdventureWorks2014_Data' on
file 1.
Processed 3 pages for database 'AdventureWorks2014', file 'AdventureWorks2014_Log' on file 1.
BACKUP DATABASE successfully processed 24539 pages in 0.464 seconds (413.165 MB/sec).

The backup set on file 1 is valid.
```

How It Works

Using the WITH CHECKSUM option in a backup will verify each page checksum, if it is present on the page. Regardless of whether page checksums are available, the backup will generate a separate checksum for the backup streams. The backup checksums are stored in the backup media and not in the database pages, which means they can be used in restore operations to validate that the backup is not corrupt.

Using the WITH CHECKSUM option in a backup command allows you to control the behavior of what will happen if an error occurs (such as an invalid checksum or a torn page). The default behavior of CHECKSUM is that if a checksum cannot be verified, the backup will be forced to stop, while reporting an error. This can be changed by adding CONTINUE_AFTER_ERROR:

```
USE master;
GO
BACKUP DATABASE AdventureWorks2014
TO  DISK = 'C:\Apress\AdventureWorks2014checkcon.bak'
WITH CHECKSUM, CONTINUE_AFTER_ERROR;
```

Using WITH CHECKSUM to ensure a backup's integrity is a good start, but it does not validate the ability to restore the backup. To better ensure the ability to restore a backup, RESTORE VERIFYONLY should also be used in tandem with the CHECKSUM option. When using RESTORE VERIFYONLY, the following checks are performed to verify the backup:

- Checking that it is a complete backup set with readable volumes
- Validating certain header fields such as page_id
- Checking the checksum, if one is present in the media
- Checking for adequate free space in the restore path

Using WITH CHECKSUM in conjunction with RESTORE VERIFYONLY helps validate a backup's integrity, but it is not fool-proof. Database backups are stored in a format called Microsoft Tape Format (MTF). This format includes MTF blocks, which contain the backup metadata, while the backed-up data is stored outside of the MTF blocks. RESTORE VERIFYONLY performs simple checks on the MTF blocks and not on the actual data blocks, which means the blocks could be consistent while the backup files could be corrupted. In such a case, RESTORE VERIFYONLY would show that the backup set could be restored, but issuing a restore would result in failure.

The moral of this solution is that you can try to ensure backup integrity, but the only sure way to test backup integrity is to restore backups and run DBCC CHECKDB on the restored database.

27-4. Transaction Log Backup

Problem

You have been tasked with creating a backup solution that includes a point-in-time recovery ability while ensuring minimal data loss in the event of a required recovery.

Solution

The solution simply requires planning so that the transaction logs for databases not in SIMPLE recovery mode are backed up routinely. The frequency of these transaction log backups should be determined in coordination with the business so as to determine the maximum acceptable data loss. In some cases, this may be a full day, and in other cases it may be no more than 15 minutes. If the database is not in SIMPLE recovery model, consider it mandatory to include the transaction logs in your backup scheme.

After performing a full backup, and after determining the desired schedule for the transaction log backups, one can then use a command such as the following to back up the transaction logs:

```
BACKUP LOG AdventureWorks2014
TO DISK = 'C:\Apress\AdventureWorks2014.trn';
GO
```

If backing up the logs, one may desire a script that is a little more complex to allow for different log backup files, rather than placing all log backups into the same backup file. To script a log backup and provide this ability, one could employ a script such as the following:

```
DECLARE @DiskPath VARCHAR(256)
      , @DBName sysname = 'AdventureWorks2014';

SET @DiskPath = 'C:\Apress\' + @DBName + '_'
      + REPLACE(REPLACE(REPLACE(CONVERT(CHAR(19), GETDATE(), 126), ' ', '_'), '-',
                                        ''), ':', '') + '.trn';

BACKUP LOG @DBName
      TO DISK = @DiskPath
      WITH INIT,CHECKSUM,COMPRESSION;
GO
```

How It Works

The backup of a transaction log follows the same basic syntax as with a database backup. The key difference with the transaction log backup is the specification of the LOG keyword in the backup statement.

The second example provided a little more complexity by adding a date and time component to the file name. This additional complexity will allow for the backup of the transaction log at a regular interval while sending each backup to a different file.

27-5. Understanding Why the Transaction Log Continues to Grow

Problem

A database transaction log has grown larger than the data files and continues to grow larger by the day. You want to know why.

Solution

The solution to this may be as simple as performing a transaction log backup for the database in question. If the database is not in the simple recovery model, then transaction log backups should be performed on a regular interval. To determine if this is the case, the backupset table in msdb should be queried and compared to the sys.databases catalog view:

```
USE msdb;
GO

DECLARE @DBName VARCHAR(128) = 'AdventureWorks2014'

SELECT d.name,ca.backup_finish_date AS LastFullBackup
            ,bs.backup_finish_date AS LastLogBackup
      FROM sys.databases d
            LEFT OUTER JOIN msdb.dbo.backupset bs
                  ON d.name = bs.database_name
                  AND bs.type = 'l'
            OUTER APPLY (SELECT TOP 1 database_name,backup_finish_date
                                    FROM msdb.dbo.backupset
                                    WHERE database_name = d.name
                                          AND type = 'D'
                                    ORDER BY backup_finish_date DESC) ca
      WHERE d.recovery_model_desc <> 'simple'
            AND bs.database_name IS NULL
            AND d.name = @DBName;
GO
```

If the database in question shows that it is in either the full or bulk-logged recovery models, and the LastLogbackup column reports a NULL value (or the time is greater than the interval for the log backups), then a log backup should be performed. See the following:

```
BACKUP LOG AdventureWorks2014
TO DISK = 'C:\Apress\AdventureWorks2014.trn';
```

How It Works

So that you get a better feel for this concept, I will cover each of the recovery models, beginning with the SIMPLE model. For performance reasons, when a transaction occurs, SQL Server will first check to see whether the affected data pages are in memory. If the necessary pages are not, then they will be read into memory. Subsequent requests for affected pages are presented from memory, because these reflect the most up-to-date information. All transactions are then written to the transaction log. Occasionally, based upon the recovery interval, SQL will run a checkpoint in which all "dirty" pages and log file information will be written to the data file.

Transaction log backups can only be performed on databases using the FULL or BULK_LOGGED recovery model. A database that is set to the SIMPLE recovery model can never be restored to a point in time, because the transaction log is truncated upon a checkpoint, and log backups are not possible in this recovery model. Aside from allowing a restore from the point that the transaction log backup completed, transaction log backups also allow for point-in-time (if no bulk-logged changes exist in the log backup under the BULK-LOGGED model) and transaction mark recovery. Point-in-time recovery is useful for restoring a database to a point prior to a database modification or failure. Transaction marking allows you to recover to the first instance of a marked transaction (using BEGIN TRAN...WITH MARK) and includes the updates made within this transaction.

The size of the transaction log backup file depends on the level of database activity and whether or not you are using a FULL or BULK_LOGGED recovery model. Again, the SIMPLE recovery model does not allow transaction log backups.

Databases that use the SIMPLE recovery model will truncate the inactive portion of the log upon checkpoint. This prevents the ability to back up the transaction log, while potentially reducing the risk of runaway log-file size.

The following script creates a database called Logging, which uses the SIMPLE recovery model and creates a single table, FillErUp:

```
--Create the Logging database
USE master;
GO
CREATE DATABASE Logging;
GO

ALTER DATABASE Logging
SET RECOVERY SIMPLE;
GO

USE Logging;

CREATE TABLE FillErUp(
RowInfo CHAR(150)
);
GO
```

Monitoring the log-file size and the reason why a log file is waiting to reclaim space can be done through the sys.database_files and sys.databases catalog views. The following queries show the initial log- and data-file sizes as well as the log_reuse_wait_desc column; keep in mind that the size column represents the size in 8KB data pages:

```
USE master;
GO
DECLARE @DBName VARCHAR(128) = 'Logging';

SELECT d.name as DBName, mf.size, d.recovery_model_desc, d.log_reuse_wait_desc
    FROM sys.master_files mf
            INNER JOIN sys.databases d
                    ON d.database_id = mf.database_id
        WHERE d.name = @DBName
            AND mf.type_desc = 'LOG';
```

Execute this query, and the results should be similar to the following:

DBName	size	recovery_model_desc	log_reuse_wait_desc
Logging	70	SIMPLE	NOTHING

The log_reuse_wait_desc field is of particular importance in this solution because it provides the reason why the log file is not being truncated. Since the database has just been created and no transactions have been posted to it, there is nothing preventing the log from being truncated.

The following query uses a loop to post 10,000 rows to the FillErUp table and again queries the log-file size and the log_reuse_wait_desc:

```
USE Logging;
GO
SET NOCOUNT ON;
DECLARE @count INT = 10000
WHILE @count > 0
BEGIN
    INSERT INTO FillErUp (RowInfo)
    SELECT 'This is row # ' + CONVERT(CHAR(4), @count)
    SET @count -= 1
END;
GO

CHECKPOINT;
GO

/* check catalog views */
USE master;
GO
DECLARE @DBName VARCHAR(128) = 'Logging';
```

```
SELECT d.name as DBName, mf.size, d.recovery_model_desc, d.log_reuse_wait_desc
        FROM sys.master_files mf
                INNER JOIN sys.databases d
                        ON d.database_id = mf.database_id
        WHERE d.name = @DBName
                AND mf.type_desc = 'LOG';
"()()
```

The results of the query show that the log-file size is relatively the same and that the log_reuse_wait_desc value is still nothing.

DBName	size	recovery_model_desc	log_reuse_wait_desc
Logging	104	SIMPLE	NOTHING

Since the database recovery model is set to simple, the transaction log will be truncated after a checkpoint, allowing the log file to remain at relatively the same size. A database being set to the SIMPLE recovery model does not guarantee that the log file will not grow. A checkpoint will truncate the inactive portion of the log, but the active portion cannot be truncated.

The following example uses BEGIN TRANSACTION (and intentionally leaves it open in order to run some additional queries prior to committing the transaction) to display the effects of a long-running transaction on log-file growth and also uses DBCC SQLPERF to display some statistics on the log file after the transaction runs:

```
USE Logging;
GO

BEGIN TRANSACTION

DECLARE @count INT = 10000
WHILE @count > 0
BEGIN
   INSERT INTO FillErUp
   SELECT 'This is row # ' + CONVERT(CHAR(4), @count)
   SET @count -= 1
END;
GO

USE master;
GO
DECLARE @DBName VARCHAR(128) = 'Logging';

SELECT d.name as DBName, mf.size, d.recovery_model_desc, d.log_reuse_wait_desc
        FROM sys.master_files mf
                INNER JOIN sys.databases d
                        ON d.database_id = mf.database_id
        WHERE d.name = @DBName
                AND mf.type_desc = 'LOG';

DBCC SQLPERF(LOGSPACE);
GO
```

The results of the query show that the log file has grown, and it cannot be truncated because of an open transaction. A portion of the DBCC SQLPERF results are included to show the size and percentage of used log space.

DBName	size	recovery_model_desc	log_reuse_wait_desc
Logging	728	SIMPLE	ACTIVE_TRANSACTION

Database Name	Log Size (MB)	Log Space Used (%)
Logging	5.679688	97.52407

The results show that the log-file size has grown and that the log space is more than 97 percent used. Issuing a COMMIT TRANSACTION and a manual CHECKPOINT will close the transaction, but you will also notice that the log file remains the same size:

```
COMMIT TRANSACTION;
GO
CHECKPOINT;
GO

USE master;
GO
DECLARE @DBName VARCHAR(128) = 'Logging';

SELECT d.name as DBName, mf.size, d.recovery_model_desc, d.log_reuse_wait_desc
      FROM sys.master_files mf
              INNER JOIN sys.databases d
                      ON d.database_id = mf.database_id
        WHERE d.name = @DBName
              AND mf.type_desc = 'LOG';

DBCC SQLPERF(LOGSPACE);
GO
```

DBName	size	recovery_model_desc	log_reuse_wait_desc
Logging	728	SIMPLE	NOTHING

Database Name	Log Size (MB)	Log Space Used (%)
Logging	5.679688	16.96183

It is obvious from the query results that the transaction has been closed, but the log-file size is the same size as when the transaction remained open. The difference between the results is the percentage of used log space. The used log space before the commit and checkpoint is more than 97 percent. However, after the commit the used space falls to just under 17 percent.

■ **Tip** There are ways by which to regain disk space from bloated log files, but the focus of this solution is to highlight maintenance. Any steps taken to shrink the log file should be performed only after careful consideration.

Unlike the SIMPLE recovery model, both the FULL and BULK_LOGGED recovery models require transaction log backups to be taken before a transaction log can be truncated.

To demonstrate, the following example will drop and recreate the Logging database, then create and populate the FillErUp table via a set-based transaction. The log-file size and log reuse wait description are then queried immediately after the creation of the database:

```
USE master;
GO

--Create the Logging database
IF EXISTS (SELECT * FROM sys.databases WHERE name = 'Logging')
BEGIN
DROP DATABASE Logging;
END
GO

CREATE DATABASE Logging
ON PRIMARY
( NAME = N'Logging', FILENAME = N'C:\APRESS\Logging.mdf' , SIZE = 4096KB  )
 LOG ON
( NAME = N'Logging_log', FILENAME = N'C:\APRESS\Logging_log.ldf' , SIZE = 512KB );
GO

ALTER DATABASE Logging
SET RECOVERY FULL;
GO

ALTER DATABASE Logging
MODIFY FILE
    (NAME = Logging_log,
    SIZE = 520KB);
GO

--Size is 101
USE master;
GO
DECLARE @DBName VARCHAR(128) = 'Logging';

SELECT d.name as DBName, mf.size, d.recovery_model_desc, d.log_reuse_wait_desc
    FROM sys.master_files mf
            INNER JOIN sys.databases d
                    ON d.database_id = mf.database_id
        WHERE d.name = @DBName
            AND mf.type_desc = 'LOG';
GO
```

```
USE Logging;
GO
SELECT TOP 10000
        RowInfo = 'This is row # ' + CONVERT(CHAR(5)
                        , ROW_NUMBER() OVER (PARTITION BY t1.autoval ORDER BY (SELECT NULL)))
    INTO dbo.FillErUp
    FROM master.dbo.syscolumns t1,
         master.dbo.syscolumns t2;
GO

CHECKPOINT;
GO

USE master;
GO
DECLARE @DBName VARCHAR(128) = 'Logging';

SELECT d.name as DBName, mf.size, d.recovery_model_desc, d.log_reuse_wait_desc
        FROM sys.master_files mf
                INNER JOIN sys.databases d
                        ON d.database_id = mf.database_id
        WHERE d.name = @DBName
                AND mf.type_desc = 'LOG';
GO
```

DBName	size	recovery_model_desc	log_reuse_wait_desc
Logging	101	FULL	NOTHING

DBName	size	recovery_model_desc	log_reuse_wait_desc
Logging	101	FULL	NOTHING

The results may be different than expected, but this is for good reason. The database was created and then altered to the FULL recovery model. After a number of transactions, the log file remained the same size. Based on the definition of the FULL recovery model, the log should have grown. The log file will continue to be truncated upon a checkpoint until a full backup is taken. This is by design, because the transaction log backup requires a full backup be taken first. After a full backup has been performed, and until a transaction log backup is taken, the log file will grow.

After taking a full backup of the database and again running the INSERT query, the results are much different:

```
USE master;
GO

BACKUP DATABASE Logging
TO DISK =   'C:\Apress\Logging.bak';
GO
```

```
USE Logging;
GO
INSERT INTO dbo.FillErUp
SELECT TOP 10000
        RowInfo = 'This is row # ' + CONVERT(CHAR(5)
                        , ROW_NUMBER() OVER (PARTITION BY t1.autoval ORDER BY (SELECT NULL)))
    FROM master.dbo.syscolumns t1,
        master.dbo.syscolumns t2;
GO

CHECKPOINT;
GO

USE master;
GO
DECLARE @DBName VARCHAR(128) = 'Logging';

SELECT d.name as DBName, mf.size, d.recovery_model_desc, d.log_reuse_wait_desc
        FROM sys.master_files mf
                INNER JOIN sys.databases d
                        ON d.database_id = mf.database_id
        WHERE d.name = @DBName
                AND mf.type_desc = 'LOG';
GO
```

DBName	size	recovery_model_desc	log_reuse_wait_desc
Logging	536	FULL	LOG_BACKUP

The end result is that the log file continued to grow, and the log reuse wait description reflects that a transaction log backup is required. The size of the transaction log can be maintained by scheduled transaction log backups. The transaction log could be backed up (and subsequently the size managed) by using a script such as the following:

```
BACKUP LOG Logging
TO DISK = 'C:\Apress\Logging.trn'
```

A database using the BULK_LOGGED recovery model still uses the log file to record transactions, but bulk-logged transactions are minimally logged, causing less growth in the log. Unlike the FULL recovery model, BULK_LOGGED recovery does not provide the ability to restore the database to a point in time if bulk-logged changes exist within the log backup. In this case, the entire log must be recovered. However, if there are no bulk-logged changes in the backup, then recovery to a point in time is possible.

Only specific operations are marked as BULK_LOGGED, such as BULK INSERT, SELECT INTO, bcp, and INSERT INTO...SELECT, to name a few. A common misconception is that the BULK_LOGGED recovery model will not cause the log file to grow, which is untrue.

The following code demonstrates that bulk operations can cause the transaction log file to grow with a database using the BULK_LOGGED recovery model:

```
USE master;
GO

IF EXISTS (SELECT * FROM sys.databases WHERE name = 'Logging')
BEGIN
DROP DATABASE Logging;
END
GO

CREATE DATABASE Logging;
GO

ALTER DATABASE Logging
SET RECOVERY BULK_LOGGED;
GO

BACKUP DATABASE Logging
TO DISK =  'C:\Apress\Logging_bulk.bak';
GO

USE master;
GO
DECLARE @DBName VARCHAR(128) = 'Logging';

SELECT d.name as DBName, mf.size, d.recovery_model_desc, d.log_reuse_wait_desc
        FROM sys.master_files mf
                INNER JOIN sys.databases d
                        ON d.database_id = mf.database_id
        WHERE d.name = @DBName
                AND mf.type_desc = 'LOG';
GO
```

DBName	size	recovery_model_desc	log_reuse_wait_desc
Logging	70	BULK_LOGGED	NOTHING

```
USE Logging;
GO

SELECT *
        INTO PurchaseOrderDetail
        FROM AdventureWorks2014.Purchasing.PurchaseOrderDetail
```

```
USE master;
GO
DECLARE @DBName VARCHAR(128) = 'Logging';

SELECT d.name as DBName, mf.size, d.recovery_model_desc, d.log_reuse_wait_desc
        FROM sys.master_files mf
                INNER JOIN sys.databases d
                        ON d.database_id = mf.database_id
        WHERE d.name = @DBName
                AND mf.type_desc = 'LOG';
GO
```

DBName	size	recovery_model_desc	log_reuse_wait_desc
Logging	136	BULK_LOGGED	LOG_BACKUP

In this example, I used a SELECT...INTO statement, which is minimally logged under the BULK_LOGGED recovery model. The results show that a database in a BULK_LOGGED recovery model will cause the log file to grow, even when using bulk operations.

27-6. Performing a Differential Backup

Problem

You have discovered that full backups are taking too long to perform and require too much storage. You would like to decrease the backup duration and reduce the storage requirement.

Solution

A differential backup contains all the changes made since the last full backup. A backup/restore strategy can use as many differential backups as desired, and since a differential contains all the changes from the last full backup, it can speed up the restoration process. After performing a full backup, a differential backup can be performed using a script such as the following:

```
USE master;
GO

BACKUP DATABASE AdventureWorks2014
TO DISK = 'C:\Apress\AdventureWorks2014_diff.bak'
WITH DIFFERENTIAL;
GO
```

How It Works

The differential backup statement is almost identical to a full backup statement, with the exception of the WITH DIFFERENTIAL. A differential backup will contain all changes in a database since the last full backup, which means that a full backup must already exist before a differential can be taken.

Although a differential backup can reduce the time required to back up and reduce the storage requirements, it is important to understand the mechanics of the backup. Consider a backup strategy that utilizes a full backup at 12 p.m. and a differential every two hours thereafter. The further away in time the differential backup gets from the full backup, the larger, based on activity, that backup would be. The 2 p.m. differential would contain all the changes from 12 p.m. to 2 p.m., the 4 p.m. differential would contain all the changes from 12 p.m. to 4 p.m., and so on.

While the differential backup will require less space and run faster initially, it can become slower over time as well as require more space than a full backup. A backup plan that involves differential backups needs to be carefully evaluated to find the balance between size, speed, and frequency of the differential backups and the full backups.

27-7. Backing Up a Single Row or Table

Problem

In preparation for a deployment, you have determined that it would be helpful to create a backup of a table that will undergo data or schema changes during the deployment.

Solution

Backup granularity within SQL Server starts with the database and then moves to the filegroup and finally to the file. Unless a table resides on its own filegroup, the backup statement does not natively support this functionality, but you can use several workarounds to meet this need.

To back up a table, or even specific records from a table, one of the easiest solutions is to utilize the SELECT...INTO statement. In this example we will perform a backup of the Person.Person table from the AdventureWorks2014 database and store it in the AdventureWorks2014_Bak database. See the following:

```
USE master;
GO

IF EXISTS (SELECT * FROM sys.databases WHERE name = 'AdventureWorks2014_Bak')
BEGIN
DROP DATABASE AdventureWorks2014_Bak;
END
CREATE DATABASE AdventureWorks2014_Bak;
GO

USE AdventureWorks2014_Bak;
GO
CREATE SCHEMA Person
GO

SELECT BusinessEntityID,
       FirstName,
       MiddleName,
       LastName
INTO Person.Person
FROM AdventureWorks2014.Person.Person;
GO
```

```
SELECT TOP 6 *
FROM Person.Person
ORDER BY BusinessEntityID;
GO
```

Executing the previous query will create the AdventureWorks2014_Bak database and the Person schema, and will populate the Person table with the result of the SELECT statement from the Person.Person table in the AdventureWorks2014 database.

BusinessEntityID	FirstName	MiddleName	LastName
1	Ken	J	Sánchez
2	Terri	Lee	Duffy
3	Roberto	NULL	Tamburello
4	Rob	NULL	Walters
5	Gail	A	Erickson
6	Jossef	H	Goldberg

Once the database is created and the table is populated, the data can then be validated with the final SELECT statement in the previous query. Once complete, you are ready to continue with the deployment, having essentially completed a table backup.

How It Works

The process behind this method is fairly self-evident. The SELECT...INTO creates a granular backup without using the BACKUP syntax of the table to be affected. Should something happen, this backup can provide the means to a quick recovery of the data or schema that had been modified without performing a database restore. Several issues may complicate method recovery using this method, such as a column that is an IDENTITY, replication, or triggers on the affected table.

This method also reduces the storage requirements you might encounter with other methods, such as a full backup (and the restore of the full backup so as to recover a single table as illustrated in this example).

27-8. Creating a Database Snapshot

Problem

In preparation for a deployment, you need to create a backup of the database, but the full backup would take longer than the maintenance window you have been given. You need a means by which to quickly back up the database and still have adequate time for the maintenance window.

Solution

You can utilize a database snapshot as a means of backing up "state" data. A database snapshot is created on a user database from within an instance of SQL and works on a "write"-on change basis. When creating a database snapshot, disk space is reserved for the snapshot that is equal to the reserved space of the data files of the user database. The disk space reserved for the snapshot remains completely empty until a data page from the user database is modified or deleted. Once this change occurs, the original data page is written to the database snapshot, preserving the data as it appeared at the point in time of the snapshot being taken.

The following code will utilize the AdventureWorks2014 database to create a database snapshot called AventureWorks2014_SS:

```
USE master;
GO


CREATE DATABASE AdventureWorks2014_SS ON
( NAME = AdventureWorks2014_Data, FILENAME =
'C:\Apress\AdventureWorks2014_SS.ss' )
AS SNAPSHOT OF AdventureWorks2014;
GO


USE master;
GO


SELECT DB_NAME(database_id) AS DBName,
    name AS FileName,
        type_desc,
        size
FROM sys.master_files
WHERE DB_NAME(database_id) LIKE 'AdventureWorks2014%'
        AND type_desc = 'ROWS';
GO
```

The results of the previous query show that the AventureWorks2014 and AdventureWorks2014_SS databases were created and that the file sizes are identical.

DBName	FileName	type_desc	size
AdventureWorks2014	AdventureWorks2014_Data	ROWS	26272
AdventureWorks2014_SS	AdventureWorks2014_Data	ROWS	26272

These results demonstrate that the snapshot has a data file that is the exact same size as the data files from the source database (AdventureWorks2014, in this case). Browsing the directory of the snapshot would reveal that a single file with a .ss extension would exist as the database snapshot.

Upon creating a database snapshot, the single snapshot file is completely empty and is used only as a placeholder. Data pages are added to the snapshot file as changes occur within the original database. This means that when directly querying the database snapshot, the requested 8KB data pages, which have not been modified since the snapshot was taken, are being returned from the original database.

How It Works

While not a traditional backup, a snapshot can serve the same purpose. A snapshot does not use the BACKUP syntax, but rather uses the CREATE DATABASE..AS SNAPSHOT syntax. This provides a very quick means to make a backup of the database by creating a sparse file on the operating system. You can validate the existence of a snapshot and the source of the snapshot via the following query:

```
USE master;
GO

SELECT d.name AS DBName,
        DB_NAME(d.source_database_id) AS SourceDB,
        d.create_date,
        d.is_read_only,
        mf.is_sparse
FROM sys.master_files mf
        INNER JOIN sys.databases d
                ON d.database_id = mf.database_id
WHERE d.name LIKE 'AdventureWorks2014%'
        AND type_desc = 'ROWS';
GO
```

This query demonstrates how to find the snapshots that may exist for a particular database within an instance. Snapshots have a few indicators to help identify them. These indicators are the is_sparse, is_read_only, and source_database_id fields. The is_sparse field can be found in the sys.master_files or sys.database_files catalog views, while the other fields are found within the sys.databases system catalog view. If all three fields contain a value, the database in question is a snapshot of another database.

27-9. Backing Up Data Files or Filegroups

Problem

Your database size is so large that it is prohibitive to complete a full database backup on a daily basis.

Solution #1: Perform a File Backup

It can become burdensome to maintain an effective and efficient backup procedure in very large databases (VLDBs) because of the time it takes to perform a full backup and the amount of space required. Rather than a full backup, backups can be made of the data files individually. This can be demonstrated by creating a database with multiple files and filegroups:

```
CREATE DATABASE BackupFiles
 ON  PRIMARY
( NAME = N'BackupFiles', FILENAME = N'C:\Apress\BackupFiles.mdf' , SIZE = 4096KB ,
FILEGROWTH = 1024KB ),
 FILEGROUP [Current]
( NAME = N'CurrentData', FILENAME = 'C:\Apress\CurrentData.ndf' , SIZE = 4096KB , FILEGROWTH
= 1024KB ),
 FILEGROUP [Historic]
( NAME = N'HistoricData', FILENAME = 'C:\Apress\HistoricData.ndf' , SIZE = 4096KB ,
FILEGROWTH = 1024KB )
```

```
  LOG ON
( NAME = N'BackupFiles_log', FILENAME = 'C:\Apress\BackupFiles_log.ldf' , SIZE = 1024KB ,
FILEGROWTH = 512KB);
GO
ALTER DATABASE [BackupFiles] SET RECOVERY FULL;
GO
```

To back up a single file from a database, simply use the BACKUP DATABASE command and specify the files to back up:

```
USE master;
GO

BACKUP DATABASE BackupFiles
FILE = 'HistoricData'
TO DISK =  'C:\Apress\Historic.bak';
GO
```

Solution #2: Perform a Filegroup Backup

Sometimes a filegroup contains multiple files that need to be backed up in a single backup set. This is accomplished easily enough using the BACKUP DATABASE command and specifying the filegroup to be backed up:

```
USE master;
GO

BACKUP DATABASE BackupFiles
FILEGROUP = 'Historic'
TO DISK =  'C:\Apress\HistoricFG.bak';
GO
```

How It Works

Backing up a file or filegroup works the same as a full database backup while providing a more focused, granular approach to the specific filegroup or file in the database. Either method can be employed to reduce the amount of time and space required for a full database backup.

It is critical to fully plan a database design if this backup/recovery method is going to be used so as to ensure that the entire database can be restored to a point in time and remain consistent. Consider the impact of placing one table on a file that references another table on a separate file. If either of the files need to be restored, and referential integrity would be violated because of the point in time of the restoration, this can cause a great deal of work when restoring the database to a consistent and valid state.

It is also important to remember that the primary file/filegroup must be backed up, because it contains all of the system tables and database objects.

27-10. Mirroring Backup Files

Problem

You want to ensure that multiple backups are written to different disks/tapes without affecting the backup media set or having to manually copy the backup files.

Solution

SQL Server 2005 Enterprise Edition introduced the `MIRROR TO` clause, which will write the backup to multiple devices:

```
BACKUP DATABASE AdventureWorks2014
TO DISK = 'C:\Apress\AdventureWorks2014.bak'
MIRROR TO DISK = 'C:\Apress\MirroredBackup\AdventureWorks2014.bak'
WITH
    FORMAT,
    MEDIANAME = 'AdventureWorksSet1';
GO
```

■ **Tip** Make sure that the `Apress` and `Apress\MirroredBackup` folders exist on the `C:` drive, or change the path in the previous query.

How It Works

During the backup, using `MIRROR TO` will write the backup to multiple devices, which ensures that the backup file resides on separate tapes or disks in case one should become corrupt or unusable. There are several limitations when using the `MIRROR TO` clause, the first being that it requires either the Developer or Enterprise edition. The mirrored devices must be the same type, meaning you cannot write one file to disk and the other to tape. The mirrored devices must be similar and have the same properties. Insufficiently similar devices will generate the error message 3212.

27-11. Backing Up a Database Without Affecting the Normal Sequence of Backups

Problem

An up-to-date backup needs to be created that will not affect the normal sequence of backups.

Solution

Using the BACKUP command and specifying WITH COPY_ONLY will create the desired backup without affecting the backup or restore sequence (particularly if differential backups are involved). See the following:

```
USE master;
GO

BACKUP DATABASE AdventureWorks2014
TO DISK =  'C:\Apress\AdventureWorks2014Copydiff.bak'
WITH COPY_ONLY;
GO
```

How It Works

The only difference in the backup process when using WITH COPY_ONLY is that the backup will have no effect on the backup or restore procedure for a database.

■ **Caution**   If COPY_ONLY is used with a transaction log backup, the transaction log will not be truncated once the backup is complete.

27-12. Querying Backup Data

Problem

You have to create a programmatic way to return backup information.

Solution

The msdb database maintains all of the backup history in the system tables. The system tables backupfile, backupfilegroup, backupmediafamily, backupmediaset, and backupset contain the full history of database backups as well as the media types and locations. These tables can be queried to return information on any database backup that has occurred.

The following query will return the database name, the date and time the backup began, the type of backup that was taken, whether it used COPY_ONLY, the path and file name or device name, and the backup size, ordering by the start date in descending order. See the following:

```
USE msdb;
GO
SELECT bs.database_name,
          bs.backup_start_date,
          CASE bs.type
              WHEN 'D' THEN 'Database'
              WHEN 'I' THEN 'Differential database'
              WHEN 'L' THEN 'Log'
              WHEN 'F' THEN 'File or filegroup'
              WHEN 'G' THEN 'Differential file'
```

```
            WHEN 'P' THEN 'Partial'
            WHEN 'Q' THEN 'Differential partial'
            ELSE 'Unknown'
        END AS BackupType,
        bmf.physical_device_name,
        bs.backup_size/1024/1024 as BackSizeMB
FROM dbo.backupset bs
INNER JOIN dbo.backupmediafamily bmf
ON bs.media_set_id = bmf.media_set_id
ORDER BY bs.database_name,bs.backup_start_date DESC;
GO
```

Your results will vary.

database_name	backup_start_date	BackupType
AdventureWorks2014	2015-03-18 17:12:33.000	Differential Database
AdventureWorks2014	2015-03-18 17:06:53.000	Differential Database
AdventureWorks2014	2015-03-18 16:45:22.000	Full Database

physical_device_name	BackSizeMB
C:\Apress\AdventureWorks2014Copydiff.bak	1.07617187500
C:\Apress\AdventureWorks2014_diff.bak	1.07617187500
C:\Apress\AdventureWorks2014.bak	192.07617187500

The results show the most recent backups in descending order by the date the backup was taken.

How It Works

Whenever a database backup is performed, it is recorded in the msdb database. The system tables that record this information are made available to query. This information can be used for a number of different purposes, including automating the restoration of a database.

27-13. Encrypting a Backup

Problem

It has been determined that the backups of a database contain some confidential information, and measures must be taken to protect that data at rest within the backup.

Solution

SQL Server 2014 has the ability to perform a backup while encrypting the data for that backup. To use encryption in a backup, an encryption algorithm and an encryptor (such as a certificate) must be specified as options in the BACKUP command. In addition to these requirements, a database master key must exist in the database that is to be backed up while utilizing the encryption option.

The following example demonstrates how to create a database master key (DMK) and a certificate, as well as how to utilize both of those to create an encrypted database backup:

```
-- Create a DMK.
-- The DMK is encrypted using the password "SQL2014Rocks"
USE master;
GO
CREATE MASTER KEY ENCRYPTION BY PASSWORD = 'SQL2014Rocks';
GO


--create our encryptor
USE master;
GO
CREATE CERTIFICATE AW2014BackupCert
   WITH SUBJECT = 'AdventureWorks2014 Backup Encryption Certificate';
GO


--backup the database
USE master;
GO

BACKUP DATABASE AdventureWorks2014
TO DISK = N'C:\Apress\AdventureWorks2014_enc.bak'
WITH
  ENCRYPTION
   (
   ALGORITHM = AES_256,
   SERVER CERTIFICATE = AW2014BackupCert
   ),
  STATS = 5
GO
```

■ **Note**　The creation of the certificate in this example will produce the following warning. Certificate backups will be covered later in this chapter.

■ **Warning**　The certificate used for encrypting the database encryption key has not been backed up. You should immediately back up the certificate and the private key associated with the certificate. If the certificate ever becomes unavailable or if you must restore or attach the database on another server, you must have backups of both the certificate and the private key or you will not be able to open the database.

How It Works

In this example, a database backup was created using encryption via the ENCRYPTION option. Performing this encrypted backup required that a DMK and a certificate be created on the instance.

The ENCRYPTION option was issued with the specification to use the AES_256 algorithm and the AW2014BackupCert that was created earlier in the script. If I wanted to validate whether a backup was encrypted, I could use the following query:

```
USE msdb;
GO
SELECT bs.database_name,
        bs.backup_start_date,
        CASE bs.type
          WHEN 'D' THEN 'Full Database'
          WHEN 'I' THEN 'Differential Database'
          WHEN 'L' THEN 'Log'
          WHEN 'F' THEN 'File or Filegroup'
          WHEN 'G' THEN 'Differential File'
          WHEN 'P' THEN 'Partial'
          WHEN 'Q' THEN 'Differential Partial'
          ELSE 'Unknown'
        END AS BackupType,
        bmf.physical_device_name,
        bs.backup_size/1024/1024 as BackSizeMB,
        bs.encryptor_type, bs.key_algorithm
FROM dbo.backupset bs
INNER JOIN dbo.backupmediafamily bmf
ON bs.media_set_id = bmf.media_set_id
WHERE bs.key_algorithm IS NOT NULL
ORDER BY bs.database_name,bs.backup_start_date DESC;
GO
```

27-14. Compressing an Encrypted Backup

Problem

The encrypted backups are consuming a lot of storage and you are running short on storage. You would like to implement a solution to maintain the current backup retention as well as reduce the storage-space requirements for the backups.

Solution

While I already discussed the ability to compress a backup in SQL Server in this chapter, I left the discussion for combining an encrypted backup with compression for this recipe. In prior versions of SQL Server, backups were encrypted either by the use of a third-party app or by having the database encrypted with TDE. In the latter of these two options, a compressed backup of a TDE-enabled database would provide no space savings. In SQL Server 2014, that has changed with the introduction of the native backup encryption option, which can be easily combined with the compression option.

The following example demonstrates the ability to encrypt and compress the same backup while achieving the desired space savings:

```
USE master;
GO

BACKUP DATABASE AdventureWorks2014
TO DISK = N'C:\Apress\AdventureWorks2014_compenc.bak'
WITH
  COMPRESSION,
  ENCRYPTION
   (
   ALGORITHM = AES_256,
   SERVER CERTIFICATE = AW2014BackupCert
   ),
  STATS = 5
GO
```

How It Works

In this example, I combined the options for encryption and compression into a single backup. I took advantage of the already existing DMK and certificate created in the prior recipe and specified the use of the AW2014BackupCert in the backup statement, as was done in the previous recipe.

The use of the COMPRESSION option reduced the overall size of the backup on disk to just over 45MB. This combination of compression and encryption can be essential to an environment tight on storage space and under the requirement of protecting the data in the backup.

To confirm the encryption and compression, the following query would be useful:

```
USE msdb;
GO
SELECT bs.database_name,
          bs.backup_start_date,
          CASE bs.type
             WHEN 'D' THEN 'Full Database'
             WHEN 'I' THEN 'Differential Database'
             WHEN 'L' THEN 'Log'
             WHEN 'F' THEN 'File or Filegroup'
             WHEN 'G' THEN 'Differential File'
             WHEN 'P' THEN 'Partial'
             WHEN 'Q' THEN 'Differential Partial'
             ELSE 'Unknown'
          END AS BackupType,
          bmf.physical_device_name,
          bs.backup_size/1024/1024 as BackSizeMB,
          bs.compressed_backup_size/1024/1024 as CompBackSizeMB,
          bs.encryptor_type, bs.key_algorithm
FROM dbo.backupset bs
INNER JOIN dbo.backupmediafamily bmf
ON bs.media_set_id = bmf.media_set_id
WHERE bs.key_algorithm IS NOT NULL
ORDER BY bs.database_name,bs.backup_start_date DESC;
GO
```

27-15. Backing Up Certificates

Problem

You have implemented certificates on your server for the purpose of creating encrypted backups. You want to ensure these certificates are available should the server crash.

Solution

SQL Server provides the ability to create a backup of the certificates that you implement within the instance. In the prior two recipes, I utilized a certificate to perform encrypted backups. When performing the backups in those recipes, a warning message was generated due to the lack of a backup of the certificate. The warning is often and easily overlooked, but should be heeded.

To perform a backup of a certificate, use the following syntax, which is very similar to what would be done for a database backup. Here is the general syntax:

```
BACKUP CERTIFICATE certname TO FILE = 'path_to_file'
   [ WITH PRIVATE KEY
     (
       FILE = 'path_to_private_key_file' ,
       ENCRYPTION BY PASSWORD = 'encryption_password'
       [ , DECRYPTION BY PASSWORD = 'decryption_password' ]
     )
   ]
```

The following script demonstrates how to use BACKUP CERTIFICATE to perform a backup of the certificate that has been used in the preceding recipes on backup encryption in this chapter:

```
USE master;
GO

BACKUP CERTIFICATE AW2014BackupCert
TO FILE = 'c:\Apress\AW2014BackupCert.cer'
WITH PRIVATE KEY ( FILE = 'C:\Apress\AW2014BackupCertKey.bak' ,
ENCRYPTION BY PASSWORD = 'SQL2014Rocks');
GO
```

How It Works

In this example I demonstrated the use of BACKUP CERTIFICATE to create a backup of the certificate used for the encrypted backups. This recipe not only applied to the certificates created for encrypted backups, but for all certificates that may have been created within the instance. Recovery plans should include the recovery of certificates, and therefore those certificates need to have backups created.

In this example, I showed how to back up the certificate and the private key for that certificate to flat files on disk. Once the backup has been created, it can be confirmed that the certificate and its private key have been backed up by querying the sys.certificates catalog view:

```
USE master;
GO

SELECT name, pvt_key_encryption_type_desc,pvt_key_last_backup_date
    FROM sys.certificates
    WHERE name = 'AW2014BackupCert';
```

27-16. Backing Up to Azure

Problem

You wish to utilize Azure to store your database backups.

Solution

SQL Server 2014 introduces the ability to create a backup to Azure blob storage via the use of a credential and the URL option. This feature requires that an Azure storage object already exist and that a credential be created in SQL Server in order to access that storage object from Azure.

This next example demonstrates how to perform this backup using the WITH CREDENTIAL and TO URL options:

```
USE master;
GO

CREATE CREDENTIAL SQL2014
WITH IDENTITY= 'Recipes2014'
, SECRET = 'SQL2014Rocks'

BACKUP DATABASE AdventureWorks2014
TO URL = N'https://Recipes2014.blob.core.windows.net/backuptest/AW2014_blob.bak'
WITH
    CREDENTIAL = 'SQL2014'
    ,COMPRESSION
    ,STATS = 10
GO
```

How It Works

Performing a backup to Azure is very similar to performing a backup to local storage. The main difference is that the TO URL option must be specified in order to perform the backup to Azure blob storage.

This example showed the creation of a credential first and then the use of that credential to perform the backup TO URL. Additionally, the COMPRESSION option was used, but was entirely optional. Also, I included another optional parameter called STATS, which prints an informational message concerning the percentage complete (in whichever increment has been specified) for that operation.

To create the credential, I specified a specific IDENTITY and a specific SECRET. These required values will be different for your specific Azure Storage object. The identity must be the name of the storage account used when creating the Azure Storage object. The secret will be either the primary or secondary access key associated with that Azure Storage object that you created.

27-17. Backing Up to Multiple Files

Problem

You wish to utilize multiple backup paths because of inadequate storage space on any single path.

Solution

SQL Server gives you the ability to perform a backup to multiple files and paths. The implementation of a backup across multiple files or paths is called a striped backup. When performing a striped backup, the blocks of the backup are written to the files in the media set in a fixed order. Each file in the backup set contains a different set of blocks and therefore a different piece of the data. This is different from a mirrored backup in that a mirrored backup is a full copy of the backup in each backup file.

In this example, I demonstrate how to perform a striped backup:

```
USE master;
GO

BACKUP DATABASE AdventureWorks2014
TO DISK = 'C:\Apress\AdventureWorks2014_01.bak'
, DISK = 'C:\Apress\AdventureWorks2014_02.bak'
WITH COMPRESSION
        ,STATS = 5;
```

How It Works

A striped backup utilizes the same basic syntax as if performing a backup to a single file or device. The difference with a striped backup is that the TO DISK option is specified multiple times. The TO DISK must be specified for each device to be added to the striped set.

The use of striped backups is limited to local media or a networked path that can be designated from within the TO DISK syntax. A striped set cannot be performed when using the TO URL option, as of SQL Server 2014.

Recovery

by Jason Brimhall

Chapter 27 discussed one of the most critical responsibilities of a SQL Server professional: backing up your data. In this chapter, I will discuss the second half of that very important topic: recovering your data. It is not enough to simply create a backup of the data; you need to also regularly restore your data to test the reliability of the backups.

This chapter will discuss how to restore a database from a backup file. A restore operation copies all data, log, and index pages from the backup media set to the destination database. The destination database can be an existing database (which will be overlaid) or a new database (where new files will be created based on the backup). After the restore operation, a "redo" phase ensues, rolling forward committed transactions that were happening at the end of the database backup. After that, the "undo" phase rolls back uncommitted transactions.

This next set of recipes will demonstrate database restores in action.

28-1. Restoring a Database from a Full Backup

Problem

You have created a full backup of your database. Now you want to test the backup to ensure it is a good backup.

Solution

Use the RESTORE command to restore a database from a full database backup. Unlike a BACKUP operation, a RESTORE is not always an online operation—for a full database restore, user connections must be disconnected from the database prior to restoring over the database. Other restore types (such as filegroup, file, or page) can allow online activity in the database in other areas aside from the elements being restored. For example, if filegroup FG2 is getting restored, FG3 can still be accessed during the operation.

■ **Note**   Online restores are a SQL Server Enterprise Edition feature.

In general, you may need to restore a database after data loss because of user error or file corruption or because you need a second copy of a database or are moving a database to a new SQL Server instance.

The following is simplified syntax for the RESTORE command:

```
RESTORE DATABASE { database_name | @database_name_var } [ FROM <backup_device> [ ,...n ] ] [
WITH ] [Option Name ] [,...n]
```

The RESTORE DATABASE command also includes several options, many of which I'll demonstrate in this chapter.

The first example in this recipe is a simple RESTORE from the latest backup set on the device (in this example, two backup sets exist on the device for the TestDB database, and you want the second one). For the demonstration, I'll start by creating two full backups on a single device.

```
USE master;
GO

Declare @BackupDate Char(8) = Convert(Varchar,GetDate(),112)
    ,@BackupPath Varchar(50);

Set @BackupPath= 'C:\Apress\TestDB_'+ @BackupDate + '.BAK';

BACKUP DATABASE TestDB
TO DISK = @BackupPath;
GO
-- Time passes, we make another backup to the same device
USE master;
GO

Declare @BackupDate Char(8) = Convert(Varchar,GetDate(),112)
    ,@BackupPath Varchar(50);

Set @BackupPath= 'C:\Apress\TestDB_'+ @BackupDate + '.BAK';

BACKUP DATABASE TestDB
TO DISK = @BackupPath;
GO
```

Now I will restore using the second backup from the device (notice that the REPLACE argument is used to tell SQL Server to overlay the existing TestDB database).

```
USE master;
GO

DECLARE @DeviceName VARCHAR(50);

SELECT @DeviceName = b.physical_device_name
        FROM msdb.dbo.backupset a
                INNER JOIN msdb.dbo.backupmediafamily b
                        ON a.media_set_id = b.media_set_id
        WHERE a.database_name = 'TestDB'
                AND a.type = 'D'
                AND CONVERT(VARCHAR, a.backup_start_date, 112) = CONVERT(VARCHAR, GETDATE(), 112)
                AND a.position = 2;
```

```
RESTORE DATABASE TestDB
FROM DISK = @DeviceName
WITH FILE = 2, REPLACE;
GO
```

This returns the following output (your results may vary):

```
Processed 296 pages for database 'TestDB', file 'TestDB' on file 2.
Processed 2 pages for database 'TestDB', file 'TestDB_log' on file 2.
RESTORE DATABASE successfully processed 298 pages in 0.038 seconds (61.073 MB/sec).
```

In this second example, a *new* database is created by restoring from the TestDB backup. It creates a new database called TrainingDB. Notice that the MOVE argument is used to designate the location of the new database files.

```
USE master;
GO

Declare @DeviceName Varchar(50);

Select @DeviceName = b.physical_device_name
    From msdb.dbo.backupset a
        INNER JOIN msdb.dbo.backupmediafamily b
        ON a.media_set_id = b.media_set_id
    Where a.database_name = 'TestDB'
        And a.type = 'D'
        And Convert(Varchar,a.backup_start_date,112) = Convert(Varchar,GetDate(),112);
RESTORE DATABASE TrainingDB
FROM DISK = @DeviceName
WITH FILE = 2,
MOVE 'TestDB' TO 'C:\Apress\TrainingDB.mdf',
MOVE 'TestDB_log' TO 'C:\Apress\TrainingDB_log.LDF';
GO
```

This restore operation results in the following (your results may vary):

```
Processed 296 pages for database 'TrainingDB', file 'TestDB' on file 2.
Processed 2 pages for database 'TrainingDB', file 'TestDB_log' on file 2.
RESTORE DATABASE successfully processed 298 pages in 0.037 seconds (62.724 MB/sec).
```

In the last example for this recipe, the TestDB database is restored from a striped backup set. First, I create a backup set that will be used to perform the restore of a striped backup set.

```
USE master;
GO
/* The path for each file should be changed to a path matching one
That exists on your system. */
BACKUP DATABASE TestDB
TO DISK = 'C:\Apress\TestDB_Stripe1.bak'
```

```
    , DISK = 'C:\Apress\StripedBacks\TestDB_Stripe2.bak'
    , DISK = 'C:\Apress\StripedBacks\TestDB_Stripe3.bak'
    WITH NOFORMAT, NOINIT,
NAME = N'TestDB-Stripe Database Backup',
SKIP, STATS = 20;
GO
```

Now, I will perform the restore of the striped backup set.

```
USE master;
GO
/* You should use the same file path for each file as specified
in the backup statement. */
RESTORE DATABASE TestDB
FROM DISK = 'C:\Apress\TestDB_Stripe1.bak'
    , DISK = 'C:\Apress\StripedBacks\TestDB_Stripe2.bak'
    , DISK = 'C:\Apress\StripedBacks\TestDB_Stripe3.bak'
    WITH FILE = 1, REPLACE;
GO
```

This restore operation results in the following (your results may vary):

```
Processed 296 pages for database 'TestDB', file 'TestDB' on file 1.
Processed 2 pages for database 'TestDB', file 'TestDB_log' on file 1.
RESTORE DATABASE successfully processed 298 pages in 0.031 seconds (74.896 MB/sec).
```

How It Works

In the first example, the query began by setting the database to the master database. This is because a full RESTORE is not an online operation and requires that there be no active connections to the database that is being restored in order to run.

The RESTORE was for the TestDB database, and it overlaid the current database with the data as it existed at the end of the second backup set on the backup device created from this command.

```
Declare @BackupDate Char(8) = Convert(Varchar,GetDate(),112)
    ,@BackupPath Varchar(50);

Set @BackupPath= 'C:\Apress\TestDB_'+ @BackupDate + '.BAK';
```

Prior to running the RESTORE command, I needed to query the msdb database to determine the name of the backup device since I created it dynamically based on the current date. The following query shows how to find the name of that backup device.

```
Declare @DeviceName Varchar(50);

Select @DeviceName = b.physical_device_name
    From msdb.dbo.backupset a
        INNER JOIN msdb.dbo.backupmediafamily b
            ON a.media_set_id = b.media_set_id
```

```
Where a.database_name = 'TestDB'
    And a.type = 'D'
    And Convert(Varchar,a.backup_start_date,112) = Convert(Varchar,GetDate(),112);
```

Having retrieved the name of the backup device, I can now restore the database using the following RESTORE command while specifying which database to restore.

```
RESTORE DATABASE TestDB
```

The next line of this example designated the location of the backup device.

```
FROM DISK = @DeviceName
```

The last line of this example designated which backup set from the backup device should be used to RESTORE from (you can use RESTORE HEADERONLY to see what backup sets exist on a backup device).

```
WITH FILE = 2, REPLACE
```

Any data that was updated since the last backup will be lost, so it is assumed in this example that data loss is acceptable and that data as of the last backup is desired. In the second example, a new database was created based on a RESTORE from another database. The example is similar to the previous query, only this time the MOVE command was used to designate where the new database files should be located (and the new database name is used as well).

```
MOVE 'TestDB' TO 'C:\Apress\ TrainingDB.mdf,
MOVE 'TestDB_log' TO 'C:\Apress\TrainingDB_log.LDF'
```

RESTORE FILELISTONLY can be used to retrieve the logical name and physical path of the backed-up database.

■ **Tip** The RESTORE...MOVE command is often used in conjunction with database migrations to different SQL Server instances that use different drive letters and directories.

In the last example of the recipe, the TestDB was restored from a striped backup set. FROM DISK was repeated for each disk device in the set.

```
USE master;
GO
RESTORE DATABASE TestDB
FROM DISK = 'C:\Apress\TestDB_Stripe1.bak'
    , DISK = 'C:\Apress\StripedBacks\TestDB_Stripe2.bak'
    , DISK = 'C:\Apress\StripedBacks\TestDB_Stripe3.bak'
    WITH FILE = 1, REPLACE;
GO
```

In each of these examples, the database was restored to a recovered state, meaning that it was online and available for users to query after the redo phase (and during/after the undo phase). In the next few recipes, you'll see that the database is often *not* recovered until a differential or transaction log backup can be restored.

28-2. Restoring a Database from a Transaction Log Backup

Problem

You need to restore a database to a predetermined time that is after the last full backup.

Solution

You can perform transaction log restores in conjunction with a full backup by using the RESTORE LOG command. Transaction log restores require an initial full database restore, and if you're applying multiple transaction logs, they must be applied in chronological order (based on when the transaction log backups were generated). Applying transaction logs out of order, or with gaps between backups, isn't allowed. The syntax for restoring transaction logs is RESTORE LOG instead of RESTORE DATABASE; however, the syntax and options are the same.

For this demonstration, the TrainingDB created in the previous recipe will be used (if it doesn't exist, we will create it).

```
USE master;
GO
IF NOT EXISTS (SELECT name FROM sys.databases
WHERE name = 'TrainingDB')
BEGIN
CREATE DATABASE TrainingDB;
END
GO
-- Add a table and some data to it
USE TrainingDB
GO
SELECT *
INTO dbo.SalesOrderDetail
FROM AdventureWorks2014.Sales.SalesOrderDetail;
GO
```

This database will be given a full backup and two consecutive transaction log backups.

```
USE master;
GO

Declare @BackupDate Char(8) = Convert(Varchar,GetDate(),112)
    ,@BackupPath Varchar(50);

Set @BackupPath= 'C:\Apress\TrainingDB_'+ @BackupDate + '.BAK';

BACKUP DATABASE TrainingDB
TO DISK = @BackupPath;
GO
BACKUP LOG TrainingDB
TO DISK = 'C:\Apress\TrainingDB_20150430_8AM.trn';
GO
-- Two hours pass, another transaction log backup is made
BACKUP LOG TrainingDB
TO DISK = 'C:\Apress\TrainingDB_20150430_10AM.trn';
GO
```

The previous RESTORE examples have assumed that there were no existing connections in the database to be restored over. However, in this example, I demonstrate how to kick out any connections to the database prior to performing the RESTORE.

```
USE master;
GO
-- Kicking out all other connections
ALTER DATABASE TrainingDB
SET SINGLE_USER
WITH ROLLBACK IMMEDIATE;
GO
```

Next, a database backup and two transaction log backups are restored from backup.

```
USE master;
GO
Declare @DeviceName Varchar(50);

Select @DeviceName = b.physical_device_name
    From msdb.dbo.backupset a
        INNER JOIN msdb.dbo.backupmediafamily b
            ON a.media_set_id = b.media_set_id
    Where a.database_name = 'TrainingDB'
        And a.type = 'D'
        And Convert(Varchar,a.backup_start_date,112) = Convert(Varchar,GetDate(),112);
RESTORE DATABASE TrainingDB
FROM DISK = @DeviceName
WITH NORECOVERY, REPLACE;

RESTORE LOG TrainingDB
FROM DISK = 'C:\Apress\TrainingDB_20150430_8AM.trn'
WITH NORECOVERY, REPLACE;

RESTORE LOG TrainingDB
FROM DISK = 'C:\Apress\TrainingDB_20150430_10AM.trn'
WITH RECOVERY, REPLACE;
GO
```

This results in the following (your results will vary):

```
Processed 1832 pages for database 'TrainingDB', file 'TestDB' on file 1.
Processed 2 pages for database 'TrainingDB', file 'TestDB_log' on file 1.
RESTORE DATABASE successfully processed 1834 pages in 0.127 seconds (112.796 MB/sec).
Processed 0 pages for database 'TrainingDB', file 'TestDB' on file 1.
Processed 1632 pages for database 'TrainingDB', file 'TestDB_log' on file 1.
RESTORE LOG successfully processed 1632 pages in 0.125 seconds (101.957 MB/sec).
Processed 0 pages for database 'TrainingDB', file 'TestDB' on file 1.
Processed 1 pages for database 'TrainingDB', file 'TestDB_log' on file 1.
RESTORE LOG successfully processed 1 pages in 0.021 seconds (0.069 MB/sec).
```

In this second example, I'll use STOPAT to restore the database and transaction log as of a specific point in time. To demonstrate, first a full backup will be taken of the TrainingDB database.

```
USE master;
GO
BACKUP DATABASE TrainingDB
TO DISK = 'C:\Apress\TrainingDB_StopAt.bak';
GO
```

Next, rows will be deleted out of the table, and the current time (after the change) will be queried.

```
USE TrainingDB;
GO
SELECT GETDATE();
GO
DELETE dbo.SalesOrderDetail
WHERE ProductID = 776;
GO
```

This query returns the following (your results will vary):

```
2015-03-20 09:15:27.047
```

Next, a transaction log backup is performed.

```
BACKUP LOG TrainingDB
TO DISK = 'C:\Apress\TrainingDB_20150430_2022.trn';
GO
```

This results in the following:

```
Processed 10 pages for database 'TrainingDB', file 'TestDB_log' on file 1.
BACKUP LOG successfully processed 10 pages in 0.010 seconds (7.470 MB/sec).
```

The database is restored from backup, leaving it in NORECOVERY so that the transaction log backup can also be restored. The NORECOVERY is used when multiple backups need to be restored. This leaves the database in a state permitting additional backups to be applied. In this example, it is necessary to use the date that was output prior to the delete operation. That date will be supplied to the STOPAT directive letting the engine know that the intent is to recover the database back to that time.

```
USE master;
GO
RESTORE DATABASE TrainingDB
FROM DISK = 'C:\Apress\TrainingDB_StopAt.bak'
WITH FILE = 1, NORECOVERY,
STOPAT = '2015-03-20 09:15:27.047';
GO
```

Next, the transaction log is restored, also designating the time prior to the data deletion.

```
RESTORE LOG TrainingDB
FROM DISK = 'C:\Apress\TrainingDB_20150320_0915.trn'
WITH RECOVERY,
STOPAT = '2015-03-20 09:15:27.047';
GO
```

The following query confirms that you have restored the data just prior to the data deletion:

```
USE TrainingDB;
GO
SELECT COUNT(*)
FROM dbo.SalesOrderDetail
WHERE ProductID = 776;
GO
```

This query returns the following:

```
228
```

How It Works

In the first example for this recipe, the TrainingDB database was restored from a full database backup and left in NORECOVERY mode. Being in NORECOVERY mode allows other transaction log or differential backups to be applied. In this example, two transaction log backups were applied in chronological order, with the second using the RECOVERY option to bring the database online.

The second example in the recipe demonstrated restoring a database as of a specific point in time. Point-in-time recovery is useful for restoring a database prior to a database modification or failure. The syntax was similar to the first example, only the STOPAT was used for both RESTORE DATABASE and RESTORE LOG. Including the STOPAT for each RESTORE statement makes sure that the restore doesn't recover past the designated date.

28-3. Restoring a Database from a Differential Backup
Problem

As a part of your backup strategy, you have implemented differential backups. You now need to restore the database to a point in time after the last full database backup, taking advantage of the differential backups that have been taken.

Solution

You will use the RESTORE DATABASE command. The syntax for differential database restores is identical to full database restores, only full database restores must be performed *prior* to applying differential backups. When restoring the full database backup, the database must be left in NORECOVERY mode. Also, any transaction logs you want to restore must be done *after* the differential backup is applied, as this example demonstrates.

First, however, I'll set up the example by performing a full, differential, and transaction log backup on the TrainingDB database.

```
USE master;
GO
BACKUP DATABASE TrainingDB
TO DISK = 'C:\Apress\TrainingDB_DiffExample.bak';
GO
-- Time passes
BACKUP DATABASE TrainingDB
TO DISK = 'C:\Apress\TrainingDB_DiffExample.diff'
WITH DIFFERENTIAL;
GO

-- More time passes
BACKUP LOG TrainingDB
TO DISK = 'C:\Apress\TrainingDB_DiffExample_tlog.trn';
GO
```

Now, I'll demonstrate performing a RESTORE, by bringing the database back to the completion of the last transaction log backup.

```
USE master;
GO
-- Full database restore
RESTORE DATABASE TrainingDB
FROM DISK = 'C:\Apress\TrainingDB_DiffExample.bak'
WITH NORECOVERY, REPLACE;
GO
-- Differential
RESTORE DATABASE TrainingDB
FROM DISK = 'C:\Apress\TrainingDB_DiffExample.diff'
WITH NORECOVERY;
GO
-- Transaction log
RESTORE LOG TrainingDB
FROM DISK = 'C:\Apress\TrainingDB_DiffExample_tlog.trn'
WITH RECOVERY;
GO
```

This returns the following (your results will vary):

```
Processed 1832 pages for database 'TrainingDB', file 'TestDB' on file 1.
Processed 3 pages for database 'TrainingDB', file 'TestDB_log' on file 1.
RESTORE DATABASE successfully processed 1835 pages in 0.122 seconds (117.451 MB/sec).
Processed 48 pages for database 'TrainingDB', file 'TestDB' on file 1.
Processed 1 pages for database 'TrainingDB', file 'TestDB_log' on file 1.
RESTORE DATABASE successfully processed 49 pages in 0.047 seconds (8.144 MB/sec).
Processed 0 pages for database 'TrainingDB', file 'TestDB' on file 1.
Processed 11 pages for database 'TrainingDB', file 'TestDB_log' on file 1.
RESTORE LOG successfully processed 11 pages in 0.010 seconds (8.203 MB/sec).
```

How It Works

Differential backups capture database changes that have occurred since the last full database backup. Differential restores use the same syntax as full database restores, only they must always follow a full database restore (with NORECOVERY) first. This full database restore must come from the full backup file that is in the same backup chain as the differential backup. This means that the differential backup can only be applied after the full backup; that is, the immediate last full backup prior to the differential backup being applied. In this recipe, the database was initially restored from a full database backup, then followed by a restore from a differential backup, and then lastly a restore from a transaction log backup. The differential RESTORE command was formed similarly to previous RESTORE examples, only it referenced the differential backup file. On the last restore, the RECOVERY option was designated to make the database available for use.

28-4. Restoring a File or Filegroup

Problem

You have a database with multiple filegroups. You need to restore one of the filegroups.

Solution

Restoring a file or filegroup uses virtually the same syntax as a full database restore, except you also use the FILEGROUP or FILE keyword. To perform a restore of a specific read-write file or filegroup, your database must use either a full or bulk-logged recovery model. This is required because transaction log backups must be applied after restoring a file or filegroup backup. In SQL Server, if your database is using a simple recovery model, only read-only files or read-only filegroups can have file/filegroup backups and restores.

To set up this recipe's example, I will create the VLTestDB database, if it doesn't exist, after which a filegroup backup is taken for the VLTestDB database.

```
USE master;
GO
IF NOT EXISTS (SELECT name FROM sys.databases WHERE name = 'VLTestDB')
BEGIN
CREATE DATABASE VLTestDB
ON PRIMARY
    ( NAME = N'VLTestDB',FILENAME =N'c:\Apress\VLTestDB.mdf'
    ,SIZE = 4072KB , FILEGROWTH = 0 ),
FILEGROUP FG2
    ( NAME = N'VLTestDB2', FILENAME =N'c:\Apress\VLTestDB2.ndf'
    , SIZE = 3048KB , FILEGROWTH = 1024KB )
    ,( NAME = N'VLTestDB3', FILENAME =N'c:\Apress\VLTestDB3.ndf'
    , SIZE = 3048KB , FILEGROWTH = 1024KB )
LOG ON
    ( NAME = N'VLTestDBLog', FILENAME =N'c:\Apress\VLTestDB_log.ldf'
    , SIZE = 1024KB , FILEGROWTH = 10%);

ALTER DATABASE VLTestDB
MODIFY FILEGROUP FG2 DEFAULT;

END
```

```
GO

USE master;
GO
BACKUP DATABASE VLTestDB
FILEGROUP = 'FG2'
TO DISK = 'C:\Apress\VLTestDB_FG2.bak'
WITH NAME = N'VLTestDB-Full Filegroup Backup',
SKIP, STATS = 20;
GO
```

Time passes, and then a transaction log backup is taken for the database.

```
BACKUP LOG VLTestDB
TO DISK = 'C:\Apress\VLTestDB_FG_Example.trn'
WITH NORECOVERY,NO_TRUNCATE,FORMAT;
GO
```

Next, the database filegroup FG2 is restored from backup, followed by the restore of a transaction log backup.

```
USE master;
GO
RESTORE DATABASE VLTestDB
FILEGROUP = 'FG2'
FROM DISK = 'C:\Apress\VLTestDB_FG2.bak'
WITH FILE = 1, NORECOVERY, REPLACE;
RESTORE LOG VLTestDB
FROM DISK = 'C:\Apress\VLTestDB_FG_Example.trn'
WITH FILE = 1, RECOVERY;
GO
```

This returns the following (your results may vary):

```
Processed 8 pages for database 'VLTestDB', file 'VLTestDB2' on file 1.
Processed 8 pages for database 'VLTestDB', file 'VLTestDB3' on file 1.
Processed 3 pages for database 'VLTestDB', file 'VLTestDBLog' on file 1.
RESTORE DATABASE ... FILE=<name> successfully processed 19 pages in 0.013 seconds (11.042 MB/
sec).
Processed 0 pages for database 'VLTestDB', file 'VLTestDB' on file 1.
Processed 0 pages for database 'VLTestDB', file 'VLTestDB2' on file 1.
Processed 0 pages for database 'VLTestDB', file 'VLTestDB3' on file 1.
Processed 5 pages for database 'VLTestDB', file 'VLTestDBLog' on file 1.
RESTORE LOG successfully processed 5 pages in 0.012 seconds (2.685 MB/sec).
```

How It Works

Filegroup or file backups are most often used in very large databases, where full database backups may take too long to execute. With filegroup or file backups comes greater administrative complexity, because you'll have to potentially recover from disaster using multiple backup sets (one per filegroup, for example).

In this recipe, the VLTestDB database filegroup named FG2 was restored from a backup device and left in NORECOVERY mode so that a transaction log restore could be applied. The RECOVERY keyword was used in the transaction log restore operation in order to bring the filegroup back online. In SQL Server Enterprise Edition, filegroups other than the primary filegroup can be taken offline for restores while leaving the other active filegroups available for use (this is called an ONLINE restore).

28-5. Performing a Piecemeal (PARTIAL) Restore

Problem

You have a database with multiple filegroups that needs to be recovered. You need to recover the primary filegroup in addition to any filegroups critical to the business based on a predetermined priority (you may recover certain filegroups at your leisure).

Solution

The PARTIAL command can be used with the RESTORE DATABASE command to restore secondary filegroups in a piecemeal fashion. This variation of RESTORE brings the primary filegroup online, letting you then restore other filegroups as needed later. If you're using a database with a full or bulk-logged recovery model, you can use this command with read-write filegroups. If the database is using a simple recovery model, you can use PARTIAL only in conjunction with read-only secondary filegroups.

In this example, the VLTestDB is restored from a full database backup using the PARTIAL keyword and designating that only the PRIMARY filegroup be brought online (with filegroups FG2 and FG3 staying offline and unrestored).

First, to set up this example, the primary and FG2 filegroups in the VLTestDB are backed up.

```
USE master;
GO
BACKUP DATABASE VLTestDB
FILEGROUP = 'PRIMARY'
TO DISK = 'C:\Apress\VLTestDB_Primary_PieceExmp.bak';
GO
BACKUP DATABASE VLTestDB
FILEGROUP = 'FG2'
TO DISK = 'C:\Apress\VLTestDB_FG2_PieceExmp.bak';
GO
```

After that, a transaction log backup is performed.

```
BACKUP LOG VLTestDB
TO DISK = 'C:\Apress\VLTestDB_PieceExmp.trn';
GO
```

Next, a piecemeal RESTORE is performed, recovering just the PRIMARY filegroup.

```
USE master;
GO
RESTORE DATABASE VLTestDB
FILEGROUP = 'PRIMARY'
FROM DISK = 'C:\Apress\VLTestDB_Primary_PieceExmp.bak'
WITH PARTIAL, NORECOVERY, REPLACE;
RESTORE LOG VLTestDB
FROM DISK = 'C:\Apress\VLTestDB_PieceExmp.trn'
WITH RECOVERY;
GO
```

The other filegroup, FG2, now contains unavailable files. You can view the file status by querying sys.database_files from the VLTestDB database.

```
USE VLTestDB;
GO
SELECT name,state_desc
FROM sys.database_files;
GO
```

This query returns the following:

Name	state_desc
VLTestDB	ONLINE
VLTestDBLog	ONLINE
VLTestDB2	RECOVERY_PENDING
VLTestDB3	RECOVERY_PENDING

How It Works

In this recipe, the VLTestDB was restored from a full backup, restoring just the PRIMARY filegroup. The WITH clause included the PARTIAL keyword and NORECOVERY so that transaction log backups can be restored. After the transaction log restore, any objects in the PRIMARY filegroup are available, and objects in the secondary filegroups are unavailable until you restore them at a later time.

For very large databases, using the PARTIAL keyword during a RESTORE operation allows you to prioritize and load filegroups that have a higher priority, making them available sooner. This could give you more breathing room while bringing the rest of the filegroups back online (via more piecemeal restores).

28-6. Restoring a Page

Problem

You have discovered that a few data pages have become corrupted in the database. You need to recover the corrupted pages.

Solution

SQL Server provides the ability to restore specific data pages in a database using a FULL or BULK_LOGGED recovery model via the PAGE argument. In the rare event that a small number of data pages become corrupted in a database, it may be more efficient to restore individual data pages than the entire file, filegroup, or database.

The syntax for restoring specific pages is similar to restoring a filegroup or database, only you use the PAGE keyword coupled with the page ID. Bad pages can be identified in the msdb.dbo.suspect_pages system table, or can be identified in the SQL error log, or can be returned in the output of a DBCC command.

To set up this example, a full database backup is created for the TestDB database.

```
USE master;
GO
BACKUP DATABASE TestDB
TO DISK = 'C:\Apress\TestDB_PageExample.bak';
GO
```

Next, a restore is performed using the PAGE argument.

```
USE master;
GO
RESTORE DATABASE TestDB
PAGE='1:8'
FROM DISK = 'C:\Apress\TestDB_PageExample.bak'
WITH NORECOVERY, REPLACE;
GO
```

This query returns the following:

```
Processed 1 pages for database 'TestDB', file 'TestDB' on file 1.
RESTORE DATABASE ... FILE=<name> successfully processed 1 pages in 0.006 seconds (1.302 MB/
sec).
```

At this point, any differential or transaction log backups taken after the last full backup should also be restored. Since there were none in this example, no further backups are restored.

Next, and this is something that departs from previous examples, a new transaction log backup must be created that captures the restored page.

```
BACKUP LOG TestDB
TO DISK = 'C:\Apress\TestDB_PageExample_tlog.trn';
GO
```

This query returns the following:

```
Processed 4 pages for database 'TestDB', file 'TestDB_log' on file 1.
BACKUP LOG successfully processed 4 pages in 0.013 seconds (2.366 MB/sec).
```

To finish the page restore process, the latest transaction log taken after the RESTORE...PAGE must be executed with RECOVERY.

```
RESTORE LOG TestDB
FROM DISK = 'C:\Apress\TestDB_PageExample_tlog.trn'
WITH RECOVERY;
GO
```

How It Works

In this recipe, a single data page was restored from a full database backup using the PAGE option in the RESTORE DATABASE command. Like restoring from a FILE or FILEGROUP, the first RESTORE leaves the database in a NORECOVERY state, allowing additional transaction log backups to be applied prior to recovery.

28-7. Identifying Databases with Multiple Recovery Paths

Problem

You want to find any backups that have been created that are not used in your RESTORE process.

Solution

Use the sys.database_recovery_status catalog view. Multiple recovery paths are created when you recover a database from backup using point-in-time recovery or when you recover a database without recovering the latest differential or chain of log backups. When there are backups created that you do not use in your RESTORE process, you create a fork in the recovery path.

This recipe demonstrates how to use the sys.database_recovery_status catalog view to get information about a database with more than one recovery path. In the first step, I will create a new database and give it a full database backup, create a table and some rows, and finish up with a transaction log backup.

```
USE master;
GO
IF EXISTS (SELECT name FROM sys.databases WHERE name = 'RoisdeFrance')
BEGIN
DROP DATABASE RoisdeFrance;
END
CREATE DATABASE RoisdeFrance;
GO

ALTER DATABASE RoisdeFrance
SET RECOVERY FULL;
GO
```

```
BACKUP DATABASE RoisdeFrance
TO DISK = 'C:\Apress\RoisdeFrance_A.bak';
GO
USE RoisdeFrance;
GO
CREATE TABLE Rois
(IDRoi int NOT NULL PRIMARY KEY IDENTITY(1,1), NomDuRoi varchar(255));
GO


INSERT INTO Rois (NomDuRoi)
    VALUES ('Charlemagne'), ('Napoleon I'), ('Louis VI le Gros'), ('Lothair');
BACKUP LOG RoisdeFrance
TO DISK = 'C:\Apress\RoisdeFrance_A.trn';
GO
```

Next, I'll query the sys.database_recovery_status catalog view to get information about the database at this point (column aliases are used to shorten the names for presentation in this book).

```
USE msdb;
GO
SELECT last_log_backup_lsn AS LastLSN
    ,recovery_fork_guid AS Rec_Fork
    ,first_recovery_fork_guid AS Frst_Fork
        ,fork_point_lsn AS Fork_LSN
FROM sys.database_recovery_status
WHERE database_id = DB_ID('RoisdeFrance');
GO
```

This query returns the following (your results will vary):

LastLSN	Rec_Fork	Frst_Fork	Fork_LSN
32000000011600001	1D5F5BF4-EF42-4AD9-A6CF-8F07902D0D0D	NULL	NULL

Notice that the first_recovery_fork_guid and fork_point_lsn columns contain NULL values. This is because I have not created a fork yet in my recovery path. The last_log_backup_lsn tells me the LSN of the most recent log backup, and the recovery_fork_guid shows the current recovery path in which the database is active.

■ **Tip**   A log sequence number (LSN) uniquely identifies each record in a database transaction log.

Next, I will perform a few more data modifications and another transaction log backup.

```
USE RoisdeFrance;
GO
INSERT Into Rois (NomDuRoi)
    VALUES ('Thiery I'), ('Thibaut'), ('Dagobert I'), ('Childebert l''Adopté');
GO
BACKUP LOG RoisdeFrance
TO DISK = 'C:\Apress\RoisdeFrance_B.trn';
GO
```

I'll now go ahead and RESTORE the database to a prior state (but not to the latest state).

```
USE master;
GO
RESTORE DATABASE RoisdeFrance
FROM DISK = 'C:\Apress\RoisdeFrance_A.bak'
WITH NORECOVERY, REPLACE;
RESTORE DATABASE RoisdeFrance
FROM DISK = 'C:\Apress\RoisdeFrance_A.trn'
WITH RECOVERY, REPLACE;
GO
```

Now if I reissue the previous query against sys.database_recovery_status, I will see that both the fork_point_lsn and first_recovery_fork_guid columns are no longer NULL.

```
/* check for forks */
USE msdb;
GO
SELECT last_log_backup_lsn AS LastLSN
    ,recovery_fork_guid AS Rec_Fork
    ,first_recovery_fork_guid AS Frst_Fork
        ,fork_point_lsn AS Fork_LSN
FROM sys.database_recovery_status
WHERE database_id = DB_ID('RoisdeFrance');
GO
```

This query returns the following (your results will vary):

LastLSN	Rec_Fork	Frst_Fork	Fork_LSN
32000000011600001	1D5F5BF4-EF42-4AD9-A6CF-8F07902D0D0D	462E6F9B-61AE-4F10-B1A4-58474C447A7E	32000000011600001

How It Works

The sys.database_recovery_status catalog view allows you to see whether multiple recovery forks have been created for a database.

In this recipe, I made one full database backup and two transaction log backups. If I restored the database using all three of the backups, I would have remained in the same recovery path. However, instead, I restored only the first full backup and first transaction log backup, putting the database into recovery before restoring the second transaction log. By recovering prematurely, I brought the database online into a second recovery path.

28-8. Restore a Single Row or Table

Problem

Some users have reported that some data within a table has been changed or deleted and therefore is inaccurate. You would like to restore the previous values without replacing the entire database.

Solution #1: Restore Rows from a Backup

Backup granularity within SQL Server starts with the database and then the filegroup and finally the file. Unless a table resides on its own filegroup, the backup statement does not natively support this functionality, but you can use several workarounds to meet this need.

To demonstrate how a full database backup can be used to restore a single row, I've created a database with a single table called Person using a SELECT...INTO statement.

```
USE master;
GO

IF EXISTS (SELECT * FROM sys.databases WHERE name = 'Granular')
BEGIN
DROP DATABASE Granular;
END
CREATE DATABASE Granular;
GO

USE Granular;
GO

CREATE SCHEMA Person;
GO

USE Granular;
GO

SELECT BusinessEntityID,
        FirstName,
        MiddleName,
        LastName
INTO Person.Person
FROM AdventureWorks2014.Person.Person;
GO
```

```
SELECT TOP 6 *
FROM Person.Person
ORDER BY BusinessEntityID;
GO
```

Executing the previous query will create the Granular database and populate the Person table with the result of the SELECT statement from the Person.Person table in the AdventureWorks2014 database.

BusinessEntityID	FirstName	MiddleName	LastName
1	Ken	J	Sánchez
2	Terri	Lee	Duffy
3	Roberto	NULL	Tamburello
4	Rob	NULL	Walters
5	Gail	A	Erickson
6	Jossef	H	Goldberg

After the database is created and the table populated, a backup is created, then a single row is deleted via the following code.

```
USE master;
GO
BACKUP DATABASE Granular
TO DISK = 'C:\Apress\Granular.bak';
GO

USE Granular;
GO
DELETE p
FROM Person.Person p
WHERE p.BusinessEntityID = 1;
GO

SELECT TOP 6 *
FROM Person.Person
ORDER BY BusinessEntityID;
GO
```

Executing the previous query creates a full backup and deletes the person with a business entity ID of 1, as illustrated in this next set of results:

BusinessEntityID	FirstName	MiddleName	LastName
2	Terri	Lee	Duffy
3	Roberto	NULL	Tamburello
4	Rob	NULL	Walters
5	Gail	A	Erickson
6	Jossef	H	Goldberg
7	Dylan	A	Miller

To be able to restore the single deleted row, the backup must be restored with a different name, and the row can then be restored using an INSERT statement.

```
USE master;
GO


RESTORE DATABASE Granular_COPY
FROM DISK = 'C:\Apress\Granular.bak'
WITH MOVE N'Granular' TO 'C:\Apress\Granular_COPY.mdf',
MOVE N'Granular_log' TO N'C:\Apress\Granular_log_COPY.ldf';
GO


USE Granular;
GO


INSERT INTO Person.Person
SELECT BusinessEntityID,
       FirstName,
       MiddleName,
       LastName
FROM AdventureWorks2014.Person.Person
WHERE BusinessEntityID = 1;
GO


SELECT TOP 6 *
FROM Person.Person
ORDER BY BusinessEntityID;
GO
```

The results of the previous query show that the row was restored.

BusinessEntityID	FirstName	MiddleName	LastName
1	Ken	J	Sánchez
2	Terri	Lee	Duffy
3	Roberto	NULL	Tamburello
4	Rob	NULL	Walters
5	Gail	A	Erickson
6	Jossef	H	Goldberg

How It Works

The process behind this method is fairly self-evident. The database backup being restored with a different name provides the ability to use a SELECT statement from the restored table. Several issues may complicate this method, such as a column that is an IDENTITY, replication, or triggers on the affected table.

Another concern is the size of the database. If the database size is 1TB, space needs to be available to restore the database, and the data and log files should be placed on separate disks from the production database to reduce disk I/O during the restore.

Solution #2: Restore Rows from a Database Snapshot

Restoring an entire database to recover lost rows or tables can be overly burdensome and definitely can be considered overkill. Another method is to utilize a database snapshot as a means of backing up "state" data. A database snapshot is created on a user database from within an instance of SQL and works on a "write" on change basis. After creating a database snapshot, disk space is reserved for the snapshot that is equal to the reserved space of the data files of the user database. The disk space reserved for the snapshot remains completely empty until a data page from the user database is modified or deleted. Once this change occurs the original data page is written to the database snapshot preserving the data as it appeared at the point in time of the snapshot being taken.

The following code will create a database called Original and populate it with a SELECT...INTO statement from the AdventureWorks2014 database and then create a database snapshot from the Original database called Original_SS.

```
USE master;
GO

IF EXISTS (SELECT * FROM sys.databases WHERE name =
'Original')
BEGIN
DROP DATABASE Original;
END
CREATE DATABASE Original;
GO

USE Original;
GO

CREATE SCHEMA Person;
GO

SELECT BusinessEntityID,
       FirstName,
       MiddleName,
       LastName
INTO Person.Person
FROM AdventureWorks2014.Person.Person;
GO

CREATE DATABASE Original_SS ON
( NAME = Original, FILENAME =
'C:\Apress\Original_SS.ss' )
AS SNAPSHOT OF Original;
GO
```

If you recall from Chapter 27 (Backups), the size of the data file for the snapshot will be exactly the same as that of the source database – which is Original in this case.

The following query directly queries the Original_SS database, but because no changes have been made, the query is actually being returned from the Original database:

```
USE Original_SS;
GO

SELECT *
FROM Person.Person
WHERE LastName = 'Abercrombie';
GO
```

The results show the original values of people with the last name of Abercrombie.

BusinessEntityID	FirstName	MiddleName	LastName
295	Kim	NULL	Abercrombie
2170	Kim	NULL	Abercrombie
38	Kim	B	Abercrombie

Updating the last name from Abercrombie to Abercromby will cause the original data page to be written to the database snapshot, while the Original database writes the updated value. The following query updates all people with the last name Abercrombie and then queries both the Original and Original_SS databases to show the different values:

```
USE Original;
GO

UPDATE Person.Person
SET LastName = 'Abercromny'
WHERE LastName = 'Abercrombie';
GO

SELECT *
FROM Person.Person
WHERE LastName = 'Abercrombie';
GO

USE Original_SS
GO

SELECT *
FROM Person.Person
WHERE LastName = 'Abercrombie';
GO
```

```
(0 row(s) affected)

BusinessEntityID    FirstName    MiddleName    LastName
----------------    ---------    ----------    --------------
295                 Kim          NULL          Abercrombie
2170                Kim          NULL          Abercrombie
38                  Kim          B             Abercrombie
```

The results show that once the Original database was updated, the last name of Abercrombie was updated, and no results were returned. Querying the snapshot database, Original_SS, shows all affected records have been written to the snapshot.

The snapshot can be used to revert the records to their original state by using a non-equi join on the desired columns.

```
USE Original;
GO

UPDATE Person.Person
SET LastName = ss.LastName
FROM Person.Person p
INNER JOIN Original_SS.Person.Person ss
ON p.LastName <> ss.LastName
AND p.BusinessEntityID = ss.BusinessEntityID;
GO

SELECT *
FROM Person.Person
WHERE LastName = 'Abercrombie';
GO
```

```
(3 row(s) affected)

BusinessEntityID    FirstName    MiddleName    LastName
----------------    ---------    ----------    --------------
295                 Kim          NULL          Abercrombie
2170                Kim          NULL          Abercrombie
38                  Kim          B             Abercrombie
```

How It Works

The results show that for all records in the Original database's People table where the BusinessEntityID matches the Original_SS database's Peoples table, the BusinessEntityID and LastName column values do not match. The net result is that the changes made to the last name are reverted to the values that are stored in the database snapshot, restoring them to the values at the time of the snapshot.

It is important to know that a database snapshot can be used to restore a database, which is referred to as *reverting* the database. Reverting a database is also typically much faster than doing a full restore because the only thing that needs to be done is to revert the data pages from the snapshot to the original data files. The following code shows how to revert the Original database from the Original_SS snapshot.

```
USE master;

RESTORE DATABASE Original
FROM DATABASE_SNAPSHOT = 'Original_SS';
GO
```

28-9. Recover from a Backup in Azure Blob Storage

Problem

You have stored backups in your blob storage account and now need to recover your database from one of these backups.

Solution

Just like performing a backup to Azure blob storage, restoring from Azure blob storage will require the use of a credential. This is done through the use of the CREDENTIAL option as a part of the restore command and is very similar both to the backup implementation of the CREDENTIAL option as well as being very similar to a traditional RESTORE statement.

To perform a restore from Azure blob storage, I will utilize the credential used in the Backup chapter (Chapter 27).

```
USE master;
GO
RESTORE DATABASE AdventureWorks2014
FROM URL = N'https://Recipes2014.blob.core.windows.net/backuptest/AW2014_blob.bak'
WITH
   CREDENTIAL = 'SQL2014'
   ,BUFFERCOUNT = 75
   ,STATS = 10
   ,REPLACE
GO
```

How It Works

The ability to restore a database from Azure blob storage is possible due to the FROM URL and WITH CREDENTIAL options with the RESTORE command. In this example, I used the backup AW2014_blob.bak that had been stored in Azure blob storage, and overlaid it on the AdventureWorks2014 database.

To perform this restore operation I utilized the SQL2014 credential that was created in Chapter 27 as a part of the backup performed to Azure blob storage.

```
WITH
   CREDENTIAL = 'SQL2014'
```

In addition to the credential, I specified the source of the backup file to be from the URL specific to the storage account created in Azure blob storage.

```
FROM URL = N'https://Recipes2014.blob.core.windows.net/backuptest/AW2014_blob.bak'
```

Being able to backup direct to Azure or restore direct from Azure offers great flexibility. With that flexibility there is some inflexibility that should be considered such as the inability to stripe the backup.

28-10. Recover a Certificate

Problem

You need to migrate an instance of SQL Server to a new server. One of the tasks for the migration is to restore the certificates used for TDE and for backup to the new server in order to maintain operations with as little change as feasible with a server migration.

Solution

Certificates do not follow the traditional restore process that would be implemented for a database restore. However, a certificate can be restored, or in this case, migrated to a new server. The method to restore a certificate is through the use of the CREATE CERTIFICATE statement (just as if creating a new certificate).

Using the certificate created in Chapter 27 on backups, I can issue a CREATE CERTIFICATE statement to use the backup file created previously. With a backup of the certificate on disk, I will use the following code to restore that certificate. Before restoring that certificate, I will first show that the certificate was present by querying the sys.certificates catalog view. Then I will drop and recreate the certificate. I will conclude with querying sys.certificates again to confirm that the certificate was indeed created.

```
USE master;
GO
SELECT c.name,c.start_date,c.pvt_key_encryption_type_desc,c.pvt_key_last_backup_date
       FROM sys.certificates c
       WHERE name = 'AW2014BackupCert';
GO

DROP CERTIFICATE AW2014BackupCert;
GO

CREATE CERTIFICATE AW2014BackupCert
FROM FILE ='c:\Apress\AW2014BackupCert.cer'
WITH PRIVATE KEY(FILE='C:\Apress\AW2014BackupCertKey.bak'
    ,DECRYPTION BY PASSWORD='SQL2014Rocks');
GO

SELECT c.name,c.start_date,c.pvt_key_encryption_type_desc,c.pvt_key_last_backup_date
       FROM sys.certificates c
       WHERE name = 'AW2014BackupCert';
GO
```

Running these statements together, I receive the following results. Prior to the Certificate drop...

name	start_date	pvt_key_last_backup_date
AW2014BackupCert	2015-03-19 04:10:42.000	2015-03-19 05:33:30.653

After dropping and recreating the certificate

name	start_date	pvt_key_last_backup_date
AW2014BackupCert	2015-03-19 04:10:42.000	NULL

How It Works

Certificates are recovered by first ensuring a backup to flat file has been performed for the certificate. SQL Server will throw warning messages if the certificate is not backed up to a flat file.. To restore a certificate, the CREATE CERTIFICATE syntax must be used.

CHAPTER 29

■ ■ ■

Principals and Users

by Jason Brimhall

Microsoft uses a set of terminology to describe SQL Server security functionality, which separates the security architecture into the following:

- *Principals*: These are objects (for example, a user login, a role, or an application) that may be granted permission to access particular database objects.

- *Securables*: These are objects (a table or view, for example) to which access can be controlled.

- *Permissions*: These are individual rights, granted (or denied) to a principal, to access a securable object.

Principals are the topic of this chapter, and securables and permissions are discussed in the next chapter.

Principals fall into three different scopes:

- *Windows principals* are principals based on Windows domain user accounts, domain groups, local user accounts, and local groups. Once added to SQL Server and given permissions to access objects, these types of principals gain access to SQL Server based on Windows Authentication.

- *SQL Server principals* are SQL Server-level logins and fixed server roles. SQL logins are created within SQL Server and have a login name and password independent of any Windows entity. Server roles are groupings of SQL Server instance-level permissions that other principals can become members of, inheriting that server role's permissions.

- *Database principals* are database users, database roles (fixed and user-defined), and application roles—all of which are covered in this chapter.

I'll start this chapter with a discussion of Windows principals.

Windows Principals

Windows principals allow access to a SQL Server instance using Windows Authentication. SQL Server allows you to create Windows logins based on Windows user accounts or groups, which can belong either to the local machine or to a domain. A Windows login can be associated with a domain user, local user, or Windows group. When adding a Windows login to SQL Server, the name of the user or group is bound to the Windows account. Windows logins added to SQL Server don't require separate password logins; in that case, Windows handles the login authentication process.

When users log on to SQL Server using Windows Authentication, their current user account must be identified as a login to the SQL Server instance, or they must belong to a Windows user group that exists as a login.

Windows logins apply only at the server operating system level; you can't grant Windows principals access to specific database objects. To grant permissions based on Windows logins, you need to create a database user and associate it with the login. You'll see how to do this when I discuss database principals.

When installing SQL Server, you are asked to decide between Windows-only and mixed authentication modes. Whichever authentication method you choose, you can always change your mind later. Microsoft Windows Authentication allows for tighter security than SQL Server logins. This is so because security is integrated with the Windows operating system, the local machine, and domain, and because no passwords are ever transmitted over the network.

29-1. Creating a Windows Login

Problem

Your SQL Server instance is configured for mixed mode authentication. Now you need to add a Windows principal as a login within that instance.

Solution

Use the CREATE LOGIN command to add a Windows group or login to the SQL Server instance. When using mixed authentication mode, you can create your own logins and passwords within SQL Server.

The abridged syntax for creating a login from a Windows group or user login is as follows:

```
CREATE LOGIN login_name
FROM  WINDOWS
[ WITH DEFAULT_DATABASE = database
| DEFAULT_LANGUAGE = language ]
| CERTIFICATE certname ASYMMETRIC KEY asym_key_name
```

Table 29-1 describes the arguments of this command.

Table 29-1. CREATE LOGIN Arguments

Argument	Description
login_name	This option specifies the name of the Windows user or group.
DEFAULT_DATABASE = database	This option specifies the default database context of the Windows login, with the master system database being the default.
DEFAULT_LANGUAGE = language	This option specifies the default language of the Windows login, with the server default language being the login default if this option isn't specified.
CERTIFICATE certname	This option allows you to bind a certificate to a Windows login.
ASYMMETRIC KEY asym_key_name	This option binds a key to a Windows login. See Chapter 30 for more information on keys.

In this recipe, I assume you already have certain Windows accounts and groups on the local machine or in your domain. This example creates a Windows *login* on the SQL Server instance, which is internally mapped to a Windows user.

```
USE master;
GO
CREATE LOGIN [PETITMOT\JeanLouis]
FROM WINDOWS
WITH DEFAULT_DATABASE = AdventureWorks2014,
DEFAULT_LANGUAGE = English;
GO
```

In the second example, a new Windows login is created based on a Windows group. This is identical to the previous example, except that you are mapping to a Windows group instead of a Windows user.

```
USE master;
GO
CREATE LOGIN [PETITMOT\Contenu]
FROM WINDOWS
WITH DEFAULT_DATABASE= AdventureWorks2014;
GO
```

How It Works

This recipe demonstrated adding access for a Windows user and Windows group to the SQL Server instance. In the first example, CREATE LOGIN designated the Windows user in square brackets.

```
CREATE LOGIN [PETITMOT\JeanLouis]
```

On the next line, the WINDOWS keyword was used to designate that this is a new login associated with a Windows account.

```
FROM WINDOWS
```

Next, the default database and languages were designated in the WITH clause.

```
WITH DEFAULT_DATABASE = AdventureWorks2014, DEFAULT_LANGUAGE = English
```

In the second example, I demonstrated how to add a Windows group to SQL Server, which again requires square brackets in the CREATE LOGIN command.

```
CREATE LOGIN [PETITMOT\Contenu]
```

The FROM WINDOWS clause designated that this was a Windows group, followed by the default database (if the default database does not exist, the user will be unable to connect).

```
FROM WINDOWS
WITH DEFAULT_DATABASE= AdventureWorks2014
```

When a Windows group is associated with a SQL Server login, it enables any member of the Windows group to inherit the access and permissions of the Windows login. Therefore, any members of this group will also have access to the SQL Server instance without explicitly having to add each of their Windows accounts to the SQL Server instance separately.

29-2. Viewing Windows Logins

Problem

You need to report on all Windows principals that have been added as logins in a SQL Server instance.

Solution

You can view Windows logins and groups by querying the sys.server_principals system catalog view. This example shows the name of each Windows login and group with access to SQL Server, along with the security identifier (sid). Each principal in the system catalog view has a sid, which helps uniquely identify it on the SQL Server instance.

```
USE master;
GO
SELECT name, sid
FROM sys.server_principals
WHERE type_desc IN ('WINDOWS_LOGIN', 'WINDOWS_GROUP')
ORDER BY type_desc;
GO
```

This returns the following results (your own results will vary):

name	sid
PETITMOT\ SQLServerMSSQLUser$ROIS$JEANLOUIS	0x0106000000000000550000000732B9753646EF90356745
PETITMOT\ SQLServerMSFTEUser$ROIS$JEANLOUIS	0x0106000000000000550000000732B9753646EF90356745
PETITMOT\ SQLServerSQLAgentUser$ROIS$JEANLOUIS	0x0106000000000000550000000732B9753646EF90356745
PETITMOT\Contenu	0x0106000000000000550000000732B9753646EF91356745
NT AUTHORITY\SYSTEM	0x010100000000000512000000
PETITMOT\Administrator	0x0106000000000000550000000732B9753646EF90356845
PETITMOT\George	0x0106000000000000550000000732C9753646EF90356745

How It Works

In this recipe, I demonstrated how to query Windows logins in the SQL Server instance using the sys.server_principals system catalog view. This view actually allows you to see other principal types too, which will be reviewed later in the chapter.

29-3. Altering a Windows Login

Problem

You have discovered that a Windows login in your SQL Server instance is configured for the wrong default database. You need to change the default database for this login.

Solution

Once a Windows login is added to SQL Server, it can be modified using the ALTER LOGIN command (this command has several more options that are applicable to SQL logins, as you'll see later in the chapter). Using this command, you can perform tasks such as the following:

- Changing the default database of the login

- Changing the default language of the login

- Enabling or disabling a login from being used

The abridged syntax is as follows (using arguments pertinent to CREATE LOGIN):

```
ALTER LOGIN login_name { ENABLE | DISABLE
WITH
DEFAULT_DATABASE = database DEFAULT_LANGUAGE = language    }
```

In the first example, a Windows login (associated with a Windows user) is disabled from use in SQL Server. This prevents the login from accessing SQL Server and, if connected, ceases any further activity on the SQL Server instance.

```
USE master;
GO
ALTER LOGIN [PETITMOT\JeanLouis] DISABLE;
GO
```

This next example demonstrates enabling this account again.

```
USE master;
GO
ALTER LOGIN [PETITMOT\JeanLouis] ENABLE;
GO
```

In this example, the default database is changed for a Windows group.

```
USE master;
GO
ALTER LOGIN [PETITMOT\Contenu]
    WITH DEFAULT_DATABASE = master;
GO
```

765

How It Works

In the first example, a Windows login was disabled using ALTER LOGIN and the login name.

```
ALTER LOGIN [PETITMOT\JeanLouis]
```

Following this was the DISABLE keyword, which removed this account's access to the SQL Server instance (it removed the account's access but still kept the login in the SQL Server instance for the later option of reenabling access).

```
DISABLE
```

The second example demonstrated reenabling access to the login by using the ENABLE keyword.

The third example changed the default database for a Windows group. The syntax for referencing Windows logins and groups is the same—both principal types are designated within square brackets.

```
ALTER LOGIN [PETITMOT\Contenu]
```

The second line then designated the new default database context for the Windows group.

```
WITH DEFAULT_DATABASE = master
```

29-4. Dropping a Windows Login

Problem

An employee has changed departments and no longer needs access to a SQL Server instance. You need to remove the employee's login.

Solution

In this recipe, I'll demonstrate dropping a login from the SQL Server instance entirely by using the DROP LOGIN command. This removes the login's permission to access the SQL Server instance. If the login is currently connected to the SQL Server instance when the login is dropped, any actions attempted by the connected login will no longer be allowed. The syntax is as follows:

```
DROP LOGIN login_name
```

The only parameter is the login name, which can be a Windows or SQL login (demonstrated later in the chapter), as this recipe demonstrates.

```
USE master;
GO
-- Windows Group login
DROP LOGIN [PETITMOT\Contenu];
-- Windows user login
DROP LOGIN [PETITMOT\JeanLouis];
GO
```

How It Works

This recipe demonstrated the simple DROP LOGIN command, which removes a login from SQL Server. If a login owns any securables (see the next chapter for more information on securables), the DROP attempt will fail. For example, if the PETITMOT\JeanLouis login had been a database owner, an error like the following would have been raised:

```
Msg 15174, Level 16, State 1, Line 3
Login 'PETITMOT\JeanLouis' owns one or more database(s).
Change the owner of the database(s) before dropping the login.
```

29-5. Denying SQL Server Access to a Windows User or Group

Problem

You need to temporarily prevent a group of users from connecting to a SQL Server instance.

Solution

Use the DENY CONNECT SQL command to deny a Windows user, or group, access to SQL Server. Here's an example:

```
USE master;
GO
DENY CONNECT SQL TO [PETITMOT\Geraud];
GO
```

To allow access again, you can use GRANT.

```
USE master;
GO
GRANT CONNECT SQL TO [PETITMOT\Geraud];
GO
```

How It Works

The GRANT command grants permissions to securables, and DENY denies permissions to them. You use DENY CONNECT to restrict the Windows user or group login from accessing a SQL Server instance the next time a login attempt is made. In both GRANT CONNECT and DENY CONNECT, it is assumed that the Windows user or group already has a login in SQL Server. Keep in mind that there are limitations to which logins you can deny permissions to. For example, if you try to DENY CONNECT to your own login with the following code:

```
DENY CONNECT SQL TO [PETITMOT\Administrator]
```

You will see the following warning:

```
Cannot grant, deny, or revoke permissions to sa, dbo, information_schema, sys, or yourself.
```

SQL Server Principals

Windows Authentication relies on the underlying operating system to perform authentication (determining who a particular user is), which means that SQL Server performs the necessary authorization (determining what actions an authenticated user is entitled to perform). When working with SQL Server principals and SQL Server authentication, SQL Server itself performs both authentication and authorization.

As noted earlier, when using mixed authentication mode, you can create your own login and passwords within SQL Server. These SQL logins exist only in SQL Server and do not have an outside Windows user/group mapping. With SQL logins, the passwords are stored within SQL Server. These user credentials are stored in SQL Server and are used to authenticate the user in question and to determine appropriate access rights.

Because the security method involves explicit passwords, it is inherently less secure than using Windows Authentication alone. However, SQL Server logins are still commonly used with third-party and non-Windows operating system applications. SQL Server *has* improved the password protection capabilities by enabling Windows-like password functionality, such as forced password changes, expiration dates, and other password policies (for example, password complexity), with Windows Server 2003 and newer.

As with Windows logins, SQL Server logins apply only at the server level; you can't grant permissions for them to specific database objects. Unless you are granted membership to a fixed server role such as sysadmin, you must create database users associated with the login before you can begin working with database objects.

As in previous versions of SQL Server, SQL Server supports principals based on both individual logins and server roles, which multiple individual users can be assigned to.

29-6. Creating a SQL Server Login

Problem

You need to create a SQL login for a user that does not have a Windows login.

Solution

To create a new SQL Server login, use the CREATE LOGIN command.

```
CREATE LOGIN login_name
[WITH PASSWORD = ' password ' [ HASHED ] [ MUST_CHANGE ],
SID = sid],
DEFAULT_DATABASE = database,
DEFAULT_LANGUAGE = language,
CHECK_EXPIRATION = { ON | OFF},
CHECK_POLICY = { ON | OFF},
CREDENTIAL = credential_name ]
```

Table 29-2 describes the arguments of this command.

Table 29-2. *CREATE LOGIN Arguments*

Argument	Description
login_name	This is the login name.
' password ' [HASHED] [MUST_CHANGE]	This is the login's password. Specifying the HASHED option means that the provided password is already hashed (made into an unreadable and secured format). If MUST_CHANGE is specified, the user is prompted to change the password the first time the user logs in.
SID = sid	This explicitly specifies the sid that will be used in the system tables of the SQL Server instance. This can be based on a login from a different SQL Server instance (if you're migrating logins). If this isn't specified, SQL Server generates its own sid in the system tables.
DEFAULT_DATABASE = database	This option specifies the default database context of the SQL login, with the master system database being the default.
DEFAULT_LANGUAGE = language	This option specifies the default language of the login, with the server default language being the login default if this option isn't specified.
CHECK_EXPIRATION = { ON | OFF},	When set to ON (the default), the SQL login will be subject to a password expiration policy. A password expiration policy affects how long a password will remain valid before it must be changed. This functionality requires Windows Server 2003 or newer.
CHECK_POLICY = { ON | OFF},	When set to ON (the default), Windows password policies are applied to the SQL login (for example, policies regarding the password's length, complexity, and inclusion of nonalphanumeric characters). This functionality requires Windows Server 2003 or newer.
CREDENTIAL = credential_name	This option allows a server credential to be mapped to the SQL login. See Chapter 30 for more information on credentials.

This example first demonstrates how to create a SQL Server login with a password and a default database designated.

```
USE master;
GO
CREATE LOGIN Gaston
WITH PASSWORD = 'Tr0isMots',
DEFAULT_DATABASE = AdventureWorks2014;
GO
```

Assuming you are using Windows Server 2003 or newer, as well as mixed authentication, the recipe goes on to create a SQL login with a password that must be changed the first time the user logs in. This login also is created with the CHECK_POLICY option ON, requiring it to comply with Windows password policies.

```
USE master;
GO
CREATE LOGIN Aurora
WITH PASSWORD = 'ChangeMe' MUST_CHANGE
, CHECK_EXPIRATION = ON
, CHECK_POLICY = ON;
GO
```

How It Works

The first example in this recipe demonstrated creating a SQL login named Gaston. The login name was designated after CREATE LOGIN.

```
CREATE LOGIN Gaston
```

The second line designated the login's password.

```
WITH PASSWORD = ' TroisMots,
```

The last line of code designated the default database that the login's context would first enter after logging into SQL Server.

```
DEFAULT_DATABASE = AdventureWorks2014
```

The second SQL login example demonstrated how to force a password to be changed on the first login by designating the MUST CHANGE token after the password.

```
CREATE LOGIN Aurora
WITH PASSWORD = 'ChangeMe' MUST_CHANGE ,
```

This password policy integration requires Windows Server 2003 or later, as did the password expiration and password policy options also designated for this login.

```
CHECK_EXPIRATION = ON, CHECK_POLICY = ON
```

29-7. Viewing SQL Server Logins

Problem

During an audit, a request has been submitted to you to provide a list of all SQL logins.

Solution

Again, you can view SQL Server logins (and other principals) by querying the sys.server_principals system catalog view.

```
USE master;
GO
SELECT name, sid
FROM sys.server_principals
WHERE type_desc IN ('SQL_LOGIN')
ORDER BY name;
GO
```

This returns the following results:

name	sid
##MS_PolicyEventProcessingLogin##	0x812190CA1F613649AAA462AE02A3BBB4
##MS_PolicyTsqlExecutionLogin##	0x3632F962FE66F7449F4467B8B36F6F94
Bayard	0xAA7CFE96239C164CA7BA3D10E68882D3
Piper	0x1063EBB4A91E7D4795A19FBEA6CD0138
Aurora	0x61E42C794BBFA34E9913F9006666D5FE
Gaston	0xF54D817AA1DE8A4781745DC7758A532E
sa	0x01

How It Works

This recipe's query returned the name and sid of each SQL login on the SQL Server instance by querying the sys.server_principals catalog view.

29-8. Altering a SQL Server Login

Problem

You need to change the password for a SQL Server login.

Solution

Use the ALTER LOGIN command. Once a login is added to SQL Server, it can be modified using the ALTER LOGIN command. Using this command, you can perform several tasks:

- Change the login's password

- Change the default database or language

- Change the name of the existing login without disrupting the login's currently assigned permissions

- Change the password policy settings (enabling or disabling them)

- Map or remove mapping from a SQL login credential

- Enable or disable a login from being used

- Unlock a locked login

The syntax arguments are similar to CREATE LOGIN (I'll demonstrate usage in this recipe).

```
ALTER LOGIN login_name { ENABLE | DISABLE
WITH PASSWORD = ' password '
[ OLD_PASSWORD = ' oldpassword '
| [ MUST_CHANGE | UNLOCK ] ]
DEFAULT_DATABASE = database
DEFAULT_LANGUAGE = language
NAME = login_name
CHECK_POLICY = { ON | OFF }
CHECK_EXPIRATION = { ON | OFF }
CREDENTIAL = credentialjiame I   NO CREDENTIAL }
```

In the first example of this recipe, a SQL login's password is changed from Tr0isM0ts to Chuch0t3r.

```
USE master;
GO
ALTER LOGIN Gaston
WITH PASSWORD = 'Chuch0t3r'
OLD_PASSWORD = 'Tr0isM0ts';
GO
```

The OLD_PASSWORD option designates the current password that is being changed; however, sysadmin fixed server role members don't have to know the old password in order to change it.

This second example demonstrates changing the default database of the Gaston SQL login.

```
USE master;
GO
ALTER LOGIN Gaston
WITH DEFAULT_DATABASE = [AdventureWorks2014];
GO
```

This third example in this recipe demonstrates changing both the name and password of a SQL login.

```
USE master;
GO
ALTER LOGIN Gaston
WITH NAME = HyBrasil, PASSWORD = 'UC@ntCMe';
GO
```

Changing the login name instead of just dropping and creating a new one offers one major benefit: the permissions associated with the original login are not disrupted when the login is renamed. In this case, the Gaston login is renamed to HyBrasil, but the permissions remain the same.

How It Works

In the first example of this recipe, ALTER LOGIN was used to change a password designating the old password and the new password. If you have sysadmin fixed server role permissions, you only need to designate the new password. The second example demonstrated how to change the default database of a SQL login. The last example demonstrated how to change a login's name from Gaston to HyBrasil, as well as change the login's password.

29-9. Managing a Login's Password

Problem

You have multiple users that are unable to log in to SQL Server. You would like to check the password settings for these users.

Solution

Use the LOGINPROPERTY function to retrieve login policy settings.

SQL Server provides the LOGINPROPERTY function to return information about login and password policy settings and state. Using this function, you can determine the following qualities of a SQL login:

- Whether the login is locked or expired

- Whether the login has a password that must be changed

- Bad password counts and the last time an incorrect password was given

- Login-lockout time

- The last time a password was set and the length of time the login has been tracked using password policies

- The password hash for use in migration (to another SQL instance, for example)

This function takes two parameters: the name of the SQL login and the property to be checked. In this example, I want to return properties for logins to determine whether the login may be locked out or expired.

```
USE master;
GO
SELECT p.name, ca.IsLocked, ca.IsExpired, ca.IsMustChange, ca.BadPasswordCount,
ca.BadPasswordTime, ca.HistoryLength, ca.LockoutTime,ca.PasswordLastSetTime,ca.
DaysUntilExpiration
    From sys.server_principals p
        CROSS APPLY (SELECT  IsLocked = LOGINPROPERTY(p.name,  'IsLocked') ,
        IsExpired = LOGINPROPERTY(p.name,  'IsExpired') ,
        IsMustChange = LOGINPROPERTY(p.name,  'IsMustChange') ,
        BadPasswordCount = LOGINPROPERTY(p.name,  'BadPasswordCount') ,
        BadPasswordTime = LOGINPROPERTY(p.name,  'BadPasswordTime') ,
        HistoryLength = LOGINPROPERTY(p.name,  'HistoryLength') ,
        LockoutTime = LOGINPROPERTY(p.name,  'LockoutTime') ,
```

```
        PasswordLastSetTime = LOGINPROPERTY(p.name,  'PasswordLastSetTime') ,
        DaysUntilExpiration = LOGINPROPERTY(p.name,  'DaysUntilExpiration')
   ) ca
   WHERE p.type_desc = 'SQL_LOGIN'
        AND p.is_disabled = 0;
GO
```

In SQL 2012, the PasswordHashAlgorithm property was added. This property returns the algorithm used to hash the password. In this next example, I want to demonstrate this property for the LOGINPROPERTY function.

```
USE master;
GO
SELECT p.name,ca.DefaultDatabase,ca.DefaultLanguage,ca.PasswordHash
    ,PasswordHashAlgorithm = Case ca.PasswordHashAlgorithm
        WHEN 1
        THEN 'SQL7.0'
        WHEN 2
        THEN 'SHA-1'
        WHEN 3
        THEN 'SHA-2'
        ELSE 'login is not a valid SQL Server login'
        END
    FROM sys.server_principals p
    CROSS APPLY (SELECT  PasswordHash = LOGINPROPERTY(p.name,  'PasswordHash') ,
        DefaultDatabase = LOGINPROPERTY(p.name,  'DefaultDatabase') ,
        DefaultLanguage = LOGINPROPERTY(p.name,  'DefaultLanguage') ,
        PasswordHashAlgorithm = LOGINPROPERTY(p.name,  'PasswordHashAlgorithm')
    ) ca
    WHERE p.type_desc = 'SQL_LOGIN'
        AND p.is_disabled = 0;
GO
```

This query returns the following:

Name	DefaultDatabase	DefaultLanguage	PasswordHash	PasswordHashAlgorithm
sa	master	us_english	0x0200...	SHA-1
HyBrasil	AdventureWorks2014	us_english	0x0200...	SHA-1
Bayard	AdventureWorks2014	us_english	0x0200...	SHA-1

How It Works

LOGINPROPERTY allows you to validate the properties of a SQL login. You can use it to manage password rotation, for example, checking the last time a password was set, and then modifying any logins that haven't changed within a certain period of time.

You can also use the password hash property in conjunction with CREATE LOGIN and the hashed_password HASHED argument to re-create a SQL login with the preserved password on a new SQL Server instance.

In each of the examples, I queried the `sys.server_principals` catalog view and then used a CROSS APPLY with a subquery that utilized the LOGINPROPERTY function.

```
FROM sys.server_principals p
CROSS APPLY (SELECT  PasswordHash = LOGINPROPERTY(p.name,  'PasswordHash') ,
    DefaultDatabase = LOGINPROPERTY(p.name,  'DefaultDatabase') ,
    DefaultLanguage = LOGINPROPERTY(p.name,  'DefaultLanguage') ,
    PasswordHashAlgorithm = LOGINPROPERTY(p.name,  'PasswordHashAlgorithm')
) ca
```

This method was used so I could retrieve information about multiple SQL logins at once. Rather than pass each login name into the first parameter of the LOGINPROPERTY function, I referenced the outer catalog view, `sys.server_principals`. This allows me to retrieve the properties for multiple logins simultaneously.

To limit the query to just SQL Server logins, I added the following in the WHERE clause:

```
WHERE p.type_desc = 'SQL_LOGIN'
    AND p.is_disabled = 0;
```

I aliased the CROSS APPLY subquery and used the aliases to reference the columns I needed to return in the SELECT clause.

```
SELECT p.name,ca.DefaultDatabase,ca.DefaultLanguage,ca.PasswordHash
        ,PasswordHashAlgorithm = Case ca.PasswordHashAlgorithm
        WHEN 1
        THEN 'SQL7.0'
        WHEN 2
        THEN 'SHA-1'
        WHEN 3
        THEN 'SHA-2'
        ELSE 'login is not a valid SQL Server login'
        END
```

Here, you will also see that I utilized a Case expression. This was done to render the output more easily understood than the numeric assignments of those values.

29-10. Dropping a SQL Login

Problem

After an audit, you discover that a login exists that should have been removed some time ago. You now need to remove that login.

Solution

Use the DROP LOGIN command to remove SQL logins.

This recipe demonstrates dropping a SQL login from a SQL Server instance by using the DROP LOGIN command.

The syntax is as follows:

```
DROP LOGIN login_name
```

The only parameter is the login name, which can be a Windows (as demonstrated earlier in this chapter) or SQL login, as this recipe demonstrates:

```
USE master;
GO
DROP LOGIN HyBrasil;
GO
```

How It Works

This recipe demonstrated the simple DROP LOGIN command, which removes a login from SQL Server. The process is simple; however, if a login owns any securables (see the next chapter for information on securables), the DROP attempt will fail. For example, if the HyBrasil login had been a database owner, an error like the following would have been raised:

```
Msg 15174, Level 16, State 1, Line 3
Login 'HyBrasil' owns one or more database(s).
Change the owner of the database(s) before dropping the login.
```

29-11. Managing Server Role Members

Problem

You have a new user account that you need to create. Upon creation of this account, the user needs to be added to the diskadmin fixed server role.

Solution

To add a login to a fixed server role, use ALTER SERVER ROLE.

Fixed server roles are predefined SQL groups that have specific SQL Server-scoped (as opposed to database- or schema-scoped) permissions assigned to them. Prior to SQL Server 2012, you could not create new server roles; you could only add or remove membership to such a role from other SQL or Windows logins. Since SQL Server 2012, you can create a user-defined server role.

The sysadmin fixed server role is the role with the highest level of permissions in a SQL Server instance. Although server roles are permissions based, they have members (SQL or Windows logins/groups) and are categorized by Microsoft as principals.

The syntax used to add a member to a fixed server role is as follows:

```
ALTER SERVER ROLE server_role_name
    ADD MEMBER server_principal
```

The first parameter (server_role_name) is the fixed server role to which you are adding the login. The second parameter (server_principal) is the login name to add to the fixed server role.

In this example, the login Gargouille is created and then added to the sysadmin fixed server role.

```
USE master;
GO
CREATE LOGIN Gargouille WITH PASSWORD = 'De3pd@rkCave';
GO
ALTER SERVER ROLE diskadmin
    ADD MEMBER Gargouille;
GO
```

To remove a login from a fixed server role, use ALTER SERVER ROLE. The syntax is almost identical to adding a server_principal.

```
ALTER SERVER ROLE server_role_name
    DROP MEMBER server_principal
```

This example removes the Gargouille login from the sysadmin fixed role membership.

```
USE master;
GO
ALTER SERVER ROLE diskadmin
    DROP MEMBER [Gargouille];
GO
```

How It Works

Once a login is added to a fixed server role, that login receives the permissions associated with the fixed server role. ALTER SERVER ROLE was used to add a new login to a fixed role membership; ALTER SERVER ROLE was also used to remove a login from a fixed role membership.

Adding SQL or Windows logins to a fixed server role should never be done lightly. Fixed server roles contain far-reaching permissions, so as a rule of thumb, seek to grant only those permissions that are absolutely necessary for the job at hand. For example, don't give sysadmin membership to someone who just needs SELECT permission on a table.

29-12. Reporting Fixed Server Role Information

Problem

You need a report on all users who are members of the sysadmin fixed server role.

Solution

You can execute the system stored procedure sp_helpsrvrolemember or query the sys.server_role_members catalog view.

Fixed server roles define a grouping of SQL Server-scoped permissions (such as backing up a database or creating new logins). Like SQL or Windows logins, fixed server roles have a security identifier and can be viewed in the sys.server_principals system catalog view. Unlike SQL or Windows logins, fixed server roles can have members (SQL and Windows logins) defined within them that inherit the permissions of the fixed server role.

To view a list of fixed server roles, query the sys.server_principals system catalog view.

```
USE master;
GO
SELECT name
FROM sys.server_principals
WHERE type_desc = 'SERVER_ROLE';
GO
```

This query returns the following:

```
name
--------------
public
sysadmin
securityadmin
serveradmin
setupadmin
processadmin
diskadmin
dbcreator
bulkadmin
```

You can also view a list of fixed server roles by executing the sp_helpserverrole system stored procedure.

```
USE master;
GO
EXECUTE sp_helpsrvrole;
GO
```

This query returns the following:

ServerRole	Description
sysadmin	System Administrators
securityadmin	Security Administrators
serveradmin	Server Administrators
setupadmin	Setup Administrators
processadmin	Process Administrators
diskadmin	Disk Administrators
dbcreator	Database Creators
bulkadmin	Bulk Insert Administrators

Table 29-3 details the permissions granted to each fixed server role.

Table 29-3. *Server Role Permissions*

Server Role	Granted Permissions
sysadmin	GRANT option (can GRANT permissions to others), CONTROL SERVER
setupadmin	ALTER ANY LINKED SERVER
serveradmin	ALTER SETTINGS, SHUTDOWN, CREATE ENDPOINT, ALTER SERVER STATE, ALTER ANY ENDPOINT, ALTER RESOURCES
securityadmin	ALTER ANY LOGIN
processadmin	ALTER SERVER STATE, ALTER ANY CONNECTION
diskadmin	ALTER RESOURCES
dbcreator	CREATE DATABASE
bulkadmin	ADMINISTER BULK OPERATIONS

To see the members of a fixed server role, you can execute the `sp_helpsrvrolemember` system stored procedure.

```
EXECUTE sp_helpsrvrolemember 'sysadmin';
```

This returns the following results (your results will vary):

ServerRole	MemberName	MemberSID
sysadmin	sa	0x01
sysadmin	NT AUTHORITY\SYSTEM	0x010100000000000512000000...
sysadmin	BUILTIN\Administrators	0x010200000000000520000000...
sysadmin	PETITMOT\SQLServerMSSQLUser$ROIS$JEANLOUIS	0x010500000000000515000000...
sysadmin	PETITMOT\SQLServerMSFTEUser$ROIS$JEANLOUIS	0x010500000000000515000000...
sysadmin	PETITMOT\Administrator	0x010500000000000515000000...
sysadmin	PETITMOT\SQLServerSQLAgentUser$ROIS$JEANLOUIS	0x010500000000000515000000...

Alternatively, to see the members of a fixed server role, you can query the `sys.server_role_members` catalog view.

```
USE master;
GO
SELECT SUSER_NAME(SR.role_principal_id) AS ServerRole
     , SUSER_NAME(SR.member_principal_id) AS PrincipalName
     , SP.sid
   FROM sys.server_role_members SR
   INNER JOIN sys.server_principals SP
      ON SR.member_principal_id = SP.principal_id
   WHERE SUSER_NAME(SR.role_principal_id) = 'sysadmin';
GO
```

This returns the following results (your results will vary):

ServerRole	MemberName	MemberSID
sysadmin	sa	0x01
sysadmin	NT AUTHORITY\SYSTEM	0x010100000000000512000000...
sysadmin	BUILTIN\Administrators	0x010200000000000520000000...
sysadmin	PETITMOT\SQLServerMSSQLUser$ROIS$JEANLOUIS	0x010500000000000515000000...
sysadmin	PETITMOT\SQLServerMSFTEUser$ROIS$JEANLOUIS	0x010500000000000515000000...
sysadmin	PETITMOT\Administrator	0x010500000000000515000000...
sysadmin	PETITMOT\SQLServerSQLAgentUser$ROIS$JEANLOUIS	0x010500000000000515000000...

How It Works

You can query the system catalog view sys.server_principals in order to view fixed server roles, or you can use the sp_helpsrvrole system stored procedure to view descriptions for each of the roles. To view members of a role (other principals), use the sp_helpsrvrolemember system stored procedure or query the sys.server_role_members catalog view. The next recipe will show you how to *add* or *remove* other principals of a fixed server role.

Database Principals

Database principals are the objects that represent users to which you can assign permissions to access databases or particular objects within a database. Where logins operate at the server level and allow you to perform actions such as connecting to a SQL Server, database principals operate at the database level and allow you to select or manipulate data, to perform DDL statements on objects within the database, and to manage users' permissions at the database level. SQL Server recognizes four types of database principals:

- *Database users*: Database user principals are the database-level security context under which requests within the database are executed and are associated with either SQL Server or Windows logins.

- *Database roles*: Database roles come in two flavors, fixed and user-defined. Fixed database roles are found in each database of a SQL Server instance and have database-scoped permissions assigned to them (such as SELECT permission on all tables or the ability to CREATE tables). User-defined database roles are those that you can create yourself, allowing you to manage permissions to securables more easily than if you had to individually grant similar permissions to multiple database users.

- *Application roles*: Application roles are groupings of permissions that don't allow members. Instead, you can "log in" as the application role. When you use an application role, it overrides all of the other permissions your login would otherwise have, giving you only those permissions granted to the application role.

In this section, I'll review how to modify, create, drop, and report on database users. I'll also cover how to work with database roles (fixed and user-defined) and application roles.

29-13. Creating Database Users

Problem

A SQL login has been created, and now you want that login to have access to a database.

Solution

Once a login is created, it can then be mapped to a database user. A login can be mapped to multiple databases on a single SQL Server instance—but to only one user for each database it has access to. Users are granted access with the CREATE USER command. The syntax is as follows:

```
CREATE USER user_name [ FOR
{ LOGIN login_name
| CERTIFICATE cert_name
I   ASYMMETRIC KEY asym_key_name
} ] [ WITH DEFAULT_SCHEMA = schema_name ]
```

Table 29-4 describes the arguments of this command.

Table 29-4. CREATE USER Arguments

Argument	Description
user_name	This specifies the name of the user in the database.
login_name	This specifies the name of the SQL or Windows login that is mapping to the database user.
cert_name	When designated, this specifies a certificate that is bound to the database user. See Chapter 19 for more information on certificates.
asym_key_name	When designated, this specifies an asymmetric key that is bound to the database user.
schema_name	This indicates the default schema that the user will belong to, which will determine what schema is checked first when the user references database objects. If this option is unspecified, the dbo schema will be used. This schema name can also be designated for a schema not yet created in the database.

In this first example of the recipe, a new user called Gargouille is created in the TestDB database.

```
USE master;
GO
IF NOT EXISTS (SELECT name FROM sys.databases
    WHERE name = 'TestDB')
BEGIN
    CREATE DATABASE TestDB
END
GO
USE TestDB;
GO
CREATE USER Gargouille;
GO
```

In the second example, a Windows login is mapped to a database user called Bayard with a default schema specified.

```
USE TestDB;
GO
CREATE SCHEMA HumanResources;
GO
CREATE USER Bayard
FOR LOGIN [PETITMOT\Bayard]
WITH DEFAULT_SCHEMA = HumanResources;
GO
```

How It Works

In the first example of the recipe, a user named Gargouille was created in the TestDB database. If you didn't designate the FOR LOGIN clause of CREATE USER, it is assumed that the user maps to a login with the same name (in this case, a login named Gargouille). Notice that the default schema was not designated, which means Gargouille's default schema will be dbo.

In the second example, a new user named Bayard was created in the AdventureWorks2014 database, mapped to a Windows login named [PETITMOT\Bayard] (notice the square brackets). The default schema was also set for the Bayard login to HumanResources. For any unqualified object references in queries performed by Bayard, SQL Server first searches for objects in the HumanResources schema.

29-14. Reporting Database User Information

Problem

You want to query to find more information about a database user.

Solution

You can report database user (and role) information for the current database connection by using the sp_helpuser system stored procedure. The syntax is as follows:

```
sp_helpuser [ [ @name_in_db= ] ' security_account ' ]
```

The single, optional parameter is the name of the database user for which you want to return information. Here's an example:

```
USE TestDB;
GO
EXECUTE sp_helpuser 'Gargouille';
GO
```

This returns the following results:

UserName	RoleName	LoginName	DefDBName	DefSchemaName	UserID	SID
Gargouille	public	Gargouille	master	dbo	5	0x3057F4EEC4F07A46...

How It Works

The sp_helpuser system stored procedure returns the database users defined in the current database. From the results, you can determine important information such as the user name, login name, default database and schema, and user's security identifier. If a specific user isn't designated, sp_helpuser returns information on all users in the current database you are connected to.

29-15. Modifying a Database User

Problem

You want to modify the default schema for a database user.

Solution

You should use the ALTER USER command. You can rename a database user or change the user's default schema by using the ALTER USER command.

The syntax is as follows (argument usages are demonstrated in this recipe):

```
ALTER USER user_name
WITH NAME = new_user_name DEFAULT_SCHEMA = schema_name
```

In this first example of this recipe, the default schema of the Gargouille database user is changed.

```
USE TestDB;
GO
CREATE SCHEMA Production;
GO
ALTER USER Gargouille
WITH DEFAULT_SCHEMA = Production;
GO
```

In the second example of this recipe, the default schema for a principal based on a Windows group is changed.

```
USE [master]
GO
CREATE LOGIN [PETITMOT\SQLTest] FROM WINDOWS
WITH DEFAULT_DATABASE=[TestDB];
GO
USE [TestDB]
GO
CREATE USER [PETITMOT\SQLTest]
FOR LOGIN [PETITMOT\SQLTest];
GO
ALTER USER [PETITMOT\SQLTest]
WITH DEFAULT_SCHEMA = Production;
GO
```

In the last example of this recipe, a database user name is changed.

```
USE TestDB;
GO
ALTER USER Gargouille
WITH NAME = FeeDauphin;
GO
```

How It Works

The ALTER USER command allows you to perform one of two changes: renaming a database user or changing a database principal's default schema. The first example changed the default schema of the Gargouille login to the Production schema. The second example changed the default schema of the PETITMOT\SQLTest principal. In SQL Server, you can modify the default schema for principals mapped to a Windows group, certificate, or asymmetric key. The last example renamed the database user Gargouille to FeeDauphin.

29-16. Removing a Database User from the Database

Problem

While maintaining a SQL Server instance, you have found a database user exists for a login that was removed the prior month. You want to now remove this database user.

Solution

Use the DROP USER command to remove a user from the database. The syntax is as follows:

```
DROP USER user_name
```

The user_name is the name of the database user, as this example demonstrates:

```
USE TestDB;
GO
DROP USER FeeDauphin;
GO
```

How It Works

The DROP USER command removes a user from the database but does not impact the Windows or SQL login that is associated with it. Like DROP LOGIN, you can't drop a user that is the owner of database objects. For example, if the database user FeeDauphin is the schema owner for a schema called Test, you'll get an error like the following:

```
Msg 15138, Level 16, State 1, Line 2
The database principal owns a schema in the database, and cannot be dropped.
```

29-17. Fixing Orphaned Database Users

Problem

You have restored a database to a different server. The database users in the restored database have lost their association to the server logins. You need to restore the association between login and database user.

Solution

When you migrate a database to a new server (by using BACKUP/RESTORE, for example), the relationship between logins and database users can break. A login has a security identifier, which uniquely identifies it on the SQL Server instance. This sid is stored for the login's associated database user in each database that the login has access to. Creating another SQL login on a different SQL Server instance with the same name will not re-create the same sid unless you specifically designated it with the sid argument of the CREATE LOGIN statement.

For this recipe, we will create an orphaned user. This is done by first creating a login and a user. Then drop the login and re-create it, leaving the user untouched.

```
USE AdventureWorks2014;
GO
If not exists (select name from sys.server_principals
            where name ='Gargouille')
Begin
CREATE LOGIN Gargouille
WITH PASSWORD = 'BigTr3e',
DEFAULT_DATABASE = AdventureWorks2014;
End
GO
If not exists (select name from sys.database_principals
            where name = 'Gargouille')
Begin
CREATE USER Gargouille;
END
DROP LOGIN [GARGOUILLE];
CREATE LOGIN Gargouille
WITH PASSWORD = 'BigTr3e',
DEFAULT_DATABASE = AdventureWorks2014;
GO
```

The following query demonstrates the link between Login and User by joining the sys.database_ principals system catalog view to the sys.server_principals catalog view on the sid column in order to look for orphaned database users in the database.

```
USE AdventureWorks2014;
GO
SELECT dp.name AS OrphanUser, dp.sid AS OrphanSid
FROM sys.database_principals dp
LEFT OUTER JOIN sys.server_principals sp
    ON dp.sid = sp.sid
```

```
WHERE sp.sid IS NULL
    AND dp.type_desc = 'SQL_USER'
    AND dp.principal_id > 4;
GO
```

This query returns the following (your results will vary):

OrphanUser	OrphanSid
Gargouille	0x40C455005F34E44FB95622488AF48F75

If you RESTORE a database from a different SQL Server instance onto a new SQL Server instance—and the database users don't have associated logins on the new SQL Server instance—the database users can become "orphaned." If there are logins with the same name on the new SQL Server instance that match the name of the database users, the database users still may be orphaned in the database if the login sid doesn't match the restored database user sid.

Beginning with SQL Server 2005 Service Pack 2, you can use the ALTER USER WITH LOGIN command to remap login/user associations. This applies to both SQL and Windows accounts, which is very useful if the underlying Windows user or group has been re-created in Active Directory and now has an identifier that no longer maps to the generated sid on the SQL Server instance.

The following query demonstrates remapping the orphaned database user Gargouille to the associated server login:

```
USE AdventureWorks2014;
GO
ALTER USER Gargouille WITH LOGIN = Gargouille;
GO
```

The next example demonstrates mapping a database user ([FeeDauphin]) to the login [PETITMOT\ FeeDauphin] (assuming that the user became orphaned from the Windows account or the sid of the domain account was changed because of a drop/re-create outside of SQL Server):

```
USE TestDB;
GO
ALTER USER [FeeDauphin]
WITH LOGIN = [PETITMOT\FeeDauphin];
GO
```

This command also works with mapping a user to a new login—whether or not that user is orphaned.

How It Works

In this recipe, I demonstrated querying the sys.database_principals and sys.server_principals catalog views to view any database users with an sid that does not exist at the server scope (no associated login sid). I then demonstrated using ALTER USER to map the database user to a login with the same name (but different sid). I also demonstrated how to remap a Windows account (in the event that it is orphaned using ALTER USER).

■ **Tip** In previous versions of SQL Server, you could use the `sp_change_users_login` stored procedure to perform and report on `sid` remapping. This stored procedure has been deprecated in favor of `ALTER USER WITH LOGIN`.

29-18. Reporting Fixed Database Roles Information

Problem

You need to provide a list of database roles and associated members per role.

Solution

To view role membership, you can use `sp_helprolemember`.

Fixed database roles are found in each database of a SQL Server instance and have database-scoped permissions assigned to them (such as `SELECT` permission on all tables or the ability to `CREATE` tables). Like fixed server roles, fixed database roles have members (database users) that inherit the permissions of the role.

A list of fixed database roles can be viewed by executing the `sp_helpdbfixedrole` system stored procedure.

```
USE TestDB;
GO
EXECUTE sp_helpdbfixedrole;
GO
```

This returns the following results:

DBFixedRole	Description
db_owner	DB Owners
db_accessadmin	DB Access Administrators
db_securityadmin	DB Security Administrators
db_ddladmin	DB DDL Administrators
db_backupoperator	DB Backup Operator
db_datareader	DB Data Reader
db_datawriter	DB Data Writer
db_denydatareader	DB Deny Data Reader
db_denydatawriter	DB Deny Data Writer

To see the database members of a fixed database role (or any user-defined or application role), you can execute the `sp_helprolemember` system stored procedure.

```
USE TestDB;
GO
EXECUTE sp_helprolemember;
GO
```

This returns the following results (the member `sid` refers to the `sid` of the login mapped to the database user):

DbRole	MemberName	MemberSid
db_backupoperator	FeeDauphin	0x0105000000000005150000000527A777BF094B3850F
db_datawriter	FeeDauphin	0x0105000000000005150000000527A777BF094B3850F
db_owner	dbo	0x01

How It Works

Fixed database roles are found in each database on a SQL Server instance. A fixed database role groups important database permissions together. These permissions can't be modified or removed. In this recipe, I used `sp_helpdbfixedrole` to list the available fixed database roles.

```
EXECUTE sp_helpdbfixedrole;
```

After that, the `sp_helprolemember` system stored procedure was used to list the members of each fixed database role (database users), showing the role name, database user name, and login `sid`.

```
EXECUTE sp_helprolemember;
```

As with fixed server roles, it's best not to grant membership to them without assurance that all permissions are absolutely necessary for the database user. Do not, for example, grant a user `db_owner` membership when only `SELECT` permissions on a table are needed.

The next recipe shows you how to add or remove database users to or from a fixed database role.

29-19. Managing Fixed Database Role Membership

Problem

You have been given a list of new users that need to be added to specific roles within the database.

Solution

To associate a database user or role with a database role (user-defined or application role), use the `ALTER ROLE` command. The syntax is as follows:

```
ALTER ROLE database_role_name
ADD MEMBER database_principal
```

The first parameter (`database_role_name`) is the role name, and the second parameter (`database_principal`) is the name of the database user.

To remove the association between a database user and role, you will also use the ALTER ROLE command.

```
ALTER ROLE database_role_name
DROP MEMBER database_principal
```

The syntax for removing a database user is similar to adding a user to a role. To remove a user, you need to use the keyword DROP in lieu of ADD.

This first example demonstrates adding the database user Gargouille to the fixed db_datawriter and db_datareader roles.

```
USE TestDB
GO
If not exists (select name from sys.database_principals
        where name = 'Gargouille')
Begin
CREATE LOGIN Gargouille
WITH PASSWORD = 'BigTr3e',
DEFAULT_DATABASE = TestDB;
CREATE USER Gargouille;
END
GO
ALTER ROLE db_datawriter
    ADD MEMBER [GARGOUILLE];
ALTER ROLE db_datareader
    ADD MEMBER [GARGOUILLE];
GO
```

This second example demonstrates how to *remove* the database user Gargouille from the db_datawriter role.

```
USE TestDB;
GO
ALTER ROLE db_datawriter
    DROP MEMBER [GARGOUILLE];
GO
```

How It Works

This recipe began by discussing ALTER ROLE, which allows you to add a database user to an existing database role. The database user Gargouille was added to db_datawriter and db_datareader, which gives the user cumulative permissions to SELECT, INSERT, UPDATE, or DELETE from any table or view in the AdventureWorks2014 database.

```
ALTER ROLE db_datawriter
    ADD MEMBER [GARGOUILLE];
ALTER ROLE db_datareader
    ADD MEMBER [GARGOUILLE];
GO
```

The first parameter (database_role_name) was the database role, and the second parameter (database_principal) was the name of the database user (or role) to which the database role is associated.

After that, ALTER ROLE was used to remove Gargouille's membership from the db_datawriter role.

```
ALTER ROLE db_datawriter
    DROP MEMBER [GARGOUILLE];
GO
```

29-20. Managing User-Defined Database Roles

Problem

You have several users that require the same permissions within a database. You want to reduce the administration overhead with managing the permissions for this group of users.

Solution

Create a user-defined database role. User-defined database roles allow you to manage permissions to securables more easily than if you had to individually grant the same permissions to multiple database users over and over again. Instead, you can create a database role, grant it permissions to securables, and then add one or more database users as members to that database role. When permission changes are needed, you have to modify the permissions of only the single database role, and the members of the role will then automatically inherit those permission changes.

Use the CREATE ROLE command to create a user-defined role in a database.

The syntax is as follows:

```
CREATE ROLE role_name [ AUTHORIZATION owner_name ]
```

The command takes the name of the new role and an optional role owner name. The owner name is the name of the user or database role that owns the new database role (and thus can manage it).

You can list all database roles (fixed, user-defined, and application) by executing the sp_helprole system stored procedure.

```
USE TestDB;
GO
EXECUTE sp_helprole;
GO
```

This returns the following abridged results (the IsAppRole column shows as a 1 if the role is an application role and 0 if not):

RoleName	RoleId	IsAppRole
public	0	0
db_owner	16384	0
...	...	...

Once a database role is created in a database, you can grant or deny it permissions as you would a regular database user (see the next chapter for more on permissions). I will demonstrate granting permissions to a database role in a moment.

If you want to change the name of the database role, *without* also disrupting the role's current permissions and membership, you can use the ALTER ROLE command, which has the following syntax:

```
ALTER ROLE role_name WITH NAME = new_name
```

The command takes the name of the original role as the first argument and the new role name in the second argument.

To drop a role, use the DROP ROLE command. The syntax is as follows:

```
DROP ROLE role_name
```

If a role owns any securables, you'll need to transfer ownership to a new owner before you can drop the role.

In this example, I'll create a new role in the AdventureWorks2014 database.

```
USE AdventureWorks2014;
GO
CREATE ROLE HR_ReportSpecialist AUTHORIZATION db_owner;
GO
```

After being created, this new role doesn't have any database permissions yet. In this next query, I'll grant the HR_ReportSpecialist database role permission to SELECT from the HumanResources.Employee table:

```
Use AdventureWorks2014;
GO
GRANT SELECT ON HumanResources.Employee TO HR_ReportSpecialist;
GO
```

To add Gargouille as a member of this new role, I execute the following:

```
USE AdventureWorks2014;
GO
If not exists (select name from sys.server_principals
                              where name ='Gargouille')
Begin
CREATE LOGIN Gargouille
WITH PASSWORD = 'BigTr3e',
DEFAULT_DATABASE = AdventureWorks2014;
End
GO
If not exists (select name from sys.database_principals
                              where name = 'Gargouille')
Begin
CREATE USER Gargouille;
END
GO
ALTER ROLE HR_ReportSpecialist
ADD MEMBER Gargouille;
GO
```

If later I decide that the name of the role doesn't match its purpose, I can change its name using ALTER ROLE.

```
USE AdventureWorks2014;
GO
ALTER ROLE HR_ReportSpecialist WITH NAME = HumanResources_RS;
GO
```

Even though the role name was changed, Gargouille remains a member of the role. This last example demonstrates dropping a database role.

```
USE AdventureWorks2014;
GO
DROP ROLE HumanResources_RS;
GO
```

This returns an error message, because the role must be emptied of members before it can be dropped.

```
Msg 15144, Level 16, State 1, Line 1
The role has members. It must be empty before it can be dropped.
```

So, the single member of this role needs to be dropped prior to dropping the role.

```
USE AdventureWorks2014;
GO
ALTER ROLE HumanResources_RS
DROP MEMBER Gargouille;
GO
DROP ROLE HumanResources_RS;
GO
```

How It Works

The CREATE ROLE command creates a new database role in a database. Once created, you can apply permissions to the role as you would a regular database user. Roles allow you to administer permissions at a group level—allowing individual role members to inherit permissions in a consistent manner instead of applying permissions to individual users, which may or may not be identical.

This recipe demonstrated several commands related to managing user-defined database roles. The sp_helprole system stored procedure was used to list all database roles in the current database. CREATE ROLE was used to create a new user-defined role owned by the db_owner fixed database role.

```
CREATE ROLE HR_ReportSpecialist AUTHORIZATION db_owner
```

I then granted permissions to the new role to SELECT from a table.

```
GRANT SELECT ON HumanResources.Employee TO HR_ReportSpecialist
```

The Gargouille user was then added as a member of the new role.

```
ALTER ROLE HR_ReportSpecialist
ADD MEMBER Gargouille;
```

The name of the role was changed using ALTER ROLE (still leaving membership and permissions intact).

```
ALTER ROLE HR_ReportSpecialist WITH NAME = HumanResources_RS
```

The Gargouille user was then dropped from the role (so that I could drop the user-defined role).

```
ALTER ROLE HumanResources_RS
```

DROP MEMBER Gargouille;
Once emptied of members, the user-defined database role was then dropped.

```
DROP ROLE HumanResources_RS
```

29-21. Managing Application Roles

Problem

You have an application that requires limited permissions in a database. Any user using this application should use the permissions of the application over their individual permissions. You need to create a database principal for this application.

Solution

You should create an application role. An application role is a hybrid between a login and a database role. You can assign permissions to application roles in the same way that you can assign permissions to user-defined roles. Application roles differ from database and server roles, however, in that application roles *do not allow members*. Instead, an application role is *activated* using a password-enabled system stored procedure. When you use an application role, it overrides all of the other permissions your login would otherwise have.

Because an application role has no members, it requires a password for the permissions to be enabled. In addition to this, once a session's context is set to use an application role, any existing user or login permissions are nullified. Only the application role's permissions apply.

To create an application role, use CREATE APPLICATION ROLE, which has the following syntax:

```
CREATE APPLICATION ROLE application_role_name
WITH PASSWORD = ' password ' [ , DEFAULT_SCHEMA = schema_name ]
```

Table 29-5 describes the arguments of this command.

Table 29-5. CREATE APPLICATON ROLE Arguments

Argument	Description
application_role_name	The name of the application role
password	The password to enable access to the application role's permissions
schema_name	The default database schema of the application role that defines which schema is checked for unqualified object names in a query

In this example, a new application role name, DataWareHouseApp, is created and granted permissions to a view in the AdventureWorks2014 database.

```
USE AdventureWorks2014;
GO
CREATE APPLICATION ROLE DataWareHouseApp
WITH PASSWORD = 'mywarehouse123!', DEFAULT_SCHEMA = dbo;
GO
```

An application role by itself is useless without first granting it permissions to do something. So, in this example, the application role is given SELECT permissions on a specific database view.

```
-- Now grant this application role permissions
USE AdventureWorks2014;
GO
GRANT SELECT ON Sales.vSalesPersonSalesByFiscalYears
TO DataWareHouseApp;
GO
```

The system stored procedure sp_setapprole is used to enable the permissions of the application role for the current user session. In this next example, I activate an application role and query two tables.

```
USE AdventureWorks2014;
GO
EXECUTE sp_setapprole 'DataWareHouseApp', -- App role name
    'mywarehouse123!' -- Password
        ;
GO
-- This query Works
SELECT COUNT(*)
FROM Sales.vSalesPersonSalesByFiscalYears;
-- This query Doesn't work
SELECT COUNT(*) FROM HumanResources.vJobCandidate;
GO
```

This query returns the following:

```
-----------
14

(1  row(s)  affected)

Msg 229, Level 14, State 5, Line 7
SELECT  permission  denied  on  object  'vJobCandidate',
database  'AdventureWorks2014',  schema
'HumanResources'.
```

Even though the original connection login was for a login with sysadmin permissions, using sp_setapprole to enter the application permissions means that only that role's permissions apply. So, in this case, the application role had SELECT permission for the Sales.VSalesPersonSalesByFiscalYears view, but not the HumanResources.vJobCandidate view queried in the example.

To revert to the original login's permissions, just close out the connection and open a new connection.

You can modify the name, password, or default database of an application role using the ALTER APPLICATION ROLE command.

The syntax is as follows:

```
ALTER APPLICATION ROLE application_role_name WITH NAME = new_application_role_name
PASSWORD = ' password '
DEFAULT_SCHEMA = schema_name
```

Table 29-6 shows the arguments of the command.

Table 29-6. ALTER APPLICATION ROLE Arguments

Parameter	Description
new_application_role_name	The new application role name
password	The new application role password
Schema_name	The new default schema

In this example, the application role name and password are changed.

```
USE AdventureWorks2014;
GO
ALTER APPLICATION ROLE DataWareHouseApp
WITH NAME = DW_App, PASSWORD = 'newsecret!123';
GO
```

To remove an application role from the database, use DROP APPLICATION ROLE, which has the following syntax:

```
DROP APPLICATION ROLE rolename
```

This command takes only one argument, the name of the application role to be dropped. Here's an example:

```
USE AdventureWorks2014;
GO
DROP APPLICATION ROLE DW_App;
GO
```

How It Works

This recipe demonstrated how to do the following:

- Create a new application role using CREATE APPLICATION ROLE
- Activate the role permissions using sp_setapprole
- Modify an application role using ALTER APPLICATION ROLE
- Remove an application role from a database using DROP APPLICATION ROLE

Application roles are a convenient solution for application developers who want to grant users access *only through an application.* Savvy end users may figure out that their SQL login can also be used to connect to SQL Server with other applications such as Microsoft Access or SQL Server Management Studio. To prevent this, you can change the login account to have minimal permissions for the databases and then use an application role for the required permissions. This way, the user can access the data only through the application, which is then programmed to use the application role.

29-22. Managing User-Defined Server Roles

Problem

You have several users that require the same permissions within an instance. You want to reduce the administration overhead ofh managing the permissions for this group of users.

Solution

Create a user-defined server role. Similar to the user defined database role, server roles allow one to manage the permissions for securables more easily than trying to manage the permissions for several users on an individual basis.

Use the CREATE SERVER ROLE command to create a user-defined role in a server.

The syntax is as follows:

```
CREATE SERVER ROLE role_name [ AUTHORIZATION server_principal ]
```

The command takes the name of the new role and an optional server principal. The server principal is the name of the login or fixed server role that owns the new server role (and thus can manage it).

In this example, I will create a new role.

```
USE master;
GO
CREATE SERVER ROLE hdserverstate AUTHORIZATION securityadmin;
GO
```

After the role is created, I will grant permissions and then I will add users to the role.

```
GRANT VIEW SERVER STATE TO hdserverstate;
GO
```

```
ALTER SERVER ROLE [hdserverstate] ADD MEMBER [Gargouille];
GO
```

I can now confirm the creation of the role and that the login has been added to the role.

```
SELECT sp.name AS RoleName, mem.name AS MemberName
      FROM sys.server_role_members rm
              INNER JOIN sys.server_principals sp
                      ON rm.role_principal_id = sp.principal_id
              LEFT OUTER JOIN sys.server_principals mem
                      ON rm.member_principal_id = mem.principal_id
      WHERE sp.name = 'hdserverstate'
              AND sp.type_desc = 'SERVER_ROLE';
```

With the login assigned to the user defined server role, I will now test the login to verify it can query DMVs that hold server state information, such as wait stats. To do so, I can either impersonate the Gargouille login or I can connect to the server with the Gargouille login.

```
EXECUTE AS LOGIN = 'Gargouille';
GO
SELECT * FROM sys.dm_os_wait_stats;
GO
```

```
REVERT
```

With the role working as desired, then more logins can now be added to the role to help minimize the administration efforts of the helpdesk group, without granting too many permissions.

If a user from the group no longer needs access, then the login can be removed from the role, as shown in this next example.

```
ALTER SERVER ROLE [hdserverstate] DROP MEMBER [Gargouille];
GO
```

To confirm that the user no longer has access, a quick query can be run similar in nature to the wait stats test just performed. Once again, this test will be performed with an impersonation of the Gargouille login.

```
EXECUTE AS LOGIN = 'Gargouille';
GO
SELECT * FROM sys.dm_os_wait_stats
```

```
REVERT
```

This query should now produce an error just as it should have prior to adding the Gargouille login to the hdserverstate custom server role.

```
Msg 300, Level 14, State 1, Line 37
VIEW SERVER STATE permission was denied on object 'server', database 'master'.
Msg 297, Level 16, State 1, Line 37
The user does not have permission to perform this action.
```

If the role is no longer needed, once all members have been removed, then the role can be dropped as shown in this next example.

```
DROP SERVER ROLE [hdserverstate];
GO
```

How It Works

The CREATE SERVER ROLE command creates a new role in the instance. Once created, you can apply permissions to the role as you would a login. Roles allow you to administer permissions at a group level—allowing individual role members to inherit permissions in a consistent manner instead of applying permissions to individual logins, which may or may not be identical.

This recipe demonstrated several commands related to managing user-defined server roles. CREATE SERVER ROLE was used to create a new user-defined role owned by the securityadmin fixed server role.

```
CREATE SERVER ROLE hdserverstate AUTHORIZATION securityadmin;
```

I then granted permissions to the new role to view the server state.

```
GRANT VIEW SERVER STATE TO hdserverstate;
```

The Gargouille login was then added as a member of the new role.

```
ALTER SERVER ROLE [hdserverstate] ADD MEMBER [Gargouille];
```

The Gargouille login was then dropped from the role (so that I could drop the user-defined role).

```
ALTER SERVER ROLE [hdserverstate] DROP MEMBER [Gargouille];
```

Once emptied of members, the user-defined server role was then dropped.

```
DROP SERVER ROLE [hdserverstate];
```

CHAPTER 30

■ ■ ■

Securables, Permissions, and Auditing

by Jason Brimhall

In the previous chapter, I discussed principals, which are security accounts that can access SQL Server. In this chapter, I'll discuss and demonstrate securables and permissions. *Securables* are resources that SQL Server controls access to through permissions. Securables in SQL Server fall into three nested hierarchical scopes. The top level of the hierarchy is the *server scope,* which contains logins, databases, and endpoints. The *database scope,* which is contained within the server scope, controls securables such as database users, roles, certificates, and schemas. The third and innermost scope is the *schema scope,* which controls securables such as the schema itself as well as objects within the schema, such as tables, views, functions, and procedures.

Permissions enable a principal to perform actions on securables. Across all securable scopes, the primary commands used to control a principal's access to a securable are GRANT, DENY, and REVOKE. These commands are applied in similar ways, depending on the scope of the securable that you are targeting. GRANT is used to enable access to securables. DENY explicitly restricts access, trumping other permissions that would normally allow a principal access to a securable. REVOKE removes a specific permission on a securable altogether, whether it was a GRANT or DENY permission.

Once permissions are granted, you may still have additional business and compliance auditing requirements that mandate the tracking of changes or knowing which logins are accessing which tables. To address this need, SQL Server introduced the SQL Server Audit object, which can be used to collect information on SQL instance- and database-scoped actions that you are interested in monitoring. This audit information can be sent to a file, the Windows Application event log, or the Windows Security event log.

In this chapter, I'll discuss how permissions are granted to a principal at all three securable scopes. In addition to permissions, this chapter also presents the following related securable and permissions recipes:

- How to manage schemas using CREATE, ALTER, and DROP SCHEMA

- How to report allocated permissions for a specific principal by using the fn_my_permissions function

- How to determine a connection's permissions to a securable using the system function HAS_PERMS_BY_NAME, as well as using EXECUTE AS to define your connection's security context to a different login or user to see their permissions, too

- How to query all granted, denied, and revoked permissions using sys.database_permissions and sys.server_permissions

- How to change a securable's ownership using `ALTER AUTHORIZATION`
- How to provide Windows external-resource permissions to a SQL login using `CREATE CREDENTIAL` and `ALTER LOGIN`
- How to audit SQL instance- and database-level actions using the SQL Server Audit functionality

This chapter starts with a general discussion of SQL Server permissions.

Permissions Overview

Permissions apply to SQL Server objects within the three securable scopes (server, database, and schema). SQL Server uses a set of common permission names that are applied to different securables (and at different scopes) and imply different levels of authorization against a securable. Table 30-1 shows those permissions that are used for multiple securables (however, this isn't an exhaustive list).

Table 30-1. *Major Permissions*

Permission	Description
ALTER	Enables the grantee the use of `ALTER`, `CREATE`, or `DROP` commands for the securable. For example, using `ALTER TABLE` requires `ALTER` permissions on that specific table.
AUTHENTICATE	Enables the grantee to be trusted across database or SQL Server scopes
CONNECT	Enables a grantee to have permission to connect to SQL Server resources (such as an endpoint or the SQL Server instance)
CONTROL	Enables the grantee to have all available permissions on the specific securable, as well as any nested or implied permissions within (so if you `CONTROL` a schema, for example, you also control any tables, views, or other database objects within that schema)
CREATE	Enables the grantee to create a securable (which can be at the server, database, or schema scope)
IMPERSONATE	Enables the grantee to impersonate another principal (login or user). For example, using the `EXECUTE AS` command for a login requires `IMPERSONATE` permissions. In this chapter, I'll cover how to use `EXECUTE AS` to set your security context outside of a module.
TAKE OWNERSHIP	Enables the grantee to take ownership of a granted securable
VIEW	Enables the grantee to see system metadata regarding a specific securable

To report available permissions in SQL Server, as well as view that specific permission's place in the permission hierarchy, use the `sys.fn_builtin_permissions` system table-valued function. The syntax is as follows:

```
    sys.fn_builtin_permissions
(  [  DEFAULT | NULL ] | empty_string |
APPLICATION ROLE | ASSEMBLY | ASYMMETRIC KEY |
CERTIFICATE | CONTRACT | DATABASE |
ENDPOINT | FULLTEXT CATALOG| LOGIN |
```

```
MESSAGE TYPE | OBJECT | REMOTE SERVICE BINDING |
ROLE | ROUTE | SCHEMA | SERVER | SERVICE |
SYMMETRIC KEY | TYPE   | USER | XML SCHEMA COLLECTION )
```

Table 30-2 describes the arguments of this command.

Table 30-2. *fn_builtin_permissions Arguments*

Argument	Description
DEFAULT | NULL | empty_string	Designating any of these first three arguments results in all permissions being listed in the result set.
APPLICATION ROLE | ASSEMBLY | ASYMMETRIC KEY | CERTIFICATE | CONTRACT | DATABASE | ENDPOINT | FULLTEXT CATALOG| LOGIN | MESSAGE TYPE | OBJECT | REMOTE SERVICE BINDING |ROLE | ROUTE | SCHEMA | SERVER | SERVICE | SYMMETRIC KEY | TYPE | USER | XML SCHEMA COLLECTION	Specify any one of these securable types in order to return permissions for that type.

In addition to the permission name, you can determine the nested hierarchy of permissions by looking at the columns in the result set for covering_permission_name (a permission within the same class that is the superset of the more granular permission), parent_class_desc (the parent class of the permission—if any), and parent_covering_permission_name (the parent covering permission—if any), all of which you'll see demonstrated in the next recipe.

30-1. Reporting SQL Server Assignable Permissions

Problem

You want to list the available permissions within SQL Server.

Solution

To view the available permissions within SQL Server and explain their place within the permissions hierarchy, you should use the system function sys.fn_builtin_permissions. In this first example, we'll return all permissions, regardless of securable scope:

```
USE master;
GO

SELECT class_desc, permission_name, covering_permission_name, parent_class_desc, parent_covering_permission_name
    FROM sys.fn_builtin_permissions(DEFAULT)
    ORDER BY class_desc, permission_name;
GO
```

This returns the following (abridged) result set:

class_desc	permission_name	covering_permission_name	parent_class_desc	parent_covering_permission_name
APPLICATION ROLE	ALTER	CONTROL	DATABASE	ALTER ANY APPLICATION ROLE
APPLICATION ROLE	CONTROL		DATABASE	CONTROL
APPLICATION ROLE	VIEW DEFINITION	CONTROL	DATABASE	VIEW DEFINITION
...				
SERVER	ALTER ANY DATABASE	CONTROL SERVER	...	...
...				
XML SCHEMA COLLECTION	REFERENCES	CONTROL	SCHEMA	REFERENCES
XML SCHEMA COLLECTION	TAKE OWNERSHIP	CONTROL	SCHEMA	CONTROL
XML SCHEMA COLLECTION	VIEW DEFINITION	CONTROL	SCHEMA	VIEW DEFINITION

The next example shows only the permissions for the schema securable scope:

```
USE master;
GO

SELECT permission_name, covering_permission_name, parent_class_desc
    FROM sys.fn_builtin_permissions('schema')
    ORDER BY permission_name;
GO
```

This returns the following result set:

permission_name	covering_permission_name	parent_class_desc
ALTER	CONTROL	DATABASE
CONTROL		DATABASE
CREATE SEQUENCE	ALTER	DATABASE
DELETE	CONTROL	DATABASE
EXECUTE	CONTROL	DATABASE
INSERT	CONTROL	DATABASE
REFERENCES	CONTROL	DATABASE
SELECT	CONTROL	DATABASE

permission_name	covering_permission_name	parent_class_desc
TAKE OWNERSHIP	CONTROL	DATABASE
UPDATE	CONTROL	DATABASE
VIEW CHANGE TRACKING	CONTROL	DATABASE
VIEW DEFINITION	CONTROL	DATABASE

How It Works

The sys.fn_builtin_permissions system-catalog function allows you to view available permissions in SQL Server.

The first example in this recipe, sys.fn_builtin_permissions, was used to display all permissions by using the DEFAULT option. The first line of code referenced the column names to be returned from the function:

```
SELECT class_desc, permission_name, covering_permission_name, parent_class_desc, parent_covering_permission_name
```

The second line referenced the function in the FROM clause, using the DEFAULT option to display all permissions:

```
FROM sys.fn_builtin_permissions(DEFAULT)
```

The last line of code allowed us to order by the permission's class and name:

```
ORDER BY class_desc, permission_name;
```

The results displayed the securable class description, permission name, and covering permission name (the *covering permission name* is the name of a permission class that is higher in the nested permission hierarchy). For example, for the APPLICATION ROLE class, you saw that the CONTROL permission was a child of the DATABASE class and ALTER ANY APPLICATION permission, but it was not subject to any covering permission in the APPLICATION ROLE class (because CONTROL enables all available permissions on the specific securable to the grantee, as well as any nested or implied permissions within).

class_desc	permission_ name	covering_ permission_name	parent_class_desc	parent_covering_ permission_name
. . .				
APPLICATION ROLE	CONTROL		DATABASE	CONTROL
. . .				

For the OBJECT class, you can see that the ALTER permission is a child of the SCHEMA parent class and ALTER permission. Within the OBJECT class, the ALTER permission is also a child of the covering CONTROL permission (as seen in the covering_permission_name column).

class_desc	permission_name	covering_permission_name	parent_class_desc	parent_covering_permission_name
...				
OBJECT	ALTER	CONTROL	SCHEMA	ALTER
...				

For the SERVER class and ALTER ANY DATABASE permission, the covering permission for the SERVER class is CONTROL SERVER. Notice that the SERVER class does *not* have a parent class or permission.

class_desc	permission_name	covering_permission_name	parent_class_desc	parent_covering_permission_name
...				
SERVER	ALTER ANY DATABASE	CONTROL SERVER		
...				

The second example in this recipe returned permissions for just the schema-securable class. The first line of code included just three of the columns this time:

```
SELECT permission_name, covering_permission_name, parent_class_desc
```

The second line included the word *schema* in order to show permissions for the schema-securable class:

```
FROM sys.fn_builtin_permissions('schema')
```

The results were then ordered by the permission name:

```
ORDER BY permission_name;
```

Permissions that control database objects contained within a schema (such as views, tables, and so on) were returned. For example, you saw that the DELETE permission is found within the schema scope and is covered by the CONTROL permission. Its parent class is the DATABASE securable.

permission_name	covering_permission_name	parent_class_desc
...		
DELETE	CONTROL	DATABASE
...		

Server-Scoped Securables and Permissions

Server-scoped securables are objects that are unique within a SQL Server instance, including endpoints, logins, and databases. Permissions on server-scoped securables can be granted only to server-level principals (SQL Server logins or Windows logins) and not to database-level principals such as users or database roles.

Since they are at the top of the permissions hierarchy, server permissions allow a grantee to perform activities such as creating databases, logins, or linked servers. Server permissions also give the grantee the ability to shut down the SQL Server instance (using SHUTDOWN) or use SQL Profiler (using the ALTER TRACE permission). When allocating permissions on a securable to a principal, the person doing the allocating is the *grantor,* and the principal receiving the permission is the *grantee.*

The abridged syntax for granting server permissions is as follows:

```
GRANT Permission [ ,...n ] TO grantee_principal [ ,...n ] [ WITH GRANT OPTION ]
[ AS grantor_principal ]
```

Table 30-3 describes the arguments of this command.

Table 30-3. *GRANT Arguments*

Argument	Description
Permission [,...n]	You can grant one or more server permissions in a single GRANT statement.
TO grantee_principal [,...n]	This is the grantee, also known as the principal (SQL Server login or logins), whom you are granting permissions to.
WITH GRANT OPTION	When designating this option, the grantee will then have permission to grant the permission(s) to other grantees.
AS grantor_principal	This optional clause specifies from where the grantor derives the right to grant the permission to the grantee.

To explicitly *deny* permissions on a securable to a server-level principal, use the DENY command. The syntax is as follows:

```
DENY  permission [ ,...n ]
TO grantee_principal [ ,...n ]
[  CASCADE ]
[  AS grantor_principal ] .
```

Table 30-4 describes the arguments of this command.

Table 30-4. *DENY Arguments*

Argument	Description
Permission [,...n]	This specifies one or more server-scoped permissions to deny.
grantee_principal [,...n]	This defines one or more logins (Windows or SQL) that you can deny permissions to.
CASCADE	When this option is designated, if the grantee principal granted any of these permissions to others, those grantees will also have their permissions denied.
AS grantor_principal	This optional clause specifies from where the grantor derives his right to deny the permission to the grantee.

To *revoke* permissions on a securable to a principal, use the REVOKE command. Revoking a permission means you'll neither be granting nor denying that permission; REVOKE *removes* the specified permission(s) that had previously been either granted or denied.

The syntax is as follows:

```
REVOKE [ GRANT OPTION FOR ] permission  [ ,...n ]
FROM < grantee_principal > [ ,...n ]
[ CASCADE ]
[ AS grantor_principal ] .
```

Table 30-5 describes the arguments of this command.

Table 30-5. *REVOKE Arguments*

Argument	Description
GRANT OPTION FOR	When specified, the right for the grantee to grant the permission to other grantees is revoked.
Permission [,...n]	This specifies one or more server-scoped permissions to revoke.
grantee_principal [,...n]	This defines one or more logins (Windows or SQL) to revoke permissions from.
CASCADE	When this option is designated, if the grantee principal granted any of these permissions to others, those grantees will also have their permissions revoked.
AS grantor_principal	This optional clause specifies from where the grantor derives the right to revoke the permission to the grantee.

The next set of recipes demonstrates some administrative tasks related to server-scoped securables.

30-2. Managing Server Permissions

Problem

You have a login in SQL Server to which you need to grant server-scoped permissions.

Solution

In the first example of this recipe, the SQL login Gargouilleis granted the ability to view session data from Extended Event sessions in order to monitor SQL Server activity. This permission is granted to a custom server role, as shown in Chapter 29. Keep in mind that permissions at the server scope can be granted only when the current database is the master, so we will start the batch by switching database context:

```
USE master;
GO
/*
-- Create recipe login if it doesn't exist
*/
IF NOT EXISTS (SELECT name FROM sys.server_principals
```

```
        WHERE name = 'Gargouille')
BEGIN
CREATE LOGIN [Gargouille]
    WITH PASSWORD=N'test!#l'
    , DEFAULT_DATABASE=[AdventureWorks2014]
    , CHECK_EXPIRATION=OFF, CHECK_POLICY=OFF;
END

--check for the server role
IF NOT EXISTS (SELECT name FROM sys.server_principals
    WHERE name = 'hdserverstate'
        AND type_desc = 'SERVER_ROLE')
BEGIN
    CREATE SERVER ROLE hdserverstate AUTHORIZATION securityadmin;
    GRANT VIEW SERVER STATE TO hdserverstate;
END

--check for the user
IF NOT EXISTS (SELECT mem.name AS MemberName
    FROM sys.server_role_members rm
        INNER JOIN sys.server_principals sp
            ON rm.role_principal_id = sp.principal_id
        LEFT OUTER JOIN sys.server_principals mem
            ON rm.member_principal_id = mem.principal_id
    WHERE sp.name = 'hdserverstate'
        AND sp.type_desc = 'SERVER_ROLE'
        AND mem.name = 'Gargouille')
BEGIN
    ALTER SERVER ROLE [hdserverstate] ADD MEMBER [Gargouille];
END
```

In this second example, the Windows login [PETITMOT\JeanLouis] (you will need to substitute this login for a login that exists on your system) is granted the permissions necessary to create and view databases on the SQL Server instance:

```
USE master; .
GO
GRANT CREATE ANY DATABASE, VIEW ANY DATABASE TO [PETITMOT\JeanLouis];
GO
```

In this next example, The Windows login [PETITMOT\JeanLouis] is denied the right to execute the SHUTDOWN command:

```
USE master;
GO
DENY SHUTDOWN TO [PETITMOT\JeanLouis];
GO
```

In the last example, the permission to use or view Extended Event session data is revoked from the hdserverstate custom server role, including any other grantees he may have given this permission to:

```
USE master;
GO
REVOKE VIEW SERVER STATE FROM hdserverstate
CASCADE;
GO.
```

How It Works

Permissions on server-scoped securables are granted using GRANT, denied with DENY, and removed with REVOKE. Using these commands, one or more permissions can be assigned in the same command, as well as allocated to one or more logins (Windows or SQL).

This recipe dealt with assigning permissions at the server scope, although you'll see in future recipes that the syntax for assigning database and schema permissions is very similar.

30-3. Querying Server-Level Permissions

Problem

You need to identify server-scoped permissions associated with a SQL login.

Solution

You can use the sys.server_permissions catalog view to identify permissions at the SQL instance level. In this recipe, we will query all permissions associated with a login named TestUser2. To start, we'll create the new login:

```
USE master;
GO
CREATE LOGIN TestUser2
WITH PASSWORD = 'abcdel111111!';
GO
```

Next, we'll grant a server-scoped permission and deny a server-scoped permission:

```
USE master;
GO
DENY SHUTDOWN TO TestUser2;
GRANT CREATE ANY DATABASE TO TestUser2;
GO
```

Querying sys.server_permissions and sys.server_principals returns all server-scoped permissions for the new login created earlier:

```
USE master;
GO
SELECT p.class_desc, p.permission_name, p.state_desc
    FROM sys.server_permissions p
    INNER JOIN sys.server_principals s
        ON p.grantee_principal_id = s.principal_id
    WHERE s.name = 'TestUser2';
GO
```

This query returns the following:

class_desc	permission_name	state_desc
SERVER	CONNECT SQL	GRANT
SERVER	CREATE ANY DATABASE	GRANT
SERVER	SHUTDOWN	DENY

Even though we explicitly executed only one GRANT and one DENY, just by virtue of creating the login, we have implicitly granted the new login CONNECT permissions to the SERVER scope.

How It Works

In this recipe, we queried sys.server_permissions and sys.server_principals in order to return the server-scoped permissions associated with the new login created. In the SELECT clause, we returned the class of the permission, the permission name, and the associated state of the permission:

```
SELECT p.class_desc, p.permission_name, p.state_desc
```

In the FROM clause, we joined the two catalog views by the grantee's principal ID. The grantee is the target recipient of granted or denied permissions:

```
FROM sys.server_permissions p
    INNER JOIN sys.server_principals s
        ON p.grantee_principal_id = s.principal_id
```

In the WHERE clause, we designated the name of the login for which we wanted to examine permissions:

```
WHERE s.name = 'TestUser2';
```

Database-Scoped Securables and Permissions

Database-level securables are unique to a specific database and include several SQL Server objects, such as roles, assemblies, cryptography objects (keys and certificates), Service Broker objects, full-text catalogs, database users, schemas, and more.

You can grant permissions on these securables to database principals (database users, roles). The abridged syntax for granting database permissions is as follows:

```
GRANT permission [ ,...n ]
TO database_principal [ ,...n ]
[ WITH GRANT OPTION ] [ AS database_principal ]
```

Table 30-6 describes the arguments of this command.

Table 30-6. *GRANT Arguments*

Argument	Description
permission [,...n]	This specifies one or more database permissions to be granted to the principal(s).
database_principal [,...n]	This defines the grantees to whom the permissions should be granted.
WITH GRANT OPTION	When designating this option, the grantee has permission to grant the permission(s) to other grantees.
AS database_principal	This optional clause specifies from where the grantor derives the right to grant the permission to the grantee. For example, if your current database user context does not have permission to GRANT a specific permission, but you have an IMPERSONATE permission on a database user that does, you can designate that user in the AS clause.

To *deny* database-scoped permissions to a grantee, the DENY command is used. The abridged syntax is as follows:

```
DENY permission [ ,...n ]
TO database_principal [ ,...n ] [ CASCADE ]
[ AS database_principal ]
```

Table 30-7 describes the arguments of this command.

Table 30-7. *DENY Arguments*

Argument	Description
permission [,...n]	This specifies one or more database-scoped permissions to deny.
< database_principal > [,...n]	This defines one or more database principals to deny permissions for.
CASCADE	When this option is designated, if the grantee principal granted any of these permissions to others, those grantees will also have their permissions denied.
AS database_principal	This optional clause specifies from where the grantor derives the right to deny the permission to the grantee.

To *revoke* database-scoped permissions to the grantee, the REVOKE command is used. The abridged syntax is as follows:

```
REVOKE permission [ ,...n ]
FROM < database_principal > [ ,...n ]
[ CASCADE ]
[ AS database_principal]
```

Table 30-8 describes the arguments of this command.

Table 30-8. *REVOKE Arguments*

Argument	Description
database_permission [,...n]	This specifies one or more database-scoped permissions to revoke.
< database_principal > [,...n]	This defines one or more database principals to revoke permissions from.
CASCADE	When this option is designated, if the grantee principal granted any of these permissions to others, those grantees will also have their permissions revoked.
AS database_principal	This optional clause specifies from where the grantor derives the right to revoke the permission to the grantee.

30-4. Managing Database Permissions

Problem

You need to alter database-scoped permissions for a database user.

Solution

You should use GRANT, DENY, and REVOKE to alter database-scoped permissions for a database user.

To begin this recipe, I'll set up the logins and users if they don't already exist or haven't already been created earlier in the chapter:

```
USE master;
GO
/*
-- Create DB for recipe if it doesn't exist
*/
IF NOT EXISTS (SELECT name FROM sys.databases WHERE name = 'TestDB')
BEGIN
CREATE DATABASE TestDB
END
GO
/*
Create recipe login if it doesn't exist
*/
```

```
IF NOT EXISTS (SELECT name FROM sys.server_principals WHERE name = 'Phantom')
BEGIN
CREATE LOGIN [Phantom]
    WITH PASSWORD=N'test!#23', DEFAULT_DATABASE=[TestDB], CHECK_EXPIRATION=OFF,
    CHECK_POLICY=OFF
END;
GO


USE TestDB;
GO
/*
-- Create db users if they don't already exist
*/
IF NOT EXISTS (SELECT name FROM sys.database_principals WHERE name = 'Gargouille')
BEGIN
CREATE USER Gargouille FROM LOGIN Gargouille
END;
GO
IF NOT EXISTS (SELECT name FROM sys.database_principals WHERE name = 'Phantom')
BEGIN
CREATE USER Phantom FROM LOGIN Phantom
END;
GO
```

This first example demonstrates granting database permissions to the Gargouille database user in the TestDB database:

```
USE TestDB;
GO
GRANT ALTER ANY ASSEMBLY, ALTER ANY CERTIFICATE TO Gargouille;
GO
```

This second example demonstrates denying permissions to the Phantom database user:

```
USE TestDB;
GO
DENY ALTER ANY DATABASE DDL TRIGGER TO Phantom;
GO
```

The last example demonstrates revoking database permissions to connect to the TestDB database from the Phantom user:

```
USE TestDB;
GO
REVOKE CONNECT FROM Phantom;
GO
```

How It Works

This recipe demonstrated how to grant, revoke, or deny database-scoped permissions to database principals. As you may have noticed, the syntax for granting database-scoped permissions is almost identical to server-scoped permissions. Schema-scoped permissions are also managed with the same commands, but with slight variations.

Before reviewing how to manage schema permissions, in this next recipe I'll demonstrate how to manage schemas in general.

30-5. Querying Database Permissions

Problem

You want to list the database-scoped permissions for a database user.

Solution

You can use the `sys.database_permissions` catalog view to identify permissions in a database. In this recipe, we will query all permissions associated with a user named `TestUser` in the `AdventureWorks2014` database. To start, we'll create the new login and user:

```
USE master;
GO
CREATE LOGIN TestUser WITH PASSWORD = 'abcdelllllll!'
USE AdventureWorks2014;
GO
CREATE USER TestUser FROM LOGIN TestUser;
GO
```

Next, we'll grant and deny various permissions:

```
USE AdventureWorks2014;
GO
GRANT SELECT ON HumanResources.Department TO TestUser;
DENY SELECT ON Production.ProductPhoto TO TestUser;
GRANT EXEC ON HumanResources.uspUpdateEmployeeHireInfo TO TestUser;
GRANT CREATE ASSEMBLY TO TestUser;
GRANT SELECT ON SCHEMA::Person TO TestUser;
DENY IMPERSONATE ON USER::dbo TO TestUser;
DENY SELECT ON HumanResources.Employee(BirthDate) TO TestUser;
GO
```

We'll now query the `sys.database_principals` to determine the identifier of the principal:

```
USE AdventureWorks2014;
GO
SELECT principal_id
FROM sys.database_principals
WHERE name = 'TestUser';
GO
```

This query returns the following results (if you are following along with this recipe, keep in mind that your principal identifier may be different):

```
principal_id
5
```

Now we can use the principal ID of 5 with the grantee principal ID in the `sys.database_permissions` table (I could have integrated the prior query into this next query, but I've separated them in order to give a clearer picture of what each catalog view does):

```
USE AdventureWorks2014;
GO
SELECT
    p.class_desc,
    p.permission_name,
    p.state_desc,
    ISNULL(o.type_desc,'') type_desc,
    CASE p.class_desc
    WHEN 'SCHEMA'
    THEN schema_name(major_id)
    WHEN 'OBJECT_OR_COLUMN'
    THEN CASE
        WHEN minor_id = 0
        THEN object_name(major_id)
        ELSE (SELECT
        object_name(object_id) + '.' + name
        FROM sys.columns
        WHERE object_id = p.major_id
        AND column_id = p.minor_id) END
    ELSE '' END AS object_name
FROM sys.database_permissions p
LEFT OUTER JOIN sys.objects o
    ON o.object_id = p.major_id
WHERE grantee_principal_id = 5;
GO
```

This query returns the following:

class_desc	permission_name	state_desc	type_desc	object_name
DATABASE	CONNECT	GRANT		
DATABASE	CREATE ASSEMBLY	GRANT		
OBJECT_OR_COLUMN	SELECT	GRANT	USER_TABLE	Department
OBJECT_OR_COLUMN	SELECT	DENY	USER_TABLE	Employee.BirthDate
OBJECT_OR_COLUMN	EXECUTE	GRANT	SQL_STORED_PROCEDURE	uspUpdateEmployeeHireInfo
OBJECT_OR_COLUMN	SELECT	DENY	USER_TABLE	ProductPhoto
SCHEMA	SELECT	GRANT		Person
DATABASE_PRINCIPAL	IMPERSONATE	DENY		

How It Works

This recipe demonstrated querying system catalog views to determine the permissions of a specific database user. We created the login and user and then granted and denied various permissions for it.

After that, we queried `sys.database_principals` to determine the ID of this new user.

Walking through the last and more complicated query in the recipe, the first few columns of the query displayed the class description, permission name, and state (for example, GRANT or DENY):

```
SELECT
p.class_desc,
p.permission_name,
p.state_desc,
```

The type description was actually taken from the `sys.objects` view, which was used to pull information regarding the object targeted for the permission. If it is NULL, we return no characters in the result set:

```
ISNULL(o.type_desc,'') type_desc,
```

The next expression was the CASE statement evaluating the class description. When the class is a schema, return the schema's name:

```
CASE p.class_desc WHEN 'SCHEMA'
THEN schema_name(major_id)
```

When the class is an object or column, nest another CASE statement:

```
WHEN 'OBJECT_OR_COLUMN' THEN CASE
```

If the minor ID is zero, we know that this is an object and not a column, so we return the object name:

```
WHEN minor_id = 0
THEN object_name(major_id)
```

Otherwise, we are dealing with a column name, so we perform a subquery to concatenate the object name with the name of the column:

```
ELSE (SELECT
object_name(object_id) + '.'+
name FROM sys.columns
WHERE object_id = p.major_id AND column_id = p.minor_id) END ELSE '' END AS object_name
```

We queried the permissions with a LEFT OUTER JOIN on `sys.objects`. We didn't use an INNER join because not all permissions are associated with objects—for example, the GRANT on the CREATE ASSEMBLY permission:

```
FROM sys.database_permissions p
LEFT OUTER JOIN sys.objects o
    ON o.object_id = p.major_id
```

Lastly, we qualified that the grantee has the ID of the user I created. The grantee is the recipient of the permissions. The sys.database_permissions also has the grantor_principal_id, which is the grantor of permissions for the specific row. I didn't want to designate this; rather, I just wanted the rows of permissions granted to the specified user.

```
WHERE grantee_principal_id = 5;
```

Schema-Scoped Securables and Permissions

Schema-scoped securables are contained within the database securable scope and include user-defined data types, XML schema collections, and objects. The object securable also has other securable object types within it, but I'll review this later in the chapter.

As of SQL Server 2005, users are separated from direct ownership of a database object (such as tables, views, and stored procedures). This separation is achieved by the use of schemas, which are basically containers for database objects. Instead of having a direct object owner, the object is contained within a schema, and that schema is then owned by a user.

One or more users can own a schema or use it as their default schema for creating objects. What's more, you can apply security at the schema level. This means any objects within the schema can be managed as a unit, instead of at the individual object level.

Every database comes with a dbo schema, which is where your objects go if you don't specify a default schema. But if you want to create your own schemas, you can use the CREATE SCHEMA command.

The abridged syntax is as follows:

```
CREATE SCHEMA schema_name [AUTHORIZATION owner_name ]
```

Table 30-9 describes the arguments of this command.

Table 30-9. CREATE SCHEMA Arguments

Argument	Description
schema_name	This is the name of the schema and the schema owner.
owner_name	The owner is a database principal that can own one or more schemas in the database.

To remove an existing schema, use the DROP SCHEMA command. The syntax is as follows:

```
DROP SCHEMA schema_name
```

The command takes only a single argument: the name of the schema to drop from the database. Also, you can't drop a schema that contains objects, so the objects must be either dropped or transferred to a new schema.

■ **Note**   See Recipe 30-6 for a review of using ALTER SCHEMA to transfer schema ownership of an object.

Like with server- and database-scoped permissions, permissions for schemas are managed using the GRANT, DENY, and REVOKE commands.

The abridged syntax for granting permissions on a schema is as follows:

```
GRANT permission [ ,...n ] ON SCHEMA :: schema_name
TO database_principal [ ,...n]
[ WITH GRANT OPTION ][ AS granting_principal ]
```

Table 30-10 describes the arguments of this command.

Table 30-10. *GRANT Arguments*

Argument	Description
Permission [,...n]	This specifies one or more schema permissions to be granted to the grantee.
schema_name	This defines the name of the schema the grantee is receiving permissions to.
database_principal	This specifies the database principal permissions recipient.
WITH GRANT OPTION	When designating this option, the grantee has permissions to grant the schema permission(s) to other grantees.
AS granting_principal	This optional clause specifies from where the grantor derives the right to grant the schema-scoped permission to the grantee.

To deny schema-scoped permissions to a grantee, the DENY command is used. The abridged syntax is as follows:

```
DENY permission [ ,...n ] ON SCHEMA :: schema_name TO database_principal [ ,...n ]
[ CASCADE ]
[ AS denying_principal ]
```

Table 30-11 describes the arguments of this command.

Table 30-11. *DENY Arguments*

Argument	Description
Permission [,...n]	This specifies one or more schema-scoped permissions to deny.
schema_name	This defines the name of the schema where permissions will be denied.
database_principal [,...n]	This specifies one or more database principals to deny permissions for.
CASCADE	When this option is designated, if the grantee principal granted any of these permissions to others, those grantees will also have their permissions denied.
AS denying_principal	This optional clause specifies from where the grantor derives the right to deny the permission to the grantee.

To revoke schema-scoped permissions from the grantee, the REVOKE command is used. The abridged syntax is as follows:

```
REVOKE [ GRANT OPTION FOR ]
permission  [ ,...n ]
  ON SCHEMA :: schema_name
{  TO | FROM } database_principal [ ,...n ]
  [  CASCADE ] [ AS principal ]
```

Table 30-12 describes the arguments of this command.

Table 30-12. REVOKE Arguments

Argument	Description
Permission [,...n]	This specifies one or more schema-scoped permissions to revoke.
schema_name	This defines the name of the schema for which the permissions will be revoked.
database_principal[,...n]	This specifies one or more database principals to revoke permissions for.
CASCADE	When this option is designated, if the grantee principal granted any of these permissions to others, those grantees will also have their permissions revoked.
AS principal	This optional clause specifies from where the grantor derives the right to revoke the permission to the grantee.

30-6. Managing Schemas

Problem

A new project is starting. Many new objects are to be created for this project. Prior to creating those objects, you need to create a schema that will own the new objects. You will also need to associate a user with this new schema.

Solution

You should use the CREATE SCHEMA command to create a new schema. When associating a user to a schema, you should use the ALTER USER command.

In this recipe, we'll create a new schema in the TestDB database called Publishers:

```
USE TestDB;
GO
CREATE SCHEMA Publishers AUTHORIZATION db_owner;
GO
```

We now have a schema called Publishers, which can be used to contain other database objects. It can be used to hold all objects related to publication functionality, for example, or be used to hold objects for database users associated to publication activities.

To start using the new schema, we use the schema.object_name two-part naming format:

```
USE TestDB;
GO
CREATE TABLE Publishers.ISBN (ISBN char(13) NOT NULL PRIMARY KEY, CreateDT datetime NOT NULL
DEFAULT GETDATE());
GO
```

This next example demonstrates making the Publishers schema a database user's default schema. For this example, we'll create a new SQL login in the master database:

```
USE master
GO
CREATE LOGIN Rossignol
WITH PASSWORD=N'test123',
DEFAULT_DATABASE=TestDB,
CHECK_EXPIRATION=OFF,
CHECK_POLICY=OFF;
GO
```

Next, we'll create a new database user in the TestDB database:

```
USE TestDB;
GO
CREATE USER Rossignol FOR LOGIN Rossignol;
GO
```

Now we'll change the default schema of the existing database user to the Publishers schema. Any objects this database user creates by default will belong to this schema (unless the database user explicitly uses a different schema in the object creation statement):

```
USE TestDB;
GO
ALTER USER Rossignol WITH DEFAULT_SCHEMA=Publishers;
GO
```

Chapter 31 reviews how to transfer the ownership of an object from one schema to another using ALTER SCHEMA. You'll need to use this in situations where you want to drop a schema. For example, if I tried to drop the Publishers schema right now, with the Publishers.ISBN table still in it, I would get an error warning me that there are objects referencing that schema. This example demonstrates using ALTER SCHEMA. to transfer the table to the dbo schema prior to dropping the Publishers schema from the database:

```
USE TestDB;
GO
ALTER SCHEMA dbo TRANSFER Publishers.ISBN;
GO
DROP SCHEMA Publishers;
GO
```

How It Works

Schemas act as a container for database objects. Unlike when a database user owns objects directly, a database user now can own a schema (or, in other words, have permissions to use the objects within it).

In this recipe, CREATE SCHEMA was used to create a new schema called Publishers. A new table was created in the new schema called Publishers.ISBN. After that, a new login and database user were created for the TestDB database. ALTER USER was used to make that new schema the default schema for the new user.

Since a schema cannot be dropped until all objects are dropped or transferred from it, ALTER SCHEMA was used to transfer Publishers.ISBN into the dbo schema. DROP SCHEMA was used to remove the Publishers schema from the database.

30-7. Managing Schema Permissions

Problem

A new user in your environment needs to be granted certain permissions on a schema that owns several objects.

Solution

You need to use the GRANT, DENY, and REVOKE commands using the ON SCHEMA option.

In this next set of examples, I'll show you how to manage schema permissions. Before showing you this, though, I would like to quickly point out how you can identify which schemas exist for a particular database. To view the schemas for a database, you can query the sys.schemas system catalog view. This example demonstrates listing the schemas that exist within the AdventureWorks2014 database:

```
USE AdventureWorks2014;
GO
SELECT s.name SchemaName, d.name SchemaOwnerName
FROM sys.schemas s
INNER JOIN sys.database_principals d
ON s.principal_id= d.principal_id
ORDER BY s.name;
GO
```

This returns a list of built-in database schemas (the fixed database roles dbo, guest, sys, and INFORMATION_SCHEMA) along with user-defined schemas (Person, Production, Purchasing, Sales, HumanResources).

SchemaName	SchemaOwnerName
db_accessadmin	db_accessadmin
db_backupoperator	db_backupoperator
db_datareader	db_datareader
db_datawriter	db_datawriter
db_ddladmin	db_ddladmin

(*continued*)

SchemaName	SchemaOwnerName
db_denydatareader	db_denydatareader
db_denydatawriter	db_denydatawriter
db_owner	db_owner
db_securityadmin	db_securityadmin
dbo	dbo
guest	guest
HumanResources	dbo
INFORMATION_SCHEMA	INFORMATION_SCHEMA
Person	dbo
Production	dbo
Purchasing	dbo
Sales	dbo
sys	sys

Within the AdventureWorks2014 database, I'll now demonstrate assigning permissions on schemas to database principals. In this example, the database user TestUser is granted TAKE OWNERSHIP permissions to the Person schema, which enables the grantee to take ownership of a granted securable:

```
USE AdventureWorks2014; .
GO
GRANT TAKE OWNERSHIP ON SCHEMA ::Person TO TestUser;
GO
```

In the next example, we'll grant the database user TestUser multiple permissions in the same statement, including the ability to ALTER a schema, EXECUTE stored procedures within the Production schema, or SELECT from tables or views in the schema. Using the WITH GRANT OPTION, TestUser can also grant other database principals these permissions:

```
USE AdventureWorks2014;
GO
GRANT ALTER, EXECUTE, SELECT ON SCHEMA ::Production TO TestUser
WITH GRANT OPTION;
GO
```

In this next example, the database user TestUser is denied the ability to INSERT, UPDATE, or DELETE data from any tables within the Production schema:

```
USE AdventureWorks2014;
GO
DENY INSERT, UPDATE, DELETE ON SCHEMA ::Production TO TestUser;
GO
```

In the last example of this recipe, TestUser's right to ALTER the Production schema or SELECT from objects within the Production schema is revoked, along with the permissions she may have granted to others (using CASCADE):

```
USE AdventureWorks2014;
GO
REVOKE ALTER, SELECT ON SCHEMA ::Production TO TestUser CASCADE;
GO.
```

How It Works

Granting, denying, or revoking permissions occurs with the same commands that are used with database- and server-scoped permissions. One difference, however, is the reference to ON SCHEMA, where a specific schema name is the target of granted, denied, or revoked permissions. Notice, also, that the name of the schema was prefixed with two colons (called a *scope qualifier*). A scope qualifier is used to scope permissions to a specific object type.

Object Permissions

Objects are nested within the schema scope, and they can include tables, views, stored procedures, functions, and aggregates. Defining permissions at the schema scope (such as SELECT or EXECUTE) can allow you to define permissions for a grantee on all objects within a schema. You can also define permissions at the object level. Object permissions are nested within schema permissions, schema permissions within database-scoped permissions, and database-scoped permissions within server-level permissions.

The abridged syntax for granting object permissions is as follows:

```
GRANT permission ON
[ OBJECT :: ][ schema_name ]. object_name [ ( column [ ,...n ] ) ]
TO <database_principal> [ ,...n ]
[ WITH GRANT OPTION ] [ AS database_principal ]
```

Table 30-13 shows the arguments of this command.

Table 30-13. GRANT Arguments

Argument	Description
permission [,...n]	This specifies one or more object permissions to be granted to the grantee.
[OBJECT ::][schema_name]. object_name [(column [,...n])]	This defines the target object (and if applicable, columns) for which the permission is being granted.
database_principal	This specifies the database principal that is the permissions recipient.
WITH GRANT OPTION	When designating this option, the grantee has permission to grant the permission(s) to other grantees.
AS database_principal	This optional clause specifies from where the grantor derives the right to grant the permission to the grantee.

To deny object permissions to a grantee, the DENY command is used. The abridged syntax is as follows:

```
DENY permission [ ,...n ] ON
[ OBJECT :: ][ schema_name ]. object_name [ ( column [ ,...n ] ) ] TO <database_principal> [
,...n ] [ CASCADE ] [ AS <database_principal> ]
```

Table 30-14 describes the arguments of this command.

Table 30-14. *DENY Arguments*

Argument	Description
[OBJECT ::][schema_name]. object_name [(column [,...n])]	This specifies the target object (and if applicable, columns) for which the permission is being denied.
< database_principal > [,...n]	This specifies one or more database principals for whom permissions will be denied.
CASCADE	When this option is designated, if the grantee principal granted any of these permissions to others, those grantees will also have their permissions denied.
AS database_principal	This optional clause specifies from where the grantor derives the right to deny the permission to the grantee.

To revoke object permissions to the grantee, the REVOKE command is used. The abridged syntax is as follows:

```
REVOKE [ GRANT OPTION FOR ] permission [ ,...n ]
ON [ OBJECT :: ][ schema_name ]. objectjame [ ( column [ ,...n ] ) ] FROM <database_
principal> [ ,...n ] [ CASCADE ] [ AS <database_principal> ]
```

Table 30-15 describes the arguments of this command.

Table 30-15. *REVOKE Arguments*

Argument	Description
GRANT OPTION FOR	When this option is used, the right to grant the permission to other database principals is revoked.
permission [,...n]	This specifies one or more object permissions to be revoked from the grantee.
[OBJECT ::][schema_name]. object_name [(column [,...n])]	This defines the target object (and if applicable, columns) for which the permission is being revoked.
< database_principal > [,...n]	This specifies one or more database principals to revoke permissions from.
CASCADE	When this option is designated, if the grantee principal granted any of these permissions to others, those grantees will also have their permissions revoked.
AS database_principal	This optional clause specifies from where the grantor derives the right to revoke the permission to the grantee.

30-8. Managing Object Permissions

Problem

After having defined permissions at the schema scope, you have determined that you need to define additional permissions for a specific set of tables.

Solution

Like server-level, database-scoped, and schema-scoped permissions, you can use GRANT, DENY, and REVOKE to define permissions on specific database objects

In this recipe, we grant the database user TestUser the permission to SELECT, INSERT, DELETE, and UPDATE data in the HumanResources.Department table:

```
USE AdventureWorks2014;
GO
GRANT DELETE, INSERT, SELECT, UPDATE ON HumanResources.Department TO TestUser;
GO
```

Here, the database role called ReportViewers is granted the ability to execute a procedure, as well as to view metadata regarding that specific object in the system catalog views:

```
USE AdventureWorks2014;
GO
CREATE ROLE ReportViewers
GRANT EXECUTE, VIEW DEFINITION ON dbo.uspGetManagerEmployees TO ReportViewers;
GO
```

In this next example, ALTER permission is denied to the database user TestUser for the HumanResources.Department table:

```
USE AdventureWorks2014;
GO
DENY ALTER ON HumanResources.Department TO TestUser;
GO
```

In this last example, INSERT, UPDATE, and DELETE permissions are revoked from TestUser on the HumanResources.Department table:

```
USE AdventureWorks2014;
GO
REVOKE INSERT, UPDATE, DELETE ON HumanResources.Department TO TestUser;
GO
```

How It Works

This recipe demonstrated granting object permissions to specific database securables. Object permissions are granted by designating the specific object name and the permissions that are applicable to that object. For example, EXECUTE permissions can be granted to a stored procedure, but not SELECT permissions.

Permissions can be superseded by other types of permissions. For example, if the database user TestUser has been granted SELECT permissions on the HumanResources.Department table but has been denied permissions on the HumanResources schema itself, TestUser will receive the following error message when attempting to SELECT from that table, because the DENY overrides any GRANT SELECT permissions.

```
Msg 229, Level 14, State 5, Line 2
SELECT permission denied on object 'Department', database 'AdventureWorks2014', schema
'HumanResources'.
```

Managing Permissions Across Securable Scopes

Now that I've reviewed the various securable scopes and the methods by which permissions can be granted to principals, in the next set of recipes I'll show you how to report and manage the permissions a principal has on securables across the different scopes.

30-9. Determining Permissions to a Securable

Problem

You want to see the permissions your connection has on a securable.

Solution

With SQL Server's nested hierarchy of securable permissions (server, database, and schema), permissions can be inherited by higher-level scopes. Figuring out what permissions your current login/database connection has to a securable can become tricky, especially when you add server or database roles to the equation.

Understanding what permissions your database connection has to a securable can be determined by using the HAS_PERMS_BY_NAME function. This system scalar function returns a 1 if the current user has been granted permissions to the securable and returns 0 if not.

The syntax for this function is as follows:

```
HAS_PERMS_BY_NAME ( securable , securable_class , permission [ , sub-securable ]
[ , sub-securable_class ] )
```

Table 30-16 describes the arguments for this function.

Table 30-16. Has_perms_by_name Arguments

Parameter	Description
securable	The name of the securable that you want to verify permissions for
securable_class	The name of the securable class you want to check. Class names (for example, DATABASE or SCHEMA) can be retrieved from the class_desc column in the sys.fn_builtin_permissions function.
permission	The name of the permission to check
sub-securable	The name of the securable subentity
sub-securable_class	The name of the securable subentity class

This example demonstrates how to check whether the current connected user has permissions to ALTER the AdventureWorks2014 database:

```
EXECUTE AS LOGIN ='testuser';

USE AdventureWorks2014;
GO
SELECT HAS_PERMS_BY_NAME ('AdventureWorks2014', 'DATABASE', 'ALTER');
GO

REVERT
```

This returns 0 if the connection is established using the login TestUser. This means the current connection *does not have* permission to ALTER the AdventureWorks2014 database.

```
0
```

This next query tests the current connection to see whether the Person.Address table can be updated or selected from by the current connection:

```
USE AdventureWorks2014;
GO
SELECT UpdateTable = CASE HAS_PERMS_BY_NAME ('Person.Address', 'OBJECT', 'UPDATE') WHEN 1
THEN 'Yes' ELSE 'No' END ,
SelectFromTable = CASE HAS_PERMS_BY_NAME ('Person.Address', 'OBJECT', 'SELECT') WHEN 1 THEN
'Yes' ELSE 'No' END;
GO:
```

This query returns the following when the connection is established by the TestUser login.

UpdateTable	SelectFromTable
No	Yes

How It Works

The HAS_PERMS_BY_NAME system function evaluates whether the current connection has granted permissions to access a specific securable (granted permissions either explicitly or inherently through a higher-scoped securable). In both examples in this recipe, the first parameter used was the securable name (the database name or table name). The second parameter was the securable class, for example, OBJECT or DATABASE. The third parameter used was the actual permission to be validated, for example, ALTER, UPDATE, or SELECT (depending on which permissions are applicable to the securable being checked).

30-10. Reporting Permissions by Securable Scope

Problem

You want to provide a list of all permissions for the currently connected user.

Solution

You can report on all permissions for the currently connected user by using the fn_my_permissions function.

In this recipe, I'll demonstrate using the fn_my_permissions function to return the assigned permissions for the currently connected principal. The syntax for this function is as follows:

```
fn_my_permissions ( securable , 'securable_class')
```

Table 30-17 describes the arguments for this command.

Table 30-17. fn_my_permissions Arguments

Argument	Description
securable	The name of the securable to verify. Use NULL if you are checking permissions for the server or database scope.
securable_class	The securable class that you are listing permissions for.

In this first example, I demonstrate how to check the server-scoped permissions for the current connection:

```
USE master;
GO
SELECT permission_name
FROM sys.fn_my_permissions(NULL, N'SERVER')
ORDER BY permission_name;
GO
```

This returns the following results (this query example was executed under the context of sysadmin, so in this case, all available server-scoped permissions are returned).

```
ADMINISTER BULK OPERATIONS
ALTER ANY CONNECTION
ALTER ANY CREDENTIAL
ALTER ANY DATABASE
ALTER ANY ENDPOINT
ALTER ANY EVENT NOTIFICATION
ALTER ANY LINKED SERVER
ALTER ANY LOGIN
ALTER RESOURCES
ALTER SERVER STATE
ALTER SETTINGS
ALTER TRACE
AUTHENTICATE SERVER
CONNECT SQL
CONTROL SERVER
CREATE ANY DATABASE
CREATE DDL EVENT NOTIFICATION
CREATE ENDPOINT
CREATE TRACE EVENT NOTIFICATION
EXTERNAL ACCESS ASSEMBLY
SHUTDOWN
UNSAFE ASSEMBLY
VIEW ANY DATABASE
VIEW ANY DEFINITION
VIEW SERVER STATE
```

If you have IMPERSONATE permissions on the login or database user, you can also check the permissions of another principal other than your own by using the EXECUTE AS command. Chapter 18 demonstrated how to use EXECUTE AS to specify a stored procedure's security context. You can also use EXECUTE AS in a stand-alone fashion, using it to switch the security context of the current database session. You can then switch back to your original security context by issuing the REVERT command.

The simplified syntax for EXECUTE AS is as follows:

```
EXECUTE AS { LOGIN | USER } = 'name' [ WITH { NO REVERT } ]
```

Table 30-18 describes the arguments of this command.

Table 30-18. EXECUTE AS Abridged Syntax Arguments

Argument	Description
{ LOGIN | USER } = 'name'	Select LOGIN to impersonate a SQL or Windows login or USER to impersonate a database user. The name value is the actual login or user name.
NO REVERT	If NO REVERT is designated, you cannot use the REVERT command to switch back to your original security context.

To demonstrate the power of EXECUTE AS, the previous query is reexecuted, this time by using the security context of the Gargouille login:

```
USE master;
GO
EXECUTE AS LOGIN = N'Gargouille';
GO
SELECT permission_name
FROM sys.fn_my_permissions(NULL, N'SERVER')
ORDER BY permission_name;
GO
REVERT;
GO
```

This returns a much smaller list of server permissions, because you are no longer executing the call under a login with sysadmin permissions.

```
CONNECT SQL
VIEW ANY DATABASE
VIEW SERVER STATE
```

This next example demonstrates returning database-scoped permissions for the Gargouille database user:

```
USE TestDB;
GO
EXECUTE AS USER = N'Gargouille';
GO
SELECT permission_name
FROM sys.fn_my_permissions(N'TestDB', N'DATABASE')
ORDER BY permission_name;
GO
REVERT;
GO
```

This query returns the following:

```
ALTER ANY ASSEMBLY
ALTER ANY CERTIFICATE
CONNECT
CREATE ASSEMBLY
CREATE CERTIFICATE
SELECT
```

In this next example, permissions are checked for the current connection on the Production.Culture table, this time showing any subentities of the table (meaning any explicit permissions on table columns):

```
USE AdventureWorks2014;
GO
SELECT subentity_name, permission_name
FROM sys.fn_my_permissions(N'Production.Culture', N'OBJECT')
ORDER BY permission_name, subentity_name;
GO
```

This returns the following results (when the subentity_name is populated, this is a column reference):

subentity_name	permission_name
	ALTER
	CONTROL
	DELETE
	EXECUTE
	INSERT
	RECEIVE
	REFERENCES
CultureID	REFERENCES
ModifiedDate	REFERENCES
Name	REFERENCES
	SELECT
CultureID	SELECT
ModifiedDate	SELECT
Name	SELECT
	TAKE OWNERSHIP
	UPDATE
CultureID	UPDATE
ModifiedDate	UPDATE
Name	UPDATE
	VIEW CHANGE TRACKING
	VIEW DEFINITION

How It Works

This recipe demonstrated how to return permissions for the current connection using the fn_my_permissions function. The first example used a NULL in the first parameter and SERVER in the second parameter in order to return the server-scoped permissions of the current connection:

```
FROM sys. fn_my_permissions(NULL, N'SERVER')
```

We then used EXECUTE AS to execute the same query, this time under the Gargouille login's context, which returned server-scoped permissions for his login:

```
EXECUTE AS LOGIN = N'Gargouille';
GO
REVERT;
GO
```

The next example showed database-scoped permissions by designating the database name in the first parameter and DATABASE in the second parameter:

```
FROM sys.fn_my_permissions(N'TestDB', N'DATABASE')
```

The last example checked the current connection's permissions to a specific table:

```
FROM sys.fn_my_permissions(N'Production.Culture', N'OBJECT')
```

This returned information at the table level *and* column level. For example, the ALTER and CONTROL permissions applied to the table level, while those rows with a populated entity_name (for example, CultureID and ModifiedDate) refer to permissions at the table's column level.

30-11. Changing Securable Ownership

Problem

A database user needs to be removed. The database user owns objects within the database. You need to change the owner of the objects that are owned by this user in order to remove the user from the database.

Solution

As described earlier in the chapter, objects are contained within schemas, and schemas are then owned by a database user or role. Changing a schema's owner does not require the objects to be renamed. Aside from schemas, however, other securables on a SQL Server instance still do have direct ownership by either a server- or database-level principal.

For example, schemas have database principal owners (such as database user), and endpoints have server-level owners, such as a SQL login.

Assuming that the login performing the operation has the appropriate TAKE OWNERSHIP permission, you can use the ALTER AUTHORIZATION command to change the owner of a securable.

The abridged syntax for ALTER AUTHORIZATION is as follows:

```
ALTER AUTHORIZATION
ON [ <entity_type> :: ] entity_name
TO { SCHEMA OWNER | principal_name }
```

Table 30-19 describes the arguments for this command.

Table 30-19. ALTER AUTHORIZATION *Arguments*

Argument	Description
entity_type	This designates the class of securable being given a new owner.
entity_name	This specifies the name of the securable.
SCHEMA OWNER | principal_name	This indicates the name of the new schema owner or the name of the database or server principal taking ownership of the securable.

In this example, the owner of the HumanResources schema is changed to the database user TestUser:

```
USE AdventureWorks2014;
GO
ALTER AUTHORIZATION ON Schema::HumanResources TO TestUser;
GO.
```

In this second example, the owner of an endpoint is changed to a SQL login. Before doing so, the existing owner of the endpoint is verified using the sys.endpoints and sys.server_principals system catalog views:

```
/* In case an endpoint does not exist let's create one */
CREATE ENDPOINT ProductMirror
    STATE = STOPPED
    AS TCP ( LISTENER_PORT = 7022 )
    FOR DATABASE_MIRRORING (ROLE=PARTNER);
/* In 2014, only the following endpoints are available
TSQL | SERVICE_BROKER | DATABASE_MIRRORING
*/

USE AdventureWorks2014;
GO
SELECT p.name OwnerName
FROM sys.endpoints e
INNER JOIN sys.server_principals p
ON e.principal_id = p.principal_id
WHERE e.name = 'ProductMirror';
GO
```

This query returns the following (your results will vary).

```
OwnerName
PETITMOT\Owner
```

Next, the owner is changed to a different SQL login:

```
USE AdventureWorks2014;
GO
ALTER AUTHORIZATION ON ENDPOINT::ProductMirror TO TestUser;
GO
```

By reexecuting the query against sys.server_principals and sys.endpoints, the new owner is displayed.

```
OwnerName
TestUser
```

■ **Note** If the ProductMirror endpoint does not exist and you attempt to change the owner to TestUser as done in this recipe, you will receive the following error:

Cannot find the endpoint 'ProductMirror', because it does not exist or you do not have permission.

How It Works

This recipe demonstrated how to change object ownership. You may want to change ownership when a login or database user needs to be removed. If that login or database user owns securables, you can use ALTER AUTHORIZATION to change that securables owner prior to dropping the SQL login or database user.

In this recipe, ALTER AUTHORIZATION was used to change the owner of a schema to a different database user and the owner of an endpoint to a different SQL login (associated to a Windows account). In both cases, the securable name was prefixed by the :: scope qualifier, which designates the type of object you are changing ownership of.

30-12. Allowing Access to Non-SQL Server Resources

Problem

You have a SQL login that must have access to a share on the operating system.

Solution

In this chapter, I've discussed permissions and securables within a SQL Server instance; however, sometimes a SQL login (not associated with a Windows user or group) may need permissions outside of the SQL Server instance. A Windows principal (a Windows user or group) has implied permissions outside of the SQL Server instance, but a SQL login does not, because a SQL login and password are created inside SQL Server. To address this, you can bind a SQL login to a Windows credential, giving the SQL login the implied Windows permissions of that credential. This SQL login can then use more advanced SQL Server functionality, where outside resource access may be required. This credential can be bound to more than one SQL login (although one SQL login can be bound only to a single credential).

To create a credential, use the CREATE CREDENTIAL command.

The syntax is as follows:

```
CREATE CREDENTIAL credential_name WITH IDENTITY = ' identity_name '
[ , SECRET = ' secret ' ] [ FOR CRYPTOGRAPHIC_PROVIDER cryptographic_provider_name ]
```

Table 30-20 describes the arguments for this command.

Table 30-20. *CREATE CREDENTIAL Arguments*

Argument	Description
credential_name	The name of the new credential
identity_name	The external account name (a Windows user, for example)
secret	The credential's password
cryptographic_provider_name	The name of the Enterprise Key Management (EKM) provider (used when associating an EKM provider with a credential)

In this example, a new credential is created that is mapped to the PETITMOT\Owner Windows user account:

```
USE master;
GO
CREATE CREDENTIAL AccountingGroup
WITH IDENTITY = N'PETITMOT\AccountUser',
SECRET = N'mypassword!';
GO
```

Once created, the credential can be bound to existing or new SQL logins using the CREDENTIAL keyword in CREATE LOGIN and ALTER LOGIN:

```
USE master;
GO
ALTER LOGIN Gargouille
WITH CREDENTIAL = AccountingGroup;
GO.
```

How It Works

A credential allows SQL authentication logins to be bound to Windows external permissions. In this recipe, a new credential was created called AccountingGroup. It was mapped to the Windows user PETITMOT\AccountUser and given a password in the SECRET argument of the command. Once created, the credential was bound to the SQL login Gargouille by using ALTER LOGIN and WITH CREDENTIAL. Now the Gargouille login, using credentials, has outside–SQL Server permissions equivalent to those of the PETITMOT\AccountUser Windows account.

Auditing Activity of Principals Against Securables

SQL Server Enterprise Edition offers the native capability to audit SQL Server instance- and database-scoped activity. This activity is captured to a target data destination using a *Server Audit* object, which defines whether the audit data is captured to a file, to the Windows Application event log, or to the Windows Security event log. A Server Audit object also allows you to designate whether the SQL Server instance should be shut down if it is unable to write to the target. Once a Server Audit object is created, you can bind a Server Audit Specification or Database Audit Specification object to it. A *Server Audit Specification* is used to define which events you want to capture at the SQL Server instance scope. A *Database Audit Specification* object allows you to define which events you want to capture at the database scope. Only one Server Audit Specification can be bound to a Server Audit object, whereas one or more Database Audit Specifications can be bound to a Server Audit object. A single Server Audit object can be collocated with a Server Audit Specification and one or more Database Audit Specifications.

In the next few recipes, I will demonstrate how to create a Server Audit object that writes event-captured data to a target file. I will then demonstrate how to associate SQL instance-level and database-scoped events with the audit file, and I'll demonstrate how to read the audit data contained in the binary file.

30-13. Defining Audit Data Sources

Problem

A new requirement from the security department will require that auditing be enabled on SQL Server. Knowing that auditing will be required and that more-specific requirements are forthcoming, you want to start setting up auditing while waiting for these requirements.

Solution

The first step in configuring auditing for SQL Server Enterprise Edition is to create a Server Audit object. This is done by using the CREATE SERVER AUDIT command. The syntax for this command is as follows:

```
CREATE SERVER AUDIT audit_name
    TO { [ FILE (<file_options> [, ...n]) ] | APPLICATION_LOG | SECURITY_LOG }
    [  WITH ( <audit_options> [, ...n] ) ]
    [ WHERE <predicate_expression> ]
}
[ ; ]
<file_options>::=
{
    FILEPATH = 'os_file_path'
    [, MAXSIZE = { max_size { MB | GB | TB } | UNLIMITED } ]
    [,  MAX_ROLLOVER_FILES = integer]
    [, RESERVE_DISK_SPACE = { ON | OFF } ]
}

<audit_options>::=
{
    [    QUEUE_DELAY = integer ]
    [, ON_FAILURE = CONTINUE | SHUTDOWN ]
    [,  AUDIT_GUID = uniqueidentifier ]
}
```

```
<predicate_expression>::=
{
    [NOT ] <predicate_factor>
    [ { AND | OR } [NOT ] { <predicate_factor> } ]
    [,...n ]
}

<predicate_factor>::=
    event_field_name { = | < > | ! = | > | > = | < | < = } { number | ' string ' }
```

Table 30-21 describes the arguments for this command.

Table 30-21. *CREATE SERVER AUDIT Arguments*

Argument	Description
audit_name	This specifies the user-defined name of the Server Audit object.
FILE (<file_options> [, ...n])] |	This designates that the Server Audit object will write events to a file.
APPLICATION_LOG	This designates that the Server Audit object will write events to the Windows Application event log.
SECURITY_LOG	This designates that the Server Audit object will write events to the Windows Security event log.
FILEPATH	If FILE was chosen, this designates the OS file path of the audit log.
MAXSIZE	If FILE was chosen, this argument defines the maximum size in megabytes, gigabytes, or terabytes. UNLIMITED can also be designated.
MAX_FILES	When specified, rollover to first file does not occur and, instead, any new events generated will fail with an error.
MAX_ROLLOVER_FILES	If FILE was chosen, this designates the maximum number of files to be retained on the file system. When 0 is designated, no limit is enforced.
RESERVE_DISK_SPACE	This argument takes a value of either ON or OFF. When enabled, this option reserves the disk space designated in MAXSIZE.
QUEUE_DELAY	This value designates the milliseconds that can elapse before audit actions are processed. The minimum and default value is 1,000 milliseconds.
ON_FAILURE	This argument takes a value of either CONTINUE or SHUTDOWN. If SHUTDOWN is designated, the SQL instance will be shut down if the target can't be written to. FAIL_OPERATION will cause the actions that triggered an audited event to fail while other actions are able to continue.

(continued)

Table 30-21. (*continued*)

Argument	Description
AUDIT_GUID	This option takes the unique identifier of a Server Audit object. If you restore a database that contains a Database Audit Specification, this object will be orphaned on the new SQL instance unless the original Server Audit object is recreated with the matching GUID.
predicate_expression	New to SQL Server 2012, this option is used to determine whether an event should be processed. This expression has a maximum size of 3,000 characters.
event_field_name	Name of the field that you want to filter as the predicate source.
number	Any numeric type; limited only by physical memory and any number too large for a 64-bit integer
'string'	ANSI or Unicode string used by the predicate compare. Implicit conversions are not permitted. Passing the wrong type will result in an error.

In this recipe, we will create a new Server Audit object that will be configured to write to a local file directory. The maximum size we'll designate per log will be 500MB, with a maximum number of 10 rollover files. We won't reserve disk space, and the queue delay will be 1 second (1,000 milliseconds). If there is a failure for the audit to write, we will not shut down the SQL Server instance:

```
USE master;
GO
CREATE SERVER AUDIT TroisMots_Server_Audit TO FILE
( FILEPATH = 'C:\Apress\',
MAXSIZE = 500 MB,
MAX_ROLLOVER_FILES = 10,
RESERVE_DISK_SPACE = OFF) WITH ( QUEUE_DELAY = 1000,
ON_FAILURE = CONTINUE);
GO
```

To validate the configurations of the new Server Audit object, we can check the sys.server_audits catalog view:

```
USE master;
GO
SELECT sa.audit_id,sa.type_desc,sa.on_failure_desc
    ,sa.queue_delay,sa.is_state_enabled
        ,sfa.log_file_path
```

```
FROM sys.server_audits sa
        INNER JOIN sys.server_file_audits sfa
            ON sa.audit_guid = sfa.audit_guid
        WHERE sa.name = 'TroisMots_Server_Audit'
GO
```

This query returns the following:

audit_id	type_desc	on_failure_desc	queue_delay	is_state_enabled	Log_file_path
65536	FILE	CONTINUE	1000	0	C:\Apress\

As you can see from the is_state_enabled column of sys.server_audits, the Server Audit object is created in a disabled state. Later, I'll demonstrate how to enable it in the "Querying Captured Audit Data" recipe, but I will leave it disabled until I define Server and Database Audit Specifications, which can be associated with it.

To see more details regarding the file configuration of the Server Audit object I just created, I can query the sys.server_file_audits catalog view.

```
USE master;
GO
SELECT  name,
log_file_path,
log_file_name,
max_rollover_files,
max_file_size
FROM sys.server_file_audits;
GO
```

This returns the following result set (reformatted for presentation purposes).

Column	Result
name	TroisMots_Server_Audit
log_file_path	C:\Apress\
log_file_name	TroisMots_Server_Audit_AE04F81A-CC5C-42F7-AE23-BD2C31D7438E.sqlaudit
max_rollover_files	10
max_file_size	500

In this next example, I will create a new Server Audit object that will be configured similar to the prior example. This time, I want to take advantage of the predicate_expression, which has been available since SQL Server 2012. In this example, I will demonstrate how a predicate_expression can be used to filter for events occurring in the AdventureWorks2014 database and the Sales.CreditCard table. If there is a failure for the audit to write, I will not shut down the SQL Server instance:

```
USE master;
GO
CREATE SERVER AUDIT TroisMots_CC_Server_Audit TO FILE
    ( FILEPATH = 'C:\Apress\',
    MAXSIZE = 500 MB,
    MAX_ROLLOVER_FILES = 10,
    RESERVE_DISK_SPACE = OFF) WITH ( QUEUE_DELAY = 1000,
    ON_FAILURE = CONTINUE)
WHERE database_name ='AdventureWorks2014' AND schema_name ='Sales'
  AND object_name ='CreditCard' AND database_principal_name ='dbo';
GO
```

I confirmed the creation of this Server Audit object with the following script:

```
USE master;
GO
SELECT  name,
log_file_path,
log_file_name,
max_rollover_files,
max_file_size,
predicate
FROM sys.server_file_audits sfs
WHERE sfs.name = 'TroisMots_CC_Server_Audit';
GO
```

This returns the following result set (reformatted for presentation purposes).

Column	Result
name	TroisMots_CC_Server_Audit
log_file_path	C:\Apress\
log_file_name	TroisMots_CC_Server_Audit_6E934469-D6A1-4B83-86D7-BA5E6C13C00D.sqlaudit
max_rollover_files	10
max_file_size	500
predicate	([database_name]='AdventureWorks2014' AND [schema_name]='Sales' AND [object_name]='CreditCard' AND [database_principal_name]='dbo')

How It Works

The first recipe demonstrated how to create a Server Audit object that defines the target destination of collected audit events. This is the first step in the process of setting up an audit. Walking through the code, in the first line we designated the name of the Server Audit object:

```
CREATE SERVER AUDIT TroisMots_Server_Audit
```

Since the target of the collected audit events will be forwarded to a file, we designated TO FILE:

```
TO FILE
```

Next, we designated the file path where the audit files would be written (since there are rollover files, each file is dynamically named, so we just used the path and not an actual file name):

```
( FILEPATH = 'C:\Apress\',
```

We then designated the maximum size of each audit file and the maximum number of rollover files:

```
MAXSIZE = 500 MB, MAX_ROLLOVER_FILES = 10,
```

We also chose not to reserve disk space (as a best practice, you should write your audit files to a dedicated volume or LUN where sufficient disk space can be ensured):

```
RESERVE_DISK_SPACE = OFF)
```

Lastly, we designated that the queue delay remain at the default level of 1,000 milliseconds (1 second) and that if there were a failure to write to the target, the SQL Server instance would continue to run (for mission-critical auditing, where events *must* be captured, you may then consider shutting down the SQL instance if there are issues writing to the target file). See the following:

```
WITH ( QUEUE_DELAY = 1000,
ON_FAILURE = CONTINUE)
```

In the second recipe, I demonstrated the use of the predicate_expression option:

```
WHERE database_name ='AdventureWorks2014' AND schema_name ='Sales'
  AND object_name ='CreditCard' AND database_principal_name ='dbo';
```

After creating the new Server Audit object, we used sys.server_audits to validate the primary Server Audit object settings and sys.server_file_audits to validate the file options.

In the next recipe, I'll demonstrate how to capture SQL instance–scoped events to the Server Audit object created in this recipe.

30-14. Capturing SQL Instance–Scoped Events

Problem

You have just received more detailed requirements from the security department about what to audit in SQL Server. You now know that you need to audit events that are instance-scoped

Solution

A Server Audit Specification is used to define which SQL instance–scoped events will be captured to the Server Audit object. The command to perform this action is CREATE SERVER AUDIT SPECIFICATION, and the syntax is as follows:

```
CREATE SERVER AUDIT SPECIFICATION audit_specification_name
FOR SERVER AUDIT audit_name
{
{ ADD ( { audit_action_group_name } )
} [, ---n] [ WITH ( STATE = { ON | OFF } ) ] }
```

Table 30-22 describes the arguments for this command.

Table 30-22. CREATE SERVER AUDIT SPECIFICATION Arguments

Argument	Description
audit_specification_name	This specifies the user-defined name of the Server Audit Specification object.
audit_name	This defines the name of the preexisting Server Audit object (target file or event log).
audit_action_group_name	This indicates the name of the SQL instance–scoped action groups. For a list of auditable action groups, you can query the sys.dm_audit_actions catalog view.
STATE	This argument takes a value of either ON or OFF. When ON, collection of records begins.

In this recipe, we will create a new Server Audit Specification that will capture three different audit action groups. To determine which audit action groups can be used, we can query the sys.dm_audit_actions system catalog view:

```
USE master;
GO
SELECT name
FROM sys.dm_audit_actions
WHERE class_desc = 'SERVER'
AND configuration_level = 'Group'
ORDER BY name;
GO
```

This returns the following abridged results.

```
name
APPLICATION_ROLE_CHANGE_PASSWORD_GROUP
AUDIT_CHANGE_GROUP
BACKUP_RESTORE_GROUP
BROKER_LOGIN_GROUP
DATABASE_CHANGE_GROUP
DATABASE_MIRRORING_LOGIN_GROUP
DATABASE_OBJECT_ACCESS_GROUP
...
DBCC_GROUP
FAILED_LOGIN_GROUP
LOGIN_CHANGE_PASSWORD_GROUP
LOGOUT_GROUP
...
SERVER_OBJECT_PERMISSION_CHANGE_GROUP
SERVER_OPERATION_GROUP
SERVER_PERMISSION_CHANGE_GROUP
SERVER_PRINCIPAL_CHANGE_GROUP
SERVER_PRINCIPAL_IMPERSONATION_GROUP
SERVER_ROLE_MEMBER_CHANGE_GROUP
SERVER_STATE_CHANGE_GROUP
SUCCESSFUL_LOGIN_GROUP
TRACE_CHANGE_GROUP
```

In this recipe scenario, I would like to track any time a DBCC command was executed, BACKUP operation was taken, or server role membership change was performed:

```
USE master;
GO
CREATE SERVER AUDIT SPECIFICATION TroisMots_Server_Audit_Spec FOR SERVER AUDIT TroisMots_
Server_Audit
ADD (SERVER_ROLE_MEMBER_CHANGE_GROUP),
ADD (DBCC_GROUP),
ADD (BACKUP_RESTORE_GROUP) WITH (STATE = ON);
GO
```

Once the Server Audit Specification is created, we can validate the settings by querying the sys.server_audit_specifications catalog view:

```
USE master;
GO
SELECT server_specification_id,name,is_state_enabled
FROM sys.server_audit_specifications;
GO
```

This query returns the following.

server_specification_id	name	is_state_enabled
65536	TroisMots_Server_Audit_Spec	1

We can also query the details of this specification by querying the sys.server_audit_specification_details catalog view (we use the server specification ID returned from the previous query to qualify the following result set):

```
USE master;
GO
SELECT server_specification_id,audit_action_name
FROM sys.server_audit_specification_details
WHERE server_specification_id = 65536;
GO
```

This query returns the following.

server_specification_id	audit_action_name
65536	SERVER_ROLE_MEMBER_CHANGE_GROUP
65536	BACKUP_RESTORE_GROUP
65536	DBCC_GROUP

The entire auditing picture is not yet complete since we have not yet enabled the Server Audit object (TroisMots_Server_Audit). Before we turn the Server Audit object on, we will also add a Database Audit Specification object, and then we'll look at actual audit event captures and how to query the audit log.

How It Works

In this recipe, I demonstrated how to create a Server Audit Specification that defines which SQL instance-scoped events will be captured and forwarded to a specific Server Audit object target (in this case, a file under C:\Apress).

We started the recipe first by querying sys.dm_audit_actions to get a list of action groups that we could choose to audit for the SQL Server instance. The sys.dm_audit_actions catalog view actually contains a row for all audit actions—at both the SQL instance and database scopes. So, in the WHERE clause of our query, we designated that the class of audit action should be for the SERVER and that the configuration level should be for a group (I'll demonstrate the nongroup action-level configuration level in the next recipe). See the following:

```
WHERE class_desc = 'SERVER' AND
configuration_level = 'Group'
```

Next, we used the `CREATE SERVER AUDIT SPECIFICATION` command to define which action groups we wanted to track. The first line of code designated the name of the new Server Audit Specification:

```
CREATE SERVER AUDIT SPECIFICATION TroisMots_Server_Audit_Spec
```

The next line of code designated the target of the event collection, which is the name of the Server Audit object:

```
FOR SERVER AUDIT TroisMots_Server_Audit
```

After that, we designated each action group we wanted to capture:

```
ADD (SERVER_ROLE_MEMBER_CHANGE_GROUP),
ADD (DBCC_GROUP),
ADD (BACKUP_RESTORE_GROUP)
```

Lastly, we designated that the state of the Server Audit Specification should be enabled upon creation:

```
WITH (STATE = ON)
```

In the next recipe, I'll demonstrate how to create a Database Audit Specification to capture database-scoped events. Once all of the specifications are created, I'll then demonstrate actual captures of actions and show you how to read the Server Audit log.

30-15. Capturing Database-Scoped Events

Problem

You have just learned that you need to audit some database-scoped events.

Solution

A Database Audit Specification is used to define which database-scoped events will be captured to the Server Audit object. The command to perform this action is `CREATE DATABASE AUDIT SPECIFICATION`, and the abridged syntax is as follows (it does not show action-specification syntax; however, I'll demonstrate this within the recipe):

```
CREATE DATABASE AUDIT SPECIFICATION audit_specification_name {
[ FOR SERVER AUDIT audit_name ] [ { ADD (
{ <audit_action_specification> | audit_action_group_name } )
} [, ---n]  ] [ WITH ( STATE = { ON | OFF } ) ] }
```

Table 30-23 shows the arguments for this command.

Table 30-23. `CREATE DATABASE AUDIT SPECIFICATION` *Arguments*

Argument	Description
`audit_specification_name`	This specifies the user-defined name of the Database Audit Specification object.
`audit_name`	This defines the name of the preexisting Server Audit object (target file or event log).
`audit_action_specification`	This indicates the name of an auditable database-scoped action. For a list of auditable database-scoped actions, you can query the `sys.dm_audit_actions` catalog view.
`audit_action_group_name`	This defines the name of the database-scoped action group. For a list of auditable action groups, you can query the `sys.dm_audit_ actions` catalog view.
`STATE`	This argument takes a value of either `ON` or `OFF`. When `ON`, collection of records begins.

In this recipe, we will create a new Database Audit Specification that will capture both audit action groups and audit events. *Audit action groups* are related groups of actions at the database scope, and *audit events* are singular events. For example, we can query the `sys.dm_audit_actions` system catalog view to view specific audit events against the object securable scope (for example, tables, views, stored procedures, and functions) by executing the following query:

```
USE master;
GO
SELECT name
FROM sys.dm_audit_actions
WHERE configuration_level = 'Action'
AND class_desc = 'OBJECT'
ORDER BY name;
GO
```

This returns a result set of atomic events that can be audited against an object securable scope.

```
name
DELETE
EXECUTE
INSERT
RECEIVE
REFERENCES
SELECT
UPDATE
```

We can also query the sys.dm_audit_actions system catalog view to see audit action groups at the database scope:

```
USE master;
GO
SELECT name
FROM sys.dm_audit_actions
WHERE configuration_level = 'Group'
AND class_desc = 'DATABASE'
ORDER BY name;
GO
```

This returns the following abridged results.

```
name
APPLICATION_ROLE_CHANGE_PASSWORD_GROUP
AUDIT_CHANGE_GROUP
BACKUP_RESTORE_GROUP
DATABASE_CHANGE_GROUP
DATABASE_OBJECT_ACCESS_GROUP
DBCC_GROUP
SCHEMA_OBJECT_ACCESS_GROUP
SCHEMA_OBJECT_CHANGE_GROUP
SCHEMA_OBJECT_OWNERSHIP_CHANGE_GROUP
SCHEMA_OBJECT_PERMISSION_CHANGE_GROUP
```

In this recipe scenario, we would like to track any time an INSERT, UPDATE, or DELETE is performed against the Sales.CreditCard table by *any* database user. We would also like to track whenever impersonation is used within the AdventureWorks2014 database (for example, using the EXECUTE AS command):

```
USE AdventureWorks2014;
GO
CREATE DATABASE AUDIT SPECIFICATION AdventureWorks2014_DB_Spec
    FOR SERVER AUDIT TroisMots_Server_Audit
    ADD (DATABASE_PRINCIPAL_IMPERSONATION_GROUP)
    , ADD (INSERT, UPDATE, DELETE ON Sales.CreditCard BY public)
WITH (STATE = ON);
GO
```

We can validate the settings of our Database Audit Specification by querying the sys.database_audit_specifications system catalog view:

```
USE AdventureWorks2014;
GO
SELECT database_specification_id,name,is_state_enabled
FROM sys.database_audit_specifications;
GO
```

This query returns the following:

database_specification_id	name	is_state_enabled
65536	AdventureWorks2014_DB_Spec	1

For a detailed look at what we're auditing for the new Database Audit Specification, we can query the `sys.database_audit_specification_details` system catalog view (I'll walk through the logic in the "How It Works" section):

```
USE AdventureWorks2014;
GO
SELECT audit_action_name, class_desc, is_group
,ObjectNM = CASE
    WHEN major_id > 0 THEN OBJECT_NAME(major_id, DB_ID()) ELSE 'N/A' END
FROM sys.database_audit_specification_details
WHERE database_specification_id = 65536;
GO
```

This query returns the following:

audit_action_name	class_desc	is_group	ObjectNM
DATABASE_PRINCIPAL_ IMPERSONATION_GROUP	DATABASE	1	N/A
DELETE	OBJECT_OR_COLUMN	0	CreditCard
INSERT	OBJECT_OR_COLUMN	0	CreditCard
UPDATE	OBJECT_OR_COLUMN	0	CreditCard

Although the Database Audit Specification is enabled, we have still not enabled the overall Server Audit object. I'll be demonstrating that in the next recipe, where you'll also learn how to query the captured audit data from a binary file.

How It Works

In this recipe, we looked at how to create a Database Audit Specification that designated which database-scoped events would be captured to the Server Audit object. To perform this action, we used the `CREATE DATABASE AUDIT SPECIFICATION` command. We started by changing the context to the database we wanted to audit (since this is a database-scoped object):

```
USE AdventureWorks2014;
GO
```

The first line of the CREATE DATABASE AUDIT SPECIFICATION command designated the user-defined name, followed by a reference to the Server Audit object we would be forwarding the database-scoped events to:

```
CREATE DATABASE AUDIT SPECIFICATION AdventureWorks2014_DB_Spec FOR SERVER AUDIT
TroisMots_Server_Audit
```

After that, we used the ADD keyword followed by an open parenthesis, defined the audit action group we wanted to monitor, and then entered a closing parenthesis and a comma (since we planned on defining more than one action to monitor):

```
ADD (DATABASE_PRINCIPAL_IMPERSONATION_GROUP),
```

Next, we designated the ADD keyword again, followed by the three actions we wanted to monitor for the Sales.CreditCard table:

```
ADD (INSERT, UPDATE, DELETE
ON Sales.CreditCard
```

The object-scoped actions required a reference to the database principal for which we wanted to audit actions. In this example, we wanted to view actions by all database principals. Since all database principals are by default a member of public, this was what we designated:

```
BY public)
```

After that, we used the WITH keyword followed by the STATE argument, which we set to enabled:

```
WITH (STATE = ON);
GO
```

We then used the sys.database_audit_specifications to view the basic information of the new Database Audit Specification. We queried the sys.database_audit_specification_details catalog view to list the events that the Database Audit Specification captured. In the first three lines of code, we looked at the audit action name, class description, and is_group field, which designates whether the audit action is an audit action group or individual event:

```
SELECT audit_action_name, class_desc, is_group,
```

We used a CASE expression to evaluate the major_id column. If the major_id is a nonzero value, this indicates that the audit action row is for a database object, and therefore we used the OBJECT_NAME function to provide that object's name:

```
,ObjectNM = CASE
    WHEN major_id > 0 THEN OBJECT_NAME(major_id, DB_ID()) ELSE 'N/A' END
```

In the last two lines of the SELECT, we designated the catalog view name and specified the database specification ID (important if you have more than one Database Audit Specification defined for a database, which is allowed):

```
FROM sys.database_audit_specification_details
WHERE database_specification_id = 65536;
```

Now that we have defined the Server Audit object, Server Audit Specification, and Database Audit Specification, in the next recipe I'll demonstrate enabling the Server Audit object and creating some auditable activity, and then I will show how to query the captured audit data.

30-16. Querying Captured Audit Data

Problem

After enabling auditing on your SQL Server Instance, you now need to report on the audit data that has been captured.

Solution

With the auditing solution provided through the previous recipes, we will need to use the fn_get_audit_file function.

The previous recipes have built up to the actual demonstration of SQL Server's auditing capabilities. To begin the recipe, we will enable the Server Audit object created a few recipes ago. Recall that we had defined this Server Audit object to write to a binary file under the C:\Apress folder. To enable the audit, we use the ALTER SERVER AUDIT command and configure the STATE option:

```
USE master;
GO
ALTER SERVER AUDIT [TroisMots_Server_Audit] WITH (STATE = ON);
GO
```

Now we will perform a few actions at both the SQL Server scope and within the AdventureWorks2014 database in order to demonstrate the audit collection process. I've added comments before each group of statements so that you can follow what actions I'm trying to demonstrate:

```
USE master;
GO
/*
-- Create new login (not auditing this, but using it for recipe)
*/
CREATE LOGIN TestAudit WITH PASSWORD = 'C83D7F50-9B9E';
GO
/*
-- Add to server role bulkadmin
*/
EXECUTE sp_addsrvrolemember 'TestAudit', 'bulkadmin';
GO
/*
-- Back up AdventureWorks2014 database
*/
BACKUP DATABASE AdventureWorks2014 TO DISK = 'C:\Apress\Example_AW.BAK';
GO
/*
```

```
-- Perform a DBCC on AdventureWorks2014
*/
DBCC CHECKDB('AdventureWorks2014');
GO
/*
-- Perform some AdventureWorks2014 actions
*/
USE AdventureWorks2014
GO
/*
-- Create a new user and then execute under that
-- user's context
*/
CREATE USER TestAudit FROM LOGIN TestAudit
EXECUTE AS USER = 'TestAudit'
/*
-- Revert back to me (in this case a login with sysadmin perms)
*/
REVERT;
GO
/*
-- Perform an INSERT, UPDATE, and DELETE -- from Sales.CreditCard
*/
INSERT Into Sales.CreditCard (CardType, CardNumber,ExpMonth,ExpYear,ModifiedDate)
    VALUES('Vista', '8675309153332145',11,2003,GetDate());

UPDATE Sales.CreditCard SET CardType = 'Colonial'
    WHERE CardNumber = '8675309153332145';
DELETE Sales.CreditCard
    WHERE CardNumber = '8675309153332145';
GO
```

Now that we have performed several events that are covered by the Server Audit Specification and Database Audit Specification created earlier, we can use the fn_get_audit_file table-valued function to view the contents of our Server Audit binary file. The syntax for this function is as follows:

```
fn_get_audit_file ( file_pattern,
    { default | initial_file_name | NULL },
    { default | audit_record_offset | NULL } )
```

Table 30-24 describes the arguments for this command.

Table 30-24. fn_get_audit_file Arguments

Argument	Description
file_pattern	Designates the location of the audit file or files to be read. You can use a drive letter or network share for the path and use the single asterisk (*) wildcard to designate multiple files.
{default | initial_file_name | NULL }	Designates the name and path for a specific file you would like to begin reading from. Default and NULL are synonymous and indicate no selection for the initial file name.
{default | audit_record_ offset | NULL }	Designates the buffer offset from the initial file (when initial file is selected). Default and NULL are synonymous and indicate no selection for the audit.

In this first call to the fn_get_audit_file function, we'll look for any changes to server role memberships. Notice that we are using the sys.dm_audit_actions catalog view in order to translate the action ID into the actual action event name (you can use this view to find which event names you need to filter by):

```
USE master;
GO
SELECT af.event_time, af.succeeded,
af.target_server_principal_name, object_name
FROM fn_get_audit_file('C:\Apress\TroisMots_Server_Audit_*', default, default) af
INNER JOIN sys.dm_audit_actions aa
    ON af.action_id = aa.action_id
WHERE aa.name = 'ADD MEMBER'
    AND aa.class_desc = 'SERVER ROLE';
GO
```

This returns the event time, success flag, server principal name, and server role name.

event_time	succeeded	target_server_principal_name	object_name
2015-01-03 05:11:36.854	1	TestAudit	bulkadmin

In this next example, I'll take a look at deletion events against the Sales.CreditCard table:

```
USE master;
GO
SELECT af.event_time,
af.database_principal_name
FROM fn_get_audit_file('C:\Apress\TroisMots_Server_Audit_*', default, default) af
INNER JOIN sys.dm_audit_actions aa
    ON af.action_id = aa.action_id
```

```
WHERE aa.name = 'DELETE'
    AND aa.class_desc = 'OBJECT'
    AND af.schema_name = 'Sales'
    AND af.object_name = 'CreditCard';

GO
```

This query returns the following result set.

event_time	database_principal_name
2015-01-03 05:11:36.854	dbo

The fn_get_audit_file function also exposes the SQL statement when applicable to the instantiating event. The following query demonstrates capturing the actual BACKUP DATABASE text used for the audited event:

```
USE master;
GO
SELECT event_time, statement
FROM fn_get_audit_file('C:\Apress\TroisMots_Server_Audit_*', default, default) af
INNER JOIN sys.dm_audit_actions aa
    ON af.action_id = aa.action_id
WHERE aa.name = 'BACKUP'
    AND aa.class_desc = 'DATABASE';
GO
```

This returns the event time and associated BACKUP statement text:

event_time	statement
2015-01-03 05:11:36.8630420	BACKUP DATABASE AdventureWorks2014 TO DISK ='C:\Apress\Example_AW.BAK'

The last query of this recipe demonstrates querying for each distinct event and the associated database principal that performed it, along with the target server principal name (when applicable) or target object name:

```
USE master;
GO
SELECT DISTINCT
aa.name,
database_principal_name,
target_server_principal_name,
object_name
FROM fn_get_audit_file('C:\Apress\TroisMots_Server_Audit_*', default, default) af
INNER JOIN sys.dm_audit_actions aa
    ON af.action_id = aa.action_id;
GO
```

This returns the various events we performed earlier that were defined in the Server and Database Audit Specifications. It also includes audit events by default—for example, AUDIT SESSION CHANGED.

name	database_ principal_name	target_server_ principal_name	object_name
ADD MEMBER	dbo	TestAudit	bulkadmin
AUDIT SESSION CHANGED			
BACKUP	dbo		AdventureWorks2014
DBCC	dbo		
DELETE	dbo		CreditCard
IMPERSONATE	dbo		TestAudit
INSERT	dbo		CreditCard
UPDATE	dbo		CreditCard

How It Works

We started this recipe by enabling the overall Server Audit object using the ALTER SERVER AUDIT command. After that, we performed several SQL instance- and database-scoped activities, focusing on events that we had defined for capture in the Server and Database Audit Specifications bound to the TroisMots_Server_Audit audit. After that, we looked at how to use the fn_get_audit_file function to retrieve the event data from the binary file created under the C:\Apress directory.

■ **Note**   We could have also defined the Server Audit object to write events to the Windows Application or Windows Security event log instead, in which case we would not have used fn_get_audit_file to retrieve the data, because this function applies only to the binary file format.

Each query to fn_get_audit_file we also joined to the sys.dm_audit_actions object in order to designate the audit action name and, depending on the action, the class description. Here's an example:

```
...
FROM fn_get_audit_file('C:\Apress\TroisMots_Server_Audit_*', default, default) af
INNER JOIN sys.dm_audit_actions aa
    ON af.action_id = aa.action_id
WHERE aa.name = 'ADD MEMBER'
    AND aa.class_desc = 'SERVER ROLE';
...
```

In the next and final recipe of this chapter, I'll demonstrate how to manage, modify, and remove audit objects.

30-17. Managing, Modifying, and Removing Audit Objects

Problem

Your corporate auditing requirements for SQL Server have changed. Now you need to modify the existing audit objects.

Solution

To modify existing audit objects, you should use the ALTER SERVER AUDIT SPECIFICATION, ALTER SERVER AUDIT, or ALTER DATABASE AUDIT SPECIFICATION commands.

This recipe will demonstrate how to add and remove actions from existing Server and Database Audit Specifications, disable Server and Database Audit Specifications, modify the Server Audit object, and remove audit objects from the SQL instance and associated databases.

To modify an existing Server Audit Specification, we use the ALTER SERVER AUDIT SPECIFICATION command. In this first query demonstration, we'll remove one audit action type from the Server Audit Specification we created in an earlier recipe and also add a new audit action.

Before we can modify the specification, however, we must first disable it:

```
USE master;
GO
ALTER SERVER AUDIT SPECIFICATION [TroisMots_Server_Audit_Spec] WITH (STATE = OFF);
GO
```

Next, we will drop one of the audit actions:

```
USE master;
GO
ALTER SERVER AUDIT SPECIFICATION [TroisMots_Server_Audit_Spec]
DROP (BACKUP_RESTORE_GROUP);
GO
```

Now I'll demonstrate adding a new audit action group to an existing Server Audit Specification:

```
USE master;
GO
ALTER SERVER AUDIT SPECIFICATION [TroisMots_Server_Audit_Spec]
ADD (LOGIN_CHANGE_PASSWORD_GROUP);
GO
```

To have these changes take effect and resume auditing, we must reenable the Server Audit Specification:

```
USE master;
GO
ALTER SERVER AUDIT SPECIFICATION [TroisMots_Server_Audit_Spec]
WITH (STATE = ON);
GO
```

To modify the audit actions of a Database Audit Specification, we must use the ALTER DATABASE AUDIT SPECIFICATION command. Similar to Server Audit Specifications, a Database Audit Specification must have a disabled state prior to making any changes to it:

```
USE AdventureWorks2014;
GO
ALTER DATABASE AUDIT SPECIFICATION [AdventureWorks2014_DB_Spec]
WITH (STATE = OFF);
GO
```

This next query demonstrates removing an existing audit event from the Database Audit Specification we created earlier:

```
USE AdventureWorks2014;
GO
ALTER DATABASE AUDIT SPECIFICATION [AdventureWorks2014_DB_Spec]
DROP (INSERT ON [HumanResources].[Department] BY public);
GO
```

Next, we'll look at how to add a new audit event to the existing Database Audit Specification:

```
USE AdventureWorks2014;
GO
ALTER DATABASE AUDIT SPECIFICATION [AdventureWorks2014_DB_Spec]
ADD (DATABASE_ROLE_MEMBER_CHANGE_GROUP);
GO
```

To have these changes go into effect, we need to reenable the Database Audit Specification:

```
USE AdventureWorks2014;
GO
ALTER DATABASE AUDIT SPECIFICATION [AdventureWorks2014_DB_Spec]
WITH (STATE = ON);
GO
```

To modify the Server Audit object, we use the ALTER SERVER AUDIT command. Similar to the Server and Database Audit Specification objects, the Server Audit object needs to be disabled before changes can be made to it. In this next example, I demonstrate disabling the Server Audit, making a change to the logging target so that it writes to the Windows Application event log instead, and then reenabling it. See the following:

```
USE master;
GO
ALTER SERVER AUDIT [TroisMots_Server_Audit] WITH (STATE = OFF);
ALTER SERVER AUDIT [TroisMots_Server_Audit] TO APPLICATION_LOG;
ALTER SERVER AUDIT [TroisMots_Server_Audit] WITH (STATE = ON);
```

Once the target is changed, audit events are forwarded to the Windows Application event log. For example, if I execute a DBCC CHECKDB command again, I would see this reflected in the Windows Application event log with an event ID of 33205. The following is an example of a Windows Application event log entry:

```
Audit event: eventjtime: 2015-01-03 05:11:36.8630420
sequence_number:1
action_id:DBCC
succeeded:true
permission_bitmask:0
is_column_permission:false
session_id:57
server_principal_id:263
database_principal_id:1
target_server_principal_id:0
target_database_principal_id:0
object_id:0
class_type:DB
session_server_principal_name:PETITMOT\Administrator
server_principal_name:PETITMOT\Administrator
Server_principal_sid:0105000000000005150000006bb13b36a981eb9a2b3859a8f4010000
database_principal_name:dbo
target_server_principal_name:
target_server_principal_sid:
target_database_principal_name:
server_instance_name:PETITMOT\JeanLouis
database_name:AdventureWorks2014
schema_name:
object_name:

statement:DBCC CHECKDB('AdventureWorks2014') additional_information:
```

To remove a Database Audit Specification, we need to disable it and then use the DROP DATABASE AUDIT SPECIFICATION, as demonstrated here:

```
USE AdventureWorks2014;
GO
ALTER DATABASE AUDIT SPECIFICATION [AdventureWorks2014_DB_Spec] WITH (STATE = OFF);
DROP DATABASE AUDIT SPECIFICATION [AdventureWorks2014_DB_Spec];
GO
```

To remove a Server Audit Specification, we need to disable it and then use the DROP SERVER AUDIT SPECIFICATION command:

```
USE master;
GO
ALTER SERVER AUDIT SPECIFICATION [TroisMots_Server_Audit_Spec] WITH (STATE = OFF);
DROP SERVER AUDIT SPECIFICATION [TroisMots_Server_Audit_Spec];
GO
```

Finally, to drop a Server Audit object, we need to first disable it and then use the DROP SERVER AUDIT command, as demonstrated here:

```
USE master;
GO
ALTER SERVER AUDIT [TroisMots_Server_Audit] WITH (STATE = OFF);
DROP SERVER AUDIT [TroisMots_Server_Audit];
GO
```

Any binary log files created from the auditing will still remain after removing the Server Audit object.

How It Works

This recipe demonstrated several commands used to manage audit objects. For each of these existing audit objects, we were required to disable the state prior to making changes. We used ALTER SERVER AUDIT SPECIFICATION to add and remove audit events from the Server Audit Specification and DROP SERVER AUDIT SPECIFICATION to remove the definition from the SQL Server instance.

We used ALTER DATABASE AUDIT SPECIFICATION to add and remove audit events from the Database Audit Specification and DROP DATABASE AUDIT SPECIFICATION to remove the definition from the user database. We used ALTER SERVER AUDIT to modify an existing Server Audit object, changing the target logging method from a binary file to the Windows Application event log instead. Lastly, we used DROP SERVER AUDIT to remove the Server Audit object from the SQL Server instance.

Objects and Dependencies

by Wayne Sheffield

Almost everything in a database is an object; this includes tables, constraints, views, functions, and stored procedures. Inevitably, there will come a time when you need to work on these at the object level: from renaming to moving to a different schema, to determining dependencies between objects. This chapter covers maintaining and working with database objects at the object level.

31-1. Changing the Name of Database Items

Problem

You need to change the name of an item in a database.

Solution

Utilize the system-stored procedure `sp_rename` to rename an item in the database as follows:

```
CREATE TABLE dbo.Test
    (
    Column1 INT,
    Column2 INT,
    CONSTRAINT UK_Test UNIQUE (Column1, Column2)
    );
GO
EXECUTE sp_rename 'dbo.Test', 'MyTestTable', 'object';
```

Executing this procedure returns the following caution message:

```
Caution: Changing any part of an object name could break scripts and stored procedures.
```

How It Works

Using the `sp_rename` system-stored procedure, you can rename table columns, indexes, tables, constraints, and other database items.

The syntax for sp_rename is as follows:

```
sp_rename [ @objname = ] 'object_name' , [ @newname = ] 'new_name'
    [ , [ @objtype = ] 'object_type' ]
```

The arguments of this system-stored procedure are described in Table 31-1.

Table 31-1. sp_rename Parameters

Argument	Description
object_name	The name of the object to be renamed
new_name	The new name of the object
object_type	The type of object to rename: column, database, index, object, or userdatatype

This example began by creating a new table called dbo.Test, and then the system-stored procedure sp_rename was used to rename the table:

```
EXECUTE sp_rename 'dbo.Test', 'MyTestTable', 'object';
```

Notice that the first parameter used the fully qualified object name (schema.table_name), whereas the second parameter just used the new table_name. The third parameter used the object type of object.

Next, let's change the name of Column1 to NewColumnName:

```
EXECUTE sp_rename 'dbo.MyTestTable.Column1', 'NewColumnName', 'column';
```

Executing this procedure returns the following caution message:

```
Caution: Changing any part of an object name could break scripts and stored procedures.
```

The first parameter was the schema.table_name.column_name to be renamed, and the second parameter was the new name of the column. The third parameter used the object type of column.

In this next example, we will build and then rename an index:

```
CREATE INDEX IX_1 ON dbo.MyTestTable (NewColumnName, Column2);
GO
EXECUTE sp_rename 'dbo.MyTestTable.IX_1', 'IX_NewIndexName', 'index';
```

The first parameter used the schema.table_name.index_name parameter. The second parameter used the name of the new index. The third used the object type of index.

Once you have successfully run sp_rename, you will receive the following caution message:

```
Caution: Changing any part of an object name could break scripts and stored procedures.
```

In this next example, we will create a new database and then rename it:

```
CREATE DATABASE TSQLRecipes;
GO
SELECT  name
FROM    sys.databases
WHERE   name IN ('TSQLRecipes', 'TSQL-Recipes');
GO
EXECUTE sp_rename 'TSQLRecipes', 'TSQL-Recipes', 'database';
SELECT  name
FROM    sys.databases
WHERE   name IN ('TSQLRecipes', 'TSQL-Recipes');
GO
```

These statements produce the following results and messages:

```
name
--------------
TSQLRecipes

The database name 'TSQL-Recipes' has been set.
name
--------------
TSQL-Recipes
```

In this example, we will build a user-defined data type and then rename it:

```
CREATE TYPE dbo.Age
FROM TINYINT NOT NULL;
SELECT  name
FROM    sys.types
WHERE   name IN ('Age', 'PersonAge');
EXECUTE sp_rename 'dbo.Age', 'PersonAge', 'userdatatype';
SELECT  name
FROM    sys.types
WHERE   name IN ('Age', 'PersonAge');
```

These statements produce the following results and messages:

```
name
---------
Age

Caution: Changing any part of an object name could break scripts and stored procedures.
name
---------
PersonAge
```

In this final example, we will build and then rename a stored procedure:

```
CREATE PROCEDURE dbo.renameMe
AS
SELECT 1;
GO
EXECUTE sp_rename 'dbo.renameMe', 'RenameMeToThis', 'OBJECT';
SELECT name FROM sys.procedures WHERE name = 'RenameMeToThis';
```

These statements produce the following messages and results:

```
Caution: Changing any part of an object name could break scripts and stored procedures.
name
--------------
RenameMeToThis
```

However, when changing code as shown in these examples, it is only the object name that is changed, not the underlying definition that includes the name. We can see this by examining the definition of this procedure:

```
SELECT  definition
FROM    sys.all_sql_modules
WHERE   object_id = OBJECT_ID('dbo.RenameMeToThis');
```

This query returns:

```
definition
------------------------------
CREATE PROCEDURE dbo.renameMe
AS
SELECT 1;
```

We can see that the original name is still present.

In a real-life scenario, in conjunction with renaming an object, you'll also want to ALTER any view, stored procedure, function, or other programmatic object that contains a reference to the original object name. I demonstrate how to find out which objects reference an object later on in this chapter in Recipe 31-3.

31-2. Changing an Object's Schema

Problem

You need to move an object from one schema to another.

Solution

You can use the ALTER SCHEMA statement to move objects from one schema to another (this example utilizes the AdventureWorks 2014 database):

```
CREATE TABLE Sales.TerminationReason
        (
        TerminationReasonID INT NOT NULL
                            PRIMARY KEY,
        TerminationReasonDESC VARCHAR(100) NOT NULL
        );
GO
ALTER SCHEMA HumanResources TRANSFER Sales.TerminationReason;
GO
DROP TABLE HumanResources.TerminationReason;
GO
```

How It Works

The ALTER SCHEMA command takes two arguments, the first being the schema name you want to transfer the object to, and the second being the object name that you want to transfer. In the above example, a table was created in the Sales schema, then was moved into the HumanResources schema, and finally was deleted.

31-3. Identifying Object Dependencies

Problem

You need to see which objects a specified object depends upon, or which objects depend upon a specified object.

Solution

Query the sys.sql_expression_dependencies object catalog view to identify dependencies between objects.

```
USE master;
GO
IF DB_ID('TSQLRecipe_A') IS NOT NULL
   DROP DATABASE TSQLRecipe_A;
IF DB_ID('TSQLRecipe_B') IS NOT NULL
   DROP DATABASE TSQLRecipe_B;

-- Create two new databases
CREATE DATABASE TSQLRecipe_A;
GO
CREATE DATABASE TSQLRecipe_B;
GO
```

863

```
-- Create a new table in the first database
USE TSQLRecipe_A;
GO
CREATE TABLE dbo.Book
      (
        BookID INT NOT NULL
                   PRIMARY KEY,
        BookNM VARCHAR(50) NOT NULL
      );
GO

-- Create a procedure referencing an object
-- in the second database
USE TSQLRecipe_B;
GO
CREATE PROCEDURE dbo.usp_SEL_Book
AS
SELECT  BookID,
        BookNM
FROM    TSQLRecipe_A.dbo.Book;
GO
```

How It Works

SQL Server provides methods for identifying object dependencies within the database, across databases, and across servers (using linked server four-part names). This following example demonstrates the use of the sys.sql_expression_dependencies object catalog view to identify dependencies in several scenarios.

I began by checking for the existence of two databases, and then dropping them if they existed. Next, I create two new databases and some new objects within them in order to demonstrate the functionality.

A stored procedure was created that references a table in another database. To view all objects that the stored procedure depends on, I can execute the following query against sys.sql_expression_dependencies:

```
SELECT  referenced_server_name,
        referenced_database_name,
        referenced_schema_name,
        referenced_entity_name,
        is_caller_dependent
FROM    sys.sql_expression_dependencies
WHERE   OBJECT_NAME(referencing_id) = 'usp_SEL_Book';
```

This query returns one row (results pivoted for formatting):

referenced_server_name	NULL
referenced_database_name	TSQLRecipe_A
referenced_schema_name	dbo
referenced_entity_name	Book
is_caller_dependent	0

This demonstrates how to determine object dependencies using the sys.sql_expression_ dependencies catalog view. In the SELECT statement, five columns are referenced. The first four columns— referenced_server_name, referenced_database_name, referenced_schema_name, and referenced_ entity_name—will contain the value utilized for each part of the four-part qualified name. If that particular value isn't specified when the referencing object is created, it will be NULL. The fifth column, is_caller_ dependent, indicates whether the object reference depends on the person executing the module. For example, if the object name is not fully qualified, and an object named T1 exists in two different schemas, the actual object referenced would depend on the person calling the module and the execution context.

Now, create another stored procedure that references an object that doesn't yet exist (which is an allowable scenario for a stored procedure and which is a common practice). For example:

```
USE TSQLRecipe_B;
GO
CREATE PROCEDURE dbo.usp_SEL_Contract
AS
SELECT  ContractID,
        ContractNM
FROM    TSQLRecipe_A.dbo.Contract;
GO
```

In versions of SQL Server before SQL Server 2008, dependencies on nonexistent objects weren't tracked. Subsequent versions corrected this behavior. You can issue the following query to check on the dependencies of usp_SEL_contract:

```
USE TSQLRecipe_B;
GO
SELECT  referenced_server_name,
        referenced_database_name,
        referenced_schema_name,
        referenced_entity_name,
        is_caller_dependent
FROM    sys.sql_expression_dependencies
WHERE   OBJECT_NAME(referencing_id) = 'usp_SEL_Contract';
```

This query returns one row (results pivoted for formatting):

referenced_server_name	NULL
referenced_database_name	TSQLRecipe_A
referenced_schema_name	dbo
referenced_entity_name	Contract
is_caller_dependent	0

Even though the object TSQLRecipe_A.dbo.Contract does not yet exist, the dependency between the referencing stored procedure and the referenced table is still represented.

31-4. Identifying Referencing and Referenced Entities

Problem

You are making changes to a database object, and you need to examine all other objects that either are referencing this object or are referenced by this object.

Solution

Utilize the sys.dm_sql_referenced_entities and sys.dm_sql_referencing_entities Dynamic Management Functions (DMFs).

How It Works

The sys.dm_sql_referenced_entities and sys.dm_sql_referencing_entities DMFs are used to identify referenced and referencing objects. The sys.dm_sql_referenced_entities DMF, when provided with the referencing object's name, returns a result set of objects being referenced. The sys.dm_sql_referencing_ entities DMF, when provided the name of the object being referenced, returns a result set of objects referencing it. Notice that these two DMFs are named very similarly, so ensure that you use the proper function.

   Let's go to an example to see how these DMFs work. This first section creates a database, and within that database a table, view, and stored procedure, where the view and stored procedure reference the table:

```
USE master;
GO
IF DB_ID('TSQLRecipe_A') IS NOT NULL
    DROP DATABASE TSQLRecipe_A;
GO
CREATE DATABASE TSQLRecipe_A;
GO
USE TSQLRecipe_A;
GO
CREATE TABLE dbo.BookPublisher
      (
       BookPublisherID INT NOT NULL
                           PRIMARY KEY,
       BookPublisherNM VARCHAR(30) NOT NULL
      );
GO
CREATE VIEW dbo.vw_BookPublisher
AS
SELECT  BookPublisherID,
        BookPublisherNM
FROM    dbo.BookPublisher;
GO
CREATE PROCEDURE dbo.usp_INS_BookPublisher
      @BookPublisherNM VARCHAR(30)
AS
INSERT  dbo.BookPublisher
        (BookPublisherNM)
VALUES  (@BookPublisherNM);
GO
```

To find all of the objects that are referenced by the dbo.vw_BookPublisher view, run the following query:

```
SELECT  referenced_entity_name,
        referenced_schema_name,
        referenced_minor_name
FROM    sys.dm_sql_referenced_entities('dbo.vw_BookPublisher', 'OBJECT');
```

This query returns the following result set:

referenced_entity_name	referenced_schema_name	referenced_minor_name
BookPublisher	dbo	NULL
BookPublisher	dbo	BookPublisherID
BookPublisher	dbo	BookPublisherNM

Notice that this function shows one row for the table referenced in the view, as well as a row for each column referenced within the view.

The first parameter passed to this function is the name of the object that is referencing other objects. The second parameter designates the type of entities to list. The choices are OBJECT, DATABASE_DDL_TRIGGER, and SERVER_DDL_TRIGGER. In this case, OBJECT is the proper choice, and the result is the name of the referenced table and specific columns used in the SELECT clause of the view. The other two options will show you the objects referenced by DDL triggers at the database or server level, respectfully. For instance:

```
SELECT  referenced_entity_name,
        referenced_schema_name,
        referenced_minor_name
FROM    AdventureWorks2014.sys.dm_sql_referenced_entities('ddlDatabaseTriggerLog',
'DATABASE_DDL_TRIGGER');
```

This query returns the following result set:

referenced_entity_name	referenced_schema_name	referenced_minor_name
DatabaseLog	dbo	NULL
DatabaseLog	dbo	PostTime
DatabaseLog	dbo	DatabaseUser
DatabaseLog	dbo	Event
DatabaseLog	dbo	Schema
DatabaseLog	dbo	Object
DatabaseLog	dbo	TSQL
DatabaseLog	dbo	XmlEvent

To find all of the objects that are referencing the dbo.BookPublisher table, run the following query:

```
SELECT  referencing_schema_name,
        referencing_entity_name
FROM    sys.dm_sql_referencing_entities('dbo.BookPublisher', 'OBJECT');
```

This query returns the following result set:

```
referencing_schema_name  referencing_entity_name
-----------------------  -----------------------
dbo                      usp_INS_BookPublisher
dbo                      vw_BookPublisher
```

As you can see, both the view and the stored procedure that reference the table are returned.

The first parameter passed to this function is the name of the object that you want to find references to by other objects. The second parameter designates the class of objects to list. The choices are OBJECT, TYPE, XML_SCHEMA_COLLECTION, and PARTITION FUNCTION. In this case, OBJECT is the proper choice, which results in the view and stored procedure being listed in the output. The other choices allow us to see the objects that reference a type, XML Schema Collection, or a partition function. For instance:

```
SELECT  referencing_schema_name,
        referencing_entity_name
FROM    AdventureWorks2014.sys.dm_sql_referencing_entities('dbo.Flag', 'TYPE');
```

This query returns the following result set:

```
referencing_schema_name  referencing_entity_name
-----------------------  -------------------------
HumanResources           uspUpdateEmployeeHireInfo
HumanResources           uspUpdateEmployeeLogin
```

31-5. Viewing the Definition of Coded Objects

Problem

Now that you have identified the objects that are referencing an object, or that are referenced by an object, you need to view the definition of those objects.

Solution #1

Utilize the OBJECT_DEFINITION function to view the definition of an object:

```
USE TSQLRecipe_A;
SELECT  OBJECT_DEFINITION(OBJECT_ID('dbo.usp_INS_BookPublisher'));
```

This query returns the following result set:

```
-------------------------------------------
CREATE PROCEDURE dbo.usp_INS_BookPublisher
    @BookPublisherNM varchar(30) AS
INSERT dbo.BookPublisher (BookPublisherNM)
VALUES (@BookPublisherNM);
```

Solution #2

Query the `sys.all_sql_modules` catalog view and examine the definition column:

```
USE TSQLRecipe_A;
SELECT  definition
FROM    sys.all_sql_modules AS asm
WHERE   object_id = OBJECT_ID('dbo.usp_INS_BookPublisher');
```

This query returns the following result set:

```
definition
-----------------------------------------
CREATE PROCEDURE dbo.usp_INS_BookPublisher
      @BookPublisherNM VARCHAR(30)
AS
INSERT  dbo.BookPublisher
        (BookPublisherNM)
VALUES  (@BookPublisherNM);
```

How It Works

In the first solution, the `OBJECT_DEFINITION` function accepted an object_id of an object, and it returned the Transact-SQL code that defines the specified object. The object_id was obtained with the `OBJECT_ID` function; this function is described in the next recipe. OBJECT_DEFINITION can be used to return the code from stored procedures, replication filter procedures, views, triggers, SQL functions, or rules.

The `OBJECT_DEFINITION` function can also be used to determine the code of system objects. For example, you can reveal the code that makes up the `sys.sp_depends` system-stored procedure with this query:

```
SELECT  OBJECT_DEFINITION(OBJECT_ID('sys.sp_depends'));
```

This query returns the following (abridged) result set:

```
create procedure sys.sp_depends   --- 1996/08/09 16:51
@objname nvarchar(776)          -- the object we want to check
as
...
select @dbname = parsename(@objname,3)

if @dbname is not null and @dbname <> db_name()
      begin
              raiserror(15250,-1,-1)
              return (1)
      end
...
```

In the second example, the definition of the view was retrieved from the sys.all_sql_modules Dynamic Management View (DMV). The view's object_id was used to filter the results to just this view.

Note that if the object that you pass in is encrypted, or if you don't have permission to view this object, you will have a NULL returned instead. This following example creates an encrypted view and then attempts to retrieve the definition with each of the above solutions:

```
IF OBJECT_ID('dbo.EncryptedView', 'V') IS NOT NULL
    DROP VIEW dbo.EncryptedView;
GO
CREATE VIEW dbo.EncryptedView
WITH ENCRYPTION
AS
SELECT  1 AS Result;
GO

SELECT  OBJECT_DEFINITION(OBJECT_ID('dbo.EncryptedView'));

SELECT  definition
FROM    sys.all_sql_modules AS asm
WHERE   object_id = OBJECT_ID('dbo.EncryptedView');
```

These queries return the following results:

```
----------------------
NULL

definition
----------------------
NULL
```

The definitions for check and default constraints, however, are not viewable with sys.all_sql_modules. Instead, we need to query the system views sys.check_constraints and sys.default_constraints directly:

```
SELECT  definition
FROM    AdventureWorks2014.sys.check_constraints
WHERE   name = 'CK_WorkOrder_EndDate';

SELECT  definition
FROM    AdventureWorks2014.sys.default_constraints
WHERE   name = 'DF_ScrapReason_ModifiedDate';
```

These queries return the following results:

```
definition
---------------------------------------------
([EndDate]>=[StartDate] OR [EndDate] IS NULL)

definition
---------------------------------------------
(getdate())
```

You can use OBJECT_DEFINITION to get the definition for check and default constraints; however, you will need to get the object_id from the system views first:

```
USE AdventureWorks2014;
SELECT  name, OBJECT_DEFINITION(object_id) AS definition
FROM    sys.objects
WHERE   name IN ('CK_WorkOrder_EndDate', 'DF_ScrapReason_ModifiedDate');
```

This query returns this result set:

name	definition
CK_WorkOrder_EndDate	([EndDate]>=[StartDate] OR [EndDate] IS NULL)
DF_ScrapReason_ModifiedDate	(getdate())

31-6. Returning a Database Object's Name, Schema Name, and Object ID

Problem

You know an object's name, and need to get its object_id (or you know an object's object_id, and need to get its schema name and the name of the object).

Solution #1

Utilize the OBJECT_ID, OBJECT_NAME, and OBJECT_SCHEMA_NAME functions:

```
SELECT  object_id,
        OBJECT_SCHEMA_NAME(object_id) AS SchemaName,
        OBJECT_NAME(object_id) AS ObjectName
FROM    sys.tables
WHERE   object_id = OBJECT_ID('dbo.BookPublisher', 'U');
```

This query returns the following result set:

object_id	SchemaName	ObjectName
245575913	dbo	BookPublisher

Note that you will most likely return a different object_id value.

Solution #2

Query the underlying system views directly:

```
SELECT  t.object_id,
        s.name AS SchemaName,
        t.name AS ObjectName
FROM    sys.tables AS t
        JOIN sys.schemas AS s
            ON t.schema_id = s.schema_id
WHERE   s.name = 'dbo'
        AND t.name = 'BookPublisher';
```

This query returns the same result set:

object_id	SchemaName	ObjectName
245575913	dbo	BookPublisher

How It Works

In Solution #1, the OBJECT_ID function accepted a schema-qualified object name, and returned the object_id for this object. This function also had an optional second parameter, which is the type of object. In the above example, the type of 'U' was specified, which is the type for a USER TABLE.

The OBJECT_NAME function accepts an object_id and returns the nonqualified name of the specified object. The OBJECT_SCHEMA_NAME function accepts an object_id and returns the name of the schema of the specified object. Both of these functions have an optional second parameter (not used in the above example), which is the database_id of the database to be searched. If the database_id is not passed in, these functions will utilize the current database.

All of these functions will return NULL if the specified object does not exist, or if the user does not have permissions on the object. Additionally, the OBJECT_ID function will return NULL if a spatial index is specified.

In Solution #2, the sys.tables and sys.schemas system views were queried directly to return the same information. This solution also provided the opportunity to perform wildcard searches with the LIKE operator.

Index

■ M

■ Z

Get the eBook for only $5!

Why limit yourself?

Now you can take the weightless companion with you wherever you go and access your content on your PC, phone, tablet, or reader.

Since you've purchased this print book, we're happy to offer you the eBook in all 3 formats for just $5.

Convenient and fully searchable, the PDF version enables you to easily find and copy code—or perform examples by quickly toggling between instructions and applications. The MOBI format is ideal for your Kindle, while the ePUB can be utilized on a variety of mobile devices.

To learn more, go to www.apress.com/companion or contact support@apress.com.

CPSIA information can be obtained
at www.ICGtesting.com
Printed in the USA
LVOW03s1829120416

483259LV00003B/6/P